Legal Issues in International Credit Transfers

Untersuchungen über das Spar-, Giro- und Kreditwesen

Abteilung B: Rechtswissenschaft

Schriften des Instituts für internationales Recht
des Spar-, Giro- und Kreditwesens an der Universität Mainz

Herausgegeben von

Prof. Dr. Walther Hadding und Prof. Dr. Uwe H. Schneider

Band 82/II

Legal Issues in International Credit Transfers

Edited by

Walther Hadding and Uwe H. Schneider

Duncker & Humblot · Berlin

Die Deutsche Bibliothek – CIP-Einheitsaufnahme

Legal issues in international credit transfers / ed. by Walther Hadding and Uwe H. Schneider. – Berlin : Duncker und Humblot, 1993
(Untersuchungen über das Spar-, Giro- und Kreditwesen : Abt. B, Rechtswissenschaft ; Bd. 82,2)
ISBN 3-428-07616-8
NE: Hadding, Walther [Hrsg.]; Untersuchungen über das Spar-, Giro- und Kreditwesen / B

Fremddatenübernahme: Werksatz Marschall, Berlin 45
Druck: Color-Druck Dorfi GmbH, Berlin 49
Printed in Germany

ISSN 0720-7352
ISBN 3-428-07616-8

Preface

The credit transfer is one of the most common forms of domestic payments. Because serious problems have generally not been encountered in the practical execution of credit transfers, the legal provisions governing transfers have only recently been given greater attention. A number of decisions by the highest courts have resolved most of the issues which have arisen. Scholarly study of this area has contributed to the developments in the case law.

The fall of borders and increasingly open markets are permitting the credit transfer to gain increasing practical significance internationally alongside the traditional forms of cross-border payments. This is true for payment transactions by companies and private customers as well as for those strictly between banks. But there are significant differences in execution between domestic and international credit transfers. Cross-border payment systems do not operate as smoothly as national systems. International transfers frequently take longer and, at least for private customers, are substantially more expensive. And above all, the international transfer involves a broad range of risks for the originator, for the credit institutions involved, and for the beneficiary. These risks can affect not only an individual transaction but can also potentially endanger the entire international payment system. Therefore, not only credit institutions and their associations and the associations protecting individual interests, but also central banks, national supervisory authorities and international institutions are increasingly concentrating their attention on the risks of international payment transactions.

It is also within this context that we view the efforts by the Commission of the European Community and an ad hoc working group appointed by the committee of EC central bank presidents. The work by the EC Commission has been directed primarily toward facilitating cross-border payments. Transparency, speed, reliability and economy of cross-border payment systems for private customers are to be improved. The Commission published its first discussion paper in this area, "Payment Transactions in the Internal Market" in September 1990. Following further deliberations, a working program with the title "Facilitating Cross-Border Payments: the Borders Are Falling". The problems are analyzed from the "perspective of the user" and the "perspective of the financial system". The objectives of the proposed measures are to improve transparency for the user and at the same time to support improvements in the infrastructure. The chief goal of the ad hoc working group of the committee of the EC central bank presidents, on the other hand, is to examine how the general stability of the European payment system structures can best be guaranteed.

Upon closer inspection, it becomes clear that the special legal problems relating to international transfers have not yet been resolved. This is true for German law and also for most foreign legal systems. In many countries, at least, efforts are underway to codify the law governing transfers. Such deliberations are not presently being pursued in the Federal Republic of Germany. Only a few scholarly studies have been done with respect to the international credit transfer as governed by German law, and most of these have dealt primarily with specific individual issues.

In the European Community and on a global level, a number of projects are pursuing the goal of restructuring the legal framework for credit transfers. The contributions in this volume should be seen in this light. The goal of this volume is not to provide an overview of the diverse forms of international payment transactions. Instead the main emphasis lies in the area of international credit transfers. Other forms of payment have been included in a supplementary manner. In addition, the national developments in some countries have been described as illustrations. Harmonization projects in Europe and worldwide are so diverse and are proceeding on such differing levels that it was possible only to examine a few of the more significant ones. The present state of deliberations within the European Community was not included because these deliberations have not yet taken on recognizable contours. After briefly describing the issues, the Commission working program of 27 March 1992 states under the heading of "Legal Issues": "The work at the level of the United Nations (in particular the draft of a Model Law of International Credit Transfers, which is being prepared by UNCITRAL) should be taken into consideration. The Commission intends to begin consideration of proposals in this area, including consumer issues, in the second half of 1992. It should also be pointed out that the examination by the Commission of legal issues relating to electronic data exchange has already begun and that the necessary coordination will begin as soon as results are available in this area which are relevant to payment transactions". This statement fixes the goal as being harmonization at the level of the European Community. It also makes clear the extent to which global and regional harmonization of commercial law are interconnected. It should not be forgotten, however, that legal harmonization within the European Community has a special character. This has already been stated in other contexts.

The initiators and editors of this volume have attempted to bring together a group of authors with outstanding qualifications in their areas of specialty. We are greatly indebted to each one of them for their efforts. We are aware that we have placed on them a heavy burden in addition to their regular work. But the gravity of problems arising in this area worldwide justify the acceptance of this challenge.

Some of the contributions were prepared in English or provided by the authors in English translation. Translations of the other contributions into the English language were prepared by Dr. jur. Frances Dielmann, Frankfurt am Main. We also express our appreciation to her for this important task.

The editors are indebted to the Gesellschaft zur Förderung der wissenschaftlichen Forschung über das Spar- und Girowesen e.V., Bonn. Without their support this research project would not have been possible.

Mainz, May 1992

Walther Hadding Uwe H. Schneider

Table of Contents

Abbreviations

ABGB	=	Allgemeines Bürgerliches Gesetzbuch für Österreich (Austrian Civil Code)
A.C.	=	Appeal Cases (Law Reports)
AcP	=	Archiv für die civilistische Praxis
AFB	=	Association Française des Banques
AGB	=	Allgemeine Geschäftsbedingungen (Standard Contract Terms)
AGBG	=	Gesetz zur Regelung des Rechts der Allgemeinen Geschäftsbedingungen (Laws Governing Standard Contract Terms
All E.R.	=	All England Law Reports
AO	=	Abgabenordnung (Tax Code)
AoA	=	Articles of Association
Art.	=	Article
ASO	=	Additional Settlement Obligations
AWG	=	Außenwirtschaftsgesetz (Foreign Trade and Payments Law)
AWV	=	Außenwirtschaftsverordnung (Foreign Trade and Payments Regulation)
BayObLG	=	Bayerisches Oberlandesgericht
BdDGesVölkR	=	Berichte der Deutschen Gesellschaft für Völkerrecht
BDGS	=	Bundesdatenschutzgesetz (Federal Data Protection Act)
B.F.L.R.	=	Banking and Finance Law Review
bfrs	=	Belgian Francs
BGBl	=	Bundesgesetzblatt (Federal Gazette)
BGE	=	Entscheidungen des Schweizerischen Bundesgerichtes (Decisions by the Swiss Supreme Court)
BGH	=	Bundesgerichtshof (German Federal Supreme Court)
BGHZ	=	Entscheidungen des Bundesgerichtshofes in Zivilsachen (Decisions by the German Federal Supreme Court in Civil Matters)
BIS	=	Bank for International Settlements
B.R.	=	Bankruptcy Reporter
BtmG	=	Betäubungsmittelgesetz (Narcotic Act)
Btx	=	Bildschirmtext (teletext)
BuB	=	Bankrecht und Praxis
CC	=	Code Civil
C. civ.	=	Codice civile (Italian Civil Code)

CCJ	=	Comité Européen de Coopération Juridique
CDCJ	=	Comité Directeur Européen de Coopération Juridique
CEPT	=	Conférence européen des Administrations des postes et telecommunications
cert. denied	=	certiorari denied
C.F.R.	=	Code of Federal Regulations
CHAPS	=	Clearing House Automated Payment System
CHIPS	=	Clearing House Interbank Payment System
Cir.	=	Circuit
CISG	=	Convention on the International Sale of Goods
Co.	=	Company
COD	=	Cash on Delivery
CoDA	=	Cash on Delivery Agreement
CR	=	Computer und Recht
D.C.	=	District Court
DDR	=	Deutsche Demokratische Republik (former German Democratic Republic)
DIN	=	Deutsches Institut für Normung
DM	=	Deutsche Mark
DNotZ	=	Deutsche Notar-Zeitschrift
DTC	=	Depository Trust Company
EAF	=	Elektronische Abrechnung durch Filetransfer (electronic settlement by file transfer)
EC	=	European Communities
ECU	=	European Currency Unit
Ed.	=	Edition, Editor
EDI	=	Electronic Data Interchange
EDP	=	Electronic Data Processing
EEC	=	European Economic Community
EFT	=	Electronic Funds Transfer
EFTA	=	European Free Trade Area
e. g.	=	exempli gratia (for example)
EGBGB	=	Einführungsgesetz zum Bürgerlichen Gesetzbuch (Introductory Law to the German Civil Code)
E.R.	=	English Reports
EUFISERV	=	European Savings Banks Financial Services Company
e.V.	=	eingetragener Verein (registered association)
EWiR	=	Entscheidungen zum Wirtschaftsrecht
EWS	=	Europäisches Wirtschafts- und Steuerrecht
f., ff.	=	following
F. 2nd	=	Federal Reporter, second series (U.S.)
FDIC	=	Federal Deposit Insurance Corporation
FIRA	=	Financial Institutions Regulatory and Interest Rate Control Act of 1978

FIRREA	=	Financial Institutions Reform Recovery and Enforcement Act of 1989
FS	=	Festschrift
F. Supp.	=	Federal Supplement (U.S.)
FXNET	=	Foreign Exchange Netting and Close-Out Agreement
GA	=	Giro Agreement
GB	=	Great Britain
GBP	=	Great Britain Pound
Gen.	=	General
Ges. Schr.	=	Gesammelte Schriften
GSCC	=	Government Securities Clearing Corporation
Harv. Int'l L.J.	=	Harvard International Law Journal
HGB	=	Handelsgesetzbuch (Commercial Code)
HSG	=	Handelsrechtliche Schiedsgerichtspraxis
H.R.	=	House of Representatives
ICC	=	International Chamber of Commerce
I.C.L.Q.	=	Internationaland Comparative Law Quarterly
IDS	=	Internationales Devisenschuldrecht
i. e.	=	id est (that is)
ILA	=	International Law Association
Inter. Fin. Law Rev.	=	International Financial Law Review
IPR	=	Internationales Privatrecht (private international law)
IPrax	=	Praxis des internationalen Privat- und Verfahrensrechts
IPRG	=	Internationales Privatrechtsgesetz (Law Governing the Private International Law)
IRG	=	Internationales Rechtshilfegesetz (Law on International Legal Assistance in Criminal Matters)
ISDA	=	International Swap Dealers Association
ISDN	=	Integrated Services Digital Network
ISO	=	International Organisation for Standardization
J.	=	Judge
J. Bus. Law	=	Journal of Business Law
JCP	=	Juriclasseur Périodique
JR	=	Juristische Rundschau
JW	=	Juristische Wochenschrift
JZ	=	Juristenzeitung
KG	=	Kammergericht (Berlin Court of Appeal)
KO	=	Konkursordnung (Bankruptcy Code)
LG	=	Landgericht (District Court)
LGDJ	=	Librairie Générale de Droit et de Jurisprudence
LLoyd's L.R.	=	Lloyd's Law Reports

Lloyd's Rep.	= Lloyd's List Report
LM	= Reference work on the German Federal Supreme Court, edited by Lindenmeier, Möhring, et al.
Ltd.	= Limited liability company
LZB	= Landeszentralbank
Mass.	= Massachusetts
MATIF	= Marché à Terme des Instruments Financiers
MDR	= Monatsschrift für Deutsches Recht
MIICA	= Model International Insolvency Cooperation Act
MOA	= Money Orders Agreement
MOCOMILA	= Money Commission of the International Law Association
MünchKomm	= Münchener Kommentar zum Bürgerlichen Gesetzbuch, 2nd ed., 1984 ff.
N.	= Note
NACHO	= North American Clearing House Organization
NBü	= Normenausschuß Bürowesen
NDFS	= Next-day Funds Settlement
NIL	= National Interface Location
N.J.	= New Jersey
NJW	= Neue Juristische Wochenschrift
N.Y.	= New York
No.	= Number
OBA	= Zeitschrift für das gesamte Bank- und Börsenwesen (Bankarchiv)
OECD	= Organization for Economic Cooperation and Development
OEEC	= Organization for European Economic Cooperation
O.J.	= Official Journal of the European Economic Communities
OLG	= Oberlandesgericht (Court of Appeal)
OR	= Bundesgesetz über das Obligationenrecht (Federal Law of Contracts)
OrgKG	= Gesetz über die organisierte Kriminalität (Organized Crime Act)
p.	= page
p.a.	= per annum
par.	= paragraph
PIN	= personal identification number
plc	= public limited company
PostG	= Gesetz über das Postwesen
PostStrukG	= Poststrukturgesetz
PostVerfG	= Postverfassungsgesetz
PostVsG	= Postverwaltungsgesetz

PTC	=	Participants Trust Company
Pub. L.	=	public law
Q.B.	=	Queen's Bench Division (Law Reports)
QFC	=	Qualified Financial Contract
r.	=	rule
RA	=	Runderlaß Außenwirtschaft
RabelsZ	=	Zeitschrift für ausländisches und internationales Privatrecht, founded by Ernst Rabel)
Repo	=	repurchase agreement
RG	=	Reichsgericht
RGRK	=	Das Bürgerliches Gesetzbuch mit besonderer Berücksichtigung der Rechtsprechung des Reichsgerichts und des Bundesgerichtshofes, Kommentar, 12th ed., 1974 ff.
RGZ	=	Entscheidungen des Reichsgerichts in Zivilsachen
Riv. dir. civ.	=	Rivista di diritto civile
RIW	=	Recht der Internationalen Wirtschaft
S.	=	Senate
S.A.	=	Société Anonyme
S.B.F.	=	Société des bourses françaises
s.c.	=	société coopérative (Belgium)
SAG	=	Schweizerische Aktiengesellschaft, Zeitschrift für Handels- und Wirtschaftsrechts
SAGITTAIRE	=	Système Automatique de Gestion Intégré par Télétransmission de Transactions avec Imputation de Règlements Etrangers
ScheckG	=	Scheckgesetz (Check Act)
SCHUFA	=	Schutzgemeinschaft für allgemeine Kreditsicherung
SDFS	=	Same-day Funds Settlement
sent.	=	sentence
SFr.	=	Swiss francs
S.I.T.	=	Système Interbancaire de Télécompensation
SJZ	=	Schweizerische Juristenzeitung
Stat	=	Statute(s) at Large
StGB	=	Strafgesetzbuch (Criminal Code)
StPO	=	Strafprozeßordnung (Code of Criminal Procedure)
S.W.I.F.T.	=	Society for Worldwide Interbank Financial Telecommunication
SWZ	=	Schweizerische Zeitschrift für Wirtschaftsrecht
TAN	=	transaction number
UCC	=	Uniform Commercial Code
U.K.	=	United Kingdom
U.N.	=	United Nations

UN/ECE	= United Nations Economic Commission for Europe
UNCID	= Uniform Rules of Conduct for Interchange of Trade Data by Teletransmission
UNCITRAL	= United Nations Commission on International Trade Law
UNIDROIT	= International Institute for the Unification of Privat Law
U.S.	= United States of America
USD	= United States Dollar
v.	= versus
VersR	= Versicherungsrecht
vol.	= volume
VVG	= Gesetz über den Versicherungsvertrag (Insurance Contract Act)
W.L.R.	= Weekly Law Reports
WM	= Zeitschrift für Wirtschafts- und Bankrecht, Wertpapier-Mitteilungen Teil IV
WuB	= Entscheidungssammlung zum Wirtschafts- und Bankrecht
ZfgK	= Zeitschrift für das gesamte Kreditwesen
ZGB	= Zivilgesetzbuch (Civil Code)
ZHR	= Zeitschrift für das gesamte Handelsrecht und Wirtschaftsrecht
ZIP	= Zeitschrift für Wirtschaftsrecht
ZPO	= Zivilprozeßordnung (Code of Civil Procedure)
ZVglRWiss	= Zeitschrift für Vergleichende Rechtswissenschaft

I. Law and Practice of International Credit Transfers in the Federal Republic of Germany

The Role of Cash in International Payment Transactions

By Jürgen Trosien, Frankfurt am Main*

Contents

I. Cash in International Transactions: Functions and Characteristics

Since the beginning of its use, money has been the medium which could most easily overcome borders between states and countries and thus penetrate countries with different currency systems (Währungsordnung). In cross-border transactions, money fulfills the following generally accepted functions:

— It serves as a means of exchange for the transfer of value in the form of goods and services.

— It is used as a means of preserving value. The proceeds for assets which are sold thus need not be spent immediately.

— It is a unit of counting and calculation and can serve as a measure of value for various exchanges.

In order that money can better fulfill its function as a means of exchange, a lawful duty to accept money is created; it is made the legal tender of a country. In its original form as notes and coins, money is thus also a reference to the national product, a voucher for all goods and services within a national economy.

---

* Translated by Dr. Frances Dielmann, Frankfurt/M.

The cited characteristics are best found in the form of cash. The characteristic as money is independent, however, from the material used and the name "money"; it can also fulfill the functions when it is recognized only by custom and thereby acquires value. In times of inflation, certain types of goods acquire the characteristics of money, such as American cigarettes in Germany after 1945. Money derives its value from the respect and the trust given it.

In the following discussion of cash money crossing currency borders, we will refer to the functions of money cited here.

II. Prerequisites for an International Exchange

At the present time, not all currency systems permit free cross-border cash transactions. In order for this to be possible, certain prerequisites must be met.

The most important requirement is that foreign instruments of payment, i.e. foreign bank notes and coins, must be accepted in one's own country, and a free exchange between one's own legal instruments of payment and the foreign money must be possible at any time. A prerequisite for the possibility of exchanging one's own currency into a different currency at any time and freely disposing of that currency is the free convertibility between the two currencies, applicable to domestic residents allowing them to transfer currency to foreign currencies and also applicable to foreigners through which they can freely exchange their assets into domestic or foreign currency. For private individuals, the purchasing power of the foreign money as a means of free choice of goods is a substantial incentive to acquire foreign notes and coins. These individuals generally accept only currencies based on market economies.

State-controlled or planned economies do not permit free cross-border exchange of cash or do so only with restrictions. By means of foreign currency restrictions, these nations officially prohibit penetration by foreign cash into the domestic currency area or the export of their own currency. These restrictions can be prohibitions, taxes, mandatory deposits, nominal maximum limits (e.g. for travel purposes) or certain procedures for foreign currency allowances or mandatory return of foreign currency.

Such obstacles are nevertheless evaded. Bank notes from hard-currency countries do invade the territories of other currency systems because they are a popular means of exchange in countries with an otherwise limited offering of goods. This money which enters unofficially often leads to a hidden safekeeping of assets, i.e. the hoarding of "black money" outside banks of the particular country. In this way, a type of competing currency develops "privately". Demand for foreign bank notes increases further when the domestic currency seriously loses value and acceptance. In the other direction, it can be observed that as soon as the political or economic circumstances stabilize or the central bank adopts a restrictive course of monetary policy, the hoarding of foreign money slows down, and the foreign bank notes flow back to their own country through the banking sector.

Some countries (such as the former German Democratic Republic or other Eastern Bloc countries) in recent times no longer put up serious obstacles to penetration by hard currencies or the creation of alternative markets; instead, they only lightly regulated these actions, by means, for example, of coupons for purchase of consumer goods in certain foreign currency shops instead of a strict duty to turn in foreign currency. On the other hand, they made stronger attempts to prevent foreigners from purchasing their goods in very short supply by means of prohibiting the export of their own currency.

In cross-border travel, the use of cash is very common. Taking German notes out of or foreign bank notes to the Federal Republic of Germany has been completely free of restrictions since 1956.[1] When the German mark was declared convertible[2], some more formal and already practically abandoned restrictions were dropped. In addition to the Federal Republic of Germany, at the end of 1958 other OEEC countries also declared the convertibility of their currencies: Belgium, Luxembourg, Denmark, France, Great Britain, Italy, the Netherlands, Norway, Austria, Portugal, Sweden and Switzerland. The Foreign Trade and Payments Law ("AWG") of April 28, 1961 (BGBl. I, p. 481), which finally replaced the Allied currency legislation in West Germany after World War II, did not contain any more changes regarding the handling of travel currency; since then travel currency has not been subject to any restrictions for domestic or foreign residents. In various other countries, however, there are still legal currency restrictions relating to the import and export of domestic and foreign currencies.

III. International Transactions in DM Bank Notes

Under normal economic conditions, DM bank notes are not a common means of payment or holding assets in foreign countries. Only in those areas of Germany's neighboring countries near the borders with Germany DM notes are often accepted as instruments of payment at a near-market

[1] Foreign trade circular RA No. 65/56 and 10. New version of the general authorization No. 12/49 of Sept. 14, 1956.

[2] RA No. 60/58 of Dec. 29. 1958.

exchange rate. DM notes are also used as a means of transfer in international capital transactions. In the case of the export of capital, DM notes are paid directly into accounts with banks in foreign countries for the purpose of purchasing securities, gold, real estate, etc. Only rarely are DM notes used by an investor as a means for preserving assets (e.g. in bank deposit boxes in foreign banks), i.e. hoarded for a certain period of time.

1. Inclusion in Balance of Payments Statistics

The German Federal Bank includes cross- border DM note transactions in the balance of payments statistics (in the balance of current transactions, there under travel transactions or transfer payments, and also in the balance of capital transactions). The entries are based primarily on reporting by domestic and foreign banks. In the case of transactions between non-banks (e.g. transport of cash by commuters in areas near borders or by foreign workers) to the extent that the DM notes do not return to banks, the German Federal Bank must rely on estimates, representative surveys or individual investigations.[3]

There are no statistical studies regarding the amounts of DM notes in foreign countries. Information on changes in these levels could theoretically be indirectly deduced: the movement of DM notes to foreign countries can be compared with the return of DM notes from those countries. The change in the total levels of DM bank notes in circulation outside the borders of the Federal Republic of Germany can be derived from the difference. But even the statistical data necessary for such calculations are not entirely available.

The outward flow of DM notes involves:

- payments by non-banks in foreign countries:
- payments connected with travel
- support payments and transfer of savings to foreign countries by foreign workers who are viewed as domestic residents for purposes of the German balance of payments, and in the past years also by Polish seasonal workers
- payments in connection with purchases of goods in foreign countries, particularly in the Netherlands and Switzerland near the German borders
- the taking in of DM notes connected with private capital transfers by German investors ("suitcase transactions")

[3] See the balance of payment statistics for the Federal Republic of Germany: Deutsche Bundesbank, Sonderdruck Nr. 8, 2nd ed. May 1990.

— the transmittal of German DM notes by domestic banks to foreign countries for the sale of travel currency to foreign tourists, for which reliable statistics are available

Most of these DM transactions can be statistically determined only indirectly through the return of DM from foreign countries where banks are involved (see below). Not quantifiable are the bank note transfers which do not take place through banks and which are also illegal: suitcase transactions by private individuals or business people primarily for tax reasons, who deposit large amounts of money in bank deposit boxes in foreign countries (hoarding without immediate spending, so that these amounts are temporarily withdrawn from circulation) or for counter trade (purchase of securities in the form of actual bonds, etc.) in order to evade registration by account in Germany. Money transactions involved in the European drug trade also play a role here. For all of these types of transactions, large denominations are usually used (500 and 1000 mark notes).

The flow of DM notes back into Germany takes place by means of transactions similar to those by which the notes move to foreign countries. These include the following situations:

— Foreign banks send their excess supplies of DM notes to German credit institutions.

— Foreign travelers spend DM notes in Germany.

— Foreigners purchase goods in Germany.

— DM notes are brought into Germany for capital investment purposes.

Not all of these transactions can be statistically assessed. To the extent that the DM notes flow back from foreign countries to German banks, these amounts are reported. In addition, foreign banks in nine countries report the amounts of DM notes sold to travelers. Some foreign banks in countries frequently visited by German tourists often do not send their excess DM notes directly to German credit institutions but instead transmit them together with other foreign notes to banks in other countries engaged in international currency exchange (e.g. in Zurich). The notes are then repatriated into Germany by means of this detour.

As we have seen, it is also not possible to close the statistical gap relating to transactions between non-banks, such as when foreigners spend DM notes acquired from non-banks for the purchase of goods in Germany. Such currency movements may be observed in areas near borders (the Netherlands, Austria, Switzerland).

2. Motives for Transporting Cash into Foreign Countries

Regarding the motives behind cross-border cash transactions, the following is apparent:

While cash expenditures in connection with international travel lead to the return of DM notes to Germany within a separate framework and usually within a short time, transfers of assets to foreign countries within the scope of investments are classified as capital transactions. The high fees charged for international transfers and long transfer times are often the reason why investors view it as advisable, particularly in areas near borders, to pack the money in a suitcase and deposit it in accounts in foreign countries or place the money in deposit boxes in foreign banks. However, these DM transactions are more often based on tax motives: under German tax laws, German credit institutions must upon the death of a bank customer inform the tax authorities if this customer had a bank deposit box. The transport of DM notes to foreign countries is a means for covering one's tracks if there is fear that the tax authorities might possibly detect a capital transfer made by means of foreign funds transfer.

Such cash transactions always increase when the tax authorities announce plans to collect data from banks from which movements to and from accounts could be deduced. This tendency was observed in Germany when the withholding tax on interest, the so-called "source tax", was introduced effective Jan. 1, 1989. The heated controversy concerning this source tax finally led to its withdrawal.[4] The substantial increases in cash withdrawals, particularly in the second half of 1988, in the high denominations of 500 and 1000 DM notes were transferred by means of suitcase transactions to neighboring countries and deposited in banks there. The high demand for notes in large denominations was seen in the reported bank note circulation which had increased by almost 15 % toward the end of 1988 (compared to 10 % at the end of 1987 and 8 % at the end of 1986).

3. Circulation Speed of Bank Notes in Foreign Countries

The length of time bank notes remain in foreign countries differs greatly. Usually, they return quickly to the issuing country. Under normal economic circumstances, this is supported by the following reasons:

Outside the country in which the cash notes are the legal instrument of payment, they can be used as a means of payment only to a limited extent. As a means of preserving assets in foreign bank deposit boxes, they are subject to exchange rate risks and also earn no interest.

[4] Of June 30, 1989.

There can, of course, be circumstances in which it is useful for foreign private individuals e.g. guest workers employed in Germany or hosts of German tourists in foreign countries to hoard DM notes in their own countries. This can make sense, for example, in countries with high rates of inflation or where currency control regulations prohibit the foreign currency deposits in banks, and where goods for which there is great demand, particularly imported goods, can be purchased only in exchange for hard currencies on a grey market. The DM bank notes then do not flow directly back to banks, but are instead used in those countries as an (unofficial) means of payment. As soon as the notes are deposited in banks, they are returned quickly to Germany.

The length of time during which DM bank notes remain in circulation in the non-bank sector is generally relatively long, even though subject to certain fluctuations depending on the particular foreign country. In accordance with expectations regarding possible change in exchange rate risks (e.g. when a drop in the value of that country's currency is expected) or a tightening of foreign currency regulations, the notes which non-banks receive from tourists for services or in connection with support payments by foreign workers are often returned to banks only following a substantial period of hoarding or not at all; sometimes they are transported to neighboring countries in suitcase transactions for illegal purposes. If unrestricted currency transactions are permitted in the country and the currency exchange rates are stable, the DM bank notes will most likely be deposited with banks immediately so that they can be invested in a profitable way. Therefore, the cash management practices by non-banks strongly influence the circulation of DM notes in foreign countries.

In practice, though, no hoarding based on expectations of drops in the value of other currencies can be observed at the present time (1991) in most of Germany's neighboring countries because the currencies of thse countries are tied to the mark: either through international treaties (European Monetary System) or voluntarily (Austria, Switzerland). In those countries, interest-earning DM currency accounts may be opened, from which DM bank notes may be withdrawn at any time. An incentive to hoard DM bank notes based on speculative expectations does not presently exist in those countries.

Instead, one can assume that the circulation time for DM notes through the banking sector is relatively short in all countries and generally fluctuates little. Because German bank notes do not earn interest, they are quickly sent to correspondent banks. In areas near borders, due to relatively low transport costs, it may be profitable to transmit even small DM amounts to credit institutions in border cities within Germany.

IV. The Circulation of DM Notes in the Former German Democratic Republic prior to 1989

Following the reunification and the establishment of the currency union with the five new "Länder" (states) in the territory of the former German Democratic Republic in the year 1990, from our present perspective it appears anachronistic to study DM note transactions in the former GDR prior to the Fall of 1989, the time of the "Wende". From a historical point of view, however, such an analysis is certainly worthwhile.

Prior to October of 1989, the DM was very popular as a second currency in the GDR. Due to the significance of the functions of DM currency, one must distinguish between the state-controlled area (including state-owned companies, such as hotels and Intershops) and the private sector. The DM notes which entered the state-controlled sector were returned quickly and directly or through third countries to the Federal Republic of Germany. By contrast, the circulation time for DM notes in the private sector was significantly longer due to hoarding.The state-controlled sector obtained DM notes by the following means:

— mandatory exchange, fees, fines, etc.

— cash amounts spent by travelers in hotels, Intershops, etc., in excess of the mandatory exchange amount

— cash withdrawals by the State Bank of the GDR, primarily from West Berlin banks.

The DM notes officially returned to the Federal Republic of Germany in the following ways:

— payments in cash for activities by the GDR in the Federal Republic

— amounts spent for travel by citizens of the GDR on visits to the Federal Republic

— deposits by the State Bank of the GDR into freely convertible DM accounts which they maintained with West Berlin banks.

This official DM circulation involved only a short time spent by the DM notes in the GDR.

The situation was different for DM note transactions in the private sector, for which the DM notes come from the following sources:

— cash payments in the GDR by visitors from the Federal Republic (e.g. as gifts to DDR residents)

— taking in of DM notes by GDR citizens who had received them as gifts in the Federal Republic or withdrew notes from their own accounts.

V. Summary

Based on the preceding observations, it can be determined that the outflow and return of DM notes with respect to countries with "normal" economic conditions generally balance out during the course of a year. The level of DM notes remaining as the "residue" in these countries changes little even in the case of large fluctuations in the volume of outflow and returns within the year. Due to hoarding and de-hoarding tendencies in certain "problem" countries with instable, weak currencies and overall economic crises, the DM note circulation outside of Germany still sometimes fluctuates greatly, i.e. large changes in the circulation of DM notes in foreign currencies can discernibly influence the overall circulation of DM cash notes. If one assumes a stable circulation time for DM bank notes in foreign countries, and a steady transfer of notes to foreign countries, the return of DM notes by foreign banks for which reliable data exist in contrast to almost all other sectors of note circulation with foreign countries, changes in the "residue" of DM notes located in foreign countries can be detected.

International Transfers under German Law

By Walther Hadding, Mainz*

Contents

I. Introduction

1. In the European internal market, and also worldwide, the transmittal of cashless payments by means of international funds transfers will increase in volume in the future. In addition to the traditional transfers for high amounts by large enterprises and payments between credit institutions, many transfers of small amounts by small business and private individuals can be expected[1]. The Commission of the European Communities[2] is

---

* Translated by Dr. Frances Dielmann, Frankfurt/M.

[1] At present, international transfers in Germany equal only 0.2 % of the volume of domestic transfers which, for example, in 1989 amounted to 19.5 trillion marks

therefore pushing for faster, cheaper and more transparent payment routes; the Commission, together with representatives from the banking sector and the central banks of the member states, is presently examining ways in which international funds transfers in particular can be improved. These deliberations are oriented primarily toward the technical establishment of additional networks for electronic data transmission. Since beginning operations in 1977 the electronic communications system S.W.I.F.T. (Society for Worldwide Interbank Financial Telecommunications, a cooperative association under Belgian law headquartered in Brussels) has made it possible to transmit messages relating to payment orders worldwide through an international transmission network between the connected banks (members of the association). After three years of experience with S.W.I.F.T. it was described as a "silent revolution" in international payment transactions[3].

Recently, the European Savings Bank Association and its member organizations from eleven European countries have founded a new company, EUFISERV (European Financial Services Company SC, likewise a cooperative association under Belgian law headquartered in Brussels) to provide financial services throughout Europe[4]. The 37 million customers who have obtained a eurocheque card, a universal credit card or an "S" customer card from their savings banks will as a first stage be given Europe-wide access to automated cash dispensers at savings banks. In several steps, access will first be provided to about 18,000 cash dispensers. Each cash withdrawal will be authorized on-line by the data processing center of the customer's home savings bank. The data transmission will take place through the network operator, the dvg data processing company of the Savings Bank Organization of Lower Saxony in Hannover, Germany. Using the on-line terminals and the settlement centers in the data processing networks, it is even possible that in the future all of the 1,930 savings banks in the EC member states with about 62,000 branches will be able to offer this transfer service based on the European Charter on Cooperation of March 1990; this service will be independent from the other payment routes and clearing centers, such as those offered by the German Telecom and the national central banks.

2. These developments can lead to excellent execution of international funds transfers worldwide or at least throughout Europe from a technical perspective. But where there are occasional misdirections of orders or other

(19,500,000,000,000). About two-thirds of the international transactions involve amounts under 5000 marks (see Klaus-Peter Schmidt, Die Zeit, No. 11 of March 6, 1992, p. 45).

[2] See the discussion paper present by the Commission, "Payment Transactions in the Internal Market" of Sept. 26, 1990 — Com (90) 447 final — (so-called Green Paper), as well as the new working document of March 25, 1992.

[3] See Leitermann, Die Bank 1980, p. 418.

[4] See Alfons Müller, Sparkasse 1991, p. 413.

types of defects in execution, it is not always easy to determine the legal situation between the participating parties[5]. One must keep in mind that cross-border transfers, as a rule, are so-called "chain transfers" with domestic and international "links". For example, a German debtor might first issue a transfer order to his credit institution, usually within the scope of a standing giro account relationship. In the simplest case, this first receiving bank maintains a giro account relationship with a correspondent bank in the foreign country, i.e. the country where the payee resides. But often other credit institutions are engaged in Germany as intermediaries, e.g. in the case of a savings bank the respective state central bank or giro center or, in the case of a cooperative savings organization (Volksbank/Raiffeisenbank), the regional cooperative central bank and/or the German Cooperative Bank, which maintains the giro relationship with the correspondent bank in the foreign country. This foreign correspondent bank is — again, in the simplest case — either the bank of the beneficiary or itself has a giro relationship with the bank which will finally credit the transfer amount to the beneficiary. Sometimes it is necessary to employ several correspondent banks in various countries, for example for a transfer from Germany to Brazil through New York. A transfer can proceed through a long "chain" of individual giro relationships. And it is necessary to determine separately for each giro relationship between correspondent banks in different countries which national legal system governs the respective transfer and which rights and duties result for the participating parties under that system of law. The result can be a different legal system for each account relationship in the chain; in addition, different general business terms can apply and can contain differing provisions regarding the obligations of the participating parties, the time of performance, the possibility of revocation, liability and compensation in case of breach of duties, allocation of risks, etc.[6]

3. For example, the German Bundesgerichtshof (Federal Supreme Court)[7] recently decided the following case:

A domestic enterprise issued to its bank a transfer order for payment of a purchase price of US $ 142,376 to the supplier in California, U.S.A. for printers which it had ordered. The transfer amount was to be "released to the beneficiary only upon presentation of the Air Way Bills". The first German bank requested the bank designated on the invoice, the Bank of America, by

---

[5] See e.g. the cases BGH WM 1976, p. 904; KG WM 1977, p. 1176; BGH WM 1978, p. 998; OLG Hamburg WM 1982, p. 249; BGH WM 198, p. 291; see also U. H. Schneider, WM 1989, p. 285, 286.

[6] See Pleyer/Wallach, „Erfüllungszeitpunkt und Gefahrtragung bei grenzüberschreitenden Überweisungen nach deutschem und englischem Recht", RIW 1988, p. 172.

[7] Decision of March 19, 1991 — XI ZR 102/90, WM 1991, p. 797 with comments by Horn in WuB I D 1.-4.91 = NJW 1991, p. 2210 = [LM] § 670 BGB No. 33.

telex to execute the order and also ordered its correspondent bank, the Chase Manhattan Bank, to provide cover for the benefit of the Bank of America. The German bank debited the enterprise's giro account as originator of the transfer. The Bank of America first rejected the execution on the grounds that it would not process a conditional payment order and gave notice of the retransfer of the covering funds to the Chase Manhattan Bank. The originator's bank gave notice of this to the enterprise and credited the invoiced amount as "reimbursement due to non-execution" back to the enterprise. Later, it turned out that the Chase Manhattan Bank had again debited the originator's bank for the dollar amount and provided this amount to the Bank of America which had made a new request for this amount, apparently on the instruction of the California supplier. The Bank of America then credited the amount to the California supplier. The originator's bank then canceled the reimbursement credit which it had provided to the originator. The German enterprise, which had not accepted the printers upon delivery but had also not received the U.S. dollar amount back from the California supplier then demanded a new reimbursement credit from its bank based on the argument that the later account debit was not properly based on the original transfer order. The Bundesgerichtshof denied this claim. The official summary of this decision reads:

> "In the case of a transfer to a foreign receiving bank, the originator's bank's claim for reimbursement arises when this bank transmits the order to another bank which the first bank engages and provides cover to that bank. If the execution of the transfer fails for reasons which are not within the sphere of the originator's bank, its claim is not affected. The foreign banks are not its servants."

4. The primary issue in an evaluation of the legal situation in cross-border transfers is — as already mentioned — often the question of whether German or foreign law applies. The respective conflict of laws rules will not be examined in detail in this context[8]. Briefly, the parties to the specific giro relationship can, as a rule, freely stipulate the applicable law (Art. 27 of the Introductory Law to the German Civil Code [EGBGB]). Often, the general business conditions used by the credit institutions stipulate that the law of place of performance shall govern. The result of this provision for German banks is that for giro relationships with customers the law of the seat of the bank branch managing the account is determinative (see e.g. No. 26 (1) sent. 2 of the General Business Conditions of the German banks in the version of January 1988 as amended; also No. 27 (1) sent. 2 of the General Business Conditions of the German savings banks in the version of 1986 as amended

[8] See Pleyer/Wallach, supra note 6 at III.1.; Etzkorn, Rechtsfragen des internationalen elektronischen Zahlungsverkehrs durch S.W.I.F.T. (1991), pp. 41 ff.; and the article by von der Seipen in this volume.

in May 1988)[9]. As of Jan. 1, 1993, No. 6 (1) of the Bank General Conditions will clearly provide that, "German law shall apply to the business relationship between the customer and the bank". This choice of law is valid when subjected to examination under § 9 of the Law on Standard Contracts[10]. If the transfer order is for a private cashless payment by a customer which is not connected with his profession or business, the choice of law may not remove the customer from the consumer protection provisions in the law of the state of his habitual residence (Art. 29 (1) EGBGB).

If no adequate choice of law is made, the applicable law is that of the state in which the credit institution performing the "characteristic obligation" is located because the contract has the "closest connection" to that state (Art. 28 (1) in conjunction Art. (2) sent. 2 and sent. 1 EGBGB)[11]. In the case of transfers, the execution of the transfer by means of proper transmittal or credit to the beneficiary is viewed as the "characteristic performance"[12]. If the transfer order is issued by a consumer with no choice of law, the law of the state in which the consumer has his habitual residence is applicable (Art. 29 (2) EGBGB).

In the following analysis, we will assume that German law applies.

II. Giro Relationship with a Correspondent Bank

Cross-border transfers which are to be executed in a foreign country for the benefit of a payee there or which come from a foreign country and are to be credited to a beneficiary in Germany are predominantly executed by German credit institutions within the scope of standing business relationships with foreign correspondent banks[13]. To the extent that the German credit institutions have their own subsidiaries or branch offices in foreign countries, the banks use these instead of other correspondent banks. But the relatively low number of such subsidiaries and branches makes it necessary to continue to work closely with other correspondent banks; in funds

---

[9] See the decision by the Bundesgerichtshof in: NJW 1987, p. 1825 = ZIP 1987, p. 693 and the short comment by Pleyer in: EWiR, No. 26 AGB Banken 1/87, p. 425.

[10] See Canaris, Bankvertragsrecht, (2d ed. 1981) at margin no. 2721.

[11] See Palandt/Heldrich, BGB (51st ed. 1992) at Art. 28 EGBGB, margin no. 21.

[12] See Kegel in: Gedächtnisschrift für Rudolf Schmidt (1966), p. 215, 225; Kleiner, Internationales Devisen-Schuldrecht (1985) at N 13.03.

[13] See Polke, Der Zahlungsverkehr der Banken im In- und mit dem Ausland — Risikoverteilung bei Schließung eines Kreditinstituts, dissertation, Munich 1978, pp. 186f.; Brüggemann, Die Banktechnik des Auslandsgeschäfts (6th ed. 1981), p. 16f.; Schmidt-Dencker, Die Korrespondenzbank im Außenhandel, dissertation, Hamburg I, 1982; on payment by letter of credit: Pleyer/Wallach, supra note 6, at II.1, with additional cites.

transfers this cooperation is based on a contractual giro relationship with the correspondent bank.

1. Nostro Account of the German Credit Institution at a Foreign Correspondent Bank

The giro relationship with a foreign correspondent is usually created contractually when the German credit institution opens an account at that bank; this is usually done in connection with payments to be made in the currency of the foreign country in which the correspondent bank is located. The German credit institution sends a simple letter to the foreign bank requesting that an account be opened and stating that an opening balance will be provided[14]. This letter constitutes an offer to enter into a giro relationship; the response by the foreign bank containing the account number and the terms of business constitutes the acceptance thereby completing the contract which establishes the giro relationship between the two parties. From the perspective of the German credit institution, this means that the foreign correspondent opens a so-called "nostro account" with a nostro balance at the German bank's disposal[15]. From the perspective of the foreign bank, this is a new so-called "loro" account.

In the letter requesting the opening of a giro account, the German credit institution also gives notice of the individuals who are authorized to submit payment orders. A corresponding list of signatures is included so that the foreign correspondent bank can verify the authenticity of the signatures on the transfer orders and in the case of check collections. When the giro agreement has been made, the foreign correspondent bank also receives a code key (telegraphic test key) and confirms receipt. For security reasons, code lists are sent separately. The codes make it possible to verify payment orders transmitted by telephone, telegraph or telex or by other means. Efforts are underway to achieve a uniform code key at least throughout Europe. The German credit institution usually accepts no liability for any misuse of codes and counterfeiting of signatures. The foreign correspondent bank has a duty to examine the validity of orders.

2. Loro Account at a German Credit Institution for the Foreign Correspondent Bank

If a foreign correspondent bank decides to enter into a giro relationship with a German credit institution, an account is opened at the German credit

[14] Regarding provision of the opening balance („Anschaffung"), see the General Business Conditions of the German banks, Section XI. A. No. 1.

[15] "Credit facilities", i.e. overdraft limits, can also be agreed from the beginning.

institution, usually in German marks. From the perspective of the German bank, this is a loro account, and to the foreign bank it is a nostro account. The giro agreement is completed by means of transmittal of the account number by the German credit institution. If the foreign bank does not object to the reference to the application of the bank's law in the general business conditions, its silence is deemed to be implied acceptance of these business conditions[16].

3. Reciprocal Account Relationship

Frequently, the giro relationship with the foreign corespondent is structured in such a way that the German credit institution maintains an account at the foreign bank in its currency and the foreign bank an account in German marks at the German bank. This creates a reciprocal account relationship in which each of the credit institutions manages an account for the other institution in what would be a foreign currency for that other institution[17]. Such a correspondent bank is known in banking practice as an "A-Correspondent". A reciprocal correspondent relationship is usually structured to include a line of credit which permits overdrafts. This enables the banks to promptly execute transfer orders before procurement of additional cover which might be necessary.

4. Agency Agreement

A correspondent relationship with a foreign bank can also be a mere agency agreement. This agreement governs the ability of the parties to directly issue a single transfer order, for which the settlement is not carried out through reciprocal accounts but instead through stipulated accounts at a third credit institution.

III. Cross-Border Transfer Order to a Foreign Country

A transfer order issued by a domestic customer of a German credit institution for a cross-border payment for the benefit of a payee in a foreign country is carried out in much the same way as a purely domestic transfer. The provisions of the German Law on Foreign Trade and Payments must, of course, be complied with. In addition, a distinction must be made between

---

[16] See the decision by the Bundesgerichtshof in: NJW 1971, p. 2126, 2127; and regarding that decision: Pleyer/Battes, DB 1971, p. 1289, 1295; Kollhosser, JR 1972, p. 26; Ungnade, WM 1973, p. 1130, 1133.

[17] See Pleyer/Wallach, supra note 6, at II. 1.

transfer orders to be carried out in German marks and those to be carried out in a foreign currency.

1. The Law of Foreign Trade

In accordance with § 22 of the German Law on Foreign Trade and Payments [AWG], the export of capital can be limited to exports for the purposes listed in that section; at present, however, it is not restricted. A restriction on capital export to a member state of the European Communities would be fundamentally inconsistent with the rules in the EEC Treaty on the free movement of capital[18]. § 26 AWG in conjunction with § 59 ff. of the Regulation on Foreign Trade and Payments [AWV] does contain reporting requirements. All payments for an amount over 5000 German marks or an equivalent amount in foreign currency must be reported[19], if they are not export proceeds which are not in connection with loans with a term of up to 12 months and are not made by natural persons for the purchase of goods for personal use or for the procurement of services for personal purposes (§ 59 (2) AWV). The reporting location is the German Bundesbank or one of its branches (§ 63 AWV).

2. Transfer Order in German Currency

a) If the customer issues an order to his domestic credit institution to carry out a transfer in German currency and this bank has a direct giro relationship with a foreign correspondent bank (if possible) in the beneficiary's country and maintains an account for that bank, then the originator's bank simply credits the correspondent bank's account. The originator's domestic account is debited; this debit is covered either by a positive balance or a cash deposit. Decisive is whether the foreign correspondent bank receives the necessary cover by means of the credit. In foreign payments it is important that the correspondent receives cover not merely in the form of a claim (on the books) but instead as fulfillment (actual value) through the credit, for example through a means of set-off (perhaps within the scope of an agreed overdraft limit). Then the correspondent bank will carry out the order issued to it at the same time by paying the transfer amount to the beneficiary in cash or by means of a credit, namely to German mark account held by the beneficiary at the correspondent bank. If the beneficiary designated in the

[18] See art. 67 and the Directive of June 24, 1988 (O. J. No. L 178, p. 5); Art. 8a and Art. 106; Diether Hoffmann, Banken- und Börsenrecht der EWG (1990), pp. 31 ff. 42; Börner, Die Fünfte Freiheit des Gemeinsamen Marktes: Der freie Zahlungsverkehr, in: Festschrift für Ophüls (1966), pp. 19 ff.

[19] Since Aug. 1, 1991; see Türke/Dortschy, Der Zahlungsverkehr mit dem Ausland (3d ed., Deutscher Sparkassenverlag 1991), pp. 24, 65, 75.

transfer order does not maintain an account at the correspondent bank, that bank will further transfer the amount to him or send him a check drawn on the correspondent bank. The latter method is frequently used in the Anglo-American common law countries.

b) If the originator's German credit institution engages a foreign bank to transfer an amount in German marks but does not manage a loro account for that foreign bank, then there are two possibilities for providing cover. First, the German institution can engage another correspondent, for which it does manage a loro account, in the transfer process as an intermediary. If the foreign bank is the account manager, the German institution can have its account at the foreign bank debited in the foreign currency. This then requires an additional conversion of currency for the execution of the transfer because the foreign bank is obligated in accordance with the transfer order to credit or pay the transfer amount to the beneficiary in German marks.

3. *Transfer Order in Foreign Currency*

A transfer order to the originator's bank which is to be carried out in a foreign currency is executed in the following way. Within the framework of the giro relationship, the German credit institution issues to the foreign correspondent bank an instruction (Weisung) to make the transfer amount available to the beneficiary in the form of a credit or cash payment and to debit the nostro account in which the German bank holds a balance in the foreign currency at the account managing correspondent bank. The foreign currency department of the German institution, which as a rule is in charge of disposition over the foreign currency accounts at foreign correspondent banks, is responsible for maintaining sufficient balances in these accounts or procuring additional amounts as needed. Under the giro agreement, the German institution is obligated to its customer to maintain sufficient foreign currency holdings for the purpose of carrying out transfer orders denominated in foreign currency[20].

The transfer originator's account at his credit institution in Germany is debited in German marks for the amount equivalent to the transfer amount based on the daily selling rate for the respective foreign currency. If the customer holds a foreign currency account with the German bank and the international transfer is to be debited from this account, then no currency conversion is necessary prior to the debit.

---

[20] See Ohse, Bank-Archiv 1924, p. 299, 300.

4. Employment of Additional Correspondent Banks

If an international transfer order is to be carried out in a foreign currency in which the German credit institution does not maintain an account balance at any correspondent bank with which its has a giro agreement, then it becomes necessary to engage an additional correspondent bank which has funds available in the respective currency. An additional correspondent bank is also necessary when the transfer is directed to a beneficiary in a country in which the German institution does not maintain a relationship with a bank. The transmittal of the transfer order to the additional correspondent bank having the "execution currency" leads to a debit by that bank of the local currency account which it manages for the German institution.

It is also possible that the originator's domestic bank directly contacts a bank for this individual case which is located in the beneficiary's country or at least has funds available in the currency in which the transfer is to be carried out. The transfer order is then carried out on the basis of a special agency agreement. The credit institution which directly issues the transfer order must provide cover for the transfer amount at a common third correspondent bank.

The exact amount to be debited from the originator of the international transfer for the expenses involved can be calculated only when the invoices from the other correspondent bank (engaged to provide the necessary amount in the third foreign currency) have been received. Only then is it possible to calculate the value necessary in German marks for the purchase of the third currency.

The customer originating the international transfer will, as a rule, designate a specific bank and account number for the beneficiary. This specifying instruction (Weisung) is binding for the originator's bank. An optional clause with respect to the receiving bank can be stipulated[21]. The selection of the correspondent bank to be employed is within the professional discretion of the originator's bank unless in an exceptional case the customer provides a specific instruction on this point. Instructions can also be provided to the first correspondent bank with regard to further routing.

5. Technical Transmission Procedures

As mentioned above, the electronic communications system, S.W.I.F.T., has attained a prominent role in international transfers from a technical perspective[22]. For example, a transfer order from Germany for a beneficiary

[21] See the decision by the Bundesgerichtshof, BGHZ 98, p. 24.

[22] On the following, see Etzkorn, supra note 8, at 10 ff.; Türke/Dortschy, supra note 19, at 32 ff.

in a different country is entered in standardized form into the existing computer system and sent through the transmission network, i.e. through the regional processor in the respective country to the operating center responsible for the beneficiary's bank. There, the transfer order is "routed". This means that the transfer order is place in a data output queue according to the receiving address for the beneficiary's bank (without regard to the sending bank) based on the degree of urgency — three categories are available with different processing times. A special code for the contents and receiving bank as well as automatic processing controls serve to provide the best possible security in connection with the transmission. The transfer order transmitted through the S.W.I.F.T. network, when received by the beneficiary's bank, appears visually on a computer monitor or — as has become most common — is printed for use by the department managing accounts; this is the department responsible for crediting the beneficiary's account. S.W.I.F.T. messages are confirmed to the sending institution and, in addition, a properly issued transfer order is also examined by the beneficiary's bank by means of the "authenticator" placed at the end of the message by the sending bank; the authenticator is a code automatically generated by the system.

The volume of international transfers is impressive: in 1988 an average of 82,000 messages were sent through the S.W.I.F.T. system each working day in Germany alone. Worldwide, more than 1,560,000 transaction messages — movements of deposit money — are sent through the system every day!

Since the introduction of the S.W.I.F.T. system in 1977 only a small portion of international transfers are still technically carried out by means of letter, telephone, telegram, telex or internal systems. In the case of a transfer sent by mail (airmail) a standard, four-language form is used. There, the transfer order is secured by data delimiters and two signatures which are deposited with the foreign correspondent bank. In the case of transmission by telephone or telex, the order is secured against falsification by means of previously agreed key codes; telegram transfers are sometimes sent in coded form.

Transfer orders sent by mail, telephone or telex are not generally confirmed by the foreign bank. Whether these international transfers have been properly executed is apparent on examination of the account statements sent by the foreign correspondent bank. Comparison of these account statements with the corresponding accounts managed internally by the German institution make it possible to detect any errors.

IV. International Transfer Orders from Foreign Countries

1. Execution of the Transfer Order in Germany

When a transfer order is issued by a debtor in a foreign country to be carried out for the benefit of a payee in Germany, the corresponding procedures take place in the opposite direction as compared to the transfer to a foreign country as described above (part III)[23].

The German receiving bank, as a rule, credits the transfer amount from the foreign country to its customer as beneficiary only when the foreign correspondent bank has provided adequate cover to the German bank. The German bank receives either credit to its nostro account held at the foreign correspondent bank in foreign currency or, in the case of a payment in German marks, the German bank is authorized by means of an instruction to debit the loro account (balance or credit line) which it manages for the correspondent bank. In the case of a foreign currency order, it is also possible to obtain the transfer amount in cash at the foreign correspondent bank. The result of the receipt of cover in one of these ways is a claim to a credit based on the giro relationship for the domestic customer as the beneficiary (§§ 675, 667 case 2 BGB). If no instruction to the contrary is given, the credit institution can credit foreign currency amounts to the domestic customer in German marks (No. 4 (1) Bank AGB). The unconditional credit for the benefit of the designated payee completes the transfer. The claim based on the credit as an abstract promise or assumpsit (§§ 780, 781 BGB) by the receiving bank increases the balance or reduces the deficit within the scope of the current account management of the giro account. The cashless payment is thus complete. A positive balance gives the beneficiary the right to withdraw the transfer amount in cash.

If the designated beneficiary does not have a direct account relationship with the domestic credit institution which receives the transfer from the foreign country, the cross-border transfer order is, in compliance with instructions, further transmitted to the designated credit institution — if necessary through a state central bank, giro central bank or central credit association — as is common in domestic transfers. If the beneficiary's account is not apparent from the transfer order, he is directly notified of the receipt of the transfer order, and his directions are followed.

A transfer order from a foreign country can also be carried out by the domestic receiving bank by means of a check drawn with the transfer beneficiary as payee. But due to the related risks this is done, as a rule, only when the originator expressly so specifies. In addition to the risk of loss of the

[23] See also Polke, ZIP 1985, pp. 11, 12 ff.

check document, the beneficiary of a foreign currency check bears the risk that the check amount may be converted at an unfavorable sight rate. If the check is, in fact, issued by the receiving bank, it is most often drawn on the bank's own branch in Germany or on an different credit institution in Germany. Where a check is drawn for a comparatively large amount on a foreign bank, and the domestic receiving bank is to transmit the transfer amount in this way, the foreign bank receives an advice regarding the drawing of the check. This informs the foreign bank of the credit institution where cover will be provided. This is done primarily with respect to amounts in German marks for which the cover amount is credited in German marks to the correspondent bank's loro account. The payee is responsible for collecting the check; his credit institution usually credits the amount to his account "conditioned upon receipt".

2. Technical Transmission Procedures

The volume of transactions through the S.W.I.F.T. electronic communications network (described above under III. 5.) is equally relevant with respect to the transmission of cross-border transfer orders from foreign countries. The transfer order is transmitted through the European operating center in Brussels to the receiving bank in Germany, at which the message is displayed on a monitor or — most frequently — printed and prepared for further processing. The confirmation to the sending credit institution in the foreign country as well as the necessary verification that the transfer order was properly issued take place in the way already described (see above, part III. 5.). The situation is similar for transmission by mail, telephone or telex (see above, end of part III. 5.).

3. Compensation for the Execution of Transfer Orders from Foreign Countries

a) When a transfer order is received from a foreign country, the domestic receiving institution often charges the beneficiary a special fee (commission) for the execution of the order. The amount of the fee is calculated as a percentage of the transfer amount. Based on the current account settlement, the beneficiary then receives credit for the remainder of the transfer amount. The claim to the fee is derived from no. 14 (2) sent. 2 or 3 of the bank AGB (likewise No. 9 (3) sent. 1 and 3 of the savings bank AGB) in conjunction with § 315 BGB. A special fee for the execution of international transfers is justified by the higher costs connected with the establishment and maintenance of giro relationships with foreign correspondent banks. It is also not unfair to tie the amount of the fee to a percentage of the transfer amount. The beneficiary who receives a larger amount of money through a foreign transfer should also bear a greater portion of the special costs of cashless foreign transfers[24].

b) Canaris[25] views as "extremely controversial" the fact that the fee "is charged to the beneficiary and not the originator". As a rule, the originator as debtor is required to transmit money to the beneficiary/creditor at the debtor's cost (§ 270 (1) BGB). Therefore, the beneficiary could demand reimbursement from the originator for the fee charged and withheld by his credit institution. This would make a new foreign transfer necessary — again with withholding of a fee — and so on. Therefore, permitting the domestic receiving bank to charge the fee to the beneficiary contradicts the needs of an efficient transfer procedure because it "generates superfluous payment transactions". This charge also contradicts "the implied will of the originator" and violates the rule of "strict compliance with the order" because the receiving bank "credits an amount less than the amount transferred by the originator". Therefore, only charging the originator and "not the beneficiary" would be compatible with § 315 BGB (equity). Finally, the originator is in control of the transfer routing and could choose the bank which carries out the foreign transfer for the lowest price, "while the beneficiary [must] accept the commission charge without any alternative".

Upon close examination, this approach is unacceptable. At least a beneficiary who expects a cashless payment from a foreign country within the scope of his business or profession knows from experience that the special fee will be charged by the domestic bank for execution of the transfer order and will include these costs in his price calculation in advance. It is therefore quite improbable in international business transactions that charging such a fee to the beneficiary will generate "superfluous transfers" in the form of new claims for reimbursement of steadily declining fees for execution of the previous foreign transfers. Therefore, the fee charged to the payee certainly does not stand in the way of "an efficient transfer system". Deduction of the fee by the receiving bank also does not violate the rule of strict compliance with the order. Instead, the contractual running account management of the customer's giro account permits a (partial) set-off of the customer's claim against the receiving bank for a credit with the bank's fee claim against the customer. This results from the giro relationship between the beneficiary and his credit institution. The execution of the transfer in accordance with instructions, which the receiving bank owes to the prior credit institution, has nothing to do with the set-off in the giro relationship with the receiving

[24] Regarding banking practice and the amount of the fees, see Frankfurter Allgemeine Zeitung (kj.) no. 38 of Feb. 14, 1991, p. 24; similar, K.-P. Schmidt, supra note 1.

[25] Canaris, Bankvertragsrecht, v. 1 (3d ed. 1988), at margin no. 461.

bank's own customer. It is certainly unclear why the lack of an "alternative" for the beneficiary regarding the fee should be decisive. Precisely the beneficiary chooses the domestic bank and establishes a giro relationship with that bank which includes foreign payment transactions. If the arrangement for a special fee for the processing of payment receipts from foreign countries does not appear reasonable to him, he can negotiate this point with his bank or — as an "alternative" — open a giro account with a different credit institution.

c) If the intermediary bank antecedent to the receiving bank has already deducted a fee from the transfer amount credited to it as cover, this is not consistent with the instruction under the giro agreement which it received from the originator's bank or a different antecedent bank. The receiving bank has a right under its giro relationship with its antecedent bank to credit for the full amount designated by the originator (§§ 675, 667 case 1 BGB). In its giro relationship with its customer as beneficiary, the receiving bank is obligated to assert its right to delivery of the full amount against the antecedent bank. But under the "prevailing view"[26] the receiving bank has the right to be released from this obligation by assigning the claim against the intermediary bank to the customer (§ 398 BGB).

V. Revocation of an International Transfer Order

Under German law, the revocation of a transfer order is to be classified as a counterinstruction to the agent by the originating customer i.e. the principal (§ 675, 665 BGB)[27]. This counterinstruction is intended to cause the originator's credit institution not to carry out the instruction in the original transfer order, i.e. not to transmit the cashless payment in question. It makes sense that such a counterinstruction in the framework of the giro relationship with the originator's credit institution can be complied with only as long as the original instruction has not yet been executed. The issue is therefore what act by the originator's credit institution constitutes compliance with the instructions given it under the giro agreement. Here, the unanimous view[28] is that the originator's credit institution in the case of an external transfer — where the beneficiary has a giro account with a different institution — has only to transmit the order in its own name for the customer's account to a diligently selected credit institution and to provide that institution with cover

[26] Id. with cites to case decisions by municipal courts (WM 1973, p. 291; WM 1979, p. 175; WM 1981, p. 1027).

[27] See Hadding/Häuser, ZHR 145 (1981), pp. 138, 147f.; BGHZ 103, p. 143, 146. See also Hadding/Häuser, WM 1988, p. 1149, 1153.

[28] See BGH WM 1991, p. 797, 798.

in the form of a credit in the amount of the transfer. The originator's bank need therefore no longer comply with a revocation if it has already transmitted the international transfer order to a domestic intermediary bank or a foreign correspondent bank and has provided the necessary cover. A revocation must be complied with if the transfer order has not yet been given to another institution or cover has not yet been provided. This is also the case if the transfer order has only been transmitted to a branch office in a foreign country.

If the originator's credit institution has already transmitted the international transfer order, it is obligated under the giro agreement only to transmit the revocation to the next credit institution, for example to the foreign correspondent bank. The revocation must, as a rule, follow the same chain of institutions as the transfer order. The decisive question is whether the revocation reaches the beneficiary's credit institution before the beneficiary has acquired a claim based on an unconditional credit given by his bank. When this credit has been given, the transmittal of the cashless payment in compliance with the originator's instructions has been completed, so that a revocation of the original transfer order "misses the mark"[29]. The success of a revocation which proceeds along the "chain" of credit institutions is usually dependent upon whether the credit institutions use faster means of communication for the revocation than for the preceding transfer order. The use of electronic transmission of messages will practically eliminate the possibility of having the revocation catch up with the original order. It is also not usually easily provable that the international transfer order had not yet been completed by means of credit to the beneficiary at the time when the revocation reached the receiving bank. A so-called direct revocation to a foreign receiving bank which does not have a giro relationship with the originator's bank is not legally binding for the receiving bank as a directly transmitted counterinstruction by the originator without a special agreement[30] because it has no statutory basis. A prior notice (avis) by the originator's credit institution directly to the receiving bank with regard to the prospective receipt of payment, for example in the form of delivery of a copy of the giro contract instruction to an intermediary bank, does not establish a right or obligation on the part of the receiving bank to provide the beneficiary with a corresponding credit; this is true even if the copy contains a specific value date[31]. So far no commercial custom has been established to

[29] See BGHZ 103, p. 143, 146; Etzkorn, supra note 8, at 56 ff., 73 ff., 96 ff. Polke views the time at which the beneficiary receives a "claim to the issuance of the credit" as determinative, ZIP 1985, p. 11, 14.

[30] See Landgericht Freiburg i. Br., WM 1976, p. 142 = NJW 1976, p. 333; NJW 1978, p. 1265.

[31] See OLG Düsseldorf WM 1979, p. 1272.

the effect that the delivery of such a preliminary notice is to be viewed as a legally binding order to enter into an agency agreement for the transmittal of a cashless payment. An (uncontradicted) receipt of the preliminary notice by the receiving bank thus does not establish a right on the part of the designated beneficiary to a credit. Final execution of the international transfer order by means of an unconditional credit is lacking. Whether a revocation must be complied with by the receiving bank is therefore independent of the receipt of a preliminary notice of a transfer.

VI. Execution of International Transfer Orders by the German Federal Bank

If a domestic credit institution which has received a cross-border transfer order does not have a giro relationship with a foreign correspondent bank, or if for any reason it does not wish to engage the correspondent bank, it has the possibility of transmitting the transfer order through the Deutsche Bundesbank, assuming that the domestic institution has a giro account at the Deutsche Bundesbank (see part XI G No. 1 of the General Business Conditions of the Deutsche Bundesbank). The details of the involvement of the Deutsche Bundesbank are stipulated in part XI G No. 2 ff. of these General Business Conditions. The Deutsche Bundesbank transmits the transfer order to the correspondent bank only when it has received the necessary cover (No. 9); it thus does not accept any risk. The Bank does not agree to any time limits (No. 11). A revocation of the transfer order is complied with only if the transfer order has not yet been further transmitted; a later revocation is issued only to the same institution to which the transfer order had been transmitted (No. 12). In addition, the Deutsche Bundesbank reserves the right to execute a written payment order by sending a check directly to the beneficiary or his credit institution (No. 13).

The International Credit Transfer and the Underlying Obligation

By Ulrich Huber, Bonn*

Contents

---

* Translated by Dr. Frances Dielmann, Frankfurt/M.

I. Payment by Credit Transfer under German Law

1. The Provisions of §§ 269, 270 German Civil Code

Payments by bank credit transfer are governed under German law by §§ 269 and 270 of the German Civil Code [BGB]. In the case of payment of the purchase price based on international sales contracts, the United Nations Convention on Contracts for the International Sale of Goods [CISG] supersedes these German provisions[1]; this Convention is applicable when the parties to the sales contract have their places of business in differing member states where the Convention is in effect (Art. 1 (1) (a) CISG).[2] Except in this special case, the applicability of §§ 269 and 270 BGB to international payment transactions depends on whether German law is the "proper law of the contract"; before German courts this issue is decided in

[1] CISG = United Nations Convention on Contracts for the International Sale of Goods of April 11, 1980. In effect for the Federal Republic of Germany based on the law of July 5, 1989 (BGBl. II, p. 586, of Jan. 1, 1991); see also the proclamation of Oct. 23, 1990 (BGBl. II, p. 1477). It thereby supercedes the prior uniform sales law, namely the Uniform Law on the International Sale of Goods of July 17, 1973 (BGBl. I, p. 856), which took effect on April 16, 1974 (BGBl. II, p. 146).

[2] In addition to Germany, the contracting states (as of Jan. 1, 1992) are Argentina, Australia, Austria, Bulgaria, Chile, China, Czechoslovakia, Denmark, Egypt, Finland, France, Hungary, Iraq, Italy, Lesotho, Mexico, the Netherlands, Norway, the former Soviet Union, Sweden, Switzerland, Syria, the Ukraine, the United States of America, Yugoslavia, and Zambia; see BGBl. 1990 II, p. 1477, 1480 and BGBl. 1991 II, p. 675. Canada, Guinea and Rumania will also be added in 1992; see Karollus, UN-Kaufrecht (1991), p. 9 f. The uniform sales law is also applicable when the parties to the sales contract do not have their places of business in different member states but in two different states and the applicable international conflict of laws rules refer the case to the law of a member state (Art. (1) b CISG). One example is where the seller's place of business is in Germany and the buyer's place of business is in the non-member state Great Britain — under Art. 28 (1) of the Introductory Law to the German Civil Code [EGBGB], German law applies.

accordance with Art. 27 and Art. 28 of the Introductory Law of the German Civil Code [EGBGB].[3] The principle of the "characteristic performance" (Art. 28 (2) EGBGB) generally leads to the result that German substantive law is primarily applied when the creditor has his business residence in Germany, and foreign law is primarily applied when the debtor has his business residence in Germany.

Under §§ 269 and 270 BGB, a money debt is a "qualifizierte Schickschuld" (limited obligation to send payment)[4], i.e. an obligation to be performed at the debtor's place of business. The debtor must "convey" the money to the creditor, i.e. must send the money to him. The debtor bears the costs and the risk of loss underway (§ 270 (1) BGB). The place of performance for the debtor's obligation is, however, the debtor's (business) residence (§ 270 (4) in conjunction with § 269 (1), (2) BGB). For the timely fulfillment of the obligation, it is therefore sufficient that the debtor send the payment by the stipulated payment date.[5] He is not required to send the money in such a way that, under normal circumstances, it will be received by the creditor prior to the expiration of the payment period. If the debtor instructs a third party to transmit the money to the creditor, the third party is not deemed to be his "special agent" within the meaning of § 278 BGB ("Erfüllungsgehilfe" — a person employed in the performance of an obligation, for whom the debtor is fully responsible).[6] Thus, if the debtor is required to make payment to a creditor by Dec. 31, it is sufficient that he put the money into a stamped

[3] The new Private International Law Act of July 25, 1986 (BGBl. I, p. 1142) which entered into effect on Sept. 1, 1986.

[4] See v. Caemmerer, in: Festschrift für Mann, p. 3, 8 = Gesammelte Schriften III, p. 108, 113 ff.; Heck, Schuldrecht, p. 24; Enneccerus-Lehmann, at § 23 I 3; Esser-Schmidt, at § 15 I 2; Fikentscher, Schuldrecht, at § 35 III 3 c; Larenz, Schuldrecht, v. I, at § 14 IV c; Gernhuber, Erfüllung, at § 2 VII 1, 2; Staudinger-Selb, at § 270 BGB margin no. 1; Münch-Komm-Keller, at § 270 BGB margin no. 1; Soergel-Wolf, at § 270 BGB margin no. 1. See generally, Staub, (3d/4th ed., 1896) at Art. 325 ADHGB, comment 7; Oertmann, at § 270 BGB, comment 3; Planck-Siber, (4th ed. 1914) at § 270 BGB, comment 1. The payment of insurance premiums is governed by the special provision in § 36 of the Insurance Contract Act [VVG], which differs from §§ 269, 270 BGB only in that the place of payment is the current residence of the debtor and not his residence at the time the contract was concluded. Under § 36 VVG, the premium debt is also understood to be a "qualified sending obligation"; see Prölss-Martin, at § 35 VVG, comment 6 B.

[5] RGZ 78, p. 137, 140; RGZ 99, p. 257 f.; BGH, NJW 1969, p. 875, 876. Now undisputed; see v. Caemmerer, Enneccerus-Lehmann, Esser-Schmidt, Fikentscher, and Larenz, supra note 4; Gernhuber, Erfüllung, at § 2 VII 4; Staudinger-Selb, at § 270 BGB, margin no. 11; MünchKomm-Keller, at § 270 BGB, margin no. 15 ff.; Soergel-Wolf, at § 270 BGB, margin no. 17; Palandt-Heinrichs, at § 270 BGB, margin no. 6; Prölss-Martin, supra note 4.

[6] Planck-Siber, at § 270 BGB, comment 1; v. Caemmerer, Festschrift für Mann, p. 3, 13 = Gesammelte Schriften III, p. 108, 118; MünchKomm-Keller, at § 270 BGB, margin no. 16; Soergel-Wolf, at § 270 BGB, margin no. 17; Palandt-Heinrichs, at § 270 BGB, margin no. 6; see also Soergel-Huber, at § 433 BGB, margin no. 205.

envelope on Dec. 31 and place it in the mail. He bears the risk that the envelope might be lost underway but not the risk that the delivery by the postal service might be delayed. The rule for resolving the issue of when the unexplained absence of the money shifts from "delay" to "loss" is that a loss may be presumed when the usual time for transmittal has been exceeded to an extent where the arrival of the money can no longer be expected.[7] The debtor must then arrange for a new payment. If the first payment is then received by the creditor after the second payment has been made, the debtor can claim restitution of this amount because it is without legal basis.

2. *Consequences for Bank Credit Transfer: Prevailing View*

According to the prevailing view, if the creditor agrees to payment by bank credit transfer[8] this transfer is viewed under the law in the same way as a cash payment. Under § 270 (1) BGB, the debtor bears the costs of the transfer and the risk that the transfer "may break down".[9] Under § 270 (4) in conjunction with § 269 (1) BGB, the place of performance remains the

[7] V. Caemmerer, Festschrift für Mann, p. 3, 10 = Gesammelte Schriften III, p. 108, 115: he must wait only a time "within the scope of normal irregularities of postal and banking operations". See also Soergel-Huber, at § 433 BGB, margin no. 195.

[8] See v. Caemmerer, Festschrift für Mann, p. 3, 12 f. = Gesammelte Schriften III, p. 108, 117 f. Accord, Schönle, Festschrift für Werner, pp. 817, 821, 824 f., n. 17; RGRK-Nastelski, at § 270 BGB, comment 10 (11th ed. 1960); Soergel-Reimer-Schmidt, at § 270 BGB, margin no. 3 (10th ed., 1967); Staudinger-Selb, at § 269 BGB, margin no. 19; MünchKomm-Keller, at § 270 BGB, margin no. 19; Prölss-Martin, at § 35 VVG, comment 6 B b; Jauernig-Vollkommer, at § 270 BGB, comment 3 b; Palandt-Heinrichs, at § 270 BGB, margin no. 7. See also Soergel-Huber, at § 433 BGB, margin no. 205.

[9] This is also true, as a rule for the frequently analyzed bank transfers which "broke down" at the end of the war. They could not be executed because following receipt of the transfer order the Soviet military government froze the debtor's account and closed the debtor's bank; see Meyer-Cording, Recht der Banküberweisung, p. 132 f. This was one — extreme — textbook case of allocation of risk under § 270 BGB. In the case of a sales shipment, the party which under law (§ 447 BGB) or contract bears the transport risk is faced with the possibility that the goods can be destroyed or confiscated in shipment by enemy troops; see Soergel-Huber, at § 447 BGB, margin no. 58, 66. In general, of course, the transfers which broke down involved the very different issue of whether bank customers which prior to the collapse had arranged for transfers from "East" accounts to "West" accounts could demand credit and payment from the bank in the West — this despite the fact that the bank in the West could no longer obtain payment based on the credit which had been posted for its benefit by the bank in the East due to the account freeze and bank closing; it was thus an issue of risk allocation between the beneficiary's bank and the beneficiary. See Meyer-Cording, at 58 f., 64 ff. (transfer between two branches of the same bank), 77 ff. (transfer between separate banks). A third problem is whether in "West-East" transfers the debtor (customer of the bank in the West) was still able to revoke the transfer with binding effect for his bank if the beneficiary's bank had already received credit for the cover but had not credited the account of the beneficiary; see Meyer-Cording, at 95 ff.

debtor's residence. The debtor's obligation is to arrange for the transfer. The bank must receive a correct and valid transfer order.[10] In addition, the necessary requirements must be met in the relationship between the debtor and the originator's bank such that the bank is then obligated to carry out the order. This means that the debtor must either have money on deposit or have credit with the bank; the transfer order should not be allowed to fail or be delayed due to insufficiency of covering funds. If these requirements are fulfilled, the debtor has done what he is required to do.[11] The payment date is met if the transfer order and the covering funds are present by that date. The debtor is not liable for mistakes made by the originator's bank, by intermediary banks employed by the originator's bank, or by a clearinghouse. Because the debtor has done his part by submitting the proper order, i.e. completed his act of performance, these other parties are not his "special agents" within the meaning of § 278 EGBGB.[12]

3. Diverging Views

This point is, however, disputed in the legal literature. Various methods are used to attempt to broaden the debtor's area of responsibility and to make him liable for the banks involved in the transfer.

— 1. Some authors assert that a transaction equivalent to the "sending" of money is not present until the debtor's bank has debited the transfer amount from debtor's account.[13] The debtor would thus be liable for a mistake by the bank managing his account in this first phase of the

[10] See BGH, NJW 1969, p. 875 and the reference supra note 8. The fact that the debtor sends the order to his bank by letter is not sufficient: contra, Enneccerus-Lehmann, at § 23 I 3.

[11] See the references supra note 8. Accord, the BFH, WM 1986, p. 631 (on the issue of whether upon receipt of the transfer order at the end of one year and execution in the new year the payment constitutes an expense in the old or the new year); OLG Hamburg, BB 1959, p. 507; OLG Celle, MDR 1969, p. 1007; OLG Hamm, VersR 1984, p. 174; OLG Düsseldorf, DB 1984, p. 2686 = WM 1985, p. 585; OLG Cologne, in NJW-RR 1990, p. 284. Contradictory, Soergel-Wolf, at § 270 BGB, margin no. 18.

[12] See RG, LZ 1926, p. 45, 46 (obiter dictum); OLG Hamburg, BB 1959, p. 507; v. Caemmerer, Festschrift für Mann, p. 3, 13 = Gesammelte Schriften III, p. 108, 118; Erman-Battes, at § 278 BGB, margin no. 28; Palandt-Heinrichs, at § 270 BGB, margin no. 6; Soergel-Huber, at § 433 BGB, margin no. 205.

[13] See Schoele, Das Recht der Überweisung, 1937, p. 257; Meyer-Cording, Das Recht der Banküberweisung, p. 136; Schönle, Bank- und Börsenrecht, at § 32 I (differing view by the same author, supra note 8); Esser-Schmidt, at § 15 I 2. — Following the BGH decision in WM 1971, p. 110 = NJW 1971, p. 380, the act of performance is completed "at the latest" when the debit is made from the debtor's account; similar, BGH, WM 1964, p. 113 = NJW 1964, p. 499; BayObLG, in ZfS 1986, p. 317; Erman-Sirp, at § 270 BGB, margin no. 2. Expressly opposed to the additional requirement that the account have been debited: BFH, WM 1986, p. 631; OLG Hamburg, BB 1959, p. 507; OLG Celle, MDR 1969, p. 1007.

transfer. As justification for this requirement that the amount must have been debited, it is asserted that this is the only objective means of determining whether the order was covered.[14]

— 2. Others, such as Hefermehl and Larenz, go further and demand that the debtor's bank have transmitted the order to the beneficiary's bank or to an intermediary bank or clearinghouse.[15] The consequence here would be that the debtor would be fully liable for delays within the business operations of the bank managing his account and that if he wishes to meet the payment date he would have to take the necessary bank processing time into account. The reason given for this view is that the bank where the debtor maintains his account still works "within the sphere" of the debtor.[16]

— 3. Canaris goes even a step beyond that view. He would have the debtor be liable for all banks and clearinghouses which the debtor's bank employs in the transmittal of the transfer, deeming these all to be "special agents" of the debtor.[17] The debtor's act of performance would thus not be completed until the beneficiary's bank had the transferred funds at its disposal. This view is based on the idea that the debtor's bank works "in the sphere" of the debtor when it transmits the transfer to the beneficiary's bank and that, therefore, when it engages a third party to carry out the transmittal to the beneficiary's bank, this third party must also be deemed to be working within the "sphere" of the debtor. Canaris is then consistent in demanding from the debtor that he initiate the transfer early enough that, in the normal course of business, the transfer will be received by the beneficiary's bank by the payment date; but even if the debtor does this, he would still be liable for a delay which is the fault of one of the instructed banks.[18]

---

[14] See Schoele, supra note 13.

[15] See Schlegelberger-Hefermehl, at § 365 HGB Anh., margin no. 197; Larenz, SchuldR I, at § 14 IV c; Gernhuber, Erfüllung, at § 2 VII 4 b, p. 47 f.; Staudinger-Karsten Schmidt, at margin no. C 25 preceding § 244 BGB. Baumbach-Duden-Hopt, HGB, Appendix 7, at comment III 4 C; Heymann-Horn, at § 372 HGB, appendix III, margin no. 34. Similar approach, Canaris, Bankvertragsrecht, at margin no. 481 (who then derives even more extensive consequences), See also (contradictory) Soergel-Wolf, at § 270 BGB, margin no. 18. Under this view, special rules apply for internal bank transfers, but these are not relevant in international transfers.

[16] See Gernhuber, Staudinger-Karsten Schmidt, Heymann-Horn, Canaris, Soergel-Wolf, supra note 15.

[17] Canaris, supra note 15, margin no. 481.

[18] Canaris, supra note 15, margin no. 480, 481. This contradicts the prevailing view; see the references supra notes 8, 11, 13, 15. Canaris corrects the result by having the receipt of the correct transfer order by the first receiving bank be sufficient, after all, in cases where non-compliance with the payment time limit would lead to serious legal problems for the debtor (non-compliance with a grace period, loss of insurance coverage). This result is consistent with the prevailing view (supra notes 8, 11) but constitutes a contradiction with Canaris' approach.

— The Reichsgericht went the furthest in requiring that the beneficiary's bank must have credited the funds to the beneficiary.[19] The reason set forth for this decision was that the order could be canceled by the debtor up until the time when the amount was credited by the creditor's bank.

The Federal Supreme Court has, on the contrary, clarified that the debiting of the amount from the debtor's account must, in any case, be sufficient for a timely payment and has merely left open the question of whether the receipt of the transfer order may already be sufficient without regard to the debit.[20]

4. Analysis

All of these diverging views should rejected. The firm basis for deciding the issue is § 270 (4) BGB : monetary debts are "Schickschulden" (obligations to send payment), not "Bringschulden" (obligations to be performed at the creditor's (business) residence), regardless of whether they are paid in cash or not. The results are the following:

a) No Requirement that the Transfer Be Received by the Beneficiary's Bank

Those views which would require that the transfer be received by the creditor's bank or, even more extremely, that the amount be credited to the beneficiary are not consistent with § 270 (4) BGB. It is true, without doubt, that the debtor's performance obligation is not discharged until the money has been credited to the creditor's account. But § 270 (4) BGB assumes that the transmittal procedure which leads to this completion of performance no longer belongs, as such, to the range of the debtor's duties but instead that the debtor carries out the performance required of him by initiating this transmittal procedure. The debtor's liability for the intermediary banks instructed to carry out the transfer[21] is not consistent; the practical result

[19] See RGZ 82, pp. 95, 96 f. Different substantively, RG, LZ 1926, p. 45, 46 (on § 278 BGB). The decision in RGZ 78, p. 137, which is frequently cited but also differs, does not involve the case of a bank transfer but instead a payment by check (mailing is sufficient for compliance with time limit). The decision in RGZ 105, p. 266 involves a special case in that the creditor there set an extension period with the stipulation that he must receive the money within this period. See below part I. 6. at note 43. The decision in RGZ 82, p. 95, involving the timeliness of a pre-payment of fees for a court appeal, may have been a mere anomaly; the court obviously assumed that cash payment to the court office was the usual case and deemed receipt in the account to be equivalent.

[20] See BGH, WM 1964, p. 113 = NJW 1964, p. 499; BGH, WM 1971, p. 110 = NJW 1971, p. 380.

[21] As called for by Canaris, supra notes 17, 18.

would be a transformation of the payment debt into a "Bringschuld".[22] The fact that the debtor can cancel the transfer order as long as the beneficiary's bank has not yet credited the funds[23] is immaterial.[24] Irrevocability is not a prerequisite for the completion of the debtor's act of performance. In the case of a sales shipment, the seller completes his act of performance by handing the goods over to a carrier, although under § 433 of the German Commercial Code (HGB) and the relevant special provisions of transport law he still has the right to instruct the carrier to retain the goods, to return them, or to deliver them to a different recipient. A different rule governs the act of performance by the buyer who transfers the purchase amount to the seller.

b) No Liability by the Originator for the Originator's Bank

It is, therefore, also not correct to make the debtor's liability and the timeliness of the payment dependent upon whether the bank where the debtor maintains his account conveys the transfer order — whether directly to the beneficiary's bank or to an intermediary bank. The stated justification that the originator's bank acts "within the sphere" of the debtor[25] has more the character of a poetic metaphor than of a legal argument. The decisive question is whether the debtor's "own" bank is to be viewed as his "special agent" within the meaning of § 278 BGB, and not in which "sphere" this bank acts.[26]

The bank would be the debtor's "special agent" only if the bank had to carry out an act which is among the debtor's acts of performance. But one can scarcely reconstruct the reasoning by which the transmittal of a transfer order by a bank is viewed as being one of the duties which the debtor should "actually" fulfill himself. If the debtor places the money in an envelope and drops it into a mailbox, he has done what he has to do; the postman who empties the mailbox is not the debtor's "special agent". If the debtor transfers the money by postal transfer and pays the covering funds in cash at the

---

[22] See also Soergel-Huber, at § 433 BGB, margin no. 205 n. 20.

[23] See RGZ 82, p. 95, 97; RGZ 107, p. 136, 139; BGH, WM 1984, p. 986 = NJW 1984, p. 2816; BGHZ 103, p. 143, 145; Meyer-Cording, Das Recht der Banküberweisung, pp. 91 ff.; Schlegelberger-Hefermehl, at § 365 HGB appendix, margin no. 25 ff.; Hadding/Häuser, ZHR 145, p. 138, 147 ff.; Canaris, supra note 15, at margin no. 352 ff.; Baumbach-Duden-Hopt, HGB, appendix 7, III 2 d; Heymann-Horn, at § 372 HGB appendix III, margin no. 7 f.

[24] BGH, WM 1964, p. 113 = NJW 1964, p. 499; see also Canarais, supra note 15, at margin no. 482.

[25] See Gernhuber, Staudinger-Karsten Schmidt, Heymann-Horn, Canaris, Soergel-Wolf, supra note 15.

[26] v. Caemmerer, supra note 4; see also Soergel-Huber, at § 433, margin no. 205.

closest post office, he has carried out his act of performance. What happens to the money and the transfer form behind the counter at the post office is not his responsibility. If he submits a single payment order to a bank instead of the post office, instructing payment to the creditor's account, and if he pays the covering funds in cash at the bank window, the situation is the same. The fact that the debtor does not submit a single payment order but instead has a standing account at the bank is irrelevant for the applicability of § 278 BGB.[27] In the case of a sales shipment, it is also recognized that the carrier whom the seller instructs to transport the goods to the purchaser is not the "special agent" of the seller.[28] Correctly, no one has had the idea that this result could change merely because the seller has a standing business relationship and running accounts with the carrier.

c) Irrelevance of Debiting the Debtor's Account

Finally, it is not clear why the "debit" of the transfer amount from the debtor's account should represent an act of performance by the debtor.[29] This act is certainly not among the duties which are actually the responsibility of the debtor; it involves only the accounting relationship between the debtor and his bank and does not affect the creditor.

d) The Practical Point of View

By contrast, a practical aspect which is of substantial significance supports the prevailing view.[30] The actual preference for the designation of the money debt as a limited "Schickschuld" in § 270 (4) BGB is based with respect to substantive law on the fact that clear relationships should be created.[31] The

---

[27] This has consistently been accepted in case decisions in a different context. If, for example, the seller makes an agreement with the buyer that the buyer is to open a letter of credit at the seller's bank, the seller's bank acts in this situation as the "servant" of the buyer; the fact that the seller maintains a standing business relationship with this bank does not make it the "servant" of the seller. See RGZ 105, p. 32, 34; see also RG, JW 1921, p. 1312; RGZ 103, pp. 376, 379 f.

[28] See Soergel-Huber, at § 447 BGB, margin no. 64 with additional references.

[29] See the references supra note 13.

[30] See supra notes 8, 11.

[31] For the historical legislators, the determinative aspect was not this one but instead that of procedural law: they did not want to structure the money obligation as a pure "bringing obligation"; they wished to prevent having jurisdiction for a suit by the creditor be established in the courts at the creditor's residence based on his residence as the place of performance (§ 29 German Code of Civil Procedure [ZPO]. See Nußbaum, Das Geld in Theorie und Praxis, pp. 73 ff.; v. Caemmerer, Festschrift für Mann p. 3, 6 = Gesammelte

debtor knows precisely what he has to do in order to pay the money debt on time: he must send the money on time. This is an act which he has under his control and for which he can secure proof. One should not sacrifice this advantage in the case of the bank credit transfer without pressing reasons.[32] The debtor, who must pay by Dec. 31 at the latest, can find out whether and at what times the banks will be open. If he submits the transfer order on Dec. 31 and receives a carbon copy stamped with the date by the bank, he has a straightforward item of evidence. It cannot be his responsibility to see that the bank debits his account on Dec. 31 and transmits the order, and he should not be required to obtain any proof of these acts from the bank. This simple rule should be retained.

It is interesting that some of the authors who would require the further transmittal of the transfer order for timely performance attempt, for reasons of fairness, to correct the result in cases where a particular hardship for the debtor is created (in particular where the debtor loses insurance coverage due to late payment of an insurance premium).[33] This means that they assert a theory which in their own — correct — estimation is not suitable under fire. It would be better to abandon such a theory from the beginning.

5. Failure and Insolvency of the Beneficiary's Bank

Despite all the differences of opinion concerning the precise time of the payment by means of bank transfer, there is agreement on at least one point. The debtor's risk definitely ends as soon as the properly transferred money is available to the beneficiary's bank.[34] The completion of the performance still requires the crediting of the funds. If, however, the funds are not credited even though the legal requirements for the credit are met, this cannot work to

---

Schriften III, p. 108, 111. It has become clear in practice (especially in the cases of insurance premium payments where mere seconds can determine whether coverage exists) how important the currently applicable law is from a substantive perspective. In my opinion, this rule is superior from a policy perspective to the foreign law rules (and Art. 57 CISG) which structure the money obligation as a "bringing obligation".

[32] See Soergel-Huber, at § 433 BGB, margin no. 195, 205 and the reference by v. Caemmerer (Festschrift für Mann p. 3, 12 = Gesammelte Schriften III, p. 108, 117) to the "problems of investigation and proof" which are the result of the opposing views.

[33] See Canaris, supra note 15, at margin no. 480a, 481; Heymann-Horn, at § 372 HGB appendix III, margin no. 35. Particularly the analysis of individual cases by Canaris demonstrates the degree of legal uncertainty and overtaxing of courts which result if no fixed, simple rules are applied in this area.

[34] See v. Caemmerer, Festschrift für Mann, p. 3, 14 = Gesammelte Schriften III, p. 108, 119; Schlegelberger-Hefermehl, at § 365 HGB appendix, margin no. 109; Staudinger-Selb, at § 270 BGB, margin no. 8; Staudinger-Karsten Schmidt, at margin no. C 26 preceding § 244 BGB; Canaris, supra note 15, at margin no. 478.

the disadvantage of the debtor. Delays in crediting by the beneficiary's bank must work against the creditor. This is recognized even by those authors who would have the debtor be liable for delays caused by the originator's bank and the intermediary banks.[35]

This has consequences particularly when the beneficiary's bank becomes insolvent after receiving the transferred amount and before it is credited. This case does not fit the transmittal risk which, in accordance with § 270 (1) BGB, must be borne by the debtor.[36] Such a categorization would contradict the purpose of that provision. The creditor who designates the bank to the debtor as being authorized to receive payment uses the bank as his "special agent" for the acceptance of the performance. If the bank does not deliver the money which it receives for the creditor, this falls within the creditor's scope of risk. The result is the same, for example, as in a long-distance purchase in which the seller contractually accepts the transport risk, and the buyer informs the seller that a warehouse or forwarding agent is authorized to receive the goods. Upon delivery to the warehouse or forwarding agent, the risk shifts to the buyer in accordance with § 446 BGB.[37] In the case of money sent at the buyer's risk by the bank instructed by the seller, the result is the same. If, on the other hand, the transfer fails due to the insolvency of the bank instructed by the debtor or an intermediary bank, this is within the debtor's risk; he must then arrange for a new transfer. This no longer involves a "delay" but instead a "loss" of the transferred money.

6. *Legal Situation where an Extension of Time Is Granted*

Where the debtor is in default on a monetary debt under a bilateral contract, and the creditor, in accordance with § 326 BGB, grants an extension of time, the new payment date is met when the debtor undertakes the "act of performance" in a timely manner.[38] It is sufficient that he arrange for the credit transfer prior to the expiration of the extension period.[39] Specifically, as discussed above[40], the transfer order must be received on time by the originator's bank and the order must be covered by adequate funds. In

[35] Canaris, supra note 33; see also RGZ 105, p. 266, 269.

[36] See Schlegelberger-Hefermehl, Staudinger-Selb, Staudinger-Karsten Schmidt, Canaris, supra note 34. Special rules, which are not relevant in international transactions, apply to internal bank transfers.

[37] See Soergel-Huber, at § 446 BGB, margin no. 42.

[38] A leasing case on sales shipments is BGHZ 12, p. 267, 269.

[39] Staudinger-Otto, at § 326 BGB, margin no. 106; MünchKomm-Emmerich, at § 326 BGB, margin no. 52; Soergel-Wiedemann, at § 326 BGB, margin no. 50. In accord despite his differing initial approach is Canaris, supra note 15, at margin no. 480a, 481.

[40] See above at I 2-4.

an older decision, the Bundesgerichtshof held that the debtor must, in addition, if he paid just before the end of the extension period, waive his right to cancel the transfer and must instruct the originator's bank to waive its cancellation rights with respect to the beneficiary's bank.[41] This restriction, which practically reverses the principle, cannot be justified.[42] The debtor also may not be required to give the transferor bank special notice of the urgency of the transaction.[43] Because, as is well-known, "money matters are serious business", credit transfers are always urgent, and such notice would only state the obvious. The creditor who agrees to payment by bank transfer must accept the fact that between the sending of the transfer and the free availability of the funds in his own account, a certain amount of time will pass; the creditor may not require from the debtor that the debtor attempt to change this system. Credit transfers are standardized, high-volume transactions with their own rules, e.g. the credit transfer order is carried out in a standard form and not based on individual agreements between the debtor and his bank. The act of performance which the debtor must carry out prior to expiration of the time limit is only this standard form; the creditor is not entitled to a different form.

According to the prevailing view, the creditor may also set the extension of time in such a way that he should receive the money prior to expiration of the time limit.[44] In this case, the extension is "reasonable" only if the normal time necessary for the transfer is taken into consideration. The setting of the time limit must be interpreted to mean that the debtor complies with the time limit only if he gives instructions for the transfer early enough that under normal conditions the money will be received by the creditor prior to expiration of the time limit.[45] The creditor cannot set the time limit for the actual receipt of the funds — i.e. stipulate that the time limit is complied with only if the money is, in fact, received by the creditor prior to expiration of the time limit.[46] He cannot, by unilaterally setting the time limit, transform the "Schickschuld" (obligation to send payment) into a "Bringschuld" (obligation to pay at the creditor's residence) and unilaterally shift the risk of delay to the debtor.

---

[41] BGH, WM 1959, pp. 624, 625 f. = NJW 1959, p. 1176.

[42] Properly critical, v. Caemmerer, Festschrift für Mann, p. 3, 12 = Gesammelte Schriften III, p. 108, 117 and n. 36; Canaris, supra note 15, at margin no. 482.

[43] See Soergel-Wiedemann, at § 326 BGB, margin no. 50; see also Palandt-Heinrichs, at § 326, margin no. 23.

[44] See RGZ 68, p. 329 (sales shipment). A similar extension of time for a bank transfer is dealt with in RGZ 105, p. 266 (with the result that the receipt of the transfer by the creditor's bank is sufficient for compliance with the time limit, and the actual credit to the creditor's account is not necessary).

[45] See RGZ 68, p. 329, 332; Staudinger-Otto, at § 326, margin no. 94, 106.

[46] RGZ 68, pp. 329, 331 f.; accord., LG Stuttgart, DB 1979, p. 787 (likewise involving a sales shipment). Ambigous, Palandt-Heinrichs, at § 326, margin no. 23.

If the money which was sent in a timely manner prior to expiration of the extension is lost underway or if it is not received for such a long time that its loss must be presumed, the debtor must arrange for a new transfer (§ 270 (1) BGB). This does not change the fact that his — unsuccessful — transfer attempt did comply with the stipulated time limit. If the circumstances under which the creditor may demand a second transfer are present, he may set a new time limit for this transfer, within which the debtor must arrange for the second transfer.

7. Conclusion

In conclusion, one may state that when the payment obligation is governed by German law (§§ 269, 270 BGB), the debtor is not liable for delays in the transmittal of the credit transfer. This also applies to delays within the scope of the first bank instructed by the debtor and, even more clearly, to delays within the scope of the intermediary banks. The creditor bears not only any loss of interest caused by the delay but also any currency exchange rate loss caused by the delay.[47] Only if the money does not arrive at all, or if its arrival has been delayed to the point where it can no longer be expected, must the debtor undertake a second transfer, including, in particular, the case where the transfer fails due to the insolvency of the originator's bank or one of the intermediary banks. The damage caused specifically by the delay must also, in this case, be borne by the creditor. An extension of time is complied with when the credit transfer order is received in a timely manner by the originator's bank; later delays are not the responsibility of the debtor.

[47] Actually — from the perspective of the concept of damage — this involves a type of damage which can be compensated. See Soergel-Wiedemann, at § 288 BGB, margin no. 26. In an international transfer, the probability of this type of damage is especially likely when the debtor pays in his own currency and this currency loses value with respect to the creditor's currency due to a delay in the transfer. The issue of damage is more problematic when the debtor pays in the currency of the creditor's country and that currency loses value due to the delay (represented, for example, by a drop in the exchange rate with respect to the debtor's country; see e.g., OLG Munich, NJW 1979, p. 2480). This does not actually involve an "exchange rate loss", but instead a "drepreciation loss" (see Staudinger-Karsten Schmidt, at margin no. D 335, 336 preceding § 244 BGB). The question of whether this constitutes damage in a legal sense is not decided differently in the case of payment in the currency of the creditor's country than in a purely domestic payment. Damage is to be found only when the creditor can prove (or, due to unusual circumstances it is to be presumed) that the creditor could have avoided further loss of value by means of exchange or investment if the money had been received on time. See Soergel-Wiedemann, at § 288 BGB, margin no. 29; Staudinger-Karsten Schmidt, at margin no. D 335 preceding § 244 BGB; both with additional references.

II. Special Forms of Payment

It is frequently the case that private, autonomous forms, in deviation from § 270 BGB, structure the payment obligation as a "Holschuld" (an obligation to be performed at the debtor's residence).

The simplest case is the payment by check. This involves an act of performance in fulfillment of the money debt. § 270 BGB is, therefore, applicable by analogy to the sending of the check.[48] The debtor bears the cost and risk of sending the check (§ 270 (1) BGB). In particular, the debtor bears the risk that the check may be stolen underway and collected by the thief or a "fence".[49] The place of performance nevertheless remains the (business) residence of the debtor (§ 270 (4) BGB). A timely sending of the check is thus sufficient for compliance with the stipulated payment date.[50] The payment by check is effective as fulfillment of the obligation, however, only if the check is paid by the drawee bank upon presentation.[51] Only the payment of the check leads to the result, so to speak, retroactively that the timely sending of the check is deemed to constitute the timely act of performance.

The actual payment transaction — the payment of the check — involves a "Holschuld". The creditor must present the check which was sent to him to the drawee bank in order to receive payment. The check collection, i.e. the transfer from the drawee bank to the creditor takes place in accordance with the creditor's instructions and at his cost and risk. He also bears the risk connected with transmitting the check to the drawee bank. If the check is lost on this route, the creditor cannot simply take recourse to the underlying obligation. The debtor would have the defense that payment had been made by check, i.e. that he is required to make a new payment of the underlying debt only in exchange for the return of the check.[52] This defense can be avoided by the creditor only if he either returns the check (Art. 59 (1) Check Statute in conjunction with §§ 946 ff., 1003 ff. German Code of Civil

---

[48] RGZ 78, p. 137, 140; BGH NJW 1969, p. 875; Canaris, supra note 15, at margin no. 779; Baumbach-Hefermehl, ScheckG, at Introduction, margin no. 20; Palandt-Heinrichs, at § 270 BGB, margin no. 6, with additional references; v. Caemmerer, Festschrift für Mann, p. 3, 13 = Gesammelte Schriften III, p. 108, 118.

[49] The view that "issues of money transport risks . . . [cannot] arise with respect to checks" (Staudinger-Selb, at § 270, margin no. 9) is incorrect as is the assertion that the application of § 270 BGB to check payments is "superfluous" (Staudinger-Karsten Schmidt, at margin no. C 23 preceding § 244).

[50] See the references in note 47. Contra, Canaris, supra note 15, at margin no. 780.

[51] Baumbach-Hefermehl, v. Caemmerer, supra note 47.

[52] Gernhuber, Erfüllung, p. 164, at § 9 I 13 b and p. 172, at § 9 II 6 d; Soergel-Huber, at § 433 BGB, margin no. 215. The view in Staudinger-Selb (at § 270 BGB, margin no. 9) that the debtor bears the risk of loss of the check even after the check has been delivered to the creditor is therefore incorrect.

Procedure) or provides reasonable security for the possibility that the debtor might otherwise be held liable based on the check.[53]

If in a sales contract, payment "cash against instruments" is stipulated, the debtor (buyer) is liable only for the fact that the money is available at no charge[54] to the creditor if the instruments are presented in a timely manner to the debtor or to the bank which the debtor has designated to the creditor as the paying agent.[55] The bank designated as the paying agent is the "special agent" (§ 278 BGB) of the debtor. By contrast, the debtor has nothing to do with the further transmittal of the funds: this takes place in practice through the bank authorized to make collection on the creditor's instructions and at his cost[56] and risk.

Where payment by means of letter of credit is stipulated, the issuing bank and the paying agent which it designates in the creditor's country are deemed to be the "special agents" of the debtor.[57] As in the payment "cash against instruments", the actual payment transaction here involves the creditor collecting the money from the paying agent at his own cost and risk. The debtor has nothing to do with this process or with the paying agent's right of indemnity against the issuing bank. The debtor's own participation in the actual payment transaction is only that he provides coverage of the amount to the issuing bank.

Where "cash on delivery" ("C.O.D.") is stipulated[58], the payment obligation is likewise a "Holschuld". Here, it is the carrier who collects the purchase price upon the delivery of the goods at the residence of the buyer or another designated location. This collection fulfills the obligation to pay the purchase price. The buyer has nothing more to do with the transmittal of the money by the carrier to the seller; § 270 (1) BGB is excluded by means of

[53] For the case of loss during the collection process, a special, simplified procedure has been developed between German credit institutions which makes possible the collection of lost checks; see the Scheckabkommen (check agreement), part III, printed in Baumbach-Hefermehl under "bank conditions" no. 11.

[54] Based on this clause, the buyer is obligated to designate a bank as paying agent in case of doubt; see BGH LM no. 7, with regard to § 346 HGB (B).

[55] See the arbitration decision, Schiedsgericht des Vereins der Getreidehändler der Hamburger Börse, March 11, 1971, in: Straatmann-Ulmer, HSG E 1 c, no. 7.

[56] Arbitration decision, Schiedsgericht des Waren-Vereins der Hamburger Börse, Jan. 27, 1981, in Straatmann-Ulmer, HSG E i c, no. 12.

[57] See RGZ 102, p. 155, 157; RG, JW 1921, p. 1312, 1313; RGZ 103, pp. 376, 379 f.; RGZ 105, p. 32, 34.

[58] See Soergel-Huber, at § 433 BGB, margin no. 127. The special characteristic of this form of payment is that the buyer does not have a right to examine the goods prior to payment (see Soergel-Huber on the C.O.D. clause; BGH, WM 1984, p. 1572, 1573 = ZIP 1984, p. 1497, 1498). Unless otherwise stipulated, the seller may, in accordance with trade custom, authorize the carrier to collect the purchase price only after he has provided the buyer an opportunity to examine the goods; see Soergel-Huber, at § 433, margin no. 126.

stipulation by the parties. Because the carrier is only obligated to hand over to the seller the amount which the carrier receives upon carrying out the order, the further transmittal — to the extent that German law governs the relationship between the carrier and the seller — is at the risk of the seller; § 270 (1) BGB also does not apply in this context.[59]

III. Payment by Means of Bank Transfer within the Scope of the International Sales Convention

1. The Duty to Pay the Purchase Price as a "Bringschuld"

Where a payment obligation is subject to the U.N. Convention on Contracts for the International Sale of Goods [CISG][60], Art. 57 CISG is applicable to the payment obligation. Unless otherwise stipulated, the buyer must pay the purchase price "at the seller's place of business" (Art. 57 (1)(a) CISG). The obligation to pay the purchase price is, thus, in German terminology a "Bringschuld".[61]

The issue of whether the buyer pays on time is thus, in contrast to § 270 BGB, dependent upon the time of receipt of the money by the seller. In general, the purchase price is due when the buyer has received the goods and has had an opportunity to examine them (Art. 58 (3) CISG). Only then must the buyer transmit the purchase price to the seller in accordance with Art. 57 (1) (a). Thus, the payment is timely when it is received by the seller within the period of time following delivery of the goods to the buyer which is necessary for the goods to be examined (which under Art. 38 (1) CISG must take place "within as short a period as is practible under the circumstances") and the time necessary to arrange for the credit transfer in the usual manner.[62] If a

[59] This is true generally for claims for delivery of money which are based on §§ 667, 675 BGB. See BGHZ 28, p. 123, 127; Coing, JZ 1970, p. 240; Ostler, NJW 1975, p. 2273; Larenz, Schuldrecht II, p. 337 n. 1, at § 56 II; Staudinger-Selb, at § 270, margin no. 3; Staudinger-Karsten Schmidt, at margin no. C 22 preceding § 244 BGB; MünchKomm-Keller, at § 270 BGB, at margin no. 3; Soergel-Wolf, at § 270 BGB, margin no. 3; Palandt-Heinrichs, at § 270 BGB, margin no. 2.

[60] See supra notes 1, 2.

[61] Art. 57 CISG governs only payment of the purchase price and not other payments based on the underlying contract (e. g. repayments if the contract is cancelled); see BGHZ 78, p. 257, 260. For these issues, the applicable law must be determined in accordance with Art. 7 (2) CISG.

[62] See Schlechtriem-Hager, at Art. 58 CISG, no. 7. The assertion that the examination to which the buyer is entitled prior to payment is not identical with the examination provided for in Art. 38 CISG, but that the buyer must instead be given the opportunity only for a "quick examination" before he pays (Bianca/Bonell/Maskow, at Art. 58 CISG, comment 2.8; accord, Herber-Czerwenka, at Art. 58 CISG, margin no. 8) lacks support in the text of the convention and is inconsistent with the legislative reasoning behind Art. 58 (3) CISG.

payment date is set for the buyer, he must see to it that the money is received by the seller by the stipulated time.

If the money is received late by the seller, he is, as a rule, entitled to compensation from the buyer in accordance with Art. 61 (1)(b) CISG. The losses caused by the delay must be compensated; these include, on the one hand, the seller's loss of interest and, on the other hand, any currency exchange loss incurred by the seller due to the late receipt of the purchase price. Fault on the part of the buyer is not a prerequisite for this compensation claim. The compensation claim is not applicable, however, where the buyer is discharged in accordance with Art. 79 CISG (see Art. 79 (1), (5)). This is the case when the failure to perform is due to an impediment which is beyond the buyer's control and when it could not reasonably have been expected of the buyer that he would foresee the impediment at the time the contract was made or that he could avoid or overcome it (Art. 79 (1) CISG). Force majeure in international credit transfers or impossibility of the transfer due to war, civil war, strikes, acts of God, etc., also can release the buyer from the duty to pay compensation. The buyer has the burden of proof in these cases (Art. 79 (1) CISG). Under the International Sales Convention, the liability for breach of contract is thus a form of guarantee liability[63], mitigated by the possibility of release under Art. 79.

If the buyer misses the payment date and if the seller in accordance with Art. 63 (1) CISG grants an extension of time, Art. 57 (1)(a) provides that the receipt of the money is decisive for compliance with this extension (and not as under §§ 270, 326 BGB the sending of the money). This circumstance must be taken into consideration in deciding whether the additional time is "reasonable" within the meaning of Art. 63 (1) CISG. If the money is not received by the seller within the extended time, he can cancel the contract (Art. 64 (1)(b) CISG) and claim compensation due to non-performance (Art. 61 (1)(a) CISG). The right to cancel the contract exists in any case; the claim to compensation is subject here to the possibility of release under Art. 79 (see Art. 79 (5) CISG).

2. Consequences for the Payment by Bank Transfer

With respect to payment by bank transfer, the result is the following: the buyer must arrange for the transfer, in the usual case of Art. 58 (3) CISG, within a short period following receipt of the goods (namely at the end of the examination period in accordance with Art. 38 CISG). If a payment date has

[63] See — regarding the liability of the seller — Honnold, at margin no. 276; Schlechtriem-Huber, at Art. 45 CISG, margin no. 43; this also applies to the buyer's liability. See also — regarding the "Hague" sales convention [EKG], which is substantively consistent here, note 1 above; v. Caemmerer, AcP 178, p. 121, 141 ff. (1978) = Gesammelte Schriften III, p. 23, 43 ff.

been set, he must arrange for the transfer in such a way that, in the normal course of business, the money will be available to the seller by the payment date. Because the payment obligation in accordance with Art. 57 (1)(a) CISG is a "Bringschuld", the debtor bears the risk connected with the transmittal even if he arranges for the transfer in a timely manner.[64] This is true not only where the transfer is lost underway, but also in case of delay.[65] The buyer's liability for loss and delay cannot actually be explained by the theory that the banks employed to carry out the transfer are his "special agents".[66] This would be a theory based too closely on the system of tort liability with which we are familiar. Here, the compensation liability established in Art. 61 (1)(b) CISG is a form of guarantee liability[67]; the guarantee is that the money will be available to the seller at the place of performance by the stipulated date.

The debtor may be released from liability under Art. 79, but mistakes by the banks employed by the debtor for the fulfillment of the payment obligation are not grounds for release within the meaning of Art. 79 CISG.[68] Where, as in the present case, the buyer uses a third party to fulfill the contract, he is released only if the fulfillment fails due to an impediment which is outside the buyer's control and also outside the scope of influence of the third party whom he has engaged (Art. 79 (2) CISG). Mistakes by the banks instructed to carry out the transfer — the originator's bank as well as the intermediary banks — thus in any case lie within the scope of the buyer's responsibility. External impediments, such as government payment freezes, war, civil war or labor disputes[69], of course, can release the buyer here as well. Overall, the situation under the International Sales Convention is very similar to that described by Pleyer for English law, which is likewise based on the principle of guarantee liability[70] and which significantly influenced the drafting of the Convention in this regard.[71]

---

[64] See Bianca/Bonell/Maskow, at Art. 57 CISG, comment 2.5; Schlechtriem-Hager, at Art. 57 CISG, margin no. 4; Herber-Czerwenka, at Art. 57 CISG, margin no. 3; Reinhart, at Art. 57 CISG, margin notes 4, 5; Soergel-Lüderitz, at Art. 57 CISG, margin no. 7; see also — regarding the predecessor provision Art. 59 EKG — Dölle-v. Caemmerer, at Art. 59 EKG, margin no. 12.

[65] See the references in note 64.

[66] But see Schönle, in: Festschrift für Werner, p. 817, 822.

[67] See supra note 63.

[68] Doubts expressed with respect to correspondent banks: Huber, RabelsZ 43 (1979), p. 413, 512. I do not agree with this doubt.

[69] Contra, Schlechtriem-Stoll, at Art. 79, margin no. 41, 42, 44. Under this view, the buyer would bear the risk of a labor dispute in the banking sector. In my opinion, this would not be consistent with the purpose of the release clause in Art. 79. Under Art. 79, circumstances beyond the debtor's control are to release him from liability — and what is more beyond the debtor's control than a labor dispute?

[70] See Pleyer/Wallach, RIW 1988, p. 172, 180.

[71] See Schlechtriem-Huber, art Art. 45 CISG, margin no. 9.

The buyer's liability is limited to delays within the course of business of the originator's bank and the intermediary banks which it engages. After the transfer is received by the bank designated by the seller, the buyer is no longer liable for delays in crediting the transfer amount or for the risk that the beneficiary's bank could become insolvent after receiving the funds and prior to crediting the amount to the seller.[72] The beneficiary's bank is not employed by the buyer/debtor but instead by the seller/creditor. Therefore, misconduct by the beneficiary's bank is governed by Art. 80 CISG. Under this provision, the creditor has no claim based on the debtor's failure to perform to the extent that the failure to perform was caused by the creditor's own act or omission. The provision also applies when the failure to perform is caused by an act or omission by a third party engaged by the creditor in performing the contract.[73] This does not differ from German law.[74]

In the case of an extension of time in accordance with Art. 63 CISG, Art. 57 (1)(a) provides that the buyer must arrange for the transfer in such a way that the money is available in the account designated by the seller prior to expiration of the time limit. Delays in the transfer — particularly including those for which the payor bank or an intermediary bank is responsible — work to the disadvantage of the buyer, in contrast to the rule under § 270 BGB. Delays caused within the business operations of the beneficiary's bank are not allocated to the buyer. The extended time period is met when the transfer arrives at the beneficiary's bank in time so that in the normal course of business the amount should be credited to the seller by the end of the additional time period.

3. Special Forms of Payment within the Scope of Application of the International Sales Convention

The definition of the place of payment as provided in Art. 57 (1)(a) CISG is considered to be subordinate. The parties may stipulate a different provision. One case which frequently occurs in international trade is governed by Art. 57 (1)(b): if under the sales contract, payment is to be made against delivery of the goods or documents, the place of payment is the location where the goods or documents are to be handed over. The payment is to be made against delivery of the goods if the parties stipulate "cash on delivery"; the place of payment here is the place of delivery for the goods, which in case of doubt is the buyer's place of business.[75] Payment is to be made against

[72] See Schlechtriem-Hager, at Art. 57 CISG, margin no. 4.

[73] See Schlechtriem-Stoll, art Art. 80 CISG, margin no. 8.

[74] See part I 5 above and notes 34, 36.

[74] Only this case is covered by Art. 57 1 b, alternative 1. In my view, this provision is misunderstood in Schlechtriem-Hager, at Art. 57 CISG, margin note 12 ff.; likewise its

presentation of documents when the parties stipulate "cash against instruments".[76] In both cases, the payment obligation is a "Holschuld"; the same rules govern as under German law.[77] Here, the buyer has nothing to do with the transmittal of the purchase price. Payment is also to be made against presentation of documents where a documentary letter of credit is stipulated.[78] The place of payment is the seat of the issuing bank or the paying agent designated to the seller by the issuing bank; the payment obligation here is also a "Holschuld".

Where the seller asserts a claim for concurrent performance as provided for in Art. 58 (1) sent. 2 and Art. 58 (2) CISG, without a special contractual stipulation, this case is not governed by Art. 57 (1)(b).[79] The statutory place of payment (Art. 57 (1)(a)) remains completely unaffected.[80] If the seller, as is his right, demands concurrent performance, the effective place of payment shifts away from the statutory place of payment under certain circumstances, perhaps even as a rule. The basis is Art. 58 (3) CISG: unless otherwise stipulated (such as "cash against instruments", letter of credit, "cash on delivery"), the buyer need not pay until he has had an opportunity to examine the goods. In the case of a sales shipment[81] the seller can also, as under German law[82], instruct the carrier to collect the purchase price against delivery of the goods, after giving the buyer a reasonable opportunity to examine the goods (Art. 38 CISG[83], Art. 57 (2), (3) CISG). In this case, the seller waives his right to payment at his place of business and instead chooses concurrent performance, and the buyer fulfills the purchase price obligation by means of payment to the carrier.[84] He has nothing more to do with the transmittal of the money to the seller. If the contract does not require

---

predecessor provision, Art. 59 (1) clause 2 EKG in Dölle-v. Caemmerer, at Art. 59 EKG, margin no. 2. See also BGHZ 74, p. 136, 141 f.

[76] See Schlechtriem-Hager, art Art. 57 CISG, margin no. 22.

[77] See part II above.

[78] See Schlechtriem-Hager, at Art. 57 CISG, margin no. 22.

[79] Incorrect, Huber, RabelsZ 43 (1979), p. 413, 512 and Schlechtriem-Hager, at Art. 57 CISG, margin no. 18. My error was based on the fact that at the time I was not familiar with the term "cash on delivery" (see BGH WM 1984, p. 1572 = ZIP 1984, p. 1479).

[80] Accord — regarding the predecessor provision in Art. 59 (1) EKG — BGHZ 74, p. 136, 142.

[81] More precisely: a purchase in which the "contract stipulates transport of the goods"; see Schlechtriem-Huber, at Art. 31 CISG, margin no. 23 ff.

[82] See Soergel-Huber, at § 433 BGB, margin no. 126.

[83] See supra note 62.

[84] What Gernhuber (Erfüllung, p. 19. at § 2 IV 2) has stated with respect to the analagous case under German law also applies here: The place of performance for the payment at the seller's location; "but the seller has the right to take on the greater burden of going to get it if he does not thereby additionally burden the buyer."

shipment of the goods, i.e. the delivery obligation is a "Holschuld"[85], then unless otherwise stipulated, the seller may give the buyer the opportunity to examine the goods where the goods are to be picked up (Art. 31 b), c) CISG) and may demand concurrent performance there (Art. 58 (1) sent. 2 CISG). The payment obligation remains a "Bringschuld", but payment need not necessarily be made at the seller's place of business (see Art. 31 b) CISG). The involvement of banks in the payment transaction is absent in this case.

If payment by check is stipulated, the rules on the payment of the purchase price apply by analogy to the transmittal of the check. The actual payment procedure is not the responsibility of the buyer; instead, the collection is the duty of the seller. To this extent, the same rules apply as under German law.[86]

IV. The Legal Situation When Foreign Law Is Applicable

If, under Art. 27, 28 EGBGB, foreign law is applicable to a contract which is the basis for a payment obligation, the place of payment must be determined under the foreign law. Many foreign legal systems provide that the payment obligation — as under the International Sales Convention — is a "Bringschuld".[87] As a rule, this would lead to the result, as under the Convention, that the debtor not only bears the risk of loss, but is also liable for damages caused by delay if the bank instructed by the debtor or one of its intermediary banks does not correctly carry out the transfer and the transfer is therefore not completed until after the stipulated payment date.[88] The details must be determined based on the particular applicable national legal system.

---

85 See Schlechtriem-Huber, at Art. 31 CISG, margin no. 48, 53.

86 See part II above.

87 See the overview in v. Caemmerer, Festschrift für Mann, p. 3 f., 15 = Gesammelte Schriften III, p. 108 f., 120. A money debt is viewed as a "Bringschuld" by: England, the U.S.A., Switzerland, Turkey, Greece, the Netherlands, Italy, Poland, and the Scandinavian countries. Under French law (art. 1247 C. civ.) money debts are "Holschulden" ("les dettes sont qué rable et non portables"); the significance for the case of payment by bank transfers appears doubtful (v. Caemmerer, supra note 11). With the reform of 1916, Austria followed the German model (§ 905 Austrian Civil Code). In contrast to v. Caemmerer, supra, I believe that with respect to future law the German system is preferable to the model of the "Bringschulden". See supra note 31.

88 Regarding English law, see Pleyer/Wallach, RIW 1988, p. 172,180.

V. Consequences for the Bank's Liability (1): Legal Situation in the Case of a "Bringschuld"

1. Legal Basis

With regard to the liability of the banks involved in international credit transfers for damages due to delay in the transfer, it is significant to determine whether the obligation is a "Bringschuld" to be fulfilled by means of payment at the creditor's residence (as under the International Sales Convention and many foreign legal systems) or a "Holschuld" to be fulfilled at the debtor's residence (such as where payment by check or "cash against instruments" is stipulated) or a "Schickschuld" to be fulfilled by sending payment (as under §§ 269, 270 BGB). In the case of "Holschuld" or a "Schickschuld", the debtor has nothing to do with the transfer procedure and is not liable to the creditor for the delay. If, however, the payment obligation is a "Bringschuld", failure to complete the order on time, in contrast to the other two cases, makes the debtor liable to compensate the creditor, in particular for loss of interest and possibly also due to currency exchange losses.[89] Here, the debtor suffers damage due to the non- punctual conduct of the bank. If compliance with the payment date depends on compliance with an addition of time or the fulfillment of a condition precedent, then in case of a "Bringschuld" additional damage may be incurred by the debtor if the payment delay causes cancellation of the contract or failure of the condition precedent in the relationship between the debtor and the creditor. In all of these cases, the debtor can attempt to recover his damages from the transferring bank; this is true when the delay takes place within the business operations of that bank, but also if it is caused within the business operations of one of the intermediary banks employed by the originator's bank.

The issue of whether such a claim exists is, in the case of international payment transactions, first dependent upon the applicable law. In this article, we can describe the legal situation only under German law. German law is, of course, applicable when the debtor and the transferor bank are both resident in Germany and, under German conflict of laws rules, also if the bank office is in Germany and the debtor is a resident of a foreign country (Art. 28 (2) EGBGB). Independently from this rule, the applicability of German law is also derived, in the case of participation by a German bank, from Art. 26 (1) sent. 2 of the General Business Conditions of German banks ["AGB"].[90]

---

[89] See supra note 47.

[90] Bank general business conditions [AGB] in the version of Jan. 1, 1988, printed, e. g. in Baumbach-Duden-Hopt, HGB, appendix 8.

2. Liability of the Originator's Bank with Respect to the Debtor

a) The Fault of the Bank

If, in a payment by bank transfer, the originator's bank violates its duty to process and transmit the transfer order in a timely manner, the bank is liable to the debtor as its principal for damages due to the delay (§ 286 BGB). A warning (§ 284 (1) sent. 1 BGB) is not a prerequisite for the default because the bank's duty to carry out the transfer order immediately is derived from the order itself. The transfer order already contains the instruction that it is to be carried out immediately; it would make no sense to require an additional warning. The bank bears the burden of proof that it was not at fault for the delay (§ 285 BGB), and, in particular, that the delay was not due to the fault of the bank personnel (§ 278 BGB); if the delay in processing takes place within the bank's operations, this burden of proof will be met only in very exceptional cases.

The bank's liability is limited by No. 7 AGB (General Business Conditions of banks). The bank is liable as a rule only for the damage suffered by its customer (the debtor) in the amount of the loss of interest, but this is true in every case of fault (even simple negligence). Thus, if the debtor is required to compensate the creditor for an interest loss incurred by the creditor due to the delay, the debtor can take recourse against the bank. The bank is liable to the customer (debtor) for further damages only in the case of gross negligence and even then only if the order does not relate to the customer's trade (No. 7 sent. 2 AGB). The bank's liability is further restricted in that the bank is liable for damages in addition to loss of interest in case of negligent delay in the transfer only if the customer (debtor) gave notice upon submission of the transfer order, in a manner separate from the standard transfer form, that the payment was subject to a time limit and that the customer might suffer damage in addition to the interest loss in case of delay (No. 7 sent. 1 AGB). This applies especially in the case where the creditor suffers an exchange rate loss due to the delay and demands compensation from the debtor[91]; another relevant case is where the debtor suffers damage because he fails to comply with an extension of time (grace period) due to late receipt of the transfer by the creditor or does not fulfill a condition precedent in his relationship with the creditor.

In most cases, notice in accordance with No. 7 sent. 1 AGB will not be given.[92] If such notice is given, however, extended liability for the bank is established only if the bank does not reply. Presumably, in the case of

---

[91] See supra note 47.

[92] E.g. OLG Düsseldorf, WM 1982, p. 575.

international transfers, the bank will state to the customer that the bank will not accept liability for the receipt of the money by the requested date or will suggest that the customer remove the transaction from routine credit transfer and choose an expedited route, whereby in accordance with § 670 BGB the customer bears the additional costs.

The purpose of No. 7 AGB is to open this possibility for the bank. Therefore, concerns regarding the validity of the clause based on § 9 of the Law Governing Standard Contracts ["AGBG"][93] are not justified.[94] The customer is not placed at an unreasonable disadvantage (§ 9 (1) AGBG). It is reasonable to require from him that he contact his bank individually, and not just by means of filling out a transfer form, if he knows that the transfer must arrive in the creditor's account within a fixed time and that he is threatened with a substantial disadvantage if this time limit is not met. Above all, one can demand from the customer that he precisely disclose this date to the bank so that the bank evaluate the risk. It should be quite clear to everyone familiar with the handling of credit transfers that this notice cannot be given on the transfer form itself[95]; the form is neither designated nor suitable for individual messages from the customer to the bank.

This clause is also not incompatible with the significant basic principles of the statutory rules (§ 9 (2) no. 1 AGBG). One basic principle in the statute is that the creditor may recover damages from the debtor only when he has notified the debtor of the danger of an unusually high loss (§ 254 (2) BGB). This concept is given specific form in No. 7 AGB. It also cannot be said that substantial duties of the bank based on the transfer order are so restricted by the clause that the achievement of the purpose of the contract would be endangered (§ 9 (2) AGBG). The clause does not permit the bank to violate its duties without sanction or leave the customer without rights. In the usual case, compensation for a loss of interest is a reasonable remedy which covers typical loss due to delay in crediting the transfer. Only in exceptional cases is the customer threatened with atypical damages. The fact that the clause is also consistent with § 11 (8) AGBG derives from the fact that in the case of gross negligence the bank must compensate the customer for all damages if the order is not connected with his trade; in the case of simple negligence, limiting the liability to loss of interest is permissible even with respect to non-merchants.[96]

[93] See Brandner, in: Ulmer-Brandner-Hensen, at appendix to §§ 9-11 AGBG, margin no. 160; Baumbach-Duden-Hopt, HGB, appendix 8, Bank AGB, no. 7, comment 2; regarding the earlier version of this clause, see Canaris, supra note 15, at margin no. 2577, 2578.

[94] Accord. v. Westphalen, WM 1984, p. 2, 6.

[95] Contra, Baumbach-Duden-Hopt, supra note 93; Heinrichs, in: Neue Entwicklungen im Bankhaftungsrecht, p. 115, 128.

[96] See Hensen, in: Ulmer-Brandner-Hesen, at § 11 no. 8 Bank AGB, margin no. 10. Contra, Baumbach-Duden-Hopt, supra note 93.

Of course, the result is that the customer who attempts to pay a "Bringschuld" by means of an ordinary bank transfer takes the risk that he may be liable to his creditor for damages and face other disadvantages, for which he will not be able to recover from the bank even when the bank is at fault. Specifically with regard to an exchange rate loss caused by delayed execution, there is an issue of whether reliance by the bank on No. 7 sent. 1 would be an abuse of rights because the risk of such losses is apparent to banks in international transfers even without any special notice.

b) The Fault of the Intermediary Banks

If the originator's bank transmits the transfer order in a timely manner to an intermediary bank (for which the originator's bank bears the burden of proof in accordance with § 285 BGB) and if the further transmittal is delayed by the intermediary bank, the originator's bank is liable to its customer only if the intermediary is deemed to be its "special agent" (§ 278 BGB). The general view in the legal literature does not consider the intermediary bank to be a "special agent" — in contrast to the Reichsgericht. The reason stated is that the originator's bank fulfills the instructions given when it transmits the order to an intermediary bank; the bank is not obligated to do more.[97] The Bundesgerichtshof has recently adopted this view specifically with regard to international bank transfers.[98]

[97] Schoele, Das Recht der Überweisung, p. 196; Meyer-Cording. Das Recht der Banküberweisung, p. 74 n. 1; Schlegelberger-Hefermehl, at § 365 HGB appendix, margin no. 46; Kümpel, WM 1977, pp. 694, 698 ff.; Hadding/Häuser, ZHR 145 (1981), p. 138, 146; v. Gablenz, Die Haftung der Banken bei Einschaltung Dritter, pp. 223 f., 242; Hüffer, in ZHR 151 (1987), pp. 93, 95; Hüffer, WM 1987, pp. 641 ff.; Koller, in: Neue Entwicklungen im Bankhaftungsrecht, p. 21, 23; Schröter, ZHR 151 (1987), pp. 118, 120 ff.; Canaris, supra note 15, at margin no. 390; Baumbach-Duden-Hopt, at HGB appendix 7, comment III 2 c; Palandt-Heinrichs, at § 278 BGB, margin no. 27. Contra, i. e. in favor of application of § 278 BGB: RG, LZ 1926, p. 45, 47 (see note 102 below); Köndgen, in: Neue Entwicklungen im Bankhaftungsrecht, pp. 133, 146 ff.; Soergel-Wolf, at § 278 BGB, margin no. 44. The prevailing view in the legal literature incorrectly cites a basis in the case decisions by the Reich Court and the Federal Supreme Court. The holding in RG, LZ 1926, p. 45 is, as stated, clearly opposite to that view. RGZ 105, p. 48, 50 (= Bank-Archiv 22 (1922), p. 261) did not involve the case of a bank transfer, but instead the totally different case where a bank was ordered to arrange for the opening of a letter of credit by another bank (the competent chamber of the Reich Court has already made reference to the incorrect interpretation of this case, apparently without success, in RG, LZ 1926, p. 45, 46). The decision in BGHZ 4, p. 244, 248 does not contain a holding on the issue of § 278 BGB but instead merely mentions that a bank may engage a giro central bank for the execution of a transfer, which no one contests. The decision in RG, LZ 1933, p. 770, also does not involve § 278 BGB. All that remains is an obiter dictum by the OLG Hamburg, (JW 1931, p. 548) which rejects application of § 278 in an unrelated context; that case involved the issue of whether the bank customer can challenge the (correct!) transmittal of the order by the first bank with respect to the receiving bank under § 119 (1) BGB. That possibility was rejected by the OLG, I believe correctly; it is not clear how a reference to the purported non-applicability of § 278 BGB could stray into this context.

This view must be rejected. The order directed to the bank does not state that the bank should instruct an intermediary bank to carry out the transfer; instead, the order states that the funds should be credited to the account of the creditor with the transferee bank.[99] If the originator's bank has a direct business connection with current accounts or an agency arrangement with the beneficiary's bank, it carries out the order by transmittal directly to the beneficiary's bank.[100] Only if this direct connection is lacking does the bank need to engage an intermediary bank in the creditor's country, which then makes contact with the beneficiary's bank.[101] If the originator's bank has no correspondent bank in the creditor's country, it must first employ an (additional) correspondent bank in its own country which has the necessary connection.[102] Taking this situation into consideration, it would severely stretch the point to say that the order directs that an intermediary bank should be instructed to carry out the transfer. The order requires transmittal to the beneficiary's bank; only because the originator's bank does not have the means to do this directly does it engage the intermediary bank. This is a typical case for § 278 BGB[103], as the Reichsgericht correctly decided. The situation is scarcely different from that in which a carrier employs a sub-carrier. The intermediary bank also does not act as a "substitute" for the originator's bank within the meaning of § 664 (1) sent. 1 BGB.[104] The bank

[98] BGH, NJW 1991, p. 2210, 2211, citing Canaris, supra note 15, at margin no. 390.

[99] Convincing, RG, LZ 1926, p. 45, 46 f.

[100] See Pleyer/Wallach, RIW 1988, p. 172, 173; v. Gablenz, Die Haftung der Banken bei Einschaltung Dritter, p. 239.

[101] See Pleyer/Wallach, id.; v. Gablenz, id.; see e.g. the facts in OLG Hamburg, JW 1931, p. 548.

[102] See Pleyer/Wallach, id.; as an example, see the facts in RG, LZ 1833, p. 770; See also v. Gablenz, supra note 100, at 240 (also concerning the use of banks in third countries).

[103] See RG, LZ 1926, p. 46, 46 f. That case was exceptional in that the originator's bank had not transmitted the transfer to a correspondent bank but instead to a branch office of the Reichsbank which arranged for the settlement between it and the beneficiary's bank. The transfer of a paper mark amount dated July 28, 1923 was delayed for 14 days by mistake, and the originator asserted a claim against the originator's bank for a depreciation loss. The Court of Appeal rejected the claim; the Reichsgericht set aside the judgment and remanded the case. In the view of the Reichsgericht, the claim should have been rejected only if the engagement of the Reichsbank branch office was the only route "which, in accordance with trade practice and the principles of good faith, was available" and if the originator "should at the time of contracting have expected as a part of the contract that this route could be selected." Only then could one say that the order was directed toward transmission to the Reichsbank branch office from the beginning and was therefore satisfied in this way.

It is obvious that this requirement set by the Reichsgericht for the case of engagement of a correspondent bank is never satisfied; it is clear that the Reichsgericht viewed correspondent banks as "servants" of the originator's bank and had doubts only of a factual nature with respect to the special function of the Reichsbank branch office.

[104] Contra, v. Gablenz, supra note 100, at 223, 242. The basic distinction between "substitution" (§ 664 (1) sent. 1 BGB) and use of a "servant" (§§ 664 (1) sent. 3 and 278

carries out the order itself with the help of the intermediary bank and does not have the order carried out by the intermediary bank in the place of the originator's bank. The version of No. 9 AGB presently in effect does not lead to a different result because that provision states only that the bank may use a substitute but not whether in a specific case a substitution is made. The question of whether the originator of an international transfer must expect that intermediary banks will be employed is also not decisive.[105] The application of § 278 BGB can simply not be dependent upon such knowledge; such knowledge by the creditor is present in most cases under § 278 BGB.

The practical advantage to the application of § 278 BGB is, above all, that the originator can recover compensation from his bank without first having to investigate whether the delay occurred at that bank or at an intermediary bank. It has been noted that the originating party in transfer transactions is faced with a "complete system".[106] It difficult to understand why one cannot reach the simple conclusion that the originator's bank should be liable to the originator for this complete system, but that one instead becomes caught up in legalistic speculation concerning "network contracts" and "compound contracts".[107]

Nevertheless, one should not overvalue the practical significance of this issue. If we assume that the originator's bank is liable for the intermediary bank in accordance with § 278 BGB, this liability is basically limited in accordance with No. 7 AGB to loss of interest, assuming that the customer did not give special notice to the bank of the particular urgency of the

---

BGB) is untenable (v. Gablenz at 122 ff.); the concept of "servant" does not refer only, or even primarily, to the agent's "own people" but instead also includes independent third parties. Under the correct view, § 675 BGB should be taken literally, and § 664 BGB should not be applied at all in connection with agency agreements for compensation. In agency agreements for compensation, it is obvious that the party obligated to perform services or the contractor cannot withdraw from his duties by assigning them to a third party; this result does not require a special legal provision. Independent third parties which the contractor employs to carry out the stipulated work under an agency agreement for compensation, are thus always "servants" and never substitutes. With regard to this disputed issue, see the references in v. Gablenz, p. 81.

105 This was held to be decisive in BGH, NJW 1991, p. 2210, 2211. The transfer was used for payment of a purchase price. The beneficiary's bank was authorized under the transfer order to make payment only against delivery of the shipping documents. The beneficiary's bank rejected this conditional transfer order and transferred the amount back to the correspondent bank. Upon request, the correspondent bank made the transfer amount available to the beneficiary's bank a second time. The beneficiary's bank then credited this amount to the beneficiary. The BGH held that the originator's bank should not be responsible for this arbitrary conduct by the correspondent bank. This result is not acceptable.

106 Möschel, AcP 186 (1986), p. 187, 211.

107 Id.

transaction. Also, the originator's bank is liable in accordance with No. 25 AGB only for gross negligence by the intermediary bank. The originator's bank bears the burden of proof that the mistake was caused by the intermediary bank and that the intermediary bank was not grossly negligent. Of course, the bank customer may have compensation claims against the intermediary bank — based either on his own rights or assigned rights which may be more extensive and may even extend to the case of simple negligence.[108] If, on the other hand, one assumes that the intermediary bank is not a "special agent", then such compensation claims by the customer against the intermediary bank are eliminated from the start. Specifically where international transfers are involved pursuit of legal remedies against the foreign intermediary bank can involve uncertainties and problems.[109] Under the general principles of § 278 BGB, this risk must be borne by the originator's bank and not the originator.

3. The Intermediary Bank's Liability to the Debtor

There is basic agreement that the debtor and customer of the transferor bank may recover damages from the intermediary bank, at least by a circuitous route, if he suffers a loss due to late transmittal of the transfer order. Here again, we can analyze only the case where the intermediary bank's liability is governed by German law. This is the case, on the one hand, when a domestic bank employs a second domestic bank in the course of a transfer to a foreign country and, on the other hand, when for a transfer from a foreign country the foreign bank employs an intermediary bank in Germany to transmit the order to the beneficiary's bank in Germany.

The firm starting point from the legal perspective is that no direct contractual relationship exists between the customer and the intermediary bank.[110] This follows from the wording and the purpose of § 164 (1) BGB: the originator's bank acts in its own name with respect to the intermediary bank; the fact that it is acting for the account of a third party is not sufficient to establish a contractual relationship between the principal party and the intermediary bank.

---

[108] See part 3, below.

[109] See e.g. BGH, NJW 1991, p. 2210; and supra note 105.

[110] See Schlegelberger-Hefermehl, at § 365 HGB appendix, margin no. 97; Canaris, supra note 15, at margin no. 392; both with additional references. Whether Möschel (supra note 106) is really attempting to assert something different with the designation "Netzvertrag" (network contract) appears unclear. This metaphor does not have any meaning as a legal concept.

a) Recovery of Third Party Damages

Based on the traditional — well-founded — view, this problem can be solved with the help of the legal theory of "recovery of third party damages".[111] Where the intermediary bank does not properly carry out the order, the originator's bank has a claim to compensation against the intermediary bank due to default (or perhaps due to collateral negligence). The loss, of course, is not incurred directly by the originator's bank but instead by its customer. As is always the case when a contracting party executes a contract not on its own behalf but as an indirect representative on behalf of and for the account of a principal, the originator's bank may claim compensation for the "third party damages" incurred by its principal.[112] The principal can then demand assignment of this compensation claim from his bank in accordance with §§ 667 and 675 BGB; by means of this detour, he can then take recourse against the intermediary. Of course, the restrictions on liability existing in the contractual relationship between the two banks also govern this claim. If they also contracted[113] on the basis of the AGB, then primarily No. 7 AGB must be taken into consideration. The intermediary bank is thus liable, as a rule, only for the loss of interest incurred by the originator. It is liable for additional damages only if it had received special notice of the urgency of the transfer and the particular risk of unusual damages or where the risk was apparent even without special notice.

---

[111] As in BGHZ 27, p. 241, 247: regarding the liability, of the receiving bank with respect to the originator's bank for damage to the originator due to violation of a breach of a duty of confidentiality; BGH, WM 1968, p. 1368 = NJW 1969, p. 320; BGH, WM 1976, p. 904, 907; OLG Hamm, WM 1979, p. 339, 341; OLG Cologne, WM 1989, p. 93, 94; Schlegelberger-Hefermehl, at § 365 HGB appendix, margin no. 100; Hadding/Häuser, ZHR 145 (1981), pp. 138, 146; Hadding, in: Festschrift für Werner, pp. 165, 174 ff.; see also Hüffer, ZHR 151 (1987), pp. 93, 98 ff.

[112] The objection by Canaris (supra note 15, at margin no. 26) that there is no "shifting of loss" but instead that by nature the damage could be incurred only by the originator and not by the originator's bank is founded on an incorrect view of liquidation of damages for third parties: with the same argument one could also deny a commission agent or freight carrier the right to third party damage liquidation; but these are the classic cases for which this legal principle was established (see H. Lange, Schadensersatz, at § 8 III 4). See, in detail, Hadding, in: Festschrift für Werner, pp. 165, 174 ff.

[113] On the basic applicability to the relationships between banks, see Canaris, supra note 15, margin no. 2518. In international transactions, the incorporation is determined under German law if the seat of the correspondent bank is in Germany (Art. 28 (1), (2) in conjunction with Art. 31 (1) EGBGB). In the case of incorporation by means of a commercial letter of confirmation, Art. 31 (2) EGBGB must also be considered.

b) Contract Protecting a Third Party's Interest

A second view, which has recently gained momentum, does not employ the detour of assignment of the first bank's claim against the second bank for recovery of third party damages. Instead, the contract between the originator's bank and the intermediary bank is viewed as a "contract protecting the interest of a third party", namely the originator.[114] Thus, based on the contract, the customer has his own direct right to compensation against the intermediary bank (§ 328 BGB). In this same sense, the Bundesgerichtshof decided a case involving check collection: where a presenting bank, which was instructed by the check payee to collect the check, then entrusted a second bank with presentment of the check, this second bank was held directly liable to the payee where the second bank presented the check late and thereby violated its duty to the presenting bank.[115] If this result is correct, then one could scarcely reach a different result in the case of delayed handling of a transfer order by an intermediary bank.

c) Relationship between the Bases of Claims

If one views the issue only from the aspect of legal interpretation, both of these methods can be supported. If one chooses the theory of a "contract protecting the interest of a third party", the traditional presumption concerning recovery of third party damages is not "incorrect" but is superfluous. The bank customer does not need to have his bank's claim assigned to him, and he does not need to assert that the bank possesses a claim for recovery of third party damages; instead, he can recover his own damages directly. The originator's bank loses the claim for recovery of third party damages; if the originator's bank asserts a claim against the intermediary bank, it can in accordance with § 335 BGB only sue for payment to its customer.[116] Only if

[114] See OLG Düsseldorf, WM 1982, p. 575, 576; OLG Frankfurt, WM 1974, p. 726, 727; OLG Munich, DNotZ 1987, p. 694; Canaris, supra note 15, at margin no. 25, 395; Hüffer, ZHR 151 (1987), p. 93, 105 also reaches the same result.

[115] BGHZ 96, p. 9, 17 (involving a certified German Bundesbank check; in the absence of a late presentment, the collection guarantee expired). This decision is also based on BGHZ 69, p. 82, 86, regarding the protective effect of a debit agreement concluded between banks for the customer who presented the debit voucher where the drawee bank failed to give timely notice to the presenting bank of the nonpayment. This was, however, an exceptional case because under the traditional view the customer of the presenting bank would not have been helped by the principle of liquidation of damages for a third party even if the presenting bank had assigned its rights (Canaris is correct to this extent, supra note 15, at margin no. 26).

[116] A claim for performance to the third party is also permissible in the case of a "third party liquidation" (BGH, WM 1987, p. 581, 582; H. Lange, Schadensersatz, at § 8 III 9; Soergel-Mertens, margin no. 259 preceding § 249); payment to the bank itself can be

the originator's bank has already compensated its customer has it suffered damage for which it may recover from the intermediary bank. Thus, when one presumes the existence of a "contract protecting the interest of a third party", the claim to recovery of third party damages is supplanted by the provision of § 335 BGB.[117]

d) Analysis

Thus the question must be whether it is correct to assume a contract protecting the interest of a third party and thereby exclude the possibility of recovering third party damages as being unnecessary. We should first remember that the legal theory of the contract protecting the interest of a third party is a construction with two different functions.[118] In one class are the cases in which the contract debtor violates a contractual duty which serves to protect health or property; the injured party is not the contract creditor, however, but instead a third party close to him. Case decisions have by means of interpretation of the contract — in fact probably through extending the objective law supporting the contract — drawn this closely related third party within the protection of the contract and developed separate rules for this purpose.[119] In another class are cases in which the duties based on an agency agreement are violated and only financial losses are incurred. The financial loss is not incurred by the creditor, however, but instead by a third party, and the question arises as to whether the third party should have a separate right to compensation based on the agency agreement. There are no general rules available for resolving this question. As Caemmerer has plausibly suggested, "there must be an ascertainable express or implied intention of the parties"; the "assumption that there should be a benefit for a third party must be supported within the meaning of the specific contract"; the principles which have been developed in the case law with respect to the completely different group of cases involving personal injury

---

claimed only it can be expected that the compensation will benefit the injured party (see RGZ 58, p. 39, 43; RGZ 90, p. 240, 247; BGH, WM 1987, p. 581, 582; Soergel-Mertens). Thus the distinction is not so important. MünchKomm-Gottwald (at § 335 BGB, margin no. 4) rejects the application of § 335 BGB to contracts with protective effect for third parties "to the extent that the recipient of the promise does not owe compensation to the third party". Precisely this can be in doubt; this restriction is impractical.

[117] See Hagen, Die Drittschadensliquidation 24 (1971); MünchKomm-Gottwald, at § 328 BGB, margin no. 75, with additional references concerning the issue disputed in the legal literature.

[118] See v. Caemmerer, Festschrift für Wieacker, p. 311, 320 = Gesammelte Schriften III, p. 189, 198 f.

[119] See v. Caemmerer, Festschrift für Wieacker, pp. 311 ff.= Gesammelte Schriften III, p. 189 ff.

and property damage are not applicable here "because, as a rule, they do not fit the factual situation".[120]

It is thus a straightforward problem of interpretation of the agreement made between the two banks, and because there is no express stipulation in the contract, it is specifically a question of the "implied intent of the parties". The interesting feature is that the contract, as the Bundesgerichtshof has correctly held, is one for "high-volume transactions of a certain type using a uniformly practiced procedure".[121] The interpretation, therefore, (in contrast to the situation where the issue involves whether a third party is to be included within the protective scope of an agreement with an attorney[122]) cannot be made based on the individual situation in the specific case but instead only based on the typical interests involved. Characteristic of these interests is, on the one hand, that the bank in transmitting the transfer order (as is apparent to the intermediary bank) acts on the instructions of and in the interest of the customer designated on the form, and, second, that the customer employs a procedure here which involves certain "typical procedural risks" against which he needs protection.[123] Under these circumstances, interpretation of the contract as one "protecting the interests of a third party" at least suggests itself[124]; such an interpretation is not excluded by the fact that reasonable protection may be provided for the customer in many cases[125] by other means (for example, under the theory of "recovery of third party damages").[126] The view that the contract between the originator's bank and the intermediary bank in the case of the bank transfer is a contract protecting the interests of the originator should, therefore, be approved.[127]

---

[120] V. Caemmerer, Festschrift für Wieacker, p. 311, 321 = Gesammelte Schriften III, p. 189, 199.

[121] BGHZ 69, p. 82, 86; BGHZ 96, p. 9, 17.

[122] Regarding such cases, see v. Caemmerer, supra note 120.

[123] BGHZ 69, p. 82, 86; BGHZ 96, p. 9, 17.

[124] See the convincing comment by the BGH that the inclusion of the customer within the protective scope "by the contract ... is required by the principles of good faith", BGHZ 69, p. 82, 86; very similar, BGHZ 96, p. 9, 17.

[125] But not in the case of BGHZ 69, p. 82; see note 115 above.

[126] Incorrect is the criticism by Hüffer (ZHR 151 (1987), p. 105) that it was "superfluous" for the BGH to "strain the contract with this protective effect" and "thus ignite the following well-known discussion". In both cases (supra, note 123), the customer filed suit based on his own rights directly against the second bank; he did not rely on rights assigned by the first bank, even where present under the facts of the case. In this situation, the principle of liquidation of third party damages could not help the plaintiff. The BGH therefore could not avoid the issue of whether a contract with protective effect for third parties was present. The issue for the BGH was not whether "development of a legal rule" was "necessary" but instead whether the claim should be accepted or rejected. "Development of a legal rule" can result from any decision regarding whether to apply a rule or traditional legal concept to a new set of facts; a court cannot avoid making a rule when faced with a specific set of facts.

e) Scope of Liability

Of course, the only advantage for the customer is that he acquires a direct right against the intermediary bank and is not dependent upon having the originator's bank's compensation claim for recovery of third party damages assigned to him. Even with the help of the legal theory of the "contract protecting the interests of a third party", the bank customer cannot acquire a broader claim than that arising out of the contractual relationship between the two banks.[128] Therefore, the rule in No. 7 AGB must be considered if the application of the AGB is stipulated between the banks. The intermediary bank is liable to the customer based on the "protective benefit" only for the loss of interest (for which the customer as the debtor in the underlying obligation must compensate the creditor due to the character of the payment obligation as a "Bringschuld"). The bank is liable for additional damages only where special notice is given regarding urgency and particular risk of damage or where the risk is apparent.

4. Liability to the Beneficiary by the Beneficiary's Bank

Basically, the originating party in the transfer can also have compensation claims against the beneficiary's bank.[129] Here, it makes no difference wheth-

---

[127] In order to avoid misunderstandings, it must again be emphasized that this involves a true contract for the benefit of a third party within the meaning of § 328 BGB. It is unusual only in that the third party does not, as in the normal case under § 328 BGB, have a right to the performance (namely execution of the transaction) but instead only a claim for compensation in the case of nonperformance or faulty performance. Such a provision is covered by the principle of private autonomy, and it can be derived from the contract by means of supplementary interpretation when this is consistent with the interests of the parties and good faith (§ 157 BGB). See v. Caemmerer, Festschrift für Wieacker, p. 311 = Gesammelte Schriften III, p. 189; see also BGH, WM 1987, p. 257, 259 = NJW 1987, p. 1758, 1759 with additional references. See the differing and unconvincing view of Gernhuber, Das Schuldverhältnis, p. 540, at § 21 III 4. The catch phrase "development of a legal rule" which he also uses does not explain anything at all, and it is not true that the supplementary interpretation is a "spurious justification". On the topic of supplementary interpretation in general, see Flume, Allg. Teil II § 16, 4, pp. 321 ff. and specifically with regard to the contract with protective effect for third parties, at § 16, 4 f.

[128] § 334 BGB is also applicable to the contract with protective effect for third parties; see BGHZ 33, p. 247, 250; BGHZ 56, p. 269, 272; Larenz, Schuldrecht I, p. 229, at § 17 II; v. Caemmerer, Festschrift für Wieacker, p. 311, 316 = Gesammelte Schriften III 189, 194; MünchKomm-Gottwald, at § 328 BGB, margin no. 78; Soergel-Hadding, at § 328 BGB appendix, margin no. 21.

[129] There is no question of liability under § 278 BGB by the originator's bank for conduct by the beneficiary's bank in breach of the order. When it transmits the transfer order and cover to the beneficiary's bank, the originator's bank has completed its compliance with the order. Correct to this extent: BGH, NJW 1991, p. 2210, 2211 (see note 105 above); see also RGZ 105, p. 48, 50 = Bank-Archiv 22 (1922), p. 261.

er the compensation claim is based on rights assigned by the originator's bank and the principle of "recovery of third party damages"[130] or on a separate right and the benefit under the contract made between the originator's bank (or the last intermediary bank) and the beneficiary's bank.[131] To the extent that the loss is incurred due to delayed handling of the transfer order by the beneficiary's bank, the originator in the transfer, i.e. the debtor in the underlying obligation, can, under the correct view, not incur such loss. Even though the money debt is a "Bringschuld", the debtor is not liable for delays caused by the beneficiary's bank; time limits, including grace periods, are met if the transfer is received by the beneficiary's bank prior to the expiration of the time period and the beneficiary's bank then delays crediting the funds until after the payment date.[132] Therefore, the debtor cannot have a compensation claim against the beneficiary's bank. The creditor must take recourse against his bank, which in the handling of the transfer has violated its duties based on the banking agreement with its customer.

5. Direct Liability to the Creditor by the Originator's Bank

a) The Issue

If we assume that the agreement made by a bank for the handling of a credit transfer can include protection for third parties, the additional issue arises as to whether the only protected third party is the originator or whether the beneficiary of the transfer can also be a protected third party. This question may not be limited to the case where an agreement for the further transmittal of the transfer has been concluded between a first bank and an intermediary bank (or between two intermediary banks). The question applies equally to the relationship between the beneficiary and the originator's bank. Only if the transfer order issued to his bank by the originator encompasses a protective effect for the creditor as the beneficiary can one also assume the same for the agreements made with intermediary banks along the route of the transfer. If the transfer is delayed, the beneficiary's loss could consist of a loss of interest (either that the creditor/beneficiary suffers a loss of interest income or owes interest) and, in the case of international transfers, a currency exchange loss.[133]

In the present case of a "Bringschuld", the creditor already has a claim to compensation against his debtor for the delay losses if the transfer is delayed

[130] See part V 3 a above. As an example, see also OLG Cologne, WM 1989, p. 93.

[131] See part V 3 b above. Examples: OLG Frankfurt, WM 1984, p. 726; OLG Munich, DNotZ 1987, p. 694.

[132] See above, part I 5, and part III 2 with note 72.

[133] See supra note 47.

by the banks and therefore not received until after the payment date.[134] As a rule, it will not be the creditor but instead the debtor who will take recourse against the banks in the case of delay. This could be different in specific cases, especially where the debtor is insolvent but also where it is easier for the creditor to sue the bank (e.g. an intermediary bank in the creditor's country). The issue can thus also have practical significance in the case of the "Bringschuld". We can only examine the case here where the bank (whether the originator's bank or an intermediary bank) is liable under German law, i.e. has its seat in Germany (see Art. 28 (2) EGBGB).

It is clear that the transfer agreement (i.e. the banking agreement with the customer in conjunction with the specific transfer order) is not an agreement for the benefit of the beneficiary (§ 328 BGB) in the sense that the beneficiary acquires his own right against the bank to have the transfer carried out.[135] The fact that the transfer is revocable until it is credited to the beneficiary would not contradict this possibility[136]; under § 328 (2) BGB, this would not be incompatible with a contract for the benefit of a third party. That it is not such a contract, however, follows from the contents of the transfer order. The bank is only instructed to transmit the amount to the beneficiary's account; the bank is not ordered to directly achieve payment to the beneficiary, and also no reasonable interest of the originator is apparent by which the beneficiary should acquire his own right against the originator's bank.

If the beneficiary thus does not have a claim to performance based on the transfer (the carrying out of the transfer), this does not mean that the same must be true for a claim to compensation based on conduct contrary to the order.[137] A contract can also be a "contract for the benefit of a third party" in the sense that it does not create a third party claim to "performance obligations" but instead contains "protective duties". This means that the instructed party must carry out the order based exclusively on the instruction of the originator but at the same time in the interest of the beneficiary and that this interest of the beneficiary should be legally protected. In this sense, in the case of non-cash credit transfers, the beneficiary can also be included within the protective scope of the contracts concluded for the handling of the payment.

---

[134] See part III 2 above with note 63, and part IV with note 88.

[135] See BGH, WM 1960, p. 346 = LM No. 19 on § 328 BGB; BGH, NJW 1961, p. 1715; BGHZ 69, p. 82, 84; BGH, WM 1982, p. 291, 294; BGH, WM 1986, p. 1409, 1410; Schoele, Das Recht der Überweisung, pp. 211 ff.; Meyer-Cording, Das Recht der Banküberweisung, pp. 13 f.; Schlegelberger-Hefermehl, at § 365 HGB appendix, margin no. 51; Canaris, supra note 15, at margin no. 398; Baumbach-Duden-Hopt, HGB, appendix 7, comment III 3 A; Heymann-Horn, at § 372 HGB appendix III, margin no. 19.

[136] See supra note 23.

[137] See BGHZ 69, p. 82, 84 ff.

The fundamental decisions by the Bundesgerichtshof regarding "benefits for third parties" involving bank contracts have in fact been for the benefit of the beneficiary and not the debtor in the non-cash payment.[138] These cases all involved the peculiarity that the beneficiary was at the same time the originator. That party submitted the debit voucher or the check to his bank for collection; the presenting bank handed the item over to the drawee bank or an intermediary bank; in handling the transaction, one of these latter banks violated its duties with respect to the presenting bank, causing the beneficiary to incur a loss. It is particularly easy here to assume that the presenting bank made the agreement with the second bank directly in the interest of its own principal and also wished to give this principal legally effective protection.

The situation regarding bank transfers is different in this respect; the creditor is not the principal of the first bank. One can ask, however, whether that fact can be decisive. As described above, it is necessary to interpret the contract[139] — primarily the first contract between the originator and his bank.

b) Inclusion of the Beneficiary within the Protective Scope of the Transfer Order

Because the credit transfer is a high-volume standard transaction based on a uniform procedure[140], the party interests typical of such transactions are decisive. But the typical characteristic of the bank transfer is that in case of delayed handling a disadvantage will with certainty be incurred by the beneficiary. The issue of whether, from a legal point of view, the beneficiary or the originator must finally bear this loss is governed by the underlying obligation, which can be structured in various ways. This is not obvious from the transfer order alone and also has nothing to do with the bank. In any case, the loss is first suffered by the beneficiary and this fact is apparent to every party involved in the transfer procedure. The late handling of the transfer is thus a "procedurally typical risk"[141] of the beneficiary. The beneficiary relies on the proper handling of the transfer[142] by agreeing with respect to the sender that payment may be made by means of a bank transfer. The sender is obligated as the debtor in the underlying obligation to act in the interest of his creditor in making the transfer; regardless of whether the risk of delay affects him or the creditor, the debtor has a natural interest in having

[138] BGHZ 69, p. 82; BGHZ 96, p. 9.

[139] See V 3 b, d above.

[140] See BGHZ 69, p. 82, 96; BGHZ 96, p. 9, 17.

[141] Id.

[142] Id.

the money received by the creditor as soon as possible after it has been sent, i.e. that it not be delayed on the way where it is of no good to him or to the creditor. The bank must comply with this typical intent of the debtor. The inclusion of the beneficiary within the protective scope of the transfer order thus appears to be "necessary under principles of good faith".[143]

It follows logically from the debit voucher and check collection decisions by the Bundesgerichtshof[144] that the protective scope of the bank transfer agreements should also include the beneficiary. There is no danger here of endless extension of the circle of protected parties because the transfer has only a single originator and a single beneficiary, who are both specifically designated on the transfer order.

c) Brief Comparison with the Legal Situation under Transportation Law

This extension of the protective scope of the transfer order to the beneficiary is not unique. It is perhaps appropriate to compare the transfer, somewhat as a transport of money, with transport of other goods. If the sender instructs a carrier to transport goods to a receiving party, the carrier violates his contractual duty to the sender if he damages the goods underway or does not carry out the transport in a timely manner (§ 429 (1) German Commercial Code [HGB]). But after the arrival of the goods at the place of delivery, the receiving party may also assert claims for compensation of losses resulting from the damage or delay (§ 435 HGB).[145] This is true "without regard to whether he acts in his own interest or in the interest of a third party"; i.e. the receiving party can claim compensation based on the shipping agreement which was made not by him but by the sender and for losses which he incurred due to improper handling of the goods or failure to comply with the stipulated delivery time. The receiving party is thus included within the protective scope of the shipping agreement. Because in accordance with § 435 sent. 1, 2 HGB he can also demand delivery of the goods from the carrier under the conditions cited there, i.e. he can demand fulfillment of the shipping agreement, the shipping agreement in its statutory form is not only a contract "with protective effect for third parties" but also, even though with some limitations, a true "contract for the benefit of a third party".[146] There is, however, in the case of the bank transfer no precise equivalent (due to the necessary involvement of the bank instructed by the

---

143 Id.

144 Id.

145 See BGHZ 82, p. 162, 170; Helm, in: Großkomm. HGB, at § 435, margin no. 13.

146 See also Soergel-Huber, margin no. 33 preceding at § 446 BGB.

originator). The relevant factor in this context is the protective effect of the shipping agreement for the receiving party who does not enter into a contractual relationship with the carrier. This protective effect exists without regard to whether the sender can issue diverging instructions to the carrier up until the time stipulated in § 433 (2) HGB, similar to the fact that the originator can cancel the transfer order until the time of credit to the creditor's account. The constellation of party interests with respect to a bank transfer is not unsimilar to the interests involved in a shipping agreement. It is true that § 435 HGB is a provision so closely tailored to the special characteristics of freight shipping that one certainly could not apply it directly by analogy in other situations. But the comparison demonstrates that the interpretation of the transfer agreement as a contract with protective effect for the beneficiary merely follows logically from a principle which the legislators have long recognized as being correct with respect to the shipping agreement.[147]

d) Legal Consequences

Logically following the case decisions by the Bundesgerichtshof, the bank transfer should be viewed as a contract with protective effect for the beneficiary. This would have the result, at least where in the underlying contractual relationship a "Bringschuld" exists, that a delay in the transfer, regardless of whether by the originator's bank or the intermediary bank, would subject the bank to two claims: one claim by the originator and one claim by the beneficiary. Both claims would have the same basis and be directed toward the same interests; the bank would have to pay compensation only one time; the originator and the beneficiary would be joint creditors (§ 428 BGB). The settlement between the originator and the beneficiary would be governed by their underlying contractual relationship (see § 430 BGB). The beneficiary would have the final right to the compensation, which is obvious in the case of a "Bringschuld" in which the debtor is liable to the creditor for losses due to delay.[148]

Of course, the beneficiary's claim for compensation would not be broader than that of the originator. Limitations on liability which the originator validly agreed to with respect to the originator's bank or between the originator's bank and the intermediary bank, would also be effective against the beneficiary if he takes recourse against the originator's bank or the intermediary bank based on the "protective effect" of the agreements made between them.[149] No. 7 AGB also has practical significance here. The

[147] § 435 traces back to Art. 405 of the ADHGB of 1861. Regarding the motives, see v. Hahn, at art. 405 ADHGB, margin no. 1-6.

[148] See part III 2 above with n. 63; part IV with n. 88.

[149] See supra note 128.

beneficiary may, as a rule, only obtain compensation for loss of interest. In the more difficult case, where there is a currency exchange loss or loss of value in the funds due to the delay[150], the bank, to the extent that it had stipulated the application of the AGB with its direct contracting partner, would be liable for such losses only if it had received special notice in accordance with No. 7 AGB or where the risk was apparent to the bank and reliance on No. 7 should therefore be viewed as an abuse of rights.[151]

VI. Consequences for the Bank's Liability (2): Legal Situation in the Case of a "Holschuld"

If the payment obligation is a "Holschuld", such as where payment by check is stipulated[152] or in case of payment "cash against instruments"[153] then if the banks involved in the payment transaction (i.e. here the banks instructed to carry out the collection) delay the processing, the only claims possible are those of the creditor. The debtor has nothing to do with the collection, i.e. the actual transfer transaction[154]; he is not liable to the creditor for the banks which the creditor has employed to carry out the collection and therefore has no reason to take recourse against these banks due to the delay.

The bank instructed by the creditor to collect the check or the documents is liable — assuming that German law applies — to the creditor at least for its own negligence. Under the principles stated above, it is also liable, in accordance with § 278 BGB, for the negligence of the additional banks which it employs in carrying out the collection order.[155] The view would also be incorrect here that the first instructed bank has already carried out its order when it transmits the check or the instruments to its intermediary bank in the debtor's country, or employs an intermediary bank in its own country to undertake this transmission.[156] If, in the case of a check collection, the first

[150] See supra note 47.

[151] Regarding the basic validity of no. 7 AGB, see V 2 a above.

[152] See part II above.

[153] Id.

[154] Id.

[155] See part VI 2 b above; see generally RG, LZ 1926, p. 45 (regarding the transfer). Contra, with respect to check collection, Canaris, supra note 15, at margin no. 742; regarding collection of documents, Nielsen, in: BuB, at margin no. 5/452; v. Gablenz, Die Haftung der Banken bei Einschaltung Dritter, pp. 261 ff.; Zahn-Eberding-Ehrlich, margin no. 3/8 (in contrast to the prior edition); Canaris, supra note 15, at margin no. 1095 with additional references. But with respect to documentary transactions as here, see Schlegelberger-Hefermehl, at § 365 HGB appendix, margin no. 270; Liesecke, Festschrift für Fischer, p. 397, 403; and the firm opinion in Heymann-Horn, at § 372 HGB appendix IV, margin no. 17.

instructed bank maintains a direct business relationship with the drawee bank, or in the case of collection of bills, with the bank designated by the debtor as the paying agent, the first bank will present the check or the documents directly to that bank and settle through their current accounts. In this way, the first bank carries out the order. If the first instructed bank lacks a direct connection to the drawee bank or paying agent and for this reason employs intermediary banks, the intermediary banks are used to carry out the order. This is actually without doubt a case for § 278 BGB. Of course, the liability is limited under No. 25 AGB to gross negligence. And, in the case of collection of documents, the presenting banks totally exclude liability for intermediary banks (Art. 3 (3) Uniform Rules for Collection).[157] That is, however, not consistent with § 9 AGBG.[158] On the other hand, the drawee bank or paying agent, where the documents are to be collected, is naturally not a "special agent" for the bank instructed to carry out the collection.[159]

Regardless of the applicability of § 278 BGB, the creditor in any case has a claim against the intermediary bank which violates its duties under the order which it accepted, based on the "contract with protective effect for third parties".[160] The result cannot be different for the collection of documents. The right to compensation is subject to the limitations of No. 7 AGB.[161]

In contrast, the drawee bank in the case of the check or the paying agent in the case of collection of documents is not liable to the creditor if it does not honor the papers or does so late. The creditor does not have a claim against the bank for payment of the check or documents; this would require a check guarantee or a letter of credit. Therefore, the creditor cannot derive rights from a delayed payment. In that case, of course, he has a claim against the debtor because the drawee bank or paying agent acts as the "special agent" of the debtor.[162] If the bank acted improperly, the debtor may then take recourse against the bank.

---

[156] But see in this sense, Canaris, supra note 15, at margin note 742, 1095.

[157] Uniform Rules for Collections of the International Chamber of Commerce, Paris.

[158] See Heymann-Horn, at § 372 HGB appendix IV, margin no. 17. Contra, Canaris, supra note 15, at margin no. 1095; Baumbach-Duden-Hopt, HGB, appendix 12, Art. 3 ERI, comment 1.

[159] Correct to this extent is Canaris, supra note 15, margin no. 742; OLG Cologne, BB 1953, p. 305 (both, however, relying incorrectly on RGZ 105, p. 32, 34); Palandt-Heinrichs, at § 278 BGB, margin no. 27. Art. 3 (1) ERI apparently includes within the definition of "collecting bank" the paying agent named by the debtor to the creditor and by the creditor to the presenting bank; the question of whether the "collecting bank" is a "servant" can, therefore, not be answered generally: the correspondent bank of the presenting bank is a "servant"; the debtor's paying agent is not.

[160] See BGHZ 96, p. 9, 17 and part V 3 b-d with note 115 above; with respect to damage due to delay, see Canaris, supra note 15, at margin no. 741.

[161] But see part VII 3 below.

[162] See part II above.

VII. Consequences for the Bank's Liability (3): Legal Situation in the Case of a "Schickschuld"

1. The Usual Case : No Loss Suffered Directly by the Debtor

If the underlying obligation is subject to § 270 BGB and the money debt is therefore a "qualifizierte Schickschuld", only in an exceptional case can the debtor who arranges for the credit transfer directly suffer a loss due to improper handling by the banks. One example, of course, is where the transfer is delayed for such a long time that it must be deemed to be "lost", and the debtor, in accordance with § 270 (1) BGB therefore arranges for a second transfer. The debtor will then cancel the first transfer and, following determination of what had happened to it, will receive credit for the first transfer. In the meantime, however, he suffers a loss of interest, for which he can claim compensation from the bank which acted improperly (or, in accordance with the correct view, also from the originator's bank).

To the extent that a straightforward loss due to delay is involved, the debtor is not liable to the creditor within the scope of § 270 BGB.[163] The loss affects the creditor directly; the debtor's assets are unaffected.

2. Debtor's Right to Recover Third Party Damages for the Creditor?

Thus, the issue arises as to whether the debtor can make a claim for recovery from the bank responsible for the damages suffered directly by his creditor due to the delay. If the bank has its seat in Germany and is therefore subject to German law (Art. 28 (2) EGBGB), the following applies:

The debtor cannot base a claim for recovery of third party damages on the theory that he arranged for the transfer as the "indirect representative" of the creditor. The debtor transferred the money in order to pay his own debt; he acted for his own account and not for that of his creditor.

One could, therefore, consider only whether this could be a case of "release from a danger of liability". It involves the situation where a debtor is obligated to transfer ownership of an object to a creditor; the risk of performance and, in case of payment for performance, the price risk has shifted to the creditor. The object is now destroyed by a third party. Normally, the debtor would bear this loss. But in the present case, the creditor had already relieved the debtor of the risk; the debtor is released from his obligation to perform, still receives the consideration from the creditor, and suffers no net loss. It is undisputed that this cannot release the

[163] See part I 2, 4 above.

tortfeasor from liability. The shift of risk to the creditor should not work to the advantage of the tortfeasor, but instead the debtor's compensation claim against the tortfeasor should be available to the creditor (see § 281 BGB).[164]

Likewise, in the case of § 270 BGB, one could at first glance think that in a comparable sense a "release from a danger of liability" could be present with respect to the risk of delay. But the cases of destruction of an object after the passing of the risk and the delay of a credit transfer are in fact not comparable. One can scarcely say that the risk of delay is "normally" a risk affecting the debtor which only as an exception is taken over by the creditor. The risk of delay only arises as a result of the transfer. This is particularly clear with respect to the example of the currency exchange risk. If the debtor transfers an amount in German marks to the U.S.A. and if the mark loses value as against the dollar during the period of delay, one cannot say that this is a risk which the debtor normally bears. Without the transfer, a fluctuation in exchange rates would not have resulted in a loss at all; the creditor's own financial situation is what leads to the loss. The result in the case of an interest loss is comparable. The debtor's assets remain the same whether the money is received earlier or later by the creditor. The loss first arises in the creditor's assets; the amount depends upon whether and in what amount the creditor loses interest income or incurs interest expenses; this loss is not something which has "shifted" from the debtor to the creditor. A recovery of third party damages is, therefore, not possible.

3. The Creditor's Own Right to Compensation?

The loss due to delay, for which the bank is actually liable, is thus compensable only if we apply our preferred view and grant the creditor his own right to compensation based on the aspect of the "contract with protective effect for third parties".[165] It can hardly be disputed that there is a practical need for this result. Otherwise, the situation would arise where both parties (the debtor and the creditor) would be improperly deprived of the amount for a certain length of time, that loss arises thereby (a loss of interest, perhaps a currency exchange loss for the creditor) and that there is nevertheless no claim for compensation only because the underlying obligation is a "Schickschuld" and not a "Bringschuld" (otherwise the debtor would have a claim against the bank and the creditor a claim against the debtor.)

[164] See Soergel-Huber, at margin no. 25, 26 preceding § 446 BGB with additional references. It is disputed whether this involves a true liquidation of "third party damage" or whether the debtor in a legal sense has suffered his own damage. This disputed issue is relevant where the damage suffered by the creditor is higher than the damage which the debtor would suffer in the absence of the shifting of the risk (e.g. transfer of risk in a sale: when the buyer's loss is greater than the purchase price). We need not settle this issue here.

[165] See part V 5 above.

In this context, we would again like to refer to the comparable problem and its solution under freight transportation law.[166] In the case of a sales shipment, the buyer usually bears the risk of shipping (§ 447 BGB). This means that the carrier is not the "special agent" of the seller within the meaning of § 278 BGB.[167] If the carrier delays the transport, the seller does not incur the damage; the risk of loss is also not "shifted" from the seller to the buyer but instead is incurred directly by the buyer. A claim by the seller, who executed the freight agreement, for compensation of his own loss would be useless; the seller is also not obligated to compensate the buyer for this loss due to delay. The gap in the liability system is closed by § 435 BGB which, following the arrival of the goods, grants the buyer his own right against the carrier to compensation for the delay damages and thus includes the buyer within the protective scope of the freight agreement. The legal concept of the contract with protective effect for third parties should lead to the same result in the case of the bank transfer.

Here, of course, the limitation of No. 7 AGB also applies.[168] Like the debtor, the creditor can normally claim compensation for lost interest, not for additional damages, even a currency exchange loss. Such recovery would be conditioned upon the special notice provided for in No. 7 AGB. Consideration should also be given, however, to the issues of whether in the case of a German mark transfer to a foreign country the creditor's exchange rate risk is perhaps so obvious that reliance on No. 7 AGB would be an abuse of rights.

VIII. Summary

1. Under German law, the place of payment is the (business) residence of the debtor. The payment debt is a limited "Schickschuld": the debtor bears the risk of loss, the creditor the risk of delay. For payments by bank transfer, this means that the debtor complies with the payment date by submitting a proper transfer order to the originator's bank, on the condition that covering funds are available. Delays caused within the scope of the banks work to the disadvantage of the creditor. The banks, including the bank directly instructed by the debtor, are not the "special agents" of the debtor; the debtor is not liable for their acts or omissions. This result should be retained despite differing views asserted in the legal literature.

2. In practice, a number of forms of payments are often stipulated which transform the actual payment obligation into a "Holschuld": e.g. payment

[166] See also part V 5 c above.

[167] See Soergel-Huber, at § 447 BGB, margin no. 64 with additional references.

[168] See part VII 5 d above; with regard to consistency with § 9 AGBG, see part VII 2 a above.

by check, "cash against instruments", letter of credit, "cash on delivery". In these cases, payment is made at the creditor's cost and risk.

3. Under the International Sales Convention, when not otherwise stipulated, the purchase price obligation is a "Bringschuld". The buyer bears not only the risk of loss but also the risk of delay. He is liable to the seller for mistakes made by the originator's bank and the intermediary banks employed by the originator's bank. He is not liable for the mistakes or insolvency of the beneficiary's bank.

4. Under many foreign legal systems, the payment obligation is likewise a "Bringschuld". The legal consequences are generally similar to those under the International Sales Convention.

5. If the payment obligation is a "Bringschuld" and the debtor is therefore liable for mistakes by the originator's bank, then to the extent that the bank has its seat in Germany and German law therefore applies, the results with respect to the debtor's recourse against the bank are the following:

a) The bank directly instructed by the debtor is liable for delays within the scope of its operations for which it is at fault. As a rule, the interest loss must be compensated; compensation for additional damages is conditioned upon whether the debtor gave special notice to the bank concerning the risk of damage. The relevant provision in No. 7 of the General Business Conditions [AGB] for banks is consistent with the Law Governing Standard Contracts.

b) The originator's bank is liable to the same extent for the misconduct of the intermediary, but limited to gross negligence (No. 25 AGB) In contrast to the prevailing view in the legal literature which has recently been adopted by the Bundesgerichtshof, but consistently with the Reichsgericht, the intermediary banks should be viewed as the "special agents" of the originator's bank.

c) The intermediary banks are also directly liable to the debtor, even for simple negligence, within the limits of No. 7 Bank AGB, based on the "contract with protective effect for third parties".

d) The originator's bank and the intermediary banks are also liable to the creditor for the loss due to delay, likewise under the "contract with protective effect for third parties". Here again, the limitations of No. 7 and No. 25 Bank AGB apply.

6. If the payment obligation is a "Holschuld" and is collected by banks, in particular in the case of payment by check or "cash against instruments", the debtor is not liable to the creditor for delays which occur within the scope of the banks instructed to carry out the collection; the debtor does not suffer a loss. In the case of fault, the creditor may claim compensation from the bank which he instructs (the presenting bank). The presenting bank is also liable within the limits of No. 25 Bank AGB for the intermediary banks which it

employs but not for the drawee bank or paying agent. The creditor may also take direct recourse against the intermediary banks under the theory of the "contract with protective effect for third parties"; he does not have a claim against the drawee bank or the paying agent.

7. If the payment obligation is a "Schickschuld", the debtor does not suffer a loss of his own due to a delay in the transfer within the area of the bank operations. He also cannot assert the creditor's loss by means of "recovery of third party damages". Here, however, the creditor likewise has his own claim against the banks instructed to carry out and transmit the transfer under the theory of the "contract with protective effect for third parties". The creditor may recover his interest loss. If the transfer is made in the currency of the debtor's country and if due to the delay the creditor suffers an exchange rate loss, the bank's reliance upon the provision of No. 7 Bank AGB that no special notice of the risk of loss was given may be an abuse of rights by the bank.

The Law Applicable to International Credit Transfers from the German Perspective

By Christoph von der Seipen, Düsseldorf/Milan*

Contents

---

* Translated by Dr. Frances Dielmann, Frankfurt/M.

I. Introduction/Statement of the Issues

It has been a long time since economic activities stopped at the borders between countries. International legal problems have become the norm. It is astounding that the discussion concerning international credit transfers has not yet been conducted with the same intensity as is common in other areas.[1] This is particularly surprising since payment plays a significant role as the culmination of a business transaction. Furthermore, cross-border fulfillment of payment obligations is obviously complicated, both legally and technically[2], and, above all, touches upon numerous areas of the law, such as that of banking transactions and bank regulation and also data protection law.[3]

There are probably various reasons why the discussion has so far appeared rather restrained. One reason is the possible view that the handling of payments is usually not problematic in practice; this view is contradicted, however, by the many disputes which have arisen.[4] On the other hand, one

[1] But see W. Lorenz, Fehlerhafte Banküberweisungen mit Auslandsberührung, NJW 1990, p. 607; U. H. Schneider, Das UNCITRAL-Modellgesetz über den internationalen Überweisungsverkehr, WM 1989, p. 285; Pleyer/Wallach, Erfüllungszeitpunkt und Gefahrtragung bei grenzüberschreitenden Überweisungen nach deutschem und englischem Recht, RIW 1988, p. 172; Polke, Der Zahlungsverkehr der Banken im In- und mit dem Ausland (1978); Brüggemann, Die Banktechnik des Auslandsgeschäfts (6th ed. 1981).

[2] From a legal perspective, many differing forms are imaginable because domestic banks often do not have branches in foreign countries; therefore, so-called correspondent banks must be employed; regarding the various forms, see Pleyer/Wallach, supra note 1, at 172 f. With respect to the technical problems, see Anu Arora, Electronic Fund Transfers and the Law, 7 The Company Lawyer 195 ff. (1986). The international computerized transmission network, S.W.I.F.T. (Society for Worldwide Interbank Financial Telecommunication) is becoming more and more important; for details, see Pleyer/Wallach, supra note 1, at 173; Etzkorn, Rechtsfragen des internationalen Zahlungsverkehrs durch S.W.I.F.T. (1991); see also U. H. Schneider, supra note 1.

[3] See Pelichet, Note on conflicts of laws occasioned by transfrontier data flows, Preliminary document No. 5 of November 1987 for the attention of the special commission of January 1988 on general affairs and policy of the Hague Conference on private international law.

[4] See Schneider, supra note 1, with the reference in n. 8 to a study by European consumer organizations (BEUC), in which defects were found to exist.

could be of the opinion that problems which arise can easily be settled using national laws governing international situations — i.e. international conflict of laws rules.

The international conflict of laws rules in effect in the Federal Republic of Germany are contained in the Introductory Law to the German Civil Code ["EGBGB"]. The specific cases which we will examine here involve primarily questions of contract law, which are governed by Art. 27 ff. EGBGB. Because there is at present no unified law on an international level[5], from the German perspective, these EGBGB rules must be used in order to determine which national system of law shall be applied to international disputes as they arise. The very character of these international conflicts rules as national law leads to many classic problems, which can, of course, not be comprehensively covered here.[6] But even simple case situations of the kind to be dealt with here can lead to substantial difficulties.

As an example, we will consider a quite normal payment, in this case from Germany to France. The German debtor instructs his German bank to carry out the payment which he is obligated to make. The payment is made to a correspondent bank in the payee's country, which then credits the amount to its customer. Even this simple case — which can be made as complicated as we wish by inserting additional banks and payment systems[7] — can lead to substantial problems. One classic problem, for example, is where the payment is received by the creditor too late and the creditor then asserts claims for lost interest or other types of damage compensation. Which law shall govern the issue of whether the banks have fulfilled their obligations? What happens if the correspondent bank, due to foreign exchange regulations, does not carry out the payment order? Another source of dispute is the situation where the originator cancels his order. Since — at least in accordance with the strongly prevailing view[8] — there is no contractual relation-

[5] Regarding legal harmonization, see part V. below; the UNCITRAL Model Law on International Credit Transfers will not have such a great effect that it will lead to a harmonization of national laws — although that would be desirable considering the significance of its subject matter; the goals are described in part V.

[6] The conflicts rules are oriented toward national substantive norms in that they use general terms derived from national legal systems, such as contract, tort, and unjust enrichment. The classification of a certain set of facts to a specific conflicts rule can be extremely complicated; see Soergel-Kegel, at margin no. 68 preceding Art. 7 of the Introductory Law to the German Civil Code [EGBGB].; Münchener Kommentar-Sonnenberger, introduction, margin no. 353 ff.

[7] Due to space constraints, we must limit the discussion to the example mentioned. The conflicts issues to be dealt with here do arise in this set of facts and would not differ significantly if additional banks or payments systems were involved in the execution of the transfer.

[8] Approaches in which such constellations of contractual relationships would be present between all of the involved parties cannot be further analyzed here; see e. g. Gernhuber, Festschrift Larenz (1973), pp. 455 ff.

ship between the originator and the correspondent bank, the legal situation is problematic when the originator's bank has already further transmitted the payment order.

This touches on one current issue which can be generalized as follows: what happens when more than one contractual relationship exists for the purpose of achieving a single economic goal — here namely a payment? Should these various contractual relationships be subject to one single system of law or should they be individually governed by differing systems of law? The German international conflict of laws rules theoretically permit both approaches (see II. — IV.). Because the application of one single system of legal rules would certainly be desirable, consultations concerning harmonization efforts have already reached quite an advanced stage. However, international treaties, which would take priority over the general conflict of laws rules, have not yet been concluded. It is uncertain whether this will ever happen. In any case, these efforts do also influence national legal systems, so that it will be helpful here to examine these efforts more closely (V.).

II. International Conflict of Laws Rules Governing Bank Credit Transfers

We will first examine the most important conflict of laws aspects relating to bank credit transfers.[9]

1. General Conflict of Laws Rules

a) The Application of Art. 27 ff. EGBGB

There are no special conflict of laws rules governing credit transfers. The relevant relationships between the customer and his bank, between the banks and the customer's relationship to the creditor are governed by the law of obligations. Art. 27 ff. EGBGB relating to payment contracts are therefore applicable.[10]

In general it should be mentioned that the EGBGB rules concerning which law governs contracts focus on individual contracts. There is no rule which

---

[9] Bank transfers can present almost all of the issues existing in the area of conflict of laws. The following selection is made from a practical perspective.

[10] It must be kept in mind that Art. 27 ff. EGBGB incorporates the EC Convention of June 19, 1980 (Convention of Rome). Art. 36 EGBGB takes this into consideration and requires a uniform interpretation. However, this form of implementation of the convention by the German legislators was not without criticism; see Matscher/Siehr/Delbrück, BerDGesVölkR (1986), p. 27.

expressly addresses cases such as ours in which multiple contracts are connected in order to achieve a common economic goal. It is, therefore, not surprising that even in these interrelated cases the discussion is carried out almost exclusively on the level of the individual contract.[11] The complex structure is thus split apart and may be governed by various systems of law.

b) Choice of Law

Art. 27 EGBGB permits the parties to stipulate the applicable law. This broad party autonomy was not created by the Private International Law Act which took effect on Sept. 1, 1986, but already existed prior to that Act. We will not at this point consider the details of this Act.[12] In the cases of interest here, a relevant choice of law clause will often be lacking. There is no need for such a clause in the relationship between the customer and his bank because they are almost always in the same country. Even between banks, usually no choice of law is stipulated in the context of handling such routine matters as credit transfers. A choice of law clause can most likely be found between the bank customers in the original contract creating the payment obligation.

c) Determination of Applicable Law in the Absence of a Choice of Law Clause

In the absence of a choice of law by the parties, we will often look to Art. 28 EGBGB, which is the actual heart of the German international conflicts law reform.[13] If no choice of law has been made in the contract, a contract is governed by the legal system with which it has the closest connection. Art. 28 EGBGB is complicated. Par. 2-5 contain a mechanism consisting of various presumptions (par. 2-4) and an escape clause in par. 5 which does, however, permit each specific case to be viewed individually.

An analysis of Art. 28 EGBGB is beyond the scope of this study.[14] For the cases of interest here, Art. 28 par. 2 contains the most significant presumption: the governing law should be that of the habitual residence or business

[11] This is the reason why it makes no difference under conflicts rules whether one or more banks or transfers systems are involved in the transfer. For more detail on the basis for the reference, see von der Seipen, Akzessorische Anknüpfung, pp. 115 ff.

[12] See W. Lorenz, NJW 1987, pp. 269 ff.; Sandrock, RIW 1986, pp. 841 ff.

[13] See Münchener Kommentar-Martiny, at Art. 28, margin no. 1 ff..; Reithmann-Martiny, at margin no. 64 ff.; von der Seipen, supra note 11, at 128 ff., with additional references.

[14] On the relationship between the escape clause and presumptions, see von der Seipen, supra note 11, at 142 ff.

residence of the party owing the characteristic performance under the contract. This long undisputed concept[15] was adopted by the German legislators and looks to the issue of which party in a contractual relationship performs the non-monetary obligation. In most cases, this makes possible a clear determination of the applicable law[16] so that, overall, Art. 28 EGBGB guarantees a substantial degree of legal certainty based on an objective determination and, thus, is an improvement over the previous less clear legal situation. This is apparent in three of the four contractual relationships in our example: between the customers and their respective banks, the law governing the bank performing the characteristic obligation is applicable, thus in this case German or French law, respectively, to the extent that a conflict of laws question even arises; the contract between the customers is governed, as a rule, by the law of the payee because he receives the non-characteristic performance, i.e. merely the payment of money, and thus himself performs the characteristic obligation (e.g. the supply of goods or services). In our example, this would be French law.

2. Problems Arising When Multiple Banks Are Involved

a) Absence of the Mechanism of Monetary Performance vs. Non-Monetary Performance

The problems with Art. 28 par. 2 EGBGB become apparent even in our relatively simple example with regard to the fourth contractual relationship because it is not easy to determine which of the banks performs the characteristic obligation. The normal mechanism of monetary performance vs. non-monetary performance does not function here.

Here one reaches a point where it is possible to assert fundamentally differing views. The issue finally comes down to which bank is able to succeed in having its own law enforced when disputes arise between the banks. In our example, there are good reasons supporting the application of both legal systems. The details of the information needed for the payment, in particular the amount, are fixed in Germany by means of the customer's instructions and the related forwarding of the order by the bank; the correspondent bank in France has no influence on these details. On the other hand, the bank in France is responsible for the decisive act, namely crediting the transferred amount to the account of the beneficiary.

[15] This was already criticized in 1913 by the Reichsgericht, RGZ 81, p. 273; recent and quite terse criticism in Roth, Internationales Versicherungsvertragsrecht (1985), 316 ff.

[16] Lists of connecting factors can be developed on this basis; relating to various banking contracts, see Reithmann-Martiny, at margin no. 534 ff. The lists of connecting factors already existed under the previous law although the case decisions did not rely expressly on the principle in Art. 28 (2) EGBGB; see von der Seipen, supra note 1, at 115 ff.

b) Application of the Law of the Beneficiary Bank

With regard to the relationships between multiple banks, the prevailing view construes Art. 28 par. 2 EGBGB in such a way that the receiving bank is the one performing the characteristic obligation.[17] In our case, this means that French law would apply because the French credit institution received payment instructions from the German bank. No extensive reasons are provided in support of this view.[18] The concept that the bank at the beginning of the chain instructs the following bank appears to be a merely formalistic argument. Apparently, more significance is given to the fact that the beneficiary's bank completes "the credit transfer" in the sense that it is the one which ultimately credits the money to the beneficiary. In the case of a longer transfer chain, in which numerous banks are involved, this idea of crediting by the "intermediate banks", i.e. those between the purchaser's bank and the seller's bank, does not directly fit; but one could at least argue that each receiving bank moves the transfer somewhat closer to the final beneficiary and thus performs a more characteristic obligation than the bank before it.

This view of the characteristic performance under an individual contract between banks should — although certainly not completely unimpeachable — generally be accepted because it provides a certain degree of legal certainty and thus serves the basic purpose of Art. 28 EGBGB.

c) Consequence: Splitting of the Factual Situation under Conflict of Laws Rules

In this last situation, it is thus possible that numerous legal systems may all govern one single credit transfer. International conflict of laws rules do not view this as unusual but instead as one means of guaranteeing a just result; conflicts rules attempt to have each factual situation governed by the law with which it has the closest connection.[19] In this sense, the splitting of factual situations which are economically closely connected is not unusual.

[17] Canaris, Bankvertragsrecht, at margin no. 2503; Schütze, WM 1982, p. 226, 228; Kegel, Gedächtnisschrift Rudolf Schmidt, p. 215, 225; Münchener Kommentar-Martiny, at Art. 28, margin n. 238; Pleyer/Wallach, supra note 1, at 174; BGH RIW 1987, pp. 476 ff.; OLG Hamburg, VersR 1983, p. 350.

[18] See e.g. Münchener Kommentar-Martiny, supra note 17: "A transaction between multiple banks is governed by the law of the party performing the characteristic obligation. Thus, as a rule, the law of the receiving bank applies." This demonstrates a danger with the principle of the characteristic performance when no payment of money is made: the more emotional determination of which party performs an obligation which is more "chararacteristic" than the other has so far not received a more profound justification.

[19] On equity in conflict of laws, see Kegel, Internationales Privatrecht, p. 72, at § 2 I; Neuhaus, Grundbegriffe des Internationalen Privatrechts, at § 5 I; 1 C. von Bar, Internationales Privatrecht, at margin no. 219.

3. The Application of Mandatory Laws

a) Presentation of the Issue

At this point, we would like to point out a further aspect involving conflict of laws which lies outside the rules just described for the determination of the applicable law. All legal systems contain mandatory rules which demand compliance regardless of which law otherwise governs the factual situation. With regard to credit transfers, this issue does not strictly arise as long as the conflicts rules result in the application to each bank of that bank's local law — as described above: the bank complies with the mandatory rules contained in its local law and, if necessary, may rely with respect to its customer, for example, on the fact that a transfer may not be carried out due to foreign currency regulations.

If, however, a bank acts under the law of a foreign country — for example, because it agreed to a choice of law clause stipulating the application of a foreign legal system — the situation is more complicated. Here it may not simply be assumed that the bank may rely on the mandatory rules contained in its local law and, for example, refuse to carry out a transfer order due to foreign currency regulations in its own country. On the other hand, it is immediately obvious that if these rules were not applied the bank would have to violate the foreign currency laws in its own country in order to carry out the transfer — with all the consequences. Such a result would be unsatisfactory.

b) The Rule in Art. 34 EGBGB

The application of mandatory rules contained in a legal system other than the one governing the contract in general is one of the classic issues of international conflict of laws. The legal literature on this issue has become quite unmanageable.[20] In connection with the reform of the German international conflicts rules, a provision was adopted in Art. 34 EGBGB which corresponds to Art. 7 (2) of the 1980 Rome Convention on the Law Applicable to Contractual Obligations.[21] This provision applies, however, only to the mandatory provisions of German law, which are declared to be applicable irrespective of the legal system generally applicable to the contract[22] and would thus take effect if the conduct of a German bank is

[20] See generally Wengler, ZVglRWiss 54 (1951), p. 168, 173 ff.; more recent, Kreuzer, Ausländisches Wirtschaftsrecht vor deutschen Gerichten (1986); Radtke, ZVglRWiss 84 (1985), pp. 325 ff.; Schubert RIW 1987, pp. 729 ff.

[21] Concerning incorporation of the convention, see supra note 10.

[22] The only exception is Art. 27 (3) EGBGB; the choice of law cannot exclude mandatory legal provisions of a state to which the factual situation has its only connection.

generally to be judged based on foreign law. The adoption of Art. 7 (1) of the 1980 Rome Convention, which provides for the application of foreign mandatory law, was rejected by the Federal Republic of Germany by means of a reservation[23]; Germany accordingly did not include a corresponding provision when implementing the Convention into national law.

c) Compliance with Mandatory Provisions of Foreign Law

This does not mean, however, that mandatory provisions of foreign law need not be complied with at all. In principle, it is recognized that foreign mandatory rules may be applied along with the substantive law of obligations.[24] In practice, this means that a German judge may apply the foreign provisions but is not absolutely required to do so. He may decide on a case-by-case basis.

The restraint shown in German international conflicts rules with respect to mandatory legal provisions of foreign states is apparently founded on the view that "legal imperialism" cannot be accepted. On the other hand, the impression should not be made that foreign mandatory law plays a role only in extremely exceptional cases. This is shown by the wealth of related case decisions.[25] Mandatory banking law provisions are often recognized because they generally pursue goals which are, as a rule, also acceptable from the German perspective. This eliminates one concern which, along with the question of legal certainty, is supposedly the reason for the theoretically restrictive handling of this special reference to foreign law: the judge is not obliged to promote a value system which is unacceptable from the perspective of the German legal system.

Under Art. 27 (3) EGBGB, foreign mandatory legal provisions can also be applicable; see Münchener Kommentar-Martiny, at Art. 27, margin no. 66.

[23] In ratifying the convention [EVÜ], the Federal Republic of Germany made the reservation against art. 7 (1) as permitted by Art. 22 (1) a. The government draft provided for adoption of the provision, but the Federal Council succeeded with its objections. The main objection was the threat of legal uncertainty caused by the special connection. Art. 7 (1) EVÜ contains an optional provision and does not force the application of foreign intervening provisions.

[24] Regarding details, see Münchener Kommentar-Martiny, at Art. 34, margin no. 46 ff., especially margin no. 48: the respective provision must be a mandatory one, must be intended to apply, must have a sufficiently close connection to the factual situation, and must pass a substantive examination.

[25] Regarding this technique, it should be pointed out that courts often permit foreign mandatory provisions to apply through domestic blanket clauses; see the references in Reithmann-Reithmann, margin no. 348, 351. Closely connected to this technique is the date theory derived from Ehrenzweig; see Jayme, Festschrift Kegel (1987), p. 254, citing Ehrenzweig, Private International Law, (1967), pp. 119 ff.; see Hessler, Sachrechtliche Generalklausel und internationales Familienrecht (1985); see also Jayme, IPRax 1983, p. 106 and IPRax 1987, p. 64.

4. Claims Based on the Law of Unjust Enrichment

a) Statement of the Issue

In addition to contract law, the law of unjust enrichment can sometimes play a role with respect to bank credit transfers. International conflict of laws rules, as already discussed, basically follow the categorization of the basis of claims as made under substantive law and contain provisions relating to each type of claim.[26] If the facts support a claim based on unjust enrichment, the issue arises as to which law of restitution should apply.

b) Connection of Claims Based on the Law of Unjust Enrichment

Conflicts rules relating to mistake and restitution were largely left out of the 1986 reform and are, therefore, still not codified. Only one sub-area is covered by Art. 32 (1) no. 5 EGBGB, providing that the consequences of the lack of or invalidity of a contract shall be governed by the proper law of the contract. In addition, a distinction is made roughly between cases of mistake (performance without obligation) and cases where the enrichment follows from a tortious act.[27] As a rule, cases of mistake should be governed by the proper law of the contract relationship to which the mistake relates.[28] Restitution based on tortious acts should be governed either by the law of the state in which the act takes place[29] or by the law of the state in which the enrichment occurs.[30]

c) Issues Relating to Multiple Participants

When more than two parties are present, substantial difficulties can arise because it is not always clear between which parties the performance obligation exists and thus which law is relevant. Since a credit transfer to a foreign country always involves at least three parties — originator, beneficiary and at least one bank — the stage is always set for problems.

Depending upon one's point of view, various solutions may be well-supported. The German Federal Supreme Court applied German law to the situation of an excess payment by an Italian bank to a German commercial

[26] See supra note 6.

[27] Reithmann, supra note 13, at margin no. 243 ff.

[28] Id. at margin no. 245.

[29] Id. ag margin no. 257.

[30] Id. at margin no. 259.

agent although the agency contract — with which the performance was connected — was subject to Italian law.[31] This decision has been both praised and criticized.[32]

d) Conclusion

Even this simple case demonstrates that as soon as unjust enrichment claims play a role in addition to contract claims, the issue of the law applicable to international credit transfers becomes very uncertain. Isolated case decisions are certain to occur because it is not always clear into which one of the numerous case groups a particular factual situation fits.

III. Possibilities under German Conflicts Rules for Reference to a Single System of Law

1. The Issue

Because the transfer chain is often much more complicated that the one presented here, in most cases there will be numerous legal systems would could be applied to parts of the chain. In addition, the situation with respect to the law of unjust enrichment leads to a completely uncertain legal situation. The question therefore arises as to whether it might be preferable to apply one set of laws to all of the connected legal relationships. This phenomenon can already sometimes be seen with respect to banking contracts.

2. Examples of Reference to a Single Law in Complex Banking Transactions

a) Confirmed Letters of Credit and Bank Guarantees

Particularly significant in this area are the bank guarantee and the letter of credit. These are instruments widely used in international business transactions.[33] As a rule, multiple banks are involved. When the letter of credit is

---

[31] BGH NJW 1987, p. 185.

[32] On the one hand, Jayme, IPRax 1987, pp. 186 f.; on the other hand, Lorenz, NJW 1990, pp. 607 ff.

[33] See Jayme, Kollisionsrecht und Bankgeschäfte mit Auslandsberührung (1977); Zahn/Eberding/Ehrlich, Zahlung und Zahlungssicherung im Außenhandel (6th ed. 1986); von Westphalen, Die Bankgarantien im internationalen Handelsverkehr (1982); Boerke, Kollisionsrechtliche Probleme internationaler Garantien (1982), especially at 92 ff. See also the references in von der Seipen, supra note 11, at 283 ff. (bank guarantee) and 299 ff. (letter of credit).

opened by the purchaser's domestic bank and is then confirmed by the seller's foreign bank, this is done in order to give the seller a direct claim which he can realize in his own country; at the same time, he also acquires a claim against the purchaser's bank.[34] The situation is similar in the case of a bank guarantee to secure the obligations of the seller.[35] In these cases, it is reasonable that a single set of laws should govern both bank obligations, namely the law of the confirming bank.[36]

b) Differences and Parallels between the Factual Situations

In the credit transfer cases of interest to us here the beneficiary in the foreign country does not acquire a claim against the bank until the amount has been credited; until that time, he only has a payment claim against the other contracting party. Bank guarantees and letters of credit do not fit this pattern. There are parallels, however, in that multiple banks work together to achieve a single economic result; it is not desirable that breaks or stresses should arise between these banks due to the application of different legal systems. Therefore, one can ask whether the strongly prevailing view preferring a consistent splitting of transactions is truly preferable. No fundamental change of direction can be expected at this time, but we would like to briefly mention the most significant arguments for reference to a single law.

3. Arguments for Reference to a Single Law

a) Basis for the "Accessory" Connection

The differences between legal systems often obstruct foreseeability of results and thus force the aspect of legal certainty into the background. One is, therefore, tempted to avoid the rifts caused by the application of differing legal systems to one factual situation. This can be done by designating one single legal system. The conflicts law technique available for this purpose is the "accessory connection". Here, one main contract is designated to which the other economically related ("accessory") contracts are tied for choice of law purposes.

Naturally, this cannot be done in every case where there is a "mere" economic relationship; one also should not overlook the fact that the system

---

[34] Jayme, supra note 33, at 34 f.

[35] Reithmann-Martiny, at margin no. 520 ff.

[36] Regarding letters of credit see Jayme, Bankgeschäfte, p. 34; in more detail and including opposing views, see von der Seipen, supra note 11, at 283 ff., 299 ff.

constructed in Art. 27 ff. EGBGB prefers, as a general rule, the isolated consideration of contracts. On the other hand, an accessory connection can be brought into the system of Art. 28 EGBGB — i.e. where no choice of law clause is present — by means of the escape clause in par. 5.[37] In this sense, a primary contract supplies the connecting factor for some or all of the economically related contracts, which are then all governed by one law. It should be pointed out again in this context that all efforts toward harmonization of substantive law for complex economic transactions seek to overcome differences between national legal systems, to subject cross-border factual situations to only one set of rules and thus to guarantee foreseeable results. As long as these goals have not been achieved at a multinational level, a national legal system can also serve the same purposes.

b) Arguments for the Accessory Connection

The accessory connection can be justified by three arguments oriented toward the interests of the parties as the basis for a comprehensive international law of contracts.[38] The strongest argument for a uniform approach, the so-called consistency argument, is derived from the problems just discussed caused by the application of multiple legal systems.[39] This means the interest of the parties in having one calculable and foreseeable law applied. The consistency argument is decisively supported by the aspect of legal certainty. A second argument is that of continuity[40], which involves the goal of having the parties be able to rely on one system of law when they maintain a business relationship over a period of time and do not wish to be subject to different legal systems for each detail. Finally, one can also refer to an interest in holding factual situations together. A mere economic context is not sufficient, however; further qualifying characteristics are needed.[41]

Especially the first aspect, the consistency argument, but also the continuity argument — at least to the extent involving the cooperation between banks and between customers and their own respective banks — can play a substantial role in the cases of interest here. There is not just a loose economic relationship between the individual contracts but instead a chain of interdependent links, which in our example lead from the German

---

[37] See von der Seipen, supra note 11, at 141 ff.

[38] See Henrich, JZ 1961, p. 262; Kreuzer, Warenkauf, p. 75, 26; Weitnauer, Vertragsschwerpunkt p. 160, 163 f. Regarding party interests, see also Kegel, supra note 19, at § 2 II 1.

[39] This term was coined by Hoffmann; see the conference report by Jayme, IPRax 1987, p. 63, 64; regarding the consistency aspect, see von der Seipen, supra note 11, at 163 ff.

[40] See von der Seipen, supra note 11, at 185 ff.

[41] See generally and with respect to cases of application von der Seipen, supra note 11, at 195 ff.

customer through his bank to banks in France and on to the customer of the French bank.

It is hardly possible and certainly would exceed the scope of this discussion to comprehensively examine the issue of whether in each factual situation reference to a single law is truly preferable. It is obvious, however, that the consistent splitting of the factual situation can be dangerous and theoretically cement solutions which in practice do not guarantee any degree of legal certainty. In our further deliberations, the accessory approach will therefore be included in our analysis of the treatment of the relevant factual situations under conflict of laws rules.[42]

c) Concerns regarding the Accessory Connection

We would like to make some remarks about the reluctance which obviously exists with regard to the accessory connection.

Before one can impartially consider reference to a single law, certain psychological barriers must be overcome. As a rule, this is because the unitary reference naturally leads to the application of a law foreign to some of the parties. This is often viewed as a disadvantage per se to those parties.[43] This view is not convincing, however, because international conflicts law is based on the principle of equal priority of all legal systems and does not permit the classification of one legal system as superior or inferior to another. Naturally it is true that everyone has an interest in having his own legal system applied, especially since the determination of the specific applicable rules is generally easier than under a foreign system of law. But this may not be permitted to sink to a merely formalistic level, which would be the case if the application of various legal systems leads to creation of a mixed legal system which no one can foresee at all. No other arguments are apparent which would force a rejection of the accessory connection.[44]

d) Fitting the Accessory Connection into the Conflict of Laws System / the Center of Gravity in the Transfer Chain

The unitary connection achieved through the use of the accessory approach may not be used rigidly and isolated from the statute but must instead

[42] Regarding general requirements for an accessory connection, see von der Seipen, supra note 11, at 305 ff. Generally, the accessory connection will more probably be found if a type of performance can be viewed as not specifically related to a single contract but falls instead within the framework of multiple contracts — depending on the purpose of the classification within the proceeding.

[43] See Vetter, NJW 1987, pp. 2124 ff., who decisively rejects the accessory connection.

[44] Regarding Vetter's reasoning, see von der Seipen, supra note 11, at 254 ff.

take place in accordance with the principles of Art. 28 EGBGB. Therefore, the proposal that one legal system — such as American law[45] — always be used for all transfers is too simplistic and must be rejected from the perspective of existing German international conflict of laws rules.

When one seeks an overall center of gravity in the transfer chain, it is quite possible to find differing solutions. Problems can always arise if the funds do not arrive in the beneficiary's account on time; therefore, there are good arguments for having the law of the bank in the beneficiary's country govern the entire complex. This would also be consistent with the classifications in Art. 28 par. 2 EGBGB because that bank — as shown above — performs the "characteristic" or contractually typical performance as related to the entire transaction.

IV. Example

At the conclusion of our look at the German international conflict of laws rules, the basic problem of referring an international credit transfer to a legal system will be illustrated based on our initial example.

If the payment is received by the beneficiary 10 days too late, the beneficiary will charge the originator interest for the delay. Here, the law governing the contract between these two parties is decisive, in our example French law. The German debtor will first turn to his bank and investigate whether his bank fulfilled its obligations under German law, in particular the timely transmittal of the order. If this obligation was fulfilled, the issue becomes whether the German bank is responsible for a possible mistake made by the French bank. This issue would also be decided under German law. For the issue of whether such a mistake was made, however, French law would govern. If the French bank acted correctly under French law, the duty of the German bank to pay damages is still not necessarily excluded because it may not have advised the customer regarding a possible — legally permissible — delay by the bank in France. The final solutions under German and French law could thus be different. The German bank could be liable to its customer but have no recourse against the French correspondent bank. Such differing results for the banks would be avoided by the uniform application of French law because then the conduct of both banks would be found to have been correct.[46]

---

[45] See part V. 3. below.

[46] This simple example is based on a firm splitting of the transaction. A similar result could be reached if a revocation of the instruction by the customer were valid and binding under German law but not under French law; if the German bank unsuccessfully attempts to stop the payment after transmitting the order, the bank is not entirely safe from a compensation claim by the customer.

V. Legal Harmonization: the UNCITRAL Model Law of International Credit Transfers

1. Contents and Significance of the Model Law

As shown thus far, it is theoretically possible to determine the applicable law using the existing tools. The practicability of the results can sometimes be rightfully criticized, however, because the various legal systems can govern the parties' obligations in different ways. Because in practice this is at least problematic, it is not surprising that great efforts are being made toward legal harmonization in the area of international credit transfers.

The U.N. Commission on International Trade Law, [UNCITRAL], has tackled this area.[47] The "Model Law on International Credit Transfers"[48] was inspired by the goal of compiling and solving the problematic issues in this area.[49] The UNCITRAL Working Group on International Credit Transfers completed preparatory work in December 1990; the draft was considered by the UNCITRAL Commission in June 1991 and adopted in May 1992.

To what extent this Model Law will achieve practical significance is still open. In particular, the inclusion of domestic credit transfers as well as possible extensive use of the rules in the U.S. could lead to an extensive range of application. Primarily, however, the character of these rules as a model should encourage the national legislators to seek harmonization in this area.[50]

2. Conflict of Laws Rules in the UNCITRAL Model Law

The Model Law contains primarily substantive rules regarding credit transfers. It also contains a conflict of laws provision, which was first found in Art. 15 (see Appendix I) and is found in the final version as a footnote to chapter I as Art. Y (see Appendix II).

Some aspects of the controversy concerning this provision will be described in the following because that controversy reflects the distinction between the single reference and the split reference.[51] The draft of Art. 15 par.

---

[47] Details regarding UNCITRAL in Ganten/Jahn, Die Bank 1987, p. 394.

[48] Dealt with in detail in U. H. Schneider, supra note 1.

[49] Id. at 285.

[50] Id. at 293.

[51] Regarding the details of the dispute relating to the conflicts rules in Art. 15/18, see the following U. N. documents: A/CN. 9/WG IV/WP 46 of May 15, 1990 (on Art. 15: p. 59 ff.); A/CN.9/341 of Aug. 13, 1990 (on Art. 15: p. 35 f.); A/CN.9/WG IV/WP 49 of Oct. 8, 1990 (on Art. 15: p. 84 ff.). The inclusion of a conflicts rule in the Model Law was disputed because UNCITRAL has so far left conflicts issues to the Hague Conference. See A/CN.9/WG IV/WP 49 of Oct. 8, 1990, comment 13 ff.

sentence 1 permitted the possibility of a choice of law clause but recommended that the parties choose the law of the originator, the payee or the state in whose currency the payment was to be made. In the absence of such an agreement, sentence 2 provided that the law of the country in which the beneficiary's bank was located should govern.

Art. 15 par. 2 governed the relationship between the originator and the beneficiary for the case in which no choice of law had been made. Here the law of the state in which the obligation was to be discharged should govern. In the situation where the transfer could be made to different accounts in one or more countries or the payment is not made for discharging an obligation, the law of the beneficiary's bank should govern.

These rules were intended to subject the credit transfer to one single system of law, without automatically extending this law to the relationship between the debtor and the creditor. Very often, however, the law of the beneficiary's bank would have been applicable to both situations.

In the final version of the Model Law, which was submitted by the UNCITRAL Working Group to the responsible U.N. Commission, Art. Y contains fewer provisions than were found in the prior draft of Art. 15.[52] Art. Y par. 1 sentence 1 still provides for a choice of law clause, and sentence 2 provides for the application of the law of the receiving bank in the absence of a choice of law. Further stipulations as contained in the original Art. 15 — with the exception of some comments — were deleted, apparently due to the general problems connected with integrating conflicts rules into a statute for the creation of uniform substantive law.

3. The U.S. Proposal: Uniform Law for the Entire Credit Transfer

a) Reasons for Designation of the Law of the Credit Transfer System

Against this background, it is also interesting to note that the United States proposed that a further section be included in Art. 15.[53] This section would have provided a credit transfer system with the possibility of choosing a national system of law to govern the rights and obligations of all parties involved in electronic high-speed funds transfers (sentence 1). Sentence 2 would have permitted the stipulated national law to take priority over the Model Law if the rules differed.

---

[52] See Appendices I and II.

[53] See A/CN.9/WG IV/WP 49 of Oct. 8, 1990, at 84 ff. and A/CN.9/341 of Aug. 13, 1990, at 6 ff.

The justification given for this conflicts rule was that differing legal systems should not be applied to a unified credit transfer. In the view of the Americans, this is particularly important for electronic high-speed funds transfers. The supporting reasons stated that the needs of high-speed funds transfer systems had not been sufficiently taken into account in the Model Law.[54] The conflicts rule is derived from American law. In the Clearinghouse Interbank Payments System [CHIPS], Rule 3 stipulates that the entire credit transfer shall be governed by the law of the state of New York whenever any part of the transfer goes through CHIPS.[55]

b) Criticism

This proposal by the United States lands directly in the middle of the discussion concerning the accessory connection — even though no reference is made to this concept. It has already been pointed out that a fully undifferentiated application of one unified law for reasons of practicability is not provided for within the German conflict of laws rules, and that even in cases involving conflicting results no general acceptance for the accessory connection approach is in sight. The reaction was similar within UNCITRAL to the United States proposal. The special needs of electronic high-speed funds transfer systems are recognized, but this recognition does not extend to the acceptance of the U.S. proposal.[56] Even if having a single law govern the relationships among the banks is viewed as reasonable, the extension of that law to the originator and the beneficiary has so far been rejected. Furthermore, there is a danger that the funds transfer system could choose a law particularly favorable to the banks in which the needs of the customers are not sufficiently regarded. And the problem would still remain as to which law would be applicable if the transfer went through more than one system; each system would make its own claim to exclusivity. All of these concerns led to the rejection of the U.S. proposal.[57]

---

[54] See A/CN.9/341 of Aug. 13, 1990, at 6, comment 26.

[55] Id. at comment 27. In this context one must keep in mind the practical background, namely that a substantial portion of the international transfers go through the U. S. The new Federal Regulation J (55 Fed. Reg. 40, 791 (1990)) provides that U. S. contract law shall take precedence, i.e. that under Art. 4 A UCC the law of the transfer system shall apply.

[56] See A/CN.9 /341 of Aug. 13, 1990, at 7, comment 28 ff.

[57] Id. at 7, comment 32; it was merely decided that the provisions would be examined to determine whether they meet the needs of high speed transfers.

c) Result

More extensive analysis of the Model Law would exceed the scope of this study. It is significant that the current conflict of laws discussion — splitting or reference to a single law — is also found here. The UNCITRAL draft attempts to reach a balance between splitting and single reference. The American proposal leans toward a radical accessory connection approach. Here again, it is clearly shown how difficult it is to find a happy medium.

VI. Conclusions

The German international conflict of laws rules relating to credit transfers must be derived from the general provisions of Art. 27 ff. EGBGB. This often leads to the application of more than one legal system to the various parts of the credit transfer. The problem of conflicting results in different parts of one contractual relationship would make it desirable to choose a uniform connection. There are in fact many good arguments for such a uniform connection, but the prevailing view in case law and legal literature prefers separate points of connection. Trends toward a unified approach must, however, be kept in mind because relevant projects, such as the UNCITRAL Model Law on International Credit Transfers are already at an advanced stage toward harmonization of the related substantive law.

Appendix I

Article 15
Conflict of laws

(1) Persons who anticipate that they will send and receive payment orders may agree that the law of the State of the sender, of the receiver or of the State in whose currency the payment orders are denominated will govern their mutual rights and obligations arising out of the payment orders. In the absence of agreement, the law of the State of the receiving bank will govern the rights and obligations arising out of the payment order.

(2) In the absence of agreement to the contrary, the law of the State where an obligation is to be discharged govern the mutual rights and obligations of an originator and beneficiary of a credit transfer. If between the parties an obligation could be discharged by credit transfer to an account in any of one or more States or if the transfer was not for the purpose of discharging an obligation, the law of the State where the beneficiary's bank is located governs the mutual rights and obligations of the originator and the beneficiary.

Appendix II

Article Y
Conflict of laws

(1) The rights and obligations arising out of a payment order shall be governed by the law chosen by the parties. In the absence of agreement, the law of the State of the receiving bank shall apply.

(2) The second sentence of paragraph (1) shall not affect the determination of which law governs the question whether the actual sender of the payment order had the authority to bind the purported sender.

(3) For the purposes of this article:

(a) where a State comprises several territorial units having different rules of law, each territorial unit shall be considered to be a separate State;

(b) branches and separate offices of a bank in different States are separate banks.

International Interbank Funds Transfers

By Winfried Holzwarth, Frankfurt am Main*

Contents

In a suit brought by a Libyan bank for payment of USD[1] 131,000,000 by the London branch of a U.S. bank, arising out of the 1986 U.S. freeze on Libyan assets, Mr. Justice Staughton decided that the payment would have to be made in London in USD notes (or in GBP[2]) because in his view every payment obligation, including one between banks, must be satisfied either in cash or by another means which the creditor requests and the debtor is obligated or willing to employ (Bankers Trust case)[3,4]. In a similar case before the High Court of Justice, the U.S. bank was required to pay ca. USD 40 ??? to the account of a third bank at the U.S. bank in London because the U.S.

* Translatd by Dr. Frances Dielmann, Frankfurt/M.

[1] International Standard Organization ("ISO") currency code for United States Dollars.

[2] ISO currency code for Great Britain Pound Sterling.

[3] [1989] 3 All ER 252 ff., 280.

[4] See also short comment in International Financial Law Review, Oct. 1987, at 23 ff.

bank could achieve this result by means of an intercompany transfer in London and no action in the U.S. would be necessary[5].

I. Payment and the Underlying Monetary Obligation

1. Payment in Legal Tender

As a rule, the debtor must offer legal tender and the creditor must accept it or breach the contract[6]. Unless otherwise stipulated and in the absence of an express or implied understanding with the creditor, under German law, a non-cash payment is not a "fulfillment" within the meaning of § 362 German Civil Code [BGB], but instead arranging for a credit to the bank account of the creditor is deemed to be "performance in lieu of fulfillment" in accordance with § 364 (1) BGB; express or implied acceptance does, like "fulfillment", discharge the underlying debt[7], or is deemed in the case of payment by check or deposit certificates to be performance "in lieu of fulfillment" in accordance with § 364 (2) BGB; in this latter case, the creditor is required to seek satisfaction using ordinary care[8] and may assert the underlying claim only if his collection attempt fails.[9]

2. Non-Cash Fulfillment

In international interbank contractual relationships, payment is made in practice only by non-cash means; this is almost always by means of arranging for credit to be made to an account at the creditor's bank; in Germany, there are a few exceptions in the form of bank checks or other documentary means of payment, but in terms of quantity and volume, these can be overlooked. In the absence of different stipulations, this established practice permits the presumption of at least an implied agreement in favor of non-cash payment in interbank transactions. § 242 BGB provides for an exception where it would not be reasonable to require the debtor's or creditor's bank to carry

---

5 Libyan Arab Foreign Bank v. Manufacturers Hanover Trust [1989] Lloyd's L.R. pp. 690 ff.

6 Germany: § 244 par. 1 BGB; Italy: Art. 1277 C.c.; Spain: Art. 11 170 C.C.; U.S.: § 1-201 (24) UCC, but extended to currencies designated by the government or a foreign government as constituting legal tender; see also Aufricht, Comparative Survey of Central Bank Law, (New York, 1965), pp. 70 ff.

7 Kindermann, Gutschrift und Belastungsbuchung im Geldüberweisungsverkehr, WM 1982, p. 318.

8 BGH BB 69, p. 698.

9 Baumbach/Hefermehl, Wechselgesetz und Scheckgesetz (17th ed.), Introduction to Scheckgesetz, margin no. 24.

out or accept payment in cash, taking into account the amounts involved (as, for example, in the cited Bankers Trust cast); this applies, however, not only in the case of a debt in millions[10], but also simply because cash can be obtained, insured, transported across borders and converted only with unreasonable expenditures of time and costs, especially considering the current problems involving money laundering[11]. Similarly, in interbank transactions to foreign countries, performance as a rule consists of arranging for credit to be made to correspondent banks in financial centers in which the relevant currencies are legal tender, although fulfillment in cash would certainly be possible there[12]; the same is true for Eurocurrency and Eurocredit transactions[13].

In the case of international interbank contractual obligations, the prevailing practice, recognized by all expert circles active in this area, is that the debtor's bank is obligated to satisfy the debt by means of an account credit and the creditor's bank is obligated to accept this act of performance as fulfillment so that in fact a commercial practice can be presumed[14], i.e. that the so-called "book transfer" represents the fulfillment of the obligation. While Staughton J. still views cash or funds transfer as alternate forms of payment[15], in practice, from the bank's point of view, only the non-cash alternative remains[16]. Since January 1991, this has become established in more than 12 states in the U.S. as state statutory law: payment obligations between banks are satisfied as soon as the receiving bank has received payment in the form of Federal Reserve Bank settlement, through a funds transfer system or by means of an account credit from the sending bank or an account debit made by the receiving bank[17].

---

[10] Canaris, Bankvertragsrecht (2d ed., Walter de Gruyter, Berlin/New York, 1981) at margin no. 466.

[11] See Steuer, Bekämpfung der Geldwäsche aus Bankensicht, Die Bank 1991, pp. 138 ff.

[12] Kleiner, Internationales Devisen-Schuldrecht (Schulthess Polygraphischer Verlag, Zürich, 1985), at margin no. 31.47.

[13] Id. at margin note 44.06 and 54.02.

[14] On commercial practices in general, see Schlegelberger/Hefermehl, HGB (5th ed., 1976), at § 346, note 1 and note 8 ff.

[15] [1989] 3 All ER, p. 269.

[16] So that the defence of abuse of rights can work against the request for cash payment; see Dach, Payment in Cashless Societies, in: Festschrift für F.A. Mann (1977), pp. 707 ff., 713.

[17] U.C.C. § 4 A-403 (a).

II. International Interbank Funds Transfers

1. The Method of Payment

Some examples of general international payment transactions are non-cash expenditures, e.g. by credit cards, by foreign tourists, the international transfers made for small amounts between private parties (which, as an April 11, 1988 study of foreign payment transactions by the Association of European Consumer Unions pointed out, are often expensive, slow, and insecure), international payments of purchase price and incidental expenses connected with import and export or transit trade with goods, services and other obligations between companies, as well as payments made by banks and non-bank participants in national and/or international financial and capital markets. The larger the amounts involved, the more significant are cost and time effectiveness and proper functioning because otherwise exchange rate, interest and other high risks threaten and can in some cases endanger the very existence of the participants and/or even the total market.

All of these international payments involve credit institutions or other financial institutions such as Eurocheck payment systems, credit card organizations, securities companies, and clearing systems (just now starting up) which are international or deal in foreign currencies. Eurochecks and credit card expenditures must be settled, importers instruct their banks to open letters of credit, to comply with collections, or to carry out payment orders in order to pay the purchase price to the exporter, and two banks involved in foreign exchange transactions must, as a rule, employ correspondent banks located in those countries where the traded currencies are legal tender.

In this context, an international interbank funds transfer is present when within the chain of payment orders and provision of cover between the originator and the beneficiary, one or more payment transactions are carried out directly between bank offices located in different countries. The presently prevailing view is that within this chain of payment transactions only those payment orders and credit arrangements which in fact cross borders are deemed to fall within the classification of international funds transfers[18]. Because this definition applies to banks, it does not include, for example, either international transfers in which the resident customer of a German credit institution orders a transfer for the benefit of a non- resident customer who also maintains an account with the same or a different German credit institution or the "local" actions preceding or following a cross-border

---

[18] Art. 2 (1), Guidelines on International Interbank Funds Transfer and Compensation, International Chamber of Commerce — Publication No. 457, Paris 1990; Art. 1 (1) of the draft of Dec. 7, 1990, "UNCITRAL Model Law on International Credit Transfers" — UNCITRAL Doc. A/CN.9/34.

payment between two banks. Furthermore, this definition does not include payment in foreign currency by a domestic credit institution to another domestic credit institution, but because — at least at the present time — as a rule, such a payment can be carried out only by means of account transactions at at least one bank located in the country of the currency involved, the payment order by the domestic bank to the foreign bank (for the purpose of providing cover) for the benefit of the other domestic bank is included within the classification of international interbank funds transfers. Under this definition, intercompany transfers also fall into this classification if the branch offices involved are located in different countries, provided that for this purpose they are deemed to be independent[19]; likewise a DEM payment by a domestic credit institution to a foreign bank for which the domestic bank provides cover by means of crediting the foreign bank's account at the domestic bank.

2. Special Characteristics

In practice, these international interbank funds transfers are classified as documentary transfers (letter of credit, collections, checks, drafts, etc.) or non-documentary transfers (so-called "clean payments"). In terms of percentage, "clean payments" make up the overwhelming bulk of the total clearing volume in international funds transfers because they include the very urgent, high volume, cost-sensitive payments in particular in connection with international sales, services, trade, foreign currency, money market, credit, investment banking, and swap transactions and other financial innovations in which large sums must be transmitted across borders by fixed dates and as quickly and cost effectively as possible. The large sums involved necessarily bring with them high risks related to exchange rate fluctuations, overdraft interest or loss of interest income, so that increasingly effective and global liquidity management requires faster and more reliable payments. Increasingly, in international banking practice, for technical and other reasons, the exact time when payments will be due is stipulated in addition to the calendar date; non-compliance with this set time can lead to immediate maturity of all claims within the scope of the underlying contractual obligation and, by means of "cross-default"[20] clauses, the immediate maturity of all obligations by the same debtor "secured" by such clauses. Certain financial instruments become attractive only in competition with each other as the fastest and most cost-effective means of payment and in competition between the various parties offering them; their increasing popularity with international enterprises, credit institutions and other financial institutions leads to constantly

[19] Bankers Trust case, supra note 3, at 267.

[20] Lew & Stanbrook, International Trade: Law and Practice, Euromoney Publ. (1983), p. 152.

rising total volume. The following analysis will be limited to these so-called high-volume, high speed, low cost international interbank funds transfers.

Between the bank offices which are directly involved in carrying out the international funds transfer, to the extent that in the underlying contractual relationship these bank offices act on their own behalf, merely a transmittal of account credit must take place. Where these banks act for the accounts of third parties, the first bank office must transmit to the second bank in a different country and currency territory its own payment order which it has transformed from the payment order made by the originator or a prior bank, and the first bank must also transfer covering funds in the form of account credit so that the second bank can credit the amount to the beneficiary or (by means of a further payment order) arrange for credit at a third bank. The international funds transfer for the account of a third party can thus be divided into a payment order (viewed under German law as a contract for discharge of business)[21] and the provision of cover between these banks (and the preceding and following payment orders and their cover). This procedure is actually also the rule in the case of payments for the bank's own account because even those branch offices located in international financial centers and active in international transactions generally have a central Loro (and Nostro) account management, relatively decentralized funds transfer departments and other business divisions in differing locations, so that even when these banks act for their own account they employ at least internal payment orders.

Due to the efficiency of liquidity management by the banks involved, the high volume and the resulting credit risks, the payment order in international interbank funds transfer is closely tied to the provision of cover, which can include procedures entirely within the bank, through mutual account relationships, through correspondent banks, and perhaps local clearing, as well. Because the branch offices of a credit institution are connected through a credit transfer network and banks maintain account relationships with their correspondent banks, within the scope of which at least the banks located within the territory of an internationally traded currency maintain Loro accounts for their correspondent banks (for which the correspondent banks make cross-entries in Nostro accounts) and local credit transfer or settlement networks or clearing systems make possible local settlement for the most

---

[21] The classification of a payment order as an instruction within the meaning of §§ 675 and 665 BGB (BGHZ 66, pp. 372 ff. 375; Hadding/Häuser ZHR 145 (1981), p. 138, 140) is based on the existing giro account relationship in accordance with §§ 675 and 611 BGB (BGH WM 1979, pp. 417 f.; Kindermann, BuB, p. 6129), which is not identical with an international correspondent bank relationship; therefore the international interbank transfer order should be classified as a separate agency contract within the meaning of §§ 675, 611 ff. BGB because debiting the sending bank's account at the receiving bank is neither necessary nor characteristic.

important local banks[22], payments in one of the currencies in use at the location of the two bank offices is, as a rule, carried out by means of account credit (for the transfer order) or debit (against the sender) in an appropriate Loro account, or payments in a third currency are carried out through a correspondent bank located in the financial center of that currency, this correspondent bank maintains accounts for both of the bank offices directly involved in the international interbank funds transfer or only for one in order to be able to carry out the payment to the correspondent bank of the other bank office either directly or through a additional bank or through a local settlement system.

In the settlement of international funds transfers, as defined under 2.2, payment orders and account statements are usually transmitted in standardized form through an international, computerized system for the transmittal of messages in international transactions between credit institutions[23], the Society for Worldwide Interbank Financial Telecommunications ("S.W.I.F.T"), and recently to an increasing extent by means of electronic funds transfers (EFT) as non-documentary payments between intelligent terminals[24]. Paperless exchange of data media, batch systems, on-line data transmission[25], and electronic clearing systems bring about more and more automated international payment transactions removed from routine individual case checks or decisions by humans, thus further reduce processing time and costs; these goals are also served within S.W.I.F.T. by firmly established standardization of format and contents in the relevant messages which are continually improved and also supplemented by relevant standards of the ISO (International Standards Organization)[26] and similar efforts.

3. The Problems

As a result of the large number of transactions[27] within the scope of which these high-volume, high-speed, low-cost international interbank funds transfers are carried out, and through which the DEM clearing by a typical

---

[22] See also Hahn, Das Zahlungs- und Inkassogeschäft der Banken (Fritz Knapp Verlag, Frankfurt, 1970), pp. 73 f.

[23] See also Schönle, Ort und Zeit bargeldloser Zahlung, in: Festschrift für Werner, pp. 836 ff.

[24] U. H. Schneider, Das Recht des elektronischen Zahlungsverkehrs (Frankfurt a.M., 1982), with additional references.

[25] Pleyer/Wallach, Erfüllungszeitpunkt und Gefahrtragung bei grenzüberschreitenden Überweisungen, RIW 1988, p. 172, 173.

[26] Art. 1 ICC Guidelines.

[27] Hellner, Rechtsprobleme des Zahlungsverkehrs unter Berücksichtigung der höchstrichterlichen Rechtsprechung, ZR 145 (1981), pp. 109, 111 f.

major German bank for other banks on a peak day can easily reach DEM 100 billion[28], the most significant problems with regard to the complex scenario described above are quite obvious. The typical problems involved with funds transfers by letter, telex, and telephone were duplicates, inexecutable or lost payment orders, as well as orders carried out for the wrong amount (namely where the amount specified in digits differs from that specified in words) or carried out late, perhaps then also involving cancellation orders[29]. These problems are now significantly reduced in comparison to the new problems of authentication, technical improvements in hardware and software, manipulation of messages (e.g. by falsification or duplicate entries), or deviation from standards, as well as the extreme urgency of the transfers.

These problems can affect a large number of payment transactions simultaneously, and the resulting risks are then multiplied by the fact that, as a rule, very high volume and the extremely short execution time result in serious risks with respect to currency exchange rates and interest and other losses. In practice, risk reduction is served by comprehensive and complex security concepts, correct operation of the systems and software involved, security within information processing, back-up systems, etc[30]. In addition, the attempt is made to further accelerate execution so that a sufficient time buffer remains for corrections and security checks. Because the increased volume of funds transfers goes hand in hand with efficient liquidity management and due to the globalization of financial markets with the constant appearance of new market participants, the other risks involved in the funds transfers, namely in particular credit (delcredere) risks[31] also grow in that payment orders are often (must be) carried out prior to receipt of the cover in order to credit payments within the stipulated time limits, and liquidity risks in the sense that in the case of failure to provide cover or the insolvency of one market participant, sufficient assets may not be available to cover open accounts. In the worst case, this can culminate in a systemic risk because the insolvency of one participant can cause other banks involved in the payment chain to be unable meet their own obligations on time[32].

---

[28] Based on experience in a major German bank.

[29] Hadding/Häuser, Rechtsfragen des bargeldlosen Zahlungsverkehrs, RWS manuscript 127, pp. 71 ff.

[30] Endres, Sicherheitsanforderungen bei kundenbezogenen EDV-Anwendungen, Bank und Markt, Sept. 1990, p. 1 ff.

[31] "In foreign trade it has become common to include in the definition of del credere risk (in addition to willingsness and ability to pay) also the higher risk regarding the possibility of collecting foreign trade claims and the political risk"; see Außenwirtschafts-Alphabet, pp. 74 ff., in: Ratgeber für das Auslandsgeschäft der Deutschen Bank AG.

[32] See Zetsch, Die Risiken im Zahlungsverkehr werden größer, Börsenzeitung, no. 224, of Nov. 18, 1989, p. 9.

4. Provisions of Law

The presently applied legal approaches are, by contrast, very rudimentary.

Staughton J. describes the interbank transfer as a procedure in which the U.S. bank fulfills its payment obligation in that Bank A creates a monetary obligation with respect to the Libyan bank which is actually not a "transfer" but instead the creation of a new obligation by a new bank[33].

This means of providing cover, described correctly here with respect to international interbank funds transfers, for an international payment order, which can be routed through banks other than those involved in the provision of cover, is based on a further payment order. In the Bankers Trust case, it is theoretically possible that the U.S. bank could instruct a French correspondent bank, which maintains an account for the Libyan Arab Bank, to credit the particular amount in USD to this account, and that the U.S. bank provides cover for the benefit of this French bank by means of instructing its correspondent bank in the U.S. to credit the account of the French bank with the sum in USD; the cover for the French bank is achieved through a further payment order to Bankers Trust in New York and its payment order to the U.S. correspondent bank for the benefit of the French bank carried out by means of bankwire, Fedwire, or CHIPS[34], i.e. through a U.S. clearing system.

a) Applicable Law

From a legal perspective, each individual payment order is a contract offer by a sender to a receiving bank; acceptance by the receiving bank results in a bilateral contract, which under German law is viewed as a "contract for discharge of business". Because in international banking practice, as a rule, no express choice of law is made in such funds transfers, under German international conflict of laws rules, and similarly under many other legal systems, the law of the receiving bank is applicable because that bank performs the characteristic obligaition, and therefore the contractual relationship has the closest connection to the law of the country where the bank is located[35]. In the example just discussed, the "actual" payment order would

---

[33] Bankers Trust case, supra note 3, at 270 f.

[34] Association of Reserve City Bankers, Report on the Payments System (Washington, 1982), pp. 133 ff., 136 ff., 146 ff.; Rowe, Electronic Trade Payments (London, 1987), pp. 9 ff.; Geva, CHIPS Transfer of Funds, 1987 JIBL 208 ff.

[35] Art. 28 EGBGB; Art. 4 of the Convention of June 19, 1980 (Convention of Rome); see also Bar, Internationales Privatrecht, v. II, at margin no. 496; from a comparative perspective, see Rabel, The Conflict of Laws, v. 3, pp. 140, 143 ff., 167.

be governed by French law[36], while the one- or two-step provision of cover would be subject to the law of the state of New York.

To the extent that the bank issuing an international payment order and the receiving bank maintain an account relationship and at least one of these banks, with the knowledge of the other bank, incorporates general terms and conditions or special conditions in its account management, the law of the location of the receiving bank would also apply; this is because in interbank transactions as a rule only the general terms and conditions of the bank performing the characteristic obligation are applicable, and these terms and conditions typically provide expressly or by implication that the law of the bank shall govern. However, the number of banks worldwide which conduct business based on such terms and conditions at all or specifically with respect to other banks is relatively small. Nevertheless, German case decisions, based in part on general considerations and in part on the proper law of the contract or a special connecting factor[37], presume that in case of doubt the general terms and conditions of the receiving bank as the bank performing the characteristic obligation are validly incorporated into the contract.[38] Otherwise, the account agreements commonly used in routine banking transactions are extremely rudimentary and can be interpreted only by implication to include a current account agreement, an accounting order, the scope of disposition of assets or perhaps a set overdraft allowance.[39]

b) Agreements between Banks

On the other hand, in the bilateral relationship between banks, agreements concerning very specific aspects or other legally relevant understandings between banks can exist; in connection with an international payment order between the particular bank offices, these can be significant. Without attempting to be comprehensive, we offer some examples: agreements regarding telegram and telex codes or S.W.I.F.T authenticator keys, "standing instructions" regarding the route for provision of cover, or other understandings stipulating the form, contents and/or means of transmittal of payment orders and other related messages, or established practices of a bilateral nature.

[36] On English law, see Dicey and Morris, the Conflict of Laws (8th ed., London, 1967), pp. 849 ff.

[37] See Drobnig, Allgemeine Geschäftsbedingungen im Internationalen Handelsverkehr, in: Festschrift für F.A. Mann (Munich, 1977), pp. 591 ff.; Jayme, Kollisionsrecht und Bankgeschäfte mit Auslandsberührung (Berlin, 1977), pp. 21 f.

[38] BGH WM 1987, pp. 530 f. and comments in WuB ID 1.-5.87.

[39] Kleiner, Vertragsklauseln bei Bank-Fremdwährungsschulden, EWS (1991), p. 53, 56.

Among the roughly 1600 S.W.I.F.T. member banks[40], the understanding applies that international payment orders shall as a rule be exchanged through this network. To the extent that international funds transfers are involved, S.W.I.F.T. substantially facilitates the paperless execution of payment orders (but not the clearing of the related payments) by means of standardized messages such as customer transfers, bank transfers, cancellation orders, etc., using standards of the International Standards Organization ("ISO")[41], an ISA currency code[42], a bank identifier code and international technical terminology. The S.W.I.F.T. User Handbook containing the by-laws, articles of association, general terms and conditions and extensive technical instructions includes only a few principles of liability relevant for international funds transfers based on Belgian law because S.W.I.F.T. is located in Belgium. Briefly, liability is created by the intentional or negligent violation of defined duties of care or general duties of conduct within defined spheres of risk.[43]

c) International Provisions

International conventions or broadly recognized provisions regarding funds transfers do not presently exist, and specific national laws regarding funds transfers appear to exist to a significant degree only in the U.S.[44] The United Nations Commission on International Trade Law ("UNCITRAL") has recently approved UNCITRAL Model Law on International Credit Transfers[45], which may possibly serve as a basis for adoption of legislation within the European Communities[46].

Toward the end of 1990, the International Chamber of Commerce in Paris recommended its new "Guidelines on International Interbank Funds Transfer and Compensation" ("Principes directeurs pour le transfer international interbancaire de fonds et pour l'indemnisation") for acceptance and application in funds transfers ("ICC Guidelines").[47]

---

[40] Etzkorn, Rechtsfragen des internationalen elektronischen Zahlungsverkehrs durch S.W.I.F.T. (Walter de Gruyter, 1991), at § 1.

[41] E.g. ISO 7982-1, Bank telecommunication — Funds transfer messages.

[42] ISO 4217.

[43] Etzkorn, supra note 40, chapter 2.

[44] Id. at 26, with additional references.

[45] See U. H. Schneider, Das UNCITRAL Modellgesetz über den internationalen Überweisungsverkehr, WM 1989, pp. 285 ff.

[46] EC Commission, Discussion Paper: Making Payments in the International Market, Doc. No. COM (90) 447/2.

[47] ICC Publication No. 457.

Although the ICC Guidelines do not — at least yet — find application in international interbank funds transfer practice and in particular have not — at least yet — been integrated by S.W.I.F.T. into its terms and conditions, we will include these Guidelines in the following legal discussion. At least in rudimentary form, these ICC Guidelines do reflect some principles of international interbank funds transfer practice and supplement the primarily technical agreements, understandings, practices and standards discussed above with fundamental legal classifications. To the extent that the applicable law does not contain specific statutes or case decisions regarding funds transfers which are inconsistent with these principles, these principles should achieve some degree of general application.

d) The Responsibilities of the Banks Involved

These principles crystallize specifically in various areas of responsibility, whereby the fundamental rule remains that the banks must act in good faith, with reasonable care with regard to established banking practices, and strictly in compliance with instructions.[48]

Included within the sphere of responsibility of the sending bank are the authenticated payment order, which must at a minimum include an unconditional order to carry out a payment, name and address and other identification (e.g. in the S.W.I.F.T. system the bank identifier code), name and address or identification of the receiving bank, the transfer amount, the transfer currency, name and address or other identification of the beneficiary, other information regarding provision of cover if not otherwise stipulated, and, if necessary in the particular case, instructions regarding the value date for cover.[49]

As a rule, authentication takes place by S.W.I.F.T. authenticator key or a code in accordance with a separate agreement, in which the originator's bank is charged with the risk of misuse of the authentication procedure, provided that the beneficiary's bank is not responsible for the misuse of the authentication procedure and could not be aware of it.[50] Although not often expressly stipulated, losses due to "decoding" of the authentication procedure and its misuse by unauthorized parties should generally be allocated equally to both banks, regardless of which bank proposed the procedure

[48] These general principles were included in various preliminary drafts of the ICC Guidelines but were later dropped because the were considered to be self-evident.

[49] Art. 5 ICC Guidelines.

[50] See UNCITRAL Legal Guide on Electronic Funds Transfer, 1986, Chapter III par. 27, for banking practice with relation to customers, which is consistent with in relation to other banks.

used, assuming that negligence by one of the banks does not provide reason for a different allocation of the loss. The originator's bank is also responsible for issuing its order in terms of form and contents completely and in compliance with the applicable standards, namely in particular those of S.W.I.F.T. or ISO 7746.[51]

Finally, the originator's bank's sphere of responsibility includes the duty to provide to the unrestricted disposal of the beneficiary's bank the cover for the related payment order by the value date at the latest, unless otherwise expressly stipulated between the two banks; such an alternative stipulation might provide that a sufficient overdraft credit would be acceptable.[52] The elementary significance of this provision of cover in banking practice is also demonstrated by the fact that the ICC Guidelines repeat the beneficiary's bank's claim against the originator's bank for cover.[53]

Within the sphere of responsibility of the beneficiary's bank is the execution of the payment order in accordance with the instructions, (a) if this payment is received with all necessary information and proper in form and contents[54], (b) if the corresponding cover has been received for its unrestricted disposal (or is available within the scope of an overdraft credit)[55] and (c) if the beneficiary's bank does not give notice to the originator's bank within a reasonable time and by suitably quick means following receipt of the order that it will not carry out the payment order because it is not able or willing to do so.[56] This means that the offer by the originator's bank contained in the payment order is not complete without the availability of the corresponding cover; it therefore need not be expressly rejected even though it could be accepted expressly or by implication; the acceptance of a complete offer may be presumed if the beneficiary's bank does not expressly reject it and return any covering funds which it had received.[57]

In addition, the beneficiary's bank is obligated to carry out an accepted payment order immediately either by crediting the beneficiary's account or by issuing a further payment order (including the procurement of cover) to a third bank. As a rule, the order should be carried out on the same day. Execution may be made on the following business day only if the payment order including cover is received by the beneficiary's bank after the time at which it is able to carry out the payment order on that day; this time must be

---

[51] Art. 6 ICC Guidelines.

[52] Art. 7 ICC Guidelines.

[53] Art. 10 ICC Guidelines.

[54] Art. 9 ICC Guidelines.

[55] Art. 13 ICC Guidelines.

[56] Art 13 in conjunction with Art. 14 ICC Guidelines.

[57] Art. 14 ICC Guidelines.

contained in notice given by the bank or based on local practice or the rules of the local settlement or clearing system.[58]

A value date indicates merely the intended time by which cover will be made available to the beneficiary's bank.[59]

The requirement that the beneficiary's bank act strictly in accordance with instructions means that the bank must exercise the care expected of banks and carry out necessary actions, without, however, being liable for delays, losses, mutilation of orders and mistakes in connection with the transfer which lie outside the scope of the bank's duties.[60] The allocation of such risks is based on applicable agreements, understandings, customs or terms and condition such as those of S.W.I.F.T. or special clearing systems.

The compensation obligations between two bank offices engaged in an international interbank funds transfer should, as a rule, be limited to the interest loss caused by a violation of duty by one of the banks within its sphere of responsibility; compensation for exchange rate losses or other damages is not expressly excluded but is generally presumed to be unfounded.[61] The type, rate and amount of interest compensation should be based on practices in the financial center of the currency involved, taking the actual time into account.[62]

This right to interest compensation and any other claims based on the ICC Guidelines are available only to the two banks involved in a particular international interbank funds transfer and not to other banks or any other third parties involved in the transactions preceding or following the specific transfer or in the provision of cover.[63]

The ICC Guidelines were first recommended in 1990. Their issuance as "guidelines" and not as "rules" or "customs and usages" indicates a lesser practical and legal weight given them by the international banking community in Paris. These principles do reflect, however, some significant usages at least as developed over some time between banks in countries with highly developed funds transfer systems for high-volume, high-speed, low-cost payments; they may therefore be viewed as potential commercial practices.[64]

---

[58] Art. 8 ICC Guidelines.

[59] Art. 1 (n) ICC Guidelines.

[60] Art. 11 ICC Guidelines.

[61] Art. 15 ICC Guidelines.

[62] Art. 17 and 18 ICC Guidelines.

[63] Art. 3 ICC Guidelines.

[64] In favor of the "Uniform Rules for Collections" and the "Uniform Customs and Practice for Documentary Credits" to the extent that their rules are not already viewed as trade customs: Nielsen, Das Inkassogeschäft (Bankverlag, Cologne, 1987), p. 14; Nielsen, Grundlagen des Akkreditivgeschäfts (Bank-Verlag, Cologne, 1985), p. 20; Zahn/Ebert/Ehrlich, Zahlung und Zahlungssicherung im Außenhandel (6th ed., Berlin/New York, 1986), at margin no. 1/23.

III. Multicurrency Netting Systems

1. Method of Function

The numerous legal and practical problems connected with international interbank payment transfers as well as the flood of risks related to the electronic automated systems and extension to formerly documentary payment transactions, which are now adapted to the system through Electronic Data Interchange ("EDI"), urgently call for a comprehensive technical and legal institutionalization.[65]

Staughton J. gives one example of what he refers to as a "complex transaction": The originator's Bank A has an account at Bank B in London, Bank B has an account at Bank C in New York, the beneficiary's bank has an account at Bank E in London which has an account at Bank D in New York; Bank C and Bank D in New York have accounts at the Federal Reserve Bank in New York. Thus a payment from the originator's bank to the beneficiary's bank involves a reduction in the obligations of the Federal Reserve Bank in New York with respect to Bank C, Bank C to Bank B and Bank B to the originator's Bank A. At the same time it causes an increase in the obligations of the Reserve Bank in New York to Bank D, Bank D to Bank E, and Bank E to the beneficiary's bank. At the level of the Federal Reserve Bank in New York, in which a settlement among all the participants in this clearing systems takes place, the actual amount to be debited from Bank C's account and credited to Bank D's account in connection with the described payment can be reduced because on the same day Bank F makes a payment to Bank C and Bank D makes a payment to Bank G through the system, so that at the end of the clearing Bank C and Bank D are debited/credited only with the net balance and provide or receive this net amount.[66]

Therefore, an institutionalized international clearing ("netting institution") would appear optimal; ideally, as many of the credit and other financial institutions very active in international funds transfers as possible should be participants, and the netting system should include as many of the internationally significant trading currencies as possible; also, taking the realistically foreseeable volume and risks on a worldwide basis into consideration, the time periods for settlements should scarcely exceed 24 hours. Such multilateral multicurrency interbank netting institutions are in the planning stage.[67]

---

[65] See also Etzkorn, supra note 40, at 125 ff.

[66] Bankers Trust case, supra note 3, at 270.

[67] Clifford Chance, EC Financial Services, Sept. 1990, p. 2: Europe: ECHO Netting System; David Lascelles, Banks hope to net a saving, Financial Times of Feb. 25, 1991.

One such netting institution which is already in an advanced stage of discussion would maintain one current account in each signficant trading currency for each bank office connected to the system; credit and other financial institutions could have numerous branches active in international payment transactions separately connected to the system. The individual bank offices would have outgoing payment orders debited by the netting institution from the appropriate currency account and incoming payment orders credited to the appropriate account. At a fixed account closing on each working day, the netting system would net each account in each currency. Here, the numerous credits and debits would be converted to a single net positive or negative balance in each of the various currencies, and would then be reported or made available to the bank offices for immediate payment between the netting institution and the bank offices. For this purpose, the netting institution and the connected bank offices would maintain corresponding currency accounts with clearing banks in each relevant financial center and would then pay the net balance in the particular currency. Thus, the netting institution would make or receive only one payment per day in each currency to each bank office regardless of the number or volume of individual transactions involving that bank office had actually been processed on that day, and regardless of the future developments in the number and volume of these payments. If a sufficient number of bank offices and currencies were included in this system, the numbers and volume of "actual" payments otherwise necessary between these bank offices could be significantly reduced. The result would be substantial savings in terms of costs and reduction of processing risks.

2. The Risks

Attempts can be made at two levels to control credit and system risks. One level involves objective criteria for admission to the system, which must, of course, permit fair and open access, requirements for original provision of security, requirements that additional cover be provided subsequently by the connected banks as needed, as well as the possibility of excluding from the netting systems any bank which is in a crisis situation. These steps can significantly reduce the risk to the system which could be caused by the failure of one of the participating banks. At the second level, the netting institution must provide reliable technical facilities, including back-up facilities, capable of handling the volume and types of transactions. This technical side would involve netting and settlement of balances at least once per day, limits on credit commitments which the system would permit individual bank offices to enter into based on internal and individual criteria, and possible obligations for additional contributions by all participants to prevent the insolvency or collapse of the netting institution — failure of the netting institution to pay its obligations could lead to the insolvency and collapse of the connected participants.[68]

3. Legal Structure

This factual and technical risk reduction would be conditioned and supported by the legal structuring of the netting institution and its contractual relationships with the connected banks. The formation and administrative headquarters[69] of the netting institution would need to be within the territory of a suitable legal system and the charter of the institution validly tied to this legal system. Also of great importance would be a proper choice of law to govern the legal relationships between the netting institution and the connected banks, as well as the legal structuring of these legal relationships within the scope of the applicable legal system, e.g. by means of general terms and conditions or uniform model contracts used by the netting institition which would need to be valid in accordance with the law of the location of each connected bank.

In addition, proper choice of law and legal structuring of agreements with the operator of the communications facilities between the netting institution and the connected banks and clearing banks in the financial centers of the traded currencies would be necessary in order to insure reliable and legally valid settlement of balances.

The express and legally effective choice of a uniform, exclusive venue for all rights and obligations with respect to the netting institution would contribute significantly to the goal of having the contractual provisions construed and applied consistently for all participants.

The contractual freedom of the parties reaches its boundaries when it confronts the mandatory bankruptcy provisions applicable at the location of an insolvent bank.[70] It is true that other mandatory provisions of a legal system other than the law chosen to govern the contract are increasingly applied[71], but we may assume that this danger can be reduced by careful legal planning. If the banks which establish the netting institution and the participants voluntarily taking part in the netting process enter into agree-

[68] Bank of International Settlements, Report of the Committee for Interbank Netting Systems of the Central Banks of the Group of Ten Countries, Basel, Nov. 1990, pp. 5 ff.

[69] Kegel, Internationales Privatrecht (6th ed.), at § 17 II, with additional references.

[70] Reithman, Internationales Vertragsrecht (4th ed., Cologne, 1988), at margin no. 977 ff., with additional references.

[71] Id. at margin no. 341.

ments which are fair and suitable for the intended purposes, the likelihood of a negative evaluation under national laws regarding provisions in standard form contracts could be substantially excluded; in an area where all of the contracting parties are experts in their characteristic area of business, it is unlikely that the contracts would be held to be inequitable.[72] The concept of netting in its broadest sense appears to be upheld even under bankruptcy laws in most of the 11 countries in the so-called Group of Ten, whereby different requirements must be met in each of these countries so that the netting concluded prior to the timepoint of the insolvency will be recognized by the bankruptcy administrator and the courts. Thus, complete elimination of all remaining uncertainties can probably be achieved only through harmonization of the relevant national legal provisions.[73]

The first step is that the netting institution must be the actual contractual partner of the bank issuing or receiving the payment order (and not merely a sham). The current account agreement is a necessary component in the execution of international payment transfers through correspondent banks and as such its legal validity is not disputed; therefore, a corresponding agreement with a netting institution should be possible in theory, at least for the purpose of netting claims and obligations in a single currency. Whether going beyond the conversion to this first net position to a "net net" position achieved by netting the current account balances in different currencies would survive bankruptcy can only be evaluated in accordance with specific national bankruptcy laws. From the German perspective, net positions in differing currencies are permissible where the individual net positions represent claims against the insolvent bank because a foreign currency claim is converted to DEM when the recognized claim is entered in the schedule of creditor's claims[74] and in case of set-off can be converted immediately.[75] Where net positions representing obligations by the netting institution are included, there should, as a rule, be no prohibition against set-off under § 55 of the German Bankruptcy Code[76] when the "net net" position is fixed in DEM against an insolvent participant bank in Germany.

Under properly structured admission criteria, the original security should be provided by the participants outside of (i.e. prior to the start of) time periods for challenging claims under bankruptcy laws. Obligations for providing subsequent additional security should be structured in such a way that they can be called upon in sufficient time prior to the crisis. The security

---

[72] See BGH ZIP 89, p. 1537, 1538.

[73] BIS Report, supra note 68, at 20.

[74] § 69 KO; see BGH WM 1989, p. 1186.

[75] § 54 (4) KO.

[76] Jaeger, Konkursordnung (8th ed., 1958), at § 53, margin no. 27, with additional references.

agreements also need to be made in such a way thay they are legally valid under the law of the location of the objects provided as security.

These examples of potential legal problems related to the concept of a multilateral multicurrency interbank netting system would increase dramatically in number and significance if the netting were extended to foreign currency, cash, forward exchange or swap contracts or other types of financial transactions in a form where the netting institution would "assume" the contractual rights and obligations of each contracting party with respect to each other party.[77] The globalization and liberalization of financial markets as well as new financial instruments have increased competition in the banking sector and reduced profit margins to the point where such plans are necessary. A multilateral multicurrency interbank settlement netting system, capable of functioning legally and technically to the satisfaction of all participants and also operating in compliance with applicable regulatory laws will represent a significant step toward this necessary goal.

---

[77] See Houghton, Netting off Agreements — The Legal Perspective, JIBL 4 (1987), pp. 241 ff.; Shea Foreign Exchange Contracts and Netting in the U.K., International Financial Law Review 1990, pp. 19 f.; Wood/Terray, Foreign Exchange Netting in France and England, International Financial Law Review 1990, pp. 18 f.

Legal Issues in the International Use of Credit Cards

By Jörg Etzkorn, Ludwigsburg*

Contents

---

* Translated by Dr. Frances Dielmann, Franfurt/M.

I. International Use of Credit Cards — a Four or More Party System

Universally used credit cards are usually characterized as a "three-party system".[1] The participants in this system are the two parties to the underlying transaction, such as a sale, and the credit card company[2] through which the payment is to be carried out. Three bilateral contractual relationships are thus created. In the underlying relationship, there is a contract between two parties directed toward mutual performance, such as a sales contract. One party to this contract, e.g. a buyer is at the same time the holder of a credit card and has entered into a contract with the credit card company for the issuance of the card. The other party to the underlying transaction, in this example the seller, has also entered into an agreement with the credit card company directed toward the acceptance of the card by a contract organization as a means of payment.

The model of the three person or three party system presumes that the two contracts with the cardholder and the contract organization were both made by one and the same credit card company. This is only rarely the case in cross-border use of credit cards.[3] Instead, where a credit card is used in a foreign country, two credit card companies are usually involved. One company acting as the card "issuer" enters into an agreement in one country with the cardholder. In a different country, a different credit card company acting as the "acquirer" enters into an agreement with a merchant, hotel, restaurant, etc. — the contract organization — which stipulates the acceptance of a certain brand of credit card and "connects" this contract organization to the particular credit card system. A credit card company may — and very often will — engage in both issuing cards and acquiring contract organizations. The reason why two credit card companies are often involved in an international transaction is that each credit card company, regardless of whether it engages in issuing, acquiring or both, enters into agreements with cardholders and contract organizations only within its own country. Cooperation between the different credit card companies, each acting within its own country, takes place when the companies represent the same brand of credit card; this technical and organizational cooperation is based on agreements binding on all credit cards companies representing that type of card.[4]

The four credit cards widely used throughout the world are Visa, Mastercard/Eurocard, American Express and Diners Club.[5] These will be referred

---

[1] Hammann, p. 22, with additional references.

[2] Regarding the term "credit card company", see Etzkorn, WM 1991, p. 1902.

[3] See part II, 2 below.

[4] See part III below.

[5] Not included here is the JCB card, which is used primarily in the Asian-Pacific region.

to here as credit card systems. These four credit card systems differ substantially not only in terms of range of distribution and volume of transactions, but also with regard to organizational and legal structure.[6]

Where credit cards are used internationally, as we have seen, a four or more party system is involved. Added to the contractual relationships present in the three party system — i.e. between cardholder and contract organization in the underlying transaction, between cardholder and credit card company, as well as between contract organization and credit card company[7] — are the legal relationships between the two credit card companies and/or between these companies and the particular credit card system. It is not apparent that the legal relationships within a credit card system have so far been extensively analyzed in the legal literature.[8] These legal relationships between credit card systems and the connected credit card companies in the various countries, by nature, have an international element. Examples of these relationships will be used to illustrate the various issues discussed here.[9] In examining the bilateral contractual relationships involved in the underlying transaction[10] and the contracts between the credit card company and the contract organization[11] as well as between the credit card company and the cardholder[12], we will consider general international conflict of laws issues and also ask to what extent these relationships may be affected by provisions governing between the credit card systems and the connected credit card companies.[13]

The provisions governing the relationships between the credit card systems and the connected credit card companies and their possible effects on the other contractual relationships involved are significant not only in connection with international use of credit cards. Even within a single country, four parties are frequently involved, namely where the credit card company making the agreement with the cardholder is not the same company which entered into the agreement with the contract organization where the card is used.[14]

---

[6] See parts II.1., 2. and III. 1. a) below.

[7] See parts IV., V. and VI below.

[8] Even the comprehensive study by Baker & Brandel (see margin no. 19.01 f.) does not include this area. In addition to the statutory bases for electronic funds transfers in the scope of the "Rights of Participants", the "Nonstatutory Rules" within the various payments systems are also discussed, but not those of the credit card systems,

[9] See part III.

[10] See part IV below.

[11] See part V below.

[12] See part VI below.

[13] See parts IV.3, V.3., VI.3 below.

[14] See Etzkorn, WM 1991, p. 1901, 1902.

II. International Credit Card Systems

The four systems active worldwide employ quite different internal organizational structures. In describing the systems, a distinction is usually made between bank-based and non-bank-based systems. From a legal perspective, this distinction has little significance. Legally, the more important question is whether the system is open to third parties.[15] If the system is open, it is necessary to structure the legal framework in such a way that it is clear to outsiders. Closed systems[16] use rules comparable to those in open systems, but it is not necessary to draft these rules in as formal a manner as in open systems.

The classification made here, more from a legal perspective, into open and closed systems in effect corresponds to the usual distinction between bank-based and non-bank-based systems because of the specific systems of interest here: the Visa and Mastercard/Eurocard systems are bank-based and at the same time open systems, while the American Express and Diners Club systems are allocated to the near-bank sector and do not offer third parties the opportunity to engage in credit card business through their systems.

1. Open Licensing Systems

The Visa and Mastercard/Eurocard systems are open licensing systems. They do not themselves engage in credit card transactions. Instead, they make available a brand of credit card which may be used by the system participant and also seek worldwide distribution through the participating organizations. Thus, each credit card company which has joined this system can offer its business partners a system with worldwide acceptance even though the company itself acts only regionally[17], i.e. enters into agreements with contract organizations and cardholders only within its own region or country.

2. Closed Systems

In the sense used here, American Express and Diners Club are closed systems. American Express does not permit any third parties to use its name for credit card transactions. To the extent possible and reasonable, the credit card operations are conducted solely by a single legal entity, American

---

[15] See the distinctions in parts II.1. and II.2.

[16] See part II. 2 below.

[17] See part I above.

Express Inc. This corporation enters into agreements with cardholders and contract organizations in Germany.[18]

The use of the Diners Club name is likewise not open to use by interested third parties. The Diners Club system does generally, however, work through one legally independent company for each country or legal territory. This means that it is possible to transfer the use rights through sale of this company — as has occurred in Switzerland. This also means that the rules for worldwide cooperation within the system must be more formally established, not only from an organizational aspect but also due to the legal autonomy of the participants.

3. *Terminology*

For purposes of clarity, the following terminology will be used consistently in this analysis. The parent organization for the particular credit card name, e.g. Mastercard International Inc. or American Express Inc., will be referred to as the "system" or "credit card system". This term will also be used directly to mean the rules issued by this organization. "Credit card company" is the general term for the organization engaging in credit card business. Within the Visa and Mastercard systems these are primarily banks and savings institutions; nevertheless the term credit card company or "company" will be used uniformly. With respect to American Express, the company is (naturally) identical with American Express Inc. To the extent necessary, a distinction will be made in the case of credit card companies between issuing companies and acquiring companies. An issuing company is a legal entity which enters into an agreement with a cardholder relating to the issuance of a credit card. An acquiring company is a legal entity which enters into agreements with contract organizations relating to the acceptance of the credit card. A single organization engaged in credit card transactions can, but need not, be both an issuing and an acquiring company.

III. Legal Relationships within a Credit Card System

As mentioned above, the various credit card systems are structured differently legally and organizationally. In the following description, we will refer to the structures and relationships in an open licensing system. We will do so for several reasons. First, worldwide, the Visa and Mastercard/

---

[18] This does not change the fact that the same legal rules and in particular conflict of laws issues apply to these contracts as to the contractual structures used in open systems; see parts V. and IV. below. Decisive for the determination of the applicable law is the seat of the business location, not the headquarters of the company.

Eurocard systems have issued by far the majority of all credit cards. Of the approximately 463 million cards issued by the four major systems in 1990, about 420 million belonged to the Visa or Mastercard/Eurocard system.[19] In Europe in 1990, the two bank-based systems issued about 77 million cards, compared with 6.1 million by American Express and Diners Club.[20] The second reason is that in open systems there is a much greater need to formally stipulate rules. In open systems, the various locations participating in the credit card system are legally autonomous entities whose legal relationships with each other must be organized. Factually, there is also a need for such organization within a closed system, and the substantive issues to be governed probably do not differ substantially from those in an open system, but the form requirements are not as great. The rules can be handled more flexibly and need not be as transparent to outside parties.

1. Membership

a) Organizational Forms of Card Systems

The prerequisite for participation in the Visa or Mastercard system is the acquisition of a "Membership" in the system, i.e. a share in the particular parent company. Both of the parent companies are headquartered in the U.S. state of Delaware and are subject to Delaware law. Both systems offer various types of membership. The differences are related to the type of participation in the system, namely whether the credit card company will engage in issuing or acquiring and whether it will also or exclusively engage in traveler's check transactions. In addition, there are horizontal dividing lines within the membership, e.g. a distinction between a principal membership and affiliate membership (Mastercard) or associate membership (Visa). An associate or affiliate can act with respect to the system, and thus within an international framework, only with the consent of its principal. Rights and duties in relationship to the systems are transmitted to the associate/affiliate by the principal. In addition, the Visa system has available a regional group membership which makes it possible for members within a region, as defined by the legal system or currency, to create rules within certain system limits which supplement or diverge from the otherwise applicable provisions.

The highest decision-making body in both systems is the annual shareholder meeting. The votes allocated to the individual members are based on

---

[19] Nilson Report 8, 1991.

[20] These figures do not include the JCB system cards; about 18.3 million cards were issued by that system in 1990, but only about 200,000 of these outside the Asian-Pacific region.

the member's significance within the system, as determined in accordance with fixed figures such as turnover volume, and also on the type of membership or authorized transactions (e.g. credit card v. traveler's checks). The next level of decision making is the Board of Directors, which is elected by the annual meeting and is given broad authority including the power to make amendments to the internal rules of the system[21], which are then binding on all members.

One special feature is contained in the Mastercard system with regard to Europe. Eurocard, a credit card system built up in and for Europe, works together with the Mastercard system. With respect to the acceptance and issue of credit cards, this is made possible by the fact that Eurocard consistently uses the Mastercard symbol together with its own symbol in issuing of cards and also in arranging for acceptance by merchants, etc. The entire European acceptance network is thus available to the holder of a Mastercard from North America because each Eurocard contract organization also displays the Mastercard symbol indicating acceptance of that card. Because the Mastercard symbol is also used on the Eurocard, a Eurocardholder can make use of the entire Mastercard acceptance network. From a legal perspective, the cooperation extends far beyond this long- established reciprocity agreement. Mastercard International Inc. has become a minority shareholder in the Eurocard International S.A., which is the parent-corporation of the Eurocard system. Eurocard International S.A., on the other hand, is a member in Mastercard International Inc. In its by-laws, Mastercard International has delegated the decision-making authority regarding membership and licensing[22] in Europe, within certain guidelines, to certain bodies within Eurocard International S.A. Eurocard International S.A. also has its own rules which are applicable to the user of the Eurocard name, whereby the Mastercard rules also apply. The Eurocard rules are supplementary in nature and do not conflict with the Mastercard rules. We will not further pursue the Eurocard distinctions.

b) Joining the System

In accordance with the articles of incorporation and by-laws of Visa and Mastercard, the enterprises which can become members of the systems are banks, savings institutions or financial institutions, which also must meet certain criteria relating to the type of business in which they are involved or permitted to transact and to their financial situation. In both systems, applications for membership must be approved by the board of directors,

[21] See parts III. 1. c) and III. 2. below.

[22] See part III. 1. c) below.

and, under certain circumstances, also by the annual meeting.[23] One prerequisite for approval of a membership application is an agreement that the applicant will comply with the rules governing the system.[24] The consequence of approval of a membership application is the right and obligation of the credit card company to enter into a license agreement governing the use of the Visa or Mastercard name and system.

There is no requirement in joining one of the credit card systems that the company not be a member of another credit card system. In North America, membership in both the Visa and Mastercard systems is common.[25] There are also overlaps with the Diners Club system.

c) The Structure of Internal System Rules

Within a credit card system, there are extensive rules which must be heeded by a credit card company in its capacity as a member of the system. Such rules are contained in various sources. In addition to the certificate of incorporation, there are also by-laws, rules, operations manuals, various other manuals and regularly published bulletins. Generally, most of these various sources are in the nature of handbooks. They are not designed as abstract rules to be applied in the case of conflicts. Instead, they serve to lay out the technical and organizational functioning within the credit card companies and the communications between the credit card companies as well as to provide the necessary level of uniformity within the system, e.g. in the design of cards or the creation of databases. Before an enterprise can become a member of a credit card system, it must agree to be bound by the articles of incorporation, the by-laws, and the operating regulations, not only as in effect at the time of joining but also in all future versions. The law of the state of Delaware governs this agreement — without which membership is not possible — as well as the articles and by-laws of the parent corporation itself. There are basically no legal objections to an agreement in advance that one will be bound by the rules of a system which one wishes to join. Whether this agreement is also valid even with respect to future rules changes is also governed by the law of Delaware and the United States. It can be assumed that a binding recognition of future rules changes would also require reference to the company law status of the member or shareholder in the system. The authority to amend the rules is, in accordance with the articles of incorporation and the by-laws, granted to the board of directors.

---

[23] Concerning the comparable procedure for admission to S.W.I.F.T., see Etzkorn, Zahlungsverkehr, pp. 22 f.

[24] See part III. 1. c) below.

[25] See Merkel, p. 166.

This authority applies to the provisions in the manuals, the rules and a major portion of the by-laws.

The provisions relevant to the company law status of members in the Visa and Mastercard systems are contained in the certificates of incorporation and the by-laws. The by-laws stipulate conditions for membership, requirements for applications, rules, and voting rights for the annual meeting, the authority of the board of directors and, for example, the provision that a new member is obligated to enter into a license agreement governing the rights to use the card name.

The "Rules" contain general provisions regarding the use of the name as well as precise regulations relating to such matters as the design and manufacture of the cards, dealings with third parties employed by the credit card company, rules to insure round-the-clock communication among the participating credit card companies (e.g. to respond to credit approval inquiries), relations with authorized dealers, accounting and security issues, and the so-called chargeback.[26] Also incorporated in the Rules are supplements attached to the individual chapters containing precise specifications within the generally regulated procedures. Following the general regulations, references are also made to the Operations Manual or other manuals — in part to reduce the expanse of the Rules.

The Operations Manual, which is the size of a large notebook, covers in detail the majority of issues and procedures relevant in the day-to-day operations of a credit card organization. The Manual also contains numerous appendices governing for example standardization of message contents in certain procedures carried out by mail or electronically.

2. Binding Regulations with Respect to Members

a) General Regulations

The by-laws and manuals of the credit cards systems do not divide the regulations into general and specific ones, as the title of this section might suggest. The distinction is chosen here for the following reasons: many regulations contained in the manuals are of fundamental significance for the basic procedures and functioning of a credit card system. They are of only secondary significance, however, to the issues of the bilateral contractual relationships between the participating parties. These regulations will be sketched briefly.

---

[26] See part III. 2. below.

Design instructions insure a certain degree of uniformity in the issuing of cards in order to be able to rely on trademark protection and consequently on the license agreements with the credit card companies. At the same time, these design instructions indicate to the credit card companies what degree of flexibility they have in presenting the trade name and mark, e.g. what amount of space may be freely used by the company. There are also extensive provisions concerning the manufacture of the card itself, which serve various purposes. Regulations regarding the design and coding of the magnetic strip apply not only to all credit cards, but in accordance with ISO norms for all bank and other payment cards worldwide, e.g. the Eurochecque card. Other mandatory provisions relate to compliance with security standards within the credit card system. These include the placement of a hologram or other security measures such as special signature strips, type and placement of raised emblems, etc. Requirements that the cards be produced only by certain manufacturers approved by the system serve security purposes and also compliance with optical quality standards.

There are extensive rules regarding communication between the members and with the systems. The first of these are the provisions regulating uniformity in technical data processing and telecommunications. But there is also need for regulations of a substantive nature. The system sets certain guidelines for an acquiring company, i.e. a credit card company which maintains contractual relations with contract organizations in a particular region. Because in certain transactions, e.g. where the amount charged exceeds a set limit, the contract organization is obligated to request approval prior to acceptance of the credit card, the acquiring company must be able to respond to such requests 24 hours every day. This requires not only appropriate data processing capacity but also personnel working round-the-clock. An issuing company, i.e. the credit card company which maintains contracts with cardholders and is responsible for their credit standing, is obligated to respond to inquiries by an acquiring company as to whether a particular amount to be charged by a cardholder is permissible, likewise on a 24-hour basis. Here, it is not necessary to employ personnel round-the-clock if the issuing company can provide electronic data parameters on which the acquiring company can base a decision. It is significant for both the acquiring and the issuing company that the system provide facilities which permit secure, economic and reliable communication at all times. This means channeling communications paths for more than 10,000 participating card companies so that bilateral communications need not be established between each of them. The regulations also stipulate that it must be possible to answer inquiries electronically within a set time limit, usually within seconds.

Also of great significance for the structural and economic functioning of a credit card system are regulations governing payment claims and obligations involving compensation, so-called fees or interchange fees. One main purpose of these fees is to finance the system, i.e. the parent organizations of Mastercard International and Visa International, which in return use these proceeds to finance the facilities used by the entire system. The other main purpose is to create a system of compensation among the various income and expenditure structures of issuing and acquiring companies. An acquiring company earns income in connection with the use of the card regardless of which company within the system issued the card. Here, interchange fees are paid to the issuing companies as compensation. In general, these fees are also used among the various participating companies within a particular economic or legal region. This section of the by-laws contains a prototype regulation from which the card companies within a particular national group may diverge by using their own binding rules.

Compliance with quality and security standards is covered by regulations made by the system for the instance where a card company wishes to employ a third party to perform its duties or obligations. These can include card manufacturers, service companies which provide additional services to the cardholders, or data processing centers to handle funds transfers.

Other regulations having less a legal than a marketing character can involve uniform product standards within a credit card system. Each system offers credit cards in special forms, for which minimum standards apply worldwide. These variations include gold, silver, and company cards. Standards here can be related to the credit standing of the cardholder or general product design.

Finally, a matter of major importance to the functioning of a credit card system from an economic perspective are uniform standards for all credit card companies with respect to security issues. These include all preventive measures to make card counterfeiting or manipulation more difficult and methods for detecting forged cards so that the card can be blocked and withdrawn when an attempt is made to use it. Provision is also made concerning the allocation of risks of falsification as well as common funds to cover resulting losses.

Other regulations binding for the members of the credit cards systems are discussed below.[27] These are not of fundamental importance for the functioning of the system but are instead more interesting from a contractual point of view.

b) Chargebacks

One feature of credit card systems which is unusual in comparison to the familiar procedures in the law of funds transfers is the so-called chargeback.

[27] See part III. 2. b)-f) below.

A chargeback is a reverse entry which an issuing company requests and has carried out with respect to an acquiring company, which had previously charged this amount to the issuing company based on a payment transaction by a cardholder of the issuing company with a contract organization of the acquiring company.

The procedure in the case of a chargeback is as follows. In initiating the reverse entry, the issuing company relies on one of the specific chargeback grounds listed in the Rules. Following the chargeback, the acquiring company can then present the amount to the issuing company again if it so chooses and if it can assert — formal or substantive — grounds which contradict the chargeback. This then leads to a new credit for the benefit of acquiring company within the system. The reasons which can justify the rejection of a chargeback are likewise listed in the Rules. Upon this second "presentment", the issuing company is again debited for the amount. It can then start a new chargeback procedure but must rely this time on a different chargeback reason. The acquiring company again has the opportunity to attempt to contradict the chargeback using one of the specified grounds. A third chargeback attempt triggers an arbitration proceeding.[28]

From a legal perspective, the chargeback does not represent merely a procedure which is initiated or carried out for the purpose of asserting a claim. The chargeback is, instead, itself a legal right. An issuing company within a credit card system has a substantive claim against an acquiring company when it initiates a chargeback based on one of the specified reasons. The acquiring company's opportunity to defend against the chargeback with a new "presentment" relying on one of the listed reasons does not legally represent a examination of the legal justification for the issuing company's claim in the chargeback procedure. Instead, a second or third presentment is substantively a new claim by the acquiring company against the issuing company, which is satisfied by a corresponding credit or debit within the scope of the system settlement between the two companies. The unusual aspect of this arrangement is that the claims involved are not substantive ones for whose assertion or enforcement certain procedures are provided; the validity of substantive claims would be dependent not on the procedure but on the underlying grounds for the claim. The claim here is already supported — and enforced — merely by carrying out the formal procedure to assert it. The examination and possible rejection of an asserted claim is replaced here by the instrument of a counterclaim whose substantiation likewise follows from the initiation of an accounting procedure relying on specified substantive reasons. We will analyze the significance of this procedure in connection with the discussion of bilateral legal relationships between the various credit card companies.[29]

---

[28] See part III, 2. f) below.

The individual chargeback grounds specified in the Operations Manual or separate Chargeback Manuals, which provide the issuing company with a claim against the acquiring company, are equally remarkable. Some examples are: late presentment or settlement of the amount claimed; the transaction was carried out following a rejected authorization request; the card number was blocked and contained in the appropriate warning lists; no authorization request was made despite the fact that the amount of the transaction would have required such a request; missing or unreadable entries on the charge slip; presentment and settlement of more than one transaction between a certain contract organization and the cardholder, where the cardholder makes an affidavit that he engaged in only one transaction with this contract organization; charge slip with no signature, where a signature was required[30]; goods or services received did not comply with the written description or characterization and were returned or rejected by the cardholder — for this purpose, noncompliance with the description can include wrong color, size, contents or amount; goods ordered by the cardholder did not arrive.

Distinctions must be made among these various chargeback grounds for the purpose of legal characterization. The legal structuring of a chargeback as a separate substantive claim and not as a formal procedure for the examination of the validity of a transaction underlying an accounting entry is evidence of the general relationship between the accounting or settlement procedure and the underlying claims. The acquiring company which initiates an accounting entry on paper or by electronic means against an issuing company does have a substantive claim. This fact is supported by the relevant provisions concerning accounting procedures which expressly provide that an entry must be honored by the issuing company even where a chargeback is possible — in other words, the acquiring company first has a claim although the basis for this claim is in fact lacking. This makes it necessary to create corrective claims for cases in which there would normally be no claim within the scope of a contractual relationship. Examples of such cases are the authorization request which is submitted but rejected or the authorization request which was required under the circumstances but not submitted. Both of these situations represent violations by the contract organization against contractual obligations existing between the contract organization and the acquiring company.[31] With respect to the contract organization, the acquiring company is not obligated to make payment for the transaction. Under usual contract law, the acquiring company would likewise not have a right against the issuing company for payment because

[29] Part III. 3. below.

[30] See part III. 2. e) below.

[31] See parts III. 2. e) and V. 1., 3. below.

there would be no basis for this claim. In the credit card system, the initiation of an accounting entry based on a claim asserted by implication already substantively represents a separate claim. Therefore, a corrective procedure is needed. The two chargebacks in the examples correct mistakes arising out of the contractual relationship between the acquiring company and the contract organization because the breach of contract occurred there.

An example of a breach of an obligation by the acquiring company is where a delayed claim for a debit is made against the issuing company; here the acquiring company does not have a right of reimbursement from the issuing company because it failed to comply with its own duties. One can also imagine the situation where the cardholder complains of violation of duties based on his contractual relationship with the issuing company, i.e. presentment of a charge slip not signed by the cardholder. This would at the same time represent a breach of duties by the contract organization which should have examined or required the signature.

The examples of chargebacks just discussed belong to a category with a formal legal nature, serving to correct a claim which exists but is not substantiated based on the facts. In addition to this type of chargeback, other, more surprising, grounds are contained in the chargeback list. For example, in case of customer complaints regarding the delivery of poor-quality or incorrect goods, the issuing company is given a substantive claim against the acquiring company, even though there was no violation of duties by the acquiring company with respect to the issuing company or by the contract organization with respect to the acquiring company. There is an (asserted) breach of duties arising out of the contract between the cardholder and the contract organization, i.e. the underlying transaction. The goal of this rule, nationally and internationally[32], is to have problems in the underlying transaction between the cardholder and the contract organization settled exclusively by those parties and to leave the rights of the credit card organizations unaffected. This rule, whose requirements would be difficult for the cardholder to understand and therefore difficult to include in the agreement with him, as well as other rules permitting a chargeback based on a substantive right of the cardholder arising out of the underlying transaction, can be explained only against the background of American law.

American consumer protection law contains extensive provisions relating to credit cards and/or electronic funds transfers.[33] One part of the Consumer Credit Protection Act called the Truth in Lending Act[34] contains provisions

[32] See part V. 3. below; see also Merkel, p. 136.

[33] See e.g. Baker & Brandel, at margin note 12.05 (2); Schneider/Merkel, in: Festschrift für Pleyer, p. 115 ff.; Merkel, p. 40 ff.; Schneider, p. 57 ff.

[34] See Merkel, p. 41; Schneider/Merkel, p. 118.

referred to as the Fair Credit Billing Act.[35] The provisions give the cardholder the right in certain cases to assert rights based on the underlying transaction directly against the card issuer.[36] We need not examine the individual stipulations in detail.[37] The important point is that these are rights for the consumer, here the cardholder, which may not be excluded by contract. A credit card system, at least to the extent that it is oriented toward American law[38], must take this into consideration in structuring the system's internal legal relationships.

Provisions regarding chargebacks resulting from rights of the cardholder based on the underlying transaction apply directly only in the context described here, i.e. as rules of the credit card system as against the individual companies. The assertion of the claim requires that the issuing company rely vis-a-vis the acquiring company on this right of the cardholder. To what extent this solution, which is consistent with American law, should influence the legal relationships between credit card companies outside the U.S. or their contracts with cardholders and contract organization will be examined later.[39]

c) Provisions for Clearing and Settlement

The legal character of the system provisions for clearing and settlement of the transactions has already become clearly apparent in the discussion of chargebacks.[40] These are not mere technical accounting rules but instead create rights on the part of the acquiring company to demand credit and obligations on the part of the issuing company to make the corresponding payments.

In addition, the credit cards systems offer a worldwide network similar to a clearing system, through which international payment transactions may be carried out. The network offered by the credit card systems is a net settlement procedure for the participating companies. Use of this network is not mandatory, however. Credit card companies can, if they wish, settle payments on a bilateral level. Diverging arrangements can be particularly suitable, for example, for the companies within a particular currency territory.

---

[35] 15 U.S.C.A. §§ 1666 ff.

[36] See Merkel, pp. 42, 113 ff.

[37] See e. g. Merkel, pp. 115 ff.

[38] Both of the open credit card systems, Visa and Mastercard, originated in the U.S. and were first used only for domestic transactions there, Merkel, pp. 158 ff.

[39] See part III. 3., V. 3. and VI. 3.

[40] Part III. 2. b) above.

d) Standards for the Legal Relationship with the Cardholder

There are no special provisions in the Rules requiring the issuing company to include certain general or special stipulations in its contract with the cardholder. The chargeback rules discussed above, relating to the cardholder's rights against the credit card company based on events in the underlying transaction[41], are not the subject of standards requiring the issuing company to grant corresponding contractual rights to the cardholder.[42] This does not affect the fact that, based on the system's mandatory provisions, the issuing company is not permitted to enter into agreements with the cardholder which would represent violations of these system provisions.

e) Standards for the Legal Relationship with the Contract Organization

By contrast, the standards set out for acquiring companies' agreements with contract organizations are quite extensive. These contracts must stipulate, for example, that the contract organization will accept all cards with the system logo; that trademark rights held by the system will be respected — here a long text is provided which is to be incorporated directly into the contract text; the duty to comply with blocking orders contained, for example, in published lists; the duty to comply with charge limits, i.e. to obtain authorization from the acquiring company prior to the transaction for charges exceeding established or individually agreed maximum limits; standards concerning the data which the contract organization must include on the charge slip and what control procedures must be used with regard to the validity of the card, the signature, etc.; a prohibition on evading the floor limits by using multiple charge slips for a single business transaction; a prohibition on accepting cards only for purchases in excess of a certain minimum amount; a prohibition on collecting extra fees from the cardholder for the use of the card — this rule was modified in order to comply with the U.S. Cash Discount Act[43]; a prohibition on exploiting credit card data. For certain types of transactions or sectors of business engaged in by the contract organization, special standards are set for the acquiring company. Examples are mail order or phone order transactions, where the cardholder is not present in person and therefore cannot present his card. There are also other types of transactions where the cardholder typically does not sign the

[41] Id.

[42] Where the contract with the cardholder is governed by U.S. law, this applies based on statute; see Part III. 2. b) above. Concerning the effects of these rules on cardholders not subject to U. S. law, see Part VI. 3. below.

[43] See Schneider/Merkel, pp. 118 ff.

completed charge slip. A hotel, for example, may offer a quick-check-out service, in which the guest does not pay his bill when leaving but the hotel instead totals the bill later and collects the amount as a credit card charge. Here, the Rules provide that the acquiring company must stipulate in the contract with the contract organization that this procedure may be used only when the hotel obtains the prior written consent of the guest. Other rules, for example, relate to how much the final amount may deviate from the originally estimated amount in case of a transaction carried out without the signature of the cardholder.

The result of these standards is that the agreement between the acquiring company and the contract organization is set out in a very extensive text. One such agreement with a Mastercard contract organization in the U.S., printed as an example by Merkel[44], extends over 15 printed pages.

f) Arbitration Proceedings

The arbitration provisions contained in both systems include procedural rules which, from a purely practical perspective, enable the divisions engaged in carrying out the international payments for a specific credit card company to assert claims against other companies in specific cases in an arbitration proceeding without having to involve their own legal staff or outside attorneys. The arbitration rules make it possible to pursue claims which one company can have against another based on violation of by-laws or rules. In addition, the arbitration procedure can be employed to review decisions in a chargeback matter.[45] The arbitration decision is made by an authority within the credit card system and can, under some circumstances, be reviewed by the board of directors. Assertion of claims against the system itself is not included in the provisions governing the arbitration proceeding.

3. Bilateral Relations between Two Members of a Credit Card System

The rules governing legal relationships within a credit card company, which we have discussed, also permit conclusions to be drawn concerning the bilateral legal relationships between credit card companies.

Two credit card companies involved in a credit card transaction, in which a cardholder of one company makes a payment to a contract organization of the other card company, generally have no bilateral contractual relationship;

---

[44] Merkel, pp. 209 ff.

[45] See part III. 2. b) below.

this is also not necessary for carrying out the subsequent payment. Their legal relationship is founded on the internal rules of a credit card system. The parent companies in these systems[46] are subject to the corporate and commercial law of the state of Delaware. Both credit card companies are "members" and therefore shareholders in the credit card system. The internal system rules in the form of by-laws, rules and various manuals are binding on both companies based on their prior consent or their status as shareholders. It is possible, of course, that the two companies involved also have a direct contractual relationship, e.g. in the scope of a correspondent bank relationship, which is governed by the law of the location of one of the banks.[47] We may assume, however, that such correspondent agreements do not contain provisions relating to credit card payments. Also, it would be permissible to make stipulations there only regarding issues not already exclusively governed by provisions within the credit card system or where the system expressly permits a diverging rule. Each of the companies is aware of and accepts the fact that they are in contact with the companies within the framework of the credit card system, an that those companies have likewise agreed to be bound by the rules of the system. Rights and duties which the credit card system establishes as binding for individual members thus also apply directly to the bilateral relationship between two member credit card companies.[48]

The binding rules within a system have a strongly technical and organizational character. From a legal perspective, the following conclusions can be drawn, however, from the rules relating to the execution of payments.[49] A credit card company which initiates a payment collection procedure aimed at receiving reimbursement for an amount which it has advanced to the contract organization, already has a substantive claim for reimbursement against the issuing company merely by initiating the procedure, providing that the formal standards for the paper or electronic settlement are met. This claim is based on participation in the payment system in compliance with certain standards. This claim must then be satisfied (provisionally) even if possible objections to the claim exist. For claims which the obligated company may have, e.g. based on cancellation of the underlying transaction, reverse payment procedures exist. The initiation of such a reverse procedure likewise establishes a new substantive right.

The rules of credit card system do not contain any provisions leading to an assignment or any other type of transfer of rights arising out of the

[46] Here only the Visa and Mastercard systems; see part III. intro. above.

[47] Etzkorn, Zahlungsverkehr, pp. 41 ff., 51.

[48] Regarding the comparable situation concerning internal rules in the S.W.I.F.T. funds transfer system as they apply to two participating banks, see Etzkorn, id. at 53.

[49] Part III. 2. b), c).

underlying contractual relationship between the cardholder and the contract organization. The claim of one credit card company against another is a pure equalization claim based substantively only on the payment procedures within the system. It is not based on the claim against the cardholder which one of the companies could have acquired from its contract organization[50] and which that company now asserts against the other company as the contractual partner of the cardholder. There is also no assignment of rights based on the underlying contractual relationship between the two credit card companies.

IV. The Contract in the Underlying Transaction between the Cardholder and the Contract Organization

1. In General

In the underlying transaction, there is a contract for an exchange of goods or services, such as a purchase or rental. In this contract, the two parties, who here are the cardholder and the contract organization, agree that the compensation owed by one party may be paid by means of a credit card, i.e. they agree to the acceptance of the credit card. Under German law, this form of payment represents "performance in lieu of fulfillment".[51] The result under Swiss law is similar.[52] The cardholder's right to substitute the credit card payment for cash payment follows from the contract between the contract organization and the acquiring company.[53]

2. International Conflict of Laws Issues

A cross-border transaction and thus a case involving an international conflict of laws is present when the contract organization and the cardholder — as the parties to the underlying transaction — have their places of business or habitual residence in different countries. The issue of which law applies to this underlying contract is, under general conflict of laws rules, dependent upon whether the parties stipulated a choice of law and, if not, other factors such as the type of contract is involved; in either case, the consumer protection laws in the legal systems with connections to the transaction may also contain provisions relating to the applicable law.

---

[50] See part V. 1.

[51] This is the prevailing view. See Hamann, p. 31 with analysis of other views; see also Etzkorn, WM 1991, p. 1902.

[52] Schluep, p. 894.

[53] See part V. 1., 3. below.

Generally, we may assume that the law of the contract organization's place of business will apply to the underlying contract, i.e. the purchase[54] or other contract for goods or services. The consumer protection laws in effect at the place of the cardholders habitual residence can also influence the contract[55] because those laws can contain provisions relating, for example, to the incorporation or validity of general terms and conditions on which the contract was based or to collateral agreements in a language not understood by the consumer.

3. Effects of the Credit Card System Rules on the Contractual Relationship

Credit card system rules have no direct influence on the contract in the underlying transaction. The two parties in the underlying transaction are not directly connected with the credit card system. When the two parties agree to the acceptance of a credit card instead of a cash payment, this represents an individual stipulation within the framework of the contract. The fact that the contract organization is obligated to agree to this stipulation if the cardholder so wishes follows from the contractual relationship between the contract organization and the acquiring company.[56]

V. The Contract Between the Credit Card Company and the Contract Organization

1. In General

The main purpose of the contract between a credit card company and a contract organization is that the contract organization agrees to accept credit cards from the system represented by the credit card company in the future in place of cash. The credit card company agrees in exchange to "pay" the contract organization's claim against the cardholder based on the underlying transaction. The credit card company and the contract organization both have their place of business in the same country[57], and the contract is therefore governed by the laws of that country. The civil law classification of this contract is substantially dependent upon the way in which the settlement by the credit card company of the cardholder's payment obliga-

[54] See Reithmann-Martiny, at margin no. 405.

[55] See the examples from foreign legal systems in Reithmann-Martiny, at margin no. 433.

[56] See part V. 1., 3. below and see Etzkorn, WM 1991, pp. 1902 f.

[57] See part II. 1. above.

tion is structured technically and within the scope of the national legal system. Contracts of this type under German law are primarily structured as a purchase of accounts receivable[58], but this is not mandatory.[59]

2. International Conflict of Laws Issues

Taken alone, the contract between the credit card company and the contract organization usually has no international connections. International aspects are present when the cardholder who makes a payment to a contract organization by means of a credit card has his habitual residence in a country other than the place of business of the contract organization. Viewed closely, this situation also does not lead to international conflict of laws issues. The acceptance of the card, the related specific obligations, honoring of the claim by the credit card company including any possible performance disputes are governed exclusively by the contract between the contract organization and the credit card company with the safeguards incorporated into that contract. Whether the cardholder is a foreigner or not, regardless of his country of origin and regardless of the legal system there is, in fact, not relevant here at all. The situation with respect to chargebacks, as discussed above[60], appears to represent an exception.

Some chargebacks against the acquiring company are, of course, based on rights of the cardholder. These rights are asserted, however, within the legal relationship between the issuing company and the acquiring company. When, in such a case, the acquiring company wishes to "pass on" this chargeback to the contract organization, suitable provision must be made in the contract with the contract organization. And this, again, is a situation with no direct international connection. The validity of such a contract clause is governed by the law of the contract.[61]

3. Effects of the Credit Card System Rules on the Contract Relationship

As we saw above[62], there are numerous and often extensive standards which an acquiring company must heed in structuring its contract with the contract organization. To a great extent, these are rules without which a

---

[58] Etzkorn, WM 1991, p. 1903.

[59] Etzkorn, WM 1991, p. 1903.

[60] Part III. 2. b).

[61] See part V. 3. at note 68.

[62] Part III. 2. e).

contract with the contract organization could not reasonably be made at all. Some of the rules, however, are tailored very closely to U.S. law and are not easy to incorporate into contracts governed by other legal systems. In addition, rules regarding possible reverse transactions in the case of chargebacks based on cardholder complaints must be included, whereby these cardholder rights originate from U.S. legal perspectives. At another location in the rules, there is provision that in making contracts the member should not violate the law governing the contract. Stipulating this obligation does not, however, solve the problems which can arise in attempting to implement all of the system standards in compliance with the particular governing national law.

This can be very clearly seen in the following simple illustration. Mere inclusion of all of the obligations to be incorporated in the contract with the contract organization, which we have only briefly sketched here[63], and also the stipulations regarding the cited chargeback rules[64] would result in an extremely long text. One American model agreement, as mentioned above[65], extends over 15 printed pages. That agreement does not even include matters stipulated directly by American statutory law, which would have to be included in a contract governed by German law; the chargeback rules are one example because some of them are based directly on provisions of American consumer protection law. Such an extensive contract text governing a relatively simple factual situation, namely substitution and reimbursement for a cash payment, would probably be invalid under the German Law Governing Standard Contracts due to its very size; a text which is disproportional to the significance of the business transaction violates the required transparency of contractual stipulations in accordance with that statute.[66]

The validity of the contract between the acquiring company and the contract organization is not affected by whether the acquiring company has complied with its obligation to incorporate all of the designated card system provisions into this contract. Violations against the system provisions directly affect only the credit card company, and that company must bear any resulting loss. On the other hand, in the case of contracts governed by laws other than the laws of the U.S., it is often not necessary to include some of these clauses. One example relates to a chargeback transaction where the reason for the chargeback also leads to the invalidity of the underlying transaction. Under German law, it would not be necessary to include this situation in the contract with the contract organization in order for the

63 Part III. 2. e).

64 See part III. 2. b) above.

65 Part III. 2. e).

66 Palandt-Heinrichs, BGB, at § 2 AGBG, comment 3c; LG Aachen, NJW 1991, p. 2159, 2160.

acquiring company to have a right of recourse against the contract organization. Because the underlying transaction is void, there is no purchase of accounts receivable and the contract organization has no right to payment.

The intended purpose of many of the provisions which are to be incorporated into the contract with the contract organization is that performance complaints should be handled exclusively within the scope of the underlying contractual relationship. Because under U.S. law the cardholder under some circumstances has a mandatory right against the credit card company based on complaints within the underlying transaction, the credit card system rules provide that corresponding methods of recourse against the contract organization be stipulated. The final effect is to return the settlement of the complaint to the underlying transaction between the cardholder and the contract organization.[67] In order to achieve this result under German law it is not necessary that this right of recourse be included in the contract with the contract organization. It is sufficient that the issuing companies stipulate in their contracts with the cardholders that performance complaints be asserted exclusively within the underlying contractual relationship, i.e. against the contract organization. This is done in Germany by all credit card companies and does not raise any objections under German law.

Problems can arise in the case of a contract organization in Germany whose contract is governed by German law and which does not include a right of recourse by the credit card company based on rights of the cardholder under American law. A cardholder may use a card issued in the U.S. to make a purchase from this contract organization and then later assert an objection to this transaction and demand reimbursement from his issuing company. The issuing company will initiate a chargeback against the acquiring company in Germany. Whether the acquiring company can then take recourse against the contract organization depends upon the specific provisions of the agreement between the acquiring company and the contract organization. The District Court of Heidelberg was presented with such a case.[68] A reverse entry was made because the contract with the contract organization provided for this possibility where the cardholder "refuses to pay due to a complaint". The court held this clause to be valid.[69]

[67] See Merkel, p. 136.

[68] LG Heidelberg, WM 1988, p. 773.

[69] But see Welter, WuB I. D. 5. — 3.88 and Heymann/Horn, HGB, appendix § 372 at margin no. 157.

VI. Contract between the Credit Card Company and the Cardholder

1. In General

The contract between the credit card company and the cardholder is likewise governed by the law of the country in which both contracting parties have their places of business or residence. Under German law, this is a contract "for the discharge of business".[70]

2. International Conflict of Laws Issues

International aspects are present in this contractual relationship when the cardholder uses his card in a foreign country, in particular when he enters into special agreements there relating to the payment transaction.

When the card is used in a foreign country, the agreement to the payment by credit card is a part of the underlying agreement between the cardholder and the contract organization. This underlying agreement and the acceptance of the card are governed by the local law where the card is used. The payment by credit card is, at the same time, an instruction to the credit card issuer, as an additional contractual partner of the cardholder, to make payment to the contract organization. This instruction by the cardholder is not expressed directly to the credit card company, but is instead received by the issuing company when the contract organization collects the amount from the acquiring company and the acquiring company from the issuing company. The fact that this instruction reaches the issuing company (indirectly) from a contract organization in a foreign country is not relevant to its validity in the relationship between the cardholder and the issuing company.

The solution of international conflict of laws problems can be more difficult when, in the scope of the underlying transaction, special agreements are made in connection with the acceptance of the credit card. It is possible that a cardholder, in agreement with the contract organization, may waive the signature.[71] This agreement might be contained in a written form contract, e.g. authorizing the contract organization to assert damage claims arising out of the underlying transaction by means of a charge slip with no signature. The validity of this stipulation would be governed by the local law. Within the relationship between the cardholder and his credit card company, this stipulation would only be an instruction within the scope of their

[70] BGH WM 1990, p. 1059, 1060 f.; Heymann/Horn, at margin no. 146; Etzkorn, WM 1991, p. 1903.

[71] See Etzkorn, WM 1991, pp. 1903.

contract, which is governed by their common national law. On the other hand, the stipulation also represents a modification of the usual method of payment, which the cardholder is expressly authorized to make.[72] If a cardholder now takes recourse against his credit card company because this issuing company bills the cardholder for a payment made by the issuing company to a foreign contract organization based on a charge slip without a signature, as stipulated in the underlying transaction, the issue arises as to whether this stipulation in the underlying transaction — which is governed by foreign law — is also a valid instruction within the scope of the contract governed by German law. The answer to this question should be yes. The credit card company makes available to the cardholder — based on a contract governed by German law — a means of payment with which he can fulfill contractual obligations governed by foreign law. It can be necessary for the cardholder to enter into payment stipulations within the scope of the contract governed by foreign law relating to the use of the credit card. These stipulations can relate not only to the card payment itself but also contain deviations from the modes of payments otherwise common, which is expressly permitted by his contract governed by German law. If such an instruction is made, the credit card company should be obligated not only to make payment within the system to the acquiring company but should also be entitled within the scope of the contract for discharge of business to demand reimbursement from the cardholder.

3. Effects of the Credit Card System Rules on the Contractual Relationship

The credit card systems do not stipulate special rules relating to the contract between the issuing company and the cardholder.[73]

Furthermore, there should be no objection if a credit card company expressly denies rights to a cardholder which would be non-waivable for the cardholder under U.S. law and on which the rules of the credit card system are conceptually based.[74] The rules which are binding for the companies within the framework of the system do not represent rights which the cardholder can assert against his issuing company.

---

[72] Etzkorn, WM 1991, pp. 1903.

[73] See part III. 2. d) above.

[74] See part III. 2. b) above.

VII. Conclusions

The international use of credit cards involves a four or more party system. The rights and obligations between the two credit card companies involved as well as between those companies and the credit card system have not yet received any significant attention in the legal literature in Germany. Problems with the contracts involved can arise particularly where the provisions are conceptually based on U.S. law and U.S. law is directly or indirectly intended to apply to the participating parties. From a legal perspective, an "internationalization" of these provisions would appear necessary and certainly justified due to the shift in volume from the American to the non-American credit card market within the past ten years.

The individual bilateral contractual relationships involved do include some international aspects. However, the resulting issues can in most cases be resolved within the scope of a single contract governed by one national legal system.

Money Laundering as a Legal Problem

By Michael Bruns, Bonn-Bad Godesberg*

Contents

---

* Translated by Dr. Frances Dielmann, Frankfurt/M.

I. The Phenomenon of "Money Laundering"

Not only illegal drug trade but also other forms of organized crime are increasing at frightening speed. Robbery, burglary, illegal export of stolen automobiles to foreign countries, illegal weapons trade, "milieu crime" and the extortion of protection money are increasing being committed as organized crime[1].

The nature and methods of criminal organizations have been forcefully described in a decision by the Bundesgerichtshof: "Activities [of criminal organizations] are structured in such a way that if possible the central figures need not reveal themselves at all. Traditional means of investigation can usually succeed only in uncovering the criminal acts of peripheral participants, who in turn have no insight into the structure and composition of the overall organization. These peripheral figures can be exchanged and replaced at will, so that arresting them does not significantly disturb the activities of the organization. Those persons who by necessity are privy to greater knowledge of the organization are prevented from revealing that knowledge by means of hush money, threats and intimidation. When a member is caught, the organization frequently provides monetary support for family members and legal fees for a defense lawyer in order to achieve cooperation and avoid having information about the organization revealed."[2]

Even this brief description makes it apparent that for criminal organizations the proceeds of crime are not merely the final goal of their criminal acitivities. Like any enterprise, these "underworld organizations" need operating capital. The proceeds are the motive and also the prerequisite for organized crime.[3]

The dimensions of illegal accumulation of capital can be illustrated as follows: Experts believe that in the illegal drug trade alone there is a turnover worldwide of between 100 and 500 billion U.S. dollars per year.[4] Based on this estimate, the international drug trade would equal the volume of the legal trade in crude oil.[5] About 10% of the budget of the European Community is believed to be illegally diverted to third parties in the form of subsidies.[6] If one takes into consideration that these are only a couple of the

---

[1] See the Begründung des Entwurfs des Bundesrates eines Gesetzes zur Bekämpfung des illegalen Rauschgifthandels und anderer Erscheinungsformen der organisierten Kriminalität [OrgKG] — Bundestagsdrucksache 11/7663, p. 19.

[2] BGHSt 32, p. 115, 120.

[3] Steinke, Kriminalistik 1990, p. 297.

[4] Pieth, Strafverteidiger 1990, p. 558.

[5] Id.

[6] Steinke, supra note 3, at 297 ff., 298.

areas engaged in by criminal organizations it becomes clear that the underworld is truly capable of moving and perhaps even shaking the foundation of national budgets.[7]

These perceptions about crime are increasingly shifting the recovery of criminal proceeds into the forefront of national and international crime policy.[8]

One substantial problem in this regard is the uncovering of the criminal proceeds. On the one hand, existing criminal law permits recovery of the proceeds of crime by means of forfeiture (§§ 73 ff. StGB) only when proof of the origin of the respective assets can be traced in an unbroken line back to the crime.[9] On the other hand, there is always a trail from the proceeds to the actual perpetrator of the crime. It is therefore not surprising that criminal organizations expend great amounts of energy on perfectly camouflaging their profits. Their goal is to return these profits back into legal commercial circulation without detection in order to wash off the stains of the criminal origin.

Here at the interface between legal commerce and crime we find the phenomenon of "money laundering".

1. Outward Forms

As a starting point we can use the American phenomenological definition: Money laundering is described as the means[10] used to conceal the existence, the illegal origin or the illegal use of income and to disguise this income in such a way that it appears to arise from a legal source.[11]

This "laundering" of criminal profits is carried out, as a rule, in several steps. In what is most likely the largest field of organized crime, the illegal drug trade, but also for example in extortion of protection money and organized prostitution, the first step is to unobtrusively feed the direct proceeds, usually cash, back into legal circulation. This money is then transformed into apparently legal profits through a number of further steps.

---

[7] See Pieth, supra note 4.

[8] See the papers from the Federal Office of Criminal Investigation [BKA] conference "Does Crime Pay — Tracing and Confiscating Proceeds of Crime" of 10-13 November 1986 in Wiesbaden — BKA-Vortragsreihe, v. 32, 1987, pp. 17 ff.; see also the report by the Federal Minister of Justice "zur Novellierung der Vorschriften über Verfall und Einziehung und anderer Vorschriften des Strafgesetzbuches sowie zu Maßnahmen zum Aufspüren von Drogengewinnen — Bundestagsdrucksache 11/5525, Appendix 2, part C II, p. 14.

[9] See Boge, in: "Macht sich Kriminalität bezahlt — Aufspüren und Abschöpfen von Verbrechensgewinnen", BKA-Vortragsreihe, v. 32, 1987, p. 89, 91.

[10] Probably meant to be "methods".

[11] Arzt, NStZ 1990, p. 1.

The laundering of large amounts of cash as the first step turns out to be the most critical moment in the entire transaction. The federal government has determined that often casinos, currency exchange dealers, gambling machines and similar cash-intensive enterprises are frequently used as "laundromats".[12]

The popular vision of the courier who travels to an foreign tax haven with suitcases full of money is also true to reality to some extent.[13] There are, of course, also other situations in which the proceeds arise in forms other than cash, such as in the case of white-collar crime. This includes broad subsidy fraud and cases of organized investment fraud. But even here a cash transfer is often interposed in order to interrupt the "paper trail" which is created in non-cash transfers.

The subsequent steps in the laundering process generally involve only transfers of "deposit money". There are no limits set here to the financial imagination which is employed. The possibilities range from payment of sham foreign debts to the acquisition and resale of real estate, securities, foreign currency or other commodities. Basically, any form of commercial activity can be used in money laundering.[14]

2. International Dimensions

It is obvious that the chances for success of a money laundering scheme rise substantially if a transfer takes place across national borders. The limitation of government jurisdiction to its own national territory, the lack of or limitations in compatibility of the legal systems involved, and the resulting problems of international legal assistance, but also the "offshore banking facilities" established by many countries with a view to their own national benefits make national borders attractive instruments for the concealment of the proceeds of criminal acts.

The criminal investigation agencies have experienced a dense network of money laundering schemes operating worldwide. In addition to Caribbean,

---

[12] See the report of 10 March 1989 prepared by the working group, "Waschen von Gewinnen aus illegalem Betäubungsmittelhandel — Abschöpfung der Gewinne aus Straftaten" under the chairmanship of the Federal Minister of Justice.

[13] See e. g. with express reference to the situation in Switzerland the report of 12 June 1989, on the amendment of the Swiss Criminal Code (Gesetzgebung über Geldwäscherei und mangelnde Sorgfalt bei Geldgeschäften) — published as an appendix to the report by the Federal Minister of Justice, "zur Umsetzung der Drogenkonvention, zur Novellierung der Vorschriften über Verfall und Einziehung und anderer Vorschriften des Strafgesetzbuches sowie zu Maßnahmen zum Aufspüren von Dorgengewinnen" — Bundestagsdrucksache 11/5525 — appendix to appendix 2, part 113, p. 33 f.

[14] See also Pieth, supra note 4.

American and Asian financial centers, European financial centers are now also suspected of being used for laundering.[15] It is estimated that worldwide the illegal drug trade alone supplies about 85 billion U.S. dollars annually in investment and "laundering" capital.[16]

Our present legal system — and also those of most other countries[17] — is to a great extent ill-equipped to face this situation. This realization against the background of steadily rising drug crime kindled numerous international and subsequent national initiatives at the beginning of the 1980's for the purpose of combatting money laundering.

II. International Initiatives

1. United Nations Convention of 20 December 1988

We will first look at the United Nations Convention Against Illicit Traffic in Narcotic Drugs and Psychotropic Substances, adopted on 20 December 1988 in Vienna ("Vienna Convention").[18]

a) Article 3 par. 1. (b) and (c) (i) of the Vienna Convention obligates the parties to the Convention to adopt laws establishing as criminal offenses certain acts directed toward the laundering of proceeds from illicit drug trade. "Money laundering" in this context is

— the conversion or transfer of property [with knowledge of its origin] ... for the purpose of concealing or disguising the illicit origin of the property or of assisting any person who is involved in the commission of such an offence ... to evade the legal consequences of his actions;

— the concealment or disguise of the true nature, source, location, disposition, movement, rights with respect to, or ownership of property [from an offence].

b) In addition, Art. 3 par. 1 (c) (i) provides that the acquisition, possession or use of property shall be made a criminal offence when done with

[15] Report by the Federal Minister of Justice, supra note 8, appendix 2, part D 1, p. 15.

[16] Report by the Financial Action Task Force on Money Laundering established by the World Economic Summit, Paris, 7 February 1990, part 1, I, A, a, p. 5; compared with the turnover figures for the international drug trade cited in part I. above, it is clear that this working group assumed a minimum figure.

[17] The U.S. must be viewed as an exception in that it created a comprehensive instrument for combatting money laundering very early. Details are discussed in the report by the Federal Minister of Justice, supra note 8, pp. 10 ff., 18 ff. See also Meyer / Dessecker/Smettan-Walther, "Gewinnabschöpfung bei Betäubungsmitteldelikten", Freiburg 1989, Landesbericht Vereinigte Staaten von Amerika, pp. 415 ff.

[18] The United Nations Convention on Illicit Traffic in Narcotic Drugs and Psychotropic Substances — E/Conf. 82/15.

knowledge of its origin. This requirement is conditioned upon compatibility with the national constitutional principles and the basic concepts of the legal system in the respective country.

The Federal Republic of Germany was one of the first nations to sign the Vienna Convention on 19 January 1988. It hat not yet been ratified. Ratification will require that new national laws be adopted, in particular with respect to the provisions of Art. 3 par. 1. (b) and (c) (i).

2. *Basel Statement of Principles*

The "Cooke Committee"[19], composed of representatives from central banks and banking regulatory authorities from the USA, Japan, the Federal Republic of Germany, France, United Kingdom, Italy, Canada, Sweden, the Netherlands, Belgium, Luxembourg and Switzerland, adopted the "Basel Statement of Principles" on 12 December 1988. The goal of these principles is the "prevention of criminal use of the banking system for the purpose of money-laundering". The principles are directed to the identification of bank customers, compliance with existing provisions of law and the rejection of questionable financial transaction as well as cooperation by financial institutions with criminal investigative authorities to the extent possible under laws regarding the banker's duty of secrecy.

The statement of principles itself has no binding legal effect. Some countries have, however, made the principles obligatory, either by means of agreements directly with the credit institutions (Italy, Austria and Switzerland) or by adopting them into law (France, Luxembourg, United Kingdom).[20]

3. *World Economic Summit*

At the 15th World Economic Summit in July 1989 in Paris, the seven participants in the Summit, together with the President of the EC Commission established a "Financial Action Task Force on Money Laundering" with the objective of developing concepts for prevention of misuse of the international banking system for the purpose of money laundering.[21]

---

[19] Committee on Banking Regulations and Supervisory Practices; see also Pieth, supra note 4.

[20] These figures are based on calculations by the Financial Action Task Force on Money Laundering, Report, Paris, 7 February 1990, part II, A, b, p. 10.

[21] In addition to the Summit participants (the United States, Japan, Federal Republic of Germany, France, United Kingdom, Italy, Canada and the EC Commission), other members of the Task Force were Sweden, the Netherlands, Belgium, Luxemburg, Switzerland, Austria, Spain and Australia.

The task force presented a report of 7 February 1990, in which it dealt with the scope and methods of money laundering as well as existing national and international programs to combat money laundering.[22]

The report included the following basic recommendations:

— Each country should without delay implement and ratify the Vienna Convention.
— Bank secrecy laws should be "conceived so as not to inhibit implementation of the recommendations" of the task force.
— "... an effective money laundering enforcement program should include increased multilateral cooperation and mutual legal assistance in money laundering investigations and prosecutions and extradition in money laundering cases".

The report also recommends the introduction of a criminal offence involving "knowing" (intentional) money laundering as dealt with in the Vienna Convention (see 1. a) above). The task force goes further than the Vienna Convention in suggesting examination of the issue of whether laundering of proceeds from criminal offenses other than drug offenses should be made punishable under criminal law. And the task force recommended that not only employees but also corporations be made subject to criminal liability (recommendations 4-7).

The group further recommended that legal measures be adopted for the confiscation of the proceeds as well as the instrumentalities of money laundering (recommendation 8).

The report also contains recommendations dealing with the extension of the role of the "financial system" in combatting money laundering. Financial institutions should

— refrain from maintaining anonymous accounts, and should instead establish and record the identity of their customers;
— take reasonable measures to check the identity of their customers, in particular in cases where there is reason for doubt as to whether the direct customer is acting on his own behalf or for the interests of a third party;
— maintain records of transactions and the identiy of customers for at least five years in order to be able to comply with requests by competent investigative authorities;
— investigate especially large transactions and those with unusual patterns and record the results of such inquiries for possible use in cooperation with competent authorities (recommendations 9-15).

---

[22] See the Task Force Report, supra note 16, at 28 ff.

Difficulties arising in connection with the so-called banker's duty of secrecy should, in the task force's opinion, be dealt with by (lawfully) permitting the financial institutions to at least report suspicion of illegal activities to competent authorities. Also, accompanying legal regulations should be established relieving the financial institutions from criminal or civil liability for violating the duty of secrecy if the report to the authorities is made in good faith. It should be permissible to make such a report without precise knowledge of the underlying criminal activity and regardless of whether illegal activity actually occurred. There should be no requirement that the customer be informed of such a report to the authorities.

To the extent that the financial institution is subject to a reporting requirement and does not report its suspicions, the institution should terminate its business relationship with the particular customer (recommendations 16, 17 and 19).

At the World Economic Summit in Houston on 9-11 July 1990, the heads of state or government of the seven participants and the representatives of the European Community urgently encouraged all states to sign and ratify the Vienna Convention and to provisionally apply the rules of the Convention in the interim.[23]

They also stated with respect to the report by the Financial Action Task Force that they would subscribe to the recommendations of the Task Force and obligate their countries to implement the recommendations without delay and to the full extent.[24]

4. *Strasbourg Convention of 8 November 1990*

Based on the realization that the existing Council of Europe conventions did not establish an adequate basis for international cooperation in the area of confiscation of criminal proceeds, the Council of Europe on 8 November 1990 opened for signature the "Convention on Laundering, Search, Seizure and Confiscation of the Proceeds from Crime"[25] ("Strasbourg Convention"). In addition to the representatives from the member states of the Council of Europe, representatives from Australia, Canada, the United States, the European Community and Interpol took part in the drafting process.[26]

---

[23] Economic statement from Houston of 11 July 1990, point 75, Presse- und Informationsamt der Bundesregierung, Bulletin of 13 July 1990, No. 91, pp. 781 ff., 790.

[24] Id at point 78.

[25] Convention on Laundering, Search, Seizure and Confiscation of the Proceeds of Crime, ETS No. 141.

[26] Grotz, JZ 1991, p. 182, 183.

Article 6 (1) of the Strasbourg Convention contains provisions largely identical to those in Article 3 par. 1 (b) and (c) (i) of the Vienna Convention requiring the establishment of certain criminal offenses (see part I. above). Due to the influence of the World Economic Summit (see part 3. above), the Strasbourg Convention goes further in that it extends to all proceeds of crime, not only those related to drug offenses. However, it also permits reservations to Article 6 in which the parties to the convention restrict its application only to certain offenses or categories of offenses, as is felt necessary from the respective national perspective.[27]

The Strasbourg Convention was immediately signed by twelve member states of the Council of Europe, including the Federal Republic of Germany.[28] It is also open to states which are not members of the Council of Europe.[29]

The Strasbourg Convention has not yet been ratified by Germany for the same reasons as those relating to the Vienna Convention (see part I. above).[30]

5. EC

The Council of the European Community on 10 June 1991 adopted a "Directive on prevention of the use of the financial system for the purpose of money laundering"[31] ("Council Directive"). The Council Directive refers to the cited international initiatives and conventions (see parts 1.-4. above). It adopts and expands upon the major provisions and makes implementation obligatory for the EC member states.[32]

Based on the definition of money laundering incorporated from Article 3 par. 1 (b) and (c) (i) of the Vienna Convention (Article 1 of the Council Directive — see part 1. above), the Council Directive provides for the following obligations:

a) Money laundering shall be prohibited (Art. 2),

---

[27] Id.

[28] Id.

[29] See Art. 36 and 37 of the Strasbourg Convention. This also applies to non-member states who did not participate in the drafting of the Convention on the condition that the Convention has entered into force and that the Committee of Ministers of the Council of Europe issues an invitation following a set consultation procedure.

[30] This has already lead to a written inquiry by a Social Democratic member of the German Bundestag (BT-Drucks. 12/43 — Frage 13). The reply by the federal government expressly refers to the necessary legislative measures which are outstanding.

[31] Council Directive 91/308/EEC of 10 June 1991 on the prevention of the use of the financial system for the purpose of money laundering, OJ No. L 166/77.

[32] The Directive is addressed to the member states (Art. 18); it thus does not apply directly as national law.

b) Credit and financial institutions[33] shall be required

- to ascertain the identity of their customers and the persons on whose behalf the customeers act (Art. 3 par. 1-6),
  - when establishing a business relationship (opening an account or safe deposit relationship — Art. 3 par. 1), or
  - in transactions involving a sum of 15,000 ECU or more in a single or linked operations or where there is suspicion of money laundering (Art. 3 par. 2, 6), if identification has not already been established under Art. 3 par. 1.
- to keep the record of the identification and original documentation of transactions for a period of at least five years after termination of the business relationship or the transaction (Art. 4).
- to examine with special attention any transaction likely to be related to money laundering (Art. 5),
- to cooperate fully with the authorities by
  - informing the authorities of suspicious transactions
  - providing all necessary information (Art. 6)[34],
- not to enter into suspicious transactions before informing the competent authorities; in compliance with national laws, the authorities may give instructions not to execute the transaction (Art. 7)[35],
- not to inform the customer or third parties that information has been transmitted to the authorities regarding money laundering (Art. 8),
- to establish adequate procedures of internal control and communication in order to prevent money laundering (Art. 11 par. 1),
- to take appropriate measures to make personnel aware of provisions of the Council Directive, and to ensure that personnel are able to recognize suspicious transactions and act accordingly (Art. 11 par. 2).

---

[33] Under Art. 1 of the Council Directive, "'financial institution' means an undertaking other than a credit institution whose principal activity is to carry out one or more of the operations included in numbers 2 to 12 and number 14 of the list annexed to Directive 89/646/EEC (OJ No. L 386, 30, 30.12.1989, p. 1) or an insurance company duly authorized in accordance with Directive 79/267/EEC (OJ No. L 63, 13.3.1979, p. 1), as last amended by Directive 90/619/EEC (OJ No. L 330, 29.11.1990, p. 50), insofar as it carries out activities covered by that Directive". We will not deal here with the special rules which apply to such enterprises.

[34] Under Art. 6 par. 3, "Information supplied to the authorities ... may be used only in connection with the combating of money laundering". The member states may make provision, however, that this information may be used for other purposes.

[35] Art. 7 sentence 3 of the Council Directive provides for an exception in cases where refraining from a transaction is not possible or would be "likely to frustrate efforts to pursue the beneficiaries of a suspected money-laundering operation"; in the cases the authorities must be informed immediately afterward.

c) A disclosure in good faith by an employee or director or a credit or financial institution to the competent authorities shall not constitute a "breach of any restriction on disclosure or information imposed by contract or by any legislative, regulatory or administrative provision, and shall not involve the credit or financial institution, its directors or employees in liability of any kind" (Art. 9).

Article 16 par. 1 provides that the directive shall be implemented by the member states before 1 January 1993.

III. The Law in the Federal Republic of Germany

The legal system in the Federal Republic of Germany is not at the present time adequate either with respect to criminal policy regarding money laundering[36] nor does it comply with the obligations under the cited international conventions.

1. Criminal Law

The criminal offenses defined under existing criminal law do not, as a rule, apply to the factual situations involved here.

a) Aiding and Abetting by the Money Launderer

An obvious approach would be to view and prosecute money launderers as accessories to the original crime (§ 25 (2) StGB) or at least as abettors (§ 27 StGB). This would require that the act in question, e. g. drug sale, be viewed as not yet completed when the money launderer does his part.[37] This is often dependent upon the specific factual situation in a given case. Decisive is that the accessory must wish to engage in a joint action[38] or that the abettor at least want the main action to occur.[39] This requirement will usually not be met. One reason is that disclosing the origin of the funds to the person responsible for disguising them would violate the principle of isolating the

---

[36] The first emphatic formulation of criminal policy demands with regard to combating money laundering was in 1986 at the BKA Conference "Macht sich Kriminalität bezahlt — Aufspüren und Abschöpfen von Verbrechensgewinnen" (supra note 3); regarding the list of demands asserted primarily by police representatives, see the paper by Boge, "Gewinnabschöpfung als 'Dritte Dimension' der Bekämpfung des illegalen Rauschgifthandels und -schmuggels", supra note 3, at 89, 92 ff.

[37] See Dreher/Tröndle, § 25, margin no. 9; § 27, margin no. 4, with additional references.

[38] Id. at § 25, margin no. 8.

[39] Id. at § 27, margin no. 8.

various participants in a criminal organization (see part 1. above). Moreover, the money launderer who is — by necessity — fully integrated in society normally does not want to have anything to do with "real" crime. His asset is his "respectability"; his guiding principle is "willful blindness". In most cases, it will not be possible to prove that he even had knowledge of the essential facts of the original crime.[40]

b) Accessory after the Fact

Under § 257 (1) StGB, an accessory after the fact is one who assists another person with the intent to help that person secure the benefits of his unlawful act. The prevailing view is that the benefits must have been acquired directly from that act.[41] This is often not the case in complex laundering schemes. An accessory after the fact must also have at least rudimentary knowledge of the main crime.[42] Proof of this knowledge is usually difficult and often impossible.

c) Interference with Law Enforcement

It is a criminal offence under § 258 (1) StGB to interfere with the prosecution and punishment of another person for an unlawful act. This provision requires that the interference occur with intent or knowledge. The perpetrator must therefore intend to aid the personal benefit of the criminal or must at least foresee the interference as a certain result of his actions.[43] These requirements likewise do not match the typical motives of a money launderer (see a) above).

d) Receiving Stolen Property

Under § 259 StGB, it is a criminal offence to purchase, to acquire for oneself or for a third party, or to dispose of or help to dispose of, for one's own benefit or the benefit of another, any property which was acquired by means of an act directed against the property of a third party. Thus, the underlying act must have been directed against the property of a third party. This excludes broad areas, in particular laundering of drug money. Even if one assumes that trading in illicit drugs is frequently connected with fraud[44],

---

[40] Id. at § 25, margin no. 8; § 27, margin no. 8.

[41] Schönke/Schröder-Stree, § 257, margin no. 23; Arzt, supra note 11, at 3.

[42] Dreher/Tröndle, § 257, margin no. 8.

[43] Id. at § 258, margin no. 1, 11 f.

[44] Due to the "double invalidity" of an agreement for the sale of narcotics under § 134 BGB, as presumed in case law, the buyer cannot acquire valid ownership of the narcotics; see also Arzt, supra note 11, at 2.

it is not a criminal offence to receive objects which have been substituted for the property acquired directly by means of the underlying criminal act. Finally, receipt of stolen goods ("Hehlerei") relates only to "things", i.e. physical objects and not to claims such as bank deposits.[45]

The cited provisions of the German Criminal Code are thus useful in the prosecution of money laundering only in exceptional cases.

2. *Acquisition in Good Faith under the Law of Property*

Laundering of the proceeds of crime is also aided by the fact that private property laws are based on the dogma of making objects of legal property rights as negotiable as possible. § 935 (1) BGB [German Civil Code] limits the possibility of good faith acquisition of personal property by creating an exception for objects which were stolen, misplaced or in some other way lost without the intent of the owner. This would apply only to the proceeds of crime which are directly acquired by means of an unlawful act such a theft or embezzlement. But even an object acquired by means of an unlawful act such as an illicit drug sale, which is void under § 134 BGB[46], is marketable without restriction where it was acquired "with the will" of the transferor — assuming the good faith of the subsequent purchaser.

At the same time, the fundamental principles of the civil law in practice create a presumption of good faith on the part of the purchaser: where no evidence is already present, the party disputing the good faith of the purchaser must prove that he acted in bad faith.[47]

This is especially true when the criminal proceeds involve money or bearer securities. In this case, § 935 (2) creates the possibility for good faith acquisition of objects which had been stolen or otherwise lost.

---

[45] Dreher/Tröndle, § 242, margin no. 2; § 259, margin no. 1 b.

[46] Case law has so far presumed the co-called double invalidity of agreements for the sale of illicit drugs. Not only is the unlawful transfer of ownership of illegal drugs invalid under § 134 BGB; the transfer of the purchase price is likewise void (BGHSt 31, p. 145 ff.; BGHSt 33, p. 233).

[47] See Palandt-Bassenge, § 932, note 5; similar thoughts probably led Arzt (supra note 11, at 6) to the interesting proposal to provide for statutory acquisition of ownership to drug sale proceeds by the state which could be prevented only by proof of good faith acquisition by a third party. The objectives of the suggestion by Arzt would be to ease the burden of proof for forfeiture of drug proceeds under criminal law and thereby avoid the constitutional problems arising in connection with the presumption of innocence (see note 65). One unresolved question is to what extent intervention into the protection of ownership under Art. 14 of the Basic Law [GG], as involved in such a statutory acquisition, could be justified here without being tied directly to a specific crime. And if the origin in a specific crime must be proven, there would be no lessening of the burden of proof as compared to the present situation (see part I. above).

3. *Banker's Duty of Secrecy*

Based on their key position in the overall system of financial transactions, credit institutions are almost inevitably involved in money laundering operations.[48] In this area, the so-called banker's duty of secrecy applies, which prohibites the credit institution and its employees and other related persons from disclosing to unauthorized parties any information relating to a customer's accounts or other facts gained by means of the business relationship with the customer, to the extent that the customer wishes these facts to remain confidential.[49] There is no consensus regarding the true legal basis for the banker's duty of secrecy in the Federal Republic of Germany; it is not governed by statute. The view which is probably the predominant one is that this duty is derived from constitutional principles, in particular as relating to the general personal rights of the customer[50], and supported as an additional legal basis by the contractual or pre-contractual relationship between the bank and the customer.[51]

Bank secrecy is not a direct legal obstacle to the tracing of proceeds from crime. Specifically, it does not create a right on the part of the credit institution or its employees to refuse to give evidence in a criminal proceeding because it is not contained in the list of professional privileges in § 53 StPO [Code of Civil Procedure].[52] Instead, the credit institution and its employees have a duty to provide evidence in criminal proceeding, which in accordance with § 95 StPO also includes the duty to turn over bank documents. Furthermore, seizure of bank documents under § 94 StPO as well as any necessary related search of the bank premises are possible unter § 103 StPO.[53]

Nevertheless, the banker's duty of secrecy in its present form facilitates the use of credit institutions for the purpose of money laundering:

— Conspicuous circumstances relating to business transactions which point directly to a criminal origin of transferred funds are generally not

[48] The Bundesverband Deutscher Banken is reported to have admitted that it is obvious that attempts are being made worldwide to misuse credit institutions for money laundering; Die Welt, 24 January 1991.

[49] Hadding/Schneider-Musielak, Bankgeheimnis und Bankauskunft in der Bundesrepublik Deutschland und in ausländischen Rechtsordnungen, Landesbericht Bundesrepublik Deutschland, Berlin 1986, p. 14.

[50] It will be necessary in this context to take into consideration the "right to informational self-determination" as found by the Bundesverfassungsgericht (Federal Supreme Constitutional Court) in its "census decision" (BVerfGE 65, p. 1) as it relates to the specific bank customer.

[51] Hadding/Schneider-Musielak, p. 13; Prost, NJW 1976, p. 214.

[52] Kleinknecht / Meyer, § 53, margin no. 3 f., with additional references.

[53] LG Hamburg, NJW 1978, p. 958 f.

reported to investigative authorities by credit institutions because the duty to maintain bank secrets creates a risk liability on the part of the credit institution with regard to the accuracy of its factual and legal assessment of its observations. If a suspicion transmitted to an investigative agency is correct, the banker's duty of secrecy is subordinated to the higher ranking interest of the state in criminal prosecution. The customer also has no rights under his contract with the bank which would override this interest. Instead, in such a case it could be assumed that the underlying purpose of the contract between the bank and the customer was money laundering. There is not presently a criminal offence of money laundering as such; therefore, the contract would not be void under § 134 BGB unless the acceptance of the "dirty" money by the bank fulfilled the requirements of some other specific criminal offence (see part 1. above). There is consensus, however, that a legal transaction which is entered into or executed in connection with an unlawful act violates public policy and is therefore void under § 138 BGB.[54] Thus, if the suspicion of money laundering is correct, there is no legal basis for liability on the part of the bank for disclosing information to the investigative authorities. Otherwise, the bank would have to fear compensation claims by the customer for any damages which the customer suffers as a result of the disclosure.

— Credit institutions are generally very reluctant to participate in pending criminal proceedings. With a view to the cited risk of liability, they exhaust all existing means of refusal. For example, the Code of Criminal Procedure provides that the prosecuting attorney or the court, but not the police, may force a witness to appear and testify (§ 48 ff., 161 a StPO). Therefore, employees of credit institutions often do not comply with a police summons.

4. *Tax Secrecy*

§ 30 AO (Tax Code) creates a duty for "officials" and equivalent persons to maintain tax secrecy. This duty had been viewed as an obstacle to drawing the tax authorities into the "investigative team" for the purpose of tracing proceeds of crime. This possible obstacle has now been removed. At least in the view of the federal government, tax secrecy does not stand in the way of such criminal investigation because there is generally an overriding public interest in disclosure within the meaning of § 30 (4) no. 4 AO. The Federal Minister of Finance in agreement with the state ministers of finance will make this position clear to the state and federal tax authorities.[55]

[54] Palandt-Heinrichs, § 138, note 1 f.

[55] See the statement in the Nationaler Rauschgiftbekämpfungsplan — Maßnahmen der Rauschgiftbekämpfung und der Hilfe für Abhängige, issued by the Federal Minister for Youth, Family, Women and Health and the Federal Minister of the Interior, as of 13 June 1990, V. 2.1.3, p. 32.

5. Problems of International Legal Assistance in Criminal Matters

Corresponding to national problems in the investigation of money laundering are the difficulties involved in providing legal and judicial assistance to other countries. In the absence of international agreements, legal assistance can as a rule be provided only when the act or offence being pursued in the requesting state is also a criminal offence in the requested state. This applies under § 3 par. 2 of the Law on International Legal Assistance in Criminal Matters of 23 December 1982 (IRG) for the extradition of an offender as well as under § 43 (3) IRG to the execution of foreign criminal judgments. Additionally, the existing laws already hinder the investigation of flows of capital within the Federal Republic of Germany: as a rule it is necessary to make searches and seize documents. § 66 par. 2 no. 1 IRG permits this to be done by German judicial authorities within the scope of judicial assistance only when the criminal actions on which the foreign proceeding is based could also be prosecuted under German law.

Requests by foreign states based on an accusation of "money laundering" cannot presently be complied with because no such criminal offence exists in Germany. This leads not only to international resentments but also holds the danger that Germany can become an attractive location operations by criminal organizations.

IV. National Initiatives

The numerous international initiatives have also begun to have an effect in Germany. For a long time the German federal government was not conscious of any need to take action with respect to the phenomenon of money laundering. Great foreign policy pressure by the U.S. at the end of the 1980's has caused higher levels of government to begin to look at the issues involved. In the U.S. at that time comprehensive provisions under the Bank Secrecy Act already were in effect regarding collection of data on funds movements; at the end of 1988, the "Kerry Amendment" introduced by Senator John Kerry added an international dimension.[56] The U.S. Treasury Department was obligated to enter into negotiations with other countries in order to achieve introduction there of provisions comparable to those in the U.S. with respect to duties to record dollar transactions as well as disclosure of these records to American criminal investigative agencies. Lack of

[56] 31 U.S.C. JJ 5311-5326 as amended by the Anti-Drug-Abuse Act of 1986, Title I, Subtitle h, pup. 1.99-570 and the Anti-Drug-Abuse Act of 1988, Title VI, Subtitle e, pup. 1100-690; see also the references in note 17 supra.

willingness to cooperate on the part of the negotiating partners could then under certain circumstances lead to exclusion from dollar clearing in the U.S.[57]

It was clear at that time that the American government would scarcely make use of such sanctions against the Federal Republic of Germany. The seriousness of the American action and the pressure exerted by the U.S. government have, however, led to initiation of a range of activities by the German government (and by other trading partners of the U.S.).

1. Report by the Interdepartmental Working Group "Laundering of Proceeds from Illicit Drug Trade — Confiscation of Proceeds from Criminal Acts" of 10 March 1989

Against the background described above, the German Federal Cabinet on 13 December 1988 resolved to establish an interdepartmental working group on "Laundering of Proceeds from Illicit Drug Trade — Confiscation of Proceeds from Criminal Acts". The working group was composed of relevant federal departments as well as the central bank, the Deutsche Bundesbank. The working group submitted its report on 10 March 1989[58], and on 11 April 1989, the Federal Cabinet resolved that laundering of proceeds from illicit drug trade should be made a criminal offence, that it should further examine the possibility of extending such a provision to other criminal acts, and that the duties of credit institutions to identify their customers and to cooperate with criminal investigative agencies should also be studied.[59]

2. Report by the Federal Minister of Justice on the Implementation of the Drug Convention to Reform the Provisions on Forfeiture and Confiscation and other Provisions of the StGB as well as Measures Regarding the Tracing of Drug Proceeds[60]

The primary political goal of the report mandate was to make publicly clear the federal government's intent to emphatically pursue the issues relating to confiscation of proceeds. Due to the brief time which had passed since the preceding working group report (see part 1. above), no substantial

[57] Anti-Drug-Abuse Act of 1988, Title I, Subtitle h, sec. 4702.

[58] Bundesminister der Justiz, Bericht der ressortübergreifenden Arbeitsgruppe "Waschen von Gewinnen aus illegalem Betäubungsmittelhandel — Abschöpfung der Gewinne aus Straftaten" of 10 March 1989; the report was not published.

[59] Bericht des Bundesministers der Jusitz, supra note 15, p. 10.

[60] Report by the Bundesregierung, Bericht des Bundesministers für Jugend, Familie, Frauen und Gesundheit über die Rauschgiftsituation und die Grundzüge eines nationalen Rauschgiftbekämpfungsplans, Bericht des Bundesministers der Justiz, supra note 15.

new results could be expected. The report did, however, deal more deeply with measures being taken by other countries to confiscate criminal proceeds.[61] Finally, the report recommended that the draft laws, above all the provisions to make money laundering a criminal offence, be completed during the 11th legislative period and that consideration be continued regarding measures to detect the proceeds of crime in the early stages of a criminal investigation, e. g. for the identification of persons making cash deposits and for reporting of transfer transactions and that interested circles, particularly credit institutions, be included in seeking acceptable solutions.[62] The Federal Cabinet considered this report along with a report by the Federal Minister of Youth, Family, Women and Health on the narcotic drug situation and the outline of a national plan for combatting narcotic drugs.[63] The Cabinet substantially followed the Minister of Justice report in its resolution of 24 October 1990 and also resolved to convene a "national drug conference" with the goal of pursuing a "national plan to combat narcotic drugs".[64]

3. National Plan to Combat Narcotic Drugs

The "National Drug Conference" was held with representatives from federal, state and city governments, churches, labor unions, welfare and charitable organizations, parent's associations and youth services. On 13 June 1990, under the chairmanship of the Federal Chancellor, it adopted the "National Plan to Combat Narcotic Drugs".[65] In the section on "legislative measures" the plan provides for the "creation of effective provisions of law for the removal of financial resources". In the context of money laundering these measures are to include:

- — a criminal offence of money laundering
- — a law regarding the tracing of proceeds from serious crimes including provisions for
- — identification of persons making cash deposits
- — exemption by law from liability for claims for damages or injunctions in connection with cooperation with investigative authorities
- — exemption from criminal penalties in connection with cooperation with criminal investigative authorities.[66]

[61] Supra note 15, p. 18 ff.; the report deals in particular detail with the Swiss proposal for a law "on money laundering and lack of care in financial transaction" which was quite advanced at that time. That proposal was attached as Appendix 2 to the report, pp. 30 ff.

[62] Id. at 29.

[63] Id. at 2 ff.

[64] Id. at 61 ff.

[65] Nationaler Rauschgiftbekämpfungsplan, supra note 55.

[66] Id. at part VI. 7, pp. 40 ff.

4. The Draft by the Federal Council of a Law to Combat Illegal Narcotic Drug Trade and Other Forms of Organized Crime [OrgKG]

In 1989 and 1990, the federal government attempted to approach the problems of "organized crime" by means of several draft laws aimed at improving the removal of criminal proceeds.[67] At the same time, the Social Democratic group in the German Bundestag introduced a bill which would make money laundering a criminal offence.[68] At about the same time, the Federal Minister of Justice received a draft of a law to amend the code of criminal procedure (StVÄG 1989); the main thrust of this law was to broaden the authority of criminal investigative agencies. Common to all of these drafts was that they called into question the traditional limits on encroachment by the state. This led to heated debate in scholarly as well as political circles[69], which blocked any swift adoption of these drafts.

Thanks to an initiative by the Federal Council (the upper house of parliament), the various drafts, which had been submitted quickly and not coordinated with one another, were combined into a draft Law to Combat Illegal Narcotic Drug Trade and Other Forms of Organized Crime [OrgKG] which also included supplementary regulations.[70] But no consensus would be reached within the 11th legislative period, in particular with regard to the changes in criminal procedure contained in this draft.[71] The draft was

---

[67] Draft of a ... Criminal Law Amendment — Criminal Fine, BT Drucks. 11/5461; Draft of a ... Criminal Law Amendment ... Expanded Forfeiture, BT Drucks. 11/6623; the instrument of a "criminal fine" (§ 43 a StGB-E) as well as the "expanded forfeiture" (§ 73 d StGB-E) pursue the goal of facilitating seizure of the criminal proceeds. In the case of the expanded forfeiture, this takes place by means of lowering the burden of proof for the origin of objects from criminal acts. It would be sufficient to show that the circumstances suggest that such an origin may be presumed (§ 73 d par. 1-E). the criminal fine involves an intervention independent of the origin of the criminal proceeds; the amount of the fine would be conditioned only upon the guilt of the offender. Even without further examining the details of these proposals here we can say that constitutional protection of property and the presumption of innocence can permit a lowering of the burden of proof or criminal law confiscation of assets only within a very restricted scope and only in connection with especially serious crimes. Therefore, even if these proposals are implemented, the emphasis in the future must remain on improving means to trace the proceeds.

[68] Draft of a ... Criminal Law Amendment — Confiscation of Proceeds, Money Laundering — BT Drucks. 11/5313.

[69] See Pieth, supra note 4, at 558 ff.; Ostendorf, JZ 1991, pp. 62 ff.; Köhler / Beck, JZ 1991, pp. 797 ff.; Arzt, supra note 11, p. 5; Steinke, supra note 3, pp. 297 ff.

[70] Entwurf eines Gesetzes zur Bekämpfung des illegalen Rauschgifthandels und anderer Erscheinungsformen der Organisierten Kriminalität [OrgKG] des Bundesrates (BT Drucks. 11/7663).

[71] Particularly the proposed provision on dragnet searches, the use of undercover agents and the use of "technical devices" such as bugging devices and video cameras — Art. 4 OrgKG-E.

reintroduced by the Federal Council on 26 April 1991[72], in a form which took into consideration the position adopted by the Federal Cabinet.[73]

Art. 1 no. 21 of the draft[74] provides for the criminal offence of money laundering to be included in the Criminal Code at § 261. This would fulfill one of the significant prerequisites for ratification of the U.N. Convention (see part II. above).[75] At the same time, it should become possible to ratify the Strasbourg Convention (see art. II. 4. above) and to comply with the standards in the resolutions of the World Economic Summit (see part. II. 3. above) and the EC Council Directive (see part II. 5.) above.

a) Under § 261 (1), it would be punishable by up to five years imprisonment or a fine to

— conceal,
— disguise the origin of or
— prevent or endanger the investigation of the origin, the tracing, the forfeiture, the confiscation or the seizure of

an item of property originating from

— a serious crime committed by another person
— a violation by another person of § 29 (1) no. 1 of the Narcotics Law [BtmG][76], or
— a crime committed by a member of a criminal organization.

The aim of these measures is to make it punishable to prevent or render more difficult attempts by criminal investigative agencies to gain control of proceeds of certain types of crime. This should facilitate the administration of justice with relation to reducing the effects of crime.[77]

b) Under par. 2 of this provision, it would also be punishable to

— obtain such an item of property for oneself or another person, or
— use, receive, accept, invest or hold for oneself or another person such an item of property with knowledge of the origin of the property at the time of receipt.

---

[72] Entwurf eines Gesetzes zur Bekämpfung des illegalen Rauschgifthandels und anderer Erscheinungsformen der Organisierten Kriminalität (OrgKG) des Bundesrates (BT Drucks. 12/989) [OrgKG-E 1991].

[73] BT Drucks. 11/7663, pp. 49 ff.

[74] Id. at 7.

[75] See OrgKG-E 1991, Begründung zu No. 21 (§ 261 StGB) — Geldwäsche — Vorbemerkung, p. 26.

[76] Under § 29 of the Narcotics Act, it is punishable to plant, deal in, produce, import, export, sale, deliver, bring into circulation, purchase or acquire narcotics.

[77] OrgKG-E 1991, Begründung zu § 261 StGB, par. 1, p. 27.

This provision is intended to implement Art. 3 1. (c) (i) of the U.N. Convention (see par. II. 1. b) above) "in a manner consistent with the constitutional principles and the basic concepts of the legal system of the Federal Republic of Germany".[78] The item of property should in practice be "frozen", i. e. be made unmarketable. This also fulfills the function of an alternative offence applicable to cases where proof cannot be brought of the intent to obstruct or hinder justice under par. 1.[79]

The criminal offence is objectively circumscribed by a further rule in par. 6 of the provision that the act (under par. 1) shall not be punishable "if a third party previously acquired the item of property without committing a crime".

The offence is limited subjectively to cases where there was knowledge of the origin of the property at the time of receipt.

c) Of fundamental significance for the entire provision is the concept of "originating" as used in par. 1, with which the connection of the incriminating property to the original offence is defined. By necessity, this attribute can include a chain of dispositions. The legislative history of the draft law indicates that the chain should be limited only where the value of the respective item is substantially the result of independent subsequent performance by a third party.[80]

Thus the provision permits the blemish of the criminal origin to extend far into the circulation of property. Taking into consideration that the property involved is primarily cash or claims ("deposit money"), the added value criterium is not likely to have any substantial practical significance. The only practical limitations on the offence will be the subjective elements.

d) The provision is given added effect by § 262 (5) E which stipulates that a person shall also be punishable if he "recklessly fails to recognize that the item of property originates from an ... unlawful act by another person".

The legislative history of the draft states that such augmentation of the offence is indispensable in order to avoid difficulties of proof and insure effective law enforcement.[81] Reference is made to the prevailing view in case law and legal scholarship where recklessness is defined as ignoring due to carelessness or particular indifference the forceful possibility that an event will occur.[82]

The draft is quite daring on this point. Criticism of the introduction of elements of a money laundering offence which are less strict than actual

---

[78] Id., par. 2.

[79] Id.

[80] Id., par. 1.

[81] Id., par. 5

[82] Id. See also Dreher/Tröndle, § 16, margin no. 20, with additional references.

intent is not without justification because

— it is not consistent to punish a subsequent offender for recklessness or negligence when the underlying offence — e. g. violation of the Narcotics Act — generally requires intent, and
— the main problem of proving the origin of the item of property is still not solved.[83]

One obvious solution would be to introduce exceptionally strict duties of care for persons engaged in businesses which are particularly suited to being used for money laundering[84].

Apparently there is a trend at the present time to employ measures of this type — but in addition to § 261 (56). This is seen in the drafting of a law regarding the tracing of proceeds of serious crimes (see part 5. below).

The relationship between duties of care to be stipulated by statute and the planned criminal liability for recklessness under § 261 (5) does not appear clear. If statutory duties of care are in fact introduced the question will arise as to whether there is even a need for separate criminal liability. There would be many reasons in favor of approaching the difficult policy issues of criminal liability for negligent money laundering by means of supplementary (non-)criminal enforcement of the duties of care directed at preventing money laundering. Instead of the difficult proof of the other elements of the crime under § 261 (1) or (2), it would then only be necessary to show that certain procedures had not been complied with by the person suspected of money laundering. The use of less drastic sanctions for enforcement of the duties of care than those used under § 261 (5) would not be problematic. In the areas of commerce and finance which are relevant here the preventive effect is dependent more on whether there are government sanctions than on how severe the sanctions are.

e) § 261 (8) stipulates that items of property originating from a crime in a foreign country can also be "laundered" within the meaning of the law if the underlying act was punishable at the place where it was committed.

This provision creates the international dimension necessary for effectively combatting transnational crime. It is based on the principle of substitute criminal enforcement (§ 7 (2) StGB). It also implements the obligation contained in Article 6 2. a. of the Strasbourg Convention.[85]

---

[83] Botschaft über die Änderung des schweizerischen Strafgesetzbuches, supra note 13, p. 51.

[84] Id.

[85] Art. 6 par. 2 a of the Strasbourg Convention provides that the question of whether money laundering is punishable in the signatory states should not depend on whether the underlying crime falls within the jurisdiction of the criminal courts of the respective signatory state.

f) Under § 261 (3) E attempted money laundering is also punishable. On this point, the draft is based on § 258 (4) and § 259 (3) StGB.

g) § 261 (4) E provides for an aggravated offence punishable by six months to ten years imprisonment for "particularly serious instances" of money laundering. These generally involve cases of money laundering as a business or by organized gangs.

h) § 261 (9) and (10) E contains grounds for suspension or mitigation of punishment when the offender

— reports the money laundering voluntarily and before it has been discovered and
— if the act was intentionally committed, has also secured the items of property in question or
— by voluntarily disclosing his knowledge has substantially aided in the detection of parts of the crime in addition to his part in it or in the detection of a criminal violation by another person under § 261 (1) E.

These provisions are substantially modelled on the existing provision with respect to assistance with criminal investigation under § 371 (2) no. 2 AO and § 31 (1) BtMG.

Emphasis must be placed on the fact that the requirement of assisting in the detection of the crime is limited to those instances where the money laundering was carried out with intent (§ 261 (9) no. 2 E). The drafting history states that this limitation is intended to take into consideration the fact that a suspicion of money laundering may not arise until somewhere far into a long business relationship, particularly in the case of credit institutions. Without this rule, a bank employee who might be accused of negligently failing to report to the authorities would not have any opportunity to report a later suspicion because normally the previously "laundered" money would already have been withdrawn by the account holder and the employee would therefore have no opportunity to "secure" the property.[86]

i) With respect to confiscation of items directly related to the criminal act (e.g. the laundered money), § 216 (7) E first refers to § 74a StGB. Under § 74a StGB, stipulation is made in deviation from § 74 StGB that the "laundered" items may be confiscated even if the money launderer does not own or have rights to the items if the person entitled to the items at the time of the decision concerning confiscation

— at least negligently contributed to the connection of the item to the crime (§ 74a (1) StGB) or

[86] OrgKG-E 1991, Begründung zu § 261 StGB par. 9 and 10, p. 28.

— acquired the item in a reprehensible manner with knowledge of the circumstances which would have permitted the confiscation (§ 74 a (2) StGB).

j) § 261 (7) E of the draft would make applicable additional new measures, namely "administrative fine" (Art. 1 no. 2 ArgKH-E — § 43 a StGB) and "Extended Forfeiture" (Art. 1 no. 9 OrgKG-E — § 73 d StGB).[87] This would have farreaching effects:

— In the case of a fine — which would be permissible only in conjunction with a prison sentence of at least two years for a money laundering offence — the maximum amount to be imposed would be limited only by the total assets of the offender. At least in theory the convicted money launderer could be completely expropriated.[88]

— Extended forfeiture would extend to items of property belonging to the money launderer for which no direct origin in the money laundering offence (e. g. as payment for the criminal act) can be proven but where the circumstances justify the presumption of this origin. This would thus also allow seizure of assets belonging to the money launderer in addition to those for which the concrete connection to the crime is found.[89]

5. *Working Draft of a Law on the Tracing of Proceeds of Serious Crimes*

For the purpose of implementing the cited EC Council Directive (see part II. 5. above), the recommendations of the World Economic Summit's Financial Action Task Force (see part II. 3. above) and the resolutions of the German Federal Cabinet of 24 October 1989 (see parts 1. and 2. above), the government is presently working on a draft of a law on the tracing of proceeds of serious crimes. In accordance with the resolution of the Federal Cabinet of 24 October 1990 on the report by the Federal Minister of Justice of 2 November 1990[90], this is being done with extensive participation by representatives from credit institutions.

---

[87] See note 67.

[88] There is presently serious controversy concerning the permissibility of such a "social death penalty" under constitutional law (see also the very explicit criticism by Köhler / Becker, JZ 1991, pp. 798 ff.).

[89] "Expanded forfeiture" is likewise not undisputed (Köhler / Becker, JZ 1991, p. 799); but here the arguments seem to be limited to the "issue of faith" regarding whether Art. 14 of the Basic Law [GG] can permit the state to stipulate a duty to prove legal acquisition of private property. Taking the reservation in Art. 14 par. 1 GG into consideration it would appear that when sufficient elements of suspicion are present it would be possible to impose such a duty on the owner.

[90] See note 60 supra.

This draft[91] is intended to supplement crime prevention by means of increasing the responsibilities demanded of the institutions and persons involved in financial transactions. The framework has been laid out in the EC Council Directive.

a) Taking these goals into consideration, a new law in this area would have to be directed primarily toward credit and other financial institutions. The definition of a credit institution will be based on the definition in Art. 1 (1) of the Credit System Act [KWG] so that primarily "banks" in the traditional sense will be involved.

In accordance with Art. 1 of the EC Council Directive, the definition of financial institutions would also include, among others, life insurance companies. Consideration is being given to permitting later regulations to expand the catalogue of activities which define "financial institutions".

b) It is presently planned that the concept of "identification" of customers and the "financial transaction", which are left open to a great extent in Art. 3 of the EC Council Directive, will be concretely defined.[92]

c) Some of the central elements of a future law will include the introduction of

— identification requirements,
— duties to make and maintain records,
— duties of care in the opening of accounts and safe deposit relationships by customers for third parties,
— reporting obligations and
— a duty to establish internal security measures.

aa) A general duty on the part of credit and other financial institutions to require identification of customers who are not regular customers of the institution and where the financial transaction involved exceeds a minimum of DM 30,000 (see Art. 3 (2) sentence 1 of the EC Council Directive — part II. 5. above). The minimum amount could also be reached by multiple transactions which are obviously connected.[93]

In the case of large cash deposits — a minimum amount of DM 50,000 to DM 100,000 is under consideration — identification should be required from the depositor even where the holder of the account involved was properly identified at the time the account was opened.[94] The duty to identify cash

[91] The present article was completed in October 1991. In the meantime, the government draft of 8 April 1992 of a law on the tracing of proceeds of serious crimes has been submitted [Gewinnaufspürungsgesetz — GewAufspG] (Bundesratsdrucksache 220/92).

[92] See § 1 GewAufspG-E.

[93] See § 2 par. 1 and 2 GewAufspG-E.

[94] See § 2 par. 4 GewAufspG-E.

depositors should also extend to other types of business, casinos and persons who professionally hold funds on behalf of third parties even though they are not ever credit or financial institutions. Exceptions would be made for attorneys in criminal defense and for firms engaged in transporting money.[95]

bb) A duty would be created on the part of insurance companies to establish the identity of customers where the premium exceeds a certain amount. Based on Art. 3 (3) of the EC Council Directive, the amount under consideration is DM 2,000 in the case of periodic payments and DM 5,000 in the case of one-time payments.[96]

cc) An exception from the identification duty should be made where the person in question is personally known and has at a prior time provided formal identification.[97]

dd) On the other hand, the identification obligation should apply without regard to a minimum transaction amount when the party required to obtain the identification becomes aware of facts which would indicate money laundering intent or a connection between the transaction and certain serious crimes. For business (see aa)), this rule would be limited only to suspicion of money laundering.[98]

ee) Under Art. 3 (5) of the EC Council Directive, the identification obligation would also have to extend to determination of the person economically entitled to the funds. The customer would at least have to be asked whether he was acting for his own account or on behalf of a third party. The name and address of the economic beneficiary would then have to be obtained. Exceptions for members of certain independent professions, such as attorneys and notaries, would have to be considered for cases where funds are deposited into their trust accounts or where new such accounts are opened.[99] Certain declarations should be required from such professionals by the credit or financial institutions when accounts are opened. These could include declarations that the person opening the account

- knows the identity of the economic beneficiary of the funds,
- the administration of the money is not for the purpose of concealing the name of the economic beneficiary,
- is not aware of any evidence that the deposited funds were illegally acquired, and
- will oversee the transactions to be carried out through the account and will inform the credit institution when the trust relationship is ended.

---

[95] See § 3 GewAufspG-E.

[96] See § 4 par. 1 GewAufspG-E.

[97] See § 7 GewAufspG-E.

[98] See § 6 GewAufspG-E.

[99] See § 8 GewAufspG-E.

If these declarations are not provided, the institution should not be permitted to open the trust account.[100]

ff) Furthermore, Art. 4 of the EC Council Directive should be implemented. Art. 4 involves the obligation to record the identification information and to maintain these records for at least five years. Consideration is being given to permitting the records to be maintained on data media such as microfilm or magnetic tape, provided that they can be provided in readable form within a reasonable time.[101]

gg) Due to the basic pinciple under data protection laws that individuals should have control over their personal data, the gathering and use of the cited types of records will require a new basis in law.[102] It must be emphasized that the types of information relevant in this context are of a particularly sensitive character. This is true not only because financial data are generally viewed as especially worthy of protection.[103] Instead, it must also be taken into consideration that these data can be particularly suited to damage the reputation and credit status of individuals because they are collected in a crime prevention context and, at least in the eyes of the public, appear at least related in some way to a criminal act.

It is thus clear that not just any purpose is sufficient to justify the collection and evaluating of such data. As is true for bank secrecy in general[104], only very significant interests can be sufficient. Mere public interest in criminal investigation is not adequate. Instead, the crimes involved must be limited to serious ones.

There seems to be a basic consensus on this point among those involved in the drafting of a law on the tracing of proceeds of serious crimes; on the other hand, there are conflicting views with respect to the factual situations which justify reporting data to the authorities. Those who place more emphasis on efficient criminal investigation would like to permit a broad range of uses of the data. Use in other criminal proceedings, with the exception of minor violations, should be permissible. § 25 of the Court Procedure Act [GVG] which governs the authority of criminal law judges, is being considered as a point of orientation. Use of the records would not be permitted in cases involving violations

— where private prosecution is available,

---

[100] See § 11 GewAufspG-E.

[101] See § 9 GewAufspG-E. The draft provides for a six-year period for preserving records.

[102] BVerfGE, p. 1; see note 51 supra.

[103] This view is clearly manifested in the concept of "banker's secrecy" and finds concrete form in the former "Bankenerlaß" now § 30 a AO.

[104] Hadding / Schneider-Musielak, p. 21; Prost, p. 215.

— where the maximum penalty is not more than 6 months imprisonment, or
— of a minor nature so that the maximum penalty would be no more than one year imprisonment, and the case is brought by the public prosecutor in criminal court.

When, on the other hand, major emphasis is placed on the interventive nature of the collection and reporting of the relevant information, the use of the records would have to be restricted to those cases in which it is absolutely necessary to law enforcement. It would be admissible only in prosecuting those violations which the law defines as the underlying basis for the duty to collect the information and in prosecuting serious crimes.[105]

Finally, balancing the costs in terms of possible loss of trust among banking customers against the investigative advantages of use of such information will be a very delicate legal policy issue.

It is still unclear whether and to what extent use of the data will be permissible in the investigation of tax offenses.[106]

hh) Implementation of Articles 6-8 of the EC Council Directive will require that credit and financial institutions be obliged to report to criminal investigative authorities without delay any facts of which they become aware which indicate a connection between a financial transaction and certain criminal offenses. The customer in the transactions may not be informed of this disclosure. The transaction in question may then be carried out only when the public prosecutor has consented or at the earliest on the second day after the disclosure is made.

Based on the present state of negotiations, this rule would be made weaker by an exception under which the financial institution would have the right to carry out urgent transactions immediately and then make the required report.[107] Article 7 of the EC Council Directive already contains this exception, and it would appear that in practice delaying execution of transactions until after reports are made to the authorities could prove to be rare. It will be almost impossible to determine subsequently with sufficient certainty that a transaction was in fact not urgent and that it also did not appear urgent to the credit institution at the time of the decision to carry it out. If one additionally takes into consideration that timely compliance with the reporting requirement will be enforceable only by means of a fine and also the requirement that the elements of offenses leading to criminal

[105] This approach is followed in § 10 par. 1 GewAufspG-E.

[106] Under § 10 par. 2 GewAufspG-E when a final court judgment has been issued based on money laundering or one of its underlying offenses, the use of information from the records which create a suspicion of criminal tax violations should be usable for purposes of reassessing taxes.

[107] See § 12 par. 1 GewAufspG-E.

sanctions be strictly construed, the rule that credit institutions should report to the authorities immediately could be substantially undermined.[108]

Another undecided issue involves the consequences the duty to report suspicion of money laundering will have with regard to the voluntariness of reporting which is required under Art. 1 no. 21 § 261 (9) OrgKG-E for exemption from criminal liability (see part 4. h. above).[109]

ii) A central issue is the necessary release of the institutions and their employees from the risk of criminal or civil liability for making a report (see part III. 3. above). Article 9 of the EC Council Directive also provides for such release by the member states. Discussions are presently in progress regarding a rule under which a party will not be liable for reporting to criminal authorities facts which point to a criminal offense which would require identification of the customer provided that an incorrect report is made with intent or gross negligence.[110]

Such a rule should give the institutions a sufficient range of discretion for open and responsible cooperation and also sufficiently meet the needs of the state's interest in criminal enforcement.

kk) Furthermore, the working draft would also implement Art. 11 of the EC Council Directive which requires internal security measures within the credit institutions. The following types of rules are being recommended: development of internal control procedures, monitoring of employees in sensitive areas with respect to reliability, education of employees with respect to the problems of money laundering and the designation of contact persons to the decision-making levels within the investigative agencies.[111]

The contents and the text of the working draft have not yet achieved a consensus among all the participants. The plans for a law on tracing criminal proceeds break the mold of traditional criminal law to such a great extent that no rapid agreement can be expected. There is, however, basic agreement on the necessity of including the credit industry within the scope of responsibility for tracing the proceeds of serious crimes.[112]

---

[108] The draft now contains no independent enforcement of the duty to report under § 12 GewAufspG-E.

[109] Under § 12 par. 4 GewAufspG-E, the duty to report does not exclude the possibility of voluntariness un § 261 par. 9 OrgKG-E.

[110] See § 13 GewAufspG-E.

[111] See § 15 GewAufspG-E.

[112] According to a newspaper article, the Bundesverband Deutscher Banken takes the following position: "For the Banking Association, this involves national enforcement of international obligations. It involves the introduction of a criminal offense of money laundering and the inclusion of credit institutions in tracing the proceeds of serious crimes. Society should be willing to accept some degree of intervention into personal freedoms in order to help achieve a greater purpose, namely the survival of the legal system". Die Welt of 24 January 1991.

V. Outlook

Finally, we should once again point out the limitations on enforcing normative conduct by means of criminal law. Combatting crime in this border area between "business" and "crime" can depend only to a limited extent on the drafting art of legislators. The extent and intensity of government cooperation, particularly on an international level, will probably always fall short of actions by business. There will always be areas in which commercial acts cannot be subjected to state regulatory control or at least only in a restricted way. It will be possible to effectively fight the phenomenon of money laundering only when the participants actively become involved instead of blinking their eyes at the proper moment so as not to see what is happening. This assumes that these participants will recognized the dangers of being smothered by criminal activity and will accept a type of business ethic based on a broad congruence of values within our society that will look beyond their own narrow interests. This type of consensus seems to be developing within the area of financial institutions.[113]

[113] See note 92.

Foreign Payment Transactions from the Perspective of a Major Corporation (Volkswagen AG, Wolfsburg)

By Eduard Kuß, Burkhardt Reichel, and
Mathias Rudnick, Wolfsburg*

Contents

---

* Translated by Dr. Frances Dielmann, Frankfurt/M.

I. In General

1. Introduction

Volkswagen AG is a major, worldwide automobile corporate enterprise and is one of the five largest auto manufacturers in the world. Volkswagen AG has manufacturing and assembly plants in almost all parts of the world. Its corporate headquarters are in Wolfsburg, Germany. Following reorganization, the management structure is now comprised of the following areas:

General Management	Production
Management of VW (trade name)	Personnel
Legal, Audit, and Economics	Control and Finance
Overseas Business and Sales Strategy	Research and Development.

A large portion of the employees in non-operational areas are located in Wolfsburg, where the financial activities of the enterprise are directed by the Group-Wide Treasury.

In 1990 the 100% subsidiary V.A.G. Bank GmbH acquired the full status of a bank, permitting it to expand the enterprise's activities in the area of financial services. While the goals of this subsidiary are directed toward promotion of vehicle sales and providing financial services to general consumers, the financial affairs of the enterprise in a narrower sense are conducted by the Treasury.

The enterprise's global activities require cooperation with banks operating worldwide which have the necessary competence and experience in foreign trade.

Among the enterprise's banking partners are first class names with branches and correspondents in all parts of the world. VW's presence on all important capital markets is ensured through this cooperation.

The international supply industry has achieved increasing importance, for VW and other auto manufacturers, due to development of modern production and transport technology. Control over funds transfers and foreign exchange as well as the processing of foreign payments have become a part of the daily routine for the employees involved in those areas. In additional to the execution of payments with foreign counterparts, current investment possibilities on international markets are naturally also given due attention. The goal of all these activities is to secure the enterprise's capabilities as an automobile manufacturer.

2. *Prior Developments in the Foreign Payments System of the VW AG*

Shortly after the end of World War II, when Volkswagen AG was still the "Wolfsburg Motor Works", the first Volkswagens were exported. As the first vehicles were delivered primarily as part of reparations payments, the first true export transaction began in 1947 by the newly named Volkswagen Werk GmbH. The first general importer was the Netherlands firm Pon. In 1948, contracts were concluded with trading partners in Denmark, Luxembourg, Sweden, Belgium and Switzerland. The export share of the Wolfsburg production was then 23 %. The resulting foreign currency receipts amounted to 21 million Deutsch marks.

A new dimension was opened through export of the VW Beetle to the U.S.A. by the Gebrüder Pon. By 1953, VW exported to 86 countries and had foreign currency receipts of 254.2 million marks. Under the leadership of Prof. Heinrich Nordhoff (1948-1968), Volkswagens were exported to over 100 countries. Subsidiaries or independent manufacturing facilities were established in all important market locations. This steady growth continues today and in 1989 led to proceeds from exports by domestic group companies of 27.6 billion marks.

Parallel to these sales trends, it has been necessary to increase the number of personnel in the Group Treasury in Wolfsburg and to expand data processing technology and communications systems to meet the company's growing needs. New methods of computerized coordination and communication with Volkswagen AG's banking partners and expansion of financial capabilities to include the creation of the company's own corporate bank will mark the path of the Treasury Division as an internal provider of financial services in the future.

3. *The Scope of Current Business Activities*

Foreign trade plays an important role in many national economies. For the Federal Republic of Germany with its numerous exporting companies, the balance of payments represents a significant determining factor in foreign trade. For a multinational industrial enterprise like Volkswagen AG, the increase in foreign trade interrelationships determines sales and profit opportunities in foreign markets. Worldwide logistics also offer chances to reduce costs in connection with the purchase of supplies and components. As a result, Volkswagen AG is also increasing its activities in the international payment sector. The volume of payments and the number of monetary transactions have steadily increased during the past years. Statistics prepared monthly with respect to the current accounts of Volkswagen AG show the current volume of payments and percentage changes in comparison with the previous month and the equivalent period in the prior year. These figures include domestic transactions as well as incoming and outgoing foreign payments in DM or foreign currency converted to marks. The statistics also show a ranking based on the turnover volume of the various banks. Account relationships with more than 20 institutions are included. Statistics concerning pure foreign currency transactions are also prepared. It would not be helpful to include a "hit parade" of the foreign currency transactions here because a data analysis is rendered more difficult by varying contract modalities — determined in accordance with exchange rate fluctuations. The preferred contract basis, especially with trading partners in countries with instable currencies, continues to involve the classic hard currencies. A list of foreign currency turnover volume for the years 1988-1990 is included in the appendix of our report.

4. *Foreign Exchange Planning*

a) Business of Foreign Currency Management

Foreign currency management involves the purchase and sale of claims against payment.

Volkswagen AG requires its own foreign currency management in order to be able to meet its international payment obligations which result from commercial transactions (sale and purchase of goods and services). Conversion of claims and obligations denominated in foreign currency into domestic currency or a third currency is the main task here. Foreign exchange management makes an increase in profits possible, but not without significant risk. It is therefore necessary to establish certain premises about the task at hand. Necessary are a clear definition of the scope of discretion of the involved parties, transparency of all business procedures, monitoring by management as well as internal and external auditors, and the strict separation (functionally and in terms of personnel and location) of working procedures into (1) placing of orders, (2) trade, (3) supervision, control and accounting, and (4) execution of payments. Strict functional separation takes place through dividing the work process into two departments. The first is Control and Payments. Here, a distinction is made between Planning (information concerning the placing of orders with currency management), Execution (booking, settlement and control of the foreign currency transactions), and Domestic/Foreign Payments (execution of payment). The second department is Foreign Currency and Position Management (actual business transactions, connected with provision of cover for the transaction). The following foreign currency transactions serve as instruments of payment: cash transactions to be covered within two working days, forward outright transactions with stipulated maturity upon conclusion of deal, and swap transactions (the exchange of maturities between two currencies upon a date fixed in advance). The positive and negative balances resulting from traded currencies result in the cash and forward trading positions. The member of the managing board in charge of Control and Finance issues standards (daily and total limits) for foreign currency transactions each day. It is not permissible to carry over unused portions of daily limits to the next trading day. Due to the high risk involved, Volkswagen AG does not allow open positions in foreign currency trade. No dealings are made in time zone arbitrage.

b) Principles of Currency Planning

aa) Organization

In addition to daily currency trading, monthly revolving currency planning is also carried out. Responsible for this longer term disposition is the "Currency Disposition Determination" body [Devisendispositionsermittlung]. This body is made up of participants from the various business sectors and the subsidiary companies which are involved in the execution of foreign currency transactions or which place orders for such transactions in connection with their purchase or sales activities. The group is chaired by the Group-Wide Treasury. The members have until the 10th working day of each month to prepare a revolving six month plan. During the meetings, prognoses for development in currencies relevant to the enterprise are presented and appropriate recommendations for currency dispositions are made. The data prepared by "Devisendispositionsermittlung" are checked by the Treasury Control, made available to the currency disposition, and serve as the basis for related transactions.

bb) Planning Volumes

The planning data for inward and outward flows of currencies are divided into three volumes in order to detect possible risks contained in the interrelated currency flows. Planning Volume I involves currency receipts from the sale of vehicles, Planning Volume II currency receipts and expenditures relating to logistics and Plannung Volume III currency receipts and expenditures from capital transactions. In the case of inconsistencies, in particular substantial variations from the planning data, the Treasury contacts the responsible sectors or affiliates. In the future, the foreign currency activities of the enterprise companies will be carried out centrally, i. e. through the Group-Wide Treasury, for the various subsidiaries.

II. Organization of the Involved Departments

1. Type of Business Transactions

Orders are placed for the processing of the following types of transactions: originating and receiving transfers (clean payments), receipt of documentary transfers, collection of checks drawn on foreign banks, collection of checks issued in foreign countries drawn on Volkswagen AG in marks or foreign currency, and receipts and expenditures of consideration for currency transactions.

2. Organization of Responsibilities and Procedures

a) Organization of the Volkswagen AG Treasury

Following a reorganization in the spring of 1991 the prior area of Finance and Capital was transformed into the Group-Wide Treasury in Wolfsburg. These measures included integration of the area of Taxes and Customs into the structural concept of the Group-Wide Treasury. As in the prior structure, there is a spatial and organizational separation of the central disposition office for money and currency transactions from the bookkeeping office. The organizational structure of the Volkswagen Treasury and the department Control and Payment Transactions are shown in the following diagrams:

b) Payment Procedures

Within the accounting system of the Volkswagen AG, the Debitor and Creditor offices are responsible for the proper settlement and posting of claims and liabilities resulting from the delivery of goods and services. The departments requesting payment transactions through the Volkswagen AG's bank accounts submit the necessary forms and information for incoming and outgoing payments to the Group-Wide Treasury. The basic processing procedure for an outgoing international payment will now be illustrated using the example of a credit transfer order.

A liability arises based on delivery of goods or services. An invoice is received containing terms for payment. The Creditor-Current Accounts department [Kreditoren-Kontokorrente] prepares a monthly time plan for payments to be executed. In a summary of maturities the sum of the outpayments for a working day is calculated; for this purpose, foreign currency outpayments are converted to DM at the official selling rate for the invoice date as a planning estimate. Consultation follows with the Group-Wide Treasury for Foreign Currency and Position Management (see also part I. 4.). The form "Payment Order in Foreign Trade" (Z1) [Zahlungsauf-

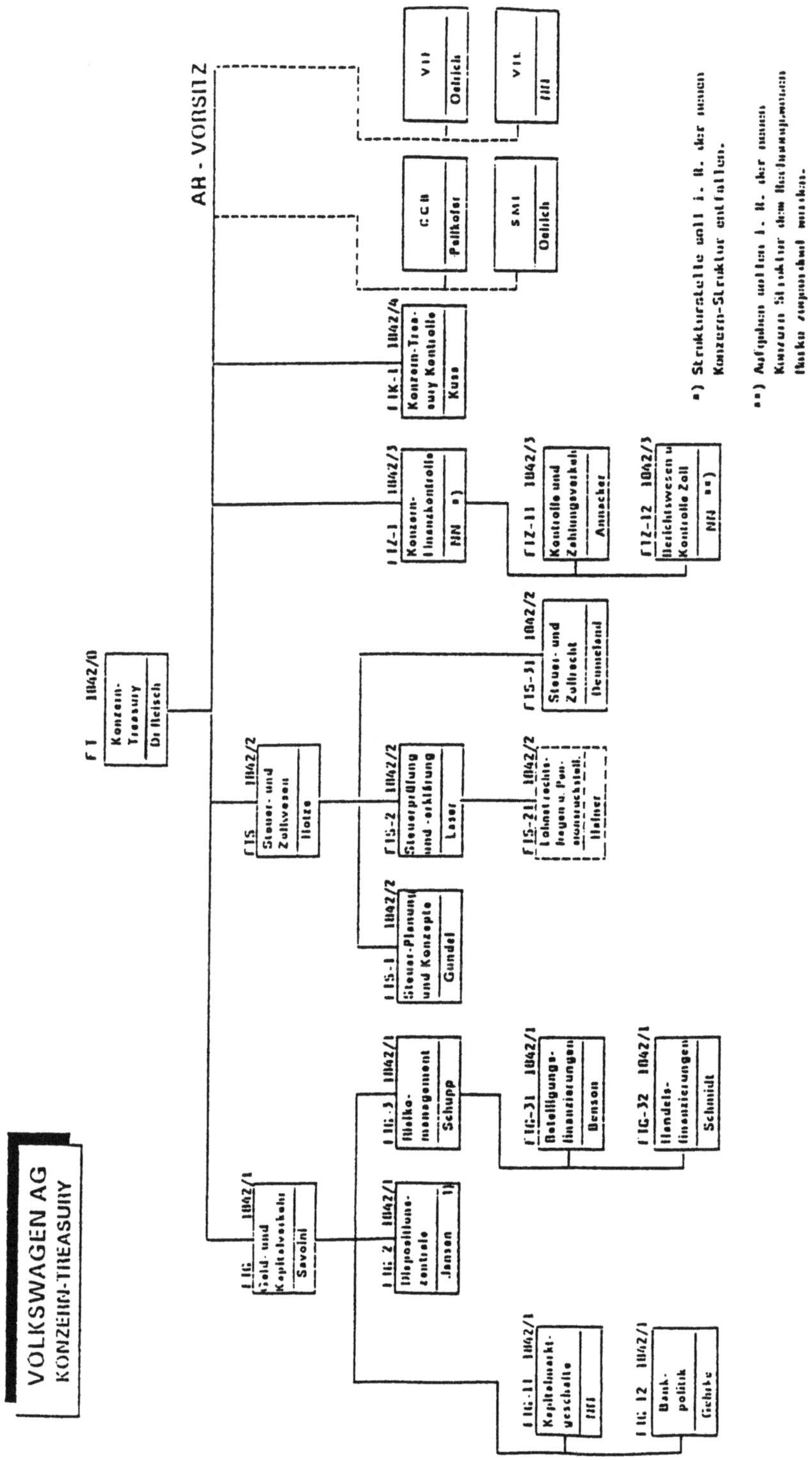
VOLKSWAGEN AG
KONZERN-TREASURY
AR - VORSITZ

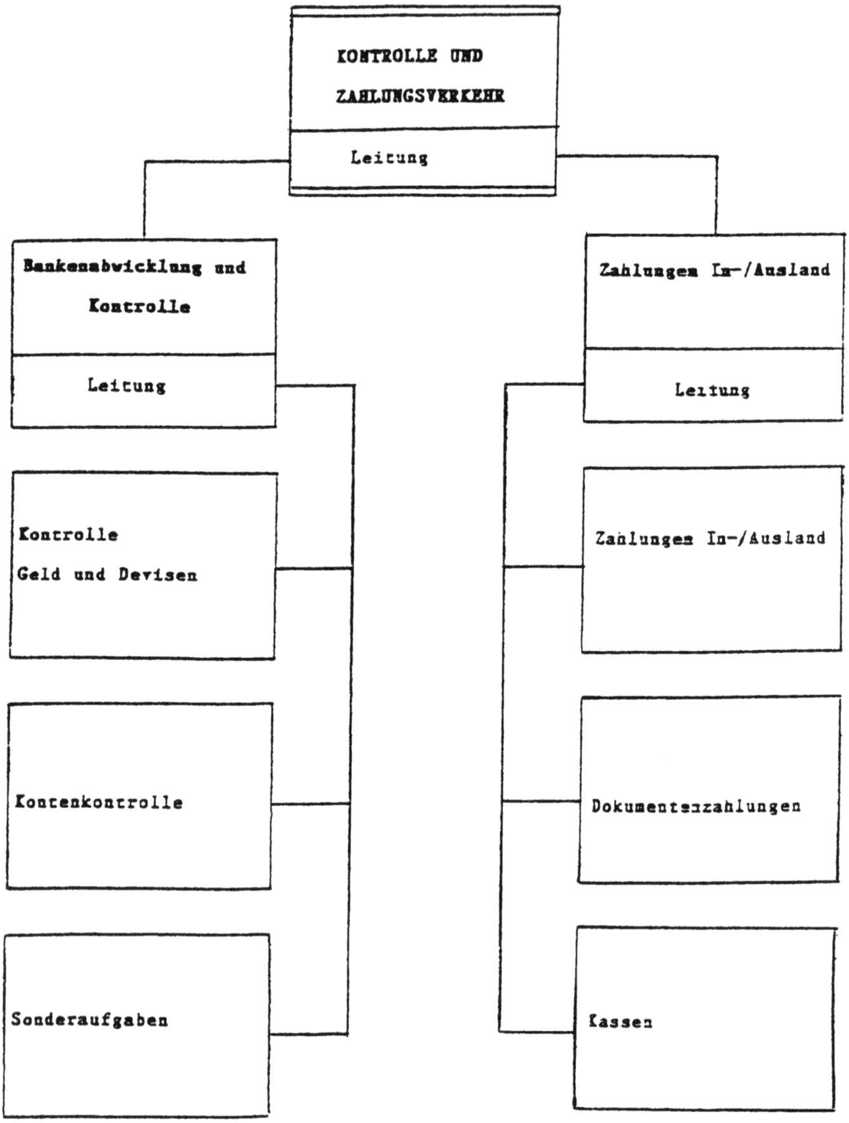

trag im Außenwirtschaftsverkehr] and the related payment lists are prepared containing the following data:

Foreign currency amounts to be paid,

Posted/planned DM amounts per currency, and

Code number to release the open payment position following execution of the payment order.

The payment order is approved by means of signature and legalization stamp (above DM 1,000 two signatures). The payment order is then transmitted to the Control and Payments department in the Treasury. In the Control and Payments department [Kontrolle und Zahlungsverkehr] — Domestic/ Foreign Payments group [Zahlungen In-/Ausland] — the entries on the payment order are examined for plausibility and the signatures are compared with the authorized signature cards. If necessary, the first selected credit institution may be changed for the purpose of achieving a quantitative balance in the orders allocated to various institutions, or orders for certain currencies or destination countries may be allocated to certain institutions. In the case of payments by check to foreign countries, the checks are delivered by the drawee bank or the correspondent bank, or the check is returned to Volkswagen AG which arranges for delivery of the check. Transfer orders in foreign currency to be debited from foreign currency accounts are submitted to the Banking and Control department [Bankenabwicklung und Kontrolle], Money and Foreign Currency Control [Kontrolle — Geld und Devisen] for disposition. Transfer orders in foreign currency to be debited from DM accounts are handled in the Account Control group [Kontenkontrolle].

The order is then transmitted to the first receiving bank by 10 am of the working day; this transmittal is carried out by mail to non-local institutions; if necessary an avis is sent by telefax. The account managing institution executes and posts the order. The Kontenkontrolle receives the account statements and undertakes the posting of the debit including related fees. The payment slip is returned to Zahlungen In-/Ausland for examination of the fees charged, and the slip is then filed. This process is shown in the following diagram:

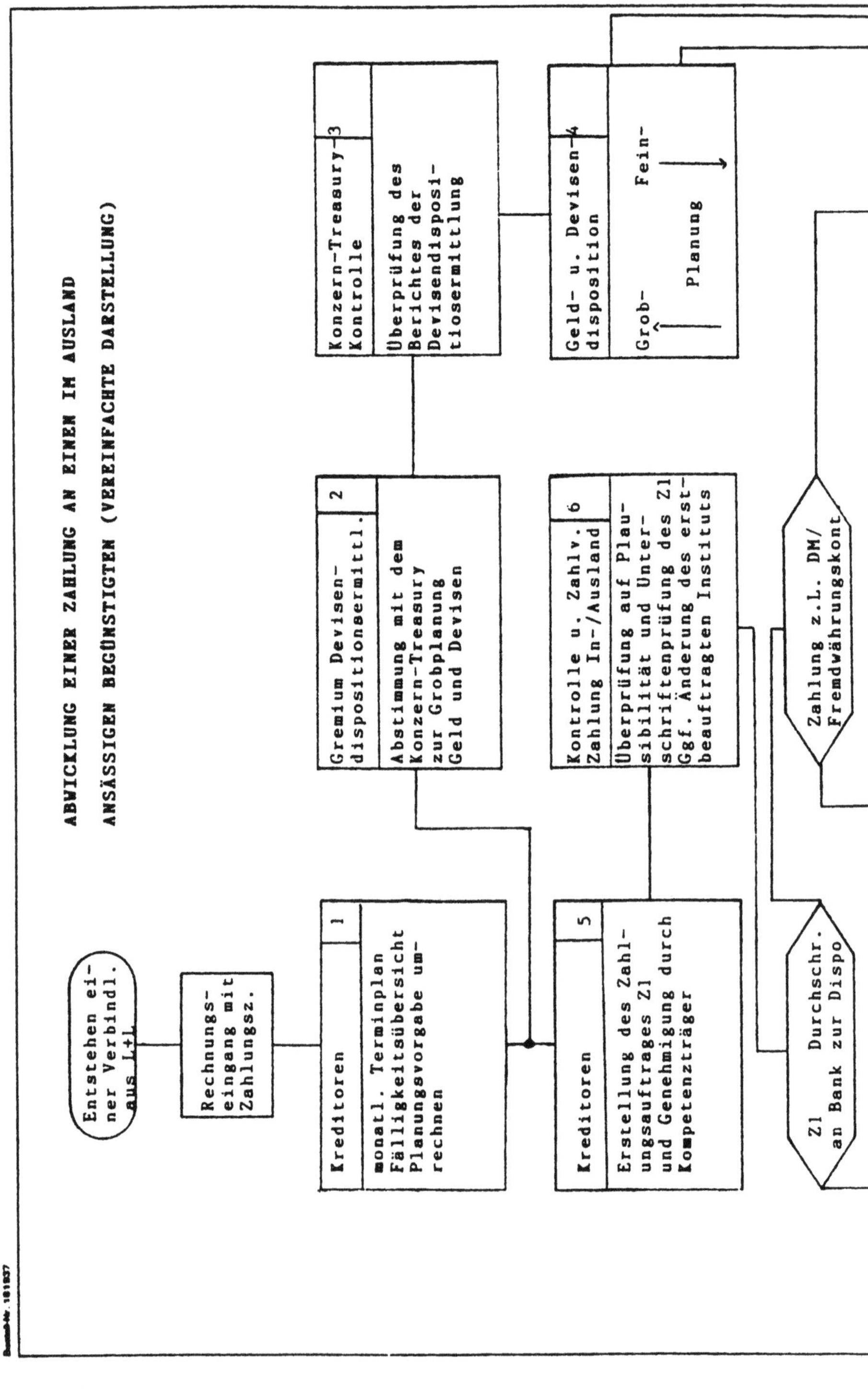
ABWICKLUNG EINER ZAHLUNG AN EINEN IM AUSLAND
ANSÄSSIGEN BEGÜNSTIGTEN (VEREINFACHTE DARSTELLUNG)
Entstehen einer Verbindl. aus L+L
Rechnungseingang mit Zahlungsz.
Kreditoren
1
monatl. Terminplan
Fälligkeitsübersicht
Planungsvorgabe umrechnen
Gremium Devisendispositionsermittl.
2
Abstimmung mit dem Konzern-Treasury zur Grobplanung Geld und Devisen
Konzern-Treasury Kontrolle
3
Überprüfung des Berichtes der Devisendispositionsermittlung
Geld- u. Devisendisposition
4
Grob-
Fein-
Planung
Kreditoren
5
Erstellung des Zahlungsauftrages Zl und Genehmigung durch Kompetenzträger
Kontrolle u. Zahlv. Zahlung In-/Ausland
6
Überprüfung auf Plausibilität und Unterschriftenprüfung des Zl
Ggf. Änderung des erstbeauftragten Instituts
Zl an Bank
Durchschr. zur Dispo
Zahlung z.L. DM/ Fremdwährungskont

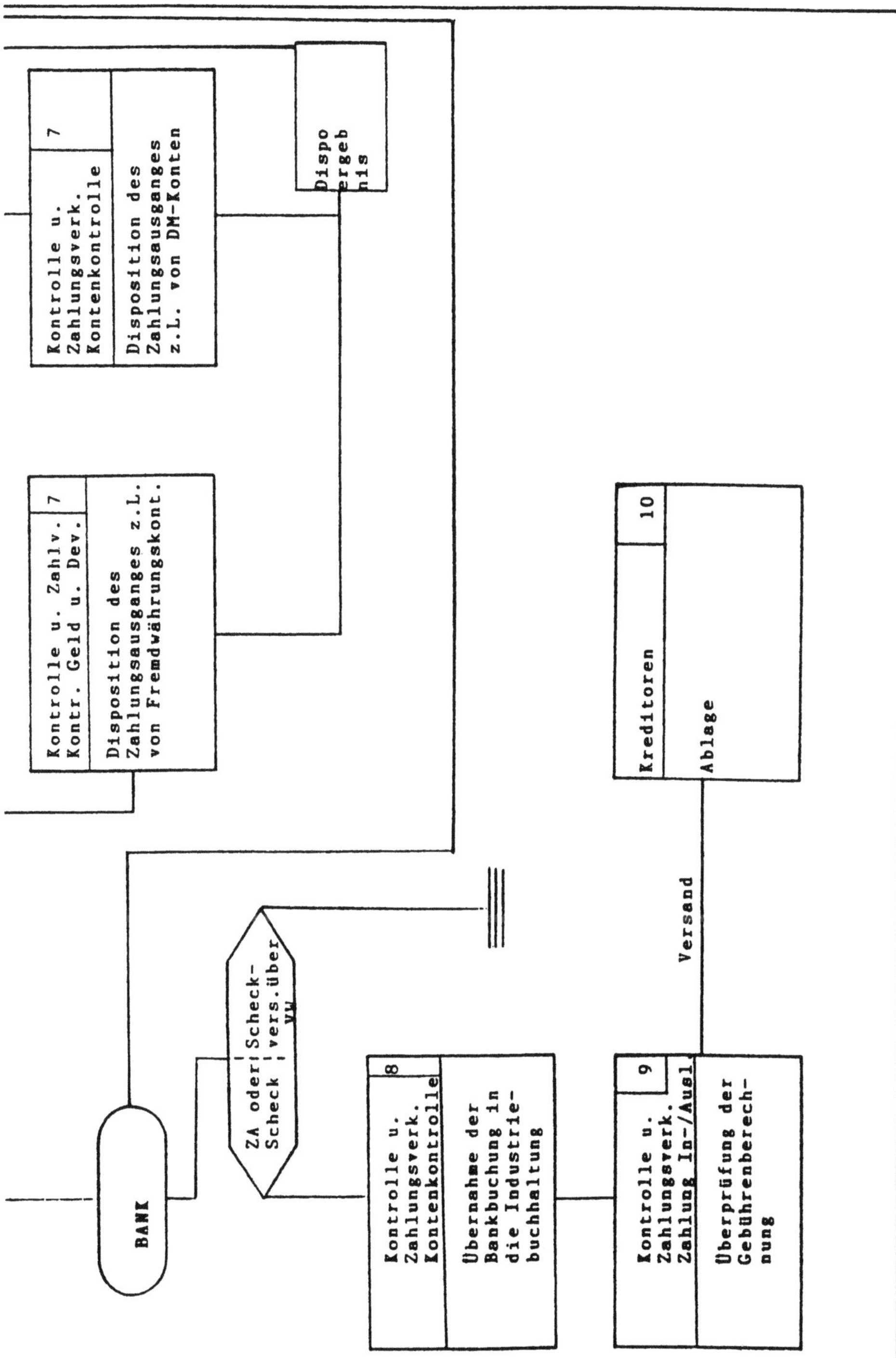

Kontrolle u.
Zahlungsverk.
Kontenkontrolle
7
Disposition des
Zahlungsausganges
z.L. von DM-Konten
Dispo
ergeb
nis
Kontrolle u. Zahlv.
Kontr. Geld u. Dev.
7
Disposition des
Zahlungsausganges z.L.
von Fremdwährungskont.
Kreditoren
10
Ablage
Versand
BANK
ZA oder Scheck
Scheck-
vers.über
VW
Kontrolle u.
Zahlungsverk.
Kontenkontrolle
8
Übernahme der
Bankbuchung in
die Industrie-
buchhaltung
Kontrolle u.
Zahlungsverk.
Zahlung In-/Ausl.
9
Überprüfung der
Gebührenberech-
nung

III. Standards Provided to the First Receiving Bank

1. Payment Route

When a payment order is submitted to a bank, it is usually left up to the first receiving bank to choose the payment route. The banks managing accounts for the Volkswagen AG maintain relationships with numerous correspondent banks in order to be able to promptly transmit payment to each recipient. Payment through S.W.I.F.T. is carried out through the national processing centers and the operating centers in Zoeterwoude and Culpeper.

2. Value Dates

Debits for payment orders are made on the value dates: same day for DM payment orders submitted by 10 am and on the second working day following submission for foreign currency payments. An exception applies for payment orders for which the Kreditoren Bookkeeping has provided a fixed value date.

3. Stipulated Dates

If necessary, the payment order may contain a fixed value date for receipt by the beneficiary.

4. Other Provisions

For some payment transactions, a divergence from the otherwise stipulated fee arrangement can be indicated (e. g. all costs charged to the originator).

IV. Criteria for the Selection of the First Receiving Bank

1. Previous Business Experience

"International payment transactions must be completed promptly and reliably. We can do this through our worldwide network and our optimal technical facilities. Above all: our employees know their job."

This slogan has been used by a well-known major German bank to advertise its involvement in international funds ransactions. And rightly. Our experience has shown that despite high technical standards in the execution of transfer orders, problems still arise in connection with international payments. Critical selection of banks by the Volkswagen AG can minimize these problems from the start. This is what experience has shown.

2. *Costs (internal/external)*

Just like every private customer of a credit institution, the Volkswagen AG incurs costs for most financial services by external providers in international transactions. These costs can be tied to the amounts transferred or can be flat-rate fees. The banks working with Volkswagen AG generally collect fees in currency exchange transactions based on their cost plus a margin of profit directly by means of the exchange rates used; for international payment transactions, a fee is usually charged based on each individual transaction. In the case of pure payments based on commercial transactions, receipts of documentary and non-documentary payments are distinguished. Receipts based on the sale of goods are, as a rule, clean payments, justified by Volkswagen AG's high credit standing. For payment receipts in the form of documents from international transactions, special terms have been stipulated with over 50 institutions. Under these conditions, the collection agents are allowed to charge the Volkswagen AG a percentage fee based on the amount of the incoming payment. No maximum fee is set. But no other costs may be charged with the exception of mailing and special expenses. Minimum fees are charged by only three institutions and are of secondary importance. A percentage fee is likewise charged for non-documentary payment receipts. Because here the risk and the processing expense to the banks is limited, a maximum fee is generally stipulated with all of the banks. Where multiple receipts are credited on the same day from one originator, the maximum fee may be charged only once for that day. The value date for receipts in DM is the date of receipt. Receipts in foreign currency are credited two working days later. Fees for outpayments are also based on a percentage of the amount of this payments, likewise limited by a maximum fee. No fee is charged for small payment orders. The value date for credit to the payment beneficiary should be compensated within two days. Additional costs based on special payment agreements with foreign trading partners of Volkswagen AG are handled individually on a commission basis and are charged to the customer in VW's international accounting. Special terms are negotiated for the foreign currency accounts managed for the VW AG. As compensation, the account managing institution is permitted a calculated float. As a rule, the total costs for clean payments are divided into domestic costs allocated to the Volkswagen AG and foreign costs allocated to the foreign originator/ beneficiary.

3. Selection Criteria

As a major enterprise constantly involved in international business, the Volkswagen AG expects a high degree of competence and capability from its banking partners. In selecting institutions — here particularly with respect to international transfers and check payments — an allocation is generally made with relation to geographic regions and/or trading partners. Payments on behalf of the Volkswagen AG's foreign subsidiaries or general importers are made through one bank each, if possible. This leads to a specialization effect at that bank which benefits the security and speed of execution of orders. For capital imports and exports in the common foreign currencies, the Volkswagen AG maintains foreign currency accounts. A large portion of the payment receipts from exports which are billed in foreign currency are directed through the VW subsidiary CCB (Coordination Center Bruxelles). Certain transfers for the benefit of the Volkswagen AG are combined here. The Group-Wide Treasury in Wolfsburg then receives only one credit per day in each foreign currency. This procedure is also used for incoming payments converted to DM. The circle of institutions involved in international business on behalf of the enterprise must all have achieved a certain standing in the banking sector as well as having foreign branches and correspondent banks available in order to be able to smoothly carry out all of the necessary transactions. It is scarcely worthy of mention that these credit institutions are connected to the S.W.I.F.T. worldwide communications network and possess the additional technical infrastructure necessary to provide all of the services needed by the Volkswagen AG. As a result, it is possible to work intensively with non-local banks in this sector. It is very important that the contact persons at the credit institutions be clearly defined. A high rate of fluctuation in the responsible banking personnel creates problems and is not viewed as being beneficial to good business. The employees in the Group-Wide Treasury in Wolfsburg must know that the responsible bank employees are competent and available. This creates an atmosphere for cooperation satisfactory to both sides.

V. Cost — Opportunity and Risk

1. Terms and Conditions

Volkswagen AG incurs substantial costs in connection with its foreign trade. These costs include the fees described in Part IV. 2. for the execution of foreign payment transactions through banks. In addition, other costs arise in connection with the fixing of payment terms for commercial transactions. Standardized delivery and payment agreements have been made with numerous purchasers and suppliers. Depending upon the credit standing of the trading partners as well as the country rating, foreign payments for commercial transactions can be structured as advance or prepayments, documentary payments, payment against simple invoice or on open terms. Reliable practices can bridge the often differing interests of the contracting parties. A substantial factor in setting payment terms is certainly the status relationship between major enterprises such as the Volkswagen AG and the various import/export firms. These latter firms have a significant interest in establishing long-term contractual relationships with the Volkswagen AG. The resulting firm basis of calculation permits our trading partners to achieve satisfactory profit margins. It is therefore unjustified to speak of an unbalanced relationship between major enterprises and small domestic and foreign suppliers and purchasers.

2. *Negotiation of Terms with Banks*

The terms and conditions negotiated with banks are an important part of the basis for the acquisition of financial services in payment transactions. The outcome of negotiations regularly reflects the cooperative climate which the Volkswagen AG constantly seeks to achieve in its agency arrangements with banks.

3. *Costs within the Enterprise*

The total costs of foreign transactions are allocated to the various relevant sectors by means of cost location accounting. It is apparent that due to the overlapping duties of employees it is not possible make a clear division in foreign payment transactions between personnel costs and other expenses. Therefore, an allocation of clearly defined transaction costs in the form of bank commissions, fees, and interest are allocated to the location originating the costs. For example, in the internal accounting the fee for factoring a forfeit is allocated to sales. The base fees for account management are borne by the Payments and Control group.

4. *Risks*

In its foreign trade activities, the Volkswagen AG is confronted with numerous well-known risk factors such as those related to foreign currency, exchange rates, conversion and transport. The goal of the VW risk management with respect to smooth execution of foreign payments must be to acquire clear information regarding the credit standing of the respective business partners and countries. Limitation of risk in connection with the liquidity, contract performance and payment morality of foreign companies is achieved through the instruments of documentary payments and export financing arrangements. In these areas, some of the universal banks and specialized credit institutions located in the Federal Republic of Germany have established themselves in the past several years. Business relationships with export financing institutions are functioning without significant problems. Payment problems resulting from events in foreign countries are much more difficult to foresee. Generally, these problems do not arise from a single cause. Observation of the economic situation, developments in domestic and foreign politics, as well as potential for social conflicts in the relevant countries is necessary, in any case, by risk management personnel in order to minimize losses. Specific gathering of information locally as well as access to relevant data through business friends throughout the world make these tasks easier.

5. Legal Consequences, Reporting Obligations

Certain international business transactions undertaken by Volkswagen AG are subject to statutory reporting duties (under the Foreign Trade Act and the Foreign Trade Regulation). These reports must be submitted to the Deutsche Bundesbank (Central Bank) which is authorized to transmit the collected data to other federal authorities. These data serve as the statistical basis for the determination of incoming and outgoing payments and in particular for preparation of the balance of payments of the Federal Republic of Germany. The responsibility at the Volkswagen AG for basic handling of these reporting duties is the Foreign Tax department [Steuerwesen Ausland]. The sectors directly involved (Group-Wide Treasury, Kreditoren, Debitor, V.A.G. Treasury) are responsible for originating the reports or turning in the reporting forms. The Treasury is responsible for reporting transactions carried out through banks using the "Zahlungsauftrag im Auslandsverkehr" form (Z1). The required data are transmitted to the Deutsche Bundesbank by the account managing banks in consultation with the affected departments. The foreign payments group [Zahlungen Ausland] receives the completed Z1 forms from other departments and checks that the data subject to reporting are complete and plausible. Reporting duties relating to financial relationships or transactions involving goods and services which are not carried out using the Z1 form are handled by Debitoren Bookkeeping. These a priori involve payments in Germany for the benefit of foreigners as well as interest, dividends and license fees. In- and outpayments in transit trade arise as vehicle and component contracts between the Volkswagen AG and certain affiliates and cooperating partners. Here, the reporting is also done by Debitoren and Creditoren. Leading managers in each special sector are made responsible for fulfilling the statutory reporting duties. Failure to comply can lead to substantial fines. The areas of responsibility in this regard are shown in the Appendix.

VI. Perspectives

The future of foreign payments in their present form appear uncertain from the viewpoint of a major enterprise. Newly developing communications systems as well as a changing sense of identity within the financial departments of large enterprises will lead to changes. Innovative applications in data processing and further development of the traditional banking department into a Corporate Finance division will open new perspectives for the Volkswagen AG. Electronic data processing can lead to improvements in the internal processing of payments, and these improvements can also extend to existing trade and banking relationships. On the other hand, innovations in external facilities in international payment systems are also being developed. The S.W.I.F.T. system begun in 1977 has revolutionized foreign transactions by banks and opened new opportunities for their business clients in the area of foreign payments. Particularly the increased speed of transfers has proved to be of great advantage for major customers who often transfer very large amounts. Now this international data network must be further improved. The system partners are working to reduce the high costs to the banks participating in the S.W.I.F.T. system for standing lines by increasing transmission speeds. Expansion of capabilities for the transmission of free data and certain special functions also appear desirable. Internally at Volkswagen AG there is a complex area where improvements and refinements of present standards can be made. These include expansion of the electronic mailbox system within the Volkswagen AG, in particular introduction of the electronic data interchange procedure (EDI). The goal is to effectively implement necessarily complex business transactions in a data network with business partners and enterprise affiliates on a national and international level. Disadvantages with the present procedures, such as double execution of processing steps (such as data entry) will be eliminated. EDI will permit faster execution of tasks by means of a drastically reduced processing time on the part of the recipient and shorter waiting time for the receipt of relevant information. Direct electronic data communication also increases data security because transmission errors between mechanical data media can be eliminated. In the future, communication between the computers of the Volkswagen AG and the data processing facilities of its business partners will take place exclusively through telecommunications networks. The circulation of magnetic tapes so far used as data exchange media will be successively reduced. The introduction of an EDI system in the area of banking is also planned by the Volkswagen AG. It is planned that a special software package designed for the network will be used. Preparatory measures, including consultation with the relevant banks, are already in progress. The changes which have already taken place in the sense of identity of Treasuries of large enterprises will also lead to new objectives for the financial management of the Volkswagen AG. The Corporate Bank as an inhouse provider of financial services has already become indispensable for major multinational enterprises. Central clearing in order to manage unused liquidity from affiliates as well as determination and analysis by a central division of risk potential to the overall enterprise are in the foreground. Increasing participation in international financial markets not only opens new opportunities for optimizing profits but also represents a source of danger to financial stability and thus to the entire enterprise. The Volkswagen AG is therefore working very carefully with its available instruments. The Volkswagen Group-Wide Treasury primarily performs a service function for the other parts of the enterprise. The goal of all the financial activities is always to secure the enterprise's capability as an automobile manufacturer: the production of the "Volkswagen".

V O L K S W A G E N A G

Geleistete Zahlungen in Fremdwährung (ohne Einbehaltungen, Anzahlungen, Kontokorrentumbuchungen).

Es handelt sich hierbei um Zahlungen aus den drei Hauptzahlungsterminen pro Monat.

Währung		Fremdwährungsbeträge	
	1989	1989	1990
USD	110.170.952,24	136.408.335,--	106.358.201,40
BEC	1.433.917.174,55	1.597.711.949,--	2.502.400.790,--
DKK	9.546.171,82	5.302.960,--	1.227.734,--
FRF	682.828.426,74	740.997.037,--	820.216.411,--
GBP	30.010.341,52	21.591.248,--	49.623.063,--
ITL	61.813.200.098,27	68.009.963.401,--	68.579.593.448,--
JPY	4.978.566.986,71	3.062.797.343,--	4.519.773.169,--
CAD	29.636.331,62	47.142.340,--	70.298.241,--
NLG	32.773.376,28	74.213.904,--	92.258.497,--
NOK	29.373.412,90	11.533.983,--	1.169.398,--
ATS	2.456.006.375,94	2.490.897.028,--	2.989.654.845,--
SEK	28.300.086,09	13.315.289,--	9.413.001,02
CHF	42.860.768,18	38.705.218,--	46.587.280,64
ESB	1.101.359.338,29	1.925.415.982,--	1.304.674.886,--
ZAR	1.212.144,88	1.212.776,--	12.365,--
FIM	2.235.824,33	769.525,--	334.494,39

Anlage 1 zur OA 221/1

Meldepflichten Kapital- und Zahlungsverkehr

Nr.	Leistungsart	Gesetzliche Grundlagen: geregelt in AWV	Gesetzliche Grundlagen: Meldeformular	Gesetzliche Grundlagen: Fristen	Betriebliche Zuständigkeiten: Veranlassung	Betriebliche Zuständigkeiten: Abgabe des Meldeformulars
2.3	ein- und ausgehende Zahlungen außerhalb des Warenverkehrs, die über ein gebietsfremdes Geldinstitut abgewickelt werden (Auslandskonten)	§ 59 § 60 Abs.2	Z2 eing. Zahlungen Z3 ausg. Zahlungen Auslandskontenmeldung	monatlich bis zum 7.Tag des Folgemonats	Konzern-Treasury	Konzern-Treasury
2.4	Forderungen und Verbindlichkeiten gegenüber Gebietsfremden (Meldefreigrenze TDM 500)	§ 62				
2.4.1	Finanzbeziehungen	§ 62 Abs.2	Z5 Forderungen und Verbindlichkeiten aus Finanzbeziehungen mit Gebietsfremden	monatlich bis zum 10.Tag des Folgemonats	Konzern-Treasury Abschluß VW AG Debitoren Kreditoren	Debitoren
2.4.2	Waren und Dienstleistungsverkehr	§ 62 Abs.3	Z5a Forderungen und Verbindlichkeiten gegenüber Gebietsfremden aus Waren- und Dienstleistungsverk.	monatlich bis zum 20. Tag des Folgemonats	Konzern-Treasury, Abschluß VW AG, Debitoren Kreditoren	Debitoren
2.5	ein- und ausgehende Zahlungen im Transithandel (Definition siehe § 40 Abs. 3 AWV)	§ 66 (verw. auf §§ 59 - 61)	Z1 oder Z4 (siehe 2.1 und 2.2)	wie unter 2.1 bzw. 2.2	Debitoren Zollangelegenheiten	Debitoren Kreditoren
2.6	Zahlungen von Gebietsansässigen aus dem Betrieb der Seeschiffahrt	§ 67	Z 8 Einnahmen und Ausgaben der Seeschiffahrt	monatlich bis zum 7. Tag des Folgemonats	V.A.G T	V.A.G T

EUFISERV — Cooperation between European Savings Banks in the Area of Funds Transfers

By Alfons Müller, Brussels*

Contents

I. Introduction

1. Structure, Functions and Market Shares of Savings Banks in Europe

The European Savings Banks Group in Brussels is made up of 1,698 savings banks with 58,133 branches in 16 European countries.[1] The structures of the savings banks in the various countries are quite diverse: some countries, such as Luxembourg, Portugal and Greece, have only one institution which acts nationwide while other countries, such as Germany, have over 500 separate and independent savings banks.

The individual member organizations in the European Savings Banks Group do not have a uniform legal structure. The palette extends from public bodies to private institutions and stock corporations, e.g. in Belgium, Denmark and the Netherlands. In most cases, the savings banks have established common facilities within the member countries, such as state

* Translated by Dr. Frances Dielmann, Frankfurt/M.

[1] At the end of 1989.

banks or central savings banks, accounting and processing centers, academies, specialized subsidiaries such as building and loan associations, investment fund companies and publishing firms.

In some countries, the scope of activities is bound by the so-called "regional principle", i.e. the business territory of a savings bank is limited to the community or region in which the bank was established. Examples are the savings banks in Germany and France. In other countries, the savings banks — primarily the large savings institutions — have dissolved their local or regional ties and have branches nationwide, as in Spain.

In most European countries, the savings banks offer universal banking services and do not differ in this respect from private banks.

Despite increasing liberalization and despite differing legal and organizational structures, the savings banks have retained common sets of values which in many cases reflect their historical goals and the purposes for which they were founded. Most of the institutions in Europe still use their profits for public and charitable purposes, such as environmental protection or patronage of cultural and leisure time facilities.

Growing national and international competition as well as economic necessity of rationalization, often related to mergers into larger institutions, are also being felt by the savings banks. This trend has accelerated in the past years and is shown by the following numbers: in the member countries of the European Savings Banks Group there were still 1,960 savings banks in 1987 but only 1,698 at the end of 1989.

2. European Savings Banks Cooperation Charter

In the uniform European Act, which entered into force on July 1, 1987, the following was stipulated: the European Community shall undertake the necessary measures in order to create, step by step, an internal market by December 31, 1992.

The fixed date and the measures undertaken in the meantime by the EC Commission have had the effect that the orientation toward a unified Europe has been pursued with great energy in all areas of the economy including the credit business. In many cases, this also includes the EFTA (European Free Trade Association) countries, with which the EC Commission has institutionalized its relationships since 1989 and attempted to achieve cooperation in the internal market through further liberalization in the flow of goods and services.

The savings banks possess substantial commercial potential in Europe. But the large number of differing and decentralized institutions impedes a concentration of power. The necessity of reaching new decisions is great, and the new circumstances are unfamiliar to many savings banks. The risks, challenges and opportunities in the European internal market are different in each country. Rapid adjustment to current and future developments is crucial.

A "Commission 1992" appointed by the European Savings Banks Group has comprehensively examined alternative adaptation strategies during the past several years. The Commission 1992 reached the conclusion that cooperation between savings banks is desirable, feasible and preferable to all other strategies.[2]

The charter adopted in 1990 may be summarized as follows:

The members of the European Savings Banks Group resolved the following:

— to use the common traditional characteristics and the close personal and institutional ties which have been created within the European savings bank sector over the years;
— to increase their business capacities through pooling of resources for the benefit of their customers;
— to cooperate actively with their partners in other countries based on the principles of priority and preference set out in the report by the Commission 1992 of the European Savings Banks Group;
— to realize open and broad cooperation directed toward multilateral and collective activities as well as the development of bilateral agreements;
— to create suitable procedures to initiate and promote cooperation between the member institutions of the European Savings Banks Group;
— to promote a savings bank image of European proportions based on a dynamic impression of common traditional values and economic and financial vitality.

II. Objectives and Tasks of EUFISERV

1. Establishment of EUFISERV

The conditions for cooperation between the European savings banks are particularly favorable in the area of transactions with private customers. The European savings banks offer their private customers a full range of banking

[2] DOC 106/89 fin — Commission 1992, p. 34.

and financial services. It appears that the area of funds transfers for private customers and for small and middle-sized businesses would be particularly well-suited for cooperative efforts.

An important sector within the private accounts market is the card-initiated bank transaction. Here, the dense network of branch banks and the highly developed technology of the European savings banks can be expanded into a strategic marketing advantage. In order to offer customers in this sector a uniform, economical and qualitatively attractive service possible in this area, representatives of the savings banks from 11 European countries established EUFISERV s.c. on February 23, 1990, in Brussels. EUFISERV is the abbreviation for European Savings Banks Financial Services Company. The shareholders of EUFISERV are savings bank associations and savings banks from 11 European countries. In order to develop a system of linked cash dispensers in Europe, a savings bank network was created with its central office in Hannover. EUFISERV s.c. entered into a long-term agreement with the dvg Hannover, Germany (data processing company of the Savings Bank Organization of Lower Saxony) concerning the establishment and operation of the network. The connection of the savings banks with the European savings bank network enables the savings banks to provide on-line cash dispensers in Europe 24 hours a day, 7 days a week.

2. Development and Operation of An Automated Cash Dispenser Network by the European Savings Banks

In an initial step, savings bank customers will be provided access to all cash dispensers belonging to European savings banks. The cash dispenser project was started in October 1990 with pilot tests conducted between Portugal, Spain and Germany. In November 1990, the system was put into operation linking the first countries. In the Spring of 1991, 5 countries were already connected to the system. By the Spring of 1992, all 11 participating countries should be connected. Additional national savings bank organizations have already expressed interest in membership in EUFISERV and in cooperation generally in the area of funds transfers. The countries which will enter the cash dispenser network during 1991 are the frequently visited EC countries France, Spain, Italy, Portugal, the Netherlands and Belgium, as well as Austria and the Scandinavian countries Norway, Sweden and Finland.

Following the introductory stage, EUFISERV will provide about 50 million holders of savings bank customer cards, Eurocheque cards or credit cards (VISA or EUROCARD) with access to about 24,000 automated cash dispensers in Europe. The European savings banks are thus the first group of credit institutions to achieve open access and reciprocity between card payment systems through the use of cash dispensers, a concept which has been supported for years.

The networking of European cash dispensers makes travel among European countries significantly easier for savings bank customers. They can obtain foreign currency as needed very simply and around the clock. The cash dispenser monitor screens display information and instructions in German, English, French and the respective local language. The system authorizes each cash withdrawal on-line by checking the customer's account at his home savings bank.

3. Development and Implementation of the Technical and Organizational Infrastructure for Execution of Funds Transfers

The design of the network and the most important functions authorization, payment and clearing are shown in the illustration below.

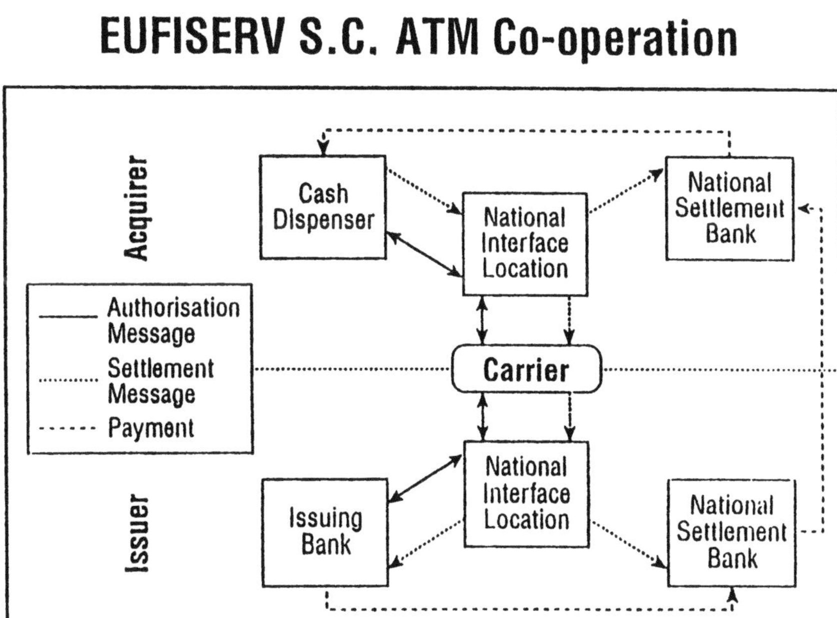

Each national member organization is connected with the dvg Hannover, the central network, through a national interface location. The realization of the cash dispenser network was preceded by two years of development and implementation in the individual member countries. This work was coordinated by a project team which was commissioned by the member states in close cooperation with the European Savings Banks Group. One important objective was to harmonize the differing conditions in the various member states. The working groups, which were employed from the beginning and which were made up of members from different countries, were especially effective. They dealt with specific areas such as data processing, message transmission, message coding and other security problems as well as clearing.

The development work led to the preparation of an Operations Manual containing the system description worked out for each of the participating countries as well as detailed technical specifications for using the system. The pilot tests carried out in 1990 were successful and affirmed the feasibility of the goals set for the project.

4. Cooperation in European Funds Transfers

Following conclusion of the cash dispenser project there are no limits to the further development of EUFISERV.

Based on the established savings bank network, other payment services can be developed in accordance with the wishes of European savings bank customers for additional electronic banking services. The savings banks view the further development of these services as a challenge which will permit them to demonstrate their competitive position with respect to other credit institutions in the European internal market. With 1800 savings banks and a network of more than 58,000 branch offices in the EC countries and most of the EFTA countries, with a turnover of over 1 trillion ECU, and 210 million savings and 80 million giro accounts, the European Savings Banks Group has an excellent infrastructure closely tailored to its customers' needs. Its greatest potential is in the area of serving private customers and mid-sized companies.

Based on a correct evaluation of the significance of funds transfers for banks and savings banks, it was not surprising that, within the scope of achieving the internal market and creating a uniform European currency, the EC Commission has also dealt with the subject of funds transfers.

Following the public discussion of its "Green Paper" on funds transfers, the Commission on March 20, 1991, issued a communication on the topic of "funds transfers in the internal market". The Vice President of the EC

Commission and Commissioner responsible for financial institutions and company law, Sir Leon BRITTAN, stated in connection with the publication of the report that the Commission sees in the improvement in funds transfers the key to opening new opportunities and advantages in the internal market after 1992.

The European savings banks and the financial services company, EUFISERV, which they have established, view the deliberations by the EC Commission on the subject of funds transfers as being greatly important. Above all, they highly value the declaration by the Commission that the growing need for qualitatively improved funds transfer opportunities should not be controlled by a single monolithic organization, but that priority should instead be given to competition among the various European credit institutions and groups. This goal is justified even though the integration of various funds transfer cultures will require a high level of cooperation among the various levels of organization in the groups of credit institutions as well as the central banks.

The Commission sees its role as that of a mediator with the goal of coordinating the differing views of the participating parties in the interest of an optimal overall result. EUFISERV, as the body created to facilitate cooperation in funds transfers between the European savings banks, will find an extensive range of work in this important sector.

III. Conclusions and Perspectives

It is already apparent from our present perspective that the establishment of EUFISERV was a farsighted and enterprising decision by the European savings banks.

The realization of the internal market starting in 1992 will further intensify the need for cooperation by savings banks in Europe in the area of funds transfers. It is, therefore, foreseeable that funds transfers for private and business customers, as well as further improvement in card-controlled payments will represent important fields of activity by EUFISERV in the interests of its member organizations well into the future.

The German Postbank in International Funds Transfers

By Klaus M. Gormanns, Bonn*

Contents

---

* Translated by Dr. Frances Dielmann, Frankfurt/M.

I. The Services Offered by the Postbank

1. Introduction

The transport of cash money is among the oldest services offered by the postal service. Money was originally transported in coaches in sealed letters, iron-mounted strongboxes or barrels. This difficult and often dangerous method of transport forced the postal service to seek other ways of transferring money. The first major step in this direction came in 1848 with the introduction of the payment order. Instead of transporting the coins and notes which had been paid in, now a voucher was delivered to the payee against which the transferred amount would be paid to him.

The search for a cashless payment system was also begun in the last century. Austria opened its postal check service in 1883. Switzerland and Japan did not follow this example until 1906, the German Reichspost in 1909. The German postal check service was renamed Postal Giro (transfer) Service in 1984, in order to more accurately reflect the broad scope of the services available.

The postal service — in 1950 renamed "Deutsche Bundespost" (German Federal Post) and in the former German Democratic Republic "Deutsche Post" — has always offered funds transfer services suited to the need of the business community and the private customer and expanded these services in accordance with its statutory mandate.[1]

Today the statutory mandate of the Bundespost is found in the Postal Charter: The Postbank must "meet the demands of citizens, business and administration for ... postal bank services".[2]

The range of services offered by the Postbank, one of three enterprises belonging to the Deutsche Bundespost, today makes it possible to make payments to almost every country in the world and to receive payments from many countries. Any person is entitled to use the facilities of the Postbank if the requirements set out for the individual services are met.[3] Customers find this service by the Postbank to be simple, secure and fast.

The scope and significance of foreign funds transfers can be illustrated by the following figures: each year, about 2.8 million foreign transfers are made,

---

[1] § 2 (3) of the Law on the Administration of the German Federal Post (Postal Administration Act [PostVwG]) of July 24, 1953 (BGBl. I, p. 676), meanwhile abrogated by § 66 (1) of the Postal Charter Act [PostVerfG] in the version of Art. 1 of the Law on the Restructuring of the Postal and Telecommunications System and the German Federal Post (Postal Structure Act [PostStrukG]) of June 8, 1989 (BGBl. I, p. 1026).

[2] § 4 (1) PostVerfG.

[3] § 8 (1) PostG in the version of the proclamation of July 3, 1989 (BGBl. I, p. 1449).

and about 1.6 million transfers are received from foreign countries. The number of postal money orders exceeds 2.4 million outgoing and 900,000 incoming orders. In addition, over 1 million payments are sent to foreign countries in the form of correspondent bank checks.

2. The Most Important Services

Because the spectrum of services offered by the Postbank is in part not typical of banks in general, the most important services will be described briefly. The holder of a Postbank giro account has the possibility of ordering payments to almost every county in the world. In addition, any person may use the postal money order and the postal order to carry out a funds transfer.

a) Funds Transfers

As in other banks, the funds transfer is the most important non-cash type of payment. By means of a transfer, money can be transmitted from a post giro account to a foreign post giro account. Here, the originator and the beneficiary in the foreign country or at least the beneficiary's bank must have a post giro account.

Post giro transfers are possible to a total of 21 countries, including all significant Western European countries and also Japan. The transfer order, which does not have a maximum limit on the amount — with the possible exception of foreign currency regulations in the receiving country — can be issued in German marks, in the currency of the country of destination, or in another common currency, whereby the U.S. dollar is the primary currency for transfer to non-European countries. The official foreign currency selling rate determined by the Frankfurt Currency Exchange is used for the currency conversion. If this rate is not available for a particular currency, the conversion is based on a usual bank rate.

If the payment is especially urgent, the transmittal can be accelerated using a telegram transfer, whereby transfers to bank giro accounts in the United States, Canada and Italy, including Vatican City, are carried out through correspondent banks. If — outside of the 21 countries mentioned above — no agreement for a transfer system has been made with the particular country of destination or if the target account is not known, the transfer is carried out by means of a postal money order, as described below. If the target country does not have a postal money order service or if the originator does not wish the amount to be paid in cash, an order check drawn on a correspondent bank with an office in the target country is sent directly to the payee.

In the other direction, i.e. from foreign countries to Germany, the transferred amount is credited to the tranferee's Postbank giro account. If the beneficiary is not a Postbank giro customer, the Postbank transmits the amount to the bank where the beneficiary maintains his account. In most cases, the transfers are received in German marks. If this is not the case, the official buying rate fixed by the Frankfurt Currency Exchange is used for the conversion to German marks. If no official buying rate is available for a particular currency, the usual bank rate is used.

b) Money Order

In addition to the transfer, the Postbank offers the money order for certain countries, which in urgent cases can also be sent by telegram. Here, the customer orders the Postbank to debit a certain amount from his post giro account and pay this amount directly to the payee.

Money orders received from foreign countries are converted to domestic money orders for settlement and sent to the payee.

c) Payment Card

Customers who do not have a giro account at a Postbank can employ the payment card service. Using the payment card, the customer instructs the Postbank to credit an amount, which the customers pays in bar at the post office, to a post giro account of the payee in the foreign country. The receiving account can also be a post giro account held by the bank where the payee maintains his account. In this way, payees in 32 countries can be reached.

The telex payment card is available for urgent payments of this type. An additional fee is charged, and the payment order is transmitted to the foreign country by telex instead of by letter.

Payment cards received from foreign countries are credited by the Postbank to the customer's post giro account or transmitted to the bank where the customer maintains his account. Because post giro accounts at the Postbank are maintained only in German marks, payment card amounts stated in foreign currency are converted to marks at the official buying rate.

d) Postal Money Order

One service offered only by the post office is the postal money order. It is the oldest form of tranmitting money after the transport of cash. The foreign postal money order allows transfer of money to recipients in countries which are not connected to the postal giro service and do not have a geographically comprehensive network of banks. 196 countries can be reached using this service.

The money to be transmitted to the foreign country is paid in cash to the postal service. Payments are accepted at all post offices, Postbank offices and other post locations. An amount up to 1,000 German marks can generally also be accepted by a rural postman.

A money order which is to be paid in cash to the payee by the postal authority in the destination country's currency is designated by the Postbank as a cash postal money order. Approximately 50 postal authorities offer this service. The postal money order amount is, in accordance with the regulations in the particular country, delivered either to the residence of the payee or — following delivery notice to the payee — paid in cash at a post office.

In addition, there is a so-called "check postal money order", which will be described in the section on payments by check.

Toward the end of the 1950's, the peak era of the foreign postal money order began, caused by the increase in the number of foreign workers who regularly sent a portion of their salary to their home countries by means of postal money order. Following a peak in the mid-1960's, the number of postal money orders to foreign countries has constantly declined. One reason for this is that more and more foreign workers have opened their own bank accounts. The increase in cashless payments in the same period of time as the decline in the cost-intensive postal money order certainly is also in the best interests of the Postbank.

The possibility of having an amount transmitted relatively quickly by telegraphic postal money order is currently possible to 32 countries.

Postal money orders are received in Germany from 62 foreign countries. The terms and conditions of the postal service are used for carrying out these payments.

e) Payments By Check

Customers may instruct the Postbank to carry out their payments in almost all countries in the world by means of sending checks.

The post giro customer merely must indicate this choice on the transfer form.

Transmittal by means of check is an alternative in the case of a postal money order when the money is to be sent to a country which does not participate in the postal money order procedure or when the maximum limit stipulated with the particular country is exceeded or if the payor expressly requests this method.

In carrying out these instructions, the Postbank draws checks on financial institutions in the country of destination in order to achieve acceptance with as few problems as possible. The customer can, to a great extent, freely choose the currency in which the check is to be drawn; 14 currencies are available.

f) Check Collection

The Postbank accepts domestic and foreign checks — including those drawn in foreign currency — from post giro customers for collection. These can be bank checks, Eurochecks, post checks or travelers' checks. The checks are collected by the usual means. The check amounts are credited to the post giro account of the presenter. Some checks can also be accepted at post offices and collected in the same manner.

g) Cash on Delivery

A letter or package mailed with a return receipt at a post office can be sent cash on delivery (C.O.D.) where the delivery is to be made in exchange for payment of a fixed amount in cash. The collected amount is credited to the sender's post giro account. In six countries, there is even the possibility of having the amount credited to a post giro account in that country. C.O.D. shipments are possible to 22 foreign countries from Germany and to Germany from 24 countries.

The General Terms and Conditions of the postal service apply to incoming and outgoing C.O.D. shipments. The Postbank undertakes only the transmittal or crediting of the C.O.D. amount.

h) Travelers' Checks and Foreign Currency

Also belonging to foreign funds transfers in a broad sense are travelers' checks and foreign currency, which will be mentioned briefly for the sake of completeness. The Postbank provides its customers with travelers' checks in 14 currencies from various issuers and accepts numerous types of traveler's checks from different issuers for payment at post offices.

The Postbank's foreign currency service can also provide its customers with most of the common currencies in the world and buys 28 different currencies at designated offices.

3. The Statutory Mandate

The banking and other financial services described above are offered by the Postbank within the scope of the authority granted to the federal government in the German Basic Law (constitution) in Article 73 no. 7 and Article 87 no. 1. In accordance with the statutory mandate cited in the introduction, the Postbank must structure its services in accordance with market needs taking economic and technical developments in consideration.[4]

II. The Technical Execution of Funds Transfers

In the technical execution of international funds transfers, the Postbank is dependent upon the technical standards of its partners, primarily postal authorities and postal banks. This means that even today funds transfers with many countries are still paper-based. Only with Switzerland can data be exchanged in both directions by means of teleprocessing; this is possible with the four Scandanavian countries only for incoming data.

The fact that international payments must still often be handled manually because no automated systems are available or the automated systems available at the national level are incompatible, is not a problem merely of the postal service. The European Commission has for a long time been engaged in efforts to achieve an acceleration of transfer procedures and related cost reductions.

It was recognized years ago by the European Conference on Postal and Communications Administrations (Conférence européen des Administrations des postes et télécommunications — CEPT), a suborganization of the Universal Postal Union made up of 32 European postal administrations, that the constantly growing volume of international funds transfers will require a shift to the use of data tranmission. The so-called telegiroprocessing was therefore agreed upon, using its own data record format, with which postal funds transfers would be executed inexpensively within Europe. But even before this goal was reached it became apparent that an opening in the direction of the S.W.I.F.T. system would be necessary to meet future needs, not least because only 12 countries had shown interest in creating a telegiro network. The payment orders issued by customers are gathered into collective orders and entered by means of magnetic tape, disk, or magnetic tape cassette.

The transfer connections with a number of countries have grown historically, and the execution of transfers is therefore structured in various ways.

[4] § 4 (1) sent. 2 PostVerfG.

In the case of funds transfers, the Postbank is responsible for seeing that the funds are already available in the target country in a reciprocal account (nostro account) at the time the order is to be carried out, so that the foreign postal authority or postal bank can receive its money at the same time or immediately thereafter. If the payment is carried out in German marks, the transferred amount is credited to the reciprocal (loro) account maintained in Germany by the foreign postal authority or Postbank.

In the case of postal or other money orders which are to be paid in cash in the target country, cover is provided by means of monthly invoices, with advance payments if necessary, or — more often in the case of money orders — through reciprocal accounts.

Corresponding arrangements apply to payments received from foreign countries.

Where checks drawn on banks are sent, the Postbank must make sure that the reciprocal account has sufficient funds to cover the volume of the checks issued within a stipulated period of time. The delayed collection of checks by the payee (time lag) works to the advantage of the correspondent, with the Postbank sometimes being allowed a floating share.

III. Legal Provisions

It is necessary in any fairly comprehensive description of the legal situation regarding postal transfers to explain what — from a legal perspective — a postal bank is, how its relationship to its customers is structured, and how the legal relationships between the postal bank and its foreign partners are governed.

1. Postbank Services in Accordance with the Provisions of the Post Office Administration Act of 1953

Prior to the reorganization of the Deutsche Bundespost in 1989, the postal bank services were a part of the general postal services. The federal administration of the Deutsche Bundespost was directed by the Federal Minister of Post and Telecommunications. In accordance with the resolutions of the executive board, he could issue regulations regarding the conditions and fees for the use of the facilities of the post and telecommunications systems based on the authority granted in § 14 of the Post Office Administration Act [PostVsG]. The use of the postal bank services was governed by the Post Office Act and the Post Giro Regulation, and the postal money order by the Post Regulation. A participant relationship under public law arises on the basis of the terms and conditions when postal services are used.

2. The Postbank under the Provisions of the Postal Charter of 1989[5]

Following the effective date of the Post Structure Act of July 1, 1989, the Deutsche Bundespost was reorganized.

a) A New Legal Identity?

During the 11th legislative period of the German Lower House of Parliament (Bundestag), the federal government resolved to fundamentally reform the post and telecommunications system because the existing institutional and regulatory structures were not flexible enough to adapt to future needs. In implementing new regulatory concepts in telecommunications and structual rearrangement of the Deutsche Bundespost, postal services were given a certain autonomy when the Postbank was created as a third enterprise alongside the postal service and Telekom; this was done by means of the Postal Structure Act, the core of which is the Post Charter contained in Article 1. The restructuring of the Deutsche Bundespost is governed by § 1 (2) of the Post Charter. The three cited enterprises within the Deutsche Bundespost were removed from the Federal Ministry for Post and Telecommunications on July 1, 1989.

Despite the establishment of the three enterprises, the unity of the Deutsche Bundespost was left intact. It remains as a unified administration within the meaning of Article 87 of the Basic Law.[6]

The special revenue fund of the Deutsche Bundespost still exists, and separate special revenue funds were created for the three enterprises.[7] The enterprises are managed independently.[8] The Postbank can transact business in its own name and function as a separate legal entitiy.[9]

b) Transformation from a Public Law Participant Relationship to a Private Legal Relationship

One major innovation provided for by the legislators in the course of the restructuring of the Deutsche Bundespost was that the legal relationships between the enterprise and its customers which had previously been gov-

[5] PostVerfG in the version in Art. 1 PostStrukG, see note 1.

[6] Argumentum e contrario § 1 (2) PostVerfG.

[7] § 2 (1) sent. 2 PostVerfG.

[8] § 37 PostVerfG.

[9] § 5 PostVerfG.

erned by public law would now be transformed into private legal relationships.[10] It was also stipulated that the public law legal relationships existing at the time of the shift in the applicable law, e.g. a post giro participant relationship, would continue in existence and take on the character of private law relationships in accordance with the new applicable legal principles.[11]

c) The General Terms and Conditions [AGB] of the Postbank including the Special Terms and Conditions

The Post Structure Act amended § 7 of the Postal Act such that the legal relationships arising through use of the facilities of the postal system would be of a private law nature. Because the Post Structure Act took effect on July 1, 1989, then based on the wording of the law, this stipulation also took effect at that time. On the other hand, the legislators were aware that the replacement of the administrative law provisions governing the public law relationship between the Postbank and its participants through provisions of private law could not be realized within a period of a few weeks — the Post Structure Act was adopted on June 8, 1989 and took effect at the beginning of the following month. § 65 (1) of the Postal Charter therefore allowed a time limit of two years for the creation of Postbank General Terms and Conditions; at the end of this time period, at the latest, the Legal Regulations of the Federal Minister for Post and Telecommunications would expire.

The new Postbank General Terms and Conditions have been in effect since July 1, 1991. Despite the clear wording of § 7 Postal Act, this provision could therefore also not take effect until that date. The provision of § 65 (3) sent. 1 Postal Charter can only be understood in this way.[12]

The drafting of the Postbank AGB did not consist merely of reformulating the contents of the previously applicable legal provisions, but instead created a new legal foundation for the relationship between the Postbank and its customers based on the German Civil Code and the Law Governing Standard Contracts. While, for example, the earlier version of the Postal Act provided in § 8 that a person without full legal capacity or fully competent to contract could still employ the services of the Deutsche Bundespost, the Postbank AGB now comply with the provisions of the German Civil Code

---

[10] § 7 PostG.

[11] § 65 (3) sent. 2 PostVerfG.

[12] See Engelbracht/Zimny, Die Auswirkungen des Poststrukturgesetzes auf die Deutsche Bundespost Postbank und auf die Rechtsbeziehungen zu ihren Kunden, in Postpraxis 1990, no. 2, p. 35. See also VGH Mannheim, decision of Mar. 6, 1990, in: NJW 1991, p. 512. Contra, A. Gramlich. Ein ungewisser Übergang: Anmerkungen zu Folgen der Poststrukturreform, die sich hätten vermeiden lassen. Verwaltungsrundschau, 1990, no. 3, pp. 82 ff.

protecting the rights of minors because the Postbank is now subject to the same limitations on its relationships with customers as are banks and savings institutions.

The Postbank AGB contain only few provisions specifically relating to the subject of international funds transfers, but the following five of the approximately 40 Special Terms and Conditions do relate to international transfers:

— Documentary orders for payments to payees in foreign countries
— Cashless transmittal of payments to accounts from foreign countries
— Money orders from foreign countries
— Transmittal of deposits to payees in foreign countries
— Collective orders in data processing form for payment to foreign countries.

The provisions of the implementing regulations for the Postal Money Orders Agreement and the Postal Giro Agreement relevant for customers were incorporated into these Special Terms and Conditions.[13]

The Postbank AGB[14], the Special Terms and Conditions[15] and the fee schedules[16] were officially published and are available for examination at the offices of the Postbank, the postal service and Telekom.[17]

d) The International Convention of the Universal Postal Union and its Implementing Regulations

The legal basis for international postal transactions is found in the Universal Postal Convention. This multilateral convention is updated approximately every five years. The version presently in effect was adopted in 1989 at the World Postal Congress in Washington. Almost all of the countries in the world with independent postal authorities are members of the Universal Postal Union.[18]

The rules for the individual service sectors are contained in separate conventions. In the present context, the conventions on postal money orders,

[13] See part III 2 d.

[14] Officially published in Postbank publik, no. 22, of May 31, 1991, pp. 309 ff.

[15] Officially published in Postbank publik, no. 25, of June 6, 1991, pp. 341-400; no. 49, of Oct. 31, 1991, p. 690; no. 55, of Dec. 12, 1991, p. 743; no. 7, of Feb. 20, 1992, p. 70.

[16] Officially published in Postbank publik, no. 26, of June 6, 1991, pp. 401-412.

[17] § 23 (2) no. 1a of the Law Governing Standard Business Conditions of Dec. 9, 1976 (BGBl. I, p. 3317), most recently amended by Art. 6 § 2 of the Law of July 25, 1986 (BGBl. I, p. 1142) in the version in Art. 4 (8) PostStrukG.

[18] See L. Kämmerer, Die Rechtsgrundlagen des Weltpostverkehrs, Archiv für das Post- und Fernmeldewesen 1958, p. 9 ff.

postal transfers and postal C.O.D. shipments are of interest. Implementation regulations also exist in connection with these conventions, which primarily supplement the conventions in the area of operations. Their legal existence is independent from the validity of the conventions whose implementation they serve.[19]

The contents of these conventions did not yet become governing national law with the signing of the conventions by the various member states of the Universal Postal Union. The conventions of the Universal Postal Union and the related implementation regulations were adopted into German domestic law by means of a formal federal statute in accordance with Art. 59 (2) sent. 1 of the Basic Law.

In the past, the implementation regulations for the Universal Postal Convention and the other conventions of the Universal Postal Union were converted into German law by regulations promulgated by the Federal Minister of Post and Telecommunications in accordance with Art. 80 of the Basic Law. The authority for such regulations was provided by § 14 of the Postal Administration Act which, as already discussed, was replaced by the Postal Structure Act.[20] This led to the problem of how to transform the implementing regulations into domestic German law. One possibility would have been to continue to transform such implementing regulations of the Universal Postal Union by domestic regulation. These regulations would constitute private law and therefore be subject to review by civil courts. This alternative was not selected because there was no legal basis available for it.

In connection with the selected method of transforming the implementation regulations into Special Terms and Conditions of the Postbank, it is not certain that the civil courts will give appropriate consideration in their decisions to the fact that due to the provisions of the international conventions the Postbank has no freedom of decision on certain points.

While international postal transactions are carried out with many foreign postal authorities on the basis of the particular international agreement, cooperation with postal authorities not members of the relevant convention of the Universal Postal Union is to a great extent carried out with no significant problems by general compliance with the provisions of the relevant convention without either of the parties expressly relying on these provisions.

e) Relationships with Foreign Non-Postal Partners

For the sake of completeness, we will mention here the legal relationships with foreign partners with whose help the Postbank executes international

[19] Id. at 14.

[20] See note 1.

funds transfers with a number of countries. The primary cooperation is with banks. Only in a few cases do contractual relationships exist; in most cases the Postbank which employs a different bank in the execution of a funds transfer which the Postbank has been instructed to carry out is itself a customer of this other bank so that the rights and obligations are governed by that bank's terms and conditions.

3. Liability by the Postbank

Any reasonably complete description of the most significant Postbank provisions applicable to its customers using international funds transfer services would be well beyond the scope of this discussion. We would merely like to attempt to sketch the liability of the Postbank, in particular because this topic is one of the main concerns of the UNCITRAL Model Law currently being drafted.

Of course, the primary provisions governing the relationship of the Postbank with its customers are contained in statutes. These include the Postal Act, the laws connected with the conventions of the Universal Postal Union and general statutory provisions. In addition, the relationships are governed in the interest of uniform procedures by the Postbank AGB and the related schedule of fees and prices. Some Postbank services are additionally governed by Special Terms and Conditions.

The provisions establishing liability by the Postbank are spread among various sources. The primary basis for liability is the Postal Act.

a) Liability under the Postal Act

§ 11 of the Postal Act provides for the principles of liability:

"(1) The liability of the Deutsche Bundespost ... Postbank for damages caused by improper executions of its services is limited to the scope stipulated under the provisions of this statute.

(2) To the extent that liability by the Deutsche Bundespost ... Postbank is excluded or limited by this statute, any party using its facilities or any other person shall have a claim for compensation against the employees involved only if those employees intentionally violated their official duties."

In addition to these principles, the Postal Act contains supplementary provisions relating to liability in the transmittal of funds and in post giro services. Finally, a separate provision relates to the supply of incorrect information.

It may be surprising that under provisions governing liability in funds transmittal services it is not the Postbank but instead the Postal Service which is liable for having an amount (which has been paid in properly) paid out or credited to a post giro account.[21] This stipulation was made in the interest of the customer. In the case of damages, the customer is able to take recourse against the location where he paid the money in cash. In almost all cases, this is a post office. The internal handling of a payment order, which is unknown to the customer and which can involve mistakes within the areas of responsibility of either the Postbank or the Postal Service, should not be decisive in establishing where the customer must turn in case of a problem.[22]

The liability provision governing C.O.D. shipments is based on this same idea.[23] The Postal Service is liable to the sender of a shipment for having the C.O.D. amount collected upon delivery and properly transmitted to the sender.

It is also consistent that the Postbank is liable to its customer for having a money order properly paid or credited because in this case the customer had issued the underlying payment order to the Postbank.[24]

And finally, this concept is also the basis for liability in post giro services.[25] The Postbank is liable in connection with post giro services for damages incurred by the post giro customer due to improper execution of his instructions (transfers, checks, debit transfers) by the post giro office, in accordance with the general statutory provisions governing the liability of a debtor for the fulfillment of his obligations. New is the fundamental liability of the Postbank for the delayed execution of orders — although only in cases of intentional misconduct or gross negligence — except those involving standing or urgent orders.[26]

For the sake of completeness, we will also mention liability for the supply of incorrect information. The Postbank is liable for damages incurred due to the provision of incorrect information in writing in connection with post giro services in accordance with the general statutory provisions governing the liability of a debtor for the fulfillment of his obligations[27]; the same is true for information in connection with postal services.[28] Otherwise, the Postbank is

---

[21] § 15 PostG.

[22] Altmannsperger, Die Neuregelung der Posthaftung durch das Poststrukturgesetz, Postpraxis 1989, no. 9, p. 204, 206.

[23] § 15 (3) PostG.

[24] § 15 (2) PostG.

[25] § 19 PostG.

[26] § 19 sent. 2 PostG.

[27] § 21 (2) PostG.

[28] § 21 (1) PostG.

liable for incorrect information given by the post giro offices only in case of intentional misconduct or gross negligence.[29]

The liability provisions just discussed do not expressly stipulate whether and to what extent they apply to international funds transfer orders. § 27 Postal Act stipulates that the provisions of that law as well as the Postbank AGB shall also apply for postal transactions with territories outside the scope of application of the German Basic Law. This is not true, of course, to the extent that the Postal Act is superceded by international agreements and conventions and related implementing laws and regulations.

b) The Liability of the Postbank under the Universal Postal Convention and the other Conventions of the Universal Postal Union

For the international transactions by the Postbank which are of interest to us in the scope of this discussion, the Universal Postal Convention and its related conventions are the most significant sources. These do not, however, comprehensively govern the area of international transactions. Existing gaps in the provisions are filled by the appropriate rules governing domestic transactions.[30] Besides this principle of subsidiarity there is also a principle of specialization: in cases in which a rule is present for domestic transactions and a rule governing the same situation is present in an international agreement or convention, the latter rule has priority.[31] Both of these rules are anchored in Article 24 of the Charter of the Universal Postal Union, which can be summarized as follows:

The provisions of these conventions do not affect the domestic legal provisions of the member states unless expressly otherwise stipulated. The provisions of the Universal Postal Convention and the related conventions and implementing regulations can only be applied in cases where the the target country has acceded to the agreement and the relevant conventions and a postal authority or postal bank received the order to execute the payment. The conventions of the Universal Postal Union and the implementing regulations govern postal services for the member states to the convention. They have mandatory application for these states.

Neither the Universal Postal Convention or the related implementing regulations govern liability claims by customers in case of faulty performance in international funds transfers. Only the conventions of the Univer-

---

[29] § 21 (2) clause 2c PostG.

[30] Altmannsperger, Kommentar zum Gesetz über das Postwesen, at § 27, margin no. 2.

[31] Id.

sal Postal Union, which govern within the scope of international funds transfers — i.e. the Money Orders Agreement, the Giro Agreement and the Cash-on-Delivery Agreement — contain liability provisions relevant in this context.

Under the Money Orders Agreement, the participating postal authorities are liable in principle for the proper payment of the amounts which were paid in.[32]

An exclusion of liability exists for any type of delay in the transmittal and payment of the money order[33] and also where the postal authority in the target country cannot provide any accounting of the payment of an order because the "official papers" were destroyed due to Acts of God[34] or where no investigation request was filed within one year.[35]

Compensation is limited to the amount paid in by the sender, i.e. there is no liability for consequential damages such as lost profits or any indirect damages.[36]

The so-called designated authority, i.e. the postal authority in the target country, is responsible for compensating the entitled party when — as in the normal case — the amount is to be paid to the payee. If the amount is to be reimbursed to the sender, e.g. in case of a timely cancellation of the payment order, the sending authority is responsible for paying compensation.[37]

The Giro Agreement contains liability rules similar to those in the Convention on Postal Money Orders. The authorities are liable to the customer for the amounts debited from his account until the funds transfer has been properly carried out.[38] The convention makes the authority against which the compensation claim is asserted liable for compensation to the entitled party. As before, in the case of a transfer the amount of compensation is limited to the amount debited from the post giro account.[39] The service offices are liable for incorrect entries in the lists. The liability includes mistakes in converting currency and in transmittal.[40] Liability is excluded for delays in the transmittal and execution of transfers.[41] Finally, the authorities are released from any liability if they are not able to provide any accounting

[32] Money Orders Agreement [MOA] Art. 9.

[33] Art. 9 § 2a MOA.

[34] Art. 9 § 2b MOA.

[35] Art. 9 § 2d MOA.

[36] Id.

[37] Art. 9 § 4.1 MOA.

[38] Art. 4 § 1.1 Giro Agreement [GA].

[39] Art. 4 § 3.1 and 3.2 GA.

[40] Art. 4 § 1.2 GA.

[41] Art. 4 § 1.3 GA.

concerning the transfer because the official papers were destroyed due to Acts of God[42] or where the issuer of the transfer order does not submit an investigation request within one year.[43]

The Giro Agreement stipulates similar rules for money orders. The postal authorities are liable for proper payment.[44] Likewise, the authorities are liable for incorrect entries by their service offices in lists and for mistakes in converting currency and transmitting orders.[45] Liability is excluded for delays in the transmittal of the money order or the payment.[46]

Finally, the Cash-on-Delivery Agreement contains liability provisions similar to those in the other conventions. The authorities are liable for the C.O.D. amount collected until its proper payment or credit to the post giro account of the sender. Any liability for delay is excluded. The maximum limit on liability is the C.O.D. amount to be collected. The authorities are liable for the fact that the shipment is not delivered without collecting or in exchange for a lesser amount.[47] An exclusion of liability is stipulated for the cases where the faulty collection of the C.O.D. amount was due to fault on the part of the sender, where the shipment is not delivered because it violates postal regulations, or where no investigation request is filed within one year.[48] Compensation is paid to the entitled party as a rule by the sending authority.

c) Liability under the General Terms and Conditions

The Postbank General Terms and Conditions (AGB) do not contain separate liability provisions; no. 13 merely cites certain provisions in the Postal Act, which have been described above in Part III 3.a).

d) Liability under the Special Terms and Conditions

The Special Terms and Conditions, which are likewise general terms and conditions within the meaning of the Law Governing Standard Business Conditions, contain several liability provisions directly applicable to international funds transfers.

---

[42] Art. 4 § 1.5a GA.

[43] Art. 4 § 1.5 b GA.

[44] Art. 9 § 1 GA.

[45] Art. 9 § 2 GA.

[46] Art. 9 § 4 GA.

[47] Art. 8 § 1 Cash-on-Delivery Agreement [CoDA].

[48] Art. 8 § 2 CoDA.

The Postbank is liable under the Special Terms and Conditions for "Documentary Orders for Payments to Recipients in Foreign Countries" to the customer for the amount debited from his giro account until the order — which may be a single, collective or standing order — is properly carried out. Proper execution is presumed where

— the amount is credited to the account of the payee,
— the amount is properly paid, or
— a check for the respective amount is properly handed over to the payee.[49]

This is a very extensive guarantee liability, which is not limited even by circumstances such as unauthorized manipulation of communications media, Acts of God, war or bankruptcy of the instructed institution.

Another liability provision is found in the Special Terms and Conditions for batch orders containing payments to be sent abroad. Here, the customer is charged with all consequences of the violations of special conditions listed there as well as all losses and disadvantages arising from the fact that the data which he provides are not in proper form or are incorrect or incomplete. The Postbank further limits its liability to gross fault and to the extent that the conduct of the Postbank contributed to the causation of the damages.[50]

Finally, the Special Terms and Conditions for the use of "Bildschirmtext", the German interactive videotex service, contain rules for allocating liability between the Postbank and the customer. The latter must bear all losses arising due to abuse or other misuse of the personal identification number (PIN) for his giro account or the transaction number (TAN).[51] The Postbank is liable — but only for gross fault — for breakdowns in the Btx system, in particular for improper transmission of data or where access to a giro account or other giro services by Btx is temporarily or permanently impossible.[52]

In contrast to the other two sets of Special Terms and Conditions just mentioned, the rules for Btx use are not expressly applicable to foreign transactions but this follows from the principle of § 27 Postal Act as described above.

The liability rules listed above, as now stipulated in the Special Terms and Conditions, represent an improvement for the customer in comparison to the rules governing the participant and user relationships prior to July 1, 1991. This is true at least for the allocation of rights because in the past the division of liability was not always clear. Fortunately, the cases of misdirect-

[49] No. 1.9, 2.7 and 3.10.

[50] No. 9.

[51] Id.

[52] No. 10.

ed or unexecuted orders were relatively rare. In the few cases which arose, the Postbank's good relations with most of its foreign contractual partners generally made it possible to find satisfactory solutions for the customer.

4. The Postbank Liability Rules in Light of the Law Governing Standard Business Conditions and the UNCITRAL Model Law

The Postbank General Terms and Conditions including the Special Terms and Conditions were drafted with consideration to the existing statutory and case law concerning banking law — primarily the Postal Act but also the Law Governing Standard Business Conditions [AGBG]. It is still possible, however, that in a particular case a civil court might hold that a provision of the Postbank Terms and Conditions is invalid under §§ 9-11 AGBG and under § 13 AGBG could issue an order to cease use of the provision. No such cases have yet arisen because the Postbank Terms and Conditions have been in effect only since mid-1991.

The duties of banks provided for in the 1990 draft of the UNCITRAL Model Law in some areas extend beyond what is presently demanded of credit institutions under German law. Even the Postbank Terms and Conditions, which have been very recently drafted taking statutes and case law into consideration, do not comply with the UNCITRAL provisions in all points. For example, the duty to provide assistance in case of a "stuck" payment order is not expressly included in the Postbank provisions; this does not mean that the Postbank does not make best efforts to assist the customer in investigating and resolving problems arising with payment orders. The scope of liability stipulated in Art. 13 of the Model Law draft for the first instructed bank in case of an unsuccessful payment order represents a guarantee liability which in this form is new. The liability of the Deutsche Bundespost is limited to reimbursement of the amount paid in or debited from an account. Liability for delays is expressly excluded under the conventions of the Universal Postal Union. Taking into consideration the extreme differences in the funds transfer systems used in the various countries, from purely manual systems to full electronic processing of orders, liability for delays applicable to all transactions does not presently appear either proper or realistic.

The path toward global adaptation of all legal provisions relevant for customers in the banking sector to the goals set by the U.N. Commission in the Model Law is still a very long one.

II. Law and Practice of International Credit Transfers in Some Other Countries

Law of International Funds Transfers in England

By Ross Cranston, London

Contents

In recent times there has been considerable discussion in England about the law of funds transfer. The speeding up of the funds transfer process and the internationalisation of banking are two particular causes of concern. In 1989, a government committee (the Jack Committee) reported on the need for a review of the law in respect of the completion and countermand of funds transfer in the light of such developments.[1] It also saw as a reason for reviewing the law the problems arising on a sudden insolvency of one or more parties to a transaction or in the event of a systems failure, error or fraud.[2]

What I aim to do in this chapter is to analyse from the perspective of English law, some of the legal problems arising in international funds transfers. The first part of the chapter examines some general aspects of funds transfer systems; the second, aspects of the timing of a funds transfer. At the outset it should be emphasised that English law is not always clear on the matters discussed. Nor does it provide unequivocally how issues are to be

[1] Banking Services: Law and Practice. Report by the Review Committee, Cm. 622, 1989, chapter 12 (Jack Committee). The Committee thought that problems could arise with both electronic and paper based systems.

[2] ibid., p. 103.

determined. The views expressed here may not win universal support, although I think they have strong justification.

There is some conflict in the authorities as to whether the resolution of disputes in the area is an issue of law or of banking practice.[3] The better view is that both must be considered. Banking practice will be influenced by a range of factors. For example, if banks are not satisfied as to the nature, the method of transfer, or the credit worthiness of transferring banks, banking practice may be that payment of the transferee occurs only after banks have settled between themselves. In the court decisions in this area, matters of practice such as these are mentioned and presumably influence the conclusions of law. That transfers are "on us" rather than "not on us", the method of transfer (telex, banker's payment etc.), the terms of transfer, the relationship between the banks — all have been commented on by the judges. Law and practice are intertwined.

I. General Matters

1. Relationship Tranferor - Transferor Bank

The basic principle in funds transfer is that a transferor as principal gives a mandate to its bank (the transferor bank), that is, an authority to take certain action.[4] If the transferor bank acts within the mandate, it may claim reimbursement from the transferor (for example, by debiting its account if it has one). If the transferor acts outside the mandate, for example paying on a forged mandate, it has no authority to claim reimbursement, although the transferor may ratify what the bank has done or the transferor may be estopped from denying the bank's right to reimbursement.[5]

It is sometimes said that the transferor must comply strictly with the terms of the mandate, but this means only that it must act within its terms.[6] If the bank construes any ambiguity in the mandate reasonably, the transferor cannot complain,[7] althouth it may be that in a case of ambiguity the bank

[3] See Momm v. Barclays Bank International Ltd. [1977] Q.B. 790, 799 (a matter of law), cf. view adopted by the Jack Committee, p. 104.

[4] See Lord Chorley, "Opening the Account, and other Problems", Gilbart Lectures on Banking 1955, pp. 40-43.

[5] This derives from cases on cheques: e. g., Lord Joint Stock Bank Ltd. v. Macmillan [1918] A.C. 814.

[6] In Royal Products v. Midland Bank [1981] 2 Lloyds L.R. 194, Webster J. thought that strict compliance excluded reasonable care and skill (at p. 199). But the two are compatible, even in letters of credit law to which he referred: see Uniform Customs and Practice for Documentary Credits, Article 15.

[7] Ireland v. Livingston (1872) 5 H.L.C. 395; Commercial Banking Co. of Sydney Ltd. v. Jalsard Pty. Ltd. [1973] A.C.

should return to its customer for clarification. Moreover, the transferor bank is not necessarily to be regarded as guaranteeing any particular result, for example, payment of the transferee. So long as it exercises reasonable care and skill in carrying out its instructions, it is regarded as fulfilling its mandate. But acting with reasonable case and skill means transferring funds on time; if a bank accepts a mandate to transfer funds by a specified date, it cannot excuse non-performance on its own part on the basis that it acted with reasonable care and skill because acting with reasonable care and skill means acting in time.[8]

One aspect of acting with reasonable care and skill of particular importance in funds transfer is choosing a reliable correspondent if the bank chooses, as it may have to, to act through a correspondent to effect a particular transfer.[9] Clearly also, if a bank executes a funds transfer order knowing it to be dishonestly given, shutting its eyes to the obvious fact of the dishonesty, or acting recklessly in failing to make such enquiries as an honest and reasonable bank would make, the bank has breached its duty.[10] Importantly, the duty to exercise care and skill can be excluded by an exemption clause, subject to the test of reasonableness laid down in the Unfair Contract Terms Act 1977.

2. *Bank-Bank Relationship; Settlement and Clearing Systems*[11]

There may be a bilateral or a multilateral contract between the transferor bank and transferee bank. Correspondent banks clearly enter a bilateral contract with each other. Payment and clearly systems like CHAPS are typically governed by multilateral contracts. The multilateral contract may arise indirectly, in the sense that a contract between a member and a payment and clearing organisation results in a contract between the former and the members as a whole. Alternatively, members of a system may agree together to comply with the rules regarding clearing and settlement. In either event, new members of an existing payment and clearing system will be admitted on the basis of adherence to the existing provisions of the contract.

Traditionally, English law regarded the rules of associations as not being justiciable. The view was that associations were established on a consensual basis, and in the absence of a clear indication that members contemplated the

---

[8] Lord Chorley, Law of Banking, 6th ed., London, Sweet & Maxwell, 1974, p. 270; E. P. Ellinger, Modern Banking Law, Oxford, OUP, 1987, p. 369.

[9] Equitable Trust Co. of New York v. Dawson Partners Ltd. (1927) 27 Lloyd's L.R. 49.

[10] Barclays Bank plc v. Quincecare Ltd. [1988] F.L.R. 166.

[11] This section is based on R. Cranston, "Payment and Clearing Systems in the European Community", in: R. Cranston (ed.), The Single Market and the Law of Banking, (London, Lloyds of London Press, 1991), pp. 207-8.

creation of legal relations, their governance was not to be treated as amounting to an enforceable contract.[12] It seems clear, however, that the rules of payment and clearing systems are legally binding — in English law either because in accordance with traditional theory, property rights or the right to trade is involved, or because in terms of basic theory there is an intention to create legal relations. In the case of some payment and clearing systems, it is clear that legal relations are intended, especially if there is an explicit provision for a governing law. Not inconsistently, however, the rules of payment and clearing systems often provide a dispute resolution procedure to avoid resort to the courts. There may be an internal conciliation, and even arbitration procedure, before resort to formal mechanisms is permitted.[13]

Typically, there will be a provision in the payment and clearing rules allowing for their variation from time to time.[14] (In English law, a contract cannot be varied without mutual agreement, but parties can bind themselves to accept variation without such agreement.)[15]

An important question is the extent to which parties which are not members of a payment and clearing system are bound by its rules. The simplest example is where a transferor requests its bank to transfer money to a third party — is it bound by the contract between the transferor bank and transferee bank? Again, will a transferee seeking payment on a debit instrument be bound by the contract between transfer bank and transferee bank in obtaining payment? The answer depends on the circumstances. Certainly it cannot be said that just because the transferor and transferee are not direct parties to a contract they are not bound by it because of notions of privity. In English law there is clear authority that one can be bound by the custom and usage of a market, irrespective of one's knowledge of them. Indeed a "man who employs a banker is bound by the usage of bankers".[16] The custom or usage becomes binding as an implied term of the transferor-bank or transferee-bank contract, although where a party is unaware of it the custom or usage can only be implied if it is reasonable.[17] There is some possibility of treating a payment and clearing rule as a custom or usage for the purposes of this principle.

---

[12] For example, see the argument in Pharmaceutical Society of Great Britain v. Dickson [1970] A.C. 403, 426.

[13] For example, Clearing House Automated Payments System, Clearing Rule, r. 1 (6).

[14] ibid., r. 1 (d).

[15] For example, Burnett v. Westminster Bank Ltd. [1966] 1 QB 742.

[16] Hare v. Henty (1861) 142 E.R. 374, 379.

[17] Sweeting v. Pearce (1861) 142 ER 210.

3. *Other Relationships*

There is no contractual relationship between a transferor and the transferee bank; English law takes a rather strict view of privity of contract.[18] Nor is there any contractual relationship between a transferor and its bank's correspondent; in English law there is no privity of contract between a principal and its agent's agent.[19] In England, for largely historical reasons, banks can be strictly liable for the tort of conversion if they collect a negotiable instrument for other than the true owner. Statute provides some defences. By contrast, in the case of funds transfer, a bank is unlikely to be liable in similar circumstances, unless it has the very high degree of knowledge required in English law of a contrustive trustee. In addition there will not be the proximity necessary for liablity in tort law.

In English law[20] a funds transfer is not effected by the assignment of any debt the transferor bank owes the transferor.[21] Consequently, a transferor can revoke after giving instructions to its debtor (that is its bank), which would not be possible if a funds transfer was by way of assignment. Moreover, transferees have no contractual claim on the basis of assignment against a transferor bank, but only in contract against their own bank. Exceptionally, however, there could be special arrangements giving rise to a contract between the transferor bank and the transferee. A contract of guaranteed payment which banks entered into with transferees would be an example.

II. Timing of a Funds Transfer

There are at least five different aspects to the timing of a funds transfer. The first is discharge of the underlying obligation. This concept involves the payer and payee and, like funds availability, applies to any funds transfer, whether or not through the medium of the banking system. A second point is

[18] Royal Products Ltd. v. Midland Bank Ltd. [1981] 2 Lloyd's Rep. 194, 198. In United States law, a different view might be taken: Evra Corporation v. Swiss Bank Corporation (1982) 673 F 2d 951.

[19] Royal Products Ltd. v. Midland Bank Ltd. [1981] 2 Lloyd's L.R. 194. J. Vroegop, "The Role of Correspondent Banks in Direct Funds Transfer" [1990] Lloyd's Maritime and Commercial Law Quarterly 547 argues against privity of contract, but this does not represent the law.

[20] Contrast US law: Delbrueck & Co. v. Manufacturers Hanover Trust Company (1979) 609 F 2d 1047, 1051.

[21] Royal Products Ltd. v. Midland Bank Ltd. [1981] 2 Lloyd's Rep 194, 198. See Dr. Mann's discussion in R. Pennington, A. Hudson and E. Mann, Commercial Banking Law, Plymouth, Macdonald & Evans, 1978, pp. 285-9, E. P. Ellinger, Modern Banking Law, Oxford, Clarendon, 1987, pp. 366-8.

completion, in other words, the stage in the process when a funds transfer by one bank customer to another bank customer becomes complete (or final), in the sense that (a) the bank making it cannot unilaterally reverse it and; (b) that the transferor's bank has fulfilled its instructions. Thirdly, there is the timing of countermand, the stage of the process up until when the initiator of an instruction has the right to countermand (or revoke) it. A fourth point relates to access to funds — when does a transferee have access to the proceeds of a funds transfer. Finally, there is the point which can be characterised as "bank reversal", the point beyond which a bank on its own volition cannot reverse a transfer. None of these points necessarily coincide, although some (e. g. countermand) cannot be latter than others (e. g. availability of funds). Let us examine each in turn.

1. Discharge of Underlying Obligations

This is a matter of contract between the parties. Commercial contracts usually provide that a funds transfer is to be made by having immediately available (or same day) funds in a specified account in a specified bank on a specified day. For example, a charterparty might read: "Payment of hire is to be made in New York in cash in United States currency to X bank [address], for the credit of the account of Z re [ship], on the first day of each month". Legally, the transferor's obligation is being discharged by the transferee bank assuming an obligation as debtor in lieu of that of the transferee.

The English courts have said that this type of clause cannot mean that payment occurs at the point when the transferee bank receives an instruction from the hirer's bank; rather the transferee bank must have at least made the decision to credit the transferee's account, even if it has not actually credited it. The transferee does not have to have been notified, although if the transferee were to contact its bank it would be told of the decision to credit. The reasoning is that the crucial point is when the instruction is executed, making funds available to the transferee.

"... when payment of a debt is effected by a transfer of funds within a bank from the account of customer A to that of customer B pursuant to an order given to the bank by customer A, the time of the payment must, in principle, be the time when the order to transfer is executed and not the time when it is given or received. According to the evidence on the bank's practice given before me, the effective time of execution of the order, from the point of view of availability of the funds to customer B, is the time of the decision to debit the one account and credit the other. That is, accordingly, in my view, the time of transfer or payment."[22]

[22] Tenax Steamship Co. Ltd. v. Reinante Transoceania Navegacion S.A. (The Brimnes) [1973] 1 W.L.R. 386, 402. Approved on appeal [1957] 1 Q.B. 929, 50-1, 963-4, 968.

Since the key point is the availability of funds, the obligation will not be discharged by provisional credit of the account.[23] Nor, at the other end of the spectrum, does it matter that after the decision to credit, there are other administrative processes (for example, the overnight processing of data by computer). The precise point of the decision to credit will not always be clear — "rarely can precision on such a matter be called for"[24] — but will depend on evidence of practices within the particular bank. For example, it may be that debits and credits are made to accounts during a day, but only at the end of the day are final decisions made. The test is an objective test: were the transferee to contact its bank, at what point would it have been told that it had an unrestricted and immediate right to funds.[25]

The key aspect of this clause, as already mentioned, is that funds must be available to the transferee. In a decision which has been criticized as adopting an unduly narrow interpretation of whether under such a clause funds are available in cash, the House of Lords has held that a funds transfer had not been effected when funds, although available, were subject to an interest liability.[26] The decision involved a funds transfer from a charterer to the owner's account with an Italian bank. On January 22nd, the owner's bank credited the owner's account with the amount, and the owner had immediate use of the money, although the evidence was that if it had withdrawn the sum then it would probably have incurred a liability to its bank to pay interest until January 26th. The court's reasoning was as follows:

"The book entry made by the owner's bank on January 22 in the owners' account was clearly not the equivalent of cash, nor was there any reason why the owners should have been prepared to treat it as the equivalent of cash. It could not be used to earn interest, e. g. by immediate transfer to a deposit account. It could only be drawn subject to a (probable) liability to pay interest. In substance it was the equivalent of an overdraft facility which the bank was bound to make available. I have put the word 'probable' in brackets because I attach no significance to its use in the arbitrator's finding. The finding of a probable liability to pay interest must connote a right in the owner's bank to charge interest, which is the decisive factor. It follows, in my view, that on January 22 there was no 'payment in cash' by the charterers of the hire then assumed to be due and accordingly the owners, having refused to accept the credit as payment in accordance with clause 5, were entitled to withdraw the ship, as they did on January 24."[27]

---

[23] cf. B. Geva, "Payment into a Bank Account" [1990] 3 JIBL 108, 110.

[24] ibid., at p. 951.

[25] Geva helpfully refers to this as the "hypothetical positive response" test: op. cit., p. 113. Geva himself argues for a "receiver finality" test, but this is not English law.

[26] A/S Awilco of Oslo v. Fulvia S.p.A. Di Navigazione of Cagliari (The Chikuma) [1981] 1 W.L.R. 314.

[27] ibid., at p. 320.

Thus the transferee must have an unrestricted and immediate access to funds if the underlying obligation is to be regarded as discharged.

So far we have considered situations where the contract provides expressly how a payment obligation is to be discharged. What if there is no express provision in the contract? The fundamental principle in English law is that a monetary obligation must be discharged in cash, unless the right to cash has been waived or varied by contract.[28] If a person has a fundamental right to be paid in cash, and he or she accepts payment by funds transfer into a bank account, it follows that the obligation is not discharged until there is an unconditional right to the immediate use of the funds transferred. In other words, the same approach as to timing applies as under the express clauses about payment in immediately available funds we have just considered. A transferee cannot sue the transferor if its bank fails after this point, since it has been paid. The transferee's remedy is against its bank in the insolvency. The transferee must take the credit risk of its bank's failure if it accepts payment by credit transfer, just as it takes the credit risk of depositing its money with that bank.

In cases where an instrument is used, instead of cash, in discharge of an obligation, the English courts have developed a number of rules governing the timing of a funds transfer. For example, a banker's payment order, which is an obligation of the transferor bank, is treated in London as equivalent to cash. Consequently, delivery of a banker's payment order to a transferee bank seems to constitute payment.[29]

Generally, the English courts will treat payment by bill of exchange or other negotiable instrument as conditional payment.[30] It is subject to a condition subsequent that the instrument be paid on presentation. If the instrument is dishonoured, the debt revives. If the instrument is paid, the better view is that the time of payment is back-dated to the time when it was given to the transferee.[31] This accords with the nature of the condition as a condition subsequent (so that if the instrument is paid it ranks as actual payment from that date); and with the fact that the instrument changes the legal relationship between the parties, giving the transferee a legal right to sue for a sum of money. Similar rules apply to payment by means of a letter

[28] Libyan Arab Foreign Bank v. Bankers Trust Co. [1989] 3 W.L.R. 314, 347.

[29] Empresa Cubana de Fletes v. Lagonisi Shipping Co. Ltd. [1971] 1 Lloyd's Rep. 7.

[30] e. g., Allen v. Royal Bank of Canada (1925) 95 L.J.P.C. 17; Tank Express A/S v. Compagnie Financiere Belge des Petroles S.A. [1949] A.C. 76; Bolt & Nut Co. (Tripton) Ltd. v. Rowlands Nicholls & Co. Ltd. [1964] 2 Q.B. 10. This presumption is rebutted if the instrument was taken in total satisfaction of the liability.

[31] cf. J. Vroegop, "The Time of Payment in Paper-Based and Electronic Funds Transfer Systems" [1990] Lloyd's Maritime & Commercial Law Quarterly 64, 66-69, 86, who concludes that the authorities are the other way.

of credit.[32] If the seller does not receive payment under the letter of credit, then generally speaking the buyer is still liable to pay the price.

In re Charge Card Services Ltd.[33] considered whether there is a general principle of English law that whenever a method of payment is adopted which involves a risk of non-payment by a third party, there is a presumption that the acceptance by the transferee of payment through a third party is conditional on the third party making the payment. The Court of Appeal decided that there is no such general principle. Each method of payment has to be considered in the light of the consequences and other circumstances attending that type of payment.

2. Completion (or Finality) of Payment

It will be remembered that this is the stage at which one bank cannot unilaterally reverse a funds transfer and the transferor's instructions have been fulfilled by the transferor bank. One reason this is relevant is if there is a crisis, for example, an insolvency of one of the banks. If a funds transfer has been completed (or is final), the transferor bank cannot reverse a transfer to a transferee bank which has become insolvent. Since at that point it has carried out its customer's instructions, the loss falls on the transferor if the transferee has not been paid (or, to put it in terms of the previous discussion, if the payment obligation is not discharged). In most cases there will not be a great gap between when payment is complete (or final) and when the transferor's payment obligation is discharged, so the transferor's risk is small.

English common law is rather sparse on the matter. There is some authority, however, for both intrabank transfers (when both transferor and transferee have accounts at the same bank) and interbank transfers (when they have accounts at different banks).

With an intrabank transfer, payment is complete when the entries are made in the bank's books debiting the transferor and crediting the transferee, or on the day when entries are made in the computer for debiting or crediting. The transferee need not have received notification of the transfer.[34] The bank itself cannot reverse the entries after this point. Momm v. Barclays Bank International Ltd,[35] the leading case, involved a German bank, which

[32] W. J. Alan & Co. Ltd. v. El Nasr Export and Import Co. [1972] 2 Q.B. 189, 212, 231: Maran Road Saw Mill v. Austin Taylor & Co., Ltd. [1975] 1 Lloyd's Rep. 156; E. D. & F. Man Ltd. v. Nigerian Sweets & Confectionery Co. Ltd. [1977] 2 Lloyd's Rep. 50.

[33] [1988] 3 W.L.R. 764.

[34] Eyles v. Ellis (1827) 130 E.R. 710; Momm v. Barclays Bank International Ltd. [1977] 1. Q.B. 790.

[35] [1977] 1 Q.B. 790.

had agreed to transfer pounds sterling to another German bank, instructing an English bank, where both German banks had accounts, to make the transfer "value June 26". One 25 June the English bank credited the transferee's account, debited the transferor's account, and prepared appropriate entries for overnight processing by the computer. That day it was learnt that the transferor bank was insolvent and had ceased trading. On 27 June, the English bank cancelled the entries, so that it would not have to claim against the transferor bank in the insolvency (its account after the transfer was in overall debit). The court held that the transfer had been complete on 26 June and that accordingly the English bank was not entitled to reverse the entries, even though the original transfer had not been notified to the transferee. The judge reasoned:

> The issue is whether or not a completed payment had been made by the defendants to the plaintiffs on June 26. ... If there were no authorities on this point, I think that the reaction, both of a lawyer and a banker, would be to answer this question in the affirmative. I think that both would say two things. First, that in such circumstances a payment has been made if the payee's account is credited with the payment at the close of business on the value date, at any rate if it was credited intentionally and in good faith and not by error or fraud. Secondly, I think that they would say that if a payment requires to be made on a certain day in fact and in law it must be that this has either happened or nor happened ...[36]

With an interbank transfer between correspondent banks, payment is complete when the transferee bank is notified that funds are made available for the credit of the customer's account. Consequently, the transferor has no claim against his bank for not effecting the transfer if the transferee bank ceases trading after such notification, since the transfer is complete at that point.[37] The transferor will have to pay the transferee again if it has not been paid by the transferee bank.

With an interbank transfer through a clearing house, a transfer is complete when the rules so provide.[38] This might be as late as when movements are made on the accounts of the respective banks with the central bank.

3. Countermand

Countermand (or revocation) involves the obligation of a bank to comply with its customer's instructions (or mandate). The bank is agent of the customer. Subject to any contractual provisions, if the bank's mandate is

---

[36] at p. 800.

[37] Royal Products v. Midland Bank [1981] 2 Lloyd's L.R. 194.

[38] Because of doubts as to whether third parties are bound by these rules — see Part I of this chapter — the Jack Committee recommended clarifying legislation: op. cit., pp. 106-7.

withdrawn, it must comply with its principal's instruction and stop the process if this is practicable. Of course it will charge the transferor for this privilege. Notice of countermand must be clear, brought to the attention of the bank (constructive countermand is not recognized in English law), and given to the branch of the bank where the account is kept.[39]

In the absence of express contract, the authorities seem to establish the following propositions relevant to an international funds transfer. Firstly, a customer who instructs its bank to holds funds to the disposal of a third party can countermand at least until the time when the funds have been transferred or credit given to the transferee.[40] Secondly, a customer who instructs its bank to transfer funds to a third party cannot revoke from the moment the bank incurs a commitment to the third party.[41] Thirdly — and this is the typical case — a customer who instructs its bank to pay another bank to the order of a third party cannot revoke once the payee bank has acted on the instructions. This may be a point prior to crediting of the payee's account.[42] In all these cases, it is irrelevant, from the point of view of revocation, whether the third party has been informed.

Countermand is often a matter of express contract between the customer and the bank in modern payment systems. Take CHAPS, which is the automated high value payment clearing system for sterling. CHAPS payments, which are normally credited to the payee in advance of settlement in the clearing, are guaranteed and "irrevocable" payments for same day settlement.[43] (Payments are not to be routed through CHAPS if they require the transaction to be completed by a deadline.[44]) It appears that payments become irrevocable once there has been a "logical acknowledgement" by the transferee bank.[45] Transferors, whose banks use CHAPS, are bound to those rules on the legal grounds considered earlier.

4. *Access to Funds*

We have seen earlier that availability of funds is the test used for discharge of an underlying payment obligation: in other words, the test is at what point would a transferee be told, were it to contact its bank, that it has an

---

[39] Again this derives from the cases on cheques: e. g., Burnett v. Westminster Bank Ltd. [1966] 1 QB 742.

[40] Gibson v. Minet (1824) 130 E.R. 206.

[41] Warlow v. Harrison (1859) 120 E.R. 920.

[42] Astro Amo Compania Naviera S.A. v. Elf Union S.A. (The "Zographia M") [1976] 2 Lloyd's L.R. 382.

[43] Clearing House Automated Payment System, Clearing Rules, r. (2) (c).

[44] r. (3) (c).

[45] See rr. (4) (c), (4) (d), (11) (c).

unrestricted and immediate right to funds. What arises under the present heading is the extent to which the availability may be modified in practice by particular arrangements between the transferee and its bank.

There are three possible ways that this modification can occur so that availability does not constitute access. Firstly, the transferee may still be indebted to the bank (or "in the red") after a funds transfer and have agreed with its bank not to draw on its account until its indebtedness is reduced still more or possibly eliminated altogether. The funds are available, but by agreement the transferee does not have access to them. Secondly, by agreement with its bank, a customer may be able to draw on its account prior to the funds being available. This is a well-known phenomenon in domestic banking, where payees of cheques are given credit before funds are cleared, and there is no reason in principle why it cannot apply to international funds transfers. Thirdly, a bank may be estopped from denying access to an account, having represented to a transferee that funds are available, even though in fact they are not. For estoppel to arise, however, the transferee must have relied somehow on the representation.[46]

5. *Bank Reversal*

Bank reversal concerns the relationship of the transferor and its bank. It is relevant to whether the transferor bank can stop a funds transfer if it decides that there are insufficient funds, discovers that the transferor has become insolvent and will not reimburse it, or for other reasons. The issue arose recently in the decision Libyan Arab Foreign Bank v. Manufacturers Hanover Trust Co. (No. 2).[47] In that case Manufacturers Hanover Trust (MHT) in New York sent a tested telex at 5.44 pm on 7th January to MHT London: "We are crediting you [$ 62 m] for the account of Libyan Arab Foreign Bank Tripoli". MHT London acted on this telex on the morning of 8th January, credited LAFB, debited MHT New York on the same sum in their Nostro account, and notified LAFB of the transfer. At 6 pm on 7th January, however, MHT New York had purported to cancel the transfer, and it was never posted in MHT New York's computerised books of account either to LAFB's account with MHT New York or to MHT London's Nostro account at MHT New York. Eventually, MHT London purported to cancel the transfer as well. The court held the cancellation ineffective:

"By parity of reasoning with Momm's case, these actions within MHT London in my judgement constituted a full completion of the payment of the $ 62 m., and were in no way affected by the absence of similar entries in MHT New York."[48]

---

[46] Skyring v. Greenwood (1825) 107 E.R. 1064.

[47] [1989] 1 Lloyd's L.R. 608.

[48] at pp. 631-2.

III. Conclusions

The Jack Committee considered in some detail aspects of funds transfer and the need for law reform. The discharge of payment obligations was outside the scope of the report. However, in relation to completion of payment, the committee broached legislative change. Its reasoning was that there is a risk of sudden failure of a non-clearing bank or non-bank involved in a transaction so large as to have repercussions on the clearings. Error and fraud were also thought to be risks. While remote, these risks were regarded as greater because of the increase in international banking transactions and the development of the single market in the European Communities. Clarifying the law would not prevent a crisis, but would assist its resolution. Jack's specific recommendation was that the rules should provide as follows:

"They should provide (a) that payment is to be regarded as complete at the point where the payee's bank (or its agent in the clearing), having actual or ostensible authority to accept payment on behalf of the payee, accepts a transfer of funds from the paying bank (or its agent in the clearing) for the payee's account — provided that the transfer is or has become unconditional; and (b) that, where the transfer is between two accounts at the same bank, payment should be regarded as complete when the bank has taken the decision to treat the instructions for transfer as irrevocable. The rules should be subject to modification by contractual arrangement among parties to a contract governing a payment system."[49]

There are obvious questions as to whether Jack is correct as regards the rules to be adopted, what they would mean, and whether they would meet the purpose for which they are proposed.

The general approach of the Jack Committee was to minimise the need for legislation. This was the approach with countermand. Jack recommended as follows:

"A standard of banking practice should require banks, when establishing countermand rules for individual payment systems, to allow customers a period of time for countermand wherever possible, only eliminating it where that is necessary for the efficient working of the system. Banks should take steps to make customers aware of the different countermand rules applying to different payment systems."[50]

In reaching this conclusion, the report said that there were no convincing arguments offered in support of a uniform rule or rules on countermand. An inflexible rule would stifle competition and technological progress. Competition might not operate strongly where banks used the same clearings but was relevant between payment systems. Nonetheless, Jack thought that customers should have an opportunity to countermand. "The principal

---

[49] op. cit., p. 109.

[50] ibid.

underlying the banking practice long applied to cheques must surely be applicable to more modern payment systems too: that is to say, the customer should be allowed a reasonable period of time for countermand, insofar as this can be reconciled with the efficient working of the system."[51] This was to be achieved by the banks formulating their own contractual rules, in accordance with a standard of best practice, only eliminating countermand when necessary for the efficient working of the system. Customers should be informed of the period for countermand in different payment systems.

On availability of funds, the Jack committee was concerned with the position of consumers. It thought that banks should give their customers a simple explanation as to the timing of the clearing cycle, and the concept of cleared balances. This would deal, especially, with the normal time taken to clear cheques and bank payment orders, should specify the "hold" period the bank is applying, and should say whether the bank has a right of reversal if the cheque or bank payment order is later returned unpaid. However, the report says that its standard should also cover other payment systems as appropriate. Moreover, it recommended that banks should consider how their customers could usefully be given more information, in periodic statements of account and in ATM slips, about cleared as well as uncleared balances on their account.

Nothing has been done in relation to the recommendations of the Jack Committee in this regard. The government has expressed doubt as to their desirability, and in any event concluded that action should be postponed pending the outcome of developments such as the current initiative of the United Nations Commission on International Trade Law Working Group on International Payments in relation to a model law.[52]

---

[51] ibid., p. 105.

[52] Banking Services: Law and Practice, Cm. 1026, 1990, p. 29.

Law and Practice of Foreign Funds Transfers in France

By Michel Vasseur, Paris*

Contents

---

* Translated by Dr. Frances Dielmann, Frankfurt/M.

Introduction

French law does not contain special statutory provisions governing domestic or international funds transfers. This is because the funds transfer is subject to the general statutory provisions governing legal transactions and also because legal disputes, whether settled in or out of court, are rare. Few case decisions are available, particularly where foreign funds transfers are involved. This observation could lead to the assumption that there is no need for statutory rules to govern the legal events connected with the funds transfer and that it can be left to practice and to the courts to formulate appropriate rules.

In this context, however, it must be mentioned that the French legislators have undertaken measures to promote the funds transfer as a means of cashless payment. For example, written transfer orders are exempt from the stamp tax. In addition, the laws of Oct. 22, 1940 and Dec. 29, 1989 stipulate that money debts which exceed a certain amount must be satisfied by means of a transfer (or by check or credit card).

For foreign funds transfers, the Decree No. 89-938 of Dec. 23, 1989, in conjunction with the Repeal of the Currency Control Order of Jan. 1, 1990, provides that the transfer of deposit currency between France and foreign countries must be carried out by credit institutions and equivalent enterprises. The Decree creates an obligation on the part of the credit institutions to submit statistics to the Banque de France concerning flows of capital so that the French balance of payments and the foreign-trade balance can be calculated. The credit institutions are also subject to further statistical and tax provisions containing certain special requirements regarding disclosure of the identity of the transferor and the transferee when a capital transfer is to be carried out for a natural person (Art. 98-3 of Act No. 89-895 of Dec. 29, 1989).

The legislators stopped here.

The transfer is a means of cashless payment which is excellently suited an as instrument for the transfer of capital. Studies have shown that the number of transfers by far exceeds the number of movements of capital carried out by other means. This observation is true within France and even more so in the international sector.

Most foreign funds transfers in France are carried out through the SWIFT network. This is also true for the 73 other countries connected to this network (as of July 1990). In France, to a limited extent, the SAGITTAIRE system is also used when the transfer can be carried out through this system.

In 1990, 16.2 million foreign funds transfers originating in France were made through the SWIFT system. These consisted of 7.6 million transfers for customers and 8.6 million transfers between banks.

2.5 million orders were executed through SAGITTAIRE for a total amount of 35,393,000,000 francs, including 600,000 for customers and 1.9 million directly between banks[1].

Due to the importance of SWIFT and SAGITTAIRE in the execution of international funds transfers, we must take a closer look at their methods of operation.

I. SAGITTAIRE and SWIFT

SAGITTAIRE stands for: système automatisé de gestion intégrée par télétransmission de transactions avec imputation de règlements "étrangers" (data processing system for integrated processing of transactions with foreign connections). It is a national, bank-internal data processing system, which enables connected banks resident in France to post in automated form items which arise out of international transactions through the SWIFT network. Only francs may be transferred through SAGITTAIRE and only where the sums are credited to or debited from accounts with banks resident in France. An additional French bank can be involved to further transmit an amount, for which it has received credit, through SWIFT to a foreign bank which should then credit the amount to its customer.

SAGITTAIRE is thus the extension of SWIFT in France for the purpose of executing transfers as effectively as possible.

For a Bank A which, for example, would like to carry out a transfer on the order of its foreign correspondent bank, one of the following situations may be present:

— the beneficiary (customer or bank) has an account with Bank A: Bank A can complete the transaction within its own accounting system;

— (more often) the beneficiary is a customer at a different Bank B, with which Bank A does not maintain a direct account relationship.

Prior to the introduction of SAGITTAIRE the execution of international transfers was especially disappointing. Transfers could come from the far ends of the world in a very short time, but the transfers arriving from foreign countries through SWIFT could not be processed in France with the same speed. There was a "break" in the transfer chain. The settlements between the banks were carried out through accounts maintained by the banks with the Banque de France, and usually not until after a fixed settlement time. One or more days could pass. New processing steps were required, under some

[1] In 1990, the domestic funds transfers (transfers for settlement, guarantees, transfers through the Banque de France) reached the astronomical sum of 143,637,000,000,000 francs.

circumstances even using an intermediate voucher which was not suitable for transmitting all of the information received through SWIFT.

Therefore, the group of SWIFT users in France had an accounting system developed for the settlement in francs which posts all entries electronically without any paper vouchers and which is open to all banks resident in France which are members or users of SWIFT.

SAGITTAIRE was put into operation on Oct. 16, 1984. The facilities are operated by the Banque de France. The legal relationships between the Banque de France as system administrator and the connected banks are governed by a common agreement, to which are attached standard rules of procedure and the basic regulations governing accounting. The transactions carried out through SAGITTAIRE are coded in the same form as is necessary for SWIFT. In addition, compliance with uniform standards which seek to make possible complete automation of procedures is required.

The system administrator, the Banque de France, is responsible for carrying out the transfer orders and informs the participants of entries made to their accounts. At the end of each day, a list of transactions is prepared and settlement is made. The Banque de France carries out the transactions on behalf of each institution in the accounts which it manages. SAGITTAIRE thus serves primarily as a system for the further execution of orders through SWIFT and for the actual settlement of payments.

These transactions may involve customers or be directly between banks. There are no upper or lower limits on amounts.

On the one hand, transactions can be connected with the execution of an order received from a foreign country. The SAGITTAIRE member acts here as the French intermediary bank for a foreign bank which has instructed it to carry out a funds transfer for a customer or to transfer funds to the foreign bank's account with a third bank (e.g. to adjust the foreign bank's accounts in francs). Finally, a transfer can be made for the benefit of a third party (e.g. to cover a foreign exchange transaction with francs, to obtain or repay a loan stated in francs, or to cover a customer transfer which was sent from the foreign bank directly to the beneficiary's French bank).

On the other hand, the payment transactions involved may have been initiated by a member itself in connection with an international transfer, e.g. payment in francs for the benefit of a nonresident or obtaining of francs for a foreign exchange transaction which the member has entered into with a foreign bank or another French bank. Here are two examples:

Example One

A British enterprise, which is a customer of Barclays Bank, purchases a machine for 100,000 francs from a French company, which maintains an account with Crédit Lyonnais.

On the order of its customer, Barclays Bank transmits through SWIFT to its correspondent bank in France, the Société Générale, a transfer order for the amount of 100,000 francs for the account of the French seller. The Société Générale transmits through the SWIFT network an instruction to debit its SAGITTAIRE account at the Banque de France; from there the amount is credited, again through SWIFT, to the account of the Crédit Lyonnais. Finally,the Crédit Lyonnais credits the amount to the account of its customer.

Second Example

The Crédit Lyonnais has bought 1 million dollars from the Société Générale in exchange for francs. The two banks each have a correspondent bank in New York, Irving Trust for the Crédit Lyonnais and Manufacturers Hanover for the Société Générale. The Crédit Lyonnais transmits through SWIFT an instruction to debit its SAGITTAIRE account in the amount of the transaction in francs; a corresponding credit is made to the Société Générale. The Société Générale instructs Manufacturers Hanover Trust, its correspondent bank in New York, to debit its account there: Manufacturers Hanover Trust then transmits the amount to Irving Trust through the American capital transfer system CHIPS, where it is finally credited to the dollar account of the Crédit Lyonnais.

This demonstrates how effectively a transaction between two banks resident in France can be carried out through SAGITTAIRE, where cover is obtained for a foreign exchange transaction and thus requires an international transfer.

The fees for the use of SAGITTAIRE are 4.39 francs for a normal transaction and 6.69 francs for a high urgency transaction (compared with 2.50 francs per transaction through SWIFT). These SAGITTAIRE fees are generally viewed as too high, and they are expected to fall as the number of transfers increases.

When looking at international funds transfers involving French banks, we cannot stop at the SAGITTAIRE system.

The only international transactions which can be carried out through SAGITTAIRE are transfers in francs between banks resident in France and this, of course, only when the banks choose to use SAGITTAIRE (which is not mandatory). Some banks — although only a few — use SAGITTAIRE only for receiving but not for sending transfers.

When foreign currency instead of francs is transferred, banks primarily use the SWIFT system. In this regard, however, we must remember that SWIFT is only a private telecommunications system between banks, i.e. a network for the exchange of data between the connected banks.

As an example, we may consider a buyer in the U.S. who owes a French seller, a customer of the Société Générale, 100,000 dollars. He turns to his bank in the U.S., the Chase Manhattan Bank. Chase Manhattan debits his account for 100,000 dollars and transmits this amount by an American funds transfer system (CHIPS or FEDWIRE) to Citibank, the New York correspondent bank of the Société Générale. Citibank informs the Société Générale in Paris through SWIFT that the 100,000 dollars have been credited to its account, and the Société Générale in Paris credits this amount to the account of its customer, the exporter.

We will see that the transfer procedure is viewed the same way legally regardless of whether it is used in a domestic or an international transaction and whether it is carried out through SAGITTAIRE or SWIFT.

II. Legal Classification of the Bank Transfer

When a credit transfer is made, money is transferred by debiting the account of one person and crediting the amount to the account of another person. The transfer is thus a means of cashless payment. A capital movement takes place by means of the debit and the credit. At the beginning of the event is a payment order, at the end a credit to the beneficiary's account, by which the transfer is completed. Under French law, the transfer is governed by the International Standardization Organization (I.S.O.) definition; a funds transfer is the "complete execution of a capital movement between an originator and a beneficiary". This means that under French law the transfer must be viewed as a unified procedure. It would not be correct to view a transfer in which multiple banks are involved as a series of individual transfers between these banks.

For a long time, the transfer was viewed differently by economists and legal scholars.

In the economic sense, the credit balance in a bank account represents deposit money, and a transfer of money takes place by means of the transfer.

The legal classification prevailing until recently assumed that the credit balance in an account represented a claim against the bank. Under this view, the transfer would represent an assignment of the claim: assignment of a claim by one party, and in most cases acceptance of an obligation by another party.

Here, the originator, who has a claim against his bank, orders his bank to enter into an obligation with respect to the beneficiary. The originator is the instructing party, the bank is the instructed party, and the beneficiary is the payee.

In accordance with Art. 1275 Code Civil this involves a perfect delegation with which the originator/instructing party is released from his debt to the beneficiary/payee. The beneficiary's claim against the bank is subsituted completely for the debt which the beneficiary had against the originator.

This classification as an assumption of debt is one of the many attempts which have been made to explain commercial transactions in commercial law using provisions of civil law. This approach, as described with respect to the credit transfer, is generally rejected today.

In an assumption of debt, the instructed party plays an active role. He is obligated to the payee to carry out the transaction. In the case of a credit transfer, however, the beneficiary's bank does not formally enter into an obligation; it merely posts the amount and credits the amount to the name of the designated person. Based on this credit to the beneficiary's account, the bank becomes a debtor of the beneficiary just as if the money had been deposited by the beneficiary. In other words, the classification as an assumption of debt is not able furnish the explanation of how the payee's claim against the payor is transformed — not into a simple claim against the bank, but instead into a claim arising out of the posting of the amount to his account. Legally, the result is the same as in the case of a deposit by the beneficiary.

Naturally, it cannot be denied that the bank becomes the debtor of the beneficiary, but the debt possesses an economic and legal peculiarity which cannot be explained using the civil law model of a debt assumption. The debt leads to a deposit in an account by means of a credit.

Above all, it must be emphasized that the classification as an assumption of debt cannot explain why, under French law, the transfer is not already completed when the beneficiary's claim against the bank is created but instead only when the transfer amount is credited to his account.

These are not the only objections to a classification of a transfer as an assumption of debt. Often, the transfer is used to carry out another transaction and not merely to make a payment; using a transfer, for example, money can be transmitted from a donor to a donee or from a principle to an agent. In these cases, no claim exists in favor of the beneficiary against the originator; one therefore cannot speak of an assumption of debt releasing the originator. A further goal is pursued. Underlying transactions which are not for the purpose of making a payment or delegating an obligation can be carried out by means of a transfer. One such case is where the originator has two accounts at the same bank and has money transferred from one account to the other, or where he has accounts at two different banks and orders one bank to transfer money to his account at the other bank. Here, the transfer is merely an instrument for the movement of deposit money.

This criticism, with its various facets, indicates that the claim — to the extent that the account has a positive balance and a claim exists at all — experiences a transformation in order to become what a money transfer attempts to accomplish. The economic events thus mold the legal classification. A transformation takes place in the course of the transfer process and again at the beneficiary at the end of the transfer.

Characteristic of the transfer is the movement of deposit money which should be equivalent to the delivery of cash. This view was first confirmed by the commercial section of the Cour de cassation in its decision of July 22, 1986[2]. This view also finds a confirmation in statutory law in that payments in excess of a fixed minimum amount must be paid by transfer (or check). At the same time, the statute provides that the transfer shall factually have the same discharging effect as payment by cash.

It is not difficult to follow the deliberations leading to this classification. The free circulation of money must be guaranteed. Payment with cash is simple and free from problems. Civil law provisions regarding assumption of debt, by contrast, are complicated. The transfer is a means of cashless payment which cannot be subjected to the provisions concerning assumption of debt. Instead, the transmittal involved is well-adapted for its purpose, as is the transmittal of cash money. In the present case, the claim, in order to properly play its role as a means of payment, is transformed into that object which was the goal of the procedure — even when carried out electronically — namely a credit to an account.

The claim is delegated by means of the interplay between two accounts: on one side, the originator's account is debited, and he irrevocably loses the right of disposition with respect to the transferred money; on the other side, the amount is credited to the account of the beneficiary, and he acquires the absolute right of disposition with respect to the money.

In this case, the object to which the right is related has priority superior to the right itself; in other words, the claim loses significance in comparison to the monetary amount to which the claim represents a right. The legal claim fades into the background, and a formalized procedure is created. This phenomenon is long-recognized in commercial law with respect to drafts. It must be emphasized, however, that the legal claim is more diversified here: it leads to a credit to an account. In any case, whether a draft under commercial law or a transfer, the delegation of the obligation requires a basis: a right and incorporation of the claim in this right. In this way, new transmittal procedures were created based on the transfer of the right. The special characteristic of the transfer is that the uniform formal procedure has

---

[2] Dalloz, 1987, p. 299, sommaires commentés; excerpts published with comments by Vasseur.

evolved independently without the legislators providing regulations, and that this has occurred in a legal area characterized by freedom from form requirements.

It is important in the case of the credit transfer to specially emphasize the formalized procedure. The transfer is based upon a double movement with respect to accounts. This means a double account transaction — possibly by electronic means; only through the precise execution of these acts can the legal goal be achieved. As long as the transfer has not been completed, i.e. as long as the double account transaction has not been carried out, and, above all, as long as the amount has not been credited to the beneficiary's account, then — even in the case of electronic execution — the intent of the parties remains without effect or least has not yet developed its full effect.

In the present case, it would not be sufficient to simplify the transmittal event so that the positive balance in an account can be used as a means of payment; instead, after the claim is transferred, it must provide the parties with the same advantages as cash. The amount credited to the beneficiary must therefore be protected from all objections and defenses based on the underlying legal relationship between the originator and his bank and between the banks. The bank which credits the transfer amount to the account of the beneficiary may not, for example, be permitted to reclaim this amount on the grounds that the originator's account did not contain sufficient covering funds. Likewise, the transfer order must, as a rule, be irrevocable.

Under this classification, it appears correct to view the funds transfer as a transfer of deposit money. The transfer is neutral, an abstract transaction like the delivery of cash.

It cannot be denied that the transfer is the most frequently used technical means of carrying out payments. Rejecting the vulnerable case law rules of the Cour de cassation, the Law of July 13, 1967 regarding compulsory winding-up and liquidation of assets provides in art. 29-4 that the transfer is a payment procedure and one — as we must particularly emphasize — which is a normal procedure equivalent to cash payment. The Law of Jan. 25, 1985 regarding compulsory winding-up and liquidation of assets for companies [bankruptcy law] contains the same rule (Art. 107-4). The statutory law thus, by implication, recognizes the credit transfer as a means of transmitting money. In addition to satisfying debts, the transfer as a means of payment can also, as already mentioned, be used to carry out transactions which are not based on an underlying obligation, such as a gift. This was expressly confirmed by the Cour de cassation in its decision of July 12, 1966[3].

3 Dalloz, 1966, p. 614.

A transfer may be made between two accounts belonging to the same person, either at the same bank or at two different banks. This represents a simple transaction within the scope of managing assets.

In the interest of a complete legal analysis of the transfer, the following should also be mentioned: the transfer was dealt with in the abovementioned decision by the Cour de cassation of July 12, 1966. That decision contains the fundamental statement "A real contract is created by means of a transfer of money", i.e. a contract arising out of the delivery of property. This classification is significant because it makes possible a gift by means of a transfer and also the creation of a cash lien by means of a transfer. It also confirms that the transfer is a formalized procedure requiring a double account transaction, i.e. the debit to the account of the originator and the credit to the account of the beneficiary.

Thus, the issue of the legal basis for making the transfer must be distinguished from the issue of the legal basis of the transfer order given by the originator to his bank.

III. The Transfer Order

Under French law, the transfer is based on the transfer order, given by the originator to his bank; in carrying out the transfer, the intermediate bank or banks employed, as well as the beneficiary's bank, act as subordinate agents (paying agents) of the originator's bank. Using this classification, which assumes a transfer order and subordinate transfer order, French law views the transfer as a single event to be judged uniformly.

1. The Various Transfer Orders

With respect to a transfer which — as shown above — is to be classified as an order, a distinction must be made between transfer orders to a normal commercial bank and transfer orders to the Banque de France.

a) Transfer Orders to a Commercial Bank

The transfer order is not subject to form requirements. It can, for example, be made orally or by telex. The usual form is in writing. The transfer order can be contained in a letter from the originator to his bank. The banks do, however, make forms available to their customers which need only be filled out. A standard form was created in 1980. Written transfer orders are not negotiable under French law; no "transfert de provision" is possible[4], nor are defenses excluded. Legally, it is possible that the transfer can be delivered as an instrument payable to order just as any other written payment order, but in practice this is rare. If the transfer order were structured as a negotiable instrument, a "transfert de provision" would be possible, and defenses against the transfer would be excluded. The principle that criminal law is to be strictly construed would then lead to the result that a transfer order without sufficient cover would not be subject to criminal prosecution under the provisions governing checks drawn without sufficient funds.

Most often, the originator submits the transfer order to his bank. The transfer order can also be given directly to the beneficiary, who must then submit it to the originator's bank for execution. The delivery of the transfer order directly to the beneficiary therefore has no discharging effect for the debtor and does not represent payment. Only when the transfer is completed by means of credit to the beneficiary's account is the payment completed[5].

Due to rapidly advancing developments in the area of data processing, the written transfer order is increasingly being replaced by orders on magnetic data media. Such automated transfers are common, particularly in the payment of salaries and pensions. The originator gives the magnetic tapes to his bank. Direct data transmission — the way of the future — will eliminate the need for magnetic tapes. For transfers within the SAGITTAIRE system, the participant electronically transmits an order to the system administrator, the Banque de France, to debit its account and credit the account of another participant. This system attempts to insure that obligations arising out of business transactions can be paid in francs by means of international transfers.

The bank transfers discussed so far involve so-called sight orders, which are to be carried out for the benefit of the beneficiary in the best way possible, but for which no fixed time is stipulated for the execution even if the order is given in automated form and processed electronically. Since January 30, 1987, transfers in automated form can also be made with a fixed time of payment. These transfers are posted not on the date submitted, as with transfers to be carried out "the best way possible", but instead at the fixed time. The transfer with a fixed payment date is an improvement. Previously, the originator and the beneficiary had no certainty as to when the transfer would be completed. For a company which expects that salaries and pensions will be paid at the end of the month, this uncertainty concerning the time of execution represented a special disadvantage. In order to be sure that

---

[4] In contrast to drafts and checks. The "provision" (i. e. the right to cover) is transferred under French law with the negotiation.

[5] Commercial section of the Cour de cassation [Cass. civ. com.], 29. Nov. 1954, Bulletin, III, p. 278.

all salaries are credited on the last day of the month, it had to submit the transfer orders several days in advance. The company could stipulate the time at which the bank would enter the orders in its accounting system, but the beneficiary's bank was not obligated to undertake the crediting of the beneficiary's account at a given time. The debit and credit took place at the originator's and the beneficiary's bank on the day on which it was posted in the accounting system of the particular bank — with a gap in between. The result was a disposition loss for the originator and the beneficiary.

In the case of the transfer with a due date, the date of the credit to the beneficiary's account is predetermined and guaranteed. The credit to the beneficiary's account is carried out shortly after the debit to the originator's account. Thus, both the originator and the beneficiary benefit. The bookkeeping procedures between the two banks are carried out one working day prior to the due date, the entry into the first bank's accounting system at the latest two (or three) days before the due date and the submission of the order three (or five) working days before the due date.

The reform of Jan. 30, 1987 probably represents only the first step. Based on the goods results achieved with these rules, the French Committee for the Organization and Normalization of Banking (Comité français d'organisation et de normalisation bancaires) is pursuing further developments. It is planned that in the near future a fixed date of execution will be stipulated for all automated transfers. The goal of this reform is the creation of an automated settlement system between the banks (système interbancaire de télécompensation = SIT), which should replace the posting systems of the individual banks.

b) Transfer Orders to the Banque de France

The Banque de France receives two different types of transfer orders.

1. Some transfer orders, the so-called "blue transfers" (due to the color of the paper), are normal transfers: they enable the customer to make a transfer between the main office and a branch office or between two branch offices. It is mandatory that these transfers be submitted to the Banque de France. Direct delivery from the originator to the beneficiary, for example, is not permitted.

2. In addition, there are "red transfers", with which transfers between accounts at a single branch can be initiated. The forms for these red transfers are made available only to certain account holders, i.e. banks, finance companies, stock exchanges and notaries.

   In Paris, all financial transactions between the societes de bourse and the notaries are carried out using these red transfers; they are also used in settlements and generally for carrying out transfers between banks. The bank can, however, also deliver these transfer orders directly to the customer.

The red transfer is a standard form which the originator can fill in and give to the beneficiary who submits it to the Banque de France.

In principle, the red transfer is not a negotiable instrument but instead designates a specific beneficiary. Very often, however, red transfers are circulated without the beneficiary's name, and the holder can have the amount credited to his account by entering his name or submitting the transfer to his bank as a bearer instrument. A red transfer without the name of the beneficiary or the beneficiary's account is thus a bearer instrument. A bank is not liable when it receives a transfer order from the bearer and credits his account[6].

2. The Underlying Legal Relationship

With regard to the issue of whether the order given by the originator is valid, the underlying contractual relationship between the originator and the beneficiary need not be considered. As discussed above, the transfer is a transaction which, like the delivery of a sum in cash, can be viewed abstractly. If the transfer order is made by a person without legal capacity or by an agent without authority, if it is made by mistake or unlawfully or in violation of a statutory prohibition, the funds transfer can, of course, be reversed, just as cash notes would have to be returned. But this is a contractual claim which does not affect the transfer transaction as such, even if the money transmitted by means of the transfer is in dispute.

At least two aspects regarding the underlying legal relationship related to the transfer must be discussed.

First: A credit transfer is possible only when the originator is the holder of a giro account and the beneficiary also maintains an account at a bank or credit institution or other institution which may accept deposits[7].

Second: A credit transfer can be carried out only when sufficient covering funds are available in the originator's account. A transfer order "without prior, freely disposable cover" does not, however, have criminal consequen-

---

[6] Commercial court of the Départements Seine, decision of July 11, 1961 in: 1962 Banque 45.

[7] A transfer cannot be carried out directly between a post giro account and a bank account. A bank which is to carry out a transfer from the account of its customer to a post giro account must first debit the customer's account and then order the post giro office to debit the bank's post giro account and credit the beneficiary's account.

ces for the originator even if the transfer order is delivered directly to the beneficiary by the originator.

The transfer is thus an independent (abstract) legal transaction, which must be distinguished from the underlying transaction to which it relates. Like every legal transaction, it requires suitable intent, legal capacity and authority, and a legal basis.

The originator's intent is demonstrated by the order which he gives. If the bank carries out a transfer without an order or for an amount in excess of that shown on the transfer order, then the transfer is carried out in whole or in part without a legal basis, and the bank can take recourse against the holder of the credited account for restitution of the amount transferred without justification. If the bank carries out a transfer by mistake even though the originator's account did not contain sufficient covering funds, the bank likewise has the right to recover the transferred amount, here from the originator; it is irrelevant whether the bank itself had made a mistake in managing the originator's account[8]. The bank cannot, however, assert a claim against the beneficiary whose account was credited, if he had a right to the amount. When credit is made to the wrong account (for example, the bank transfers funds to the account of X where the account of Y should have been credited), the transfer itself is not invalid but there is no legal basis for the payment of funds and thus for the transfer. It is undisputed that the originator and the bank may recover the amount which was credited to the recipient by mistake.

The legal basis for the transfer order is the underlying transaction which the originator wishes to carry out and which, as a rule, is unknown to the bank. The transfer is isolated from the underlying transaction and is abstract. Therefore, the invalidity of the underlying transaction has no effect on the transfer itself. The consequences of invalidity exist only within the relationship between the originator and the beneficiary. The originator may seek restitution from the beneficiary. The legal validity of the transfer is not drawn into question[9].

In the sense just discussed, a person is legally competent to initiate the transfer if he has lawful control of the funds.

3. Legal Consequences of a Transfer Order

The legal consequences for the originator and the beneficiary must be examined separately from those for the bank.

---

[8] See Vasseur, note Dalloz, 1980, p. 172.

[9] Cour de cassation, July 22, 1986, Dalloz 1987 p. 299, sommaires commentés, excerpts published with comments Vasseur.

a) Originator and Beneficiary

Because the transfer involves an order, then like any other order it should be revocable[10]. It must be emphasized, however, that a revocation is possible only until the transfer order has been carried out.

In accordance with a decision by the commercial section of the Cour de cassation of Jan. 26, 1983[11], the transfer is deemed to be completed with respect to the originator on the day when his account is debited. As a result, the originator loses the right to the "provision" (the right to the covering funds) at that time. Therefore, the originator can revoke the transfer order only until this time and not until the time at which the amount is credited to the beneficiary's account. The beneficiary's claim to payment of the amount does not, however, already arise at the time when the originator's account is debited but instead not until the amount is received by his bank (or, more accurately, when the credit is made to his account). Thus the transfer is completed with respect to the beneficiary when the amount is credited to his account.

The time period during which a revocation by the originator is possible is extended, by way of exception, when the originator makes the execution of the transfer order subject to a condition which the beneficiary must fulfill and when the fulfillment of this condition is a prerequisite for the credit[12].

The time period for a revocation is, in effect, also extended in the case of a transfer with a fixed due date (see above) because the originator's account is not debited until the stipulated due date.

The general business conditions of the SAGITTAIRE system provide that "the administrator of the system (the Banque de France) will not accept any revocation ... " (Art. 48) and that "the participant who has wrongly issued a legally valid payment order for the benefit of another participant must take recourse against this other participant so that restitution may be made through SAGITTAIRE or in a different form outside of SAGITTAIRE" (Art. 49). The SWIFT User Handbook contains a similar provision (Part VII, Chapter 92).

Finally, it must be emphasized that for the beneficiary the delivery of the transfer order to him is not equivalent to payment of the amount due. The transfer can be viewed as a payment only when the amount has been credited to the account of the beneficiary.

---

[10] Art. 2004 C. civ.

[11] Dalloz, 1983, Informations Rapides, p. 469, note Vasseur.

[12] 1986 Revue trimestrielle de Droit commercial [Rev. T. D. Com.] 418.

b) The Originator's Bank

The primary obligation of the bank is to carry out the transfer order in accordance with the instructions given. Its secondary duty is to carry out this order without delay; it is liable for damages which arise due to a delay.

1. As just mentioned, the originator's bank must carry out the transfer in accordance with the instructions given. The originator can make the execution of the transfer — essentially the credit to the beneficiary — subject to a condition which the beneficiary must fulfill before the amount is to be credited to him. The originator's bank is obligated to inform the beneficiary's bank of the wording of this condition[13].

   The obligation to carry out the transfer means that the bank must monitor the transaction. In the case of an order in writing, it must examine the authenticity of the originator's signature, and it may not carry out an order where there is doubt concerning the legal validity of the order. This relates to the problem of forged or falsified orders. It is undisputed that the bank is liable when it violates its duties of care, in particular when it carries out a transfer where the originator's signature was recognizably forged.

   The legal situation is more difficult to judge where the bank cannot be charged with fault because the originator's signature was excellently forged and no circumstances were present in connection with the delivery of the order which should have caused the bank to use increased caution.

   Here, the issue is which party must bear the loss arising out of the execution of a forged or falsified transfer order. The parties in question are the bank and the originator. This issue is disputed in the case decisions and the legal literature. Hamel, Lagarde and Jauffret[14] correctly suggest that a forged or falsified transfer order be handled like the forged or falsified check. The statutes do not contain express provisions for this situation for the transfer or for the check. There is, however, a substantial body of case law concerning the check. The application of these case decisions to the transfer would lead to a distinction between a transfer order false from the beginning (forged) and one which was properly issued and later falsified.

   In the case of the forged transfer order, the alleged originator has no connection to the order; in reality, he did not issue the order. The issue must therefore be decided in his favor. The bank must bear liability for a loss and must return the amount debited from the account of the presumed originator. This is conditioned upon the fact that the customer

---

[13] Paris, Jan. 31, 1986, 1986 Rev. T. D. Com. 418.

[14] 2 Droit commercial at no. 1737 (1966).

was not at fault, e.g. for making his confidential bank data available to a third party.

If, on the other hand, the transfer order was first properly prepared and later falsified (e.g. by changing the amount or the name of the beneficiary), the result must, as a rule, be different. The originator must bear the loss; the bank is not responsible because it could not detect that the order was falsified[15].

2. The bank must carry out the transfer in accordance with the instructions which it receives and without delay, i.e. as quickly as possible, whereby the due date must be heeded in the case of a transfer with a fixed due date. If we put this special case aside, "without delay" means that the bank must proceed with the necessary speed even if the originator has not specifically requested this of the bank. In a decision of April 24, 1981, the Cour de cassation held that a time lapse of three days "did not constitute an unreasonable delay".

3. With respect to international funds transfers using SAGITTAIRE, two basic concepts must be distinguished for purposes of clarity; the SAGITTAIRE posting date (also to be distinguished from working day) and the value date.

   The SAGITTAIRE posting date begins at 1 pm of the previous working day and ends at 1 pm on the current working day.

   The value date is the date of the actual debit and credit to accounts of the system participants. With respect to the posting day, only the values D (= day), D + 1, or D + 2 are permissible. The great majority of transactions are completed on the value date D.

   The posting day must be distinguished from the working day, which is approximately 7 am until 6 pm. After the closing, the orders are collected and transmitted on the following day.

   SWIFT, with whose network SAGITTAIRE is connected, is technically able to comply with maximum time limits for transmission. At present, these transmission times vary depending on the level of urgency designated by the originator and on the current workload in the network. In urgent cases, transmission may take from a few seconds to a few minutes.

[15] It is generally recognized that electronic funds transfers are much safer than written transfer orders, especially due to the security procedures employed by SWIFT and SAGITTAIRE.

IV. The Execution of the Transfer Order

1. Legal and Substantive Conditions for the Execution: Consent and Double Account Transactions

Multiple parties are involved in the execution of the transfer, the transmittal of deposit money. The transfer is a legal transaction. It requires the consent of the parties, i.e. in the usual case the consent of the originator, the beneficiary and the bank(s). At the same time, we must keep in mind that the transfer is a formalized transaction, which is substantively carried out by means of account transactions. Without the debit and credit of the accounts, the transfer cannot be completed.

As long as this double account transaction has not taken place, the intent of the parties has not been fully satisfied. The execution of the transfer thus consists of: 1. mutual consent of the parties, and 2. double account transaction (debit and credit to the accounts).[16]

a) Consent

With regard to the consent of the parties, the consent of the originator does not present any problems. His consent is demonstrated by the order which he issues. There are also no problems with the consent of the bank(s). The consent of the bank(s) managing the accounts is demonstrated by the action which it takes, i.e. the debit or the credit. The banks are not authorized to reject the order except in specific cases, e.g. where the transfer appears to be related to illegal transactions, as in the laundering of money acquired by means of criminal acts.

The beneficiary gives his express consent to the transfer if he submits the transfer order, which he receives from the originator (not often the case), to his bank. Otherwise, legal doctrine assumes that the beneficiary's consent may be implied from the fact that he is the holder of a bank account and that the payments involved are of a nature typically made by means of check or transfer for his benefit[17]. A different legal view, which does not conflict with the first, views the beneficiary's bank, which credits the beneficiary's account, as acting as an agent with the retroactive approval of the beneficiary; this approval is demonstrated by the fact that the beneficiary makes no objection after receiving notice of the transfer[18]. Regardless of which of the legal approaches, express or implied consent, is used, the beneficiary's

[16] See II Ripert & Roblot, Droit commercial at no. 2306.

[17] Ripert & Roblot, id. at no. 2310.

[18] Hamel, et. al., supra note 14 at 1739.

approval of the transaction is obvious. It is not possible that the beneficiary receives money without his knowledge and against his will.

b) Double Account Transactions

As long as the transfer has not been carried out on both sides, the intent of the parties has not been satisfied. The double account transaction is a necessary component of the execution of the transfer. The result is that the transfer transaction is not completed until the credit has been made to the account of the beneficiary. Until this time, the transferred amount has not become his property[19], even though, under the decisions of the Cour de cassation, the amount is no longer the property of the originator after it is debited from his account[20]. We must look closer here at the time period between the debit from the originator's account and the credit to the beneficiary's account.

In the case of a transfer between two accounts at the same branch of a bank, the legal situation is clear. The debit from the originator's account and the credit to the beneficiary's account are made simultaneously.

The same is true for a transfer between two accounts at two different branches of one bank, although there can be a small gap between the actual time of debiting the originator's account and crediting the beneficiary's account. In a computerized accounting system, this time gap is practically excluded, but even if there should be a delay, the transfer is not completed until the credit is made to the beneficiary's account. The same is true for transfers between accounts at different banks. The Cour de cassation[21] decided that the transfer is not completed until credit is made to the beneficiary's account. In this case, the beneficiary's bank acts as the agent of the first bank in the transfer of money to the beneficiary[22]. With respect to the originator, the beneficiary's bank is a subagent; the beneficiary's bank also holds certain funds for the beneficiary. The fact that two banks are involved instead of only one makes the situation more complicated because the money must get from the originator's bank to the beneficiary bank. This occurs either by means of a transfer, which the first bank makes to the account of the second bank (if the two banks have an account relationship with each other) or by means of a "red" or "blue" transfer through the Banque de France where both banks hold accounts, or with the help of a

---

[19] Cass. civ. com., decision of May 3, 1984, in: 1985 Rev. T. D. Com. 341.

[20] Cass. civ. com. Jan. 26, 1983.

[21] Feb. 7, 1944, in: II Jurisclasseur Périodique [J. C. P.] at 2.604 (1944); see also Cass. civ. soc. of May 3, 1984 in: 1985 Rev. T. D. Com. 341.

[22] Also Paris, decision of Jan. 31, 1986, in: 1986 Rev. T. D. Com. 418.

settlement computer in the case of transfers transmitted on magnetic tape or through a bilateral or multilateral accounting system.

Despite all these various means of execution, the complete execution of the transfer still requires the double account transaction.

The beneficiary's bank must precisely comply with the instructions received from the originator's bank. As already pointed out, the originator's bank can instruct the beneficiary's bank to make the credit to the beneficiary's account subject to a condition which the beneficiary must fulfill. If the beneficiary's bank does not comply with this instruction by the originator's bank, it violates its contractual duties to the originator's bank and must reimburse it for the transferred amount[23].

2. Consequences of the Debit for the Originator

When the debit is made from the originator's account, he loses his property right to the "provision", i.e. the covering funds. The consequences are obvious. It was shown above that the originator can revoke the transfer order as long as his account has not been debited. Until this point in time, a creditor of the originator could execute an attachment order. If an insolvency (bankruptcy) proceeding is commenced against the originator before the transfer amount is debited from his account, the debit can no longer be carried out. In accordance with Art. 33 of the Law of Jan. 25, 1985 on insolvency proceedings, no claim arising prior to the court order may be satisfied.

But the transfer is not completed at the place where and the time when the debit is made from the originator's account; instead, it is not completed until credit is made to the beneficiary's account. The transfer is thus deemed to be executed at the place where and the time when the beneficiary's account is credited[24].

It should be particularly emphasized in this context that the originator is unable to revoke the transfer order from the day on which his account is debited, but that the transfer is not carried out and completed until the credit has been made to the beneficiary's account. We must therefore still examine the time period in between. The basis of deliberation is that with the debit from the originator's account, the money no longer is the property of the debtor, even though it is not yet the property of the creditor, but has at least been made available to him for satisfaction of his claim. Therefore, a reorganization or bankruptcy proceeding opened by a court after this time

---

[23] Id.

[24] Supra, note 19.

can no longer prevent the payment. The money made available for the purpose of satisfying the creditor's (beneficiary's) claim is the property of the bank between the time when the originator's account is debited and the creditor's account is credited. It follows that during this time period the beneficiary has two debtors — the originator and the bank(s) through which the money is transferred.

3. Execution of Transfer Orders Through SAGITTAIRE

In each accounting event carried out through SAGITTAIRE, two transactions are carried out simultaneously — the debiting of an "interim account" of the originator and the crediting of an "interim account" of the beneficiary, who immediately receives a message concerning the amount credited to his "interim" account as well as additional data concerning the posting. At this time, even prior to the settlement at the end of the day, he has this amount at his disposal.

The "interim accounts" are maintained for each of the three permissible value dates (D, D + 1, D + 2; D = day). Using the proper inquiry order, the participant can ascertain the current balance in his "interim account" at any time. SAGITTAIRE operates in real time, message for message and can transmit the balances in the "interim accounts" to the connected banks.

In addition, the Banque de France, as system administrator, transmits reports on the current interim balances to all participants at certain fixed times.

The Banque de France also transmits to each participant at the end of the posting day an account statement of all transactions in the SAGITTAIRE "interim accounts" listed by value date. The participants are required to compare this statement prior to the start of the next working with the debit entries which they initiated and the credits which they received, in order to lodge complaints with the Banque de France, if necessary.

At the end of the working day, the balances of the SAGITTAIRE entries are registered, as debits or credits, in the accounts which the credit institutions hold at the Banque de France. SAGITTAIRE can therefore be characterized as a "net accounting system".

To this extent, the postings made through SAGITTAIRE are a subcategory of transactions which take place in the accounts at the Banque de France. These SAGITTAIRE transactions are deemed revocable (Art. XI of the SAGITTAIRE general business conditions). The revocability referred to here should not be misunderstood, however. The execution is revocable, not the order. That the execution is revocable means that the Banque de France can in whole or in part cancel payments made on the order of the customer if the customer's account at the Banque de France does not contain sufficient funds to cover his balance at the end of the day's transactions and sufficient cover is not immediately provided. If payments are canceled by SAGITTAIRE, the reverse entries due to lack of sufficient funds are carried out in reverse chronological order from the original postings. In such cases, the Banque de France as system administrator notifies the delinquent participant and the affected beneficiaries of the cancellation.

This "netting" system with the possibility of revocation is to be replaced soon by a "gross" accounting system which will permit an immediate funds transfer which is irrevocable and final. This is to be done through accounts opened with the central bank based on the model of the American FEDWIRE system, using a risk coverage and guarantee system. The "net" accounting system at the end of the day with the possibility of revocation will be replaced by a continuous "gross" accounting system with no possibility of revocation but using certain guarantee mechanisms.

By using an appropriate algorithm for incoming data, SAGITTAIRE is well-equipped in the execution of transactions and is able to carry out effective monitoring of data (authentication). Double transactions can also be monitored in real time. Incoming data are also stored for use in possible investigations or for renewed transmission in case messages are lost by the recipient. Transactions not yet executed are also entered and stored in the system.

V. The Liability of the Originator's Bank

It has already been stated that the originator's bank is obligated to carry out the transfer order in accordance with the instructions which it receives from the originator and without delay. Therefore, the bank is liable if it does not carry out the order at all or does so incorrectly. It is also possible, however, that omission or incorrect execution of a transfer order is not the fault of the bank. The issue then arises as to the extent of the bank's liability for intermediary banks.

First, it must be determined whether there is a claim for compensation.

1. Claim for Compensation

a) In Case of Delayed Execution

The damage suffered by the originator in case of a delay can take many different forms. It is possible that he thereby violates criminal laws. It is also possible that the originator could lose rights due to failure to make a timely payment. Or the originator's right to enter into an agreement, for which an option was granted on the condition that a sum of money be paid by a certain time for exercise of the option, might be frustrated if the bank does not comply with this time limit. In the case of international funds transfers, the damage can also consist of an exchange rate loss.

1. In practice, the courts hold the originator's bank liable for damages if an exchange rate loss occurs due to devaluation of the Franc and this devaluation takes place between the issuing of the transfer order and the late execution. In a decision of Nov. 10, 1962, the Paris court[25] held that "the bank which did not carry out the order, which it had received, with the proper speed ... must compensate the originator for the damages suffered in the delayed transfer because the bank did not carry out the order until more than a week after it was issued and the equivalent sum in Italian currency dropped due to a devaluation of the Franc which took place in the meantime".

   In a decision by the Paris court of Sept. 22, 1988[26], compensation was likewise awarded for an exchange rate loss. In that case, the exchange rate loss arose in connection with an incorrectly executed international transfer order by the late repayment of foreign currency (dollars) whose exchange rate had fallen. The originator was also obligated to take out a loan for the full amount of the dollar value. Here, compensation had to be paid not only for the exchange rate loss but also for the loan interest which the originator was forced to pay.

2. Compensation is also awarded in the case where, due to the delay, the originator loses the profit from a purchase option. The following brief summary is a good example of such a case:

   A Greek citizen enters the Paris branch of a French bank with a check for 13,000 U.S. dollars. He requests payment of $ 3000.00 in travelers checks and the balance in the form of three checks, for $ 5000, $ 3000 and $ 2000, payable in Mexico. The customer needs the $ 10,000 in Mexico by Dec. 19, 1976 in order to exercise a purchase option for which he has already advanced $ 5000. Because the $ 10,000 are not paid in time, the customer loses the $ 5000 already paid and must also pay a penalty of $ 10,000.

   The French bank issued the three checks for $ 5000, $ 3000 and 2000 drawn on its correspondent bank Banamex in Mexico; to cover the checks it initiated a transfer of $ 10,000 for the benefit of the Mexican bank.

   When the customer arrived at the Banamex in Mexico on Dec. 17, 1976

---

[25] II Semaine Juridique 13.016 (1963).

[26] Dalloz, Sommaires commentés, p. 30; excerts published with comments Vasseur.

(two days prior to the date on which he had to exercise the option and pay the $ 10,000), he was not able to obtain payment of the three checks. The $ 10,000 had not been paid to the Banamex on time.

The reason was that the French bank in transferring the $ 10,000 to the Mexican bank to cover the checks had not included an attribute of the transfer in that the transfer did not include the designation of the beneficiary. Therefore, the Mexican bank refused to honor the three checks drawn on it.

Upon his return to France, the customer first claimed reimbursement from the French bank of the $ 10,000 which he had provided to the bank in Paris and for which he had not received the equivalent in Mexico.

The customer then also claimed compensation for his additional losses in the amount of $ 16,782, consisting of the $ 5000 which he had advanced for the option, the $ 10,000 which he had to pay as a contract penalty, and $ 782 for his travel costs to Mexico.

This claim in the amount of $ 16,782 must be classified as compensation for damages because the $ 10,000 which the customer had originally provided to the French bank had at this time already been reimbursed.

In its decision of Nov. 26, 1981, the Paris court of appeal held the French bank liable for these damages; this decision was confirmed by the Cour de cassation on June 7, 1983[27]. The Cour de cassation held that the French bank had agreed to make $ 10,000 available to the customer in Mexico. The bank had thereby assumed an obligation to achieve a result; it was liable because it did not achieve this result. The customer therefore had to be fully compensated for his losses.

This example involves an incorrect execution of the transfer order by the bank, but above all the fact that the bank did not fulfill its contractual duty to achieve a specific result, namely to make $ 10,000 available to the customer in Mexico. The damage resulted from the incorrect execution of the transfer which was intended to provide covering funds to the Mexican bank. The French bank was therefore required to compensate the customer for his damages down to the last penny.

b) Direct and Indirect Damages

It is remarkable to what extent the courts award compensation for losses suffered by the originator.

---

[27] 1984 Dalloz, Informations rapides 90, note Vasseur.

In a case decided by the Paris court on Sept. 22, 1988, the originator, who had to take out a loan for the full amount of dollars which were repaid late, was awarded compensation for the loan interest which he had to pay.

Likewise in the "Mexican" case, confirmed by the Cour de cassation on June 7, 1983, the originator received compensation to the full extent on the grounds that he no longer had the opportunity to exercise his option because he could not pay the seller the stipulated price. He succeeded in having the French bank compensate him for the $ 5000 which had already been paid to the seller for the option as well as the $ 10,000 penalty which he had to pay due to the failure to exercise the option and the $ 782 in travel costs.

Such extensive compensation for damages would appear to exceed the usual compensation based on contract liability as governed by Articles 1150 and 1151 French Civil Code. Under Art. 1150, compensation is to be paid only if the extent of damage was foreseeable or could have been foreseeable at the time the contract was made. Art. 1151 states that compensation shall include only losses which were the direct result of the carrying out of the contract.

We are thus presented with the issue of whether in the Mexican case the originator's French bank had been notified of the special urgency of complying with the time limit within which the option had to be exercised by means of the payment. Could the bank foresee the damages which incorrect execution of the transfer would cause? Were the costs of travel to Mexico "a direct result of the execution of the contract"?

The answer to these questions must be no. The scope of compensation awarded to the originator by the French courts is too high and legally unfounded because this compensation also covers damages which were not foreseeable and which were indirect.[28]

2. The Originator's Bank's Liability for the Intermediary Banks

Above all, it must be emphasized to what a broad extent the courts hold the originator's bank liable for mistakes made by the other banks involved.

1. First, the decision by the Cour de cassation of Nov. 30, 1983[29]: A customer of the Finindus Bank, who had purchased land in Brazil, instructed the bank to carry out the capital transfer. In order to carry out the transac-

---

[28] The SWIFT User Handbook, in SWIFT Policy, Part V. — Responsibility and Liability, Art. 23-4-3, excludes all liability on the part of SWIFT for indirect damages.

[29] Dalloz 1984, Informations rapides, p. 308, note Vasseur.

tion, the bank turned to the Sudameris-France Bank, which had the transaction executed by its agent in Sao Paulo.

It turned out that the money was transferred to a different person and not to the intended beneficiary. It was unclear who had made the mistake and whether the transmitted instructions had been sufficiently precise. In any case, the originator's bank, Finindus, was held liable to reimburse the originator for the transfer amount.

2. The decision, mentioned above, by the Paris Court of Sept. 22, 1988[30] is even more clear: In December 1984, a French company gave its bank an order to transfer 2 million francs for the benefit of its branch in the U.S. The bank, which could not carry out the transfer itself, gave the order to the Société Générale, which then transmitted the order to an American bank. The order was to be carried out in French francs because the transferor company in the U.S. wanted to have French francs available. Unfortunately, the American bank converted the 2 million French francs into $ 203,000. The dollar exchange rate, which reached a peak at the beginning of 1985, then fell. The French company refused to accept the dollars. Finally, the dollars were exchanged back into francs in October 1985. Due to the exchange rate loss, only 1,624,474 francs still remained from the original 2 million.

   The Paris Court of Appeal held the originator's bank liable for damages because, in the court's view, "a bank is responsible to the originator for the agent which it employs; it cannot use the defense that it is not responsible for the mistakes of others".

   This very broad rule is disputed.

Art. 1994 C. civ. provides that an agent is not responsible for one whom he employs to carry out business if he was authorized to employ third parties to carry out the business.

In evaluating the use of third parties in the transfer, the fact that international transfers were involved must be given special consideration. The Cour de cassation did decide that an agent — even with the authorization of the principal — who employs a third party to carry out the transfer must monitor this third party[31]. These decisions did not, however, involve banks. Furthermore, it can scarcely be imagined how the originator's bank should oversee the French bank to whom it transmitted the transfer order (the Société Générale) and the Société Générale should then oversee the large American bank to whom it passed the transfer order. the Paris Court of Appeal decided on July 6, 1990 — although not in connection with a funds

[30] Supra note 26.

[31] Cour de cassation, Dec. 10, 1912, Dalloz 1914. v. I, p. 97 (1914 D. P. I); Cass. civ., May 29, 1980, Bull. Civ. I, no. 183.

transfer — that a bank which engages a foreign correspondent bank to carry out the collection of a bonded debt is not in a position to oversee the foreign bank and therefore cannot be held responsible for the fault of that bank.

As a logical consequence, in the case of an international credit transfer which is carried out incorrectly or not at all, application of Art. 1994 C. civ. should lead to the result that the originator's bank which did not commit the mistake itself should only be obligated to assist the customer in his efforts to recover from the bank actually responsible for the mistake. As long as no legal provision exists to the contrary, the principle applies that each party is responsible for his own mistakes.

This legal view is also supported by the fact that electronic transfers can be reconstructed, making it possible to localize the mistake and determine which party was responsible, even if this search is difficult and costly. This is possible, at least for the data transmitted through SAGITTAIRE, which are continuously documented. Sources of mistakes can also be other intermediary banks or the SAGITTAIRE or SWIFT transmission systems, over which the originator's bank has no influence. Specifically, the originator's bank cannot be held liable for mistakes which interfere with the transmission system and thus lead to delays.

The general business conditions for SAGITTAIRE do not contain any provisions relating to the liability of the originator's bank, but do include detailed provisions regarding the liability of the system administrator, the Banque de France, to the system participants, originators and beneficiaries[32], as well as their liability to the Banque de France as administrator.

In particular, where the Banque de France is at fault it is improbable that the originator's bank could be held responsible for violating a duty of oversight with respect to the Banque de France.

The SWIFT User Handbook (Part V., Responsibility and Liability) also contains provisions regarding the liability of the network operator; in case of delay (Art. 22-4) and also in case of irreparable loss of the transferred funds (Art. 23-4), whereby a maximum liability limit is stipulated for the case of loss.

It would not appear appropriate to make the originator's bank responsible when using SWIFT and hold it liable to the originator for the full amount of damages although maximum liability limits apply to SWIFT itself. In

---

[32] In accordance with Art. 74 of its general business conditions, the Banque de France is responsible for the performance of the stipulated services in accordance with the agreements entered into with the participants. It is liable for duplicate transfers and where the participant is not informed quickly enough of mistakes by the system or where a change in participant data is not registered. A special provision excludes liability if an order could not be carried out within the stipulated time period due to force majeure.

addition, SWIFT insures its risks. The cases in the past 13 years where insurance coverage has had to be paid — due to delays and interest losses — can be counted on one hand, despite the fact that almost 1.8 billion transactions have been carried out between banks during this time period.

VI. Legal Consequences of the Credit Transfer

Based on the legal evaluation of the credit transfer as presented here, namely as a transfer of deposit money, the legal consequences are easy to determine.

The credit transfer has the same effect as the delivery of cash; deposit money is transferred to pay for the transaction which the originator wishes to execute, thereby replacing the delivery of cash: payment, gift, capital transfer, etc.

When the transfer is executed, the bank becomes the depository of the money credited to the beneficiary. The bank authorized by the customer to manage his account has the duty to accept and safeguard all amounts which it receives for the customer. The execution of the transfer has the effect that a claim is created for the benefit of the beneficiary against his bank for the full amount credited to his account, while the originator's claim against his bank for the full transfer amount is extinguished.

There is no legal connection between the two claims, so that the bank holding the beneficiary's money cannot raise defenses against the beneficiary which it could raise against the originator. Therefore, a bank which has carried out a transfer despite the lack of sufficient cover in the originator's account cannot assert this lack of cover with respect to the beneficiary and demand repayment of the credited funds. Interference in the legal relationships between the banks likewise cannot be asserted against the beneficiary. The beneficiary bank which has credited the account of its customer cannot cancel this credit on the grounds that events have occurred in the international transfer which make it impossible for the beneficiary's bank to collect funds which were credited for its benefit at the originator's bank.

VII. Difficulties Based on Differing Legal Systems

French courts have not yet been confronted with the conflicts between different legal systems which can occur in connection with international funds transfers. This is evidence of the fact that malfunctions in international transfers are not usually taken as grounds for recourse to the courts.

It is, therefore, not surprising that legal literature has devoted little attention to the very difficult issues which can arise.

In general, at the present time, a distinction is drawn between the actual transfer procedure and the underlying transfer order.

Under the prevailing view, the law of the originator's bank is applicable to the issue of the transfer order — in the absence of an express stipulation to the contrary, which is possible based on the principle of freedom to contract. As a rule, it may be assumed that the law of the location of the particular branch involved is determinative for banking transactions.

The prevailing view is that for the transfer procedure itself, which as shown serves to transmit deposit money, the law of the place of delivery governs. Thus, the law of the beneficiary's bank would apply, whereby this law governs primarily the relationships between the beneficiary and his bank and the relationship between the originator and the beneficiary (with respect to the transfer, not to the legal relationship underlying the transfer order).

The most difficult issue is that regarding the law applicable to the relationship between the originator and the beneficiary's bank. This includes the relationships with other banks which might be employed, both between the banks and also between the originator or beneficiary and an intermediary bank.

One view would apply the law of the bank instructed to carry out the next step in the transfer because this law would have the strongest interest in deciding whether this transfer was carried out or not. This proposal appears to be in conflict with the unified payment transaction on which the transfer is based.

Therefore, a different view should be preferred, one which attempts to avoid the application of different laws to the individual segments in a credit transfer and would subject the entire transfer procedure to a uniform law. This would appear particularly proper in the case of electronic transfers in which it is very difficult to bring the extreme speed of the execution into harmony with segmentation of applicable laws. The question still remains as to which single legal system should govern.

Even prior to the development of electronic funds transfers, the proposal was made by legal scholars that the law of the beneficiary's bank should apply. This view is based on the principle — stated above — that the transfer is completed at the location of the beneficiary's bank. In the case of an originator who gives an order to transfer money to a foreign country, one can assume that he accepts the possible application of foreign law to this transfer. The same is true for intermediary banks as soon as they become involved in the execution of the transfer order[33].

[33] See Hamel, Opérations de banque, v. II. 1943, no. 861.

We still must examine whether the legal system which governs the beneficiary's bank is really the one most suited to provide answers to the questions raised. Consideration has not been given to whether the law of the originator's bank should perhaps govern instead because the originator and his bank are the ones who initiate the transfer procedure. Is not the law of the place where the transaction is initiated the most appropriate, and are not all acts following the issue of the order done merely to carry out this order?

Questions upon questions. None of the views mentioned above is able to solve the issues regarding the law applicable to a transfer procedure in a fully satisfactory manner.

VIII. The Role of the Credit Transfer in the Future

The future of the funds transfer in France in foreseeable: on the one hand, the transfer will continue to grow in importance within the category of written payment instruments; on the other hand, this written transfer order will continue to be replaced by electronically supported automated transfers.

In France in 1989, only 108 million written transfers were carried out, compared with over 1 billion automated transfers. The automated transfers made up 91,4 % of the total number (in 1985 only 85.7 %). This development can also be observed in the area of international funds transfers. It can be assumed in international transfers that with improvements in the data networks the automation will proceed even faster and more comprehensively than with domestic transfers.

The Actual Significance of and the Law Relating to Foreign Funds Transfers in Italy

By Concetto Costa, Messina*

Contents

I. Basic Principles: the Italian Practice of Funds Transfers with Foreign Countries. Issues of Currency Control Law. Applicable Law

In Italian business practice, the bank transfer is, without doubt, the most widely used, the most economical and the most suitable form for transmitting money to persons in a different country from the person for whom the transmittal is carried out.[1]

While the excution of such a transfer can be for a variety of reasons, the most frequent case is the payment of the purchase price in connection with commercial transactions.

---

* Translated from the German version by Dr. Frances Dielmann, Frankfurt/M.

[1] Regarding the more technical aspects of this banking operation, see: A. Di Meo, I pagamenti internazionali (Ipsoa, Rome 1990), pp. 15 ff.; Le operazioni bancarie (R. Ruozi, ed., 3d ed., Guiffré, Milan 1989), pp. 225 f.; G. C. Marchesi, Finanza e tecnica delle esportazioni (Ipsoa, Rome 1985), pp. 54 ff.; G. C. Lecchi, Il servizio estero merci (Iceb, 1982), pp. 71 ff.; one fundamental work is the publication by the Banca d'Italia, Libro bianco sul sistema dei pagamenti in Italia (Rome 1987), p. 145 ff.

In this case, the direct transfer of funds by a bank represents a means of international payment, without being the only one.[2] The procedure is generally as follows: one party (the "originator") gives an order to his bank to transfer a certain amount to a foreign party (the "beneficiary"). If the bank has a branch in the beneficiary's country, it carries out the order through this branch; otherwise it employs an intermediary bank. The transferred amount is paid to the beneficiary in the stipulated currency by a bank in his own country (which in general is stipulated by the parties and reported to the beneficiary's bank with the transfer order)[3] or, if he has an account with that bank, it is credited to his account.

At the time he gives the order, the originator must pay the transfer amount to his bank, or if he has an account with the bank must have the amount debited from his account.

The entire operation can be structured as a pure accounting transfer of book deposits between banks, whose purpose is the transmittal from the originator's account to the beneficiary's account. In this case, one speaks of a "giroconto bancario" or "bancogiro" (bank transfer, wire order).[4] But if the operation is not carried out strictly by accounting means because somewhere in the procedure a direct payment of money is necessary (e. g. where the originator or the beneficiary does not have an account with the relevant Bank), one speaks of a "bonifico bancario".

As we have shown, in international funds transfers there are usually several banks involved.

The banks usually employ foreign banks with which they have a "correspondent relationship", i. e. a standing working relationship. If the bank designated by the beneficiary does not have a correspondent relationship with the originator's bank, a third bank which has a correspondent relation-

---

[2] In addition to checks, drafts, documentary letters of credit and documentary collection: for a broad overview from a banking perspective, see Di Meo, supra note 1 at 4 ff.

[3] In Italian banking practice, the related amounts are generally posted to an "interim account"; a check for the transfer amount which has already been drawn is made available to the beneficiary if he does not have an account at the bank, so that the beneficiary can make it payable to his order and present it.

[4] G. Santini, Il bancogiro (UPEB, Bologna 1948); G. Ferri, Bancogiro, in: Enciclopedia del diritto, v. V. (Giuffré, Milan 1959), pp. 32 ff.; G. Santini, Giroconto, in: Novissimo digesto italiano, v. VII (Utet, Turin 1965), p. 861; G. F. Campobasso, Il bancogiro Profili strutturali, in: Le operazione bancarie, v. II (G. Portale ed., Giuffré, Milan 1978), pp. 633 ff.; G. F. Campobasso, Bancogiro e moneta scritturale (Cacucci, Bari, 1979), pp. 1 ff.; G. Molle, I contratti bancari (Giuffré, Milan 1981), p. 496; M. Spinelli & G. Gentile, Diritto bancario (Cedam, Padova 1991), p. 309; G. F. Campobasso, Bancogiro, in: Enciclopedia giuridica Treccani, v. IV (Rome 1988); N. Salanitro, Conto corrente bancario, in: Digesto delle discipline privatistiche [D.D.P.], Sezione commerciale, v. IV (Utet, Turin 1989), pp. 15 ff.; concerning international post giro transfers, see G. Falcone, Conto corrente postale, in: IV D.D.P. (Utet, Turin 1989), pp. 28 ff.

ship with the first two banks is engaged.[5] The order can be sent to the correspondent bank by means of letter or telex or through the SWIFT system.[6] In most cases, Italian banks presently use the SWIFT system. The other means of communication, which are slower and less certain, are used only if expressly requested by the originator or if the beneficiary's bank is not connected to the SWIFT system.[7] Within the scope of cooperation between the correspondent banks, the settlement of the reciprocal claims and obligations is not made by means of a direct flow of money. Instead, a "clearing house" is used, which settles the reciprocal claims and obligations between the banks immediately or at regular intervals; this is done either by crediting a balance to one or the other of the banks[8] or by means of a procedure stipulated in agreements directly between the individual banks, such as the widely used system of reciprocal "nostro" and "loro" accounts.[9] Italian banks today primarily use the system of reciprocal accounts for their foreign transactions and work with traditional bookkeeping methods, while clearing houses and fully computerized procedures are rarely used.[10] For this reason, the view has been asserted that in Italy in interbank transactions, even with foreign banks, one cannot really speak of "electronic funds transfers" at all.[11]

[5] A third bank is also employed when the reciprocal accounts of the two banks are not maintained in the same currency as that designated in the transfer order. The third bank is then referred to as the "covering" or "intermediary" bank.

[6] Di Meo, pp. 16 ff.

[7] Banca d'Italia, Libro bianco, pp. 149 ff.

[8] On electronic bank settlement systems, see Banca d'Italia, Libro banco, pp. 153 ff.; V. Zeno-Zencovich, Clearing Houses informatizzate e irrevocabilità del pagamento, in: Il diritto dell'informazione e dell'informatica (1987), pp. 555 ff.; on settlement systems generally, see L. Nivarra, Stanza di compensazione, in: Enciclopedia del diritto, v. XVIII (Giuffré, Milan 1990), pp. 651 ff.

[9] See Ruozi, pp. 223 ff.

[10] Banca d'Italia, Libro bianco, pp. 153 ff.

[11] R. Maccarone, I trasferimenti elettronici di fondi nel diritto italiano, in: Le operazioni della banca tra norme e prassi (Giuffré, Milan 1988), pp. 352 ff.; R. Maccarone, I trasferimenti elettronici di fondi, in: Bancaria (1981), p. 792; Banca d'Italia, Libro bianco, pp. 154 ff. It should be pointed out that at present in Italy great efforts are being made toward "computerization" of funds transfers; in addition to the Libro bianco of the Banca d'Italia, see D. Qualeatti, Struttura e prospettive di sviluppo del sistema italiano dei pagamenti, in: Temi di discussione del servizio studi della Banca d'Italia, no. 60, 1986; F. Passacantando, Il sistema dei pagamenta in Italia, in: Il mutamento dell'attività vancaria: nuovi problemi monetari ed organizzativi (Cedam, Padova 1988), pp. 29 ff., and M. Sella, Intervento, in: Il mutamento dell'attività vancaria: nuovi problemi monetari ed organizzativi (Cedam, Padova 1988), pp. 43 ff.; A. Tarola, D. Qualeatti, P. Di Blasi & P. Salamone, Sistema dei pagamenti, prodotti bancari e retitelematiche, Aspetti tecnologici, realizzativi di sicurezza e giuridici, Quaderno ASSBB; Banca d'Italia, Il sistema dei pagamenti in Italia: progetti d'intervento (Rome 1988); Il sistema de pagamenti italiano: progetti in corso e prospettive di sviluppo (Banca d'Italia, Rome 1990).

A sketch of how these problems are dealt with in other countries is found in the well-known "libro rosso": Sistemi di pagamento in undici paesi industrializzati (Banca dei Regolamenti internazionali, ed. Banca d'Italia, Rome 1990).

It must be emphasized that in international commercial transactions, payment by means of bank transfer, just like payment with checks or drafts, involves risks for the seller if the transfer is to be made after delivery of the goods: as in all other cases of "subsequent payment", the seller here bears the risk that the payment might be made late or not at all. This payment method involves risks for the buyer when the transfer is made prior to receipt of the goods. Here, as in other cases of "anticipatory payment", the buyer pays the purchase price before he acquires control of the goods and therefore bears the risk that the seller will not perform or will deliver defective goods. For this reason, Italian business, at least when they do not sufficiently know or trust the foreign contractual partner, prefer payment forms other than direct bank transfer; these include the documentary letter of credit and the collection of documents, which are more expensive but significantly limits the risks for both parties.[12]

So far, we have looked only at the execution of cross-border funds transfers by banks. In fact, prior to the recent reform of the Italian currency control law, transfers to foreign countries and foreign currency transactions could only be carried out by certain authorized banks ("banche agenti")[13] and in compliance with strict regulations. These regulations precisely stipulated the requirements for execution of these transactions and prohibited the holding of accounts in foreign currency. Now, however, Art. 7 (1) of the Testo unico in materia valutaria (D.P.R. of 31 March 1988, No. 148) provides that foreign funds transfers to and from Italy and foreign exchange transactions can be carried out not only by the Ufficio Italiano Cambi, the Banca d'Italia, the authorized banks, or, within certain limits, other authorized enterprises, but also by the postal authorities within the limits set by the Foreign Ministry in accordance with international conventions and agreements. This innovation is part of a legal reform implementing the EC Directive on free movement of capital of 24 June 1988[14], which has eliminated most of the restrictions on capital transactions in effect under prior law.[15]

---

[12] See C. Costa, "Astrattezza" ed eccezioni opponibili nel credito documentario irrevocabile (Giuffré, Milan 1989), pp. 114 ff., with additional references; see also A. Frignani, Il contratto internazionale, in: Trattato di diritto commerciale e di diritto pubblico dell'economia (F. Galgano, ed., 12, Cedam, Padova 1990), pp. 212 ff.

[13] The number and amounts of the transfers carried out by other "authorized" banks, post offices, the Banca d'Italia, and Ufficio italiano Campi were quite modest.

[14] G.U.C.E.L. 178 of 8 July 1988; regarding the Directive, see A. Santa Maria, Diritto commerciale communitario (Giuffré, Milan 1990), pp. 179 ff., with additional references.

[15] Analysis of applicable foreign currency law is found in G. Garioni, Articolo per articolo il decreto valutario, in: Commercio internazionale, 1990, No. 11, Inserto, III; E. Capossela, Liberalizzazione valutaria e direttiva CEE: un confronto, in: Commercio internazionale, 1990, No. 11, Inserto, IX; U. Perucci, Dalla "canalizzazione" al "monitoraggio", in: Commercio internazionale, 1990, No. 11, Inserto, XVI; G. Bialetti, Deregulation valutaria: luci ed ombre, in: Commercio internazionale, 1990, No. 11, Inserto, XIX;

Finally, with regard to the applicable law — it is anticipated that the subject of international funds transfers will soon be governed by a uniform law[16] — there is the problem of determining — using international conflict of laws rules — which law is applicable to the relationships between the various parties involved in the transfer. The prevailing view in Italy is that in the case of complex international banking transactions, which consist of numerous economically interconnected legal relationships, the law applicable to each legal relationship (originator/bank, first/second bank, bank/beneficiary, etc.) is to be determined separately, so that each "segment" of the transaction can be governed by a different law.[17] We must now look at the criteria used to determine the law applicable to each of the individual legal relationships. The Rome Convention of 19 June 1980 on the Law Applicable to Contractual Obligations, which entered into effect on 1 April 1991, provided that where no express choice of law is made by the parties, the contract is to be governed by the law of the state of residence of the party owing the "characteristic performance" (Article 4). The general view is that the law of the bank governs.[18] Thus, in the relationship between the originator and the

---

G. Toma, Il nuova look della "dichiarazione valutaria", in: Commercio internazionale, 1990, No. 11, Inserto, XXII; G. Garioni, Posizione netta ed in cambi: cadono i divieti, in: Commercio internazionale, 1990, No. 11, Inserto XXIII. It should be kept in mind that in addition to the rule already mentioned there is another regulation requiring a domestic resident or intermediary to report to the Ufficio Italiano Cambi the execution of and reasons for amounts exceeding 20 million lire; this is for tax and statistical reasons (Law no. 227 of 4 Aug. 1990 converting Regulation no. 167 of 28 June 1990; the former Regulation no. 91 of 27 April 1990 expired when not converted into statutory law on time).

[16] The UNCITRAL Model Law on International Credit Transfers was adopted in May 1992 after completion of this article. The text cited in this article is the draft used by the UNCITRAL Working Group in its meeting of 7 Dec. 1990. (See U. H. Schneider, Das UNCITRAL Modellgesetz über den internationalen Überweisungsverkehr, WM 1989, pp. 285 ff.; and U. H. Schneider, in this volume). Mention should also be made of the initiatives by the EC Commission, the International Chamber of Commerce in Paris and other international organizations involved in payment transactions. But these initiatives are generally limited to regulation of electronic funds transfers [EFT] and do not, with the exception of the UNCITRAL Model Law extend to the entire range of transfer transactions. Especially worthy of mention is the Recommendation by the EC Commission of 14 Feb. 1990 on Transparency of Banking Conditions used in International Financial Transactions (90/109/CCE in O.J. L 67/39 of 15 March 1990).

[17] See L. Radicati di Brozolo, Operationi bancarie internazionali e conflitti di leggi (Giuffré, Milan 1984), pp. 178 ff., with additional references; on documentary letters of credit, see Costa, p. 17, note 38; an opposing view, with respect only to international bank guarantees, is found in A. Giardina, Conflitti di leggi in tema di garanzie bancarie, Banca, borsa, titoli di credito (1983), pp. 447 ff.; A. Giardina / U. Villani, Garanzie bancarie, commercio internazionale e diritto internazionale privato (Cedam, Padova 1974), pp. 79 ff.; in the same sense, see Art. 18 of the UNCITRAL Model Law draft.

[18] Radicato di Brozolo, Operazioni, pp. 1144 ff.; Radicati di L. Brozolo, La legge regolatrice delle operazioni bancarie secondo la convenzione di Roma del 19 giugno 1980, in: Verso una disciplina comunitaria della legge applicabile ai contratti (T. Treves, ed., Cedam, Padova 1983), pp. 83 ff.; F. Bonelli, La convenzione di Roma del 19 giugno 1990 e

first bank, the law of the bank applies[19], in the relationship between the correspondent banks, the law of the second bank as the one performing the "typical bank obligation"[20], and in the relationship between the beneficiary's bank and the the beneficiary, the law of the bank[21].

II. Relationship between the Originator and the Bank. Duties and Liability of the Bank. Bankruptcy, Death or Legal Incapacity of the Originator

In Italy in the past few years the question of which general legal structure under civil law could encompass the entire process of a bank transfer was often discussed[22]. Possibilities were the assignment of claims[23], contract for the benefit of a third party[24], "delegatio promittendi"[25], and "delegatio solvendi"[26]. The problem of the "legal nature" of the bank transfer appears in more recent legal literature to have moved into the background; instead of classifying the entire bank transaction under an existing concept, an atomistic approach is used which concentrates on the analysis of the individual "segments" of the contractual relationships.[27] This approach fits into a general and widespread trend in Italian commercial law, which asserts the independence of legal institutions of commercial law from those of the general civil law, and thus emphasizes the originality and special character of commercial law.[28] In this respect, reference to the legal concept of the

---

la legge applicabile alle operazioni bancarie, in: Verso una disciplina comunitaria della legge applicabile ai contratti (T. Treves, ed., Cedam, Padova 1983), pp. 115 ff.

19 Radicati di Brozolo, Operazioni, pp. 144 ff.

20 Id. at 169 ff.

21 This is the case under the Convention of Rome when a specific contractual relationship exists between the bank and the beneficiary or under Art. 25 (2) disp. prel. C.c. when, as can be the case with transfers, no contractual relationship exists between the bank and the beneficiary; see Radicati di Brozolo, Operazioni, pp. 186 f.

22 Italian legal scholars have dealt less with transfers in general than with the specific situation of the bank giro; the remainder of this article will likewise focus primarily on the bank giro.

23 P. Mossa, Il diritto dello check, v. I (Sassari, 1919), p. 45.

24 F. Messineo, Punti di vista sulla natura dell'accreditamento bancario, Banca, borsa, titoli di credito, v. I (1963) pp. 309 ff.

25 Santini, Il bancogiro, pp. 140 ff.; Santini, Il giroconto, pp. 862 f.; Molle, p. 501; Spinelli / Gentile, p. 310; most recently: E. Giannantonio, Trasferimenti elettronici di fondi e adempimento, Foro italiano, V (1990), pp. 165 ff.

26 Ferri, p. 34.

27 Campobasso, Bancogiro e moneta scritturale, pp. 36 ff.

28 This problem is particularly acute in Italy due to the reconsolidation of the civil and commercial codes in 1942; see G. Portale, Tra responsabilità della banca e "ricommercializzazione" del diritto commerciale, in: Funzione bancaria, rischio e responsabilità della

instruction in judging commercial law concepts with a character similar to an instruction is not generally rejected, but the application of the related civil law rules is considered to be subsidiary, i. e. should be made only when they do not conflict with special rules or with the nature and purposes of the individual commercial law legal institutions.[29]

In the absence of legal provisions specifically governing bank transfers and funds transfers in general[30], the relationship between the originator and the bank is legally analyzed using the concept of the mandate (Art. 1703-1730 Codice civile [C.c.]).

It must be kept in mind that when the bank transfer is ordered by a person who does not have a giro account at the instructed bank, an independent contract is created (here it is therefore a true mandate), while in the case where the originator has a giro account, under the prevailing view, no independent contract is made in the relationship originator/bank (in contrast to the situation under German law), but instead the transfer is a part of the mandate which is given to the bank with the current account agreement.[31] The bank's obligation to carry out the transfer orders of its own customer is derived from this current account agreement[32], even when the beneficiary's bank, as is usually the case with transfers to a foreign country, is a different one.[33]

---

banca (A. Nigro / S. Maccarone, ed., Giuffré, Milan 1981), pp. 271 ff.; G. Portale, Diritto privato comune e diritto privato dell'impresa, in: Dento anni dal codice di commercio (Giuffré, Milan 1984), pp. 227; C. Angelici, La contrattazione d'impresa, in: L'impresa (Giuffré, Milan 1985), pp. 185 ff.; Costa, pp. 117 ff., with additional references.

29 Campobasso Bancogiro e moneta scritturale, pp. 46 ff.; Costa, pp. 117 ff.

30 No rule governing the bank transfer can be derived from the Norme Bancarie uniformi [NUB]. The NUB only represent general terms of business, which are drafted by the Associazione Bancaria italiana [ABI] and incorporated by banks in their contracts with customers; see N. Salanitro, Le banche e i contratti bancari (Utet, Turin 1983), pp. 35 ff.

31 Santini, Il Bancogiro, p. 134; Ferri, p. 32; Molle, pp. 496 f.; Campobasso, Bancogiro e moneta scritturale, pp. 77 ff.; M. Porzio, Il conto corrente bancario, il deposito e la concessione di credito, in: Trattato di diritto privato, no. 12 (P. Rescigno, ed., Utet, Turin 1985), p. 887; the view that the legal concept of the order could not be applied is asserted by V. Santoro, Il conto corrente bancario (Giuffré, Milan 1988), pp. 25 ff.; he does, however, view the statutory rules governing the order as being applicable to the bank transfer based on the reference in Art. 1856 C.c.

32 Santini, Il bancogiro, p. 22; Santini, Giroconto, p. 862; Ferri, p. 32; Molle, p. 497; Campobasso, Bancogiro e moneta scritturale, pp. 135 ff.; this is true only when the necessary liquid assets or credit are available; the transfer would thus not fall within the tasks for which the bank reserves the right of acceptance or rejection based on Art. 19 of the "Norme Bancarie Uniformi in materia di conticorrenti di corrispondenza" and Art. 14 of the "Norme bancarie uniformi in materia di depositi in contocorrente" (see Campobasso, Il bancogiro. Profili strutturali), p. 669; contra, Salanitro, Conto corrente bancario), p. 15).

33 Campobasso, Bancogiro e moneta scritturale, pp. 141 ff.

In the relationship between the originator and the bank, the transfer order is a disposition with respect to the account from which the transfer amount is debited.[34] While the transfer order can be made in any form[35], it is common in Italian banking practice to have the originator sign a standard form which contains the beneficiary and his bank, the payment order, the designation of the means of execution of the order, and the authority to debit the account (if not paid in cash). From the similarity to the legal figure of the mandate and the related legal provisions, Italian legal scholarship and case decisions derive a number of consequences which are not specifically directed to international transactions but can be applied to them:

a) In carrying out the order, the bank must comply with the duties of care of an agent, for which the law stipulates especially strict requirements (Art. 1710 (1) C.c.; Art. 1856 C.c.).[36] Banks have been held liable, for example, for not making sure that the transfer order was carried out by the correspondent bank[37], or where under the particular circumstances the bank should have suspected that the order was counterfeit[38].

b) The bank has the duty to inform the customer promptly of any circumstances which occur after the transfer order is submitted and which could influence the execution of the transfer agreement, such as the closing of the beneficiary's account or the bankruptcy of the beneficiary (Art. 1710 (2) C.c.).[39] The bank cannot simply rely on the instructions which it is given but must stop the execution of the transfer, if possible, if circumstances arise which are unkown to the originator or cannot be reported to him in time and which are discernibly of substantial significance for him.[40]

c) The bank has the duty with respect to the originator to provide an accounting (Art. 1713 C.c.), which in the case of a giro account holder is specifically the duty to send a periodically prepared account statement containing the relevant debit.[41] Furthermore, the bank has the duty (which in banking practice is not always performed) to inform the originator of the

---

[34] Molle, p. 533.

[35] Id. at 534.

[36] Id. at 533; among the duties of care of the beneficiary's bank are the requirements that the bank obtain additional information from the sender if the transfer order is insufficient or unclear (Art. 10 of the UNCITRAL draft provides that the order should be executed on the day it is received).

[37] See Trib. Torino, 16.05.1949, Rivista bancaria, 1949, p. 366; Trib. Foggia, 14.07.1987, Giurisprudenza di merito, 1989, p. 65.

[38] Cas., 20.02.1988, No. 1764, Banca, borsa, titoli di credito 1989, II, p. 440.

[39] Santini, Bancogiro, p. 156; Campobasso, Bancogiro e moneta scritturale, p. 146, note 28; Santoro, p. 63; Cass., 20.02.1988, No. 1764, Banca, borsa, titoli di credito, 1989, II, p. 440.

[40] Campobasso, Bancogiro e moneta scritturale, p. 149, note 28.

[41] Santoro, p. 64.

execution of the transfer order, i. e. the completion of the credit or payment to the beneficiary.[42]

d) In the case of bankruptcy of the originator, Art. 78 1. fall., provided for the termination of the contractual relationship, is viewed as being applicable: the bank which receives the order to transmit an amount of money (or to arrange for credit of an amount by a correspondent bank) from a customer who subsequently becomes bankrupt must then stop the execution of the transfer if it has not yet been completed.[43]

If the bank carries out the transfer without knowledge of the bankruptcy, it cannot claim the related amount from the bankruptcy estate (and must credit back to the account any amount which has been debited). This follows from the principle, which is strictly followed in Italian case decisions, that knowledge of the order opening the bankruptcy proceeding is generally presumed.[44] Where the transfer is completed prior to the opening of the bankruptcy proceeding, it must be determined whether the bankruptcy administrator can file a claim against the beneficiary to avoid the transaction. Assuming the payment in giro transactions is equivalent to payment in cash[45] and that it is therefore a payment "using normal means", which is governed by Art. 67 (2) and not by rt. 67 (1) 1. fall.[46], a distinction must be made between an uncovered ("allo scoperto") and a covered ("sul debito") transfer. The prevailing view in the literature concerning the relationship between the legal transactions similar to an instruction and bankruptcy

---

[42] Campobasso, Bancogiro e moneta scritturale, p. 150, note 28; this is also true under Cass. 06.02.1982, No. 693 (unpublished) when a substitute is used; see also part a. below and note 34.

[43] Santini, Bancogiro, p. 154; Campobasso, Bancogiro e moneta scritturale, pp. 151 ff.; Molle, p. 533.

[44] In this case, the bank can seek reimbursement from the beneficiary unless the bankruptcy administrator elects to proceed directly against the third party under Art. 44 case 1 instead of against the bank; see also G. Paoli, Operazioni di bancogiro e dichiarazione di fallimento, Diritto e Giurisprudenza, 1981, pp. 274 ff., 279 f.; Campobasso, Bancogiro e moneta scritturale, p. 153, with additional references; Salanitro (Le banche, pp. 184 ff.) views this principle as being applicable to all banking agreements; under a different view, followed in the literature only by Molle (p. 533, note 145), is that where a bank which has executed a transfer in good faith, i. e. without knowledge of the bankruptcy of the customer, the transfer is valid.

[45] See parts IV. and V. below; one should remember in this context that the analogous case of payment by checks is regarded as a payment "by normal means".

[46] Santini, Bancogiro, p. 125; Campobasso, Bancogiro e moneta scritturale, p. 251; Paoli, pp. 281 ff.; see also the decision — involving a transfer between customers of the same bank — Cass. 11.07.1989, No. 3265 (Giurisprudenza commerciale, 1990, II, pp. 28 ff., with a comment by Marinoni R., Adempimento del debito altrui e gratuità dell'attribuzione: una nuova pronuncia della Cassazione sul temp = Diritto fallimentare, 1990, II, pp. 55 ff.), which classified the transfer without sufficient cover as fulfillment of an obligation for a third party and therefore held that Art. 67 case 1 was applicable with respect to the bank and Art. 64 case 1 was applicable with respect to the beneficiary.

proceedings is that when the transfer is made "allo scoperto", i. e. the bank has not received the cover from the originator prior to the opening of bankruptcy, the bank can assert the transferred amount against the bankruptcy estate by registering the claim in the schedule of the bankrupt's debts. This has the consequence that the estate suffers no damage because the bank registers a claim in place of the beneficiary for the same amount, so that there are no grounds for challenging the claim.[47] On the other hand, in the case of a transfer "sul debito", in which the bank carries out the transfer prior to the opening of bankruptcy and has already received the transfer amount from the originator (for example, by debiting his account which still had funds to cover this amount) the bankruptcy administrator can file an action for avoidance against the beneficiary in accordance with Art. 67 (2) 1. fall.[48]

With regard to the death or legal incapacity of the originator, the view that Art. 1728 C.c., under which the mandate is void in these cases, is not applicable. It is felt that the nature and purpose of the bank transfer better fit the principle expressed in Art. 1270 (1) C.c. for the instruction and in Art. 31 1. ass. for the bank check, under which the subsequent legal incapacity or death of the originator does not affect the execution of the transfer order. This would mean that the bank is obligated to carry out the transfer order in these cases.[49]

III. Relationship between Correspondent Banks. Relationship between Originator, Beneficiary's Bank and Any Intermediary Bank

It has already been emphasized that in international funds transfers, as a rule, two banks are involved, i. e. the originator's bank and the beneficiary's

---

[47] This would also have to apply in the case where the order is executed by a second bank; if, however, the second bank issues the order but it has not yet been executed, one could scarcely assert the view that Art. 78 case 1 could be applied to this relationship; instead, the first bank should have issued a revocation order to the second bank.

[48] The basis here is that a "detriment" to the bankruptcy estate is a condition of avoidance under bankruptcy law; see F. Vassalli, "Delegatio solvendi", adempimento di terzo e revocatoria fallimentare, Rivista di diritto commerciale, 1967, II, pp. 107 ff.; U. Apice, Revocatorio falolimentare e pagamento fatto dal terzo, Fallimento, 1982, pp. 1232 ff.; M. Libertini, Pagamento cambiario e revocatoria fallimentare (Giuffré, Milan 1983), p. 119; G. Portale, Delegazione "allo scoperto" e revocatoria fallimentare, Giustizzia civila, 1984, II, pp. 451 ff.; Costa, p. 151, with additional references; it should be pointed out that in Italian law not all scholars view a "detriment" as a condition of avoidance: see Maffei Alberti A., Il danno nella revocatoria (Cedam, Padua 1970).

[49] Santini, Bancogiro, pp. 151 ff.; Santini, Giroconto, p. 863; G. Augenti, Contocorrente bancario, disposizioni di pagamento mortedel correntista, in: Notaro, 1972, pp. 1 ff.; Campobasso, Bancogiro e moneta scritturale, pp. 148 ff.; Molle, p. 533.

bank. If a correspondent relationship is in effect between them[50], the beneficiary's bank is obligated in most cases to accept and to carry out the payment order which it receives because mutual performance of services, including transfers, is stipulated in the correspondent agreement.[51] Settlement of payments is carried out through a clearing house or through reciprocal accounts.[52]

If there is no correspondent agreement between the banks, the originator's bank can make an offer regarding the specific transfer, which the beneficiary's bank can accept or reject.[53] The common banking practice is to engage a third bank which maintains correspondent relationships with these two banks.[54] In this case, the transfer agreement between the originator and his bank is joined by two additional separate legal relationships, one between the originator's bank and the intermediary bank and one between the intermediary bank and the beneficiary's bank.[55]

We can assume that each of these banks is liable to the bank from which it received the order in accordance with the provisions of law governing the order as described in the preceding section[56]; the problem then becomes the determination of what legal relationships exist between the originator and the banks which, subsequent to the originator's bank, are involved in the execution of the transfer and with whom the originator has no direct contractual relationship. One alternative is that where more than one bank is involved the object of the order by the originator to his bank is deemed to be the payment of the designated amount; the result here would be that the other banks would have a substitute function (subagent)[57]. The second alternative is that in this case the object of the order is simply to entrust another bank with the execution of the payment.[58] If the first alternative is

[50] Regarding correspondent banks, see Molle, pp. 843 ff.; M. Porzio, I contratti bancari in generale, in: Trattato di diritto privato (P. Rescigno, ed., 12, Utet, Turin 1985, p. 838 ff.).

[51] Molle, p. 501; Campobasso, Bancogiro e moneta scritturale, pp. 128 ff.

[52] See part I above.

[53] Molle, p. 501.

[54] Or even with a "chain" of banks — although this is quite rare.

[55] Molle, p. 501.

[56] Under the decision by Trib. Padua, 22.05.1982, Banca, borsa, titoli di credito, 1983, II, pp. 491 ff., the originator's bank cannot revoke the order with respect to the beneficiary's bank after credit has been made to the beneficiary's account.

[57] The issues related to the relationship between the correspondent banks are highly disputed; see, e. g. G. Minervini, Mandato, submandato, esostituzione del mandatario nella prassi bancaria e nella giurisprudenza, in: Le operazione bancarie (G. Portale, ed., I, Giuffré, Milan 1978), pp. 217 ff., and in: revista di diritto civile, 1976, I, pp. 473 ff.; Molle, pp. 70 ff.; Salanitro, Le banche, pp. 118 ff., with additional references.

[58] Under this view, the relationship between the originator's bank and the third party's bank would not be a form of "substitution of agent" and certainly not a form of "subcontract", but instead a new and distinct legal construction, the "mandato per con di

correct, the originator's bank would be responsible to the originator for the selection of the agent and his performance within the scope stipulated in Art. 1717 and Art. 1856 C.c.[59] If the second alternative is correct, the originator's bank would be liable only for mistakes in the transmittal of the order and the formulation of instructions.

Under the first alternative, the originator could also cancel the order issued to the intermediary bank or the beneficiary's bank directly (or through his bank) and in case of non-performance by those banks could claim compensation from them directly (Art. 1717 (4) C.c.). Under the second alternative, the originator could not take any action within the scope of the legal relationship between his bank and the correspondent banks because his only contractual partner would be his own bank.

In banking practice, the originator always designates the beneficiary's bank in the transfer order, and generally, based on recommendation by his bank, also the intermediary bank or banks to be engaged. This circumstance led in the legal literature to the view prevailing so far that a delegation order is involved, in which the duty of the originator's bank consists of the transmittal of the order.[60] This view has been criticized by its opponents because the delegation of the execution to the second bank on behalf of the originator has more a technical character, while the true intent of the parties to the original transfer agreement (the originator and his bank) is that the transfer will be executed "through" other banks, with the result that these other banks should be viewed as the agents of the first bank.[61]

The latter view, which appears to most closely do justice to the economic bases of this banking operation, does not lead to extended liability for the originator's bank because, as has been pointed out, the originator designates the agent with the consequence that Art. 1717 (1) and (2) C.c. are not applicable.[62] Instead, this view leads to an extension of the liability of the other banks, against which the originator can take recourse directly based on Art. 1717 (4) C.c.[63]

---

terzo", which is not governed by statute; see A. Luminoso, Mandato, commissione e spedizione, in: Trattato di diritto civile e commerciale (Cicu e Messineo, eds., Giuffré, Milan 1984), pp. 105 f.

[59] The relationship between the two provisions is known to be highly disputed; see Salanitro, Le Banche, pp. 118 ff.

[60] Santini, Bancogiro, p. 171; Santini, Giroconto, p. 863.

[61] Campobasso, Bancogiro e moneta scritturale, pp. 141 ff., 163 ff.

[62] It should be pointed out that Art. 2 of the "Norme bancarie Uniformi in materia di servizio incassi" expressly releases the bank from any liability for the conduct of the agent.

[63] Campobasso, Bancogiro e moneta scritturale, pp. 163 ff. and 174 ff., who also emphasizes that the different rule under German law is due to the specific statutory provision governing the mandate; in France and Spain, on the other hand, where the laws are more similar to those in Italy and action by the originator against the substitute is

IV. Relationship between the Paying Bank and the Beneficiary. Credit. Legal Status of the Beneficiary and Liability by the Bank. Cancellation of the Transfer Order. Possible Defenses. Bankruptcy of the Beneficiary

With respect to the relationship between the bank instructed to make the payment and the beneficiary, a distinction must be made based on whether the beneficiary maintains a giro account at this bank. If not, no special problems arise because, unter the generally prevailing view, the beneficiary does not have a direct contractual relationship with this bank and cannot assert any contractual claims against it (the bank is responsible only to the preceding bank or to the originator for diligent execution of the order)[64]. If, however, the beneficiary does have an account with the bank, which in domestic as well as international transfers is more often the case, the situation is more difficult.

In this second case, the bank is bound by obligations based on two legal relationships: to the originator based on the transfer order (within the scope of the legal transaction "similar to an instruction") and to the beneficiary based on the current account agreement. Banking practice views this banking operation as completed when the transferred amount has been credited to the beneficiary's account. From this point in time the beneficiary acquires the right of disposition over the funds (Art. 1852 C.c.).

There is dispute, however, concerning which rights the beneficiary has against his bank prior to the credit. The Uniform Banking Norms (Norms Bancarie Uniformi [NUB]) of the Italian Banking Association (Associazione Bancaria Italiana [ABI]) governing current account relationships, on which the banks base the individual contracts with their customers, provide in Article 4 that "all transfers and deposits undertaken by third parties for the benefit of the account holder shall be credited to his account". This provision is construed to mean that the bank is obligated to accept the transfer order by a third party for its giro account holder.[65] The question remains open as to

permissible. The view is followed in Italy, however, that the substituted bank, can proceed with the "actio mandati contraria" only against the represented bank because in Art. 1717 par. 4 C.c. is an exception (Molle, p. 679; Minervini, p. 227).

[64] In the case of a payment which is delayed or not executed, one could only envision some form of noncontractual liability on the part of the bank; Art. 16(8) of the UNCITRAL drafts seems to choose this approach in that it provides for liability without regard to "a pre-existing relationship between the parties, whether contractual or otherwise". It must be pointed out, however, that the prevailing view in Italian case law and scholarship relating to the parallel issues of payment by bank check which is delayed or not executed excludes any noncontractual liability on the part of the bank (see R. Maccarone, Problemi in tema di responsabilità della banca per mancato pagamento di assegni, in: Funzione bancaria, rischio e responsabilità della banca (Maccarone & Nigro, eds., Giuffrè, Milan 1981, pp. 177 ff.).

[65] Porzio, Il conto corrente, p. .885, note 127; Salanitro, Conto corrente bancario, p. 15.

whether, prior to the crediting of the transfer amount to his account, the beneficiary has a right against the bank for payment of this amount based merely on receipt of the transfer order by his bank, and whether this right can be judicially enforced by means of an action for payment filed directly against the bank.

The majority of Italian legal scholars are of the opinion that no such claim exists and that prior to the credit the beneficiary is only entitled to have the bank participate in the execution of the transfer. In court, this right can only take the form of a claim for compensation for failure to credit or for late credit of the transfer amount.[66] In this regard, Italian case decisions have determined that the bank is not free to post credits without any time limits but must instead credit amounts as quickly as their technical means permit.[67]

It should also be mentioned that as a result of the Italian currency law reform, through which Italian citizens are now permitted to hold accounts in foreign currency, the problem arises in banking practice as to how to handle payment orders which originate in foreign countries and denominated in foreign currency. Previously, the banks converted the foreign currency amounts to Italian currency and then credited this amount to the beneficiary's account; they have now begun to inform the customer of the receipt of the order and to request his instructions, whereby the timing of the credit is delayed.

A further problem is whether the legally binding completion of the transfer is dependent exclusively on the posting of the credit or whether an additional element related to the beneficiary should be added: namely knowledge of the credit, or rather his approval of or failure to object to the credit.[68] This problem arises from the perspective of formal theory because the credit is viewed by the majority of scholars not as a mere factual act but instead as a legal transaction, which can be classified as a unilateral promise (Art. 1334 C.c.) or as a contract with unilateral obligations for the originator (Art. 1333 C.c.).[69]

Italian scholars are of the opinion that the crediting of the amount alone is sufficient to complete the transfer process. Depending on the approach

---

[66] Campobasso, Bancogiro e moneta scritturale, p. 183 ff.

[67] Cass., 26.07.1989, No. 3507, Foro italiano, 1990, I, p. 128 ff., with a comment by G. Carriero, Bonifico bancario ed onere di diligenza; Art. 16 of the UNCITRAL draft contains a comprehensive rule which includes liability on the part of the bank causing the delay.

[68] The widespread view in other European countries that the fulfillment effect takes place prior to the credit to the beneficiary's account, namely at the time the transfer order is transmitted to the beneficiary's bank or when it is accepted, is decisively rejected in Italy (see Campobasso, Bancogiro e moneta scritturale, pp. 153 ff.; but see Art. 17 of the UNCITRAL draft).

[69] Spinelli & Gentile, p. 310; Campobasso, Bancogiro e moneta scritturale, pp. 200 ff.

taken, the reason given is that in this case the general theory relating to legal transactions must yield priority to the private contractual autonomy of the parties or, more concretely, to the current accounts agreement in effect between the bank and the beneficiary, which contains an order to collect payments.[70] The result is that the bank's obligation takes effect at the time when the credit is made.[71] A possible rejection of the payment affects the relationship with the originator, and the beneficiary can only order his own bank to cancel the transactions.[72] The notice of the credit, which the bank sends to the beneficiary in accordance with its obligation under the current accounts agreement, thus has primarily a function as information and evidence.[73]

Italian case decisions have reached conclusions similar to the legal literature in this area on the basis of the now accepted premise that transfer credit is equivalent to delivery of money.[74] This view, which was already justified when cash payments were substantially replaced by "paper-based transfers", is even more so now that "electronic funds transfers" are beginning to replace paper-based ones.[75]

Significant conclusions can now be drawn with regard to some specific problems:

a) If the transfer is carried out by a single bank, the unanimous view in Italy is that a cancellation (or an amendment) of the transfer order is possible up until the time when the order is completed, and this is, as we have shown, the time when the amount is credited to the beneficiary's account.[76] Prob-

[70] Santini, Bancogiro, p. 58; Santini, Giroconto, p. 862; Ferri, p. 33; Molle, p. 535; F. Giorgianni, I crediti disponsibili (Giuffré, Milan 1974), p. 299; Caltabiano A., L'accreditamento bancario, in: Le operazioni bancarie (G. Protale, ed., II, Giuffré, Milan 1978), p. 725; G. Cavalli, Conto corrente, in: Enciclepedia giuridica Treccani, VIII, Rome 1988); Campobasso, Bancogiro e moneta scritturale, pp. 299 ff., who does however diverge from a transactional view of the execution of the individual credit.

[71] Santini, Bancogiro, pp. 55, 89 ff.; Ferri, p. 33; Molle, p. 535; Campobasso, Bancogiro e moneta scritturale, p. 201; regarding application of these principles to electronic funds transfers, see Giannantonio, Trasferimenti elettronici di fondi e adempimento, pp. 175 ff.; Maccarone, I trasferimenti elettronici di fondi nel diritto italiano, pp. 349 ff, 366 f.

[72] Ferri, p. 34; Molle, p. 535; Salanitro, Conto corrente bancario, p. 15; but it is possible for the account holder to issue a preventive instruction to the bank that any transfer addressed to him should be rejected.

[73] Santini, Bancogiro, p. 5; Campobasso, Bancogiro e moneta scritturale, p. .201.

[74] Cass. 02.08.1956, No. 3020, Banca, borsa, titoli di credito, 1957, II, pp. 173 ff.; Cass. 12.01.1971, No. 38, Banca, borsa, titoli di credito, 1971, II, pp. 179 ff.; Cass. 25.07.1972, No. 2545, Banca, borsa, titoli di credito, 1972, II, pp. 341 ff.; Cass. 23.01.1979, No. 517, Banca, borsa, titoli di credito, 1980, II, pp. 145 ff.; Cass. 26.07.1989, No. 3507, Foro Italiano, 1990, I, pp. 128 ff.; Trib. Padua, 22.05.1982, Banca, borsa, titoli di credito, 1983, II, pp. 491 ff.; Dir. fall., 1983, ii, pp. 518 ff., Bancaria, 1984, pp. 106 ff.

[75] On this issue, see Santoro, pp. 35 ff.

[76] Santini, Bancogiro, p. 146; Feri, p. 33; Campobasso, Bancogiro e moneta scritturale, pp. 153 ff., where the various views under which the order can be revoked as long as the

lems with the cancellation will, therefore, not arise in the fully electronic, online funds transfer sytems, in which the credits and the debits take place simultaneously with entry of the transfer order.[77]

If, on the other hand, as is usually true in international funds transfers, more than one bank is involved in the transfer procedure, the problem arises as to whether the originator's right to cancel the order exists until the time when the transfer amount is credited to the beneficiary's account or only until the time when the first bank transmits the order to the second bank. Furthermore, returning to the point mentioned above, it is not clear whether the right of cancellation can be asserted directly against each of the banks involved in the transfer or whether the originator can exercise this right only with respect to his own bank, which in the opinion of some scholars can refuse to transmit its customer's cancellation order.

The solution of these complex problems is closely tied to the issue of classification of the relationships between the originator and the banks engaged in the transfer procedure.[78]

If one follows the view that the order issued to the originator's bank is exclusively that an equivalent order be issued to the correspondent bank, then one would reject the existence of a direct relationship between the originator and the following links in the chain because the originator can exercise his right of cancellation only with respect to his own bank — and only as long as his bank has not transmitted the order to a correspondent bank.[79]

---

originator's account has not yet been debited or the beneficiary has not received knowledge of the credit, are critically analyzed. But this view seems to be followed in the UNCITRAL draft; Art. 11 permits a revocation up to the time the transfer is executed provided that the revocation order is received in sufficient time for the bank to act on it. Normally in banking practice the transferor's account is debited before credit is made to the beneficiary's account, and the interest on the transfer amount in the meantime (so-called float) represent a profit for the banks. On this basis, the decision Cass. 05.03.1980, No. 1483, Banca, borsa, titoli di creditor, 1980, II, pp. 388 ff., in which the transfer order can be revoked only based on "cogent grounds" because it involves an order for the benefit of a third party (Art. 1723 par. 2 C.c.), must be severely criticized: if this approach were followed, it would lead to the paradoxical result that practically all transfer orders would be irrevocable.

[77] See Giannantonio, Trasferimenti elettronici difondied adempimento, p. 174, which also discusses some exceptions to this rule, showing that these problems can also arise in EFT systems; see also Maccarone, I trasferimenti elettronici di fondi, pp. 795 ff.; Donadi M. Problemi giuridici del trasferimento elettronico di fondi, Contratto e impresa, 1988, pp. 559 ff.; Zeno-Zencovich, p. 561; E. Giannantonio, Trasferimenti elettronici difondi e autonomia privata (Giuffré, Milan 1986). Regulations of EFT systems connected with clearing houses generally stipulate that transfer orders are irrevocable.

[78] See part III. above.

[79] Santini, Bancogiro, p. 168; Santini, Giroconto, p. 863; Molle, p. 534. This view is aimed primarily at protecting banks which have an interest in excluding customers from

If, instead, one follows the — preferable — view that the object of the order is the transfer of a fixed amount of money and that the various legal relationships are to be classified as "agency relationships within the order relationship", this leads to the result that the originator can exercise his right of cancellation directly with respect to all of the banks — until the final credit is made to the beneficiary's account.[80]

b) When the credit has been made, the bank can undertake a retransfer only with the consent of the beneficiary, i. e. the account holder. A retransfer (or a refusal to credit the amount or a claim against the beneficiary for restitution of the amount already paid to him) can be undertaken when there are justified objections to the payment made to the beneficiary.

The Italian legal literature, which to this extent refers to the principles governing the instruction, views as permissible objections based on the cover relationship between the originator and the bank or between the correspondent banks as well as objections based on the underlying transaction between the originator and the beneficiary.[81]

It is disputed, however, whether objections can arise out of the simultaneous invalidity of the underlying transaction and the cover obligation (defence of the so-called "double defect") and from defects based on the giro order (so-called "issum"), which creates the basis for charging the originator for the amount transferred to the beneficiary: the still prevailing view in Italy, based on the legal principles governing the instruction, is that these defenses can also be asserted against the beneficiary.[82]

The defects involving the "issum" include the absence of a giro order, voidability of the giro order (due to mistake, threat, fraud, or legal incapacity) and counterfeit giro order.[83]

---

intervening in their internal affairs to the greatest extent possible; this approach does, however, leave the transferor without protection, with respect to monitoring the execution of the banking transaction as well as with regard to the bank's liability.

[80] Campobasso, Bancogiro e moneta scritturale, pp. 163 ff.; one should be able to make the same argument with regard to the revocation rights of the individual banks with respect to the correspondent banks; Art. 11 of the UNCITRAL draft, on the other hand, appears to limit the possibility of revocation to the direct partner in each contractual relationship.

[81] Campobasso, Bancogiro e moneta scritturale, pp. 212 ff., with extensive references.

[82] Santini, Bancogiro, pp. 157 ff.; Campobasso, Bancogiro e moneta scritturale, pp. 214, 223 ff., who is of the opinion that the bank may not assert defects in the giro relationship if the beneficiary upon timely inquiry provides convincing evidence of the existence of lawful grounds against the transferor (in this case, due to lack of an actio mandati contrario, the bank can proceed against the transferor by means of an unjust enrichment action or based on implied agency).

[83] Campobasso, Bancogiro e moneta scritturale, pp. 225 ff.

If, however, as the rule in international funds transfers, more than one bank is involved in the transfer, objections based on defects in a giro order directed to a bank which is in the chain of banks involved in the transfer prior to the beneficiary's bank cannot be asserted against his bank because the order relationships between the individual banks represent independent legal transactions regardless of how their relationship to the order issued by the originator is viewed: the objections to one transaction therefore cannot be carried over to the next one. In this context, one can speak of a special form of "abstractness" of the legal transactions.[84]

It should be emphasized that in the Italian legal literature in the past few years an attempt has been made to extract some legal transactions in international commercial transactions with an "abstract character similar to an instruction" from the general legal concept of the instruction. Due to the requirements of speed and efficiency in commercial transactions, with respect to the respective underlying transaction a much higher degree of "abstractness" is required of these than of the instruction in the actual sense: absolutely no defence based on the underlying transaction should be effective against the beneficiary, with the exception of the defence of fraud founded on "liquid evidence".[85] It does not appear unreasonable to predict that this approach will be applied to international funds transfers.

It is fully undisputed, on the other hand, that all defenses based on the direct legal relationship between the paying bank and the beneficiary can be asserted against the beneficiary: defenses arising out of the current accounts agreement, the settlement procedures and mistakes made in crediting the amount.[86]

c) In the case of the bankruptcy of the beneficiary, until the credit is made the beneficiary's bank is obligated, based on the existing order relationship, to inform the correspondent bank so that it can inform the originator.[87] If no

---

[84] This would appear to me to be the logical conclusion from the approach followed by Santini, Bancogiro, pp. 181 f., and Campobasso, Bancogiro e moneta scritturale, p. 226, note 94. One case in which the specific facts proved to be decisive Trib. Verona, 16.02.1990, Foro italiano, 1990, I, pp. 2972 ff. The approach followed in this article would certainly apply where the relationships between the banks are viewed as entirely independent; doubts could arise however when one assumes a legal connection between them.

[85] Concerning international bank guarantees, see G. Portale, Le garanzie bancarie internazionali (Giuffré, Milan 1989), pp. 22 ff., 35 ff., 71 ff., with additional references; on documentary letters of credit, see Costa, pp. 1 ff., with additional references.

[86] See Campobasso, Bancogiro e moneta scritturale, pp. 234 ff.; on mistakes by the bank with respect to the existence of covering funds, see Trib. Milan, 18.04.1985, Banca, borsa, titoli di credito, 1987, II, p. 94, with a comment by G. Rescio, Clausola di modifica unilaterale del contratto e bancogiro di somma erroneamente accreditata — that author views the defect, I believe incorrectly, as one involving the cover relationship rather than as one involving the payment relationship, as was actually the case.

[87] Santini, Bancogiro, p. 155, note 57; see part II. above. Paoli, pp. 284 ff., on the other

cancellation follows, the bank can carry out the credit but the full amount becomes part of the bankruptcy estate[88], so that the bank cannot set off its own claims.[89]

If the credit has already been made at the time of the bankruptcy, the transfer procedure is completed. In this case, the general problem of the treatment of bank current accounts in the bankruptcy proceeding remains.[90]

V. Relationship between Originator and Beneficiary

The nature of the relationship between the originator and the beneficiary, the "underlying transaction", on which the transfer is based, can vary greatly (sales contract, gift, loan, etc.). As we have shown, the bank is totally outside this legal relationship.[91] If the parties agree to payment by transfer, and the execution of the transfer is made in compliance with the agreement, the credit to the beneficiary's account (or the cash payment of the amount to the beneficiary, if he does not have an account) represents an indirect fulfillment of the payment obligation, and the debtor is discharged.[92]

If, instead, no such agreement is made, an issue arises regarding the requirements which must be met in order for the debt to be discharged.

Various views relating to this issue are found in Italian legal scholarship: some authors are of the opinion — and this appears convincing — that payment by transfer should be deemed equivalent to payment in cash, so that

---

hands, believes that the respective amount must immediately be brought into the bankruptcy estate.

88 Molle, p. 535.

89 Cass., 25.07.1972, No. 2545, Banca, borsa, titoli di credito, 1972, II, p. 341 = Foro italiano, 1973, I, p. 2211.

90 See Caltabiano, pp. 732 ff.; specifically relating to the bank transfer: Campobasso, Bancogiro e moneta scritturale, p. 251; E. Bonavera, Plurailità di conti dello stesso corentista, giroconto e revocatoria fallimentare, Giurisprudenza commerciale, 1989, II, p. 848; Cass. 12.01.1917, No. 38, Banca, borsa, titoli di credito, 1971, II, p. 484 (comment by G. Pico, Ordine di bonifico ed accreditamento in conto) = Giurisprudenza italiana, 1972, I, 1, p. 1122 (comment by D. Maltese, Azione revocatoria fallimentare e rimessa di terzo in conto corrente); also involving the bank transfer is the famous case Cass. 18.10.1982, No. 5413, Foro italiano, 1983, I, p. 69 (with a comment by A. Nigro, Scoperto di conto, conto corrente assistito da apertura di credito e revocatoria fallimentare delle rimess) = Banca, borsa, titoli di credito, 1983, II, p. 8 (comment by G. Terranova, Effetto estintivo e funzione solutoria delle rimesse in conto corrente bancario) and 1984, II, p. 168 (comment by G. Rescio, Revocatoriadelle rimesse in conto corrente e situazione giuridica dell'accreditato) = Fallimento, 1982, p. 1429 (comment by Danovi R., In ricordo della revocatoria fallimentare degli accreditamenti sui conti correnti bancari).

91 Molle, p. 535; Ferri, p. 33; Campobasso, Bancogiro e moneta scritturale, pp. 240 ff.

92 Molle, p. 535; Ferri, p. 33; Campobasso, Bancogiro e moneta scritturale, p. 249.

Art. 1188 (2) C.c. would be applicable; under this article, payment to a party not authorized to receive the payment discharges the debt if the creditor subsequently approves the payment or derives a benefit from it. This provision is construed to mean that it is sufficient for discharge of the debt if the creditor gains an advantage.[93]

Another group takes the approach that the bank transfer without prior agreement is a personal novation of the debt, so that the much stricter provision of Art. 1268 C.c. applies under which the express consent of the creditor is required with respect to the substitution of the person of the debtor. On the other hand, this group of scholars would construe the cited provision in such a manner that for the bank transfer forms of "implied consent" such as use of the transferred amount, approval of the credit, or failure to make objection to the bank for a long period of time[94], as well as use of the account number on invoices and other correspondence[95] would be recognized.

Post Script

With the Law No. 197 of 5 July 1991 (Gazetta Ufficiale of 6 July 1991, No. 157), implementing EC Directive 91/308/CEE of 10 June 1991 (G.U.C.E. of 28 June 1991, L 166), a comprehensive system of rules has been created in Italy with the goal of preventing the financial system from being used to return to circulation proceeds from unlawful acts. This Law includes provisions which are significant for funds transfers (Art. 1):

a) The transfer of funds or bearer instruments with a value of more than 20 million Italian lire can be carried out only by intermediaries expressly authorized by law (banks, post offices, etc.), and these intermediaries are required to preserve the documents relating to the transaction.

b) The beneficiary has the right to receive the payment by the third working day following the day on which the authorized intermediary accepted the order. (This provision was drafted into the law with regard to the cases where only one intermediary exists, but must also be extended to those cases where a "chain" of intermediaries exists, i. e. in connection with the relationship between the last intermediary and the beneficiary.)

---

[93] Campobasso, Bancogiro e moneta scritturale, pp. 248 ff., 258 ff.; Porzio, conto corrente, pp. 885 f.; it must be pointed out that in Italian case law the credit and the payment are held to be equivalent (see part IV. above); see the similar approach in Art. 17 par. 2 of the UNCITRAL draft.

[94] Molle, p. 537; Ferri, p. 33.

[95] Santini, Giroconto, p. 863; Giorgiani, p. 300.

c) The debtor is discharged at the time when he notifies the creditor that the order has been accepted by the intermediary.

d) Checks for an amount over 20 million lire must designate the payee and must be "non-negotiable".

A further innovation of interest is that beginning in 1992 in Italy almost all bank transfers will be carried out through the newly established computer network "Sitrad", which was designed with a view to future connection to similar networks in foreign countries.

The Italian Banking Association [ABI] has in this regard drafted a set of rules for the banks connected to the network "bonifico veloce" (memorandum by the ABI of 11 June 1991), of which the most significant is: urgent transfers must be carried out within one day, normal transfers within four days; if these time limits are not met, the bank is obligated to return the transfer fee to the customer.

The Practical Execution and Legal Framework of International Funds Transfers in Japan

By Shinsaku Iwahara, Tokyo*

Contents

---

* Associate Professor of Law. The University of Tokyo, Faculty of Law, Visiting Professor of Harvard Law School, Vice-Chairman of the Ministry of Finance's Electronic Fund Transfer Act Drafting Committee and the Japanese delegate to the United Nations Commission on International Trade Law.

The author is grateful to Professor Richard F. Dole, Jr., University of Houston Law Center; Professor Uwe Schneider, University of Mainz; Professor Hal S. Scott, Harvard Law School and Ms. Kathryn Heraty who is an LLM candidate at the University of Tokyo. The author also is grateful to several bankers including Mr. Katsuto Iida, Bank of Tokyo,

I. Introduction

1. Methods of Making International Funds Transfers

There are five methods used to initiate international funds transfers in Japan: banker's drafts; mail transfers; telegraphic transfers; in-house electronic transfers and SWIFT transfers[1]. In addition, travelers' checks and travelers' letters of credit are used by people who go abroad.

Banker's drafts are used by a person who wishes to remit money overseas but does not know the payee's bank or by a person who wishes to transfer a large amount to his overseas bank account. In mail transfers, telegraphic transfers, in-house electronic transfers, and SWIFT transfers, a customer (the originator)[2] instructs his own bank (the originator's bank) to remit a specified amount to a designated person (the beneficiary)[3] overseas[4].

The differences between these four methods involve the execution of an originator's payment order. The payment order is transmitted by mail in mail transfers, by a telegram or a telex in telegraphic transfers, by an in-house telecommunications network in in-house electronic transfers and by the SWIFT telecommunications network in SWIFT transfers.

Mail transfers, telegraphic transfers, in-house transfers, electronic transfers and SWIFT transfers are so-called giro transactions[5]. An originator's bank that is not also the beneficiary's bank typically will execute a payment order through a bank with which it has a correspondent relationship. If the correspondent bank is the beneficiary's bank, the correspondent

---

and Mr. Sadao Matsumoto, The Federation of Bankers Association of Japan, who provided invaluable information and advice. However, any errors or misinterpretation are the author's alone.

[1] See, N. Penny & D. I. Baker, The Law of Electronic Fund Transfer Systems (1981, with 1987 Cum. Supp. by D. I. Baker and R. E. Brandel assisted by D. E. Feld) para. 24.01; E. P. Ellinger, "The Giro System and Electronic Transfer of Funds" [1986] Lloyd's Mar. & Com. L. Q. 178, 190 et seq.

[2] "Originator" means an issuer of the first payment order in a credit transfer (see infra, note 7). This definition borrows from the definition of originator in Article 2, Subparagraph (c) of the UNCITRAL (United Nations Commission on International Trade Law), Draft Model Law on International Credit Transfers (A/CN.9/346, 15 May 1991, hereinafter cited as the UNCITRAL Draft Model Law). Terminology adopted here borrows heavily from the UNCITRAL Draft Model Law.

[3] "Beneficiary" means the person designated in an originator's payment order to receive funds as a result of the credit transfer (see, Article 2, Subparagraph (d) of the UNCITRAL Draft Model Law).

[4] Ellinger, supra, note 1 at 192 et seq.

[5] Ellinger, supra, note 1 at 180. See also generally about giro transactions, Penny & Baker, supra, note 1, para. 25.02; C. W. Canaris, Bankvertragsrecht (3. Aufl. 1988), Rdn. 300 et seq. and its citated materials.

bank will be instructed to credit the beneficiary's account with the amount of a payment order or to inform the beneficiary of funds received and to ask for instructions when the originator's bank does not know details of the beneficiary's account. The correspondent bank otherwise will execute the payment order either through issuing a payment order to its own correspondent bank or through another method of transmitting the payment order to the beneficiary's bank, for example use of local clearing channels. Settlement between a sender and a receiving bank will be effected through the debiting or crediting of a bank account. Either a sender's account with a receiving bank will be debited or a receiving bank's account with a sender, a correspondent bank, or a central bank will be credited[6].

Japanese banks recently have minimized their depositary-correspondent relationships with foreign banks in order to decrease costs. International funds transfers are carried out mainly through foreign local clearing channels either by a Japanese bank's own overseas branch network or by an international in-house electronic transfer system.

Among these five methods of international funds transfers in Japan, mail transfers are rarely used. Banker's drafts and telegraphic transfers are not often used. In-house electronic funds transfers and SWIFT transfers are most often used in Japan. These are mainly used for credit transfers from Japan to abroad and from abroad to Japan, but are seldom used for debit transfers[7].

The SWIFT system, for example, is a computerized world telecommunications network that operates a global data processing system for transmitting both international and domestic financial messages over dedicated lines among member banks and other connected users[8]. In 1990, the 175 Japanese banks that were members of SWIFT sent 15,057,000 messages and received

---

[6] See, Uniform Commercial Code (UCC), Article 4A-403 of the United States of America; the UNCITRAL Draft Model Law, Article 6; H. S. Scott, "Where Are the Dollars? — Off-Shore Funds Transfer", 3 Banking & Finance Law Reviews (B.F. L.R.) 243, 252 et seq. (1989); B. Geva, "International Funds Transfers — Performance by Wire Payment", 4 B.F. L.R. 111, 120 et seq. (1990).

[7] "Credit transfer" means a fund transfer in which a person who is to make payment sends a payment order directly to a bank and instructs the bank to pay. "Debit transfer" means a fund transfer in which a person who is to receive payment sends a payment order to a bank and instructs the bank to pay. See, UNCITRAL Legal Guide on Electronic Funds Transfers, A/CN. 9/SER. B/1, 1987, pp. 12 et seq.

[8] For an overview of SWIFT see Penny & Baker, supra, note 1, paras. 9.05, 16.04 and 24-5; H. F. Lingl, "Risk Allocation in International Interbank Electronic Fund Transfers: CHIPS & SWIFT", 22 Harv. Int'l L. J. 621, 624 et seq (1981); E. U. Byler & J. C. Baker, "SWIFT: A Fast Method to Facilitate International Financial Transactions", 7 J. World Trade L. 458 (1983): D. Jueterbock, "SWIFT II für die 90er Jahre", in: Die Bank, 1988, S. 329 ff.; Geva, supra, note 6 at 116 et seq.; S. Etzkorn, Rechtsfragen des internationalen elektronischen Zahlungsverkehrs durch S.W.I.F.T., 1991.

15,579,000, 4.5% of the aggregate 1990 SWIFT transactions[9]. Considering the involvement of Japanese banks in world banking, this was not a large percentage. It is explained in part by the establishment by major Japanese banks of their own in-house international electronic funds transfer systems and by a preference for use of domestic electronic funds transfer systems, like the Foreign Yen Settlement System (FEYSS), in the Japanese segments of international funds transfers.

2. *The Organization of This Chapter*

Because mail transfers, banker's drafts and other types of debit transfers are seldom used to initiate international funds transfers in Japan, this chapter focuses upon the practical execution and legal framework of electronic international credit transfers, including in-house electronic funds transfers, SWIFT transfers and telegraphic transfers. Part II surveys the Japanese domestic electronic funds transfer systems. In conjunction with a SWIFT transfer, a telegraphic transfer or an in-house transfer incoming international credit transfers are often transmitted by these systems, and, although less frequently, so are outgoing international fund transfers. Through surveying these systems we can realize how international funds transfers are executed in Japan. Part III examines the principal Japanese legislation, regulations, contract provisions and case law applicable to international credit transfers. Finally, Part IV discusses the major legal issues in Japan concerning international credit transfers.

II. Japanese Electronic Funds Transfer Systems

1. *The FEYSS*

The Foreign Yen Settlement System (FEYSS), also known as the Gaitame Yen Settlement System, is used domestically for yen-denominated wire payments from abroad[10]. The FEYSS, which is managed by the Tokyo Bankers Association (TBA), provides same-day settlement for, inter alia, transfers to a correspondent bank's yen account; yen-denominated remittan-

---

[9] The Federation of Bankers Association of Japan (FBAJ) & Tokyo Bankers Association (TBA), Annual Report 1990 on Clearing Houses (1991), p. 60.

[10] This part of the article greatly relies upon Bank for International Settlements (BIS), Large-Value Funds Transfer Systems in the Group of Ten Countries (1990), pp. 65 et seq. and The Federation of Bankers Association of Japan (FBAJ), Payment Systems in Japan, 1990. For an overview of the FEYSS see also T. Mimuro, "Gaikokukawase Yen Kessai Seido no Sôsetsu to Sono Toriatsukai (The Establishment and Organization of the FEYSS)", 404 Kinyû (Finance) 62 (1980).

ces; yen payments for export/import transactions; and yen transfers involving either the foreign exchange market or securities foreign exchange[11]. The FEYSS is an embryonic system that corresponds to CHIPS in the United States and CHAPS in the United Kingdom. In 1990, 6,270,417 credit transactions with a total value of 7,257,783 billion yen (about 54 trillion US dollars) were carried out through the FEYSS[12].

When the FEYSS was launched in 1980 paper-based funds transfer instructions were brought to the Tokyo Clearing House for exchange and the net balance calculated in the system was settled through current-account funds transfers in Bank of Japan accounts. In 1989 the FEYSS was merged with the Bank of Japan Financial Network System (BOJ-NET), which is owned and operated by the Bank of Japan. Since then, the FEYSS is one of the services offered through BOJ-NET. BOJ-NET ist a completely electronic on-line processing transfer system used mainly for interbank transactions, which provides same-day settlement.

Members of the FEYSS are those financial institutions with current accounts at the Bank of Japan that can be used to conduct current account transactions through BOJ-NET and are authorized foreign exchange banks under the Foreign Exchange and Foreign Trade Control Law[13]. Branches of foreign banks also can be members. There are a total of 162 members of the FEYSS, 64 of which are branches of foreign banks, with transactions by foreign bank branches constituting about 30% of all FEYSS transactions.

A FEYSS transfer can be initiated by either a domestic or an overseas originator. Suppose that ABC Shipping Company in New York (the originator) wishes to pay 1 billion yen to XYZ Ship Building Company in Tokyo (the beneficiary). ABC Company orders the head office of Citibank in New York (Citibank, New York: the originator's bank) to transfer 1 billion yen to XYZ Company's account with the head office of Fuji Bank (the beneficiary's bank). On May 1 1991, Citibank, New York debits ABC Company's account for approximately 72 million dollars at the rate of 138.00 yen to the dollar. Citibank, New York then instructs the Tokyo branch of Citibank (Citibank, Tokyo) to transfer 1 billion yen to XYZ Company's account with the head office of Fuji Bank through SWIFT or a telex. Citibank Tokyo executes the payment order through the FEYSS. After the merger of FEYSS with BOJ-

---

[11] Article 8 of Enforcement Bylaws of the Regulations for Foreign Exchange Yen Settlement System (hereinafter as the FEYSS Bylaws).

[12] FBAJ & TAB, supra, note 9 at 58.

[13] Foreign Yen Settlement System Regulations, Article 3 (cited as the FEYSS Regulations); FBAJ & TBA, supra, note 9 at 58; The Bank of Japan (BOJ) Banking Bureau, "Nichigin Net no Kinô to Yakuwari — Wagakuni Kessai System no Infrastructure — (The Function and Role of BOJ-NET — The Infrastructure of Japanese Payment Systems —)", Nichigin Geppo (The Bank of Japan Monthly Bulletin) [Feb., 1991] 23, 35.

NET as follows: Citibank Tokyo sends a payment order from its BOJ-NET terminal to the Bank of Japan's computer. The Bank of Japan forwards the payment order to the head office of Fuji Bank, which subsequently credits 1 billion yen to XYZ Company's account and sends a credit advice to XYZ Company. The Bank of Japan calculates the net settlement position of all system members at approximately 2 p.m. and then settles the balances through debit and credit entries to the members' Bank of Japan current accounts at approximately 3 p.m. upon the same business day. Transfers are final upon settlement.

2. BOJ-NET

BOJ-NET is a completely computerized nationwide payment system owned and operated by the Bank of Japan. BOJ-NET links the head office and branches of the Bank of Japan as well as banks, securities firms and call-loan brokers that have current accounts with the Bank of Japan. The 448 participants include 80 branches of foreign banks[14].

Participating institutions can access the host computer at the Bank of Japan's head office from the exclusive BOJ-NET terminals that have been installed in their offices, and request on-line funds transfers, FEYSS transfers and various securities transfers. BOJ-NET processes in real time funds transfers between offices of the Bank of Japan, interbank funds transfers, funds transfers resulting from clearing conducted by private payment systems — the FEYSS, the Zengin System and the bill and check clearing systems —, as well as the FEYSS transfers and various securities.

BOJ-NET can be used not only for fund transfers between participants but also for third-party transfers between customers of the participants. BOJ-NET third party transfers, which are different from the FEYSS transfers effected through BOJ-NET, for example, can be used for the funds transfers between ABC Company and XYZ Company in the previously discussed hypothetical case. However, BOJ-NET third party transfers are usually used for domestic wholesale third-party transfers; retail funds transfers are usually executed through the Zengin System which is another computerized clearing system managed by TBA for retail transactions. There also are some restrictions upon BOJ-NET third-party transfers involving securities firms and other non-bank participants. Because non-banks are not allowed either to take deposits or to engage in the funds transfer business by the Banking Act of 1981, a non-bank participant cannot be an originator's bank nor a beneficiary's bank[15].

---

[14] BOJ, supra, note 13 at 35. For an overview of BOJ-NET see BIS, supra, note 10 at 65 et seq.; FBAJ, supra, note 10 at 15 et seq.; Geva, supra, note 6 at 143; BOJ, supra, note 13 at 33 et seq.

The total value of Bank of Japan current account transactions in 1990 was 73,740,032 billion yen (about 543 trillion US dollars). Most of the amount was carried out through BOJ-NET[16].

Transfers are settled individually through participants' current accounts with the Bank of Japan in real time or at times designated by the participants. Daylight overdrafts are not permitted so that no credit risk is involved.

3. The Zengin System

The Zengin System is a totally electronic funds transfer system that is owned and operated by the TBA and is used mainly for retail credit debt funds transfers[17].

Depositary institutions, including branches of foreign banks with current accounts with the Bank of Japan directly participate in the Zengin System. Small financial institutions and various co-operatives that engage in banking indirectly participate through their agency institutions. If indirect participants are included, with the exception of post offices, almost all depositary institutions in Japan participate in the Zengin System. Non-depositary institutions, like securities firms and insurance companies on the other hand, cannot participate. In 1990, 44,281 offices of 4,737 institutions were participating, and the Zengin System carried out 626,682,000 with a total value of 1,889,821 billion yen (about 13.9 trillion US dollars)[18].

A participating institution accesses the Zengin Center host computer through its Zengin Terminal. The Zengin Center host computer and Zengin Terminals are linked by an on-line network. The Zengin System and the Bank of Japan likewise are linked by an on-line network.

An incoming international credit transfer is processed by the Zengin System as follows. A Japanese bank, which is a correspondent of a foreign originator's bank, transmits a payment order received from the originator's bank to the Japanese beneficiary's bank through the Zengin System. The beneficiary's bank credits the amount of the payment order to the beneficiary's account upon receipt. At the end of the day, the Zengin System

[15] Article 1 of the Bank of Japan Rules on Third Party Fund Transfers.

[16] The Bank of Japan Monthly Bulletin [July 1991] 99; BOJ, supra, note 13 at 36.

[17] For an overview of the Zengin System see S. Matsumoto, "The Zengin System", in: Kinyû Torihikihô Taikei (The System of Financial Transactions Law), vol. 3 (R. Suzuki & A. Takeuchi (ed), 1983), pp. 21 et seq.; BIS, supra, note 10 at 69 et seq.; FBAJ, supra, note 10 at 10 et seq..

[18] Naikokukawase Uneikikô (The Domestic Fund Transfer Management Institute: DFTMI), TBA & Zenkoku Ginkô Data Tsûshin Center (The National Bank Data Telecommunication Center; NBDTC), Zengin Shisutem Unyôjôkyô Hôkôku (Report on Activities of Zengin System) (4 March 1991), p. 4.

calculates each participant's net settlement position. Upon the following business day, the Zengin System sends a settlement summary to the Bank of Japan, which settles each participant's clearing balances through its current account with the Bank of Japan.

4. The Tokyo Dollar Clearing System

The Tokyo Dollar Clearing System settles US dollar transactions, including US dollar-denominated international credit transfers, upon a bilateral basis by transferring funds between participants' accounts with the Chase Manhattan Bank, Tokyo Branch (Chase Tokyo). In his article "Problems of Risk in International Electronic Fund Transfer Systems", Mr. Haruyuki Toyama presents the following hypothetical case[19]:

Suppose that on 1 June 1991, the head office of Fuji Bank buys 5 million dollars from the head office of Mitsubishi Bank at the rate of 138.00 yen to the dollar. On 3 June 1991, Mitsubishi Bank electronically instructs Chase Tokyo, through either SWIFT or a telex, to transfer $ 5 million to Fuji Bank, and Chase Tokyo debits Mitsubishi Bank's account and credits Fuji Bank's account as instructed. After 3 : 00 p. m. on 3 June, Chase Tokyo calculates a net debit or credit position of the account of each participant in the Tokyo Dollar Clearing System. Chase Tokyo then electronically transfers these positions, typically by SWIFT or telex, to its sub-account in the head office of Chase Manhatten Bank in New York, reducing all participants' balances with Chase Tokyo to zero. If Fuji Bank receives 25 million dollars more than it sends, Chase Tokyo transfers the 25 million dollars net credit to the account of Fuji Bank's New York Branch with the Federal Reserve Bank of New York. If Mitsubishi Bank has a 40 million dollar net debit position, Mitsubishi Bank, Tokyo instructs the New York Branch of Mitsubishi Bank to transfer 40 million dollars through CHIPS to Chase New York's account with the Federal Reserve Bank of New York for the account of Chase Tokyo.

III. The Japanese Law Applicable to International Credit Transfers

1. Existing Law

Although Japan adheres to the Giro Agreement of the Universal Postal Union, there is no specific Japanese statute dealing with either domestic or international credit (giro) transfers. The legal rights arising from international credit transfers are determined by private contracts, case law, and

[19] H. Toyama, "Problems of Risk in International Electronic Fund Transfer Systems, 2 Financial Services Yearbook (29, 138-139 (1989)).

general provisions of the Japanese Civil Code, Commercial Code, and Ordinance of Conflict of Laws.

Japanese banks usually do not enter into written contracts containing detailed standard terms of dealing with their foreign correspondent banks. The precise nature of any agreement that has been made, whether a governing law has been chosen, and, if so, which country's law governs the correspondent relationship, frequently is uncertain.

With respect to international funds transfers that are carried out through SWIFT, SWIFT by-laws provide that Belgian law governs SWIFT and its members[20]. It can be implied, therefore, that Belgian law applies between member banks. Except to the extent that Belgian law is contrary to the public order of Japan, Articles 8 and 33 of the Ordinance of Laws, recognize the validity of this choice-of-law.

With respect to both international and domestic credit transfers, an originator's relationship with an originator's bank and a beneficiary's relationship with a beneficiary's bank ordinarily are subject to the very simple standard bank terms of dealing (Geschäftsbedingungen) that appear upon the application form for an international remittance, which do not include a choice-of-law provision.

The legal framework for international funds transfers is provided primarily by the rules and agreements governing paticipants in the electronic funds transfer systems that are utilized in a transfer. The legal framework for the FEYSS, for example, is provided by two private contracts. One contract, "The Regulations", is between TBA and FEYSS members. The second contract is between the TBA and the Bank of Japan. The legal framework for BOJ-NET similarly is provided by a private contract, the "Rules", which is entered into by the participants and the Bank of Japan. Finally, the legal framework for the Zengin System is provided by the TBA rules, which constitute a contract between the TBA and its members, and by Bank of Japan Regulations, which constitute a contract between the Bank of Japan and TBA members. None of these contracts apply to customers of TBA members.

There are presently two Japanese court decisions involving international credit transfers[21] and approximately twenty Japanese court decisions involving domestic credit transfers. In order to clarify Japanese law, the Electronic Banking Committee of the Financial System Research Council of the

---

[20] S.W.I.F.T. General Terms and Conditions, Clause 10, paragraph 1.

[21] Unidentified Plaintiff v. Sanwa Bank, 794 Kinyûhômuji jô 30 (Tokyo District Court, 26 Jan. 1976); Sato v. Joyo Bank, 698 Kinyû Shôji Hanrei 16 (Tokyo High Court, 14 Feb. 1984).

Ministry of Finance is drafting a bill on Electronic Fund Transfers[22]. Upon enactment by the Diet, the new law will govern most international credit transfers in Japan.

2. Conflict of Laws Problems

As previously observed, no specific Japanese statute or standard contract provision displaces general principles of conflict of laws with respect to international credit transfers. However, there have been no court decisions or concrete discussions by commentators concerning application of these general principles in specific situations. For example, there has been no discussion concerning either an implied contract with respect to choice of law or the locus of an international credit transfer. Moreover, some commentators argue that it is inappropriate to apply different laws to discrete segments of a single international credit transfer. General principles notwithstanding, these commentators assert that the law of a single jurisdiction should be applied to a transfer[23].

IV. Legal Issues concerning International Credit Transfers

1. The Legal Characterization of Credit Transfers

There have been so many discussions and several court decisions concerning the legal characterization of credit transfers under Japanese law. Influenced by previous German case law[24], most commentators[25] and a judicial decision[26] have taken the position that a credit transfer is a contract for the

---

[22] The Electronic Banking Committee, established in January, 1987, published an interim report in 9 June 1988 (Report on Electronic Fund Transfers — Interim Report by the Electronic Banking Committee of the Financial System Research Council); the subcommittee, Electronic Fund Transfer Act Drafting Committee, is drafting a bill on Electronic Fund Transfers which is expected to be completed in 1992.

[23] T. Sawaki, K. Ishiguro & Foreign Control Department of Mitsui Bank Kokusai Kinyû Torihiki (International Financial Transactions), vol. 2 (1986), pp. 190-194, 237-241; K. Ishiguro, Kinyû Torihiki to Kokusaisoshô (Financial Transactions and International Litigation) (1983), pp. 117 et seq., 159 et seq.

[24] RGZ 102, 65; 105, 398; 141, 287; BGH, NJW 1951, 437.

[25] J. Matsumoto, Shôkôihô (Commercial Transactions Law: Das Handelsgeschäftsrecht) (1929), p. 345; S. Wagatsuma, Saiken Kakuron Jôkan (Die Einzelheiten des Obligationsrechts, der erste Band) (1954), p. 119; E. Hoshino, Minpô Gairon (Introduction to Civil Law: Die Einleitung in das Zivilrecht) (1975), p. 65; T. Maeda, "Furikomi (Credit Transfers)", in: Ginkô Torihikihô Kôza Jôkan (Bank Transactions Law Course I: Der Kurs des Bankgeschäftsrechts, der erste Band) (ed. by I. Kato, R. Hayashi & I. Kawamoto, 1976), p. 313.

[26] Unidentified Plaintiff v. Kyôwa Bank, 660 Kinyûhômujijô 24 (Tokyo District Court, 7 April 1972).

benefit of a third person (Vertrag zugunsten Dritter), and a beneficiary acquires direct rights against a beneficiary's bank based upon either the contract between an originator and an originator's bank or the contract between an originator's bank, acting as an agent of the originator, and a beneficiary's bank.

Influenced by recent German case law and German commentators[27], recent Japanese court decisions and a majority of current commentators[28], on the other hand, take the position that a credit transfer is a mandate (entgeltlicher Auftrag) and not "a contract for the benefit of a third party (Vertrag zugunsten Dritter)". Under this view, a beneficiary's rights are based upon his contract with a beneficiary's bank which requires the bank to credit the amount of a payment order to the beneficiary's account after the bank has received cover (settlement).

2. *Obligations of Sender*

a) Unauthorized Transfers

Under the Japanese Civil Code a purported sender is bound by a payment order issued by either him or his agent (including agency by estoppel or ostensible agency: Scheinvollmacht)[29]. In international credit transfers by individual originators, however, unauthorized payment orders rarely occur in Japan. An individual originator usually goes to his bank in person and pays for a payment order in full without using an electronic transfer system. The terms and conditions on a Japanese bank's application for remittance, which govern the relationship between an originator and an originator's bank, usually do not even mention unauthorized payment orders. On the other hand, unauthorized payment orders, are more common in interbank international funds transfers, and electronic funds transfer system rules dealing with interbank relationships frequently address liability for unauthorized payment orders.

If an unauthorized payment order contains the correct Bank of Japan identification number for the purported sender, the BOJ-NET rules provide that the order is deemed to have been issued by the purported sender, and

---

[27] BGH, NJW 1969, 320; H. Schönle, Bank und Börsenrecht (1971), § 31 I 1; F. Schlegelberger & W. Hefermehl, Handelsgesetzbuch (5. Aufl. 1976), Anh. zu § 365, Anm. 13; C. W. Canaris, Bankvertragsrecht (3. Aufl. 1988), Rdn. 315.

[28] Unidentified Plaintiff v. Kyôwa Bank, 773 Kinyûhômujijo 32 (Tokyo High Court, 8 Oct. 1975); Moroe Seisakusho Corp. v. Mitsui bank, 1097 Hanreijihô 62 (Tokyo District Court, 18 April 1983); K. Nishihara, Kinyûhô (Law of Finance) (1968), p. 217; S. Tanaka, Ginkô Torihikihô (Bank Transactions Law) (rev. ed. 1979), p. 216; K. Gotô, Furikomi, Furikae no Hôri to Shiharai Torihiki (Legal Principles on Credit and Debit Transfers, and Payment Transactions) (1986), p. 27.

[29] Japanese Civil Code, Article 99-116.

that the Bank of Japan is not responsible for any loss or damage caused by the execution of the unauthorized order[30]. Unless a prejudiced party proves that SWIFT could not reasonably have assumed an order to be valid, the SWIFT General Terms and Conditions similarly provide that SWIFT is not responsible for any loss or damage caused by the execution of an unauthorized order[31]. The SWIFT rules also make member banks responsible both for the authentication of messages on their terminals and for the security of the transmission lines between their terminals and a Regional Processor[32]. A member bank that breaches these duties bears the loss from resulting unauthorized transfers. If an unauthorized transfer was due to other causes, Belgian law determines whether a sending bank or a receiving bank is liable. The Zengin System rules, on the other hand, do not deal with unauthorized payment orders.

If a payment order was subject to authentication and the authentication both provided and complied with by the receiving bank was a reasonable method of detecting unauthorized payment orders, many Japanese commentators contend that the purported sender should be bound by the payment order, whether or not it was in fact authorized[33]. Civil Code Article 478, which states that a good faith payment to an apparent creditor discharges a debtor's obligation, and comparable standard terms of dealing utilized by the Japanese ANSER System, which provides business and home banking services, are cited in support of this position[34]. The common view that Article 478 of the Civil Code applies to payments of forged or altered checks, notes or bills by a payor bank[35] provides additional support.

---

[30] BOJ-NET, Basic Rules, Article 4, Pargraph 2.

[31] S.W.I.F.T. General Terms and Conditions, Clause 7.

[32] SWIFT II Policy Part V 21. 5. 2, 22. 1. 2.

[33] R. Hayashi, "CD Torihiki (Automated Teller Machine Transactions)", in: Ginkô Torihikihô Kôza Jôkan, supra, note 25 at 293; N. Sawano, "Electronic Banking to Hôteki Shomondai (Electronic Banking and Legal Problems)", in: Ohtori Tsuneo Sensei Kanreki Kinen, Hachijû Nendai Shôjihô no Shosô (Festschrift forTsuneoOhtori's60th Birthday, Aspects of Commercial Law in the 1980's) (ed. by K. Egashira, 1985), pp. 745, 767; S. Matsumoto, "Furikomiki tô Kikai Niyoru Furikomi to Furikomikitei (Credit Transfers through Automated Clearing Machines and Proposed Standard Terms of Credit Transfers)", 1153 Kinyûhômujijo 32, 36-37 (1987); N. Sawano, "Mukengen Shikinidô to Sonshitsu Futan (Unauthorized Funds Transfers and Loss Allocation)", in: Takeuchi Akio Sensei Kanreki Kinen, Gendai Kigyôhô no Tenkai (Festschrift für Akio Takeuchi's 60th Birthday, Developments in Modern Business Law) (ed. by S. Iwahara, 1990), pp. 353, 383.

[34] Matsumoto, supra, note 33 at 36-37.

[35] K. Tanaka, Tegatahô Kogittehô gairon (Introduction to Bills and Notes Act and Check Act: Die Einleitung in das Wechselgesetz und Scheckgesetz) (1935), p. 445; M. Yazawa, Jishû Shôhô 30 Mon (30 Questions for Independent Study of Commercial Law (1963), p. 176; T. Suzuki (ed.), Futsu Yokin, Teiki Yokin (Ordinary Deposits and Time Deposits) (1963), pp. 44 et seq. (I. Kato, M. Horiuchi, T. Suzuki and A. Takeuchi).

Historical and comparative studies of Article 478, however, have resulted in strong criticism of this position[36], which, from a consumer protection view point, can impose liability upon a party less able to bear a loss. A government committee and some commentators contend that even if a reasonable authentication procedure is provided and complied with by the receiving bank, a purported sender of a credit transfer or a purported drawer/maker of a check, note or bill should not bear the loss of unauthorized transfers or forged or altered checks, notes or bills if there was no fault on the part of the purported sender or drawer/maker[37]. Imposing liability for unauthorized

---

Many Court decisions have ruled that a purported drawer of a forged or altered check, note or bill should bear, in accordance with commercial custom, the loss caused by the forgery or alteration (Taishô Bank v. Tôkai Bank, 880 Hôritsushinbun 23 (Tokyo District Court, 4 July 1913): Taishô Bank U. Tôkai Bank. 1042 Horitsushinbun 28 (Tokyo Appeal Court, 22 June 1915): Nippon Shikifu Corp. v. 77 Bank, 2654 Hôritsushinbun 11 (Tokyo Appeal Court, 12 Nov. 1926); Hayashi v. Bank of America, 8/7 Kôsai Minshu 479 (Tokyo High Court, 20 Sep. 1955); Unidentified Plaintiff v. Tokyo Bank, 547 Kinyûhômujijô 26 (Yokohama District Court, 4 March 1969: New Baratt Trading Co., Ltd. v. Tokyo Bank, 577 Hanreijihô 93 (Tokyo High Court, 28. Nov. 1969)). Some commentators take the same position (S. Komachiya, Hanrei Shôhô (Case Decisions on Commercial Law) II (1953), p. 95; H. Maeda, Tegata Koggitte Hô Nyûmon (Introduction to Bills, Notes and Checks Law: Die Einleitung des Wechsel- und Scheckrechts) (1983), p. 421). Some case decisions have ruled that a payor bank is not liable for payments of forged or altered checks, notes or bills under the payor bank's standard terms of dealing (Meiji Bank v. Ohkura Mining Corp., 3947 Hôritsushinbun 11 (Tokyo District Court, 30 Nov. 1935); Miura v. Shinwa Bank, 9/3 Kaminshû 542 (Fukuoka High Court, 29 March 1958)). But a few case decisions ruled that a payor bank was liable for payments of forged checks (Kanayama v. Tokyo Bank, 79 Horitsushinbun 6 (Tokyo District Court, 25 Feb. 1892); Maeda v. The 100th Bank, 1022 Horitsushinbun 14 (Tokyo District Court, Unidentified Ruling Day)), and many case decisions, including Supreme Court decisions, held that a payor bank was liable for payment of forged checks, bills or notes because of fault on the Part of the payor bank (Fujibayashi v. Fuji Bank, 25/4 Minshu 492 (Supreme Court, 10 June 1971); Umeda Denki Corp. v. Kyowa Bank, 37/3 Minshu 219 (Supreme Court, 7 April 1983 etc.).

[36] These studies made it clear that the model of Article 478 was Article 1240 of the French Civil Code, which is only applicable to a dispute about the identity of a proper creditor (S. Kurusu, "Saiken no Junsenyû to Menseki Shôken (Der Scheingläubiger und das Legitimationspapier)", 33/4 Minshôhô Zassi 477, 482 (1956); T. Niizeki, "France Minpô Niokeru Saiken Senyû (Apparent Creditors under the French Civil Code", 41 Nagoya University Hô Sei Ronshû 84 (1967). Therefore, Article 478 should not be applied to forged or altered checks, bills, notes or payment orders (K. Uchiike, "Saiken no Junsenyû to Uketori Shôshô (Apparent Creditors and Receipts)", 34/1 Hogaku Kenkyu 49 (1961); E. Hoshino, Minpô Gairon (Introduction to Civil Law) III (1978), p. 246).

[37] Kokumin Seikatsu Shingikai Shôhisha Seisaku Bukai (The Consumer Policy Committee of the National Life Council), Shôhisha Torihiki ni Mochiirareru Yakkan no Tekiseika Nitsuite (Report on the Standard Contract Terms in Consumer Transactions) (1984) — II2 (1); S. Maeda, "Shôhisha Hogo no Kanten Karamita Electronic Banking Nitaisuru Hôkiseijôno Mondai (Problems of Electronic Banking Laws from the Consumer Protection View Point)", in: Kôdo Jôhô Shakai no Hôritsu Mondai (Legal Problems in Technologically Informed Society) (1984), pp. 236, 241; S. Iwahara, "Shikin Idô Torihiki no Kashi to Kinyûkikan (Unauthorized or Voidable Funds Transfers and Financial Institutions)", in: Kokka to Shimin (State and Citizens), vol. 3 (1987), pp. 167,

payment orders upon originator's banks, moreover, would stimulate those banks to provide improved authentication procedures and methods for detecting forged or altered checks, notes or bills. It is also argued that a limitation on losses incurred by a purported sender who is a consumer should be introduced as suggested by the 50 dollars rule under Article 909 of the Federal Electronic Fund Transfer Act of the United States[38]. The new legislation on electronic funds transfers now being drafted at the Ministry of Finance may reflect the newer opinion upon this issue.

3. Disability, Duress and Mistake (Geschäftsunfähigkeit, Beschränkte Geschäftsfähigkeit, Drohung und Irrtum)

There has been a dispute in Japan as to whether a sender can avoid his obligation to pay a receiving bank for a payment order by asserting the defenses of disability, duress or mistake (Geschäftsunfähigkeit, Beschränkte

---

222-231; T. Yamashita, "Ginkô Torihiki to Menseki Yakkan no Kôryoku (Bank Transactions and the Validity of Liability Exemption Provisions in Standard Contracts)", in: Kinyûhô no Kadai to Tenbô (Problems and Perspectives of Finance Law), pp. 189, 194-202.

The latter article further argues that, even if the bank standard terms of dealing exempt a bank from liability for executing an unauthorized payment order or paying on a forged or altered check, bill or note, unless a purported sender or drawer/maker was at fault, he should not be liable (Yamashita, supra, at 200-202).

[38] The UCC Article 4A and the UNCITRAL Draft Model Law on International Credit Transfers take a similar position but allow related parties to contract out bank liability for executing unauthorized payment orders (UCC §§ 4A-202, 203, 501; UNCITRAL-Modellgesetz, Articles 4 and 5. But see the next footnote). For an overview of this problem in Germany the United Kingdom and the United States, see C. W. Canaris, Vertrauenshaftung im deutschen Privatrecht (1971), S. 468 f.; I. Koller, Die Verteilung des Scheckfälschungsrisikos zwischen Kunde und Bank, NJW 1981, 2433, 2435; A. Baumbach & W. Hefermehl, Wechselgesetz und Scheckgesetz (16. Aufl. 1988), Art. 3 SchG, Rdn. 7, 8; Schönle, supra, note 27, § 32 II 4; Schlegelberger & Hefermehl, supra, note 27, Anh. zu § 365, Anm. 39; Canaris, supra, note 27, Rdn. 710, 368-371, D. Joost, Die Verteilung von Scheckfälschungen, ZHR 153 (1989), S. 238 ff.; U. Blaurock, Haftung der Banken beim Einsatz neuer Techniken im Zahlungsverkehr, CR 1989, S. 567 ff.; R. Pennington, "Fraud, Error and System Malfunction, A Lawyer's Viewpoint", in: Electronic Banking. The legal implications (ed. by R. M. Goode, 1985), pp. 67, 70-72; S. B. Dow & N. S. Ellis, The Proposed Uniform New Payment Code: Allocation of Losses Resulting from Forged Drawer's Signatures, 22 Harv. J. on Leg 399, 409 et seq. (1985); Gaffney v. Com. Fed. Sav. & Loan Ass's, 706 S. W. 2nd 530 (Mo. App. 1986): Bradford Trust Co., v. Tex. American Bank — Houston, 790 F. 2nd 407 (5th Cir. 1986).

Many countries, for example, Australia, Denmark and New Zealand, have adopted rules similar to the 50 dollars rule (15 U.S.C., § 1693 g; 12 C.F.R., § 205.6). The United Kingdom plans to adopt a similar rule called 50 pounds rule. See Banking Services: Law and Practice Report by the Review Committee (Chairman: Professor R. B. Jack CBE), Cm 622 (1989), pp. 89-94; Banking Services Law and Practice: The Government's Response, Cm 1026 (1990), pp. 5, 20.

Geschäftsfähigkeit, Drohung und Irrtum) etc.[39]. Electronic funds transfer system rules and bank standard form contracts do not deal with this. Although three judicial decisions indirectly relate to the issue[40], no decision deals directly with it.

According to one argument, at least the availability of the defenses of duress or mistake should be limited to situation in which a receiving bank was grossly negligent in executing an unauthorized payment order. This restriction upon the defenses would be comparable to Bills and Note Act Article 40, Paragraph 3, which is equivalent to Geneva Convention of Bills and Notes Article 40, Paragraph 2[41].

---

[39] A majority of commentators contend that the Civil Code provisions and general principles on disability, duress or mistake etc. (Geschäftsunfähigkeit, beschränkte Geschäftsfähigkeit, Drohung und Irrtum) are applicable to electronic funds transfer payment orders and that a sender can assert these defenses (Maeda, supra, note 25 at 320; Isomura, supra, note 38 at 85-100; I. Makiyama, Comments on Kagoshima District Court Decision on 27 Nov. 1989, 1267 Kinyûhômujijô 14 (1990)). It is also asserted that these provisions and general principles are mandatory and can not be contracted out of (Isomura, supra, note 38), at 87-90).

On the other hand, Professor Gotô insists that a sender should not be allowed to assert these defenses because a payment order is merely an abstract contract between a sender and a receiving bank and is independent of underlying relationships between a sender (originator) and a beneficiary. Professor Gotô insists further that a sender is sufficiently protected by and should be limited to defenses arising from the underlying relationship with a beneficiary. Professor Gotô opines that if a sender is allowed to assert defenses against a receiving bank based upon a payment order, the sender will be overly protected by the receiving bank's "deep pockets". Professor Gotô also argues that, if a disability defense is allowed, banks will not accept a payment order from an unknown sender or will increase funds transfer service fees (Gotô, supra, note 28 at 93, 97. See also S. Matsuoto, "Furkomi Torihiki Niokeru Shimuke Ginkô no Sekinin to Kumimodoshi no Toriatsukai (An Originator's Bank's Liability and Revocation in Credit Transfers) II", 1138 Kinyûhômujijô 1820 (1986)).

There might be an argument that legal relationships in an electronic funds transfer or a funds transfer generally are based on the German legal doctrine called "sozial-typisches Verhalten" (see K. Larenz, Allgemeiner Teil des deutschen Bürgerlichen Rechts, 6. Aufl. 1983, § 28 II), in which case a sender can not assert these defenses. However even admitting the doctrine, it is doubtful if a legal relationship in an electronic funds transfer or a funds transfer generally constitutes a "sozial-typisches Verhalten" (Iwahara, supra, note 37 at 235. See Canaris, supra, note 27 at Rdn. 377).

For an overview of "automatisierter oder vollelektronischer Willenserklärungen" and their legal principles see H. Köhler, "Die Problematik automatisierter Rechtsvorgänge, insbesondere von Willenserklärungen", AcP 182 (1982) 126, 132 et seq.; W. Möschel, "Dogmatische Strukturen des bargeldlosen Zahlungsverkehrs", AcP 186 (1986) 187, 192 et seq.

[40] Unidentified Plaintiff v. Fuji Bank, 795 Kinyûhômujijô 44 (Nagoya High Court, 28 Jan. 1957); Sharp Finance Corp. v. Kagoshima Bank, 718 Hanrei Times 124 (Kagoshima District Court, 18 April 1989); Benkan v. Genda, 862 Kinyû Shôji Hanrei 24 (Tokyo District Court, 25 Oct. 1990), See infra, note 82 and UCC, §§ 4A-207 and Official Comment to UCC, §§ 4A-211.

[41] Iwahara, supra, note 37 at 239-24. An originator's bank which executes an originator's payment order is in a similar position as a payor bank which pays for a check and

4. Revocation

Countries have differing views concerning the reversibility of a payment order[42]. The SWIFT rules seem to allow revocation until a receiving bank has acted upon a payment order. Thereafter, a beneficiary must agree to a sender's request for a reversal of a transfer[43].

Unless an error was made and the receiving bank consents, the FEYSS Regulations provide that a sending bank may not revoke a payment order after it has been transmitted[44]. The BOJ-NET rules also generally do not allow revocation of a payment order that has been received by the Bank of Japan[45]. However, if an originator's bank has designated the time for settlement, the BOJ-NET rules permit revocation of a payment order prior to the designated settlement time by means of a revocation order through BOJ-NET with respect to a two party credit transfer and by means of a "new payment order in the opposite direction" with respect to a third party transfer[46].

In contract to these BOJ-NET rules, which basically make a payment order irrevocable, the Zengin System rules provide that an originator can revoke a payment order until a beneficiary's bank has credited a beneficiary's account. Upon an originator's request for revocation, an originator's bank must send a "revoke request message" to a beneficiary's bank. If the

---

requires protection in executing the order because an originator's bank and a payor bank must both determine within a limited time period whether or not the order or check is voidable for duress or mistake. For an overview of arguments in Germany, see Schönle, supra, note 27, § 32 II 3a; Schlegelberger & Hefermehl, supra, note 27, Anh. zu § 365, Anm. 37; Canaris, supra, note 27 at Rdn. 377-379, and OLG Karlsruhe, JW 1938, 662.

Concerning the defense of disability, Japanese legislation needs a provision such as UCC, § 4A-211, Paragraph (g) or the UNCITRAL Draft Model Law, Article 11, Paragraph 8. See also BGHZ 52, 61, 63; BGH WM 1966, 973; Canaris, supra, note 27 at Rdn. 708, 2711 ff.; R. Schlenke, Allgemeine Geschäftsbedingungen der Banken und AGB-Gesetz (1984), S. 76 ff.

[42] See Loi no 85-695 du 11 juillet 1985; BGH WM 1988, 321; Canaris, supra, note 27 at Rdn. 354, 420 ff.; P. Ellinger, "Electronic Funds Transfer as a Deferred Settlement System", in: Goode ed., supra, note 37 at 37; Ellinger, supra, note 1 at 198; 12 C.F.R., § 210.35 (b); UCC, § 4A-211; Rules Governing the Computerized Clearing House Interbank Payments Systems, § 2 (1990); Delbrueck & Co. v. Manufactures Hanover Trust Company, 609 F. 2d 1047 (2d Cir. 1979), aff'g, 464 F. Supp. 989 (S.D.N.Y. 1979); The UNCITRAL Model Law, Article 12.

[43] Standards-1, Part VII, Chapter 92, in: S.W.I.F.T. User Handbook. See Etzkorn, supra, note 8 at 75.

[44] The FEYSS Regulations, Article 19.

[45] The Bank of Japan (BOJ), Rules on Current Accounts, Article 5, Pargraph 3.

[46] BOJ-NET Rules on Current Accounts, Article 3, Paragraph 2; BOJ-NET Rules on Third Party Transfers, Article 1 (3) and 6 and its Enforcement By-laws. See R. F. Dole, Jr., A Japanese Insight With Respect to the Finality of Wholesale Wire Transfers (31 Juli 1990), pp. 74 et seq. (unpublished).

beneficiary has not yet received credit, the beneficiary's bank must respond with an "acceptance and funds return" message[47]. After a beneficiary's bank has credited a beneficiary's account, a beneficiary, however, must consent for revocation of a payment order to be effective[48].

Although Japanese case law supports the well-established proposition that an originator can revoke a payment order in a domestic credit transfer until a beneficiary's bank has credited a beneficiary's account[49], it is not clear whether this also is true in an international credit transfer. The standard terms and conditions of an international remittance application form allow an originator to request that an originator's bank cancel a payment order, but do not indicate the extent to which an originator has a right to cancellation.

5. Obligations of a Receiving Bank

a) Creation of Receiving Bank Obligations

In Japan, a receiving bank's obligation to execute a payment order is based upon its contract with a sender. This contract can be either ad hoc, and limited to a single transaction, or a long-term contract governing the relationship between a sender and a receiving bank[50].

In an international credit transfer, an individual originator usually contracts in person and on an ad hoc basis with an originator's bank for execution of a payment order. Because an electronic transmission is not used, under Article 526 of the Civil Code an originator's bank incurs an obligation when it expresses acceptance of an originator's request. In interbank international credit transfers, on the other hand, a long-term contract usually stipulates when a receiving bank incurs an obligation to a sending bank. This long-term contract can be included in the rules of an electronic funds transfer system or in an agreement with a correspondent bank.

With respect to third-party transfers, the BOJ-NET rules establish a long-term contract among member banks, by deeming that a sending bank requests a receiving bank to credit the amount of a payment order to a beneficiary's account and that a receiving bank accepts a payment order

---

[47] DFTMI & TGBA (see notes 9 and 18), Rules on Domestic Funds Transfer Management, Part 2, Chapter 3, Subchapter 2, 1 (1) C, (2) D, 2 (1) B (B), C (B), Chapter 7 (hereinafter cited as the Zengin Rules); S. Matsumoto, Shokai Naikoku Kawase (Details of Domestic Fund Transfers) (rev. ed. 1988), pp. 130-134; do, supra, note 39 at 19.

[48] Matsumoto, supra, note 47 at 131; do, supra, note 39 at 19.

[49] The Bankruptcy Trustee of Fuji Shôji Corp. v. Sumitomo Bank, 998 Hanreihihô 87 (Osaka District Court, 30 September 1980).

[50] See Iwahara, supra, note 37 at 177, 180.

upon receipt[51]. A receiving bank's receipt of a payment order consequently obligates both the receiving bank to carry out the order and the sending bank to pay the receiving bank. When settlement is effected upon a real time basis through a sending bank's and a receiving bank's accounts with the Bank of Japan, a receiving bank has no settlement risk. The Zengin System has a similar rule[52].

Agreements between correspondent banks, on the other hand, usually do not state when a receiving bank incurs an obligation. In the absence of an express agreement between a sender and a receiving bank, under the general rule of Article 526 of the Civil Code, a receiving bank is obliged to execute a sender's payment order when it notifies the sender of acceptance of the order. However, under Commercial Code Article 509, if a sender is a merchant (Kaufmann), including a bank, with a continuing business relationship, with a receiving bank, for example, a correspondent bank, the receiving bank, must reject a payment order promptly after receipt in order to preclude a deemed acceptance of the order.

b) Nature of the Receiving Bank Obligations — "Network Liability"

The nature of a receiving bank's obligation also is determined by the agreement between a sender and a receiving bank. In domestic credit transfers there is no standard form bank contract (Geschäftsbedingungen) between an originator's bank and an originator[53], and there is a heated controversy concerning the nature of the implied agreement between them. The principal dispute is whether an originator's bank is responsible to an originator for the proper execution of a credit transer with "network liability"[54] for any loss caused by another participant in the transfer, including an intermediary bank, a beneficiary's bank, a telecommunications company, and a funds transfer system.

---

[51] BOJ-NET Rules on Third Party Fund Transfers, Article 6.

[52] The Zengin Rules, Part 2, Chapter 3, Subchapter 2, 1 (2) A, 2 (1) C (A).

[53] Some banking law practitioners proposed a draft bank standard contract on credit transfers ("Draft Bank Standard Contract on Credit Transfers", 1153 Kinyûhômujijô 6 et seq. (1987)). But it was not adopted by the banking community.

[54] "Network liability" was suggested by UNCITRAL Legal Guide on Electronic Fund Transfers (1987), pp. 124-125 (hereinafter cited as UNCITRAL Legal Guide).

The common law takes the same position as network liability that an originator's bank is vicariously liable for the negligence or default of its correspondent (Equitable Trust Co., of New York v. Dawson Partners Ltd., (1927) 27 Ll. L. Rep, 49; Ellinger, supra, note 1 at 200-202). However there is usually an exclusion of such liability in the underlying contractual document (Calico Printers' Association Ltd. v. Barclays Bank Ltd (1930), 36 Com Cas 71, aff'd, ibid., 197; Ellinger, supra, note 42, at 36).

See also infra, note 61.

Proponents of network liability contend that an originator ordinarily expects an originator's bank to be responsible for the proper execution of a credit transfer[55]. Because an originator deals only with an originator's bank, proponents also argue that an originator has a limited ability to identify why a funds transfer has not been carried out properly and to put pressure to settle losses upon third parties with whom the originator has no contractual relationship. On the other hand, an originator's bank, which usually chooses intermediary banks and means of interbank telecommunication, often deals directly with these third parties in arranging for the proper execution of a credit transfer. An originator's bank also is better able to identify the reasons why a credit transfer has not been executed properly and to put strong pressure upon a third party to compensate losses that it has caused. Further, it is easier for an originator's bank to cover the loss with insurance or self-insurance during the credit transfer process than for an originator to do so. Also, the network liability rule provides an incentive to an originator's bank to provide safer credit transfer services[56].

Theoretically it is contended that an originator's bank is an independent contractor who promises proper completion of a credit transfer to an originator and, in the absence of proper completion, is not entitled to cover from an originator (Werkvertrag)[57]. According to another theory, an intermediary bank, a beneficiary's bank, a telecommunication company, a funds transfer system and other third parties participate in a credit transfer as subagents (Erfüllungsgehilfen) of an originator's bank; which is liable for the losses that they cause[58].

---

[55] S. Iwahara, "Denshiteki Shikin Idô (Electronic Funds Transfers) (EFT): 385 NBL 14, 21 (1987).

[56] S. Iwahara, "Computer o Mochiita Kinyû Kessai to Hô (The Law of Computerized Financial Settlements)", 1 Kinyûhô Kenkyu 9, 26-31 (1985), see also UNCITRAL Legal Guide at 124; Yamashita, supra, note 37 at 203-208.

Reasons for advocating network liability may be stronger in international credit transfers than in domestic credit transfers, because a beneficiary bank, an intermediary bank or other third party participants to a credit transfer transaction are often located in foreign countries making it difficult for an originator in an international credit transfer to negotiate with the parties. See UNCITRAL Legal Guide at 124; S. Iwahara, "Denshi Shikin Torihiki Nikansuru Hôseiseibi no Hitsuyôsei to Kadai (The Need for and the Problems Associated with Enacting A New Electronic Fund Transfer Act) I, II", 1203 Kinyûhômujijô 6, 9 (1988), 1204 Kinyûhômujijô 17, 23 (1988).

For the above-cited reasons, a network liability rule should be mandatory. See Iwahara, supra, 1 Kinyûhô Kenkyu 29-30, Yamashita, supra, note 37 at 203-208.

[57] Iwahara, supra, note 56, 1204 Kinyûhômujijô 23. In Germany, old case decisions held that a Girocontract (Girovertrag) is a Werkvertrag (RGZ 107, 136, 139 etc.), Professor Canaris still understands that it is a mixture of Werkvertrag and Dienstvertrag (Canaris, supra, note 27 at Rdn. 315).

[58] S. Iwahara, supra, note 56, 1 Kinyû Kenkyu at 26-31. Professor Köndgen deems an intermediary bank as an Erfüllungsgehilfe (agent) of an originator's bank (J. Köndgen, "Bankenhaftung — Strukturen und Tendenzen —, Generalarbeit, in: Neue Entwicklungen

Even some commentators who otherwise support "network liability", acknowledge that an originator should bear losses caused by a beneficiary's bank or an intermediary bank that had been designated by the originator[59]. This view, typically immunizes an originator's bank from losses caused by a beneficiary's bank which ordinarily is selected an originator. There also is an argument that an originator's bank should be exempt from liability for consequential damages caused by all third parties[60].

The opponents of network liability maintain that an originator's bank's duty should be limited to sending a proper payment order to a proper receiving bank. These commentators reject an originator's bank's liability for losses caused by other parties[61]. For several reasons: First, vicarious liability is contrary to general principles of private law. Second, an originator who chooses a beneficiary's bank should be responsible for losses caused by the bank selected. Third, since a direct agency relationship between a beneficiary's bank and an originator can be implied under Article 105, Paragraph 2 of the Civil Code (see Sato v. Joyo Bank, infra), an originator is entitled to recover from a beneficiary's bank losses that the bank has caused.

In order to retain the confidence of bank customers, the banking community nevertheless acknowledges that an originator's bank should not be entirely absolved from responsibility for losses caused by third parties[62]. Under Article 654 of the Civil Code, notwithstanding fulfillment of its obligations under its "Inin-contract (entgeltlicher Auftrag)", which creates an agency relationship between an originator and an originator's bank, an originator's bank must assist an originator to recover damages. An agent or its successors that has fulfilled its own contractual obligation, also must deal with urgent matters until a principal or its successors are able to do so[63].

A Zengin System rule dealing with liability for errors in credit transfers states that: "Member banks share joint responsibility for losses incurred as a result of failures due to the interruption of the Zengin System or manage-

---

im Bankhaftungsrecht (J. Köndgen (ed.), 1986), S. 133, 146 ff.). However, German case law and a majority of commentators do not agree. See infra, note 61.

[59] Iwahara, supra, note 55 at 21; Interum Report by the Electronic Banking Committee, supra, note 22 at 76. See alo UCC, § 4A-402 (e).

[60] Iwahara, supra, note 56, 1204 Kinyûhômujijô 23.

[61] Sawano, supra, note 33, in: Festschrift for Ohtori at 762; Gotô, supra, note 28 at 39, 52-54. They are influenced by German case law and a majority of comentators who oppose network liability. See RGZ 105, 48, 51; Canaris, supra, note 27 at Rdn. 391; U. Hüffer, "Die Haftung gegenüber dem ersten Auftraggeber im mehrgliedrigen Zahlungsverkehr", ZHR 151 (1987), 118 et seq.; U. Schneider, "Das UNCITRAL-Modellgesetz über den internationalen Überweisungsverkehr, WM 1989, S. 285 ff.

[62] M. Hayashibe, "Songai no Futan tô (Loss Allocation etc.)", 1153 Kinyûhômujijô 26, 29 (1987).

[63] Id.

ment error"[64]. This implies that an originator's bank has primary responsibility to an originator for failures caused by the Zengin System and that the Zengin System should compensate the originator's bank[65]. The terms and conditions of a typical international remittance application form, on the other hand, provide that an originator's bank is not liable for any loss or damage arising either from the acts or omissions of another bank or from delayed delivery, non-delivery, etc., that is attributable to faulty telecommunications.

Sato v. Joyo Bank alone of the three Japanese judicial decisions dealing with an originator's bank's liability for losses caused by other participants in a credit transfer, involves an international credit transfer[66]. In the Sato case, an originator (the plaintiff) had instructed an originator's bank (the defendant) to credit a beneficiary's account at Banker's Trust Company and to notify the beneficiary, who was a U.S. citizen, that the credit could be withdrawn. Banker's Trust Company, however, failed to notify the beneficiary and the originator incurred a loss that included consequential damages.

The other two cases deal with domestic credit transfers, and take different positions. In Imasa Corp., Tokiwa Mutual Bank, an originator (the plaintiff) had instructed an originator's bank to credit a beneficiary's account with an agricultural society with the assistance of two intermediary financial institutions, both of which had been designated by the originator[67]. Because of an error by one of the designated intermediary institutions, the wrong account was credited. Because the originator had selected the intermediary financial institutions as well as the beneficiary's financial institution, the Tokyo High Court ruled that the originator's bank's duty was limited to transmitting the payment order to the designated intermediary financial institution and providing cover. The originator's damage claim against the originator's bank was rejected.

In Yamaguchi v. Fukuoka Bank, an originator (the plaintiff) had instructed an originator's bank (the defendant) to credit the beneficiary's account at the beneficiary's bank. The beneficiary's bank, however, mistakenly had credited the wrong account. The credit had been withdrawn from the account by the wrong person, and the originator had incurred a loss. The Takamatsu High Court allowed the originator's damage claim against the

---

[64] The Zengin Rules, Part 1, Chapter 1, 12.

[65] Hôritsu Mondai Kenkuyûkai Hôkokusho — EFT Torihikini Okeru Hôritsu Mondai no Meikakuka — (Report of the Study Group on Legal Issues — Examination of Legal Issues in EFT Transactions) (1986), p. 39.

[66] Sato v. Joyo Bank, 698 Shûkan Kinyû Shôji Hanrei 16 (Tokyo High Court, 14 Feb. 1984).

[67] Imasa Corp. v. Tokiwa Mutual Bank, 1260 Hanreijihô 15 (Tokyo High Court, 28 Oct. 1987).

originator's bank, ruling that the bank was liable to the originator for a loss caused by an error of the beneficiary's bank, which was a subagent (Erfüllungsgehilfe) of the originator's bank[68].

As previously discussed, the court decisions and commentators sharply disagree concerning the desirability of "network liability". The courts' ultimate reaction to the standard terms and conditions of international remittance application forms negating "network liability" consequently is unclear. There also is a current debate at the Ministry of Finance as to whether the new electronic funds transfer act should protect originators, especially those who are consumers, by incorporating either the mandatory money-back guaranty rule of Article 4 A of the American Uniform Commercial Code or "the network liability rule" in international and domestic credit transfers[69].

6. Receiving Bank Liability: to A Third Party

Under Article 105, Paragraph 2 of the Civil Code, the previously mentioned Sato v. Joyo Bank case raises the issue of whether a beneficiary's bank and an intermediary bank have a direct agency relationship with an originator and are liable to an originator for any losses that they cause. The general issue is liability to a party with whom there is no direct contractual relationship.

Although there also is support for the ruling in Sato v. Joyo Bank[70], many Japanese commentators believe that an originator does not have a direct agency relationship with a beneficiary's bank and an intermediary bank, which consequently should have only restitution and tort liability to an originator[71]. If an originator has a direct agency relationship with a beneficiary's bank and an intermediary bank, a beneficiary's bank and an interme-

---

[68] Yamaguchi v. Iyo Bank, 839 Kinyû Shôji Hanrei 3 (Takamatsu High Court, 18 Oct. 1989).

[69] According to the money-back guarantee rule, a sender of a payment order is guaranteed that a beneficiary's bank will accept the payment order or, if not, the sender will be refunded the payment order account (and interest) (see UCC, § 4A-402; the UNCITRAL Draft Model Law, Article 14). The money-back guarantee rule imposes upon an originator's bank a similar liability as network liability with respect to the payment order amount (and interest).

[70] M. Tanabe, "Furikomi Torihiki no Hôteki Shomondai (Legal Issues of Credit Transfers) I", 790 Kinyûhômu 4, 8 (1976); K. Kato, "Kawase Torihiki Niokeru Tôjisha no Hôritsu kankei (Legal Relationships Among Participants in Fund Transfer Transactions)", in: Hanrei Senrei Kinyû Torihiki Hô (Case Law and Precedents in Financial Transaction Law) (ed. by M. Horiuchi, 1979), p. 327; K. Hattori, K. Kato & J. Shibazaki, Kaisei Naikoku Kawase (Domestic Fund Transfers) (rev. ed. 1975), p. 218.

[71] Gotô, supra, note 28 at 50-51; Iwahara, supra, note 56. 1 Kinyu Kenkyu 24; Sawaki, Ishiguro & Mitsui Bank, supra, note 23 at 214-215.

diary bank could claim payment from an originator under Article 107 of the Civil Code, regardless of whether or not the originator's bank is insolvent (however, see: Moriyama v. Yanagi, 30/2 Minshu 208 (Supreme Court, 9th April, 1976)). An originator is not in a direct contractual relationship with a beneficiary's bank and an intermediary bank, and therefore should be exempt from liability upon payment to the originator's bank.

However, two legislative policy issues remain to be resolved: whether the "skip rule" should be legislated which would require an originator's bank to pay a beneficiary's bank upon an intermediary bank's insolvency[72], and whether originators and beneficiaries should be protected by legislating intermediary bank liability to originators and beneficiaries.

7. Receiving Bank Liability for Foreseeable Damages

Article 416 of the Japanese Civil Code provides that the obligor is liable for an obligee's ordinary or foreseeable losses. Two Tokyo District Court decisions accordingly hold an originator's bank liable for an originator's foreseeable consequential damages that were caused by the bank's delay in executing an electronic credit transfer[73]. In the well-known Sanwa Bank case, which involved an international credit transfer, a shipping company (the originator and plaintiff) instructed Sanwa Bank, Tokyo (the originator's bank and defendant) to credit a New York account of an agent of the originator (the beneficiary). Because the originator's bank misidentified the originator to the beneficiary's bank, the agent was unable to comply with payment terms of charter money to a New York shipowner, who cancelled the originator's contract for a ship charter. After determining that the originator's bank should have foreseen the originator's consequential damages, the Tokyo District Court allowed the originator's damage claim for approximately three million dollars[74].

As the Sanwa Bank case illustrates, the foreseeable damages that can be caused by a failed or a delayed credit transfer are disproportionate to the low

---

[72] An early draft of the UCC Article 4A proposed the skip rule as a means of reducing systemic (bank solvency) risk in a fund transfer system. It stipulated that if an intermediary bank between any originator's bank and any beneficiary bank became insolvent, the intermediary would be skipped over, and the originator's bank would be required to pay the beneficiary's bank directly. By moving the liability for insolvency of an intermediary bank back upstream to the originator's bank, this rule attempted to limit the intermediate impact of such insolvency. See Interum Report by the Electronic Banking Committee, supra, note 22, Part II, Chapter 1 C. 2.4.

[73] Unidentified Plaintiff v. Fuji Bank, 660 Kinyûhômujijô 26 (Tokyo District Court, 29 June 1972); Unidentified Plaintiff v. Sanwa Bank, 794 Kinyûhômujijô 30 (Tokyo District Court, 26 Jan. 1976).

[74] 794 Kinyûhômujijô 33.

fees that customarily are charged by a bank for a transfer.[75] Because an originator is in a better position than an originator's bank to assess potential consequential damages and to obtain insurance, an originator's bank arguably should not be responsible for them[76]. Neither the standard terms of a Japanese bank's form contract nor Japanese funds transfer system rules, however, address an originator's bank's liability for an originator's consequential damages. Even the SWIFT rules limit SWIFT's liability alone[77]. Limitation of receiving bank liability for an originator's consequential damages is one of the topics under consideration by the Ministry of Finance in connection with a new electronic funds transfer act.

8. Rights and Obligations of a Beneficiary's Bank — Finality of Credit Transfers

a) Beneficiary — Beneficiary's Bank Relationships

Subsection 4(1) discusses all receiving banks', including beneficiary's banks', obligations to their senders. This subsection deals with a beneficiary's bank obligations and rights with respect to a beneficiary. Under Japanese law, a beneficiary's bank's obligation to a beneficiary to execute a payment order ordinarily derives from a contract with the beneficiary. With respect to current accounts on which checks, bills, and notes can be drawn, the standard contract terms provide that the credit transfer amount is not withdrawable by a beneficiary until a beneficiary's has entered the credit upon its ledger[78]. The standard contract terms for ordinary deposit accounts state merely that credit transfers can be credited to an account[79]. These standard bank contract terms constitute the contractual basis of a beneficiary's rights against a beneficiary's bank.

The significance of these standard provisions in bank contracts seldom has been discussed. One important issue, is whether a beneficiary's bank has discretion to reject as well as to accept a payment order. The wording of the standard current account contract implies that a beneficiary's bank has discretion whether to credit a beneficiary's account. This implies that a similar discretion exists with respect to rejection of payment orders. However, the wording can also be interpreted to mean that no discretion exists and

---

[75] See Official Comment 2 of UCC, § 4A-305; Evra Corp. v. Swiss Bank Corp., 673 F. 2d 951 (7th Cir. 1982).

[76] Even banker who proposed a bank standard contract for credit transfers opposed limiting bank liability for consequential damages. See Hayashibe, supra, note 62 at 30.

[77] S.W.I.F.T. General Terms and Conditions, Clause 7.

[78] The Standard Contract Terms for Current Accounts, Articles 3, 4.

[79] The Standard Contract Terms for Ordinary Deposit Accounts, Article 2, Paragraph 1.

the beneficiary's bank must credit funds except in certain circumstances such as when final settlement has not been received or when payment has been suspended by court order.

Influenced by German law[80], some commentators consider that a beneficiary's right to credit for the amount of a payment order (Anspruch auf Gutschrift) should be distinguished from the rights arising from a credit entry (Anspruch aus Gutschrift)[81]. Although the former right depends upon the terms of a contract with a bank, the latter rights arise from a beneficiary's bank's entry of credit. An abstract action of entering credit is not affected by the relationships between an originator and an originator's bank, a beneficiary's bank and its sending bank, or an originator and a beneficiary. The main purpose of this argument is to defend the validity of credit entries against defenses which may arise from these relationships and to protect a beneficiary's reliance upon credit entries. By restricting the revocation or amendment of credit to a beneficiary's bank's own defenses, like disability, duress or mistake (Geschäftsunfähigkeit, beschränkte Geschäftsfähigkeit, Drohung und Irrtum) and by disregarding the defenses of other participants in a credit transfer, a German law approach protects a beneficiary's reliance upon credit entries. Japanese decisional law, however, gives greater protection to the interests of an originator than German law. Three Japanese courts have ruled that a beneficiary who was not entitled to payment by an originator had no right to credit that erroneously had been entered in his account[82]. In all three cases, an originator had misidentified a beneficiary, and the account of a person to whom the originator had no underlying obligation had been credited. The decisions uniformly invalidated the entry of credit and ordered a refund to the originator reasoning that a beneficiary can receive payments only when he has a claim against an originator based on their underlying relationship.

The standard terms of a bank contract do not deal with a beneficiary's bank's right to reverse or to amend credit that has been entered in a beneficiary's account. The Zengin System rules alone provide that a beneficiary's bank can reverse or amend credit that has been entered as a result of an error by either an originator's bank or a beneficiary's bank[83]. By allowing a beneficiary's bank to act upon the basis of an originator's bank's defense of

---

[80] Schönle, supra, note 27, § 31 III 3C; Schlegelberger & Hefermehl, supra, note 27, Rdn. 41 et seq.; Canaris, supra, note 27, Rdn. 398 et seq.

[81] M. Tanabe, "Doitsu Niokeru Furikae Torihiki (Funds Transfers in Germany)", 11/2 Hannan Ronshû-15 (1975); M. Matsui, "Nishi Doitsu Furikae Torihiki Niokeru Kashikata Kichô Nitsuite (Credit Entries in Funds Transfers in West Germany)", 161 Dôshisha Hôgaku 361 (1980); Gotô, supra, note 28 at 57-65.

[82] See supra, note 40.

[83] The Zengin Rules, Part 2, Chapter 7; Matsumoto, supra, note 39 at 22.

mistake, the Zengin System rules seem to adopt the questionable premise that claims of mistake by an originator's bank always are meritorious.

The circumstances in which a beneficiary's bank should be allowed to reverse or to amend a credit to a beneficiary's account are being considered in the drafting of a new law on electronic funds transfers by the Ministry of Finance. Retention of the present case-law rule allowing cancellation of credit if an originator was not indebted to a beneficiary is under review.

b) Reversals of Credit Because of Bank Failure

Another issue with respect to the finality of a credit transfer is the reversibility of a credit to a beneficiary's account in the event that a beneficiary's bank does not receive cover from its sending bank. In some countries, banks can enter provisional credit in their customer's accounts that is subject to reversal for a designated period. Germany, on the other hand, does not allow reversal of credit entries[84].

With the exception of the Zengin System, Japanese law is unclear. A contract between banks that are members of the Zengin System and the Bank of Japan provides that the Bank of Japan is to settle a failed member bank's debit balance and obtain reimbursement by selling the collateral that has been provided by the failed bank[85]. The Zengin System rules provide that if the amount realized from the collateral is insufficient, all other member banks in the failed bank's classification, e. g., national banks, credit unions, jointly are to share the cost of reimbursing the Bank of Japan[86]. By precluding Zengin System settlement risk to a receiving bank, these contracts and rules explain why a credit entry to an account can not be reversed because of the failure of a sending bank in a credit transfer through the Zengin System[87].

As discussed in subsection II (2), when BOJ-NET settles funds transfers in real time through Bank of Japan accounts, daylight overdrafts are not permitted; therefore there is no BOJ-NET settlement risk. Consequently in

---

[84] Canaris, supra, note 27 at Rdn. 420 et seq. See Etzkorn, supra, note 8 at 63.

[85] The Bank of Japan, Regulations on Funds Transfer Settlements, Article 20.

[86] The Zengin Rules, Part 1, Chapter 2 12 (2).

[87] Iwahara, supra, note 56, 1 Kinyû Kenkyû 52.

From the viewpoint of protecting receiving banks, settlement of a failed member bank's net debit balance by the Bank of Japan is desirable. However, this settlement removes a receiving bank's incentive to reduce large credit balance risks and to monitor a sending bank's financial soundness. This problem is similar to moral hazard in insurance. In order to avoid this problem the Zengin System recently introduced net debit limits of each member bank which set limits to each member banks' net debit balance arising from the Zengin transfers (S. Minowa, "Zengin System Niokeru Shimuke Chôka Kanri Seido no Dônyû (Introduction of Net Debit Limits in the Zengin System)", 519 Kinyû 11 (1990)).

real time settlements, a sending bank's failure also does not justify reversal of a credit entry to a beneficiary's account in a credit transfer through BOJ-NET.

However credit transfer settlement risk is present in the FEYSS, telegraphic transfers, SWIFT transfers, Tokyo Dollar Clearing System transfers and BOJ-NET transfers when the settlement time is designated by an originator's bank (non-real time settlements). Yet there has been little discussion about the significance of this settlement risk[88], and the standard terms of bank form contracts ordinarily do not deal with the problem. Although the standard current account and ordinary deposit account contracts allow a depositary bank that does not receive settlement for a check, a bill or a note to reverse credit that previously had been given[89], one court decision has denied a bank's right to a refund with respect to credit that had been withdrawn prior to the failure of settlement[90].

The policy issue is whether the law should protect a beneficiary's reliance upon a credit entry or should protect a beneficiary's bank from settlement risk in order to create an incentive for the bank to give a credit prior to receipt of settlement. With respect to check collection, Japanese case decisions and commentators support the reasonableness of the standard contractual terms allowing reversal of credit upon failure of settlement[91]. They contend that when settlement cannot be effected the payee should be aware that the credit

---

[88] S. Iwahara, "Denshi Shikin Torihiki Nikansuru Hôseiseibi no Hitsuyôsei to Kadai (The Need For and the Problems Associated with A New Electronic Fund Transfer Act) III", 1206 Kinyûhômujijô 6 et seq. (1988); A. Kinami, "Shikin Idô System Niokeru Risk Eno Hôteki Taiô Notameno Ichishiten (A Viewpoint of Legal Strategies to Deal With Risks in Funds Transfer Systems)", 1213 Kinyûhômujijô 6 (1989); The Bank of Japan, Japanese Transfer Systems in the Era of Financial Deregulation and Globalization, The Bank of Japan Report (No. 1) (July 1989), pp. 29 et seq.; Kinyû Risk to Sono Taiô Nitsuite — Kinyû Seido Chôsakai Senmon Iinkai & Gaikoku Kawase Tô Shingikai Senmonbukai (How to Deal With Financial Risks — Report by Special Committee of Financial System Research Council and Special Committee of Foreign Exchange Council) (1989), pp. 19 et seq.

[89] The Standard Contract Terms for Ordinary Deposit Accounts, Article 3, Paragraph 2; The Standard Contract Terms for Current Accounts, Article 2-5. However these provisions only deal with dishonored bills, notes and checks. It is not clear if these provisions also apply to insolvency of a sending bank. Tokyo Clearing House Rules provide that if a net debit balance member bank cannot settle a balance, the clearing house will unwind the settlement between the failed bank and other member banks (Tokyo Clearing House Rules, Article 51). This is similar to the unwinding provision of CHIPS (Rules Governing the Computerized Clearing House Interbank Payment System, § 13 (1990)). See CHIPS Settlement Finality Rules and Documents, New York Clearing House Association (1990).

[90] Fuji Bank v. Mizuno, 1123 Kinyûhômujijô 45 (Nagoya District Court, 15 Nov. 1985).

[91] Izeki Food Corp. v. Tokyo Mutual Bank, 273 Kinyû Shôji Hanrei 6 (Supreme Court, 1 July 1971); I. Kawamoto, "Kogitte no Ukeire to Yokin no Seiritsu (Checks, Deposits and Depositor's Claims)", 176 Jurist 72 (1959).

entry is reversible. In order to lessen the systemic risk[92], that is inherent in settlement risks upon systems other than BOJ-NET and the Zengin System, a bilateral obligation netting scheme will be introduced in the near future[93].

In Japan there has been no discussion on the problems related to reversals of credit entries due to bank failures. However, the general principle may be that losses caused by a bank failure should be allocated to the party who has chosen the bank. For example, between an originator and a beneficiary, an originator bears the loss caused by in originator's or intermediary bank's failure, and a beneficiary bears the loss caused by a beneficiary's bank failure because an originator chooses an originator's bank, the originator's bank chooses an intermediary bank, the intermediary bank chooses any other intermediary bank, and a beneficiary chooses a beneficiary's bank. Between an originator and an originator's bank the loss caused by an intermediary bank's failure should be allocated to an originator's bank unless the originator has designated the intermediary bank under the "network liability" rule (see IV 4 b)).

V. Conclusion

Most international funds transfers in Japan are electronic credit transfers. These transfers typically are carried out through the Japanese domestic electronic funds transfer systems: BOJ-NET, the FEYSS, the Zengin System, and the Tokyo Dollar Clearing System, supplemented by SWIFT and in-house transfer systems.

No specific Japanese statutes apply, and, it is rare for a specific standard form contract to be utilized by a bank in either international or domestic credit transfers. The legal framework of international credit transfers is provided by the mandate contracts (entgeltlicher Auftrag) between the participants in a credit transfer and by the SWIFT, the FEYSS, the BOJ-

---

92 For an overview of "systemic risk" see E. J. Stevens, Risk in Large-Dollar Transfer Systems, Federal Reserve Bank of Cleveland Economic Review (fall 1984), pp. 2 et seq.; E. G. Corrigan, Remarks Before the Federal Reserve Bank of Richmond (25 May 1988), pp. 1 et seq.; D. L. Mengle, "Legal and Regulatory Reform in Electronic Payments: An Evaluation of Payment Finality Rules" and Commentary by H. S. Scott, and G. R. Faulhaber, A. Phillips and A. M. Santomero, "Payment by R. E. Litan, in: The U.S. Payment System: Efficiency, Risk and the Role of the Federal Reserve (ed. by D. B. Humphrey, 1990), pp. 145-218.

93 "Shiharai System no Hôritsumondai Nikansuru Kenkyûkai Hôkokusho — Obligation Netting no Hôritsu Mondai Nitsuite (Report by the Study Group on Legal Problems of Payments Systems — Legal Problems of Obligation Netting)", 6/1 Kinyû Kenkyu 135 (1987); H. Maeda & H. Kanda, "Obligating Netting", 6 Kinyûhô Kenkyû (Shiroyôhen) 1 (1990).

NET, and the Zengin System rules. As a matter of Japanese mandate contract law, an originator, for example, can revoke a payment order until a beneficiary's bank has credited a beneficiary's account. The FEYSS and BOJ-NET rules, however, make payment orders basically irrevocable.

With respect to unauthorized transfers, if a payment order was subject to authentication and the authentication provided and complied with by a receiving bank was a reasonable method of identifying authorized payment orders, there has been a great deal of discussion as to whether a purported sender should be bound. According to some commentators, a receiving bank should have strict liability for unauthorized transfers, if there is no fault on the part of a purported sender even though a reasonable authentication procedure was provided and complied with by a receiving bank. There also is a debate as to whether a sender should be able to avoid his obligation to pay a receiving bank upon the basis of the defenses of disability, duress or mistake.

The creation and nature of a receiving bank's obligations presently are determined by its agreement with a sender. Nevertheless, there is debate as to whether an originator's bank is contractually responsible to an originator for the proper execution of a credit transfer with network liability for losses caused by such other participants in a transfer as an intermediary bank, a beneficiary's bank, a telecommunication company and a funds transfer system. There also is debate as to whether a new electronic funds transfer act should require either mandatory "network liability" or the American mandatory money-back guarantee. Another area of controversy is the nature of the liability that should exist between participants in a credit transfer transaction who do not have a direct contractual relationship. In view of the large amounts of consequential damages that can occur, the Japanese case law making a receiving bank liable for all foreseeable damages to its sender also is a subject of contention.

A beneficiary's bank's obligation to a beneficiary is based upon its contract with the beneficiary. Under the standard contract terms for current accounts, a beneficiary's bank may not be obliged uniformly to credit the amount of a payment order to a beneficiary's account. There also is debate as to whether a beneficiary's bank can reverse a credit entry to a beneficiary's account and recover a refund with respect to credit that has been withdrawn. The policy issue is the extent to which a beneficiary's reliance upon a credit entry should be given greater protection than an originator's intent in making a credit transfer and a beneficiary's bank's receipt of settlement.

Until new Japanese electronic funds transfer legislation is enacted, there will continue to be many unresolved legal issues concerning international credit transfers. For example, presently there are no specific governing statutes, no contract provisions and no detailed discussions by commentators with respect to conflict of law issues. In view of the many difficult legal problems concerning international credit transfers in Japan that presently are unresolved, it is to be hoped that a new electronic funds transfer act that reflects both international and national developments will be enacted by the Diet in the near future.

Factual Significance and Legal Regulation of International Funds Transfers in Switzerland

By Jacques Bischoff, Zürich*

Contents

---

* Translated by Dr. Frances Dielmann, Frankfurt/M.

I. The Significance and Practical Execution of International Funds Transfers in Switzerland

1. Definitions / Distinctions

The term "cross-border funds transfers" is very generally used to mean all business transactions which "move cash or non-cash money values across the borders of a defined currency territory — as a rule identical with the national borders of a country".[1] The cross-border (or international) funds transfer differs from the domestic one primarily in that a currency territory is exceeded and the execution of the payment transaction usually takes place in two currencies.[2]

This article will not deal with international cash payments[3] but will instead concentrate on non-cash cross-border payments, which in commercial practice are far more significant and for which a diverse system of execution has been developed.[4] Among the primary instruments (such as the documentary letter of credit, the check or the credit card), the transfer order plays a leading role for all types of cross-border payments.

The execution of non-cash payments on an international level requires, as a rule, an intermediary between the payment originator and the beneficiary. This function is usually carried out by banks[5], which have their own branches or a network of correspondent banks in foreign countries. They

---

[1] Albisetti (ed.), Handbuch des Geld-, Bank- und Börsenwesens der Schweiz, (cit. Handbuch) p. 706.

[2] Heini, part 4, chap. 1; Handbuch, p. 706, where the lack of a giro network for payment processing is used as an additional criterium.

[3] This arises primarily in connection with travel, where "foreign currency is acquired in the home country or exchanged in a foreign country for another currency" (Handbuch, p. 706).

[4] See Handbuch, p. 706.

[5] International payments through banks will not be examined here. See Lehmann, p. 36, and K. Gormanns, in this volume.

usually have standing business relationships with correspondent banks, within the scope of which in addition to other banking transactions (e.g. stock exchange transactions) non-cash payment orders are executed.

The following examination will be restricted to the description of the cross-border, non-cash payments carried out by banks, specifically as understood, i.e. actually executed and legally governed, in Switzerland.

2. Function and Actual Significance

It is characteristic of Switzerland and its economy that at the beginning of this century foreign commercial relationships were established and have since then continuously been expanded. Foreign commerce plays a traditional and central role in the Swiss economy today. Over 40 % of the Swiss national product is achieved in this area.

These intensive foreign commercial interrelationships are reflected in the banking sector, above all, in the very significant foreign transactions and related extensive payment transactions at an international level.[6] Of primary significance is the function of cross-border payments in the financing and financial execution of Swiss exports and imports; in 1991 Switzerland exported goods and services valued at 116 billion Swiss francs and imported SFr. 113 billion.

Parallel to steadily growing world trade, international financial and capital markets have developed into factors of very high economic importance during the past few decades. In 1990, the gross Swiss capital export amounted to SFr. 47 billion, and the corresponding import SFr. 34 billion. The share of pure financial transactions in international payments grew exceptionally, and the function of the banks as payment intermediaries "reached new qualitative and quantitative dimensions".[7]

3. The Practical Execution of International Payments from the Swiss Perspective

a) Bank Payment Transactions

aa) International Bank Payment Transactions

International payments between banks in differing currency territories, to the extent that the currencies of the participating banks are involved, are

[6] See also Handbuch, p. 708.

[7] Id.

carried out through local currency accounts, which are managed by banks within the currency territory for banks outside of this territory within the framework of bilateral account relationships.[8] In the case of a payment in the currency of the payor bank, this bank credits the (local currency) account — the so-called "vostro" or "loro" account of the payee bank and provides that bank with the corresponding claim in local currency. If payment is to be made in the currency of the payee bank, this bank debits the (local currency) account — the so-called "nostro" account — of the payor bank, which the payee manages for the payor.

In the case of payments in third currencies — currencies outside the currency territories of the payor and the payee banks — the actual accounting is carried out through common correspondent banks in the country of the currency involved. A payment order in U.S.$ by a Swiss bank to a German bank is carried out through their common U.S. correspondent bank by having that bank debit the U.S.$ nostro account of the Swiss bank and credit the loro account of the German bank.

The banks maintain account balances with their foreign correspondent banks at the levels necessary to carry out the volume of international payments transactions which they can expect based on past experience. These funds are obtained on currency markets, and unneeded surpluses are sold there.[9]

Banks with branch offices in the respective currency territory or at the foreign place of payment can carry out foreign payment transactions in the same way through their branches — so to speak "internally" — provided that the branches are authorized by regulatory authorities to carry out the payments and have the necessary technical facilities; in other words, where "the respective type of transaction is within the scope of business of the particular branch".[10]

In addition to the pure accounting aspect as described, the practical execution of cross-border payment transactions also involves the means of transmission of the relevant data and information. Various methods of transmission are available to banks, but the international telecommunications system S.W.I.F.T. has replaced the traditional telegram and telex systems to a great extent.

---

[8] See Kleiner, Internationales Devisen-Schuldrecht (cit. IDS), p. 267; Lehmann (p. 146); Emch/Renz (p. 327) refer in this contest to "foreign currency accounts", which may be correct from the perspective of the bank whose account is being debited; but technically, it is always a domestic currency account which is credited or debited. The necessity of reciprocal account management in international banking transactions is due to the fact that there is presently no clearing system or giro network on an international level for payment processing.

[9] See Kleiner, IDS, p. 267; Lehmann, p. 146.

[10] Kleiner, IDS, p. 33.

bb) Domestic Bank Payment Transactions

Banks without their own international network of correspondent banks — primarily those with a low volume of foreign payments — engage domestic intermediary banks (domestic correspondent banks) for the execution of cross-border payment orders. The same is true for banks which do not maintain a correspondent relationship with a bank in a particular country involved in a transaction. These banks maintain relationships as customers of their domestic correspondent banks; the execution of international payments by these banks is carried out in the same way as the customer payment transactions described below.[11] At this point it must only be mentioned that the currency transactions made necessary by the execution of the international payments are carried out by the banks within the scope of the usual bank payments in local currency. In Switzerland, these interbank payments in Swiss francs have been carried out since mid-1987 primarily through the Swiss Interbank Clearing (SIC) System[12], operated by the Swiss National Bank (SNB) in cooperation with the Telekurs AG.[13] The banks participating in the SIC maintain giro accounts with the SNB based on appropriate agreements; within the framework of this agreement, they authorize the SNB to "debit payments to other banks from their giro accounts and credit transfers from banks to their accounts".[14] The transactions initiated by these banks by means of direct electronic transmission are posted by the SNB within the scope of its account management.

b) Customer Payment Transactions

Banks undertake cross-border payments not only for their own accounts but also instead primarily for their customers. The method of execution of customer payment transactions is dependent upon the account relationship between the bank and the customer. If the customer maintains a foreign currency account, payment orders issued in this currency are debited from this account and incoming transfers credited to this account.[15] If the

---

[11] See part 3. b) below.

[12] See generally Vital, pp. 9 ff.; Hess, pp. 31 ff.; Hess, SZW, following note 53; Lehmann, pp. 53 ff. Most of the Swiss banks are presently directly or indirectly (e.g. through a banking association) connected to SIC, as are many Swiss subsidiaries of foreign banks. The banks not participating in SIC carry out business with their national correspondent banks by means of direct account relationships.

[13] A service company with headquarters in Zürich which is owned by the Swiss banks and which is active primarily in the areas of payment systems and financial information. Its capital is held by more than 280 banks.

[14] Hess, p. 35.

[15] See Kleiner, IDS, p. 268.

customer does not maintain an account in the relevant foreign currency or has an account only in local currency, he purchases the needed foreign currency amount when issuing the payment order in the foreign currency; likewise, incoming payments in foreign currency are usually[16] converted by the bank by means of a sale of foreign currency and the local currency amount is then credited to the customer's account. Cross-border payments in local currency do not lead to currency transactions between the customer and his bank, but instead between the beneficiary and his bank in the foreign country.[17]

The transactions arising out of the customer payment transactions are carried out between banks in the form of bank payments, as described above.[18]

II. Legal Regulation of Cross-Border Payment Transactions under Swiss Law

1. Preface

The following description of the regulation of international payment transactions under Swiss law proceeds from the premise that the Swiss legal system is applicable for the evaluation of the legal relationships and issues being examined. Whether and under what circumstances this is the case must be decided under conflict of laws principles; these principles will be examined at the end of this article.[19] We will now look at the situation where Swiss law applies.

2. Legal Relationships between the Parties Involved in a International Funds Transfer

a) The Legal Relationship between the Customer and his Bank

aa) Current Account and Giro Agreements

aaa) In General

The account relationship represents the nucleus of the business relationship between the bank and the customer. It consists of a conglomerate of

[16] I.e. unless otherwise stipulated between the bank and the customer; see part II. 2. a) aa) ccc) below.

[17] Kleiner, IDS, p. 269.

[18] See part 3. a) above.

[19] See part III. below.

individual agreements governing the types of transactions carried out between the bank and the customer.[20] As a rule, no comprehensive agreement covering all of the individual banking transactions is made; instead, the General Conditions [AGB] commonly used by the Swiss banks — in contrast to the AGB of the German or Austrian banks — contain rules regarding specific critical issues which can arise in connection with widely differing types of banking transactions. In evaluating a specific transaction, reference must be made to the applicable AGB as well as to specific supplementary agreements and provisions of contract law.[21] The agency character of the account management leads to the application, above all, of the provisions governing the mandate (Art. 394 ff. Swiss Law of Obligations [OR]). The agreements most significant to bank payment transactions are the current account agreement and the giro agreement which, as a rule, are entered into simultaneously and usually by implication.[22]

In the current account agreement, the customer and the bank agree that settlement for the mutual claims arising out of the various banking transactions will be made by means of a running account — following each account operation a new balance is calculated. This running account is made without special notice and based on the settlement agreement contained in the overall current account agreement.[23] The parties are obligated to include mutual claims in the current account relationship and to waive the right to assert the claims individually.[24] The inclusion of the individual items in the running account, in accordance with express provision of law[25], does not lead to a novation except where the balance is calculated and approved. In Swiss

---

[20] Von der Crone, p. 27. There is a doctrine in German legal literature referred to as the "general banking agreement", designating a comprehensive master agreement obligating the bank to perform every act which is within the scope of and common in banking. This doctrine is altogether rejected in Swiss legal scholarship on the grounds that no such comprehensive intent of the parties is present. See Kleiner, Festschrift für Schuep (cit. Festschrift 1), p. 275; von der Crone, pp. 19 ff.; Guggenheim, p. 11.

[21] On the interpretation and supplementation of contracts through recourse to contract law, see Schuep, pp. 781 ff.; on the interpretation of contracts generally, see e.g. Merz, pp. 53 ff. and Zeller, v. a., pp. 525 ff., both with additional references. On the issue of validity of general contract terms overall and with regard to specific general contract terms, see Forstmoser, p. 14; Guggenheim, pp. 38 ff.; Kleiner, pp. 9 ff.

[22] Kleiner, p. 79.

[23] See Kleiner, pp. 82 ff.; Kleiner, Festschrift für Max Keller (cit. Festschrift 2), pp. 715 f.; von der Crone, pp. 27 ff.; Guggenheim, pp. 226 ff.

[24] On this so-called current account obligation, see Kleiner, p. 82; Kleiner, Festschrift 1, p. 275; Handbuch, p. 429, von der Crone, p. 29.

[25] Art. 117 (1) and (2) OR. This is also the only provision of Swiss private law which is specifically directed to current account transactions. In Art. 124 (3) OR (effect of settlement) and Art. 314 (3) OR (calculation of loan interest), the current account relationship is mentioned, but these provisions only govern where there is no other trading practice.

banking practice, the approval by the bank can consist of a binding notice to the customer or, in any case, the account statement[26]; approval by the customer can consist of the express acceptance of a negative balance — such as by signing a notice of account — or of a lack of response within a time limit of 30 days following delivery of an account statement by the bank.[27] The novation creates a new claim in the amount of the resulting balance.[28] In addition to the authorization for the running account, the current account agreement also creates a duty on the part of the bank to keep accounts, including the posting of the individual claims and calculation of the balance as well as the preparation and delivery of account statements.

The giro agreement is a continuing agency agreement under which the bank is obligated to handle payment transactions for the customer, in particular to carry out payments and to accept transfers.[29] The prevailing view in legal scholarship and case law qualifies the giro agreement, based on its typical form as an agency agreement or agreement to perform work, as a mandate within the meaning of Art. 394 OR.[30] Under the provisions governing the commission, the bank is liable to the customer for loyal and diligent execution of payment transactions (Art. 398 (2) OR), but under Art. 100 OR the bank can contractually exclude or at least limit its liability for helpers which it engages.[31] In their AGB, the banks regularly exclude all liability for damages caused by transmission errors or the failure to recognize authorization defects except in the case of gross negligence by the bank. This division of risk led to heated controversy among scholars which culminated in a 1986 decision by the Federal Supreme Court holding that the banking

---

[26] Kleiner, Festschrift 1, p. 276. This unilateral acceptance contains an abstract admission of debt under Art. 17 OR.

[27] This brings about a novation: von der Crone, p. 34; Kleiner, Festschrift 1, p. 276 f.; the time limit of 30 days which has become established in legal literature and case law is also stated in most general business terms and account statements. On the fundamental issue of tacit acceptance, see Art. 6 AR and the literature and case decisions referring to that article.

[28] On the issue of whether this new balance legally derives from the abstract admission of debt or on the novation, see Kleiner, Festschrift 1, p. 277; von der Crone, p. 34; von Tuhr/Scher, p. 184; Guggenheim, p. 228 ff.; BGE 104 II 196.

[29] Handbuch, p. 335; Guggenheim, pp. 232 ff.; Kleiner, pp. 18 ff.; Helbig, pp. 14 ff.; BGE 100 II 370, where the current account agreement is, however, viewed as a part of the giro agreement.

[30] See Kleiner, p. 20; Guggenheim, p. 234; Nobel, p. 255; BGE 111 II 449, 110 II 283. Under Art. 394 OR, contracts for services which do not fall within a specific statutory category of contracts, are governed by the provisions regarding the mandate. But see more recent practice which differentiates to a greater extent and despite the wording of Art. 394 (2) OR would permit a classification as e.g. a mixed or "Inominat" agreement (BGE 109 II 462 ff. in contrast to BGE II 305 ff. and 104 II 108 ff.).

[31] On the bank's duties of care in executing payment transactions, see Kleiner, Festschrift 1, pp. 281 ff.; Guggenheim, p. 245 f.

sector is to be classified as a government concessioned sector within the meaning of Art. 100 (2) and Art. 101 (3) OR.[32] The result is that in the case of incorrect conduct by banking officials a judge can declare a limitation on liability invalid and that for incorrect conduct by bank employees a liability limitation is permissible only with respect to minor negligence.

Viewed as a single factual situation, the account relationship between the customer and the bank can be classified in the usual cases in practice as an "Innominat" contract, the main elements of which are the current account agreement, the duty to keep accounts and the giro agreement.[33]

bbb) The Foreign Currency Account in Particular

A foreign currency account relationship between a bank and a customer likewise consists of the elements described above; here, these elements have certain special characteristics specific to foreign currency.[34] Within the scope of the current account agreement, all foreign currency transactions are to be carried out exclusively through the respective foreign currency account. In addition to keeping accounts, the customer commissions the bank to maintain funds in the territory of the respective currency in the amount of the account balance. These funds are held by the bank — together with its own foreign currency holdings — in the bank's nostro account at its correspondent bank in the respective currency territory; the customer is usually informed of this in the AGB. The bank must insure that orders by the customer can be carried out at any time or that the customer can obtain payment of a corresponding amount in the country of the respective currency at the payment location of the correspondent bank.[35] Within the scope of this commission, the bank has the duty with respect to the customer to diligently select, instruct and monitor the foreign correspondent bank through which it carries out the foreign transactions (see Art. 399 OR). The bank does not

[32] BGE 112 II 455. The Bundesgericht thus deviated from its prior practice and followed what is apparently the prevailing view among legal scholars; see Forstmoser, p. 26; Bucher, recht, pp. 97 ff.; Guggenheim, p. 45. Reaching the same result but on different grounds: Weber, SJZ 81, pp. 87 ff. Contra, and critical of the cited BGE, Kleiner, Festschrift 1, p. 281.

[33] Heini, part 2, chap. 1 § 1 II; Kleiner, Festschrift 1, p. 279; Kleiner, Festschrift 2, p. 715. A different view is justified with respect to foreign currency transactions carried out through local currency accounts; see bb) below.

[34] See Kleiner, IDS, pp. 262 ff.

[35] Kleiner, IDS, p. 264. In contrast to an account relationship in local currency, no cash transactions in the respective foreign currency are carried out at the location of the acount managing bank. Deposits to the withdrawals from a foreign currency acount in local currency can thus take place only indirectly by means of corresponding foreign exchange transactions; see Kleiner, IDS p. 264.

have duties exceeding this duty of care under the law governing the commission (cura in eligendo, instuendo et custodiendo). Where the bank is not at fault, it is not liable for damages resulting, for example, from the insolvency of the correspondent bank.[36] This and other risks, such as those related to statutory and administrative measures or restrictions in the foreign currency territory are borne by the customer based on the contractual stipulations — the AGB used by the Swiss banks all contain a risk allocation clause to this effect.

The giro agreement also contained in the foreign currency account relationship obligates the bank to carry out payment transactions for the customer in the respective currency. The law governing the commission applies here as well.[37]

ccc) Foreign Currency Transactions through Local Currency Accounts

The duties of the bank under the giro agreement extend, as a rule, to the execution of payment transactions for the customer in foreign currencies, even where the customer does not maintain a corresponding foreign currency account with the bank but instead only a local currency account.[38] In this case, the bank, based on the necessary authorization contained in the usual bank AGB, carries out credits and debits in local currency converted from the foreign currency amounts, provided that the customer has not given instructions to the contrary to the bank in a timely manner. The execution of payment orders in foreign currency as well as the conversion of incoming foreign currency amounts always involve parallel, separate currency transactions.[39]

bb) The Individual Bank Transfer

aaa) The International Bank Transfer as a Multiphase Transfer

The focal point of international funds transfers is the multiphase transfer, i.e. a transfer through at least two banks, because in practice the originator and the beneficiary in an international payment are by nature customers of different banks in different currency territories. A single phase transfer in a

---

[36] Kleiner, IDS, p. 84 and 265; Gautschi N 11 b on Art. 466 OR. Contra, Emch/Renz, p. 327.

[37] Kleiner, IDS, p. 263.

[38] See Kleiner, IDS, p. 268, who does reject, however, this duty on the part of the bank where exotic currencies are involved.

[39] See part I, 3. b) above. Regarding determination of the exchange rate to be used with respect to the customer, see Kleiner, IDS, pp. 217 f.

legal sense can be presumed in international transactions only where the beneficiary is a customer of a foreign branch of the bank instructed by the originator; this situation will not be dealt with here.[40]

bbb) The Individual Transfer Order

The prevailing view in legal literature and case law views the individual transfer order not as an independent contract in a legal sense but instead as a mere specifying instruction to the bank based on the giro agreement. The bank is obligated to convey an instruction to the beneficiary's bank or an intermediary bank for the benefit of the beneficiary.[41] At the same time, there is a separate delivery order (Anweisung) within the meaning of Art. 466 ff. OR: The customer instructs the bank to credit an amount to the beneficiary or the beneficiary's bank as payee.[42] The instructed bank accepts this instruction by means of conveying an instruction to the next bank in the transfer chain to carry out the payment; this payment procedure is also governed by the statutory provisions on the delivery order (Anweisung) (Art. 466 ff. OR).[43] In the interest of consistency with the terminology usage common in banking practice, the instruction based on the giro agreement will be referred to in the following as the transfer order or payment order.

cc) Legal Basis and Time of Debit and Credit of Accounts

The bank must carry out the payment orders of its customer if the customer has the necessary assets with the bank (in the form of a positive account balance or sufficient line of credit). In carrying out the payment order, the bank debits the customer's account for the transfer amount and any fees for the transfer. The prevailing view in Switzerland is that the bank's right to debit the account is based on Art. 402 (1) OR, under which correct execution of the commission entitles the bank to claim from the customer reimbursement for its expenses.[44] In the case of international transfers, "if

---

[40] The legal nature of a single phase transfer also differs from that of a multiphase transfer; see Guggenheim, pp. 234 ff.; von der Crone, pp. 42 ff.; Heini, part 2 chap. 1 § 2.

[41] Kleiner, pp. 52 ff.; Guggenheim, p. 238; Wettstein, p. 50; Heini, part 2, chap 1 § 2 I; BGE 110 II 285, 77 II 369. This view has always been disputed; see e.g. Gautschi, N 11 a on Art. 466 OR, who views this as a substitution within the meaning of Art. 398 (3) and 399 (2) and (3) OR, and Weber, SJZ 81, p. 88, who views the transfer order as an isolated mandate.

[42] See Hess, SZW, p. 103 f. See also von der Crone, pp. 45 ff. Critical: Kleiner/Schmid, p. 179.

[43] See part 2. b), bb) below.

[44] Heini, part 2. chap. 1 § II 2; Handbuch, p. 335; Guggenheim, p. 238; Bucher, recht, p. 99 ff.; BGE 110 II 285.

the amount to be expended is certain" the debit is made "upon transmittal into the foreign currency territory or on the day on which the next instructed bank may debit" the originator's bank.[45]

Under the giro agreement, the bank is obligated to accept incoming payments for the customer and to credit these payments to the customer's account. The duty to credit these amounts is based on the bank's obligation to repay in accordance with Art. 400 (1) OR[46]; from the time the payment is received by the customer's bank, the customer has a right to the credit, which is subject to the condition subsequent that a revocation of the payment order could be made by the sender.[47] With the actual credit or posting of the credit, the bank agrees definitively to make payment to the customer[48]; with the credit, the customer acquires an abstract claim based on the credit. Under the law of instruction, the bank as the receiver of the instruction states to the customer by means of the credit that the bank accepts the instruction; the customer is then not affected by any defenses based on the underlying obligation or the adequacy of covering funds between the banks but instead only by the "personal relationship" between the bank and the customer or based on the contents of the instruction itself (Art. 468 (1) OR). In this sense, the bank instruction is abstract. According to KLEINER, the credit for an international payment is made at the time "when the bank receives notice that credit has been made to the bank's account at a correspondent bank for the customer's account and the bank has this amount at its disposal".[49]

b) The Legal Relationship between the Sending and the Receiving Bank

aa) Current Account and Giro Agreements

As described above[50], cross-border payments between banks are carried out through reciprocal accounts, while domestic payments are carried out

---

[45] Kleiner, IDS, p. 262.

[46] Guggenheim, p. 240.

[47] Guggenheim, p. 237; Kleiner, o. 50. The still undecided legal issue regarding the exact time at which the bank receives the payment and the customer's claim to payment thus arises must probably be decided case by case, depending on the type and modality of the technical accounting procedures used in transfers between banks.

[48] See Thalmann, SZW, pp. 258 ff.; Kleiner, p. 46 f.; Guggenheim, p. 237. Contra, von der Crone, p. 38, who views as determinative either the notice to the customer, the sending of notice, or, where the customer has a direct electronic connection to his bank, the time at which the customer is first able to acquire knowledge of the accounting entry by data processing means.

[49] Kleiner, IDS, p. 261 f.

[50] See part I. 3. a) above.

primarily through local clearing systems. But under Swiss legal doctrine, the use of bank clearing does not influence the fundamental structure of the bank transfer. Participation in bank clearing permits the presumption that each clearing bank has a giro agreement with each other participating institution established by implication.[51] A contract existing between two banks with direct account relationships is also classified as a current account and giro agreement.[52] Therefore, what we have said in regard to the contractual relationship between the customer and the bank[53] also applies here. With regard to the reciprocal account management commonly employed in interbank transactions, the issue can be raised as to whether and to what extent the AGB of these banks are incorporated into the contract and how conflicts between the AGB are to be resolved. Whether the AGB of the banks apply must be determined for each individual case; if this is the case, the general view is that the applicable AGB are those of the bank which performs the characteristic obligation.[54]

An independent contract therefore exists between the sending and the receiving bank, and not merely a subcontract. A subcontract would require that the performance agreed to by the sending and the receiving bank was already the object of the giro agreement between the originating customer and the sending bank. The presently established view rejects this theory: the sending bank is responsible to its customer in transfer transactions only for the proper transmission of the payment order and not for the actual credit to the beneficiary's account.[55] The originating customer, therefore, has no direct claim against the beneficiary's bank based on a subcontract or contractual substitution within the meaning of Art. 399 (3) OR.

Finally, the receiving bank is not the servant of the sending bank; as stated, the sending bank fulfills its obligation to the customer with the proper transmission of the payment order. The receiving bank, in crediting the transfer amount, thus does not undertake the sending bank's act of performance but instead the receiving bank's own act.[56]

---

[51] Von der Crone, p. 59; Kleiner, p. 55; Guggenheim, p. 239. On account management in the Swiss Interbank Clearing (SIC) and its legal structure, see Hess, pp. 42 ff.; Hess, SZW, following note 73. Clearing system refers here to a payment system and not to a "net settlement system".

[52] Guggenheim, p. 238; Kleiner/Schmid, pp. 179 f.; von der Crone, p. 57.

[53] See part 2. a) aa) above.

[54] Kleiner, IDS, p. 31; Etzkorn, p. 45, which additional references to German scholarship; regarding conflict of laws, see Bührer, pp. 27 ff., 94 ff.

[55] Canaris, p. 329; Kleiner/Schmid, p. 179; Kleiner, p. 52; Heini, part 2, chap. 3 § 1. What is owed is prudent care in carrying out the order but not the specific result in accordance with Art. 368 f. OR.

[56] Heini, part 2, chap. 3 § 1, with additional references. Contra, Schönle, p. 823.

bb) The Individual Bank Transfer

An individual transfer order by the sending bank to the receiving bank is classified as delivery order (Anweisung) within the meaning of Art. 466 ff. OR[57]. In my opinion it at the same time represents an instruction within the scope of the giro agreement. The sending bank as the instructing party sends to the receiving bank as the instructed party an instruction to credit the account of the beneficiary as payee. Based on its giro agreement with the sending bank, the receiving bank is then obligated to carry out the instruction and credit the beneficiary's account, provided that the sending bank provides cover, such as through an account held with the receiving bank. The sending bank is obligated to provide cover in accordance with Art. 402 (1) OR.[58] In the case of foreign currency transfers, the cover is to be paid to the sending bank's nostro account at the receiving bank; cover for domestic transfers is to be paid in local currency to the receiving bank's vostro account with the sending bank.

c) Legal Relationship between the Originator and the Beneficiary (Underlying Obligation)

aa) Object of the Performance Owed by the Originator

aaa) Preface

The origin of the bank transfer is in the legal relationship between the originator and the beneficiary. The originator issues a transfer order to his bank in order to satisfy a money debt owed to his creditor as the beneficiary. The money debt can have various legal (contractual or statutory) bases, which need not be examined here. The significant issue is that of the actual object of performance in the case of payments in local or foreign currency.

bbb) Money Debts Which Are Denominated in Swiss Currency and to be Paid in Switzerland

In accordance with Art. 84 (1), money debts are to be paid in local currency. For historical reasons, there is no statutory answer to the question of whether money debts can also be satisfied by the provision of deposit money.[59] The views asserted in legal scholarship are conflicting; it does

---

[57] Kleiner, p. 53; Guggenheim, p. 238. Contra, von der Crone, pp. 45, 59.

[58] Guggenheim, p. 238.

[59] This form of money, which is the most important in practice, is viewed as a constantly

appear that there is a consensus that deposit money is not money in a legal sense and that a bank transfer is therefore not a payment of a money debt.[60] But this principle is not absolute; various authors presume that the transfer has the effect of fulfillment of the debt where large amounts are owed and it would therefore be unreasonable to require the debtor to pay in cash.[61] Also, the bank transfer is deemed to have the direct effect of satisfying the debt where the beneficiary as creditor consents to payment by means of deposit money either expressly or by implication. This is the case, for example, where the creditor provides his bank connection and/or account number to the debtor on letterheads, delivery bills, invoices or similar documents[62], if he accepts an incoming payment of deposit money without objection within a reasonable time[63], or when he opens a bank account.[64] If the transfer does not meet the requirements for direct satisfaction of the debt it is viewed as performance in lieu of specific fulfillment.[65]

ccc) Satisfaction of Foreign Debts

Foreign debts are usually to be satisfied in the form of foreign currency; only rarely are they deemed to be obligations for goods or property, namely only where it is expressly stipulated that payment is to be made in certain forms of bills or coins.[66]

If the debtor must satisfy a foreign currency debt in Switzerland, he has the option under Art. 84 (2) OR of paying in Swiss currency instead of in foreign currency, except where a special stipulation makes mandatory the payment in foreign currency.[67] Such a stipulation can be expressed, e.g. in the word "effective" or an equivalent, unambiguous term. If the debtor has the option,

---

due bank deposit, which is entered on the books — book money — in electronic account lists, magnetic tape or microfilm, and over which dispositions can be made by means of transfers; see Guhl/Merz/Kummer, p. 80; see generally, Weber, N 32 on Art. 94 OR. According to Kleiner (IDS, pp. 45 ff.) monetary debts are to be paid in currencies with a legal rate of exchange.

[60] Weber, SJZ 78, pp. 138 f.; Kleiner, p. 68; von der Crone, p. 60.

[61] Weber, N 163 on Art. 84; Schönle, p. 820; von der Crone, p. 60 note 115.

[62] Kleiner, p. 68; Becker, N 7 on Art. 74 OR; Weber, N 164 on Art. 84 OR; BGE 55 II 201 f.

[63] Weber, note 165 on Art. 84 OR ("reasonable" time); Guggenheim, p. 235; Heini, part 3, chap. 1 § 2 II (relating to the function of money as legal tender). Contra, Kleiner, p. 68.

[65] Kleiner, p. 68; Guggenheim, p. 235.

[66] See Kleiner, IDS, pp. 45 ff. Regarding the issue of whether foreign currency debts are "monetary debts" or merely contractual obligations, see Nobel, Devisenschuld, pp. 289 ff.; Kleiner, IDS, p. 74; Weber, notes 147 ff. and note 332 on Art. 84 OR.

[67] See Kleiner, IDS, pp. 61 ff.; Weber, notes 346 ff. on Art. 84 OR; von Tuhr/Peter, pp. 64 f.

and he decides to pay in Swiss currency, the applicable exchange rate is that in effect at the place of payment at the time the debt becomes due. Under the prevailing view and case law, if the debtor is late making payment, he is liable for losses due to changes in the exchange rate, under Art. 103 ff. OR.[68]

The debtor has the statutory option only when payment is to be made in a currency which "has no statutory value at the place of payment" (Art. 84 (2) sent. 1 OR). Therefore, he has no option if the currency stipulated is legal tender at the place of payment even if it is a currency foreign to the debtor. If, however, the debtor agrees to make payment at a foreign location in the currency of that location, he must in fact make payment in that currency. The cited statutory provision does not extend to payments to be made in foreign currency territories; the debtor cannot rely on the fact that "the obligation does not comply with the statutory requirements for the actual payment clause" which would permit him to satisfy the debt in his own currency.[69] Likewise, this statutory provision does not apply to the issue of the fulfillment of foreign currency debts in equivalent value; based on the applicable principle of nominalism, the debtor bears the risk of deterioration of the value of money in international payment transactions as well.[70]

The satisfaction of foreign money debts across national borders can be impeded by governmental or economic interference or foreign currency controls on either side of the border. Performance obstacles of this type and their effects on the underlying contractual obligation have been extensively examined in legal literature.[71] It is not necessary to look at them in detail here.

bb) Place of Performance and Time of Performance in Non-Cash Payment Transactions

aaa) Money Debts and Foreign Currency Debts as "Bringing Obligations" — Obligations to be Performed at the Creditor's (Business) Residence

Unless otherwise stipulated by the express intent of the parties or by implication based on the circumstances, money debts are to be paid at the place where the creditor has his residence at the time of the payment (Art. 74 (1) and (2) no. 1 OR). The purpose of this statutory provision leads to the

---

[68] Weber, note 360 on Art. 84 OR; von Tuhr/Peter, p. 65; Bucher, p. 269; BGE 76 II 376.

[69] Kleiner, IDS, p. 62.

[70] Weber, note 340 ff. on Art. 84 OR. In the case of a true currency collapse, a judge would have discretion to adjust the purchase price; see Bischoff, pp. 187 ff.

[71] See Kleiner, pp. 96 ff. and Weber, notes 238 ff. on Art. 84 OR, with additional references.

result that in the case of non-cash payment of money debts the bank branch which manages the creditor's account substitutes for the creditor's residence.[72] This principle of performance at the creditor's residence creates a duty on the part of the debtor to give due consideration to the processing and transmission time needed for the transfer so that the transfer amount can be credited to the beneficiary's account by his bank on the due date for payment at the latest.

As a rule, foreign currency debts are also debts to be performed at the creditor's residence, as described, although a distinction must be made between debts in the debtor's currency and debts in a foreign currency.[73]

bbb) The Time at which the Debt is Discharged

In the underlying contractual relationship between the originator and the beneficiary, the effect of discharge occurs in the case of a non-cash transfer when the creditor has the money at his disposal.[74] This occurs — as described above[75] — when the sum of money to be transferred is credited to his account and he therefore has an unconditional and irrevocable claim against his bank based on the credit. The time at which the bank gives the beneficiary notice of the credit is not decisive; in other words, the notice of the credit has a declaratory character, not a constitutive effect.[76]

ccc) Allocation of Risk of Delay or Loss

The prevailing view in legal scholarship and case law is that the debtor satisfies the debt by means of a non-cash payment transaction in a timely manner only when the credit or electronic posting of the credit is made to the creditor's account within the time period for performance; the submission of the payment order within the time limit is not sufficient.[77] The result is that

---

[72] Schönle, p. 822; Guggenheim, p. 238; Heini, part 3 chap.. 1 § 3 II.

[73] See Kleiner, ISA, pp. 69 f.

[74] Schönle, p. 826; Weber, note 123 on Arts. 84 OR; Kleiner, p. 69; Thalmann, SZW, p. 258.

[75] See part 2. a) cc) above.

[76] Guggenheim, p. 237; see also Thalmann, SZW, p. 259; Weber, note 123 on Art. 74 OR.

[77] Weber, SJZ 78, p. 143; Weber, notes 124 ff. on Art. 74 OR; Thalmann, p. 162; Heini, part 3, chap. 1 § 3 III. Contra, Helbig, pp. 92 ff.; Guhl/Merz/Kummer, p. 213. The credit is thus determinative not only for the determination of the fulfillment of the contractual obligation but also for determiniation of whether payment was made on time: Thalmann, SZW, p. 258. If the debtor has agreed with the creditor that payment will be made to a

the debtor bears the risk of delay or loss of the payment because his debt is not yet discharged. The debtor may have claims for compensation against the bank responsible for the delay or loss.[78]

d) Other Legal Relationships

There are no additional contractual relationships between the parties involved in a multiphase transfer, such as between the originator and the receiving bank or between the sending bank and the beneficiary.[79] Each party may, however, assert claims based on the principles of tort, governed by Art. 41 ff. OR, against other parties with whom they have no contractual relationship. It is not apparent that such non-contractual claims have been asserted in connection with non-cash payment transactions, probably due in part to the shift in the burden of proof — the party asserting the claim must prove all the elements of the claim, including the fault and the unlawful conduct of the defendant.

3. Revocation, Avoidance or Cancellation of the Transfer

a) Revocation of the Transfer

aa) Revocation by the Originator

The originator can revoke the order to the bank as long as the bank has not indicated its acceptance of the order to the receiving bank (Art. 470 (2) OR), i.e. so long as no credit has been made.[80] A revocation by the originator must therefore be judged not only in accordance with the law governing the delivery order (Anweisung) but also — due to the nature of the giro agreement as a mandate — in accordance with the law of the mandate. It is to be classified as a counterinstruction under the giro agreement.[81] The origina-

collecting agent, or if payment is made to a collecting agent through a clearing system, then it is not the time of the account credit which is determinative but instead the actual time at which the payment is received by the collecting agent; from this point on the creditor bears the rsik of delays by the collecting agent. See also Kleiner, IDS, p. 83 and 85 f.

[78] Contractual compensation claims can be asserted only with respect to the individual links in the chain for which contractual relationships exist, e. g. by the originator against his bank but not against the beneficiary's bank. It must also be kept in mind that in their general business conditions banks usually exclude liability for any damages due to delay or failute to execute transfer orders, except loss of interest or where in a specific case the bank was informed of the risk of additional losses. See Thalmann, pp. 164 ff.

[79] Guggenheim, o. 240; Kleiner/Schmid, p. 179.

[80] Guggenheim, p. 240; Kleiner, p. 55.

[81] Accord, Heini, part 2 chap. 4 § 1 I; Hadding/Häuser, pp. 1153 f. on German law. But these authors classify every revocation, not just one issued by the originator, as a counterinstruction. On revocation by the originator's bank, see part 3. a) bb) below.

tor's bank has the duty based on the giro agreement to act immediately on this counterinstruction and must carry out the revocation measures which can be achieved using reasonable effort. These include an internal search for the payment order which may have been entered into the data processing system but not yet transmitted to the receiving bank; if the order has already been transmitted to the receiving bank, the originator's bank is obligated to immediately transmit the revocation order[82], i.e. it must revoke the transfer under the law of the delivery order (Anweisung).[83]

bb) Revocation by the Sending Bank

As the instructing party, the sending bank can revoke the transfer with respect to the receiving bank as the instructed party as long as the receiving bank has not yet declared its acceptance of the instruction to the beneficiary as payee (see Art. 470 (2) OR). In non-cash payment transactions, this acceptance is declared by means of the credit to the beneficiary's account by the receiving bank; consequently, the revocation must be honored if the credit has not yet been made.[84] Normally, the sending bank will revoke the transfer only when it receives a corresponding revocation or (counter)instruction from the originator.

Because the revocation is a statement of intent requiring receipt, it is effective only when received by the receiving bank.[85] If one or more intermediary banks are engaged to carry out the transfer, the sending bank must direct the revocation to the first intermediary bank, which must then revoke the transfer with respect to the following bank. The revocation must thus take place within the framework of the individual giro agreements, i.e. within the individual links in the transfer chain.[86]

A revocation by the instructing party directed to the beneficiary of the instruction, which basically is possible (Art. 470 (1) OR), need not be

[82] Kleiner, p. 56. This duty to convey revocation also applies to other intermediary banks later in the transfer chain.

[83] See part bb) below. Regarding the classification of the (chain) transfer initiated by the bank as a delivery order (Anweisung), see part 2. b) bb) above.

[84] See part 2. a) cc) above, and Kleiner, pp. 55 f.; von der Crone, p. 67; BGE 100 II 373. Various authors look to the time at which the beneficiary acquires knowledge of the credit; e. g. Emch/Renz, p. 328; Handbuch, p. 126.

[85] von der Crone, p. 67. In my opinion this must also apply to the counterinstruction by the originator, analogously to the instruction under the giro agreement (see part 2. a) bb) bbb).

[86] The direct revocation which skips a bank must be rejected; see Hadding/Häuser, p. 1154. In my view, maintaining the order in the chain for a revocation is also justified by practical considerations; for example, where there is no contractual relationship it may not be possible for a bank to correctly identify the party issuing the revocation.

examined here because the prevailing view of the scholars[87] is that it does not, as a rule, come into question in non-cash payment transactions.

cc) Effects of the Revocation

A valid revocation made in a timely manner leads to the removal of the transfer initiated by the sender and thus to the reversal of the transfer. The sending bank must initiate the necessary legal steps for the repayment of the covering funds or assign the respective claims to the sender.[88]

With respect to the relationship between the beneficiary and his bank, as already stated[89], the revocation cancels any claim the beneficiary has to have the transfer amount credited. but if the revocation was possible only because the beneficiary's bank was at fault in delayed processing of the transfer, the bank is liable to the beneficiary under Art. 398 (2) OR for any resulting damages.[90]

b) Avoidance of the Transfer by the Sender

Under the prevailing view, the sender has the basic right with respect to his bank to avoid the transfer order on the grounds of significant mistake (Art. 23 f. OR), intentional deception (Art. 28 OR) or threat (Art. 29 OR), but the avoidance does not impede the effect of the completed credit to the beneficiary's account.[91] The avoidance can, therefore, can have practical and legal significance only so long as a valid revocation would still be possible, namely so long as the credit has not yet been made. Thereafter, defects of intent can be asserted only against the beneficiary within the scope of the underlying contractual relationship.

c) Cancellation of the Transfer by the Receiving Bank

The right of the receiving bank to cancel a credit to the account of the beneficiary which was made by mistake or incorrectly and to correct the credit by means of a reverse transaction is generally recognized although the opinions on the legal theory justifying this action differ. The prevailing view,

---

[87] See Heini, part 2, chap. 4 § 1 I; see also von der Crone, p. 67; Guggenheim, p. 241.

[88] Kleiner, p. 56; see also Heini, part 2, chap. 4 § 1 II 2.

[89] Part. 2. a) cc) above; see also von der Crone, p. 68.

[90] von der Crone, p. 68.

[91] Guggenheim, pp. 241 ff.; Heini, part 2, chap. 4 § 2; Kleiner, p. 60. Contra, von der Crone, pp. 65 f.

which I believe is correct, is probably that the credit is a legal declaration of intent[92] which can, therefore, be avoided by the receiving bank with respect to the beneficiary on the grounds of defective intent.[93] The primary situation involved is that of avoidance due a mistake regarding the identity of the beneficiary, the account to be credited or the amount of the transfer.

The issue of the defective intent must be asserted by means of a unilateral declaration of intent which requires receipt; it must be expressed in the cancellation with appropriate notice to the beneficiary. The legal basis for the credit is retroactively removed from that point, and under the principles in Art. 62 ff. OR governing unjust enrichment, the bank is entitled to annul the entry or reverse the entry as of the date of the credit. It is not necessary under Swiss law that the defective intent, or rather the claim based on unjust enrichment, be asserted by means of a court action in order for the annulment or reverse entry to be effective.

III. Conflict of Laws Issues

1. Basic Principles

a) Preface

In cross-border payment transactions, various parties in various countries with differing currencies are involved. This constellation necessarily leads to conflict of laws issues, which will be examined here as they relate to the topics discussed above; it will be presumed that Swiss private international law applies.

Swiss conflict of laws rules have been comprehensively codified. The new Private International Law Statute [IPRG] has been in effect since January 1, 1989. This statute contains rules relating to determination of the applicable law in the narrower sense as well as provisions relating to jurisdiction. Because cross-border payment transactions are based on contractual relations between the participating parties, we will first look at the statutory provisions relating to contracts in general and then at their specific application to the contractual relationships of interest here.[94] The primary focus is more on issues relating to the applicable law than to jurisdiction.

[92] The beneficiary's bank declares its acceptance of the instruction by means of the credit; see part 2. a) cc) above.

[93] Guggenheim, p. 243; Kleiner, p. 58. Contra, Helbig, pp. 130 f.; von der Crone, p. 40.

[94] Because there can also be claims based on tort (part II. 2. above) or unjust enrichment (part II. 3. c) above), we will refer here only to the relevant provisions of the Private International Law Act (Art. 129 ff. and Art. 127 ff.)

b) Jurisdiction

With respect to the evaluation of issues of contract law, reference must first be made to the fact that the parties may freely stipulate the location of jurisdiction[95] (Art. 5 IPRG). If the parties do not exercise this opportunity, then under Art. 112 (1) IPRG the Swiss courts at the domicile of the defendant or, in the absence of this domicile, at his habitual residence, have jurisdiction to hear claims based on contract. "For claims based on the activities of a branch in Switzerland, the courts at the location of the branch shall also have jurisdiction" (Art. 112 (2) IPRG).[96] If there is no domicile or habitual residence, then under Art. 113 a claim can be brought before a Swiss court at the place of performance if performance is to be made in Switzerland.

These rules of jurisdiction will be subject to the Convention on Jurisdiction and Enforcement of Judgments in Civil and Commercial Matters (the so-called Lugano Convention) concluded on Sept. 16, 1988, which entered into force in Switzerland on Jan. 1, 1992; this convention contains rules of jurisdiction significant for international contracts which in part differ from the IPRG.[97]

c) Applicable Law

aa) Subjective Connection

The basic connecting principle contained in Art. 166 (1) is that a contract is governed by the law chosen by the parties. The intent of the parties is expressed in the so-called reference agreement which is a part of the contractual relationship governed by the choice of law.[98] The requirements for the choice of law clause set out in Art. 116 (2) IPRG are that it must be express or must be clearly implied based on the terms of the contract or the circumstances. This provision also stipulates that the issue of the existence and the validity of the choice of law clause shall be governed by the law chosen. Art. 123 ff. IPRG provides for special rules of reference in the case of silence in response to an offer and with respect to the required form of a contract.

The parties can agree to make or amend the choice of law at any time; a choice of law made or amended after conclusion of the contract is effective

[95] Regarding the exceptions, see Schnyder, pp. 22 ff.

[96] The issue of whether a company has its seat or a branch in Switzerland must be decided in accordance with Art. 21 IPRG.

[97] See Schnyder, p. 21, 105.

[98] Kleiner, IDS, p. 10, with additional references; BGE 102 II 145. Regarding the limitations on the freedom of choice, see Schnyder, p. 106.

retroactively from the date of the contract, subject, however, to any rights of third parties which had arisen in the meantime (Art. 116 (3) IPRG).

bb) Objective Connection

If no choice of law is made by the parties, the contract is subject, in accordance with Art. 117 (1) IPRG, to the law of the state "with which it has the closest connection". As a blanket clause[99], this connecting rule must be further specified. The most important criterium is provided in the IPR Act itself; the contract is referred to the law of the state in which the party performing the characteristic — i.e. functionally typical[100] — contractual obligation has his habitual residence or business residence (Art. 117 (2) IPRG). The IPRG includes an extensive but not exclusive list of types of performance to be viewed as characteristic (Art. 117 (3)).

cc) Currency as a Special Connecting Factor

The IPRG contains in Art. 147 a special reference to the law of the currency.[101] Under this special provision, the law of the currency governs the concept and the content of the currency (par. 1). The issue of the effects of the currency on the amount of the debt is subject to the law governing the debt (par. 2). The determination of the currency in which payment is to be made "is governed by the law of the state in which payment is to be made" (par. 3).

2. The Law Applicable to the Contractual Relationship between the Customer and the Bank

a) Common Choice of Law Clauses Used in Banking

The issue of the law applicable to the contractual relationship between the bank and the customer usually arises only when the customer and the bank have their residence or place of business in two different countries. If this is not the case, the transactions are purely domestic, and the law of the common country governs the current account and giro agreements (as a contractual relationship with no international connection).[102]

---

[99] Schnyder, p. 108.

[100] Id.

[101] See Fischer, pp. 425 ff.

[102] Etzkorn, p. 91. The issue of whether the parties to a purely domestic contract can choose to have the contract governed by foreign law rather that Swiss contract law is

The AGB used by the banks commonly contain a choice of law clause stipulating the law of the seat of the bank.[103] It is also necessary to determine whether the current account and giro contract is a consumer contract within the meaning of Art. 120 (1) IPRG, which would exclude the possibility of a choice of law by the parties (Art. 120 (2) IPRG).[104] Under this provision, consumer contracts are contracts for "ordinary consumer goods and services intended for the personal or family use of the consumer and not in connection with the profession or business of the consumer". Whether the services generally or specifically offered by banks in connection with payment transactions for customers are to be deemed "consumer services" is not apparent from the IPRG or from the (still sparse) legal literature and case decisions on this issue. There is a recognizable trend to include service contracts within the scope of application of Art. 120 IPRG. For this reason and also based on the protective purpose of the cited provision, I believe that it would be justified to subject the current account and giro agreement to the application of Art. 120 IPRG; this would be true, of course, only for the banking services intended for personal or family use and where, in addition, one of the other requirements of Art. 120 (1) IPRG is met.[105] If these requirements are met, the law of the state where the consumer has his habitual residence would have mandatory application.[106]

In all other cases, in particular in commercial transactions, the choice of law clause in the AGB commonly used by the banks stipulating the law of the seat of the bank is permissible under Art. 116 (1) IPRG. The chosen law governs the current account and giro agreement, including the foreign currency account relationship[107] as well as the services performed by the bank based on this agreement (in particular the execution of payment transactions, i.e. the making and acceptance of payments for the customer).

---

probably of mere academic significance. According to Schnyder (p. 106) such a choice of law may be made only when the contract has international connections. We need not attempt here do decide whether the bank's basic willingness to carry out foreign transfers or manage a foreign currency account for the customer is a sufficient foreign connection.

[103] Kleiner, IDS, p. 34.

[104] Schnyder, p. 111, with references to various court decisions.

[105] When the supplier receives the order in the consumer's country of residence (a.), an offer or advertising preceded the conclusion of the contract there, and the legal acts necessary to conclude the contract were undertaken there by the consumer (b.), or the supplier induces the consumer to go to a foreign country and place his order there (c.).

[106] Here the mandatory provision of Art. 114 (1) IPRG also applies to complaints by consumers; based on his choice, the courts at his domicile or residence or at the seat of the bank have jurisdiction. He cannot contractually waive the jurisdiction of the courts at his domicile or residence (Art. 114 (2) IPRG). The issue of whether the usual bank general business conditions violate this rule of jurisdiction or the exclusion of the choice of law must be decided in the individual case depending on whether the respective contract must be classified as a consumer contract, taking all circumstances into consideration.

[107] Kleiner, IDW, p. 262; Etzkorn, p. 92, See part II, 2. aa) bbb) above.

b) Reference in the Absence of a Choice of Law by the Parties

If no choice of law is made by the parties, the determination of the law applicable to the account relationship between the customer and the bank depends upon which party performs the characteristic obligation under the contract. Under the statute, the characteristic obligation is "in the case of a commission (Auftrag), a contract for work or similar contract for services, the service obligation" (Art. 117 (3) c IPRG). The giro agreement is classified as a simple commission[108], and the current account agreement does not alter the agency character of the contractual relationship between the customer and the bank. The current account and giro agreement is therefore subject to the cited provision of the IPRG. Because the bank performs the typical obligations, i.e. the execution — making and acceptance — of payment transactions for the customer, then for this reason as well the contract is governed under Art. 117 IPRG by the law of the seat of the bank or contracting branch of the bank.[109]

The law determined in accordance with these rules governs all legal issues arising in connection with the contractual relationship, namely the validity of the AGB, the revocation and recourse against a bank for errors[110] as well as the contents and legal effects of foreign currency obligations.[111] By contrast, HEINI views it as justified with respect to the issue of the point in time at which the money creditor's claim arises to use a special connecting factor to the law of the state "in which the branch of the credit institution managing the account for the beneficiary is located".[112]

3. The Law Applicable to the Contractual Relationship between the Sending Bank and the Receiving Bank

The contract between the sending and the receiving bank is substantively the same as that between the customer and the bank[113]; therefore, the conflicts issues are resolved basically in the same way as describe above.[114] Special elements are present here in particular with regard to the special connecting factor: first, the choice of law prohibition in Art. 120 IPRG is not

[108] See part II. 2. a) aa) aaa) above.

[109] This was the determinative connecting factor prior to the new IPRG; see Kleiner, IDS, p. 34.

[110] Heini, part 4, chap. 2 § 4 and § 5.

[111] Kleiner, IDS, p. 77. This is conditioned upon possible application of mandatory foreign currency provisions outside the applicable law of contract: Art. 18 f. IPRG.

[112] Heini, part 4, chap. 2 § 3.

[113] See part II. 2. b) aa) above.

[114] See part II. above.

relevant here because the managing of accounts as well as the specific payments transactions between the banks are always related to their business and thus cannot be consumer contracts within the meaning of that provision. On the other hand, there can be a conflict of choice of law clauses here if the AGB of both banks are validly incorporated and contain conflicting provisions on the applicable law. The prevailing view is that the AGB of the bank which performs the characteristic obligation in the specific transaction are determinative.[115] The same connecting factor is used in the absence of a choice of law by the parties.[116]

---

[115] Kleiner, p. 44; Etzkorn, pp. 45 ff., with additional references.

[116] Kleiner, p. 34; Etzkorn, pp. 49 ff. Regarding the difficulty of determining the characteristic performance in a foreign exchange transaction, see Kleiner, SAG, pp. 70 f.

Article 4 A of the United States Uniform Commercial Code

By Carl Felsenfeld, New York

Contents

I. Introduction

The case of *Evra Corp. vs. Swiss Bank Corp.*[1] brought chills to the hearts of United States bank lawyers in 1982. Although the banking bar generally considered the result satisfactory,[2] it was frightening to realize that trillions of dollars were being transmitted electronically on a daily basis through the banking system and that there was no established body of law, neither case

---

[1] 673 F. 2d 951 (7th Cir.), cert. denied 459 U.S. 103 (1982).

[2] The originator of an electronic funds transfer was not awarded $ 2.1 Million in consequential damages — the lost value of his ship charter — when a bank negligently lost the payment order that was intended to pay the ship charter rental to the owner.

law nor statutory law, to regulate these transfers. Those positioned to draft statutes in this area of law[3] generally agreed that something had to be done.

After an initial abortive effort,[4] the National Conference of Commissioners on Uniform State Laws (hereinafter called "Commissioners"), established a drafting group in January 1986 and Article 4 A of the Uniform Commercial Code (hereinafter called "UCC") was the result. It will be immediately noted that the Commissioners and their drafting group intended from the start that their statutory product be part of the UCC, a collection of statutes that the Commissioners had created in the late 1940's. That collection, designed to be the core of United States commercial law, was written, as is all work of the Commissioners, to be adopted as United States state — not federal — law.

The UCC, with some minor variations, has been adopted by all states and can now fairly be described as the law of the United States. The expectation of the Article 4 A drafters was that 4 A would be incorporated into this body of law and would also become uniform United States state, as contrasted with federal, law. Article 4 A was officially approved by its drafters in the summer of 1989 and the optimistic expectations about its acceptance appear to be justified.[5]

II. Principles Behind 4 A

When the 4 A drafters surveyed the rapidly growing electronic payment scene, they sensed a general desire, at least among the banking community, to retain through Article 4 A the essential structure of the payment system whose contours could already be seen in place. It was considered neither a desirable nor a practicable effort to try and change the payment system into a form that might have been considered preferable by the drafters as contrasted with the practitioners.

The existing payment system was generally acknowledged to have three principal ingredients. First, it involved high volume, commercial payments. This is not to say that low balance, consumer-related electronic payments were not also present. As a result of an intense consumer movement that

[3] Principally the American Law Institute and the National Conference of Commissioners on Uniform State Laws.

[4] A committee of the American Law Institute sponsored something called The New Payments Code. Largely because of changes it made in the methods of payment by check it was, without formal action, disapproved by the bar at large and it died a quiet death in 1984.

[5] Article 4 A has, as of this writing, been adopted by 17 states including California, Connecticut, Illinois and New York. There is no political opposition to it and it appears that it should be adopted within a reasonable time by all of the states.

dominated much legislative activity in the United States through the 1960's and 1970's, however, a federal statute called the Electronic Funds Transfer Act (hereinafter called "EFTA")[6] was already on the books for the specific protection of consumers in their electronic funds transfers. Thus, the thrust of 4 A was from the start in the direction of the large volume, commercial funds transfer.

Second, the goal was a high-speed system. One might conceive, on the one hand, a meticulously handled funds transfer with skilled employees monitoring each step of the way and reporting on and dealing with minor variations from a perceived norm. If such a system were contrasted with one where the primary goal of each participant was to receive and transmit messages with speed and accuracy, the greater benefits were seen in the latter. This is not to say that transfers would be handled casually,[7] but rather that the system to be memorialized by statute would establish a series of simple and precise standards that could be met clearly and immediately.

Finally, the goal was low cost. Currently, electronic transfers are typically being handled, regardless of their amount, at a cost to the original sender of between ten and twenty dollars. The implications of this factor bear upon the preceding principle as well as upon the risk that the banking system should be asked to sustain in effecting an electric funds transfer. Keeping the risk potential in line with the relatively low price was a serious consideration throughout the drafting process.[8]

III. Inclusions and Exclusions

Article 4 A is basically restricted to what bankers call "credit transfers". Under 4 A-103 (a), to be covered by the Article, a transfer must start with an order to a bank to make the transfer. In honoring the order and moving the transfer, the bank debits an account of the ordering party. By way of contrast, a bank may effect what is called a "debit transfer" by which the bank, instead of making a transfer, orders another bank to make a payment to it and then credits the account of the receiving party. Such a transfer is not covered by 4 A. The reason for this is that the United States banking system has had considerably more experience with credit than with debit transfers (although we understand that the European systems have explored debit transfers more deeply). The 4 A drafters did not want to subject a system to

---

[6] Title 15 U.S.C., Sec. 1693 et seq.

[7] See, in this connection, the "money-back guarantee" of Section 4 A-402, discussed infra at note 24.

[8] This will appear most plainly in the discussion infra notes 20 and 21 on liability for negligence and other forms of misbehavior.

statutory requirements until more about it was understood. It is not inconceivable that 4 A will be expanded at some time in the future to accommodate the debit transfer method.

In line with the principle that 4 A will concentrate on high balance transfers, consumer-related transfers — defined as those covered by the EFTA — are excluded from coverage. This makes for an odd division. Many issues (such as when is payment made) are covered by 4 A that are not covered by the EFTA. Nevertheless, since a transaction may be covered by EFTA and, therefore, not by 4 A, a question such as when a payment is made will not be covered at all.[9] This is not to say that only large payments are covered by 4 A; if a payment is not a consumer / EFTA transaction it is, by definition, covered under 4 A. Its actual size is not relevant.

Article 4 A is designed for the banking system. Thus, to be under its coverage, the electronic transfer must be handled in whole or in part by banks. Money may be moved electronically by entities that are not banks, but unless a bank is involved, the transaction will not be governed by Article 4 A. If a transaction involves institutions that are banks and those that are not, the relationships between banks and those between banks and other entities will be governed by 4 A; those among the other institutions will not.

IV. The Funds Transfer and the Payment Order

In structuring 4 A, the underlying electronic transfer is defined under Sec. 4 A-104 as a "funds transfer". A funds transfer is the movement of funds that the originator of the transfer (perhaps someone owing a debt) has in mind: a movement to the ultimate beneficiary (the person to whom the debt is owing). Actually, under 4 A, a funds transfer does not have to get to that beneficiary to be completed. It only has to get to the beneficiary's bank. One can easily see, if the beneficiary has money in the bank, it is, for all practical purposes, his. Sec. 4 A-104, therefore, defines a funds transfer as ending with the beneficiary's bank, not the beneficiary. If the bank fails to honor its customer's demand for funds in his own bank account, that is a matter for local banking law, not 4 A.

The originator usually does not care what route the payment takes from originator's bank to beneficiary's bank. Each step of the way is called a "payment order" under 4 A-103. All payment orders necessarily involve the movement of funds and must have banks as the receiving party. The order of the originator to his bank is a payment order. The final relationship between the beneficiary's bank and the beneficiary is, as noted just above, outside the

[9] Whether full thought was given to this matter is unclear.

defined funds transfer. It also does not necessarily involve a movement of funds (the bank may just hold the funds for the beneficiary) and also does not necessarily involve a bank (the beneficiary may, but need not, be a bank). It is not, therefore, a payment order.

V. Acceptance and Rejection of Orders

When a bank receives a payment order (including the order that the originator's bank receives from the originator) it may accept or reject the order.[10] A bank typically incurs a risk when it accepts a payment order. If it accepts an order without sufficient knowledge about the sender, it might not get paid. It is important to realize that a payment order does not conceptually include a passage of funds. A payment order is only a message. When a bank accepts a payment order, it is assuming that it will be paid by the sender. If, for example, it does not know the sender (which might be a non-bank originator such as a business paying an obligation electronically or might be a prior bank in the payment chain) it might want simply to reject the order and be safe rather than incur the risk of non-payment. Two brief scenarios illustrate:

1. The receiving bank may neither accept nor reject. The funds transfer is not moved along and expires at that point. If the receiving bank has no money on deposit from the sender to cover the order, it owes the sender nothing. The unaccepted order is cancelled by operation of law after five days.[11]

2. If the receiving bank does have money on deposit from the sender and neither accepts nor rejects the order, it must pay interest on the money until the sender learns of the non-action or the five days expire.

We see here one working of the principle that minimal burdens should be put upon the banking system. If the receiving bank neither accepts nor rejects, it really does not suffer any penalty. It must only pay interest on money that it has. The concept is that if the sender is really interested in knowing whether the payment order has been accepted or rejected, it is the job of the sender to find this out. It is not a duty of the receiving banks.

VI. Method of Payment Order Acceptance

More typically, because of established relationships among banks or because of funds sent in advance to cover orders, a payment order will be

[10] Sec. 4 A-208 covers acceptances and 4 A-209 rejections.

[11] Sec. 4 A-211 (d).

accepted. Acceptance of an order is entwined with the idea of sending it on to someone else. In fact the only way a bank (other than a beneficiary's bank to which we shall return) can accept an order is through the act of sending it on its path towards the beneficiary's bank.[12]

In general, the duty of the receiving bank in accepting/sending is to comply with the instructions it has received from its sender.[13] If, for example, the originator's bank accepts/sends, it also has the duty to transmit the instructions it received from the originator to the next sender, and so on down the line. An intermediary bank is not, however, required to use a funds transfer system[14] despite an instruction to that effect if it decides in good faith that "it is not feasible to follow the instruction or that following the instruction would unduly delay completion of the funds transfer".[15]

Only the beneficiary's bank does not accept by sending. It may not be appropriate for the beneficiary's bank to send at all. It may merely hold the money in the beneficiary's account. Thus, any one of a designated series of acts or communications between the beneficiary's bank and the beneficiary, including merely informing the beneficiary of the receipt of the funds for its benefit, will suffice for an acceptance. A beneficiary's bank is also deemed to accept if it has received full payment from the sender before it has had a chance to reject. In that event, since the bank is covered in full by funds, it has no credit risk, its only duty is thereupon to honor the will of its own customer and there would seem to be no legitimate reason for it any longer to reject the funds transfer.[16]

VII. Security Procedures

The duty of all banks between the originator of the funds transfer and its ultimate beneficiary is to move the funds in accordance with the originator's original order. The question necessarily arises: how do the various sending banks along the path of the payment know whether or not they are receiving a legitimate order. The question is answered through the technique called a security procedure.

Article 4 A begins by establishing the fundamental rule that if a payment order is in fact the order of the person identified as the sender or if that person is otherwise bound by that order under the law of agency, that person

---

[12] Sec. 4 A209 (a).

[13] Sec. 4 A-302.

[14] Like CHIPS or S.W.I.F.T. or some other association of banks organized for the transmission of payments. See Sec. 4 A-501 (b) and text infra at note 32.

[15] Sec. 4 A-302 (b).

[16] Sec. 4 A-209 (b).

is bound by it. Accordingly, the receiver is justified in relying upon it as the legitimate and legally binding order of the named sender. The problem, however, is that in the typical case the receiver will have neither the time nor the amount of information that may be required to make this determination. Both sender and receiver are now able, pursuant to Article 4 A, to rely upon the operations of a "security procedure" agreed upon by them both.

A security procedure between sender and receiver is defined by Sec. 4 A-201. The definition is deliberately broad in scope and less than specific in order to accommodate whatever sort of technical development may be found appropriate. The procedure is defined to be one for the purpose of verifying that the order is that of the customer or that it is free of error. Sec. 4 A-202 then provides that if the security procedure has been agreed upon by sender and receiver, it may be relied upon by the receiver as the sender's order if (a) the procedure is commercially reasonable and (b) the receiving bank complied with the procedure and any accompanying order or instruction of the sender.

In relying upon this procedure, the receiving bank need not establish that the order is in fact the order of the sender. The payment order may in fact have been sent by a completely unauthorized interloper. The task of the receiving bank thus becomes simpler and less expensive. It must, in the original establishment of the security procedure, ensure that the procedure is commercially reasonable. But this must be done only once. It must then ensure that in its receipt of every payment order it has followed the requirements of the procedure that the parties have put in place.

The principal problem inherent in the system just described is that an interloper may have gotten information concerning the security procedure and how to defeat it through the receiver itself. In this event, it was agreed that the sender should not be responsible for any resulting loss. Sec. 4 A-201 (2) provides that if the sender proves that any improper interference in the system was not caused by the sender or by a person entrusted to act through the sender, then the sender does not bear responsibility for the loss.

If a receiving bank receives funds from a sender under a payment order that is not enforceable as the order of the sender under the rules just described, the bank must, under Sec. 4 A-204, return the money and pay interest upon it for long as it holds it. The sender has a duty itself, however, of using ordinary care to shorten this time. To the extent that the sender does not honor this duty, the receiving bank is relieved of its duty to pay interest.

Sec. 4 A-205 deals with various situations where a payment order may be erroneously transmitted because a security system was not properly used by a receiving bank. In that event, the sender is generally not obliged to pay the amount of the order to the receiving bank to the extent that the error was caused by the receiving bank's mistake. Here, Sec. 4 A-205 puts upon the sender a corresponding burden of reasonable behavior that is similar to the burden placed above under Sec. 4 A-204. In Sec. 4 A-205 (b), before the sending bank will be relieved of its duty to pay the receiving bank, it must again demonstrate that it has exercised "ordinary care".[17]

VIII. Names and Numbers

Some of the more frequent errors that occur in existing funds transfer system relate to inconsistencies between names and numbers. That is, a beneficiary may be described by its name and also by some identifying number. The two may not match. This problem is dealt with in Sec. 4 A-207. The approach of the Article is to deal with the issue through the approach of the modern, high speed systems: the numbers count, not the names. Sec. 207 says that if a beneficiary is described by name and by number and if the beneficiary's bank does not know that the name and the number refer to different persons, the bank may rely upon the number.

Increasingly the modern computerized systems do not include the name, as contrasted with the number, at all. To the extent that a sender may even be able to send a name to a receiving bank, the 4 A approach is that the bank is entitled to consider the name irrelevant information and ignore it. In this manner, 4 A again honors the principles outlined at the beginning of this article that the techniques of modern, high speed systems should be honored; hand-operated devices designed for the special protection of system users are to be avoided. If a beneficiary's bank relies (properly under the Article) upon the number it has received, but the number was a mistake of a prior sender, and if the beneficiary's bank makes a payment to the holder of that number, the prior sender who made the mistake may recover against the recipient (that is, the holder of the wrong number). But the recovery is "to the extent allowed by the law governing mistake and restitution". That is, it is under the law other than Article 4 A.

The problem of inconsistent descriptions of banks by name and by number receives similar treatment under the succeeding section, 4 A-208. If the sender is a bank, the receiver may rely upon the number if it does not know that different banks are identified; it need not affirmatively determine whether the name and number refer to different banks; the sender must compensate the receiving bank for any loss incurred by the receiving bank as a result of its reliance upon the number. If the sender is not a bank, the rules

[17] We note the similarity between this requirement and a roughly equivalent requirement applicable to checks in Sec. 3-406 of the UCC. Under that provision, any person who contributes to a check forgery by his negligence may not hold the bank responsible.

are essentially the same, but there is a somewhat heavier burden upon the receiver; it must prove that the sender had notice first that the receiver might rely upon the number in its handling of the message.

IX. Cancellation and Amendment of Payment Order

Funds transfers and payment orders are, when measured by the time we customarily relate to payment transactions, particularly payment by check, very swift. The traditional "stop" order that has developed in checking transactions is, therefore, of equally short duration when applied in electronic transactions. Under Sec. 4 A-211, to be effective, a stop order or an order amending a prior order must be received in time to give "the receiving bank a reasonable time to act on the communication before the bank accepts the payment order". Stops or amendments after this time may be effective, but only if the receiving bank affirmatively accepts or is subject to an overriding payment system rule requiring the practice.

If the relationship between sender and receiver is subject to a security procedure, the stop or amendment must also be subject to the procedure. It need not necessarily be the same procedure that governed the original payment order. But the doctrine that controlled the original transaction that an order is effective, regardless of a security procedure, if it was in fact the order of the sender[18] seems to have no place here. To the extent that the drafters considered this possibility (or even likelihood), they might have concluded that there was no time within the compressed time of the system even to look for underlying facts; they may also have decided that if the order was in fact legitimate there would probably be no issue.

The ability to stop or amend an order in the hands of the beneficiary's bank is even narrower than when it is with other banks. The order may be stopped or amended only if it were somehow an improper order to start (a duplicate, directed to a wrong beneficiary etc.). If the stop or amendment does come in time, that is before acceptance,[19] then the beneficiary's bank that may have jumped the gun, that is paid over before acceptance, may recover outside 4 A under local law dealing with issues of mistake and restitution.

X. Liability for Late or Improper Execution

Rules of liability are interspersed throughout the Article. We will select two fundamental doctrines of liability to illustrate the operation of 4 A.

[18] See text under "Security Procedure" supra and Sec. 4 A-202 (a).

[19] See note 16 supra for acceptance by a beneficiary's bank.

First, assume that a receiver has made an error and as a result the payment has gotten to the intended beneficiary late. Under 4 A-305 (a), the error-making receiver is liable for the payment of interest only.[20]

Second, assume that a receiver mishandles a transfer and the funds do not reach the beneficiary at all. In this case, under subsection (b) of the same section, the damages are also interest to which are now added the expenses of the originator and incidental expenses. In other words, the damages in this second hypothetical are very similar to those in the first.

Sec. 4 A305 is unusually specific about these limitations. After describing the measure of damages, subsections (a) and (b) of the section each end with the sentence, "Except as provided in subsection (c), additional damages are not recoverable". The reason for the specificity here is that we have returned to the sensitive and difficult problem raised by the Evra case[21] that stimulated the early dedication to the concept of a funds transfer law. Consistent with the Evra result,[22] the 4 A drafters resolved that the standard measure of damages for misbehavior would be interest and would not include consequential damages. Under this conservative approach, damages would not be greater even if the misbehavior were deliberate, performed with gross negligence, with malice or with whatever adverse description tort law could devise for it.

It is useful to present by way of comparison an analogous test for misbehavior from Article 4 of the same UCC, applicable to the checking system:

> "The measure of damages for failure to exercise ordinary care in handling an item is the amount of the item reduced by an amount which could not have been realized by the use of ordinary care, and where there is bad faith it includes other damages, if any, suffered by the party as a proximate consequence." (emphasis added)[23]

It is incontestable, and it is uncontested, that the drafters knew of the concept of consequential damages ("other damages" in the above extract) and were accustomed to working with it in a payment system context. They nevertheless refused to apply it to electronic funds payments. The principles stated at the beginning of this article were applied instead. The volume of the payments made over a typical electronic network were very high and the costs typically imposed by the banking system for making them were very low. It was consequently accepted that, however remote the likelihood of consequential damages and however limiting the definition of the situations

---

[20] Interest is payable to either the originator or the beneficiary, whoever turns out to have been adversely affected by the delay.

[21] See note 1 supra.

[22] See note 2 supra.

[23] Sec. 4 A-103 (5).

in which those damages might be imposed, the risk of a recovery measured in the millions, conceivably billions, was simply too overwhelming to be bought with a fifteen dollar charge.

The disagreements in the drafting process were occasionally heated, but even the businesses that used bank networks to make their payments and might perceive consequential-damage remedies as being for their legitimate protection agreed that overall low cost was preferable to such potential recovery. It was actually a secondary consideration that there had been insufficient experience to evaluate the extent of the risks in order to underwrite what an appropriate bank fee might be. If a bank did want to sustain greater risk than the law requires, it could do so, but only under "an express written agreement" with its customer pursuant to subsection 4 A-305 (c).

Expressing the idea in somewhat different form, the banking system handles innumerable funds transfers. A business handles relatively few where time is a particularly crucial ingredient. If a business wants to ensure that the crucial transfer will arrive where it is intended to go, Article 4 A implicitly suggests that the business monitor it manually. The low cost of the transfer makes this extra precaution a bargain.

The right of a bank customer to obtain consequential damages appears only once in Article 4 A. The relationship of a beneficiary and its bank is dealt with in Sec. 4 A-404. The basic prescription is that, once the beneficiary's bank has accepted the payment order directed to it, it "is obliged to pay the amount of the order to the beneficiary". If, however,

"the bank refuses to pay after demand by the beneficiary and receipt of notice of particular circumstances that will give rise to consequential damages as a result of nonpayment, the beneficiary may recover damages resulting from the refusal to pay to the extent the bank had notice of the damages, unless the bank proves that it not pay because of a reasonable doubt concerning the right of the beneficiary to payment."

Thus, within carefully limited circumstances and with a right in the bank to receive advance notice and a defined opportunity to avoid the damages, consequential damages do take their place in the structure of Article 4 A.

XI. The Money-Back Guarantee

At this point, the question may be asked whether the banking system has gone to an extreme and abdicated its responsibility to ensure dependable and careful payment of its depositors' funds. Article 4 A stops short of such a posture. Sec. 4 A-402 starts by assuring that both an intermediary bank and a beneficiary's bank that accepts a payment order will be paid by the sender of that order. It adds to this the provision that the sender's obligation to pay is excused, and if payment has already been made it must be returned, if the funds transfer is not ultimately accepted by the beneficiary's bank.

Since every payment order except the first is necessarily based upon a previous payment order, this structure means that (i) if the payment order is not accepted by the beneficiary's bank the originator need pay nothing and (ii) if the originator has already made payment it will be returned. This obligation of the banking system directed towards the originator has been dubbed the "money-back guarantee".[24] As we have already seen, the goal of the originator is to get the funds to the beneficiary's bank. Acceptance by the beneficiary's bank means that, in generally accepted economic terms, the beneficiary has its money. Short of that acceptance, the originator has not succeeded in making the transfer and the banking system has failed it. The system, therefore, guarantees that it will accomplish this by returning the originator's money if it falls short. Consistent with the related damage provisions of 4 A, interest is payable upon the sum to be returned.

XII. Payment of the Underlying Obligation

The originator is generally deemed to make payment to the beneficiary when the beneficiary's bank accepts the payment order directed to it.[25] This is deemed to be consistent with the concept of when one has received "money". Generally one is satisfied when it is in one's bank. Discharge of the underlying obligation is also deemed to occur at that time unless (i) the underlying contract prohibited payment by this means, (ii) the beneficiary notified the originator that it was refusing payment, (iii) the beneficiary did not withdraw or apply the money, and (iv) the beneficiary would suffer a loss that could have been avoided if payment had been made by a means complying with the contract.

The final requirement is illustrated in the Official Comment by the example that an originator who is directed to pay by a cashier's check on Bank A pays by a funds transfer accepted by Bank B. Before the beneficiary withdrew the funds from Bank B, however, Bank B failed. In this event, the beneficiary was led to take a risk, the solvency of Bank B, that the beneficiary did not intend to take and it may reject the payment. Originator must pay the insolvent Bank B (because Bank B accepted the originator's order) and it must also pay the beneficiary a second time. The final sentence of 4 A-406 provides that the originator is then subrogated to the beneficiary's rights against its own, now insolvent bank; and whatever rights the beneficiary has

---

[24] The term is used in the Official Comments to Article 4 A.

[25] Sec. 4 A-406 (a).

to derive funds from the insolvent institution may be availed of by the twice-paying originator.

XIII. Variation by Agreement

Section 4 A-502 provides that "the rights and obligations of a party to a funds transfer may be varied by agreement of the affected party". Although straightforward in its language and its apparent intent, the provision has already stimulated some controversy. For example, may rights clearly given by the Article simply be taken away, not just varied, by an agreement of the parties. The right to make a stop order is given by Sec. 4 A-211. Given the swiftness of payment orders and the very brief time within which stop payment orders will have any effect, it seems a natural likelihood that banks will attempt to relieve themselves of this burden by agreeing with their customers that no stop orders will be permitted. There is less than complete certainty in the American bar that such agreements will be effective, although the better opinion seems to be that they will.

In addition, to what extent will the general rules of the UCC concerning good faith, reasonable behavior and the like carry over into agreements entered into under 4 A? An early section in the general provisions of the UCC says, for example, that no agreement modifying the UCC may disclaim the obligations of good faith, diligence, reasonableness and care prescribed by the UCC.[26] One would think that this requirement applies to Article 4 A. However, Article 4, dealing with check collections, also has a provision prohibiting a bank from disclaiming its responsibility for its own good faith or failure to exercise ordinary care.[27] Should we draw any inference from the absence of such a provision from 4 A? Common sense and a general understanding of the principles behind the UCC suggest that we should not. Then, there are some recent cases holding that more will be required than "honesty in fact" (a test that has sometimes been accused of requiring only a pure heart and an empty head) when good faith is required.[28] On top of this, in Sec. 4 A-105, Article 4 A creates a definition of "good faith" that differs from the definition of that term applicable to the remainder of the UCC. The definition has some specific applications inside Article 4 A,[29] but whether it creates an implication for 4 A generally and the parties' general duty of good gaith remains, along with the other questions raised in this paragraph, to be seen.

---

[26] Sec. 1-102 (3).

[27] Sec. 4-103 (1).

[28] See the test of good faith in UCC Sec. 1-201 (19) and its amplification for negotiable instrument situations in such cases as Savings Bank Trust Co. v. Federal Reserve bank of New York, 738 F. 2d 573 (2d Cir. 1984).

[29] See Sec. 4 A-202 (b).

The provisions of Article 4 A may be superseded by regulations of the Board of Governors of the Federal Reserve System and operating circulars of Federal Reserve Banks.[30] Since the Federal Reserve System operates the FedWire system, such regulations and circular can be consequential in setting rules for wire transfers.[31] In addition, a funds-transfer system rule can supplant an inconsistent provision of 4 A.[32] A funds transfer system is an association of banks handling funds transfers; the most significant insofar as United States law is concerned are the New York Clearing House Interbank Payment System ("CHIPS") and the Society for Worldwide Interbank Financial Telecommunications ("S.W.I.F.T.") system. To a modest extent, as provided in 4 A, funds transfer system rules, despite having the general characteristics of contracts among the banks in the association, are provided by Sec. 4 A-501 (b) to bind parties outside the association.

XIV. Conflict of Laws

The concentration of the 4 A drafters was upon funds transfers within the United States. Within this context, it was assumed throughout the drafting process that all states would adopt the Article. The essential goal of the choice of laws section, Sec. 4 A-507, was therefore to establish which of a group of essentially identical legal rules would apply to a given transaction at issue. Presumably, if one state's laws did not apply, another's would govern.

In the international arena, a different structure prevails. If 4 A does not apply through the operation of its own choice of law rules, it is certainly possible that no statutory law will be established as applicable to the transaction. How this dilemma will be handled must await presentation of the issue. Among significant and affecting factors will, of course, be the country in which the issue arises and its approach to question of conflicts of laws. All this is beyond the scope of this paper. We may note, however, that courts in the United States have shown strong inclination to apply 4 A by analogy, even when it is not the law of the affected jurisdiction.[33]

The conflicts rules are:

1. In an issue between a sender and a receiving bank, the receiving bank's law applies.

2. Issues between the beneficiary's bank and the beneficiary are governed by the law of the beneficiary's bank.

---

[30] Sec. 4 A-107.

[31] Most significant here is Federal Reserve Regulation C.

[32] Sec. 4 A-501 (b).

[33] See Shawmut Worcester County Bank v. First Amer. Bank, 731 F. Supp. 57 (D. Mass. 1990).

3. The issue of when payment is made from the originator to the beneficiary is governed by the law of the beneficiary's bank.

Parties may agree upon the law of any jurisdiction of their choosing, whether or not it has any relationship to the transaction. Funds transfer systems may also select governing law. The degree that such law selected binds third parties is the subject of Sec. 4 A-507 and is largely based upon the third party's advance notice that the system will be used and of its choice of law rules.

XV. Conclusion

Over the course of months of concentrated drafting the leading electronic payment experts in the United States gathered together and hammered out a set of rules to govern electronic payment. Article 4 A of the UCC is the result. Perhaps no one is entirely satisfied, but everyone acknowledges that the difficult problems were addressed and resolved in a manner that represents understandable and generally acceptable compromise. If the task were to be begun again today, it would probably not result in a significantly different product. Article 4 A will undoubtedly soon become the law of all, or at least substantially all, the United States.

The significant problem being faced today is the harmonizing of 4 A with the rest of the world. The United Nations Commission on International Trade Law ("UNCITRAL") has been laboring during much of the period that 4 A was drafted with an international approach to electronic funds transfers. It is unfortunate that, as of this writing, there are grave inconsistencies between the approach of 4 A and that of what is now called the UNCITRAL Model Law. Concentrated efforts over many months have been unable to resolve those differences. At this crucial time in the development of an international legal system for funds transfers one sincerely hopes that the result of the overall process will not be a splintered regulatory structure where a funds transfer can move in a fraction of a second and legal experts must with uncertainty ponder the law that governs.

III. Legal and Financial Issues Relating to Netting

Financial Risks and Legal Problems of International Netting Schemes From the United States Point of View*

By Ernest T. Patrikis and Debra W. Cook, New York

Contents

---

* The views expressed in this chapter do not necessarily reflect the views of the Federal Reserve Bank of New York or any other component of the Federal Reserve System.

I. Introduction

Dealing with the financial risks and legal problems of netting are essential to moving today's financial markets forward in an efficient, liquid, and safe and sound manner and are topics of great interest in the United States. This chapter discusses the motivating forces behind netting, describes examples of netting arrangements, and examines the legal issues regarding netting.

II. Motivating Forces behind Netting

Several forces operate in today's financial markets to encourage a financial institution to combine its payment and other financial transactions into one net amount due to or from that institution. Among them are the influence of the cost of capital and transaction costs, the requirements of the Federal Reserve Payment System Risk-Reduction Program, and the impetus to do more business, more prudently on a global basis.

1. Capital Costs

The capital-adequacy guidelines applicable to banks in the United States[1] follow the standards prepared by the Basle Committee on Banking Supervision ("Basle Accord"). At the time the Basle Accord was reached, netting by novation was the only form of netting considered by the supervisors. The United States' capital adequacy guidelines also recognize netting by novation. The guidelines establish minimum ratios of capital to weighted-risk assets, but banks are generally expected to operate well above the minimum risk-based ratios at a level corresponding to the degree of risk to which they are exposed. Off-balance sheet items such as foreign-exchange transactions and swaps are included in the capital-adequacy guidelines. Banks can be expected to seek to use netting as a way of reducing the capital charge on certain transactions.

2. Transaction Costs

Transaction costs, such as the cost of maintaining accounts with correspondents to facilitate payments, also is a factor motivating institutions to net their transactions. Netting provides institutions with a means of reducing the number of settlement payments in a given area of operations and, thereby,

[1] E. g., Capital Adequacy Guidelines for State Member Banks, I Federal Reserve Regulatory Service ¶ 3-1506.1, 12 C.F.R. Part 208, App. A (1991).

reduces the use of correspondent facilities frequently necessary to accomplish individual payments.

3. *Federal Reserve Risk Reduction Policy Program*

A further impetus to net is the Federal Reserve's Payments System Risk Reduction Policy Program (the "Risk Reduction Policy").[2] The Risk Reduction Policy relates to both the transfer of book-entry securities against payment and funds payment and focuses on credit and liquidity risk. The Risk Reduction Policy imposes discipline on the United States banking system, especially senior management of banks, to be more aware of the risks involved in payment and settlement systems. Payments system participants are encouraged by the Risk Reduction Policy to implement various tools to better manage their risk, including setting bilateral net-credit limits, sender net-debit caps, cross-system caps, and a cap for daylight overdrafts on Fedwire. In addition, the Risk Reduction Policy provides guidance on credit and liquidity risk management for securities delivery-against-payment systems that settle on a net, same-day basis directly or indirectly on Fedwire.

4. *Management of Global Counterparty Risk*

Finally, today's bank management is cognizant of the value of managing risk as a means to better manage and expand business. A financial transaction can involve market risk, credit risk, and settlement risk. No participant in such a transaction looks forward, for example, to losing the principal amount of the transaction as a result of a settlement-risk event. In the global marketplace, the better a bank is able to manage global counterparty risk, the more business it is able to do within its prudential limits.

Indeed, what banks are experiencing in the United States is the adoption of trade-comparison and netting arrangements for over-the-counter transactions similar to those used by the clearing corporations serving the securities, futures, and options exchanges.

In addition, these over-the-counter markets have now become accustomed to the use of master agreements to govern their transactions. The International Swap Dealers Association's ("ISDA") interest-rate and currency swap master agreement is well known and accepted and has certainly contributed to the growth of the swap market. Other groups of market participants are in the process of preparing master agreements. In the United States, a master agreement for foreign-exchange options is in its final polishing stages and

---

[2] III Federal Reserve Regulatory Service ¶¶ 9-1000 to 9-1008 (1989).

work has been underway for some time on a master agreement for spot and forward foreign-exchange transactions.

III. Examples of Netting Arrangements

The following is a brief description of some of the netting arrangements in which United States banks and other entities participate. The description summarizes the operation of each arrangement and discusses how the arrangement deals with liquidity, credit and systemic risk. Simply stated, credit risk is the risk that an institution will never be able to pay its obligation, while liquidity risk is the risk that an institution will not be able to make its settlement at the time settlement is due. Credit risk is frequently measured as market risk — that is, the value that will be lost on a transaction if a counter-party fails to perform. Settlement risk is the risk that a party might turn over to its counterparty its agreed-upon consideration for the transaction yet does not receive from the counterparty its consideration. Systemic risk refers to the possibility that a series of counterparties will suffer loss from the inability of a single market participant to cover its intra-day debit position vis-à-vis one or more counterparties. The ability of a netting arrangement to deal with each of these types of risk reflects upon the integrity of the arrangement.

1. The Federal Reserve Wire Transfer System

The Federal Reserve Wire Transfer System, commonly referred to as "Fedwire", is the large-value electronic funds transfer service provided by the Federal Reserve Banks. It is used primarily for domestic payments, including bank-to-bank and third-party transfers, such as interbank overnight funds sales and purchases and settlement transactions, and corporate-to-corporate payments made through banks.

Fedwire is a payments system. That is, the payment made over Fedwire may represent an amount that has been netted outside of the system, but the process of making payments over Fedwire itself does not involve the netting of payments. The amounts of Fedwire payments are debited and credited to the accounts of Reserve Bank depositors. When amounts are posted to a demand deposit account, the bank at any given point in time is either a debtor or a creditor vis-à-vis its customer. It is interesting to note that, in many banks, the amounts resulting from transfers of funds to and from customer's accounts during the day do not necessarily reflect the balance of customer's accounts. The reason for this is that many banks have disaggregated operations and the sums resulting from these operations are aggregated into a single account statement which is prepared well after the close of business. The Reserve Banks are moving to online, real-time accounting systems, such that a Reserve Bank will be able to ascertain its overall debtor/creditor position vis-à-vis its depositor at any time during the day.

A description of Fedwire is included in this discussion because several of the netting systems discussed below involve payments of the netted obligations from their systems over Fedwire. Fedwire links the twelve Federal Reserve Banks with depository institutions, including foreign banks with a United States branch or agency, United States Government departments and agencies, and foreign central banks and international organizations that maintain accounts with a Reserve Bank.

Fedwire represents a bilateral payments system. Funds are sent through Fedwire only upon the request of the sender of funds. Thus, it represents a credit transfer system. A Fedwire funds transfer is final at the earlier of the time the amount of the payment order is credited to the receiving bank's account or when the payment order is sent to the receiving bank.[3] Each Fedwire funds transfer is settled individually.

Because finality of payment is virtually instantaneous, if the sending bank or its customer requests that a transfer be revoked (due to an error, for example), the sender and receiver must resolve the dispute themselves. However, the Reserve Bank bears any financial loss associated with the failure of an institution whose account is overdrawn at the Reserve Bank. To control this type of risk, the Reserve Banks may prohibit or limit overdrafts by high-risk institutions and can require collateral against such overdrafts. Daylight overdrafts — overdrafts which occur during the course of the day — are not uncommon as a result of the large volume and type of transactions involved; however a depository institution's account with its Reserve Bank must have a positive balance by the end of the day.[4] At the end of a business day, any institution with an overdraft must resolve the overdraft. The institution is expected to borrow funds in the overnight or Federal funds market. If it is unable to do so, it may borrow from the Federal Reserve discount window and is subject to the collateral requirements associated with such borrowing.

Both credit and liquidity risk exist in the Fedwire payments system. Credit risk involves direct credit risk to the Reserve Bank or a depository institution's direct credit risk from interbank lending or incurring overdrafts on behalf of its customer.

The Risk Reduction Policy addresses these risks. The Risk Reduction Policy requires depository institutions using Fedwire to adopt a cap or limit

---

[3] Regulation J, 12 C.F.R. § 210.31 (a) (1991).

[4] Federal Reserve Bank of New York Operating Circular No. 2, ¶ 19 (1987).

on the total amount of overdrafts they incur at any time of the day in Fedwire.[5] The cap represents a multiple of capital according to the institution's self-assessment of its creditworthiness, operational controls, and credit policies and procedures. The cap is evaluated and monitored by the bank supervisors and the Federal Reserve. The Risk Reduction Policy permits a Reserve Bank to monitor on a real-time basis the actual position of any depository institution which in the Reserve Bank's consideration poses an undue risk. If a transaction will either overdraw an institution's account with a Reserve Bank or exceed a predefined level of permissible overdraft, the transaction is rejected; it may be resubmitted and will be acted upon when covering funds are received. Institutions also may be required to pledge collateral to the Reserve Bank to cover the amount of an overdraft as a result of book-entry security transactions. The Reserve Bank can terminate an institution's access to Fedwire if necessary.

Liquidity risk, while it exists, is not an issue for other participants in Fedwire because settlement occurs as each transaction is executed. The failure of an institution to have sufficient liquidity to cover an end of day overdraft on its account with the its Reserve Bank is a credit risk for the Federal Reserve but does not pose a risk to settlement for other participants.

The Risk Reduction Policy is undergoing evolution. One might regard it as having entered adolescence. Further developments are anticipated. One such development involves on-line, real time accounting. As mentioned earlier, effort is also underway to consolidate Reserve Bank accounting with the operations of Fedwire. The purpose is, as much as possible, to have an institution's account with its Reserve Bank reflect their debtor/creditor relationship real time. Another is to better ascertain the amount of the daylight overdraft against which to impose a charge for daylight overdrafts in an institution's account. These proposals present complex policy and operational issues for the Reserve Bank.

Transfers of funds through Fedwire are governed by an unusual blending of law. The wire transfer of funds operations of the Reserve Banks are governed by a regulation promulgated by the Board of Governors of the Federal Reserve System, Subpart B of Regulation J, 12 C.F.R. §§ 210.25-210.32. However, that Federal regulation explicitly incorporates State law, Article 4-A of the Uniform Commercial Code. To the extent that Subpart B and Article 4-A conflict as to a funds transfer involving a Reserve Bank, Subpart B governs.[6]

[5] III Federal Reserve Regulatory Service ¶ 9-1000 (15 June 1989).

[6] 12 C.F.R. § 210.25 (b) (i) (1991); N.Y. U.C.C. § 4-A-107 (1991).

2. *The Clearing House Interbank Payment System*

The Clearing House Interbank Payment System ("CHIPS") is a true multilateral netting system and is owned and operated by the New York Clearing House Association. While payments of all types may be sent over CHIPS, a large portion of the payments transferred over that system are in settlement of international transactions. Participants of CHIPS must be commercial banks, Edge corporations, or a banking affiliate of a commercial banking institution located in New York City. The parent of an Edge corporation, or an Article XII investment company may become a substitute participant.[7]

Participants are either settling participants or nonsettling participants which rely on the settling participants as correspondents to settle for them. The Federal Reserve Bank of New York is not a participant in CHIPS but does maintain a settlement account only available to the participants of CHIPS for settling purposes.

CHIPS represents a "true" multilateral netting system in that it is not a legally interposed intermediary between the participants (if it were, then the transactions would be bilateral transactions between Participant A and CHIPS and CHIPS and Participant B). CHIPS functions only as a message handler and a calculator and recorder of the value of payments messages sent between participants. Transactions occur between CHIPS participants on their behalf and on behalf of their customers, yet each CHIPS participant has only one net debit or net credit position at the end of the day.

All payment messages are initiated by the participant sending the funds and can be entered into the system for immediate release or for storage during the day. Same-day messages are processed immediately, unless they would cause the sender to exceed the risk-control parameters which are established on a bilateral and system-wide basis. Same-day messages that are not processed immediately are queued and released automatically upon receipt of cover within the system. Until released, a message may be deleted by the sender. Once released to the receiver, the message is irrevocable and represents an unconditional obligation of the sender regardless of error, settlement failure, or bankruptcy of the sender or the sending institution.[8]

A CHIPS participant may obtain the status of all the incoming and outgoing payment messages, the status of its net debit or credit position or that of any other participant, and its current net debit or credit position vis-à-vis all other CHIPS participants (its "net net position"). Although payment

---

[7] N.Y. Clearing House Association, CHIPS Rules and Administrative Procedures Rule 19.a (1991) (hereinafter "Rule").

[8] Rule 2.

messages are sent throughout the day, participants are aware that there is no exchange of value until settlement time. Once the system is closed, CHIPS informs each participant of that participant's net net position and each settling participant of the net positions of those for which it settles. If the net net position is negative, a "net net debit" position, the settling participant must transfer funds to the CHIPS Settlement Account at the Federal Reserve Bank of New York in order to settle its position. Once all funds have been transferred into the account, the New York Clearing House, as agent of the Federal Reserve Bank of New York, transfers funds via Fedwire to those settling participants in net net positive, or "net net credit", positions. At that time settlement is complete.[9]

There are two procedures under CHIPS for settlement in the case of a failure to settle depending on who fails to settle. If a participant is unable to settle because the settling participant is unwilling to settle that participant's net balance, the settling participant must so inform the president of the New York Clearing House Association. The president notifies the participant, and the participant has one hour to arrange for either its settling participant or a new settling participant to settle its net balance.[10] If a participant is unable to settle, the net debit of the failed participant is divided up into prorata shares, known as Additional Settlement Obligations ("ASO"), for each remaining participant.[11]

The ASO calculation is based on the highest bilateral credit limit actually extended to the failed participant during the day for which settlement is to be made.[12] The ASO liability on any participant may not be higher than five percent of that participant's maximum bilateral credit limit or any other liability in excess of that otherwise provided by CHIPS rules. A failed participant ceases to be a participant, but its obligations continue in force until performed or legally discharged.

Each remaining participant is informed of its ASO and obligated to cover it. A settling bank is obligated to settle the aggregate balance of ASOs of participants for which it settles. Should a remaining participant fail to settle its ASO with its settling participant, that participant is in default. In accordance with the CHIPS Pledge and Security Agreement, the settling participant then purchases at market value the collateral of the participant in default and uses the proceeds to settle the uncovered ASO. Any remaining funds are transferred to CHIPS for the benefit of the participant in default.

[9] Rule 13.c.

[10] Rule 13.d.

[11] Rule 13.e.

[12] Rule 13.h.

If a settling participant, on the other hand, fails to satisfy its obligation to settle, then one of the following will occur. The settling participant may be treated in the same way as a nonsettling participant and become a failed participant. The settling participant may be required to make alternative arrangements with another settling participant to settle its net debit balance. Each participant for which the settling participant is obligated to settle may be required to make alternative arrangements to settle. CHIPS may issue revised settlement or ASO reports, reflecting any changes. Or, the collateral of the settling participant may be sold and the proceeds used to cover the settlement obligations. If, in an extreme situation, settlement could not be completed by any of these means or other measures, all payment messages would be "returned to storage", effectively unwinding the entire settlement and all transfers of funds.

The CHIPS settlements account begins and ends each day with a zero balance. The risk that a participant will not have funds available to pay its net debit position is a recognized liquidity risk of the system. However, CHIPS participants are required to maintain a reasonable level of liquidity, and, as noted above, participants can monitor their positions and the positions of those for which they settle. CHIPS also imposes a net-debit position limit for each participant.

Credit risk is contained in the CHIPS system by requiring each participant to limit its exposure to every other participant by a series of bilateral credit limits on the maximum net payments it will accept from that participant. These bilateral credit limits are provided to CHIPS and are periodically reviewed by bank supervisors. Because of the bilateral nature of the net credit limits, they can be negotiated between participants and backed by collateral if a higher limit is desired. In addition, the net debit cap imposed by CHIPS on each participant limits a participant's net debit position in the overall system. The net debit cap is based upon bilateral credit limits and effectively limits the risk exposure of all CHIPS participants collectively to a single participant.

CHIPS monitors all transactions in the system on a real-time basis against the caps and limits. If a message would result in the violation of a cap or limit, that message is queued until the net positions of the parties change so as to permit payment to be sent without such violation.

Up to 1991, CHIPS was governed by its rules and the agreement between the Clearing House and CHIPS participants. Relationships between participants and between participants and their customers were governed by a confusing blend of contract and tort law and perhaps the statute law relating to the collection of checks and other items. This state of affairs has been clarified by Article 4-A of the Uniform Commercial Code, which has been enacted by New York State. The CHIPS rules contain a choice of law provision which states that the rights and obligations of participants and other parties to a funds transfer involving CHIPS are governed by the law of New York State.[13] Article 4-A-501 (2) of the Uniform Commercial Code states that, except as otherwise stated in the Article, a funds-transfer system rule governing the rights and obligations between participating banks may be effective even if the rule conflicts with the Article or indirectly affects another party to the funds transfer who does not consent to the rule.

The legal efficiency of true multilateral netting in the United States is not perfectly clear. At least three levels of legal support can be cited in support of the binding nature of a CHIPS participant's net net position. First, Section 151 of the New York Debtor and Creditor Law provides for a statutory right of setoff of any indebtedness of a debtor against any indebtedness of a creditor to that debtor, in the circumstances provided in the statute. Section 151 seems to contemplate mutual debts. It is possible that a court might construe this as including a net net position, where mutual obligations are netted. Second, the participants' agreement to the CHIPS Rules constitutes a contractual right of setoff. To date, no New York court has opined on the validity of such a contractual arrangement. Third, as mentioned earlier, the CHIPS participants are governed by new Article 4-A of the New York Uniform Commercial Code. Section 4-A-302 (2) provides that the obligation of the sender which is a member of a funds-transfer system to pay the amount of a payment order transmitted through that system may be satisfied, to the extent permitted by the rules of that systems, by setting off and applying against the sender's obligation the right of the sender to received payment from the receiving bank of the amount of any other payment order transmitted to the sender by the receiving bank. This is the net position. Section 4-A-302 (2) then continues by stating that the aggregate balance of obligations owed by each sender to each receiving bank may be satisfied by setting off and applying against that balance the aggregate balance of obligations to the sender by other members of the system. This aggregate balance (the net net position) is determined after the right of setoff leading to the net position has been exercised.

Finally, it should be noted that the proposed Financial Institutions Safety and Consumer Choice Act of 1991, prepared by the Bush Administration and introduced as H. R. 1505 in the House of Representatives and S. 713 in the Senate addresses payments-system risk reduction by means of multilateral netting. Section 504 of that proposal is intended to eliminate the risk that the receiver or liquidator of a failed member of a clearing organization could negate the netting rules of the clearing organization. This section would provide statutory validation of netting to the extent provided by the clearing

---

[13] Rule 3.

organizations rules. If a member fails, its claim with respect to payment orders received through the clearing organization would be limited to the excess, if any, of the amount of payment orders received over the amount of payment orders transmitted. This proposed Federal rule would have an effect similar to that of Section 4-A-203 (2) discussed above.

3. *Off-Shore U.S. Dollar Payment Systems*

Concerns related to off-shore U.S. dollar payment systems are reflected in the Board's Interim Policy Statement of 15 June 1989 (the "Offshore Policy Statement").[14] These include a concern that increased pressure on domestic clearing and settling systems to adopt measures to reduce systemic risk will result in the development of dollar payment systems outside of the United States. Such "offshore" dollar payment systems may operate without comparable management of risk or oversight. Thus, offshore U.S. dollar payment systems which are settled through Fedwire or CHIPS could introduce payment risks in the U.S. banking system. For example, allocation of credit and liquidity risks may be different in the country where the transactions are cleared than in the United States where the payments would be netted as a part of CHIPS or prior to payment in Fedwire.

These concerns can best be addressed through the cooperative efforts of central banks and bank supervisory authorities on an international level. The Federal Reserve's Offshore Policy Statement will be revised to reflect the November 1990 Report of the Committee on Interbank Netting Schemes of the central banks of the Group of Ten Countries. Pending the results of that report, the Federal Reserve set out certain general principles in its Offshore Policy Statement similar to risk reduction procedures. An offshore dollar-clearing or netting system, which settles directly or indirectly through CHIPS or Fedwire, should be subject to oversight or supervision as a system by a relevant central bank or supervisory authority. The participants should be responsible for clearly identifying and prudently managing the operational, liquidity, and credit risk created within the system. The system should include arrangements providing for finality of settlement in a timely manner. Finally, the direct or indirect settlement of the systems obligations through CHIPS or Fedwire should be conducted by an identified settlement agent.

4. *Fedwire Securities-Against-Payment System*

Fedwire also acts as a securities transfer network over which depository institutions send United States Government, certain Federal agency, and

---

[14] III Federal Reserve Regulatory Service ¶ 9-1008 (15 June 1989).

international organization securities in book-entry form and receive the corresponding payments.[15] Depository institutions eligible to maintain a book-entry account at a Reserve Bank directly are those institutions which also maintain a funds account at the Reserve Bank, including foreign banks with branches or agencies and all domestic commercial banks, trust companies, saving banks, savings and loan associations, and credit unions that are eligible for Federal deposit insurance. Institutions may maintain accounts on their own behalf and for holding and transacting their customer's book-entry securities.

In addition, book-entry accounts exist for other entities, but they are intended for safekeeping accounts and are not to be used to hold or transfer securities other than those of the account-holders. Also, each State is permitted two book-entry accounts with the Reserve Banks for the segregation and safekeeping of book-entry Treasury securities investments held by State and local governments. Many foreign central banks and official international organizations have book-entry securities accounts in their own names at the Federal Reserve Bank of New York.

Requests for transactions typically are made "on-line", that is, entered directly into Fedwire by the institution sending the securities without any intermediate processing by the Reserve Bank. "Off-line" transactions are those that involve manual processing by the Reserve Bank. An example of an off-line transaction would be a telephone request, done under special arrangements with the requestor's Reserve Bank, that must be authenticated by code or some other procedure established by the Reserve Bank and must be entered into the Reserve Bank's computer by Reserve Bank personnel.

A securities trade may be for "same-day" (or "cash") delivery or for "next-day" delivery. On the day of delivery, the sender will instruct the Reserve Bank to transfer the securities from its account to the account of the receiver. Typically, such a transaction will be accomplished on-line with the Reserve Bank's computer verifying that the securities to be transferred are present in the sender's account and automatically debiting that account and crediting the securities to the account of the receiver.

Book-entry securities are sent against immediate payment. Usually, the instruction from the sender will contain price information and the payment instruction will be processed simultaneously with the securities transfer. In this way, at the same time the Reserve Bank debits the securities account of the sender, it credits the sender's funds account on the Reserve Bank's books for the sale price. Correspondingly, at the same time that the Reserve Bank

[15] Securities also may be transferred "free", i. e., not against payment. When securities are transferred "free", the Reserve Bank debits the securities account of the sending institution and credits the securities account of the receiving institution, without corresponding debits and credits to the institutions' funds accounts.

credits the securities to the receiver's account, it debits the receiver's funds account for the sale price of the securities.

After receipt of securities transferred against payment, the receiver can either accept the transaction or reverse it. A "reversal" is a separate new wire transfer of the security to the first sender. If a depository institution accepts a transaction for the account of a customer and the customer has insufficient funds to cover the payment, the institution has extended daylight credit. If the customer's failure to pay persists, daylight credit becomes an outright or term loan. To comply with restraints on lending and protect themselves against the risk of loss associated with that type of credit, a depository institution might agree to process customer transactions only on a secured basis.

A message to transact book-entry securities must unambiguously specify the particular securities issue to be transferred, the face amount to be transferred, the payment amount, and the party to whom the securities are to be transferred (which must be a party that has both a securities and a funds account with a Reserve Bank). The message may contain further information identifying other parties to the transaction, for instance, a customer of the receiving institution who is the ultimate intended receiver of the securities.

Fedwire securities transfers create a risk for the Reserve Banks similar to the risk involved in funds transfers over Fedwire. If a depository institution receives a dollar value of securities greater than the dollar value of securities it has sent over Fedwire, then the debits to that institution's Reserve Bank funds account would exceed the credits to its account (the cost of the securities purchased could exceed the price received for securities it has sold) creating a daylight overdraft in that institution's Reserve Bank funds account. While there can be a funds overdraft, there cannot be a securities overdraft — that is, the sender cannot send a security it does not have in its securities account.

As of January 1991, overdrafts arising out of wire transfers of funds and book-entry securities are combined for purposes of measuring a depository institution's daylight overdraft against its Fedwire cap. While financially healthy depository institutions are permitted to exceed the cap due to book-entry securities activities, institutions that frequently exceed the cap as a result of book-entry transactions must collateralize that portion of the Fedwire overdraft related to the book-entry activity.

One current issue regarding this book-entry arrangement involves the interplay between Federal regulations issued by the United States Department of the Treasury which govern the issue, transfer, and redemption of United States Treasury book-entry securities[16] and State law governing the

[16] Treasury Department Circular No. 300, 31 C.F.R. Part 306 (1990).

same transactions in securities, Article 8 of the Uniform Commercial Code. The Federal regulation preempts the State law. In addition, notwithstanding its title the Uniform Commercial Code is not uniform. Different states have enacted different uniform versions. Moreover, some states have enacted nonuniform provisions. The result can be a complex conflicts of laws case.[17] As a step toward reducing conflicts in State law, a newly-enacted Federal law granted authority in certain circumstances to the Securities and Exchange Commission to promulgate regulations preempting State law to provide for more certainty in the transfer of securities not processed over Fedwire.[18]

5. *Government Securities Transaction Netting System*

The Government Securities Clearing Corporation ("GSCC") is a clearing agency providing automated trade comparison and netting services for the U.S. Government securities market. GSCC is owned by Government securities dealers and brokers. Members of GSCC are "Netting Members", "Comparison-Only Members", or "Clearing Agent Bank Members". Because it is a securities clearing corporation, GSCC is regulated as such by the Securities and Exchange Commission.

Comparison-Only Members include Government securities brokers or dealers, clearing agent banks that are obligated to GSCC on behalf of a person that is a nonmember, and certain other entities approved by GSCC's board. Netting Members are either Government securities brokers or dealers of clearing agent banks that are obligated to GSCC on behalf of a person that would be eligible to apply to become a Netting Member and have been Comparison-Only Members for at least six months (unless this requirement is waived). Netting Members also are required to have a net worth of at least $ 50 million and excess net capital or excess liquid capital of at least $ 10 million, except inter-dealer brokers which are required to have a minimum of only $ 4.2 million in liquid or net capital and banks which are required to have a minimum of $ 250 million in equity capital.

Clearing Agent Bank Members are members of the Federal Reserve System that are currently regularly engaged in the business of providing clearing services in eligible securities for members that have agreed to provide GSCC, upon request and under mutually agreeable terms, with clearing services, and that meet the same requirements as those for Comparison-Only Members.

---

[17] See, e. g., In the Matter of Bevill, Bresler & Schulman, Inc., 59 Bankr. 353 (DC NJ 1986).

[18] Market Reform Act of 1990, Pub. L. 101-432, § 1, 104 Stat. 963 (16 Oct. 1990) (enacting 12 U.S.C. § 1831 l and amending 15 U.S.C. §§ 78 i, 78 l, 78 m, 78 q, 78 q-1, 78 y and 78 o-5).

Trade comparison consists of reporting, validating, and matching the buy and sell sides of a securities transaction to result in a compared trade. Comparisons generated by GSCC constitute the "sole comparison" for trades in eligible securities for which members have submitted data and which GSCC has identified as compared trades. Each trade comparison generated by GSCC is a valid, binding, and enforceable contract between the members. Data entered into the system remains pending until it is compared, deleted pursuant to a schedule, or deleted by a member to correct a mistake. Uncompared data can be deleted unilaterally, but compared data may only be deleted with the consent of both parties.

There are several types of trades in GSCC. A regular trade is a trade entered into today for settlement tomorrow. A forward trade is a trade that has been compared on a final price basis one or more business days prior to its scheduled settlement date. A yield comparison is a trade compared only on a yield basis. If the trade involves securities eligible for netting, the trade data must be resubmitted after auction for comparison on a final price basis. If the data on a trade are submitted to GSCC for comparison on or after its scheduled settlement date, it is referred to as an "as-of" trade and is not eligible for netting.

A trade is eligible for netting and settlement through the Netting System if it has been compared, its scheduled settlement date is no more than 15 business days after the date of comparison, the netting will occur on or before its scheduled settlement date, both parties to the trade are Netting Members, the underlying securities are eligible for netting, and the trade has not been excluded from the net.

Each day, GSCC reports to a Netting Member the status of that member's net settlement positions and deliver and receive obligations. Net settlement positions and any resultant deliver and receive obligations of a Netting Member are fixed at the time that the report of such positions and obligations is made available by GSCC to the member. At that time, all deliver, receive, and related payment obligations between members that were created by the trades that comprise the net settlement positions are terminated and replaced by the settlement obligations issued by GSCC. Thus, GSCC is interposed as a counterparty in each net settlement obligation. GSCC is obligated to deliver securities to a member in a net receiving position, but not until the day on which GSCC receives from a member in a net deliver position securities with the same CUSIP number that are least equal in quantity to the net receiver's position and that have not been allocated for delivery to another member.[19] All deliveries and receipts must be made

[19] GSCC may accept partial deliveries, in its discretion and with the consent of the net receiving members.

against simultaneous payment or receipt in Federal funds at that day's system value for the obligations.[20] If GSCC receives securities late in the day that it cannot redeliver, the resultant financing costs are shared by the non-inter-dealer-broker Netting Members on a pro rata basis.

Each business day, each Netting Member must pay or is entitled to collect an aggregate funds-only settlement amount across all CUSIPS, i. e., on a net-net basis. A Netting Member that has an obligation to pay to GSCC a funds-only settlement amount must do so via GSCC's designated depository institution in Federal funds. GSCC will make the funds-only payments it owes to members on a timely basis irrespective of whether it has received all funds-only settlement payments due to it on that day, using Clearing Fund assets to collateralize any necessary credit extensions.

Because every net-settlement obligation involves GSCC as a counterparty on a bilateral basis, GSCC has an incentive to monitor and manage risk in the system. GSCC protects itself and its members by strict membership standards and continuous monitoring of periodic financial reports of members. In addition, daily marking-to-market is designed to limit GSCC's credit exposure to no more than one day's market movement in the underlying securities comprising the net settlement positions of a member. A Clearing Fund contains assets from each Netting Member sufficient to satisfy any losses that may be incurred by GSCC as the result of the default by the member and the resultant close out of that member's settlement positions. The Clearing Fund maintains a total asset amount sufficient to satisfy potential losses to GSCC and its members resulting from the failure of more than one member and the failure of such members' counterparties to pay their pro-rata allocation of loss. Through the Clearing Fund, GSCC has access to liquidity to meet its payment and delivery obligations. Members can gain ready access to particular securities pledged as collateral upon appropriate notice. GSCC also may allocate losses to original counterparties of a failed participant. This provides incentive for participants themselves to manage credit risk bilaterally.

In order to ensure the appropriateness of the risk protections provided by the Netting System and GSCC's margin collections, GSCC maintains an automated system for the assessment of price volatility, based on maturity ranges, that takes into account historical and implied volatility. This enables GSCC to assess, on an on-line-basis, historical and potential price movements and the implications that those price movements could have for the risk profile of GSCC members and, thus, to be able to sufficiently protect

[20] System value is the par value of securities multiplied by their system price plus interest accrued to date. System price is the uniform price established by GSCC for each CUSIP, which currently is set based on a par-weighted average of trade data.

itself from the financial exposure associated with the potential liquidation of a member.

GSCC, based on the judgement of its board that adequate cause exists to do so, may cease to act for a member, with regard to the comparison service or both comparison and netting and either generally or with respect to specific transactions, in order to protect GSCC and other members or to help ensure an orderly clearance and settlement process. If the determination is made for GSCC to cease to act for a member, GSCC will decline to accept or process data from that member or from other members with regard to any transactions to which that member is a party.

If a member is determined to be insolvent, trade data received by GSCC regarding transactions to which the insolvent member is a party that have not yet been reported by GSCC to members as compared will be deleted from the Comparison System. Compared trades involving the insolvent member that have not yet been reported as included in a net settlement position will not be eligible for netting (unless otherwise determined by GSCC's board in order to promote an orderly settlement process). All net settlement positions of the insolvent member will be closed out by GSCC's establishing, by CUSIP, consolidated net settlement positions and buying in or selling out securities in order to close out the positions. This close-out will be completed as promptly as practicable unless GSCC's board determines that the immediate close-out of positions in a security may be disadvantageous to GSCC or may promote a disorderly market in that security.

6. *Other Securities-Against-Payment Systems*

a) Participants Trust Company

Participants Trust Company ("PTC") is a New York chartered limited-purpose trust company and a member of the Federal Reserve System. PTC is also registered as a clearing corporation with the Securities and Exchange Commission. It acts as a depository for asset-backed securities, in particular Government National Mortgage Association securities ("GNMAs"). Applicants to become participants in PTC must demonstrate sufficient financial ability to make anticipated contributions to the "Participants Fund" and meet anticipated obligations to PTC. Banks are required to have minimum capital of $ 100 million, and broker dealers must have minimum capital of $ 50 million to participate in PTC; however, the capital requirements can be waived. All participants must have access to an institution that uses Fedwire because money-settlement payments are made over Fedwire.

While PTC is a delivery-against-payment system, the securities are transferred during the day from the transferor to PTC. Securities are not delivered by PTC to the ultimate transferee until settlement is completed.

PTC calculates net positions and communicates those positions to its participants via computer terminal. Closing positions are confirmed by telephone. Closing balances are manually transcribed and debits and credits are checked on a cash position sheet. The cash position sheet is transmitted by facsimile to a bank which provides settlement services for PTC. Upon notification of their net positions, participants in a net debit position provide Federal funds to that settling bank for the account of PTC. At the end of the day, PTC places a hold on securities for accounts in a debit position for which funds have not been remitted. When all funds from net debtors have been received, PTC instructs the settling bank to wire funds to net creditors; if any net debtor has not remitted funds, then PTC draws on its line of credit and advances the funds necessary to complete the settlement. Any securities on hold are assigned as collateral to PTC's banks.

Positions are netted continuously as transactions are entered and accepted into the system. All payment for net debits and net credits are transacted over Fedwire and so are irrevocable once the funds are sent. System settlement and payment finality occur when PTC has received all payments over Fedwire to its account at its settling bank and has sent out payments to settling banks in a net-credit position.

PTC also imposes risk management measures such as net-debit caps, collateral monitoring, and haircuts on securities in the system.

The concern with regard to securities-against-payment systems such as Depository Trust Company, discussed below, and PTC is that failure of a participant should be addressed as a liquidity problem rather than resulting in an unwinding of the trades of that participant. Within these two systems, an "unwind" occurs if a participant fails and is unable to meet its system obligations. All transactions by and with that participant may be "unwound" as though they never occurred. But, dealing with failures in a system by unwinding results in uncertainty about the true finality of transactions. The systemic risk of an unwind with its potentially harmful effects on other participants is an undesirable aspect of such systems. PTC has modified its rules to limit the circumstances under which an unwind can occur.

If a failure of a participant were addressed by a system as a liquidity problem, on the other hand, then appropriate measures could be taken to provide the system with liquidity to cover a potential failure (for example, by requiring the clearing house to have a line of credit available, or by requiring the participants to share the burden of the failed participant's obligations in some allocated manner). In this way, finality of transactions could be assured and the system would be more stable.

7. Depository Trust Company

The Depository Trust Company ("DTC") is a New York chartered limited purpose trust company and a member of the Federal Reserve System. It also is regulated as a clearing corporation by the Securities and Exchange Commission. DTC operates a same day funds settlement system ("SDFS") and a next day funds settlement system ("NDFS"). Both systems involve the transfer of securities[21] against payment.

A large number of the participants in the systems are banks and broker-dealers (and, in NDFS, clearing agencies), although partnerships, corporations, or other organizations which meet DTC's standards for financial condition, operational capability, and character may become participants. No organization may apply for participant in SDFS unless it applies to, and intends to participate in NDFS. Applicants for membership must be able to demonstrate sufficient financial ability to contribute to the "Participants Fund" and meet anticipated obligations to DTC. DTC does not have a minimum capital requirement.

All intra-day funds net-debit positions must be collateralized in an account with DTC. Any transactions which would result in a participant being undercollateralized is blocked and recycled through the system until sufficient collateral is available. Participants in SDFS are required to have a settling bank participant with on-line access to Fedwire. Settling banks must contribute at least $ 1 million to a "Settling Bank Fund" to serve as a first source of liquidity for DTC in a failure-to-settle situation. DTC may draw on the Fund to complete settlement when a settling bank is unwilling or unable to settle on behalf of a participant. The amount drawn from the Fund is collateralized with securities and funds from the collateral account of the participant which failed to settle.

Positions are netted continuously as transactions are entered and accepted into SDFS. DTC incorporates each participant's net position into the participant's settling bank's position. Settlement is initiated by DTC's making available to settling banks the final net debit or net credit position of each participant and the settling bank's net net debit or net net credit position. Settling banks acknowledge their positions and, if the position is a

---

[21] The following securities are eligible for deposit in SDFS: municipal notes; municipal variable-rate demand obligations; zero coupon bonds backed by U.S. Government securities; auction-rate and tender-rate preferred stock and notes; medium-term notes; collateralized mortgage obligations; Government trust certificates; Government Agency securities; and commercial paper. Securities eligible for deposit in NDFS include: municipal issues that settle in same-day funds; exchange-listed securities; over the counter equities; corporate debt securities; units; warrants; American depository receipts; unit investment trusts; certificates of deposit; registered municipal bonds; bearer municipal bonds; municipal notes; and U.S. Treasury and Agency issues.

net net debit figure, wire funds to DTC's account at the Federal Reserve Bank of New York. Because the payments for net net debits are made over Fedwire, the payment is irrevocable once sent.

If a settling bank has not wired the necessary funds to DTC by the daily deadline, it must send a message to DTC either acknowledging its intention to settle its net net debit position, or indicating its refusal to settle for particular participants. Once a refusal is sent, the settling bank must send DTC a message acknowledging its new net net position and intention to settle. The same procedure is required of a settling bank in a net net credit position that sends a refusal to settle for particular participants. If the funds or a message are not received by DTC by the deadline, DTC begins failure-to-settle procedures against that settling bank. When DTC has received all funds, it wires funds to all settling participants in net net credit positions.

In SDFS, at a participant's level, delivery is final if, at the end of the day, the receiver is not in a net debit position, the receiver has paid its net debit position, or the receiver made an offsetting transfer intraday. System settlement and payment finality occur when DTC both has received from and sent to the settling banks all necessary payments over Fedwire.

If a participant in a net debit position is unable to settle its position at the end of the day, DTC can use the securities to be transferred to that participant as collateral under a standby funding facility it must maintain with a bank. This serves as an assured means of liquidity and ensures that reversal or unwind is not the first wall of defense in the case of participant failure. If the participant is unable to cover its position on the following day, DTC can liquidate in the market the securities determined to be the failed participant's or return them against payment to the transferor.

DTC's SDFS is also unique in the United States in that it is the first delivery-against-payment system settling on a same-day basis involving securities not issued or guaranteed by the Federal Government or a Federal agency. DTC's rules for SDFS provide for the situation where the issuer of the security transferred over the system has failed.

In DTC's NDFS, securities are not transferred from the transferor to the transferee until settlement is completed. Net positions in NDFS are calculated in batches until 2 : 00 p. m. and are on-line thereafter. Payments for NDFS transactions must be made by check drawn on a New York Clearing House bank. Some out-of-town participants in the system settle through the New York Clearing House banks in a net-net arrangement provided by DTC; others use their New York correspondent banks to obtain the check and deliver it directly to DTC.

In NDFS, DTC provides a "Preliminary Settlement Statement" of participant's positions to which adjustments are made until the system closes.

Participants with net debit positions deliver their New York Clearing House bank checks payable to DTC. If a participant does not pay its settlement balance by the daily deadline, the balance is suspended and the participant must deliver Federal Funds by the morning of the next day. Participants with net credit positions present drafts on DTC for signature payable through a New York Clearing House bank.

Settlement is final in NDFS when DTC releases its "Final Settlement Statement", which may not be until sometime during the night. The Final Settlement Statement can be adjusted up until it is released even though participants have submitted checks based on the Preliminary Settlement Statement. The timing of the finality of settlement is generally not an issue because settlement is for next-day funds.[22]

DTC imposes risk management measures including net debit caps, collateral monitoring, and haircuts on securities in the system.

8. FXNET

FXNET involves the bilateral netting of foreign exchange transactions between a pair of banks by obligating each party to an FXNET agreement to either make or receive one payment for each currency on each settlement date. The development of the FXNET system was funded by a group of banks in a limited partnership in the United Kingdom. FXNET has no United States offices, however, U.S. banks are users of FXNET.

Counterparties enter into netting agreements based on bilateral netting by means of novation and close-out agreements provided by FXNET. All communications flow between the two parties over FXNET software without any centralized processing step. As the parties enter into each transaction, the FXNET computerized system transforms the obligation into a stream of net payments over the forward settlement dates.

The FXNET system works by matching transactions and confirmations between two parties, extinguishing the two matched payments and replacing them with an obligation to make a net payment on the settlement date. The netted obligations are maintained in running accounts which are continuously novated with new transactions until a settlement time is reached. The

---

[22] Payments of more then $ 5,000 must be by certified check and are not final until entered on the books of the Federal Reserve Bank of New York. Legally, certified checks are the obligation of the paying bank. Checks that are not certified (settlement checks for under $ 5,000) are subject to the stop payment provisions of the Uniform Commercial Code, which permits the dishonoring of checks until midnight on the day following the day the checks are presented for payment. However, DTC and its participants appear to perceive the funds as final when the Final Settlement Statement is issued on the morning of the day after settlement.

parties agree to a pre-established settlement time when the FXNET system sends the counterparty final settlement amounts and settlement instructions. Thus, settlement occurs between each pair of users of the system rather than for the system as a whole. Consequently, failure of one party to meet one or more net obligations does not affect other settlement obligations with or between other parties using FXNET. Instructions for the payment of matched transactions and payments instructions for unmatched transactions (the parties remain obligated to pay any transactions not matched) are delivered by FXNET, typically in a standard SWIFT format statement.

In the case of a close-out, such as in the event of a default or a liquidation proceeding, the FXNET model agreements provide for the termination of all of a participant's existing payment obligations (both matched and unmatched) under the agreement and their replacement by a net amount payable by one party to the other. A payment pursuant to a close-out event involves converting the net payments due for each settlement date into a common currency, then combining and discounting those amounts to a present value.

Decisions regarding credit worthiness, exposure and risk management are under the control of each counterparty. The FXNET software, itself, sets no bilateral credit limits. There is no obligation to net with any other counterparty using the system. The benefit of FXNET is the ability of a party to reduce the number of payment obligations it must make with each counterparty for each currency on each settlement date. In addition, the intention of novating all of the transactions into one netting agreement is to prevent a liquidator from being able to pick and choose among profitable and unprofitable transactions to uphold.

The FXNET model agreements do not specify how or where payments on the settlement date are to be made. The netted obligations are finally discharged only when payment is made.

Various counsel for FX Net have prepared reasoned legal opinions regarding the efficiency of the novation and close-out provisions provided in the FX Net Master Agreement. These opinions can be obtained from FX Net.

9. Foreign Exchange Clearing House

The North American Clearing House Organization ("NACHO") is a current effort to organize a clearing house for foreign exchange transactions. Members of NACHO will be commercial banks or trust companies or regulated non-banking business organizations that demonstrate operational and managerial capacity in foreign exchange. In addition, members will be subject to a minimum capital requirement and short-term and minimum long-term deposit ratings from rating agencies.

NACHO will be a decentralized clearing house in which the clearing house will be the counterparty on both sides of a trade (as opposed to a true multilateral system, such as CHIPS). Loss as a result of a default by a participant would be passed through to the original counterparties with positive bilateral exposures to the defaulting party. Losses under this system would be of two types: settlement losses and forward placement losses. Allocations for each type of loss would remain separate.

Trading by participants will be subject to credit limits. Credit limits will likely be determined as a percentage of a participant's capital. Thus, the exposure of NACHO to any participant will be limited. The primary loss allocation for forward exposure, plus the primary loss allocation for settlement exposure (together "Net Loss Allocation"), from the default of a single counterparty will be subject to the credit limit as will Net Loss Allocation from the default of any two counterparties. The clearing house would reject any trade which would result in a settlement's exceeding its credit limit. Presumably there would still be a valid contract between the two parties.

The NACHO system involves settlement risk because there will be an interval of time between the payment of one currency and finalized receipt of a second currency. This interval could extend to up to 24 hours in jurisdictions governed by a bankruptcy law in which transactions entered into immediately after a bankruptcy is declared are void or voidable. To account for this risk, NACHO will include settlement risk in determining credit limits.

IV. Legal Issues Regarding Netting

There are certain legal issues which must be examined in any discussion regarding the legality of netting. One issue involves whether novation is legally effective. Another concerns the concept of set-off. A third issue is whether the netting agreement will be given recognition under bankruptcy law.

1. Novation

The legal concept of "novation" refers to substituting a new contract for an existing contract by changing an element of the contract, such as a party or trade.[23] "Netting by novation" refers to combining subsequent trades into a

---

[23] As a technical matter, "novation" involves modifying a contractual relationship by adding a third party and "contract substitution" refers to replacing previous contractual

contract such that, in effect, when each trade is added a new contract exists that provides for a single net amount for all of the trades included. Netting by novation can reduce the number of settlements to one net settlement and, thereby, reduce settlement risk.

As a general rule, novation is a legally enforceable contract principle in the United States. The validity of novation in a true multilateral system is uncertain, however, because it has never been legally challenged. There is no reason to believe that the concept would not be legally enforceable in a multilateral setting.

2. *Set-Off*

Netting by novation represents a method by which two or more parties can set off debts or obligations. In the United States, set-off may be a right available to parties as a matter of State statutory law or common law and may be available even if no prior agreement between the parties exists. The United States Bankruptcy Code[24] (which, while it does not govern the insolvency of a bank, can provide guidance as to the equitable principles involved in bank closings as well as governs the bankruptcy of most other corporations) preserves any right of set-off existing under State statutory or common law. New York State's Debtor and Creditor Law[25] permits an insolvent or bankrupt debtor to set off against any indebtedness of the creditor to the debtor the amount owing from the debtor to the creditor. Common law supports the right to set-off as an equitable principle.

Thus, even if a court in the United States were to find a netting agreement invalid, the cancelling of certain mutual debts or obligations between the parties may still be legally enforceable according to the right to set off. However, because the law of set-off generally refers to situations between one debtor and one creditor, it is less clear that set-off in a true multilateral netting system (where there is no interposed intermediary to transform the obligations to bilateral transactions between the intermediary and each individual party) would be upheld.

---

obligations with a new set of obligations between the same parties. However, in case law in the United States the term generally are used interchangeably. In the context of this chapter, therefore, "novation" refers to altering the contractual relationship between parties by either replacing obligations (netting additional obligations into existing obligations to come up with new obligation) or altering a contract by adding a third party (such as interposing an intermediary), or both.

[24] 11 U.S.C. §§ 1 et seq. (1982.)

[25] N.Y. Debtor and Creditor Law §§ 151, 192 (McKinney's Supp. 1991).

3. *Bankruptcy Law*

a) Nonbank Counterparties

Section 362 of the Bankruptcy Code prohibits a creditor's exercise of a right of set-off against a debtor once a petition in bankruptcy is filed and operates automatically upon such filing (the "automatic stay" provision). Recent amendments to the Bankruptcy Code, however, provide protection for securities clearing agencies, commodity clearing organizations, forward contract merchants and certain other financial institutions (including banks) having open positions with a bankrupt debtor, by relieving them from the automatic stay.[26] These provisions operate to balance the equities between creditor's rights and protection of the United States financial markets and market participants.

For example, the Bankruptcy Code now recognizes swap master agreements and prohibits a trustee in bankruptcy from picking and choosing among the contracts included under a swap master agreement which ones the trustee will assume or reject[27] (swaps are discussed in detail below). As a result, swap participants who are parties to otherwise valid swap settlements may offset or net out termination values arising in connection with their swap agreements, notwithstanding the automatic stay and other limitations of the Bankruptcy Code.

b) Bank Counterparties

Similar protections exist under the Federal law governing the receivership of an closed bank.[28] The Financial Institutions Reform Recovery Act of 1989 ("FIRREA") amends the Federal Deposit Insurance Act ("FDI Act") and provides the framework for the receivership of banks by the Federal Deposit Insurance Company ("FDIC"). FIRREA prohibits the FDIC from repudiating Qualified Financial Contract ("QFCs") of a failed insured institution.[29]

Under the FDI Act, as amended, counterparties to QFCs of an insured depository institution may not be prohibited from exercising their right to terminate or liquidate the QFCs where such right arises upon the appointment of a receiver. In addition, the counterparties may not be prohibited from exercising any right under any security agreement relating to a QFC or any right to offset or net out the termination value, payment amount, or

[26] 11 U.S.C. § 362 (b) (6) (Supp. 1919).

[27] 11 U.S.C. §362 (b) (14) (Supp. 1991).

[28] The following discussion of Qualified Financial Contracts was prepared with the assistance of Karen R. Dacher, Attorney, Federal Reserve Bank of New York.

[29] 12 U.S.C. § 1821 (e) (8) (1988).

other transfer obligation arising in connection with the QFCs, including such rights incorporated in a master agreement.[30] The FDIC, however, may transfer the failed institution's QFCs to another depository institution upon notice to the counterparties.[31]

The FDI Act defines a QFC as a "securities contract, commodity contract, forward contract, repurchase agreement, swap agreement, and any similar agreement tht the [FDIC] determines by regulation to be a qualified financial contract...".[32] The definition of each of these terms, except for the term "swap agreement", includes a reference to its definition in the Bankruptcy Code, reflecting a parallel between the principles of general bankruptcy law and the provisions governing the insolvency of financial institutions.

The term "securities contract", therefore, has the same meaning under the Bankruptcy Code and the FDI Act. It refers to a contract for the purchase, sale, or loan of a security, and includes options, certificates of deposit, and indexes of securities, options relating to foreign currencies and settlement guarantees by or to a clearing agency.[33] Notes, stock, bonds, debentures, collateral trust certificates, voting trust certificates, certificates of deposit, investment contracts, and limited partnership interests are all types of securities[34] and, for the purposes of the FDI Act, so are mortgage loans, any mortgage-related security and any interest in any mortgage loan or mortgage-related security.[35] Specifically excluded from the definition, however, are currency, check, draft, bill of exchange, or bank letter of credit instruments and certain leveraged transactions.[36]

Commodities are bulk goods such as grains, metals and foods traded on a commodities exchange or on the spot market. On the spot market, goods are bought and sold at current market values. Trades on the commodities exchange markets anticipate future fluctuations in the prices of these goods. The FDI Act definition of commodities contracts is constructed to cover contracts with a variety of market participants and applies to contracts for

---

30 12 U.S.C. § 1821 (e) (8) (1988).

31 12 U.S.C. § 1821 (e) (9) (1988).

32 12 U.S.C. § 1821 (e) (8) (D) (1988).

33 A securities contract is a:

contract for the purchase, sale, or loan of a security, including an option for the purchase or sale of a security, certificate of deposit, or group or index of securities (including any interest therein or based on the value thereof), or any option entered into on a national securities exchange relating to foreign currencies, or the guarantee of any settlement of cash or securities by or to a securities clearing agency.

12 U.S.C. § 1821 (e) (8) (d) (ii) (1988) (citing 11 U.S.C. § 741 (7) (Supp. 1991)).

34 See 11 U.S.C. § 101 (49) (A) (Supp. 1991) (description of what constitutes a "security").

35 12 U.S.C. § 1821 (e) (8) (D) (ii) (1988).

36 11 U.S.C. § 101 (49) (B) (Supp. 1991).

commodities futures, foreign futures, leverage transactions, clearing, or commodity options.[37]

A "forward contract" is a contract, other than a commodity contract, for the purchase, sale, or transfer of a commodity and has a maturity date of more than two days after the contract is entered into.[38] Unlike futures contracts which contain standardized time periods, the time periods contained in forward contracts are negotiated by the contracting parties. Repurchase transactions, consignments, leases, swaps, hedges, deposits, loans, options, and allocated and unallocated transactions may all be structured as forward contracts. Foreign currency is commonly traded using forward contracts.

A "repurchase agreement" (repo) and reverse repurchase agreement[39] refers to an agreement to transfer certificates of deposit, eligible bankers' acceptances, or Government securities (those fully guaranteed as to principal and interest by the United States or any agency of the United States) at a certain price with the simultaneous agreement to transfer the same type of certificates of deposit, eligible bankers' acceptances, or Government securities back, either on demand or on a specified date no later than one year from the original transfer, for a certain price.[40] The FDI Act specifically expands

---

[37] A commodity contract is defined as:

(A) with respect to a futures commission merchant, contract for the purchase or sale of a commodity for future delivery on, or subject to the rules of, a contract market or board of trade;

(B) with respect to a foreign futures commission merchant, foreign future;

(C) with respect to a leverage transaction merchant, leverage transaction;

(D) with respect to a clearing organization, contract for the purchase or sale of a commodity for future delivery on, or subject to the rules of, a contract market or board of trade that is cleared by such clearing organization, or commodity option traded on, or subject to the rules of, a contract market or board of trade that is cleared by such clearing organization; or

(E) with respect to a commodity options dealer, commodity option.

12 U.S.C. § 1821 (e) (8) (D) (iii) (1988) (citing 11 U.S.C. § 761 (4) (Supp. 1991)).

[38] A forward contract is:

contract (other than a commodity contract) for the purchase, sale, or transfer of a commodity ... or any similar good, article, service, right or interest which is presently or in the future becomes the subject of dealing in the forward contract trade, or product or byproduct thereof, with a maturity date more than two days after the date the contract is entered into, including, but not limited to, a repurchase transaction, reverse repurchase transaction, consignment, lease, swap, hedge transaction, unallocated transaction, or any combination thereof or option thereon.

12 U.S.C. § 1821 (e) (8) (D) (iv) (1988) (citing 11 U.S.C. § 101 (24) (sic.) (Supp. 1991)).

[39] Repos and reverse repos have the same definition. The difference lies in who initiates the transaction relative to the dealer. If the dealer transfers securities for funds and then funds for securities, the transaction is a repurchase transaction. If the dealer transfers funds for securities and then securities for funds, the transaction is a reverse repurchase.

[40] A repurchase agreement

provides for the transfer of certificates of deposit, eligible bankers' acceptances, or

the definition of repurchase agreement to include mortgage-related securities, mortgage loans, and any interest in any mortgage loan interests, but not any participation in a commercial mortgage.[41]

Swap agreements are of two basic types, although there are a number of variations on the two. Interest rate swaps involve an agreement by one party to pay the other party interest on an agreed amount during a specified period based on one type of interest rate and an agreement by the other party to pay the first party interest on that amount during that period based on another type of interest rate (for example, fixed and floating rates of interest). Currency swaps involve an agreement by parties to pay each other a specific amount in different currencies over the same or different periods of time. The definition of swap agreement adopted in the FDI Act includes the basic interest rate and currency swaps in addition to many of the variations offered on such swaps in the market today.[42]

Most swap market participants use the International Swap Dealers Association ("ISDA") master agreement to document their transactions. The default provisions of the ISDA master agreement allow counterparties to net out their positions in the event of a default. By including swap agreements as QFCs in the FDI Act, a counterparty to a swap transaction is not prohibited from netting out its position against an insured institution for which the FDIC has been named receiver (appointment of a receiver constitutes a default under the ISDA master agreement).

The current definition of QFC and the provisions of the Bankruptcy Code do not appear to include federal funds transactions, spot contracts, and certain option contracts or master agreements for these types of contracts. As a result, if the FDIC is appointed receiver of an insured institution which

---

securities that are direct obligations of, or that are fully guaranteed as to principal and interest by, the United States or any agency of the United States against the transfer of funds by the transferee of such certificates of deposit, eligible bankers' acceptances, or securities with a simultaneous agreement by such transferee to transfer to the transferor thereof certificates of deposit, eligible bankers' acceptances, or securities as described above, at a date certain no later than one year after such transfers or on demand, against the transfer of funds.

12 U.S.C. § 1824 (e) (8) (D) (v) (1988) (citing 11 U.S.C. § 101 (49) (Supp. 1991)).

[41] Id.

[42] The FDI Act defines "swap agreement" to include:

any agreement, including the terms and conditions incorporated by reference in any such agreement, which is a rate swap agreement, basis swap, commodity swap, forward rate agreement, interest rate future, interest rate option purchased, forward foreign exchange agreement, rate cap agreement, rate floor agreement, rate collar agreement, currency swap agreement, cross-currency rate swap agreement, currency future, or currency option purchased or any other similar agreement, and ... any combination of such agreements and any option to enter into any such agreement.

12 U.S.C. § 1281 (e) (8) (D) (vi) (1988).

is a party to these transactions, the insured institution's counterparty remains vulnerable to an automatic stay and may be prohibited from exercising rights of termination or liquidation. The same is true for nonbank counterparties subject to the Bankruptcy Code. The FDIC does have the authority, however, to bring these uncovered transactions within the definition of QFC.[43]

V. Cross-Border Legal Issues when a Participant is Foreign-Chartered

The legal certainty as to whether netting will be binding takes on an added dimension when one or more of the parties to the netting is chartered in a foreign country. When foreign-chartered participants are involved in one of the described netting schemes, an issue arises as to which law governs the netting arrangement when a foreign-chartered participant is closed. Governing law could be the law of the forum, the law selected by the parties, the law of the place where the netting agreement was entered into, or the law of the country of the closed participant. Without having the facts at hand, it is difficult, if not impossible, to determine which country's law governs the netting arrangement and transactions if a participant is closed; this then introduces uncertainty as to the rights of all participants in the netting system.

In addition to the issue of governing law, when a foreign-chartered participant in a netting system is closed, the bankruptcy law of the chartering country must be examined to determine if it would supersede the law otherwise governing the netting arrangement and transactions. For example, while a foreign country's conflicts of laws principles may allow the parties to select the law governing a netting agreement entered into by the foreign-chartered party, the foreign country's bankruptcy laws may prohibit application of that governing law if it is incompatible with the foreign country's public policy.

Because of these concerns, legal certainty regarding the rights of participants in netting schemes depends upon whether neting is legally binding both in the country where the netting scheme is located and the home country of each of the participants in the scheme.

---

[43] 12 U.S.C. § 1821 (e) (8) (D) (i) (1988).

VI. Conclusion

As this discussion reveals, the legal issues arising from netting are currently being explored. While the ramifications of netting between two participants in one country such as the United States may be determinable, netting between more than two participants and netting on an international basis present more complex legal issues. In the United States, whether the net amount will be upheld as the legally enforceable result of multilateral netting arrangements is reasonably, but not perfectly, clear. The legal results of netting between domestic- and foreign-chartered participants is even less clear. As netting arrangements evolve, their incumbent risks are addressed and statutory law is enacted to deal with unsettled issues, participants in the netting arrangements and supervisors of those participants will have more confidence in the integrity of the arrangements as prudent methods of transacting business.

Financial Risks and Legal Problems of International Netting Schemes seen from a French Point of View

By Hervé Le Guen, Paris

Contents

"Netting" is not a legal concept in French law. "Compensation" or "set-off" in English, on the other hand, has been part of the French Civil Code since its promulgation in 1804. But netting is not the same as set-off. Netting is merely the calculation of a net position, whereas set-off goes beyond that, being a method of cancelling out debts, a function that corresponds to "settlement" in the English speaking world. There is no name for netting in French law, nor even a satisfactoriy translation[1], so much so that the English term is frequently inevitable.

Compensation proper is a method of settlement long used by banks, either among themselves or in their dealing with customers. For example, it serves as the basis for the running account familiar in the Romano-Germanic law countries since the Middle Ages.

It also underlies the workings of the clearing houses, through which the banks exchange payment instruments, recovering or executing them on behalf of their customers. This may be done either in the form of traditional exchanges of paper or in the modern, electronic form. In France, there are still 104 paper clearing houses, managed by the Chambre de Compensation des Banquiers de Paris, in Paris, and by local branches of the Banque de France in the provinces. There are also nine Centre Regionaux d'Exchanges d'Images-Cheques (regional truncation centers), which handle checks in dematerialized form, and nine Clearing Computers, one in Paris, eight in the Provinces through which the banks exchange payment orders on magnetic media other than cheques. These clearing computers are currently being replaced by a new national system, SIT[2], which also operates on the clearing principle.

In the international payment sphere, SAGITTAIRE[3] in France handles interbank netting and settlement of French franc operations transmitted via the SWIFT network. An Ecu netting system also operates through the Bank for International Settlements under the aegis of the Ecu Banking Association.

---

[1] According to a decision of the Minister of the Economy dated 18 February 1987 published in the Journal Officiel of the French Republic on 2 April 1987, the official French translation of the English term "netting", proposed by the Commission on Terminology of Ministry of the Economy, Finance and Budget, is "compensation monétaire de groupe". This expression only partially conveys the nature of the mechanism; it also has the disadvantage of being far more cumbersome than the word netting however, the expression "compensation monétaire de groupe" is not mandatory in official enactments and publications (as, on the contrary, are the terms "déchéance du terme" for "event of default" or "gestion de trésorerie" for "cash management") but is merely recommended.

The French version of the "Report of the Committee on Interbank Netting Schemes of the Central Banks of the Group of Ten Countries" published by the Bank of International Settlements in November 1990, is entitled "rapport du comité sur les systèmes de compensation interbancaires des banques centrales des pays du groupe des dix". Both versions are official.

[2] SIT: "Système Interbancaire de Télécompensation"(interbank remote clearing system) was inaugurated in May 1990, and entered its deployment phase in February 1991. The system is designed to permit continuous exchange of batch operations (bank transfers, bank card payments and cash withdrawals, debit notices and "titres interbancaire de paiements" — interbank payment slips).

[3] SAGITTAIRE: "Système Automatique de, Gestion Intégrée par Télétransmission de Transactions avec Imputation de Règlements Etrangers."

Netting has also long been used in other areas of concern to banks. In France, it has been used in the RELIT[4] system handling the delivery and settlement of securities, and certain financial futures contracts traded on the MATIF[5]. Banks have recently shown renewed interest in netting. Several projects — some already in their implementation phase — designed to establish international bilateral or even multilateral netting schemes for financial contracts such as currency or interest rate swaps, have come into being[6].

The international monetary authorities have become involved in the question: the Basle Committee on Banking Supervision, formerly known as the Cooke Committee and now as the Muller Committee, has acknowledged the efficiency in this type of netting to some extent, authorizing credit institutions to take account of "net" cleared operations in calculating their international solvency ratio, provided they use the "set-off by novation" technique[7]. The European directive on the European solvency ratio incorporates the same rule[8].

A report on netting systems published by the Bank for International Settlements in February 1989, known as the Angell Report[9], highlighted the potential risk of such systems and recommended that the Committee of Governors of the Central banks of the Group of Ten order further study of the question by an ad hoc committee.

The proceedings of this committee were also published by the Bank for International Settlements and are known as the Lamfalussy Report, named after the General Manager of the B.I.S. who chaired this group of experts[10].

[4] In France, the Société des bourses françaises (S.B.F.), a credit institution established by the 22 January 1988 Act on securities exchanges, is responsible for ensuring the unwinding of trades between brokerage firms on the stock market by making arrangement for the netting of securities (most of which are in book-entry form) and the corresponding financial amounts. The RELIT system, operational since May 1991, permits simultaneous settlement and delivery of securities via a computerized netting system.

[5] Under the 31 December 1987 Act on Financial Futures Markets (modifying a previous Act of 28 March 1885), financial futures contracts must be recorded by a clearing house having credit institution status.

[6] The more significant of these include FXNET (Foreign Exchange Netting and Close-out Agreement), the ISDA (International Swaps Dealers Association Agreement), and the ECHO NETTING (European Clearing House Organization) and NACHO (North American Clearing House Organization) projects.

[7] July 1988 Declaration on "International Convergence of Capital Measurement and Capital Standards" known as the "Basle Agreement" of July 1988.

[8] Council Directive of 18 December 1989 on a solvency ratio for credit institutions (89/647/EEC), Appendix II, transposed into French law by regulation no. 91-05 of the Comité de réglementation bancaire.

[9] Report on netting schemes prepared by the "Group of Experts on Payment Systems of the Central Banks of the Group of Ten Countries", Basle, February 1989.

[10] "Report of the Committee on Interbank Netting Schemes of the Group of Ten Countries", Basle, November 1990.

This report contains several recommendations for central banks and provides a list of minimum standards on the design and operation of cross-border multicurrency netting and settlement schemes. The first recommendation is that netting schemes should have a "well-founded legal basis under all relevant jurisdictions".

Certain countries already have enacted specific legislation to provide a "well-founded legal basis" for netting schemes, even when one of the participating banks is subject to a bankruptcy procedure. This is the case, for example, in the United States[11]. In other countries, netting is expected to fit into a legal framework not specifically designed for the purpose. This is what has happened in France, where legal analysis of netting draws heavily on the law on clearing.

As is to be expected, the effectiveness of netting schemes depends heavily on the law on bankruptcy applicable to the participants. If it is accepted that netting is both a method of cancelling out obligations and a form of surety it becomes readily apparent why the institution of bankruptcy proceedings against a bank participating in such a system could raise problems. That is because most bankruptcy legislation is not designed to enable creditors to extricate themselves as quickly and as unscathed as possible (by means of more or less sophisticated clearing mechanisms as in the case of a netting scheme), but rather to avoid paying off preferential creditors or even to keep the company's assets as intact as possible so as to avert final liquidation and keep it operating with a view to some future takeover.

Consequently, after a reminder of the salient features of netting schemes, including the risks that they entail if their promoters fail to take the basic precautionary measures [I], this paper will then examine how these systems can be incorporated into French law when the parties are in bonis [II], and will examine in closer detail the effectiveness of netting in relation to the law on bankruptcy [III].

I. Characteristics and Risks of Netting Systems

Netting systems serve three main purposes: to reduce the number, and hence cost, of interbank settlements; also, they are designed to reduce commitments, i. e. in banking language, to reduce exposure to other participants; lastly, netting schemes are intended to lower participants' liquidity requirements, this third objective being as it were a by-product of the first two. To achieve these objectives, netting schemes must meet a certain

[11] FIRREA: Financial Institutions Reform Recovery and Enforcement Act of 1989.

number of criteria [1]. Indeed, they may entail dangers if certain precautions are not taken [2].

1. Main Characteristics

Netting schemes are generally based on either a cross-border or a purely national interbank agreement of varying form and name. It is highly desirable that any such agreement be made in writing.

Certain schemes apply exclusively to payment netting, such as the Ecu netting scheme. Others will (or intend to) go beyond that and arrange for netting of unexpired contracts (obligation netting); this is the case notably when the netting concerns debts or claims arising from currency or interest rate futures or swaps contracts. There are two possible techniques for this: either a single framework for different types of operations[12], or a specific framework for each type of operation[13]. The common feature of these systems is that they arrange for netting of debts arising from each participant's operations with all the other participants in a single currency and at a single maturity. According to estimates cited in the Lamfalussy Report, bilateral netting reduces exposure by approximately 50 per cent, while multilateral netting may reduce it by up to 80 per cent.

These schemes also provide procedures for payment of the netting balance and, in some cases they stipulate the manner in which operations are to be concluded.

Most schemes contain a clause under which occurrence of an objective event constituting a case of default (failure to make a payment due, bankruptcy judgment, etc.). Contracts between the defaulting party and the other parties become due immediately. This clause then provides for calculation of a netting balance and immediate or accelerated payment of that balance (i. e. close-out and acceleration clauses) Multilateral systems presuppose a minimum degree of common organization to administer (notably for the calculation of net positions, etc.) and organize them. This may be handled by an outside services provider. They may also be designed with a central intermediary to substitute legally for the initial counterparties of each of the participants.

---

[12] That is what the International Swaps Dealers Association — ISDA — has opted for.

[13] As opted for by the French Banker's Association, which has a standard contract for each broad category or products (a standard contract for currency or interest rate swaps, another for caps and floors operations, yet another for interest rate futures operations, etc.), with a possibility of over-netting the netting balances arising from these different contracts.

The systems contain mechanisms to safeguard participants against the risk of failure by one of them. Here too, two variants are possible: either prior guarantees are given, generally in the form of deposits involving securities or even cash (so-called "defaulters prepay"), or rules are laid down for the allocation of losses in the event of failure (so-called "survivors pay" systems). "Defaulters prepay"-type systems are more likely to be found in a centralized systems in which a central organ administers the prepaid guarantees. A "survivors pay"-type organization corresponds more to the logic of a decentralized over-the-counter market operating within bilateral limits. Bankers currently appear to favor the latter[14].

2. *Minimum Risks and Safeguards*

While netting schemes at first sight offer advantages in terms of effectiveness (cost reduction) and security (reducing credit and liquidity risks) of payment systems, they also entail additional risk factors. The Angell and above all Lamfalussy reports state these risks very clearly[15]. To sum up, the international monetary authorities' fears are twofold. First, if netting schemes are not sufficiently legally sound, and if they are not effectively capable of producing binding net positions when they are needed most, i. e. in case of serious failure (bankruptcy of a participant), they may do no more than provide an illusion of security which merely "obscures the level of exposures"[16]. Moreover, even assuming that net positions are binding, netting may lead certain banks to take risks on one or another counterparty than would not be considered acceptable for un-netted amounts. This could actually increase the likelihood that one institution's failure may lead to failure of another and thus trigger a chain reaction (systemic risk) by encouraging an accumulation, shift or concentration of commitments.

That is one reason why the Group of Ten Central Banks adopted the recommendations of the Lamfalussy Committee. Given the risks entailed by unchecked development of netting schemes, the Committee framed two recommendations for the central banks. The first calls for these schemes to be designed and implemented in accordance with certain "minimum standards"[17]; the second considers it desirable for the central banks to institute a process of "cooperative oversight"[18]. Taking "cooperative oversight" first, this begins by establishing the principle of a division of labour among central

[14] The ECHO NETTING and NACHO projects incorporate this decentralized model.

[15] See in particular the Lamfalussy Report, Part B.

[16] Lamfalussy Report, Part A, para. 2.4.

[17] Lamfalussy Report, Part A, Section 3, paras. 3.2.-3.6 and Part C.

[18] Lamfalussy Report, Part A, Section 3, paras. 3.7-3.10 and Part D.

banks. The host-country central bank i. e. the country on whose market the scheme is established or operates, receives prime responsibility for reviewing the design and operation of the system and ensuring that it complies with the "minimum standards". The central bank vested with this responsibility should however consult with other central banks and supervisory authorities that may have an interest in the system's prudent operation.

Moreover, central banks should use this "oversight" to "discourage" institutions subject to their authority from participating in systems of unsound design or management.

There are six "minimum standards": 1 — netting schemes should have a sound legal basis; 2 — participants should have a clear understanding of the impact of the particular scheme on each of the financial risks affected by the netting process; 3 — multilateral systems should have clearly-defined procedures for the management of credit and liquidity risks which specify the respective responsibilities of the netting provider and the participants as well as procedures for limiting counterparty risks; 4 — netting systems should, at a minimum, be capable of ensuring completion in the event of inability to settle by the participant with the largest single net-debit position; 5 — they should have objective criteria for admission permitting fair and open access; lastly, 6 — they should be based on reliable technical systems and equipped with standby facilities.

The fact that a firm legal foundation is ranked first among these minimum standards demonstrates the importance of legal issues in the organization and operation of netting systems. The following section looks more closely at this legal aspect.

II. Netting When the Parties are in Bonis

When the parties are in bonis and bankruptcy law is not involved netting schemes may be fully effective under French law by dovetailing with the set-off framework. A few explanations of the legal framework of set-off [1] are required before showing how netting schemes can operate — without major difficulty in the case of bilateral netting, and at the cost of some conceptual effort in the case of multilateral netting applying the classic techniques of the law on set-off [2].

1. The Legal Framework of Set-Off under French Law

Under French Law, and in other civil law systems, set-off is generally defined as the operation whereby two reciprocal debts are cancelled out, in full or in part, depending on whether or not they are for the same amount.

Specifically, Article 1234 of the French Civil Code classifies set-off as a method of cancelling out obligations; it is listed alongside payment proper, novation, voluntary forgiveness of debt, merger or even prescription, to cite but some of the commonest methods of extinction of obligations.

In practice, French law recognizes three types of set-off.

a) Legal set-off, governed by Articles 1289-1299 of the French Civil Code. Legal set-off takes place automatically, by force of law "and even without the debtors' knowledge", according to the Code (Art. 1290), without requiring any act or even demand on the part of the parties. At most, they can refuse legal set-off if they wish to be paid differently. For legal set-off to operate, claims must meet four conditions: they must be reciprocal, fungible, liquid and payable.

Reciprocity signifies that legal set-off cannot apply between claims that the two parties concerned do not have on each other.

The condition of fungibility is explained in the Civil Code itself (Art. 1291): set-off can only occur between "two debts both of which concern a sum of money or a certain quantity of fungible things of the same kind". Concerning set-off of monetary debts, longstanding jurisprudence established by a decision of the Paris Court of Appeal of 19 July 1943[19], rejected the set-off of debts expressed in different currencies. The ruling concerned a debt in French francs to be set off against a debt in dollars. This decision was unanimously criticized by doctrine, and the courts themselves today consider that developments in international financial relations render this jurisprudence totally outdated[20]. Moreover, since the publication of a ministerial circular of 21 May 1987 (even before exchange controls were fully removed in France), residents are no longer required to obtain special authorization to settle their debts to non-residents by means of set-off. Residents are merely required to provide documents relating to these operations to the French Customs on demand[21]. By referring to "fungible things of the same kind",

[19] Revue Trimestrielle de Droit Civil 1944, 117, obs. H. & L. Mazeaud.

[20] French law requires in principle that all debts payable in France be paid in French francs (Chambre des Requêtes de la Cour de Cassation, 17 February 1937, and many more recent rulings, including for example: Cour de Cassation, 11 October 1989, Jurisclasseur Periodique JCP 1990, 21393; Cour d'Appel de Bordeaux, 8 March 1990, Dalloz 1990, IR, 119). However, it is also accepted that this requirement is mandatory only in the case of purely internal obligations, with one legal exception for payments relating to bonds denominated in Ecus (S. 44 II of the 1989 Finance Act). For contracts comprising an international element, French jurisprudence readily accepts specification of payment in foreign currency.

[21] Circular of 21 May 1987 on commercial and financial operations with foreign countries by residents on their own account or under a management contract (Journal Officiel, 23 May 1987), para. IV-B: "Residents (...) may also pay their debts to non-residents by means of set-off of claims and debts. They shall hold available to the Customs administration documentary proof of these operations."

Article 1291 also opens the door to the set-off of pecuniary obligations not yet due, such as obligations arising from financial contracts, for example.

The liquidity required for claims and debts to be set off signifies that their amount should be determined exactly. In the case of setting off claims in different currencies, the liquidity requirement raises no problem provided the said currencies are quoted either against each other or against a third currency.

Lastly, claims must be payable i. e. matured. This condition of payability presupposes that claims must be certain, i. e. that they must not be either future or hypothetical claims nor, of course, contested claims.

b) If all the conditions of legal set-off are not fulfilled, set-off may nevertheless operate either by agreement or through judicial proceedings.

Set-off can be provided for in a contract when not all of the conditions of legal set-off are fulfilled. For example, the parties may provide for the set-off of claims that are not reciprocal, or are not payable, or are not liquid.

Judicial set-off is imposed on the parties by the courts, since judges also have the possibility of waiving one or more of the conditions of legal set-off, primarily payability and/or liquidity.

c) Regardless of whether it is legal, by agreement or judicial, set-off produces two effects. First, it allows the parties to wipe out their debts or claims definitively for the amount set off, i. e. for the lower of the debts or claims in question. Which allows the courts to claim that set-off is a means of payment or, more precisely that it represents a dual payment.

However, set-off is more than just a mode of payment. It is also a form of surety. The French Civil Code does not say so explicitly, and does not deal with set-off as it deals with sureties, pledges, preferential claims and mortgages under special "titres". However, if one defines a surety as "a provision intended to guarantee payment of a debt at maturity"[22], set-off undeniably acts as a surety insofar as it guarantees to anyone who can claim to be covered by such an arrangement that his claim will be paid up to the amount of his own debt towards his creditor. Certain court decisions explicitly describe set-off as a surety[23]. This opinion is generally shared by French legal doctrine[24].

---

[22] Vocabulaire Juridique CORNU, PUF (Presses Universitaires de France), 1987.

[23] Cour d'Appel de Paris, 27 September 1977, Dalloz 1978, IR 250; Revue des Sociétés 1978, 728; Revue Trimestrielle de Droit Commercial 1979, 256.

[24] See in particular Mendegris, "La nature juridique de la compensation, Libraire Générale de Droit et de Jurisprudence", LGDJ and DUBOC, "La compensation et les droits des tiers", LGDJ, 1989. Divergent opinion, Martin-Serf, "L'interprétation extensive des sûretés rélles en droit commercial", "Revue Trimestrielle de Droit Commercial 1980, 677, spéc. no. 11.

2. Application of the Principles of the Law on Set-Off to Netting Schemes

As we have seen, the advantages of netting are far more attractive when multilateral rather than merely bilateral, in terms of reducing risks.

Yet the French Civil Code primarily envisages set-off as a relationship between two parties and two parties only. Article 1289 states that "when two persons are in debt to each other, they shall set off their respective debts ..."; Article 1290 stipulates "the two debts shall cancel each other reciprocally", and Article 1291 goes further in stating that "set-off may only occur between two debts, both of ...".

While traditional law on set-off does provide a satisfactory legal framework for bilateral netting, it is insufficient for multilateral netting. French law contains no ready-made legal framework for the latter, and an effort will have to be made to conceptualize one.

a) For bilateral netting of debts or claims for sums of money, legal set-off or set-off by agreement (for the most part contractual set-off in fact, since a netting scheme can only be contractual, even if the contract is informal) provides a perfectly suitable and effective legal framework. So there is no point in dwelling on the issue. The only possible question mark concerns the possibility of setting off claims expressed in different currencies, but as we have seen, the jurisprudence of 1943 which ruled against this set-off may now be considered to have become outdated. Promoters of international netting schemes may ignore this jurisprudence.

Concerning bilateral netting of obligations other than sums of money (financial contracts e. g. currency contracts, swaps, etc.), i. e. debts or claims not yet due, there is no need in French law to resort to the notion of novation as in Anglo-Saxon law: if legal set-off can only apply where debts are due and payable, set-off by agreement allows this condition of payability to be waived. Set-off between parties bound by a running account agreement (in which neither the balance nor any of its articles is payable prior to final closure) can already be construed as a kind of set-off in futurum[25]. Jurisprudence has allowed that the parties may stipulate a set-off concerning non-payable debts outside of the case of a running account[26].

b) The foregoing on bilateral netting applies equally to multilateral netting. But this raises an additional problem which is precisely the question of its multilateral character. The problem varies according to whether or not

[25] See Mendegris, op. cit., para. 131, p. 162.

[26] Cour d'Appel d'Amiens, January 6, 1883, Dalloz Periodique D.P., 1885-2-205 et, sur pourvoi, Cour de Cassation, Chambre Civile, 9 June 1886, D.P. 1887-1/40.

the multilateral netting system comprises a central intermediary. Where there is a central entity between the primary participants, the netting is not truly multilateral. In law, it is construed as a series of bilateral nettings between the central body and each of the participants in the system. The Lamfalussy Report[27] expresses the concept very clearly, explaining that "when the netting is conducted through a central entity which is legally substituted for the original counterparty to each payment or contract, the net-net position will, in fact, constitute a bilateral net position between each participant and the central counterparty".

Under this arrangement, so-called multilateral netting boils down to a juxtaposition of bilateral nettings. This kind of arrangement has been used successfully in France for operations processed on the MATIF[28].

The only real question raised by the organization of a multilateral netting of this kind concerns the status of the central entity. The 24 Januar 1984 Banking Act (S. 1-1) in effect classifies not only the granting of credit and taking of deposits from the public among operations reserved for approved credit institutions, but also the "provision or management of means of payment for customers". The French banking authorities tend to equate the management of a netting scheme with the administration of means of payment and, once this administration is placed in the hands of a legally constituted entity, that entity must obtain approval as a credit institution[29]. In that case, it is bound by oversight by the supervisory authorities (Commission Bancaire). The fact of having banking status indeed represents a safeguard for the system.

The question is rather more awkward in the case of multilateral netting without an intermediary, or at least without an intermediary legally substituting for the original counterparty. Here, the obstacle lies in the condition of reciprocity of debts required for performance of the set-off.

The reason for this is that multilateral netting without an intermediary implies that a situation could arise in which one of the participants may be obliged to make a payment to another participant with whom he has never directly entered into a contract, and therefore to whom he has never been indebted. All that is necessary for that is that the solvens (the person obliged to pay) must himself be in debt to the debtor of the accipiens (the person who is to receive the payment). If A owes 100 to B, who himself owes 100 to C, and if C in turn owes 50 to B, who owes 50 to A, multilateral netting will allow all

[27] Part B., para. 2-9.

[28] Section 9 of the 28 March 1885 Act, modified by the 31 December 1987 Act abovementioned.

[29] For example entities that organize the clearing of settlements and deliveries of securities (the Société des Bourses Françaises, S.B.F.) and trading on the financial futures market (MATIF S.A.) are both approved credit institutions.

of these debts to be unwound with a single direct payment of 50 by A to C. But it is immediately plain that there is no reciprocity between the debts and claims of A and the debts and claims of C. The set-off technique by itself, which requires reciprocity of debts, is therefore not sufficient to provide an adequate legal basis for A's payment to C. In a word, it does not provide a sufficient legal basis for multilateral netting without an intermediary.

One solution to this problem would be to call in the notion of novation, and precisely that of novation by change of debtor as provided in Article 1271-2° of the Civil Code. However, in Franch law, recourse to novation raises more problems than it settles. While novation is just as effective as netting or gross payment as a means of cancelling out debts (as mentioned above, it is one of the methods of cancelling obligations listed in Article 1234 of the Civil Code) when the parties are in bonis, it is much less acceptable when one of the parties is bankrupt (see below).

The technique of novation can be ruled out all the more readily since simpler, less risky mechanisms are available. One explanation of multilateral netting has been proposed in which it is viewed as a conventional bilateral netting coupled with an order (if necessary tacit) by the net debtor to his own debtors to pay their debts into the hands of his creditor[30]. This analysis draws attention to similarities between the proposed procedure and a familiar institution in French law, the "indication of payment" provided in Article 1277 of the Civil Code[31].

So there is no reason for not supposing that the most traditional mechanisms of French Civil Law (netting + order to pay) could provide the valid legal foundation required by the promoters of multilateral netting.

To be sure, this construction has yet to be tested in practice, and no jurisdiction has yet had occasion to rule on the legal nature of multilateral netting in the absence of a central entity.

Netting systems are supposed not only to allow debts and claims between parties in bonis to be settled validly. They must also demonstrate their ability to withstand the chief test which they are intended to confront, namely the law on bankruptcy.

---

[30] Jean-Pierre Mattout, paper on netting presented to the Deauville Symposium in June 1989, Revue de Jurisprudence Commerciale, special issue, November 1989.

[31] Article 1277 of the French Civil Code provides that "simple indication by the debtor of a person who shall pay in his place does not represent a novation. The same is true in the case of simple indication by the creditor of a person to receive payment in his place".

III. Netting and Bankruptcy Law

The Lamfalussy Report rightly stresses the fact that, in order to achieve the desired results, netting schemes must have a sound legal basis. In the worst case, this basis must allow for bankruptcy on the part of one of its participants[32]. Consequently, because such schemes are designed chiefly, if not exclusively, to reduce counterparty risks, it is only when one of these counterparties fails that the system needs to be able to produce its effects in full.

The question is all the more important since the aims of bankruptcy law are frequently opposed to those of netting schemes. Whereas the latter seek the most favourable and quickest possible unwinding of operations with a failed institution, bankruptcy law takes a dim view of anything resembling preferential or accelerated payment. It prefers to preserve the maximum assets, to pay as little debt as possible, and even to encourage the parties to perform their unexpired contracts in order to maximize the chances of recovery of the failed business. French bankruptcy law goes to considerable lengths in this respect. One merely has to consider the title of the 25 January 1985 Bankruptcy Act to grasp the point: "law on the judicial recovery and liquidation of business", and Section I of the Act: "This act institutes a procedure for judicial recovery intended to permit the preservation of the company, its business and jobs, and the repayment of debts".

Nor is the issue confined to application of one national legal system. In the case of bilateral netting, care should be taken to ascertain that the law on bankruptcy applicable to each of the two parties is not incompatible with implementation of that netting. In the case of multilateral netting, one needs to review the law on bankruptcy in "all the jurisdictions concerned", according to the Lamfalussy Report[33], to see whether netting will effectively reduce risks. "The jurisdictions concerned" are those in each of the participants' countries, including that of the central entity. In addition, in the case of branches of banks whose headquarters are located in another country, the "jurisdiction concerned" may be either that of the branch or that of the headquarters, or of both, depending on the international law on bankruptcy applicable.

There is no question of discussing the issue of bankruptcy law as it applies to netting exhaustively here due to this international aspect. This paper confines itself to considering the question from the standpoint of French law alone.

---

[32] See in particular the Lamfalussy Report, Part B, paras. 2-23, 2-25 and 2-26.

[33] Lamfalussy Report, minimum standard no. 1.

From the French point of view, some clarification of terms is required. When one speaks of bankruptcy law, the reference is to the 25 January 1985 Act mentioned earlier, on the judicial recovery and liquidation of businesses, and to that alone[34]. Being of recent origin, jurisprudence relating to this Act is only now beginning to be established. So any attempt to discuss its possible consequences on netting schemes amounts to little more than an exercise in future legal studies.

The 25 January 1985 Act lays down a judicial procedure applicable both to banks and to all other businesses. There is no specific legislation in France for bank failures, these being subject to ordinary law.

However, not all difficulties that a bank may encounter necessarily or immediately result in the opening of the legal proceedings provided by the 1985 Act.

In practice, difficulties encountered by banks are handled in the first place by the bank supervisory authority (the Commission Bancaire), which has the power, among others, to appoint a receiver who is vested with the necessary powers to run and manage the credit institution[35], and to appoint a liquidator if the institution's approval is withdrawn[36]. This administrative or disciplinary phase in the treatment of the bank's difficulties is independent of the opening of judicial bankruptcy proceedings laid down in the 25 January 1985 Act, although it may result in such proceedings. The possibility of both administrative and judicial procedures proceeding in parallel is not a mere hypothesis. The coexistence of the two procedures may raise problems, but so far these have been more theoretical than truly serious[37]. As a consequence of all that, a bank to which a receiver or liquidator has been appointed by the Commission Bancaire is in no way affected by the law on bankruptcy insofar as its activities are concerned. The law only begins to apply, if ever, after judgment, generally handed down by a commercial court, ordering the opening of judicial recovery procedures.

Normally, application for the opening of judicial recovery procedures must be made to the court from the moment of "cessation of payment" and at the latest 15 days after recognition of this cessation of payment[38]. The

---

[34] Article 2 of the 25 January 1985 Act states in very general terms that it applies to "all traders, craftsmen, farmers and all private law corporations".

[35] Section 44 of the 24 January 1984 Act on the activities and supervision of credit institutions, referred to as the Banking Act.

[36] Section 46 of the Banking Act.

[37] See S. Peltier, "L'étendue des pouvoirs des administrateur provisoires ou liquidateurs nommés par la Commission Bancaire", Banque et Droit no. 14, November-December 1990, and comments by M. Vasseur on cour d'appel de Paris, 3e chambre B, 2 March 1990, Dalloz 1990, jurisprudence 569 and ff.

[38] Section 3 of the 25 January 1985 Act on the judicial recovery and liquidation of businesses.

experience of the handful of bank failures that have occurred in France shows that cessation of payment generally corresponds to the closure of the bank's windows decided by the Commission Bancaire's appointee. Having clarified these points, French bankruptcy law essentially raises two problems for netting schemes: that of the ban on making payments from the date of commencement of proceedings [1], and that of the event of default [2]. Some further remarks are required on other equally important, though less difficult points, in addition to the above two questions [3].

1. The Prohibition on Making Payments from the Date of Commencement of Proceedings

Section 33 of the 25 January 1985 Act states that "the order to open proceedings automatically entails a prohibition on the payment of all debts arising prior to the said judgment". The prohibition laid down in Section 33 takes effect at "zero-hours" on the date of pronouncement of the court order opening bankruptcy proceedings[39]. This rule concerns the operation of netting schemes in two ways: it can affect the set-off that operates inside netting schemes insofar as set-off is equated with a payment; it can also affect payment of the netting balance.

a) Regarding the validity of set-off itself from the date of the judgment opening proceedings, the plain application of the rule laid down in Section 33 should lead to the conclusion that no set-off is any longer possible as from zero hours on the date of the bankruptcy judgment, at least if that set-off concerns prior debts. Indeed, the Section 33 rule could even bring into question a set-off that has already taken place between zero hours and the pronouncement of the judgment.

In their wisdom, the judges apply the rule flexibility, however, and jurisprudence does in effect allow the netting to continue to operate validly if the debts and claims are connected, i. e. if they are sufficiently interdependent in economic terms to be incapable of being treated separately in legal terms. Their connexity is a de facto notion on which the substantive judge's ruling is final; the "Cour de Cassation" (French Supreme Court) has not considered it necessary to define the concept precisely, but it has nevertheless

[39] The moment at which the bankruptcy judgment takes effect is not laid down in the January 25, 1985 Act, but in the statutory instrument taken in application of the Act: Article 14-2 of the statutory instrument of 27 December 1985 (modified in 1988) provides that "the judgment pronouncing the opening of proceedings shall take effect from the date of pronouncement". Jurisprudential interpretation of this rule (which is traditional in French bankruptcy law, as it has been taken over from the earlier legislation) is that the judgment takes effect from zero hours on the day on which it is pronounced. The rule whereby bankruptcy judgments are retroactive to zero hours is indeed common to other legal systems, Belgian, Dutch and Italian law appear to take a similar line.

set the conditions for it. Doctrine, meanwhile, has sketched out several definitions of connexity, calling in notions such as the common allocation of reciprocal obligations or their common origin[40].

By invoking this notion of connexity, the courts bring the law into line with reality. It is interesting to trace the evolution of jurisprudence on this question.

The possibility of setting off connected debts was recognized under the bankruptcy legislation prior to the 1985 Act, i. e. the former 13 July 1967 Act.

Since the 1970s, the "Cour de Cassation" has adopted an increasingly extensive interpretation of the notion of connexity[41]. In several decisions handed down starting in 1980, the "Cour de Cassation" considered that the fact of setting off after the opening of proceedings did not impair the rights of third parties on condition that the claims concerned could be connected with a more comprehensive economic operation.

In the initial decisions of the Cour de Cassation, connexity was allowed only if the netted debts or claims resulted from a single contract[42]; it then allowed that connexity may exist between debts and claims forming part of a comprehensive economic operation[43] and, finally, between debts and claims arising from distinct contracts but concluded within the framework of a master agreement[44].

For many years, the whole question was whether this jurisprudence dating from the old 1967 law on bankruptcy would be given a new lease on life under the new 25 Januar 1985 Act. One part of the doctrine did in effect consider that the 1985 Act represented a radical change of viewpoint compared with the earlier legislation, by placing greater emphasis on recovery of the failed business at the expense of the rights of creditors, to the extent that even in cases of connexity there was no longer any reason for the set-off to take place[45]. Other jurists took a different view and considered that the jurisprudence derived from the 1967 Act would not be modified[46].

---

[40] DUBOC, op. cit., no. 309 and ff.

[41] See in particular comments by M. Ghestin on Cour de Cassation, Chambre Commerciale, 4 July 1973, deux arrêts, Dalloz, 1974, 425 et 426.

[42] Cour de Cassation, Chambre civile, 18 October 1938, Dalloz Hebdomadaire 1938, p. 593; Cour de Cassation, Chambre Commerciale, 5 October 1983, Dalloz 1984, IR 130 obs. A. Honorat, and 22 June 1983, Bulletin Civil IV, no 186; Dalloz 1983, 560 comments by A. Honorat; Gazette du Palais 1984-1, pan. 24, obs. J. Dupichot.

[43] Cour de Cassation, Chambre Commerciale, 9 November 1982, Dalloz 1983, 466 comments by A. Honorat.

[44] Cour de Cassation, Chambre Commerciale, 17 May 1989, Dalloz, annotated contents 1989, p. 369.

[45] See in particular Derrida, Godé and Sortais, Redressement et liquidation judiciaires des entreprises, 2nd edition no. 285, 3rd edition no. 380; Jeantin, Précis Dalloz, p. 517, no.

The jurisprudence handed down under the new 25 January 1985 Act was not all that clearcut to begin with: certain courts of appeal have handed down decisions which appear to be capable of being interpreted as tending to uphold the earlier jurisprudence which favored set-off in case of connexity[47]. Other courts of appeal, on the other hand, took a negative stand[48]. However, the "favourable" decisions slightly outweighed the "unfavourable" ones.

This trend has recently undergone a new development. The Cour de Cassation recently heard a case which involved the validity of a set-off of connected debts in a case of bankruptcy governed by the 1985 Act. A decision handed down on 19 March 1991[49], validates the set-off after recognizing that the debts and claims in question were connected. This decision may be interpreted as confirming the continuing validity of the traditional jurisprudence. It is important to note, moreover, that in the case involved in the 19 March 1991 decision, connexity was acknowledged even though the claims and debts concerned resulted from separate contracts not even bound by a master agreement.

The jurisprudence described did not concern set-off of bank operations, nor even failures involving banks: for the simple reason that there are very few bank failures in France, and that the rare cases of bank failures have not given rise to this kind of dispute.

So it is necessary to make an effort of transposition in order to see what conclusions can be drawn for netting schemes from the jurisprudence discussed above. The first conclusion one can draw is that, notwithstanding the rule laid down in Section 33 of the 25 January 1985 Act, the bankruptcy of a participant in a netting scheme governed by French law is not in itself an obstacle to effective operation of the system, provided it is possible to establish the existence of a relationship of connexity between the debts and claims netted.

623; Chaput, Droit du redressement et de la liquidation judiciaires des entreprises, p. 126, no. 114; Saint-Alary, Houin obs., Revues des Procédures Collectives 1989, 157-161, no. 15-27; Legras de Grancourt, Revue des Procédures Collectives 1990, 119.

[46] Soinne, traité, p. 535, no. 623; Calendini, note Revue de Jurisprudence Commerciale 1990, 256, spéc. no. 11-14; Ripert et Roblot, Traité, tome 2, 11e edition, p. 872-874, no. 3040; Bac et Mathieu, La compensation pour dettes connexes, Banque et Droit, suppléement au no. 484 de la Revue Banque, June 1988; Montradon, La compensation pour dettes connexes après le jugement déclaratif peut-elle survivre à la loi du 25 janvier 1985 Jurisclasseur Périodique JCP 1991, I, p. 458 and ff.; Peltier, Banque et Droit, no. 12, July-August 1990, p. 183.

[47] Cour d'Appel de Versailles, 20 May 1987, Dalloz 1988, Annotated contents, 8, obs. Derrida; Revue de Jurisprudence Commerciale 1988, p. 30 obs. Gallet; Cour d'Appel de Paris, 28 March 1987, Dalloz 1989, IR 125; and, subject to distinct reservations, Cour d'Appel de Paris, 30 September 1988, Revue de Jurisprudence Commerciale 1989, p. 125.

[48] See in particular Cour d'Appel d'Amiens, 21 February 1991, Dalloz 1991, IR, 103.

[49] Cour de Cassation, Chambre Commerciale, 19 March 1991, Dalloz 1991, IR, 115 and La Semaine Juridique 1991, 481.

In the case of a netting system concerning financial contracts (swaps, etc.), connexity may flow from formal elements, the existence of a master agreement, and from substantive elements such as the fact that the operations in question form part of a comprehensive risk management system concerning a currency, maturity or counterparty. In other words the fact that, above a certain volume of operations, certain contracts are concluded only because of the existence of earlier ones (e. g. to reduce risk on a counterparty, or to reduce or increase a currency or maturity hedge), and would have no economic justification if taken in isolation. In that sense, the fact that a netting scheme provides for the monitoring of bilateral limits even in a multilateral system, and even if there is an intermediary entity, would certainly be taken into consideration by the courts when seeking to establish the existence of a relationship of connexity.

According to information gathered from banks actively involved in foreign exchange or interest rate markets, it does indeed look as if this is the way operations are concluded.

Consequently, once it has been established that the operations to which the netting refers are economically linked, indissociable even, there is every reason to believe that the courts would acknowledge the conditions of legal connexity, allowing them to validate the mechanism on which the netting is based in spite of the opening of bankruptcy proceedings.

However, while the condition of connexity can be met within the framework of a netting concerning contracts, this is not the case for netting concerning payment orders, for which the notions of comprehensive management and bilateral limits are not always referred to in current practice. For netting of payments, the prohibition on setting off resulting from Section 33 is likely to be fully operative.

The French monetary authorities are now aware of this drawback and have called for a start to work on modifying the legislation. So this problem could shortly be solved if Parliament passes a bill to do away with the undesirable effects of Section 33 and thus confer greater security on interbank settlement systems in general, and not only ones that operate by means of set-off[50].

b) Regarding the validity of payment of the set-off balance, the prohibition on all payments of prior debts from the date of commencement of the bankruptcy procedure would, a priori, prevent a defaulting bank from settling the said balance.

---

[50] Independently of the drawback that it entails for netting schemes, the rule laid down in Section 33 of the 25 January 1985 Act renders the setting up of settlement systems highly risky regardless of whether these take the form of net settlements after set-off or gross settlements, with the Central Bank guaranteeing irrevocability.

However, if the payment takes place despite the Section 33 prohibition (which may occur notably between zero hours and pronouncement of the bankruptcy judgment), this can only be overruled if the receiver so requests, and if he can prove that a fraud has been committed against the rights of creditors. Furthermore, a decision of the Paris Court of Appeal on 28 March 1989[51] considered that nullities likely to hit acts ocurring after the date of cessation of payment do not concern acts performed on the same day as the said cessation of payment, and that, in this particular case, the dispute did indeed concern a payment by set-off.

Whatever the case may be, if the amendment designed to remedy the drawbacks of section 33 does go through, the question of the validity of payment of the set-off balance on the day of commencement of bankruptcy proceedings will be resolved.

2. *Event of Default*

Netting systems for financial contracts generally contain a clause stating that, in case of default by a participant, or even simply in case of occurrence of an unfavourable event concerning a participant, all contracts outstanding shall be either cancelled or shall become payable before term. These are the "termination in case of default"[52] or the "close-out" and "acceleration" clauses under Anglo-Saxon law.

a) These clauses are more or less built on the same model. Briefly, they list a certain number of "cases of default" such as, for example: non-payment of an installment, non-performance of a clause in a netting contract, misreporting of legal situation or solvency, administrative or judicial granting of a stay of execution, appointment of a receiver or liquidator, withdrawal of approval to operate as a bank, pronouncement of disciplinary sanctions by the supervisory authorities, or opening of bankruptcy procedure.

The occurrence of any of these cases of default entails cancellation of contracts governed by the netting agreement and immediate payment of an indemnity, to be calculated on an appropriate basis corresponding to the balance on the netting of operations in progress. The debtor or debtors pay the creditor or creditors, and implementation of the event of default clause could equally well result in a payment by the defaulting party as in a payment to the defaulting party.

---

[51] Op. cit., note no 47.

[52] This kind of clause is found, for example, in the master agreement framed by the French Bankers' Association "Standard AFB Terms for Currency of Interest Rate Swap Transactions" (art. 8), "Standard AFB Terms for Options Transactions" (art. 9), "Standard AFB Terms for Interest Rate Cap/Floor Guarantee Transactions" (art. 8), "Standard AFB Terms for Future Rate Agreements (FRA)" (art. 8).

b) These clauses are perfectly licit in principle under French law; they are merely an expression of the autonomous will on which contract law is based: what the free will of the parties may institute (the initial contractual terms) the same free will (expressed in an event of default clause) may undo. There is abundant jurisprudence to validate event of default clauses together with acceleration or termination clauses in case of default. It has even been ruled that the courts cannot suspend application of an event of default clause in the name of equity[53]. French law does, moreover, contain a legal event of default clause, in addition to ones entered into by agreement. For example, Article 1188 of the Civil Code provides for event of default, even if not stipulated by the parties, when the debtor "diminishes by his own acts the sureties given by him (...) to his creditor".

However, one provision in bankruptcy law raises some doubts as to the effects of a cancellation clause in case of judicial recovery of the party to whose detriment such a clause might be invoked.

First, Section 56 of the 25 January, 1985 Act provides that "the judgment ordering judicial recovery shall not render claims not yet due payable". Above all, Section 37, Clause 5 of the same act states that "notwithstanding all legal provisions or all contractual clauses to the contrary, no indivisibility, cancellation or termination of a contract may result from the simple commencement of a judicial recovery procedure". In other words, the event of default clauses, which are accelerated cancellation clauses, are liable to be inoperative if they are invoked as a result of the opening of bankruptcy proceedings.

This conclusion needs to be qualified, however. Section 37, Clause 5 refers to cancellation resulting "exclusively" from the opening of bankruptcy proceedings. Yet, if the netting agreement has taken care to stipulate other "cases of default" than the opening of judicial bankruptcy proceedings (such as, for example, non-payment of an installment, the opening of administrative or disciplinary proceedings by the supervisory or control authorities, or again the appointment of a receiver by that supervisory or control authority) the fact of the subsequent opening of bankruptcy proceedings should not affect the validity of the event of default recorded in application of a different case of default.

In France, for example, since the 1984 Banking Act came into force, bank failures have always begun with the appointment of a receiver by the Commission Bancaire, and only several weeks later have judicial proceedings been opened, where appropriate. In that type of case, the event of default clause which would have been invoked as a result of the appointment of a receiver would not have been governed by the aforementioned Section

[53] Cour d'Appel de Paris, 14e chamber, 25 February 1977, Juris. Data no. 177.

37, Clause 5. It is true that, however theoretical, the possibility of a sudden bank failure occurring without the supervisory authorities having time to intervene cannot be ruled out entirely.

Which is why it is important to consider another aspect of the question. Section 37, Clause 5 only applies in fact to the judicial recovery phase of the bankruptcy procedure. This recovery phase is intended to facilitate implementation of a solution to the company's difficulties, which explains why the law contains provisions such as that found in Section 37. This recovery phase is compulsory before the second phase of the procedure, liquidation, can be initiated.

Unlike recovery, liquidation renders all debts not yet payable automatically so. Section 160, Clause 1 of the 25 January 1985 Act is perfectly clear on this point: "the judgment ordering judicial liquidation shall render payable all debts not due on the date of the judgment opening judicial recovery". The rule is both traditional and logical: since the company is to be liquidated, there is no point in waiting: the quicker what can be paid of the liabilties is paid (if necessary by set-off) the better. Even if there is no contractual event of default clause, here it is the law itself which imposes this event of default. However, the two phases of the procedure may follow in very quick succession if the failed company really is beyond recovery. Jurisprudence has even gone so far as to allow opening of the recovery and liquidation phases on the same day, provided this takes place through distinct judgments and the liquidation judgment is clearly subsequent to the recovery judgment[54].

Moreover, in the case of banks, the rationale of the French system is such that recovery is sought not through the judicial bankruptcy procedure, but through the oversight exercised by the supervisory authorities. It is up to the Commission Bancaire to explore possible recovery solutions for failed credit institutions, and judicial bankruptcy proceedings are usually opened once liquidation is the sole solution possible. To conclude on the subject of event of default clauses, the French method of handling bank failures makes little room for the judicial recovery phase of bankruptcy law and should, therefore, if the netting agreements are properly drafted, avoid triggering Section 37, Clause 5 of the 1985 Act, which is so contrary to the event of default clauses.

3. *Other Aspects of Bankruptcy Law*

Three further important aspects of bankruptcy law are: nullities which may render certain actions void during the so-called "période suspecte" prior

[54] Cour de Cassation, Chambre Commerciale, 17 May 1989, Jurisclasseur Periodique JCP 1989, 11, 21464 obs. Beaubrun; Cour de Cassation, Chambre Commerciale, 6 March 1990, Dalloz 1990, Jurisprudence, p. 321.

to opening of bankruptcy procedures, the question of "cherry-picking"; and that of the effectiveness of guarantees.

a) Nullities during the "période suspecte"

When a company files for bankruptcy, the court must set the date for cessation of payment when opening judicial recovery; this date may be the date of the judgment, but it may also be backdated up to eighteen months prior to the date of the judgment (Section 9 of the 25 January Act). The period between the date of the judgment and the date of cessation of payment is known as the "période suspecte".

No action (payment, creation of guarantees, contracts, etc.) by the company prior to the date of cessation of payment may be challenged.

On the other hand, certain actions during the "période suspecte" may be challenged if liable to be declared null in any of the cases provided by the 1985 Act. The Act provides two types of nullity: mandatory nullity, which the court is obliged to order (S. 107 of the Act), and optional nullities, which may be ordered at the court's discretion (S. 108).

Section 107 declares void a whole series of actions that might be thought to have been designed to favour a creditor (unequal agreements, sureties given for prior debts, etc.) or to hide away part of the assets (donations, etc.). One of these nullities may concern netting, namely the one provided in Section 107-4°, which nullifies payments made in any abnormal fashion[55]. The question that arises here is: can set-off within a netting system be regarded as an abnormal means of payment and thus be rendered void under Section 107-4°?

The answer is not obvious in the case of non-banks that do not practise set-off as a customary means of settlement. In their case, jurisprudence has so far provided only a partially positive reply, ruling that set-off is not an abnormal means of payment when it occurs between connected debts or claims[56].

Where banks are concerned, on the other hand, set-off is a traditional and everyday means of payment. Most banking lawyers therefore consider that it can be held to be a "customarily accepted means of payment in business relationships" and that it is definitely exempt from the nullity applicable to abnormal means of payment. There are grounds for fearing, on the other hand, that novation may not be accepted as a normal means of payment under Section 107-4°.

[55] More precisely, Section 107-4° provides that "any payment for a debt due made other than in cash, bills of exchange, transfers, receiveable-related promissory notes referred to in the 2 January 1981 Act (Law no. 81-1) facilitating credit to business, or any other means of payment commonly accepted in "business relationships" shall be declared void".

[56] Cour d'Appel de Paris, 28 March 1989, op. cit., note no. 47.

Section 108 of the 1985 Act renders voidable (no longer mandatorily null as in the preceding case) all "actions in return for a consideration accomplished" during the "période suspecte" "if persons that have done business with the debtor have been aware of the cessation of payment".

The rationale behind Section 108 seeks to rectify actions accomplished with persons having knowledge of the company's bankruptcy and who were aware that, in doing so, they were causing injury to the interests of the other creditors. The nullity provided in this section can be invoked only if it can be established that a counterparty has perpetrated a kind of fraud. The burden of proof is diametrically opposed to that in Section 107.

Consequently, the fear that operations conducted within the framework of a netting scheme may be voided under Section 108 is negligible, or at any rate no greater than for any other operation. Moreover, jurisprudence has confirmed that netting per se is not liable to be nullified under this section.

b) "Cherry Picking"

"Cherry picking" occurs when the receiver of a bankrupt business performs only those contracts outstanding that are profitable to the business while repudiating those that are unprofitable.

"Cherry picking" poses a threat to the functioning of netting systems. That is because they are based on the principle of comprehensive treatment of a set of operations of the same kind, and the fact of being able to choose to continue to perform profitable operations while repudiating the unprofitable ones runs counter to this notion of comprehensiveness.

Yet the fact is that French bankruptcy law does contain a bias in favour of "cherry picking". In its concern to facilitate recovery and to keep the company running in spite of its financial difficulties, the 25 January 1985 Act allows the receiver (a) to select the contracts he wishes to continue and those he wishes to determine, and (b) to impose his decision on the co-contracting parties. He derives these twin powers from Section 37, Clause 1: "The receiver alone has the power to demand execution of contracts outstanding".

Moreover, the Act adds that the co-contracting party "must meet his obligations despite failure by the debtor to perform prior commitments" if the receiver orders him to continue to perform a contract in progress (S. 37, Clause 2) and that, if the receiver does not use his power to require continuation, non-performance of the contract in question shall simply give rise to damages, whose amount shall be charged to the bankrupt company's liabilities as an unsecured debt (S. 37, Clause 4).

These conditions are not particularly favourable, a priori, to the effective operation of a netting scheme. In practice, they are likely to have no effect for several reasons.

The first is that the provisions designed to encourage "cherry picking" concern the judicial recovery phase only; once the liquidation phase has been reached, the question of picking between contracts scarcely arises[57]. However, as pointed out earlier, the French method of handling banking crises tends to give responsibility for the recovery phase, barring judicial proceedings, to the Commission Bancaire, leaving virtually only the liquidation phase to the courts.

The second reason is that if the receiver chooses to perform a contract, he must do so in full; if he chooses to repudiate it, the operations must be unwound in accordance with the terms of the contract. He cannot choose to continue certain terms of a given contract while not performing others. It must be the whole contract or nothing. One can see why it is useful for netting systems themselves to be based on a contract or at least on a master agreement.

Lastly, the third point to be considered is that the rules laid down in Section 37 do not apply when contracts are legally inseparable, as may occur in the case of currency contracts or, more generally, financial contracts forming part of a comprehensive risk management system. It only requires a little more than simple connexity between these contracts — a sufficiently strong link to ensure that, for example, cancellation or transfer of one contract would jeopardize the overall equilibrium[58]. It is up to the bankers to say whether any such link exists on the economic level.

c) The Effectiveness of Sureties

Netting systems frequently provide for sureties to guarantee commitments entered into by the participant. It is essential to know whether these sureties will hold good on the day they are called into play, i. e. in case of failure of a participant.

The 25 January 1985 Banking Act is by no means favourable to creditors holding sureties, or at least real sureties, their rights being regarded as

[57] However, Section 153 of the 25 January 1985 Act does authorize the continuation of some business even after commencement of liquidation, for a maximum of three months, but "exclusively for the purpose of liquidation", and jurisprudence has accepted that the provisions of Section 37 relating to the receiver's powers also apply in case of liquidation. Cour de Cassation, 17 October 1989, Bull. civ. IV, p. 169; Dalloz 1990, Somm. 2, obs. Derrida; Revue Trimestrielle de Droit Commerciale 1990, 101, obs. Martin-Serf.

[58] F. Peltier, op. cit., note no. 46, holds that connexity and indivisibility are an obstacle to "cherry picking".

secondary in relation to continuing a firm's business, which takes priority. Once the recovery procedure has begun, preferential creditors can no longer exercise their right of individual action to realize their sureties[59], and they are superseded by those creditors whose claims arise out of continuing operations, known as "Section 40" creditors[60].

There again, however, these general rules are applied flexibly in jurisprudence, and the main types of surety liable to be used by netting schemes are precisely those that qualify for this flexible treatment.

For example, because money is totally fungible, cash deposits in French law imply a transfer of ownership of funds to the pledge-holding creditors, which makes this type of surety totally effective. Once they are owners of the thing pledged (the cash deposited), and that thing itself being useable as such for making all types of purchase, there is no need to realize the pledge, keeping possession of it is enough, provided of course one has taken the precaution of transferring the funds either to the creditor's own books or to those of a third party such as the central entity of the netting system, for example.

The other most commonly used type of guarantee is the pledging of securities. In France, because practically all securities are now in book-entry form, pledged securities can no longer entail a right of withholding: in order to withhold something, it must exist in reality; it must be possible to dispossess the owner of it, which cannot happen to things that have no material existence. Theoretically then, the creditor holding a pledge in the form of securities ought to secure payment solely out of the sale price of the securities in question and thus take second rank behind those creditors whose claims arise from the firm's continuation in business. However, the Cour de Cassation recently allowed a pledge-holding creditor, even though holder of a pledge without dispossession and therefore without right of withholding, to apply for attribution of the pledged securities through the courts[61]. This judicial power allows the creditor to order the sale of the securities and receive payment out of the proceeds of the sale without being superseded by the so-called "Section 40" creditors[62].

[59] Section 47 of the 25 January 1985 Act.

[60] Section 40 of the 25 January 1985 Act provides that creditors whose claims arise out of the fact of continuation of business after commencement of judicial recovery shall take priority over creditors holding prior claims.

[61] Cour de Cassation, Chambre Commerciale, 6 March 1990 (three decisions in one day), see in particular Jurisclasseur Périodique JCP, 1990, II 15815, Amlon.

[62] A very recent decision of the Cour de Cassation suggests oddly that although the pledge-holding creditor may be paid out of the proceeds of the sale, the funds must be placed in an escrow account on his behalf either until a recovery plan has been approved, or until liquidation has been ordered if recovery proves impossible (Chambre Commerciale, 9 April 1991, not published at the time of writing).

As can be seen from this, the jurisprudence now emerging in respect of the 25 January 1985 Act bears the stamp of realism. Of course one must acknowledge the aim of the legislator, which is to help companies on the road to recovery, but the demands of business deserve consideration too and the wishes of the parties must also be respected. If the latter, by common consent, wanted their operations to be treated comprehensively (connectedly) and if they are effectively so treated, then the courts cannot ignore them. This concern accounts for the flexibility with which the commercial courts — which are the source of jurisprudence on bankruptcy, being themselves made up of businessmen — apply the law on bankruptcy.

To conclude, while netting schemes can find a sound legal basis in whatever legal systems apply to them, including in case of bankruptcy, as probably will be the case in French law, the consequences in terms of banking regulation and, more precisely, the calculation of risks in solvency ratios still remain to be drawn.

The current rules, derived both from the July 1988 Basle accord and the European directive of December 1989, allow banks to calculate their ratios on the basis of the net amount of netted operations only if the netting scheme works through novation, i. e. according to the legal technique used in Anglo-Saxon law. Logically, once other techniques are capable of producing comparable results, notably the traditional French set-off technique bolstered by a relationship of connexity, banking regulations ought to recognize this and allow risks to be based on net amounts, and should no longer confine this possibility to systems based on novation alone. The Muller Committee, formerly the Cooke Committee, is now looking into the problem and is expected to reach a conclusion shortly.

IV. International Legal Rules and Initiatives

The S.W.I.F.T. Rules

By Jörg Etzkorn, Ludwigsburg*

Contents

* Translated by Dr. Frances Dielmann, Frankfurt/M.

I. S.W.I.F.T. as an International Electronic Funds Transfer System

1. S.W.I.F.T. s.c.

a) Formation

S.W.I.F.T. is a company founded in 1973 by banks from 15 countries for the purpose of creating and operating a computerized network for the transmission of data in connection with international funds transfers. The official abbreviation S.W.I.F.T. stands for Society for Worldwide Interbank Financial Telecommunication. The seat of the company is La Hulpe near Brussels. The company is a Société Coopérative, a cooperative association under Belgian law. The associates are credit institutions and equivalent organizations which engage in foreign transactions. S.W.I.F.T. began operations in 1977, and by the end of that year over 500 banks were already participating in the S.W.I.F.T. information exchange.[1] In the meantime, S.W.I.F.T. is a geographically widespread information system which connects all of the world's significant financial markets. On Dec. 31, 1990, S.W.I.F.T. had 1812 member banks (3049 users)[2], and over 332.6 million messages were exchanged in 1990.[3]

b) Membership and Governing Bodies

S.W.I.F.T. s.c. is subject to Belgian company law (Art. 197 of the Lois coordonnées sur les Sociétés commerciales [Lois coord.] of Nov. 30, 1919).[4] The associates and thus equity owners are credit institutions but not associations.[5] At the annual meeting in 1989 the prerequisites were created to permit institutions related to the banking sector, such as brokers, to use the S.W.I.F.T. system in the future[6]; for this purpose, the status of "participant" was created.[7]

---

[1] See Schürenkrämer, pp. 23 ff.

[2] See S.W.I.F.T., Report 1990, pp. 6 f.

[3] Id.

[4] See Rigaux, No. 1329, p. 504 and No. 1396, p. 508.

[5] Art. 8 Articles of Association [AoA]; see also Loh, pp. 19 ff. The AoA are printed in Etzkorn, Zahlungsverkehr, pp. 143 ff.

[6] S.W.I.F.T., Minutes of General Meeting 1989, pp. 5 ff.

[7] S.W.I.F.T., Minutes of General Meeting 1989, p. 6; see also Clause 1, No. 5 and No. 6 and Clause 3c Gen. Terms. The General Terms and Conditions are printed in Etzkorn, Zahlungsverkehr, pp. 153 ff.

The most important governing bodies are the General Meeting and the Board of Directors (Conseil d'administration under Belgian cooperative association law). The daily management is carried out by the Executive Committee under the direction of the Chief Executive Officer, all appointed by the Board of Directors.

One factor significant to the internal expression of views within S.W.I.F.T. is the coordination of the S.W.I.F.T. members into "National Groups"[8], which are organized in various ways in the different countries; their responsibilities include nomination of candidates for the Board and delegation of experts to "Working Groups". In addition, there are "User Groups" at the national level for institutions who use S.W.I.F.T. but are not members, such as branch offices and subsidiaries of members. Since 1985 these institutions have been designated "Sub-Members".[9] The National Groups deal with issues of international interest within S.W.I.F.T., e.g. economic policy and organization, while the National User Groups are oriented more toward technical telecommunications issues.[10] The National Group in Germany included 130 banks and savings banks at the end of 1988; the National User Group consisted of 190 institutions.[11]

2. *The Operation of S.W.I.F.T.*

The goals of S.W.I.F.T. are substantially the paperless execution of international funds transfers, acceleration of exchange of messages between banks and reduction of risks in international funds transfers. S.W.I.F.T. maintains its own worldwide network through which data, such as those necessary for the execution of a transfer order, can be transmitted.

This S.W.I.F.T. network consists of various interconnected operating and switching centers. In addition to the two original operating centers in Brussels and Leiden (the Netherlands), a third center was put in operation in 1980 in Culpeper, Virginia, U.S.A.[12] The participating banks are connected to this network through national data processing centers, the "regional processors". The regional processors in the participating countries are connected by a "primary line" to "their" operating centers (e.g. for Germany the center in Leiden), and by a "fall back line" to another center. The connection of the individual members to the particular regional processor is

---

[8] See Loh, pp. 37 ff.; Schürenkrämer, pp. 45 ff.

[9] Clause 1, No. 5 Gen. Terms.

[10] Lehmann, pp. 147 ff.

[11] German S.W.I.F.T. Group, Minutes 1989, pp. 2 ff.

[12] See also Störzbach, BI 3/88, pp. 35.

by means of a dedicated line or a dial line, which does not belong to the S.W.I.F.T. shared facilities.[13]

Use of this network results in the following means of execution of a payment order: A S.W.I.F.T. member bank gathers the data needed for an international transfer and transmits them in the form of address standards for the sending and receiving bank, the currency code and the necessary message standards (including beneficiary designation, amount, purpose) to the regional processor. This processor acts as a mere relay station in transmitting the data to the proper switching center, which sends confirmation of receipt of the data to the sending institution. The message is then sent to the regional processor in the beneficiary's country — if necessary first through a different switching center — and from there is immediately sent to the (S.W.I.F.T.) receiving bank. The entire transfer procedure, including encoding and decoding as well as confirmation, as a rule takes less than 5 minutes, for urgent messages less than 1 minute, regardless of whether the receiving bank is in a neighboring European country, in the U.S. or, for example, in China.

This tremendous speed represents the greatest usefulness of S.W.I.F.T. for banks. In contrast to the present execution time measured in minutes, prior to the introduction of S.W.I.F.T. 80-85 % of all international transfer orders were transmitted by mail[14]; for overseas transfers each segment of the transfer process required 3-4 days travel time.[15] Without even considering the postal risks in some countries, it often could take 3- 4 weeks to complete a transfer.

In the meantime, international transfers by letter or telegram are the exception. In Germany, the standard form "Payment Order in Foreign Trade" (Exhibit 1 to the Report under § 59 of the Foreign Trade Act) still contains a choice of transmission by letter or telegram, but only "to the extent [the transfer] is not carried out through S.W.I.F.T.". In addition, payments to banks not connected to S.W.I.F.T. are "swifted" as closely as possible to the receiving location and processed there conventionally.[16]

Use of the S.W.I.F.T. system has also contributed to an improvement in security in international funds transfers.[17] Messages are given output sequence numbers with which the completeness of the message can be determined upon receipt. In addition, an authenticator number is included which

---

[13] Schürenkrämer, pp. 25 ff., with technical details.

[14] Loh, p. 8.

[15] In a case decided by the Kammergericht (WM 1977, p. 1176), the mailing time including two intermediary banks added up to 27 days.

[16] V. Gablenz, p. 44.

[17] Godschalk, Computergeld, p. 105; see also Loh, pp. 125 ff.; Schürenkrämer, pp. 61 ff.

is automatically calculated based on the contents of the entire message using a complex algorithm. For the actual transmission, the data are electronically scrambled so that they are not accessible to unauthorized parties. Using the authenticator, the recipient can determine whether the message has been falsified. Finally, for urgent messages which are not delivered within 15 minutes, interim reports are sent to the sending bank. A report is prepared each day of all transfer orders which have not yet been completed so that rapid clarification of errors can at least help to minimize interest losses.

Additional risks have thus not arisen through the use of an electronic transmission network, and the traditional risks in international funds transfers, such as misdirected orders, incorrect readings, etc., have been substantially reduced.

In addition to pure funds transfers, S.W.I.F.T. is also capable of carrying out communications for other banking services. Banks can have their account statements from other banks sent through the S.W.I.F.T. network, which is especially useful in nostro account settlements. Money and currency trade as well as collections can be carried out through S.W.I.F.T. These additional services by S.W.I.F.T. are not, however, the focus of interest here.[18]

For some time, S.W.I.F.T. has been planning the implementation of a new system, the so-called S.W.I.F.T. II.[19] The original date for the "cut-over" in June 1986 could not be achieved. Based on new hardware and software, the system will offer substantially extended capacities. Decentralization of network technology is intended to provide additional protection against breakdowns.

Within the framework of S.W.I.F.T. II, it will be possible to broaden the offering of general financial services. During an extended transitional phase, the previous (S.W.I.F.T. I) system will continue in service alongside S.W.I.F.T. II, in particular for funds transfers.

No changes in the duties of the participants or the S.W.I.F.T. s.c. provisions relating to company and liability law are planned in connection with the introduction of S.W.I.F.T. II.

3. Execution of a Transfer

Not only the communications network maintained by S.W.I.F.T. is significant for the issues regarding the effects of S.W.I.F.T. norms on the allocation

[18] See Etzkorn, Zahlungsverkehr, p. 5 with additional references.

[19] See also Haney, Financial Times of Oct. 21, 1985, p. VII; Störzbach, BI 3/88, pp. 35 ff.; Jueterbock, Bank 1988, pp. 329 ff.; Tutt, Banking Technology, Sept. 1988, pp. 14 ff.; Cane, Financial Times of Oct. 5, 1988, pp. 22.

of liability in connection with funds transfers. Other communications paths and internal bank operations relating to transfers must be examined in order to determine the liability relationships among the participants. The following description should serve as an illustration of these procedures as well as to introduce the legal and especially the liability relationships.

Messages to be sent through S.W.I.F.T. are divided into so-called customer transfers and bank transfers — whether for the bank's own account or for a third bank — and handled as two different types of messages. The execution of a foreign transfer involving multiple banks is viewed by S.W.I.F.T. as one customer transfer and the relevant number of bank transfers. The terminology used by S.W.I.F.T. — e.g. sender, receiver (sending and receiving bank), ordering bank (originator's bank), "account with" bank — or rather the codes for these parties relate to the specific message and not to the underlying business transaction. The result is that in the various messages necessary for carrying out a foreign transfer a single bank can also have various designations.

S.W.I.F.T. is not a supranational clearinghouse; the actual posting and settlement of payments require the traditional network of correspondent banks.[20] This also means that in providing cover there are no fundamental differences from traditional international funds transfers.[21] The sending bank must provide the value of the order out of its own currency balance or credit line or must purchase the needed currency and make this available to an account of the beneficiary's bank. The messages which must be exchanged concerning the accounting are transmitted through S.W.I.F.T.

An order in the currency of the originator or the beneficiary is carried out in the following way when the two involved institutions[22] maintain a direct account relationship with each other. The sender (originator's bank) sends a message classified as a customer transfer to the receiver (beneficiary's bank); this message contains all the necessary information (beneficiary, amount, etc.). This message is also used as the basis for entries to the loro or nostro account. The provision of cover also takes place within the direct bilateral relationship; otherwise, the sending bank must make cover available in a third account.

If an order is executed using a common correspondent bank of the two banks in a third country[23], e.g. because the transfer is denominated in a third currency or because the necessary account relationship with banks in the

---

[20] See Brüggemann, p. 23.

[21] See Etzkorn, Zahlungsverkehr, pp. 6 ff.

[22] The usual procedure in normal transfer transactions using correspondent relationships is described in Etzkorn, Zahlungsverkehr, pp. 6 ff.

[23] Id.

receiving country is lacking, the originator's bank sends a message of the classification "customer transfer" to the beneficiary's bank (receiver) in which the necessary information including the intermediary bank to be engaged is contained. In addition, a computer program at the same time automatically sends a message of the classification "bank transfer for the benefit of a third bank" from the originator's bank as sender to the intermediary bank as receiver, in which the beneficiary's bank is designated as the beneficiary of this bank transfer. By means of these two messages (and the accounting entries undertaken by the respective institutions), the transfer is completed. Finally, the intermediary bank as sender confirms to the beneficiary's bank through S.W.I.F.T. that the amount has been credited to the correspondent account.

If the originator's bank and the beneficiary's bank do not maintain a correspondent relationship with a common third bank[24], further correspondent banks must be engaged, whereby two correspondents must be located in one currency territory. For execution through S.W.I.F.T., the originator's bank (sender) sends the beneficiary's bank (receiver) a message of the type "customer transfer", naming the other correspondent banks. At the same time another message of the type "bank transfer for the benefit of a third bank" is automatically sent to the sender's correspondent bank. This message contains, for example, the instruction by the originator's bank (sender) to its correspondent bank (receiver) that an amount should be credited to the beneficiary's bank's correspondent (second correspondent or "account with" bank), whereby the beneficiary's bank is designated in this message as the beneficiary bank. From the originator's bank's correspondent, which receives the S.W.I.F.T. message, an accounting instruction is now sent to the correspondent of the beneficiary's bank. These two correspondents are both in the same country. The beneficiary's bank's correspondent now sends a credit notice to the receiving bank through S.W.I.F.T., and the respective accounting is undertaken at these banks.

Thus a transfer using S.W.I.F.T. takes place according to the following scheme: the originator's bank sends a message (customer transfer type) directly to the beneficiary's bank, and settlement is made using the (automatic) sending of messages (bank transfer type) to the respective intermediary banks.

Accounting notices relating to the provision of cover to accounts which the beneficiary's bank maintains with other banks are also sent using the "bank transfer" message. The bank at which cover will be provided can also be provided as information in the other S.W.I.F.T. messages.

---

[24] Id.

Within the scope of a giro chain in an international transfer, segments of the transfer process can occur within a currency territory.[25] These segments can also take place through S.W.I.F.T. An example is where a Paris bank sends an order denominated in French francs to another Paris bank through the S.W.I.F.T. network in the Netherlands.

But it is also possible to use domestic funds transfer methods or systems. These are used particularly when national or regional clearing systems are available which work entirely without documents. Examples are CHIPS (Clearing House Interbank Payment System)[26] in New York and CHAPS (Clearing House Automated Payment Systems)[27] in England.

In these cases, all of the segments of the transfer can be executed electronically, but individual (domestic) segments do not use the S.W.I.F.T. network and the S.W.I.F.T. system.[28]

II. S.W.I.F.T. Rules and Their Effects on the Contractual Relationships between the Participants

In order to answer the question of what liability rules are applicable to a transfer executed through S.W.I.F.T., two areas must be dealt with. First, it is necessary to determine which liability rules have been established by S.W.I.F.T. Second, one must clarify what effects these internal S.W.I.F.T. rules have on interbank relationships. The issue of possible application of S.W.I.F.T. rules to an existing contractual relationship between two correspondent banks can be decided only when it is clear in what areas and to what extent S.W.I.F.T. has issued mandatory rules.[29] In the following, the company law relationships among the S.W.I.F.T. associates will first be discussed[30] followed by the internal S.W.I.F.T. rules of conduct and liability provisions. The applicability of S.W.I.F.T. rules to pre-existing contractual relationships will be illustrated using an example of contractual structures in an international transfer, including the issue of applicable law.[31] Only then can the nature and extent of applicability of S.W.I.F.T. rules to international transfer transactions be evaluated.[32]

---

[25] Id. at 8 ff.

[26] Id. at 109 ff.

[27] Id. at 116 ff.

[28] Id. at 121 ff. concerning the legal consequences.

[29] See part II. 2. below.

[30] See part II. 3. below.

[32] See part. II. 4. below.

1. Legal Relationships among the Associates

In the General Terms and Conditions in the By-laws, which are not part ("extrait") of the of the Articles of Association (Actes de société; Art. 7 Lois coord.) which must be made public, it is stipulated that a potential new associate must agree to these General Terms and Conditions before he is admitted (Clause 3 Gen. Terms). Clause 10 provides that Belgian law shall govern the relations between the company and each member[33]; this is not merely a reference to Belgian company law but instead an autonomous, explicit choice of law for the relationships within the company.[34] This is an express choice of Belgian law made by the parties and binding on all of the member banks of S.W.I.F.T. s.c. for the legal relationships between the company and each associate.

Clause 10 (2) Gen. Terms also contains an arbitration clause which provides that disputes in connection with the General Terms and Conditions which cannot be settled amicably shall be decided with final effect in accordance with the Rules of Conciliation and Arbitration of the International Chamber of Commerce [ICC] in Paris by arbitrators appointed in accordance with those Rules.[35]

Clause 8 Gen. Terms provides that for issues of interpretation the English language text of the General Terms and Conditions and also of the User Handbook shall be determinative. The same is true, in accordance with Clause 8 Gen. Terms, for the text of the Articles of Association, regardless of the fact that under Belgian law the Articles must be published or deposited in French and Flemish.

General liability issues are governed by Clause 7 Gen. Terms[36] in such a way that S.W.I.F.T. is authorized to delegate the transmission of messages to third parties.[37]

Liability for force majeure and for non-authorized use of the facilities is excluded except where the company should not have reasonably accepted the transfer order.[38] Liability for failure to carry out a transfer or delay due to

---

[33] Clause 10 (1) Gen. Terms (formerly Art. 12 (1)) reads: "All relations between the Company and each member shall be governed by Belgian law."

[34] See Rabel, pp. 119 f.

[35] ICC Publication No. 291 of Sept. 1980.

[36] Formerly Art. 8 Gen. Terms.

[37] See also v. Gablenz, p. 247.

[38] Clause 7: The Company shall not be responsible for any loss or damage caused be failure to carry out, or delay of, messages resulting from technical failure, unless otherwise provided in the User Handbook, or force majeure. Force majeure shall include acts of authorities including P.T.T. authorities, strike or industrial dispute, political disturbance, catastrophes in nature, fire, war, epidemics and all other circumstances which prevent the

technical disturbances is limited to the instances specified in the User Handbook.

Finally, Clause 11 Gen. Terms cites the quorum with which the General Terms and Conditions can be amended at the General Meeting[39] in a manner binding for all associates.

2. Internal S.W.I.F.T. Norms

a) General Principles of Liability

aa) Allocation of Duties

In deciding how to allocate responsibilities and resulting liability among the S.W.I.F.T. participants, S.W.I.F.T. s.c. was faced with the task of developing its own "system". There were and are no provisions of law in Belgium governing electronic funds transfers which could have been used at least for subsidiary support.[40] But even the Electronic Funds Transfer Act[41] adopted in the U.S. — after the formation of S.W.I.F.T. — focuses primarily on consumer protection problems so that consequences regarding interbank relationships can scarcely be derived from such statutory provisions.[42] International rules of law are completely lacking.

The S.W.I.F.T. "system" had to, on the one hand, basically stipulate who would assume responsibility for the transmission network through which all internal S.W.I.F.T. communication would flow, including the necessary hardware. The main task was to establish general principles of liability with regard to fault consisting of intentional misconduct and negligence, including that of third parties, and to formulate elements which, related to specific working procedures, would establish rules of conduct as precise as possible which could be referred to in case of damages.

During the early time of operation it became clear that it was not sufficient to create bases for claims against S.W.I.F.T. for the irreplaceable loss of

Company against its will from carrying out its activities. Moreover, the Company shall not be responsible for any loss or damage caused by the performance of non-authorised transmission orders unless the prejudiced party proves that the Company could not reasonably assume the validity of those orders. The Company shall be entitled to make use of any reputable third party with regard to the transmission of messages, at the risk of the ordering user.

[39] See Loh, pp. 27 ff.

[40] On the necessity of legal rules, see Vasseur, in: Revue de la Banque 1982, p. 596.

[41] For more detail, see U. H. Schneider, Elektronischer Zahlungsverkehr, pp. 57 ff.

[42] Other rules of this type include, e.g., the "Consumer Credit Act" of 1974 (GB), the Consumer Protection Act of Nov. 1, 1980 (Quebec), or — even more specialized — the Danish Credit Card Law of July 6, 1984 and the Israeli law on debit cards of July 1, 1986.

transfer amounts. Instead, there was a stronger need for allocation of responsibility for interest losses resulting from delayed transfers.

bb) Responsibilities

The liability system in S.W.I.F.T. is based on the principle of fault liability, in which duties of care by the participants and penalties for breach of these duties are stipulated. This fault liability is also consistent with the basic principles of Belgian civil law.

With respect to the communications network, S.W.I.F.T. is responsible for the security of regional processors and operating centers and their data transmission facilities and lines. The banks are responsible for their terminals including modems and scrambling devices as well as for data transmission facilities and lines to the respective regional processors.

The duties of conduct whose breach can establish liability primarily serve the smooth flow of transfer transactions and the prevention of foreseeable damages. The duties of the sending and receiving banks are tied to the various stages of the transfer procedure and the possible complications relating to those stages in such a way that it was believed that blanket clauses would hardly be necessary. This may also have resulted from the intent of the User Handbook to provide concrete operating instructions for the bank employees using the S.W.I.F.T. system. In contrast to the former situation, the legally binding nature of the User Handbook is now also established in the by-laws. Nevertheless, general principles can be derived from the specific rules of conduct, and these general principles could be applied to any occurrences for which specific rules do not exist — though such occurrences are unlikely. It should be emphasized that the duties of a receiver include the availability of sufficient capacity at peak loads to handle at least urgent messages even in case of technical disturbances.[43]

S.W.I.F.T.'s responsibilities are also tied to specific rules of conduct. These, however, represent applications of the general — although subsidiary — liability of S.W.I.F.T. for mistakes or failures by the personnel or the system.[44] This is remarkable in that it reflects S.W.I.F.T.'s faith in the security of its system and, furthermore, because the next most significant electronic funds transfer system after S.W.I.F.T., a national system, the New York Clearing House Interbank Payment System (CHIPS), expressly excludes liability for system failures.[45]

---

[43] Part II. 2. b) bb) below.

[44] Id.

[45] Lingl, in: 22 Harv. Int'l L. J. 634 (1981).

It is also striking that S.W.I.F.T. faces up to the problem of computer crime in that it expressly creates elements of liability in case of fraud by S.W.I.F.T. employees, agents, and sub-contractors.[46] In the meantime, this liability has been extended in part to persons who — without specifically belonging to the cited groups — are in some way active within S.W.I.F.T.'s sphere of responsibility.

cc) Limitation on Liability

The extent of liability is characterized by maximum ceilings and floor limits whose precise amounts vary depending on the specific elements of liability involved.

Damages exceeding the maximum limits are not allocated to the participants or to the Company but instead must be borne by the individual party suffering damage. Maximum liability for the final loss of a payment is 400 million Belgian francs for an individual case, and 1 billion Belgian francs if caused by fraudulent acts (with only half the floor limit). The limit on liability by S.W.I.F.T. for loss of interest to 20 million Belgian francs annually appears quite low by contrast. But because this form of liability was introduced only subsequent to the start of operations and has not yet been increased by the Annual Meeting, which must approve this type of expenditure, it must be assumed that this amount has been sufficient for practical needs.

With respect to the floor limits (depending upon the element of liability, 100,000 — 800,000 Belgian francs) in transfers for the order of the participating banks (e.g. in currency transactions), these in fact represent a mere fraction of the loss.

b) The Individual Rules of Liability

The liability rule in Clause 7 Gen. Terms, which is formulated more as a blanket clause, is structured in detail in two chapters in the first volume of the User Handbook (Chapter 6: Bank Responsibility and Liability, Chapter 7: S.W.I.F.T. Responsibility and Liability; both in Volume 1 — Policy Section 4: Security Procedures). These are based on decisions by the Board of Directors, whose authority in Art. 22 of the Articles of Association [AoA] covers the specific formulation of the rules of liability and conduct as well as — due to the binding nature of the budget set by the General Meeting — a limitation of liability by S.W.I.F.T. to fixed maximum amounts.[47] Thus, they represent binding rules for the users of the system and for S.W.I.F.T.

---

[46] Part II. 2. b) aa) below; id. at 641 ff.

[47] Lingl, supra note 45, at 624.

The original provision, namely that claims against S.W.I.F.T. would be possible only in case of irrevocable loss of a sum of money[48] (this liability also extended to interest losses arising out of the primary loss), but by contrast interest losses due to delayed payments would — except in the case of enrichment of the recipient — always, i.e. even in the case of fault by S.W.I.F.T., be borne by the sender[49], was amended by a decision of the Board of Directors in February 1979.[50] With respect to losses due to late payments, a provision now applies which distributes responsibility among the sender, S.W.I.F.T., and the receiver and ties liability consequences to these responsibilities so that now a system of differentiated liability requirements and limitations exists depending upon whether a case of "direct loss" (irrevocable loss of a transfer amount) or "consequential loss" (interest loss due to delayed payment) is involved.[51]

aa) "Direct Loss"

α) Prerequisites for Liability

αα) Liability by S.W.I.F.T.

In case of an irrevocable loss of a transfer amount (regardless of whether in a customer transfer or a bank transfer), S.W.I.F.T. is liable[52]:

(a) in case of a negligent act, an error or an omission by S.W.I.F.T. where services are not performed in compliance with the provisions in the User Handbook,

(b) in case of negligence, error or omission by S.W.I.F.T. where the security provisions in the User Handbook are violated,

(c) in the case of fraudulent acts by persons who are not directly or indirectly employed by S.W.I.F.T. but who engage in unlawful acts within S.W.I.F.T.'s area of responsibility, but only where S.W.I.F.T. should have been aware of the fraud or the fraud was possible due to violations of data security principles.[53]

---

[48] S.W.I.F.T., Special Newsletter, April 1979, p. 4.

[49] Loh, p. 129.

[50] Board Paper No. 185, in: S.W.I.F.T., Special Newsletter, April 1979, p. 2.

[51] Penney & Baker (at margin no. 16.04) describe only the case of "consequential loss" and state that this is the only liability provision; this mistake may have resulted from reliance on Board Paper No. 185 which dealt only with the (new) element of "consequential loss".

[52] The elements listed in (a) — (d) correspond to the points in the User Handbook, v. I. chap. 7, at 7.2.2.1.

[53] This rule was adopted later as an extension of the liability under the present rule (d).

(d) in case of fraudulent acts by S.W.I.F.T. employees, agents or subcontractors in the operation or maintenance of the regional processors, data transmission facilities, or transmission lines.

ββ) Liability of the Sender or Receiver

The provision that liability by S.W.I.F.T. is conditioned upon the securing of the data by means of the authenticator leads to the result that the sender is liable where such security is lacking.

Other rules of conduct for the sender and receiver were not originally specially defined, but in the meantime are derived from the conduct requirements for the participants in a message, i.e. S.W.I.F.T., sender and receiver, relating to liability for interest losses (consequential loss).[54]

β) Scope of Liability

Included within the scope of liability are the loss of the transfer amount as well as a resulting loss of interest. The liability is restricted by a floor limit and a maximum in each case. In cases of fraud by employees, the floor limit per instance amounts to 400,000 Belgian francs and the maximum liability per instance is 1 billion Belgian francs; in other cases, the floor limit is 800,000 Belgian francs and the liability for damages based on a single transfer is limited to 400 billion Belgian francs, with an overall maximum of 600 billion francs per year.

It must also be kept in mind that S.W.I.F.T. is responsible, in addition to the correct performance of the services designated in the User Handbook, for the security of system elements controlled by S.W.I.F.T., such as regional processors, operating centers and data transmission facilities and lines between the regional processors and the operating centers and between the different operating centers.

bb) "Consequential Loss"

α) Prerequisites for Liability

Liability for losses due to delayed payments (so-called consequential losses)[55] depends upon whether one of the participants has violated the

---

[54] See part. II. b) bb).

[55] See also Penney & Baker, supra note 51; Board paper No. 185, supra note 50.

specifically enumerated duties of conduct. In order to concretely state the provisions, some terms used in daily practice (such as value date and close of accounting) were clarified or redefined.

No express allocation of causality for the damage is stipulated in the rules, but generally only violations of the enumerated rules of conduct technically make the occurrence of damage possible.

αα) Responsibility of the Sending Bank

The sender of a message is responsible for interest losses:

(a) where a message is not confirmed by S.W.I.F.T.[56]

Each message entered (i.e. a transfer for the bank's own account or for the account of a customer or correspondent institution) is confirmed by S.W.I.F.T. in accordance with a fixed procedure.

If the confirmation is not received, the sender is obligated to send the message again — designating it as a possible duplicate entry. Liability is tied to violation of this duty to resubmit the message.

(b) when a message is confirmed by S.W.I.F.T. but does not then appear in the list of delivered messages.

This list represents an additional level of security. If a message reaches S.W.I.F.T. from the sender and is confirmed, but then — for whatever reason — is not delivered, the sender is notified of the non-delivery. This creates a duty on the part of the sending bank to become active in accordance with the relevant rules. Violation of this duty establishes liability.

(c) if, in the case of an urgent message, it does not receive a notice of delivery prior to the receiver's close of accounting.

This sanction again arises from an omission relating to the sender's duty to act. The notice of delivery transmitted to the sender contains the time the message was delivered to the receiver (expressed in accordance with the receiver's local time zone).

The close of accounting is defined as the latest possible time in a country or time zone at which the receiving bank can post the value of a transfer for the benefit of a third bank on the same day. S.W.I.F.T. lists these times in a special S.W.I.F.T. Directory, so that the sender is informed of the last posting time in the particular receiving country.

(d) if the sender transmits a message other than in the prescribed format.

---

[56] These elements correspond to the User Handbook, v. I, chap. 6, at 6.5.

Format here means a specific application for the individual type of message.

The reason for this provision is that the three-digit code (e.g. MT 202 Bank Transfer in Favour of a Third Bank) used for the message type is frequently also used by the receiving bank in its further internal organizational transmission[57], so that an incorrect type designation could lead to delays.

(e) if the sender does not respond immediately to a notification by S.W.I.F.T. that the system at a bank, a regional processor or an operating center "is down", and

(f) where the sender uses address codes not contained in the S.W.I.F.T. directory.[58]

ββ) Responsibility of the Receiving Bank

In case of a loss due to delayed payment, the receiving bank is responsible:

(a) when a message is not processed with the proper value date even though it was received prior to the close of accounting and sent to the address listed in the S.W.I.F.T. Directory.

This liability provision contains two elements. The duty to bear responsibility for delays arising due to the fact that the receiver reported an incorrect "address" for inclusion in the S.W.I.F.T. Directory is based directly on the principle of fault.

Alongside this element is the duty to carry out a transfer in accordance with the designated value date if the message containing the transfer order is received prior to the close of accounting.[59] The value date is defined as the date on which the transfer amount is available to the receiving bank[60], i.e. the date on which the sending bank wishes its account with the receiving bank to be debited or, respectively, the date on which the sending bank provides credit to an account of the receiving bank.

It is particularly significant that this provision applies only to the category of "bank transfer" but not to the category of "customer transfer".[61] The value date rule thus applies only to the participating banks. It does not have any direct effect on when the money will be available to a customer. Under a prior

---

[57] S.W.I.F.T., Special Newsletter, April 1979, p. 3.

[58] This liability provision was later added to the User Handbook; it was not yet contained in Board Paper no. 185 (and is therefore missing in Penney & Baker, supra note 51). It corresponds substantively to provision (a) for the receiving bank.

[59] On the close of accounting, see part II. 2. b) bb) α) αα).

[60] Board Paper, supra note 50, p. 2.

[61] Regarding terminology, see part I. 3.

rule, which has in the meantime been abandoned, it was possible to designate a so-called "payment date". This created a duty on the part of the receiving bank to credit or pay the amount to a (non-bank) customer on the designated date. National practices and also correspondent agreements did, however, have to be taken into consideration.[62]

The receiving bank's duty with respect to the value date is binding for the creation of liability only when the S.W.I.F.T. message is received prior to the close of accounting which is agreed among all of the participants in advance and is therefore available for use by the sending bank.

(b) where the receiving bank does not respond directly to system messages — equivalent to the sender's liability described under (e) above.

(c) where the receiving bank fails to check the completeness of the incoming orders using the output sequence number[63], and

(d) where the receiving bank does not comply with its duties based on the so-called terminal principles.

The terminal principles are likewise stipulated in Volume 1 of the User Handbook. They create the following duties for each S.W.I.F.T. user[64]:

Terminals must be suited to the peak capacities common for the respective bank. Reserve capacities must be available which are sufficient to handle at least urgent messages in case of failure of the main terminal. On bank working days at least 7 hours of receiving time between 8 am and 6 pm are required for messages, and it must be insured that all messages present in the switching centers[65] can be received prior to the close of accounting.

These duties are intended to prevent delays due to technical breakdowns at the receiver and exclude liability by the receiver with reference to these measures.

(e) when the receiving bank does not exercise the care expected of a prudent bank.[66]

This provision is one of the few blanket clauses: In the second phrase of the clause two cases are listed which — without being expressly described as such — can be viewed as illustrations.

---

[62] Regarding this abandoned rule, see also Etzkorn, Zahlungsverkehr, p. 97.

[63] Part I. 2. above.

[64] Board Paper, supra note 50, p. 4.

[65] Part I. 2. above.

[66] This rule was added later.

γγ) Responsibility of S.W.I.F.T. s.c.

In case of interest lost due to late payment, S.W.I.F.T. is responsible[67]:

(a) when messages are confirmed to the sender and do not appear in the list of undelivered messages but have in fact not been delivered,

(b) in case of errors by the S.W.I.F.T. system or its personnel,

(c) when S.W.I.F.T. fails to give immediate notice of breakdowns at banks, operating centers and regional processors.

The liability provision cited under (a) corresponds to the provisions (a) and (b) of the sender, (c) with (e) of the sender and (b) of the receiver.

Viewed systematically, (a) and (c) represent specific applications of the general provision (b), namely liability for errors by the system or the personnel.

As can be concluded from the procedure for asserting a claim against S.W.I.F.T., S.W.I.F.T.'s liability is meant to be subsidiary liability. The rules[68] prescribe that the sender and receiver can take recourse against S.W.I.F.T. only if both have complied with their duties, as described above[69], and the receiving bank has not been enriched.

β) Scope of Liability

Liability for interest losses due to late payment is restricted by floor and maximum limits.

The floor limit is 100,000 Belgian francs per instance of damage, which is, however, the total for the sending and the receiving bank, who must assert the claim jointly. Multiple claims which are individually under this limit can now[70] be asserted cumulatively. If an asserted claim proves to be unjustified, a penalty in the amount of 30,000 is charged.

Compensation claims against S.W.I.F.T. are satisfied out of an "interest loss contingency" fund which since 1979 has been included in the annual budget and consists of 20 million francs.[71] If claims in a business year should exceed this contingency, they are satisfied proportionately.

---

[67] These elements correspond to the User Handbook, v. I, chap. 7, at 7.1 (3).

[68] Board Paper, supra note 50, p. 2.

[69] See part II. 2. b) bb) α) αα).

[70] This differs from the Board Paper, supra note 50, pp. 2, 4.

[71] See part II. 2. a) aa) above.

cc) Provisions for the Assertion of Claims

The assertion of claims due either to a direct loss or a consequential loss is made in accordance with uniform provisions which again refer to the application of Belgian law and contain primarily time limits, procedures, and arbitration rules.

If S.W.I.F.T. does not reach a decision with respect to a claim within a fixed time limit, the claim is deemed to be accepted. If S.W.I.F.T. rejects the claim, the applicants have the right to submit the dispute to a board of arbitration. The provisions relating to arbitration stipulate that Belgian law shall be applied. In addition, the arbitration court is required to decide in accordance with "ordinary prescriptions of the law", unless these rules of law are in the view of the court of arbitration in conflict with the principles of equality or with the respective transaction.

In particularizing Clause 10 (2) Gen. Terms (application of the ICC Rules of Conciliation and Arbitration), modalities such as the constitution of the arbitration board, means for forcing a judgment, legal remedies, Brussels as the seat of the board, and the subsidiary application of Belgian arbitration law[72] are stipulated.

3. Correspondent Bank Relationships and Applicable Law

An examination of the legal relationships between the banks involved in a cross-border funds transfer is not the purpose of this article.[73] But we must look at least briefly at the issues and results of how these relationships are governed because the question of the effect of S.W.I.F.T. rules can only be decided on the basis of these existing correspondent relationships.

In the execution of an international transfer, various credit institutions in different currency territories and legal systems come into contact with each other; this contact takes the form of a chain in which each link consists of two banks between which a current account or giro relationship exists.[74]

From a legal perspective, each respective giro relationship is an individual unit, a bilateral contract.[75] There is in each instance between an instructing

---

[72] Art. 167 ff. Code Judiciaire.

[73] See Etzkorn, Zahlungsverkehr, pp. 39 ff. and the articles by von der Seipei Holzwardt and Hadding in this volume.

[74] See Etzkorn, Zahlungsverkehr, pp. 8 ff.

[75] See generally, Kleiner, Devisen, at margin no. 13.04; Germany: Kegel, Festschrift Schmidt, pp. 237 ff.; MünchKomm-Martiny, at margin no. 275 preceding Art. 12 EGBGB; Austria: Schinnerer, ZZ 1984, p. 205; U.S.A./N.Y.: Delbrueck & Co. v. Manufacturers Hanover Trust, 464 F. Supp. 989, 993 (1979).

and an instructed bank a contractual relationship whose fate is primarily determined by the provisions of banking contract law or agency law in the legal system applicable to the respective transfer (segment). To the extent that individual transfer segments take place within a currency or legal territory, the particular rules of a local clearing house or funds transfer system may also have to be considered.[76]

In cases with foreign connections — such as cross-border transfers — the determination of the applicable law is made in accordance with international conflict of laws principles. Under German law, the conflict of laws rules relating to the international contract law of interest here are based on the principle of party autonomy, i.e. the right of the parties to choose the law applicable to the contract, stipulated in Art. 27 of the Introductory Law to the German Civil Code [EGBGB].[77] Under the internationally prevailing view[78], the validity of such a choice of law clause is to be decided in accordance with the lex fori. The principle of party autonomy is substantially recognized in all other legal systems[79], so that the law applicable to international transfers is to be determined primarily in accordance with the will of the parties. In most international commercial transactions no choice of law is expressly made in the individual contract but instead within the scope of general business terms and conditions. This is particularly true for banks.[80] And it can be assumed that the respective user of the general terms and conditions will choose the law of his own business location.[81]

It can usually be assumed that the general terms used in interbank transactions are validly incorporated into the contracts between the banks. The general terms applicable to a specific transaction are those of the bank performing the obligation characteristic of the particular contract, and the applicable law is thus the law of the seat of that bank. In the case of transfers — regardless of where the accounts are maintained — the applicable general terms are those of the bank which, on the instruction of its correspondent bank, carries out the transfer order (in its country).

Instead of an express choice of law, an implied choice is also possible under international contract law.[82] It must be derived from the particular circum-

---

[76] See Etzkorn, Zahlungsverkehr, pp. 8 ff., 13 f., 131 ff.

[77] Regarding previous legal rules, see Kegel, Internationales Privatrecht, p. 421; Sandrock-Sandrock/Steinschulte, at margin no. A1; Lüderitz, at margin no. 266.

[78] Kleiner, Devisen, at margin no. 11.09.

[79] Vischer, pp. 39 ff.; Wood, at 1.4 (1), pp. 7 f.; Kleiner, Devisen, at 11.09; Reithmann-Martiny, at margin no. 26; Sandrock-Sandrock/Steinschulte, at margin no. A 263 ff.

[80] Zahn/Eberding/Ehrlich, at margin no. 1/28.

[81] Kleiner, Devisen, at margin no. 13.03.

[82] Etzkorn, Zahlungsverkehr, p. 48, with additional references.

stances of the individual case or from typical circumstances.[83] If no general terms are applicable, then the factors which would typically permit the implication of a choice of law, such as jurisdiction or arbitration clauses[84], are generally also lacking. If the contract is not based on general terms, an implied choice of law cannot usually be presumed.

If no choice of law is made by the parties, the applicable law must be determined objectively.

Under German law, Art. 28 (1) EGBGB provides that the applicable law shall be that to which the contract has the closest connection. This use of an objective connection is a change from the principle of hypothetical party intent which was the German conflicts rule previously in effect.[85] The presumptions enumerated in Art. 28 (2) — (4) lead to the result that banking services contracts are to be governed by the law of the state of the bank which performs the obligation characteristic of the contract.

As a rule, the characteristic obligation is the performance which distinguishes the contract from other contracts[86]; the payment of money is, thus, not characteristic of the contract. With respect to the relationship between two banks in the execution of a funds transfer, the typical and characteristic performance within the meaning of Art. 28 (2) EGBGB is fulfilled by the bank which is instructed by a correspondent bank to carry out a transfer order in its own country, regardless of which of the two banks is the account manager.[87]

Other legal systems also use the characteristic performance as the basis for the (objective) reference to a system of law.[88]

4. Incorporation of the S.W.I.F.T. Rules into the Correspondent Relationship

On the one hand, the S.W.I.F.T. By-laws and the User Handbook prescribe the duties and rights of S.W.I.F.T. in relation to the individual associates, i.e. the sender and the receiver, and make these subject to Belgian law; this must also affect the direct relationship between the sender and the

---

[83] Kegel, Internationales Privatrecht, 424 ff.

[84] Etzkorn, Zahlungsverkehr, p. 8.

[85] Heymann-Horn, at margin no. 85 preceding § 343; regarding the prior German conflict of laws, see Reithmann-Martiny, at margin no. 64; with respect to the hypothetical intent of the parties, see also Vischer, pp. 99 ff.

[86] Heymann-Horn, at margin no. 86 preceding § 343.

[87] Etzkorn, Zahlungsverkehr, pp. 45 ff.

[88] Great Britain: Re United Railways of Havanna and Regla Warehouse (1961) A.C. 1007.

receiver. On the other hand, the sender and receiver of a message, as participants in an international transfer (segment), are always additionally involved in a correspondent relationship, with the result that this relationship is governed by the law of the seat of the instructed bank, i.e. the law of the receiver, and perhaps by the receiver's general business terms.[89]

The question therefore arises regarding the way and extent to which the S.W.I.F.T. rules can affect the contractual relationship between two correspondent banks in an international transfer.

a) Application of S.W.I.F.T. Rules to the Individual Contractual Relationship between Banks

It cannot be assumed that correspondent agreements between banks contain express provisions regarding the question of incorporation of S.W.I.F.T. rules of conduct or liability norms. Even general terms and conditions, to the extent that they serve as the basis for business relationships, do not — as far as is known — contain such stipulations.

The legal relationships in connection with S.W.I.F.T. are structured as company law and contract law relationships between individual associates and the company, S.W.I.F.T. s.c.; they are not bilateral agreements between two individual associates, such as a sender and a receiver. S.W.I.F.T. rules are also not expressly incorporated into the legal relationship between two correspondent banks; instead an implied incorporation would have to be presumed.

When a bank becomes a member of S.W.I.F.T., it agrees unconditionally by means of prior acceptance of the General Terms and Conditions and the related acceptance of the rules contained in the User Handbook[90] to receive and to process[91] messages from other members — which can also include their correspondent banks — and to do so in accordance with the rules in effect for S.W.I.F.T. members.

A bank which sends messages as a S.W.I.F.T. member can do so only within the scope of and governed by the S.W.I.F.T. provisions; the bank also knows that these rules govern equally for the receiver — e.g. a correspondent bank. The rules and provisions governing legal statements of intent are fundamentally applicable to these messages which are exchanged between the banks by means of electronic media.[92]

---

[89] See part II. 3. and in more detail Etzkorn, Zahlungsverkehr, pp. 41 ff.

[90] See Clause 3 (1) and Clause 1 No. 8 Gen. Terms and Etzkorn, Zahlungsverkehr, pp. 21 ff.

[91] See also Köhler, AcP 182 (1982), pp. 138 ff.

[92] See part II. 2. a) aa); see also part II. 2. b) bb) α) $\alpha\alpha$) and $\beta\beta$).

The unconditional willingness of a bank, on the one hand, to receive messages within the framework of the S.W.I.F.T. rules and the bank's decision, on the other hand, to transmit a message through S.W.I.F.T. governed by S.W.I.F.T. rules with the knowledge that this message will be processed in accordance with the S.W.I.F.T. rules at the same time represents an agreement between two correspondent bank partners, acting here as sender and receiver of a S.W.I.F.T. message, that they will accept the S.W.I.F.T. rules for their bilateral correspondent relationship and mandatorily incorporate these rules into their relationship.[93]

This result is not contradicted by the fact that the contractual relationship, the instructing of one bank by its correspondent partner, which is subject to the law of the seat of the instructed bank[94], is by agreement governed in part by Belgian law. It is entirely permissible that, if the parties so desire, parts of a contractual relationship can be governed by a law different from that generally applicable to the contract.[95]

b) Scope of Incorporation of Rules

In accordance with general principles, the incorporation of S.W.I.F.T. provisions into the correspondent relationship extends to those areas for which comprehensive rules for the relationship between the correspondent partners can be derived from the S.W.I.F.T. provisions.

The S.W.I.F.T. rules contain as a particularization of general principles of fault liability detailed rules of conduct for all stages of the execution of a transfer, which even extend to the duty to maintain specified data processing and reserve capacities.

In the General Terms and Conditions[96], it is bindingly stipulated that all disputes regarding liability issues[97] shall be decided by a board of arbitration, substantively in accordance with the S.W.I.F.T. regulations. From this provision is derived the duty for the members to proceed in accordance with the S.W.I.F.T. rules likewise in the case of issues concerning the allocation of responsibility between the sender and receiver, i.e. between two correspondent banks. Proceeding in accordance with the S.W.I.F.T. arbitration rules and general S.W.I.F.T. provisions is not only reasonable but is also necessary in order to establish possible liability by S.W.I.F.T. s.c. The subsidiarity of

---

[93] See also Penney & Baker, at margin no. 24.03 (1) (b).

[94] See part II. 3.

[95] Delaume, at § 1.03; Rabel, p. 390 with references to specific countries.

[96] Clause 10 Gen. Terms.

[97] Clause 7 Gen. Terms.

liability by S.W.I.F.T. leads to the result that issues of possible liability by the sender and the receiver must first be clarified, and this must be done in accordance with the S.W.I.F.T. rules.[98]

S.W.I.F.T. rules thus contain not only provisions concerning the elements of liability for all phases of execution of a transfer. The rules regarding the legal process and scope of liability are also comprehensive so that the incorporation of S.W.I.F.T. rules in the correspondent relationship between two banks extends to all areas of the practical execution of a transfer by the sender and the receiver.

c) Decision by the German Federal Supreme Court of March 9, 1987

In a decision of March 9, 1987[99], where the Federal Supreme Court expressly mentioned that a transfer in dispute had been made through S.W.I.F.T., the Court did not deal with the issues discussed here concerning the incorporation of S.W.I.F.T. rules and the (at least subsidiary) incorporation of Belgian law. The Court held that in the disputed case — order by a French bank to a German bank, transfer to be carried out in German marks — the general terms and conditions of the German correspondent bank, as the bank performing the characteristic obligation, were effectively incorporated into the agreement and that the application of German law was therefore agreed to by the parties.[100]

German law was then applied in examining the issue of whether in the case of proper execution of the transfer but defects in the underlying contractual relationship a claim existed between the banks based on unjust enrichment.[101]

But based on the views supported here, the issue of whether the transfer had been properly carried out should have been decided not based on the general business terms and German law but instead in accordance with the S.W.I.F.T. provisions and Belgian law.[102]

---

[98] If the liability issue involved is one only between the sender and the receiver, it is possible that instead of the arbitration procedure suit could be filed in a court of law; even in this case the S.W.I.F.T. provisions should govern substantively; see part c) below.

[99] In: WM 1987, pp. 530 ff., comment by Hadding, in WuB ID of May 1, 1987.

[100] BGH WM 1987, p. 531; see Etzkorn, Zahlungsverkehr, pp. 45 ff., 51.

[101] Issues concerning the underlying contractual relationship — where the order is otherwise properly executed — are not covered by the provisions between S.W.I.F.T. s.c. and its associates; here, neither S.W.I.F.T. rules nor Belgian law apply, but instead the law at the seat of the originator's bank.

[102] This would not have changed anything significantly; under S.W.I.F.T. rules, the decisive criterium is the beneficiary's name and not the account number.

d) Result

Where a specific execution of a S.W.I.F.T. transfer is involved, the law otherwise applicable between two correspondent banks should not govern, but instead the S.W.I.F.T. rules and Belgian law. The banks participating in a transfer through S.W.I.F.T. have so agreed by means of acceptance of the S.W.I.F.T. rules.

These rules are comprehensive — in a technical and organizational manner — for all phases of the execution of a transfer transaction, the related liability norms and the provisions concerning the assertion of claims. These special comprehensive rules therefore legally replace the rules based on contracts and national law which would otherwise apply to the correspondent relationship in general.

III. S.W.I.F.T. — an International System of Rules?

This formulation as a question may appear surprising, especially with regard to the fact that this article is combined with four others in this volume under the title "International Legal Rules and Initiatives". But in order to answer this question, we must look at the results of the analysis up to this point[103] which illustrate the character of the various types of S.W.I.F.T. rules from a legal perspective and also in comparison with other systems of rules or initiatives. Of particular legal interest in this context is the question of to what extent the S.W.I.F.T. rules constitute "international law", such as in the sense of a transnational commercial law.[104]

1. Results of the Analysis to this Point — Special Characteristics of S.W.I.F.T. as an International System of Rules

The internal S.W.I.F.T. rules which have been used to illustrate the S.W.I.F.T. system from a legal perspective, in particular with respect to issues of liability, have clearly shown that the creation of S.W.I.F.T. and thus also its character were molded by efforts to find practical solutions to technical and organizational questions involved in international funds transfers; S.W.I.F.T. is not primarily an attempt to create an internationally binding legal framework for funds transfers. However, it has also been shown that the rules established by S.W.I.F.T. do, at the same time, have unifying effects from a legal perspective. The fact that these rules directly apply only for users

[103] See part 1. below.

[104] See part 2. below.

of the system actually has little significance when we look at the number of participating institutions and the volume of transactions[105] carried out through S.W.I.F.T.

On the other hand — as shown in this analysis[106] — the technical use of S.W.I.F.T. leads to uniform legal practices. Independently from the law generally applicable to the correspondent relationship between two banks, a specific transfer is governed by the S.W.I.F.T. system of rules and, in a supplementary manner, Belgian law. This set of rules — as shown[107] — contains a comprehensive system of liability.

In addition, from the perspective of substantive law, the S.W.I.F.T. rules also contribute significantly to a legal harmonization and thereby to the solution or prevention of problems in international funds transfers. These effects cannot be shown in detail within the scope of this article.[108] As examples, we should mention that the issues of when the payment is final[109] and at what time a transfer order may still be revoked[110] are handled in a uniform way through application of the S.W.I.F.T. rules and thereby substantially resolved. These issues of finality of payment and permissible revocation were objects of the study by UNCITRAL[111] which preceded the drafting of the UNCITRAL Model Law on International Credit Transfers. The same effect is achieved with respect to the issues of the legal effects of engaging third parties, i.e. issues arising from differing structures under national laws of compensation for damage, scope of liability and shifting of damages.[112] Also eliminated by S.W.I.F.T. rules are possible uncertainties relating to the use of an advice.[113] It cannot be ignored, however, that one possibility desirable from a technical perspective, namely the use of local electronic clearinghouses means, at the same time, from a legal perspective that for the respective segment of the transfer which is carried out through the local clearing system, the (contractual) legal rules of this system take priority over the S.W.I.F.T. rules.[114]

---

105 See part I. 1. a) above.

106 See in particular part II. 4.

107 See part II. 4. b), d) and II. 2.

108 See Etzkorn, Zahlungsverkehr, pp. 56-58.

109 Id. at 56 ff.

110 Id. at 73 ff.

111 UNCITRAL (ed.), Legal Guide on Electronic Funds Transfers (New York, 1987).

112 See Etzkorn, Zahlungsverkehr, pp. 78 ff.

113 Id. at 84 ff.

114 Id. at 121 ff. and part III. 2. b) below.

2. *Transnational Law and International Funds Transfers through S.W.I.F.T.*

Even though designed as a technical and not as a legal set of rules, S.W.I.F.T. today clearly influences efforts to create international systems of rules relating to cross-border funds transfers.[115] A completely separate issue is whether the S.W.I.F.T. rules possess an independent character as international law of funds transfers.

a) Transnational Commercial Law and the New Law Merchant

In the area of international commercial law, a theory is increasingly pursued in international legal scholarship under which, alongside classic international law and public international law, an independent substantive international commercial and economic law is emerging on the model of the historical "law merchant".[116] The distinctive feature of this body of law is the attempt to achieve internationally uniform rules independent from national legal systems.[117] The sources of this new law[118], also referred to as lex mercatoria or transnational (commercial) law[119], are international agreements and conventions as well as commercial customary law.[120] Customary law consists of unwritten rules which are followed within a particular community over a long period of time with awareness of their legal significance; such a definition can also claim validity in a comparative law context.[121] The possible existence of transnational commercial law must be examined with respect to the ability to link sanctions to it[122] and also under criteria such as ability to determine the relevant community, actual practices and the intent to give it legal effect.[123]

---

[115] See in particular the articles by Schneider and Blaurock in this volume.

[116] Schmitthoff, 5 J. Bus. Law 105 (1968); Schmitthoff, 17. I.C.L.Q. 55 (1968); Schmitthoff, Transnational Law, pp. 20 ff.; Horn, Internationale Anleihen, pp. 513 ff.; Horn, Codes of Conduct, pp. 59 ff.; Goldstajn, Festschrift Schmitthoff pp. 171, 174 ff.

[117] Horn, Internationale Anleihen, p. 513.

[118] Critical: v. Bar, pp. 75 ff., especially p. 79 f.

[119] Regarding distinctions between the terms, see Horn Transnational Law, pp. 11 ff.; Heymann-Horn, Introduction III, margin no. 16.

[120] Horn, Internationale Anleihen, pp. 513 f.

[121] Id. at 518, n. 48, 49.

[122] Id. at 520.

[123] Id. at 522, 524, 527.

b) Transfers through S.W.I.F.T. as International Customary Law

If the rules applicable to international transfers through S.W.I.F.T. are to be viewed as transnational rules in the sense of a new law merchant for the area of international funds transfer, these rules must fulfill the criteria cited above.

aa) The Community Establishing the Law

The community within which such a customary system of law may develop must be viewed here as including all of the banks and financial institutions for which the statutes of S.W.I.F.T. s.c. and the related elaborations in the User Handbook are binding. The community establishing the law thus consists of all of the member institutions of S.W.I.F.T. s.c. as well as the additional non-member institutions included in the national user groups[124], but not the non-bank originator or beneficiary of a particular transfer because they are not associates or "users" of S.W.I.F.T.

The fact that this community is one organized under private law on the basis of a national company law is not an obstacle because it is entirely possible that transnational rules can develop within this form of a community.[125] The fact that the rules which may rise to the level of transnational commercial law are the rules of the company — or are influenced by the company rules — is likewise not an obstacle. But whether these company law rules in fact lead to transnational law must be determined based on the additional criteria — actual practice and intent to view the rules as having legal effect.

bb) Actual Practice

Determinative of actual practice is the length of time as well as the uniformity of the practice.

With respect to time, it is certainly possible to expect differing views. Due to the fact that the rules have applied in substantially the same form for over 10 years, and thus since the very beginning of electronic international funds transfers, this requirement should be viewed as fulfilled.[126]

The issue of uniform usage must be differentiated. On the one hand, the S.W.I.F.T. provisions are binding as company rules for all participants; on the other hand, as shown above[127], transfers are in part not carried out under

---

[124] See part I. 1. b) above.

[125] See Horn, Internationale Anleihen, pp. 522 f.

[126] See Hinsch/Horn, Konsortialkredite und Projektfinanzierungen, p. 198; Horn, id. at 526.

[127] See part III. 1. above and Etzkorn, Zahlungsverkehr, pp. 13 f., 123 f.

S.W.I.F.T. rules, namely to the extent that other systems are engaged. This leads to the result that where segments of transfers are executed, for example, in the financial centers of New York, London or Zurich, these segments are governed not by S.W.I.F.T. rules but instead by the rules of the local systems, e.g. rules relating to finality of payment, revocation or liability of the system operator and other participants.

cc) Intent to View the Rules as Having Legal Effect

The issue of intent to view the rules as legally binding is likewise characterized by a certain ambivalence. On the one hand, S.W.I.F.T. provides detailed rules which, without the necessity of referring to other provisions, comprehensively govern the issues of allocation of liability among the participants[128], finality of payment and revocation[129]. Compliance with these rules is made compulsory — without the necessity of recourse to national courts — through an arbitration clause in accordance with the ICC Rules, which make decisions possible independently from national legal systems.[130] On the other hand, S.W.I.F.T. as an organization — and thus its members as well — do not wish to intervene in national structures of funds transfer law, as was shown by an attempt to provide for designation of a value date.[131] In order to solve an existing problem in international funds transfers, S.W.I.F.T. had decided to adopt provisions regarding the designation of value dates, but formulated these provisions in such a way that existing legal structures should not be interfered with. Later, it was found necessary to eliminate this provision without replacement because it was not possible to achieve a satisfactory rule without interfering in such national structures.

dd) Result

S.W.I.F.T. provisions are fundamentally suitable for the development of customary commercial law for the participating banks. But at the present time, the existence of such a customary commercial law in the area of funds transfers should not yet be presumed, for two reasons. One reason is that the S.W.I.F.T. rules do not apply throughout due to use of local transfer systems. The second reason is that S.W.I.F.T. has not (yet) decided to establish rules for the participants where it would be necessary to push aside conflicting provisions in the individual countries.

---

[128] See part II. 2. b) above.

[129] Etzkorn, Zahlungsverkehr, pp. 56 ff. and 73 ff.

[130] See part II. 2. b) above.

[131] See Etzkorn, Zahlungsverkehr, p. 34.

c) International Commercial Practice and International General Business Conditions

It is possible that transnational law could (first) develop in the form of international commercial custom or international general business conditions[132], whereby international customs can also be drafted as general business conditions.[133] These forms of international commercial law will be mentioned only briefly.

The community within which commercial custom could develop through S.W.I.F.T. rules would not be that of banks generally or even of all internationally active banks, but instead only those banks using S.W.I.F.T. To the extent that the establishment of a transnational law in the form of international customary law cannot yet be presumed, the establishment of international general business conditions appears under the present circumstances more likely than the establishment of international commercial custom.

In contrast to other internationally common general business terms such as Incoterms or ICC Uniform Rules and Practices[134], the S.W.I.F.T. rules, if viewed as general business conditions, are applicable only to a portion of the parties using S.W.I.F.T., namely the connected banks, but not to the other users such as private companies.

Overall, the significance of the S.W.I.F.T. rules — as long as they do not rise to the level of transnational law — will be in harmonization from a practical perspective.

---

[132] Heymann-Horn, Introduction III, margin no. 16.

[133] Horn, in: Wolf/Horn/Lindacher, at § 24, margin no. 23.

[134] Id.

The Uniform Rules for International Credit Transfers under the UNCITRAL Model Law

By Uwe H. Schneider, Darmstadt/Mainz*

Contents

---

* Translated by Dr. Frances Dielmann, Frankfurt/M.

I. Drafting History

Following long preparations, the UNITED NATIONS COMMISSION ON INTERNATIONAL TRADE LAW (UNCITRAL) resolved in 1986 to establish a Working Group with the task of drafting a model law on international credit transfers.[1] The Working Group was comprised of representatives from the various member states. These representatives included government officials, banking practitioners, representatives of associations, attorneys, and university professors. The Working Group met for eight days twice each year and concluded its work in December 1990. The draft of the Model Law was presented to the Commission in the summer of 1991 and was adopted during the following Commission meeting in May 1992.

The text is available in each of the six UNCITRAL negotiating languages, namely Arabic, Chinese, English, French, Russian and Spanish. There is no authorized German, Danish or Italian translation. This is a significant difference from the legal instruments of the European Communities, in which German, Danish, Italian etc. are also official languages. And the text of the Model law itself is understandable only upon additional examination of the Commission Report. It is clear from the Report only that no consensus was reached on a number of critical issues. So, for example, rules regarding the underlying contractual relationship, such as the time of discharge of money obligations, and conflicts of laws issues were included as a "compromise" in footnotes, despite serious criticism by many delegations. This is not apparent from the introduction to this article.

---

[1] See also Schinnerer, Zeitschrift für Rechtsvergleichung, 1985, p. 226; Bergsten, Revue de Droit des Affaires Internationales, 1987, p. 649; Patrikis, Bank Administration, Sept. 1987, pp. 30 ff.; Bradley Crawford, The Legal issues in EFTS, unpublished speech delivered at the annual meeting of FELABAN, San José, Costa Rica, May 30, 1988; Bradley Crawford, in: 4th Singapore Conference on International Commercial Law (Coh, ed., 1988); Effros, The Banking Law Journal 1988, p. 510; Vasseur, Banque de Droit 1989, p. 61; Uwe H. Schneider, WM 1989, p. 285; *Heinrich,* Universal Payments Law, Summer 1991, p. 4; *Dole,* U. Pa. J. Int'l Bus. L. Vol. 12 [1991], p. 661; *de Boer,* Nederlands Juristenblad 1992, 1289; *Bergsten,* A Payments Law for the World: UNCITRAL Model Law on International Credit Transfers (unpublished).

II. Difficulties in the Harmonization of Banking Transactions Law

Every harmonization of laws is subject to the same general problems. Differing legal cultures and legal systems, differences in the relationships between regulatory law and private law and between mandatory rules and contractual freedom make the search for common rules more difficult.

In the present case, there are additional problems: first, substantial differences between the individual countries with respect to funds transfer practices, in the practical significance of the funds transfer as a means of payment, in the technical execution of transfers, in the training level of the personnel carrying out the transfers, etc., and second, differences in the level of development of laws governing the transfer. Cashless funds transfers are carried out in very different ways in the various countries. In some, such as the United States, the check is the dominant means of payment while the credit transfer is gaining importance in interbank payments and also increasingly in commercial transactions. In some cases, particularly with respect to large payments, transfers are carried out by fully electronic means; in other cases — especially in many developing countries — credit transfers are still paper-based. The U.S. delegation was primarily interested in the "high speed, high volume electronic credit transfer". Other delegations attempted to comprehensively include all types of transfers within the scope of the rules, whereby their thoughts were directed toward transfers by private customers.

And in addition: Only a few countries have comprehensive laws governing credit transfers. A codified law governing transfers, Art. 4A UCC[2] has recently been adopted by numerous states in the U.S. It is commonly known that commercial law in the U.S. is not primarily federal law but lies instead within the competence of the individual states. In many European countries, there is at least a more or less well-developed body of case law from the highest courts. But in many cases, even this is lacking. "Harmonization" in this area therefore means not only adaptation of differing national laws; it means for many countries that a completely new body of law must be created. These circumstances led to the need for a careful analysis of the practice of credit transfers, the related risks, the obligations of the parties, the scope of responsibilities, the typical contract conditions, etc.

---

[2] See the articles by Miller/Davenport, Ballen/Diana, Fry, French, Baxter/Bhala, Nelson, and Goldstein, in: The Business Lawyer, 1990, pp. 1389 ff. On the influence of Art. 4A UCC on the Model Law, see Ballen/Diana, Banking Technology, July/August 1991, p. 38, and Crawford, 19 Canadian Business Law Journal (1991), p. 166.

III. The Conceptual Approach

Although general conceptual approaches were not always discussed with the necessary breadth in the meetings of the Commission, a number of the initial deliberations can still be clearly recognized.

1. Certainty, Speed, Cost Reduction

The Model Law is designed to make clear to all participants their obligations and responsibilities. There are two reasons for this. On the one hand, international awareness of the massive volume of payment transactions — it is estimated that in New York alone transfers amount to between 1.5 and 2 trillion dollars each working day — and of the existing systemic risks has grown.[3] The establishment of the duties and responsibilities of the participants is intended to contribute to the achievement of "good order in international transfers". And on the other hand, the participants themselves should be made aware of their rights and obligations.

At the same time, the quality of execution of transfers should be promoted. For example, legally binding, short time limits for execution should speed up transfers. Restrictions on liability should make it possible to limit the costs, which are decisive for the setting of fees for transfers. Whether this last aspect has been fully achieved is rather doubtful, due to the mandatory "money-back guarantee".

2. Uniform Rules for the Entire Contractual Chain

The Model Law attempts to insure that equivalent legal rules will be applied to the entire contractual chain, even if these rules are derived from differing national legal systems. Proposals that only the cross-border "segments" be governed by the Model Law were, therefore, rejected. The Model Law contains rules relating to:

— the relationship between the originator and his bank,

— the relationships between the banks, including the beneficiary's bank, and

— the relationship between the intermediary bank or the beneficiary's bank and the beneficiary.

a) In order to assess these rules, we should first look at the current practices:

[3] Bank for International Settlements, Report on Netting Schemes, Basel, 1989; Zetschke, Die Risiken im Zahlungsverkehr werden größer, Börsenzeitung, Nov. 18, 1989.

International credit transfers are, as a rule, chains of transactions with domestic and cross-border segments. From the perspective of German law[4], the German customer as the originator enters into an agency agreement (Geschäftsbesorgungsvertrag) with his bank, the originator's bank contracts with its foreign correspondent bank, which contracts with the beneficiary's bank. The beneficiary's bank creates certain rights to payment on the part of the beneficiary. By engaging further intermediary banks in various countries, a long chain of contracts can be created. A separate determination must be made for each contractual relationship with respect to the law applicable to that relationship[5] and to which rights and duties exist. This is especially true for the contracts made by the beneficiary's bank, which enters into contractual relationships with the preceding bank and also with the beneficiary. Assuming that the contract is subject to the law chosen by the parties, the result can be that each contractual relationship in the chain can be subject to a different system of law; in addition, various sets of general business conditions containing different provisions regarding the obligations of the participants, the time of performance and finality, liability in case of breach of obligations, allocation of risks, etc., can apply.[6]

If the entire procedure is viewed as a unit, it is completely unclear which system of law should be applied in a specific case, for example, relating to a revocation order given by the customer to one of the intermediary banks or relating to issues of liability.

b) UNCITRAL cannot create international commercial law. UNCITRAL is not a legislator. However, UNCITRAL can and wishes to contribute to equivalent national laws. Achievement of this goal will enable the participants to better plan their transactions.

Of course, this concept can be successful only if the Model Law is adopted by a large number of countries. It would be particularly problematic if a small number of states gave up their long- established legal rules to adopt the Model Law, other countries did not do so, and no real harmonization effect were achieved.

---

[4] See Canaris, in: Großkomm. HGB (4th ed., 1988), Bankenvertragsrecht, part 1, margin no. 300 ff., with additional references; Hadding/Häuser, ZHR 145 (1981), pp. 138 ff.; Hellner, ZHR 145 (1981), pp. 109 ff.; Schröter, ZHR 151 (1987), pp. 118 ff. Contra, Möschel, AcP 186 (1986), pp. 187 ff.: network contract within the entire chain.

[5] See Pelichet, Note on Conflicts of Laws Occasioned by Transfrontier Data Flows, unpublished manuscript of the Hague Conference on Private International Law, 1987; Pelichet, Note on the Problem of the Law Applicable to International Credit Transfers (1991).

[6] On the issue of the applicable law when a transfer is executed through S.W.I.F.T., see Etzkorn, Rechtsfragen des internationalen elektronischen Zahlungsverkehrs durch S.W.I.F.T. (1991), p. 54.

Two other issues are significant:

- First, consideration was given to the possibility of including general rules of interpretation in the Model Law. This was not done. But — assuming that the Model Law will be implemented as national law — one must remember in the future that such laws, which serve the goal of creating an international law of commercial transactions, are subject to special rules of interpretation.[7]
- Second, the conflict of laws issues gain significance due to the fact that various countries will make more or less substantial changes to the Model Law. There was a systematic and substantive consensus that no rule should be included in the Model Law itself. As the result of a "compromise", a footnote was included containing the recommendation that additional legal policy discussions should focus on the possibility of adopting a choice of law rule. The rules maintain free choice of law by the parties and provide, in the absence of a choice of law, that the law of the state in which the receiving bank has its place of business shall apply.

3. The Principle of Freedom of Contract

The Model Law is based on the principle of freedom of contract (Art. 4). This was by no means undisputed in the discussions. There was a consensus that the Model Law should not be a consumer protection law. It is applicable without distinction to transfers by private customers, interbank transfers and transfers by enterprises. Of course, this does not exclude the possibility that national legislators may choose to add supplementary consumer protection provisions.

Independently from this principle, the view was asserted by some parties that "good order in funds transfers" and protection of small and middle-sized enterprises, artisans, and professional occupations would require a mandatory regulation of contractual duties and responsibilities in some cases. Divergent contractual stipulations could also restrict the rights of third parties. The response to this view was that the Model Law as an element of "international commercial law" should be governed by the principle of freedom of contract and that necessary latitude to permit future developments could be achieved only if the contracting parties are able to react to these developments by means of adapting their contracts. One could also contemplate whether some mandatory provisions might be needed to protect

[7] On this issue, see also the UN Convention on Contracts for the International Sale of Goods; v. Caemmerer/Schlechtriem, Komm. zum Einheitlichen UN-Kaufrecht, 1990, Art. 7, margin no. 11 ff.

small and middle-sized credit institutions which could be forced to adopt unreasonable contract conditions due to the competitive force of large customers.

4. Statutory Duties

In addition to rules relating to the contractual relations between the participants, the Model Law also contains a number of "statutory duties" which are made mandatory for the credit institutions based merely on the fact that they take part in payment transactions and carry out credit transfers. The justification given for these professional duties is that this is the only way to insure good order in international transfers. One example relates to the duties of a credit institution receiving a transfer order from which it is apparent that the order has been misdirected.[8] In this case, one could at least seriously question whether a credit institution must become active and make the originator aware of the misdirection. The Model Law requires the credit institution to inform the sender. It must be pointed out, however, that the sanctions for breach of this duty are insignificant.

5. Limitation of Liability

Transfer transactions represent risks for all the participants which can be substantial. This is especially true for international transfers (e.g. exchange rate risk, insolvency of an intermediary bank, delays due to political causes, currency control regulations, delays caused by negligent employees, breakdown of the electronic systems, etc.). In this context, the Model Law distinguishes between risks relating to the transfer amount itself and risks relating to consequential damages. The Model Law provides for guarantee liability for the transfer amount itself, which will be presented in more detail below.[9] On the other hand, the Model Law also contains a broad limitation on liability for consequential damages.

6. No Provisions Governing the Underlying Financial Obligations?

One of the questions decided was whether the Model Law should also govern issues arising out of the underlying legal relationship between the

[8] During the negotiations, the representative of the then existing German Democratic Republic stated with a sly grin that not infrequently payment orders intended for the Deutsche Bank AG, Frankfurt, were directed to the Deutsche Außenhandelsbank of the GDR.

[9] See part IX. below.

originator and the beneficiary. The primary issues relate to the point in time when money debts are discharged if the amount is transferred and to which contractual partner should bear the risk of delay or loss of the transfer amount; these questions are presently not governed in a uniform way in the various national legal systems. There is hardly any doubt that uniform rules are needed.[10] But the Model Law on International Credit Transfers would certainly not be the proper location for these uniform rules.

IV. The Sphere of Application of the Model Law

1. Paper-Based and Electronic Transfers

The incentive for the development of "Model Rules" resulted from special problems with large payments using electronic media in cross-border transactions. Consideration was, therefore, given at times to the possibility of limiting the scope of application of the Model Rules to electronic transfers. This is understandable when we keep in mind that it was particularly the U.S. banking regulatory authorities who advocated codification of such rules.

The Model Law goes well beyond this area. It deals with the order or instructions by the customer to a credit institution to make a payment to a third party ("credit transfer"), regardless of the amount and regardless of whether the instructions are issued within the framework of an existing business relationship or as a single order — and regardless of the form in which the order is issued. Not included are debits from the account of a debtor or payment by check ("debit transfers"). But the law applies not only to banks but to all entities that as an ordinary part of their business engage in executing payment orders (Art. 1).[11] It is not relevant whether the institution is also a "credit institution" in a regulatory law sense.[12] Here, the scope of application of the Model Law differs from that of Art. 4A UCC. Art. 4A UCC governs only transfers employing a bank in the regulatory law sense. In addition, under the Model Law, the first sender can also be a credit institution, so that the Law governs pure interbank transfers.

---

[10] See e.g. Schönle, in: Festschr. für Werner (1984), p. 817, and Pleyer/Wallach, RIW 1988, p. 172.

[11] By contrast, the Guidelines of the International Chamber of Commerce deal only with transfers by banks accepting deposits (Art. 1A ICC Guidelines).

[12] In most countries, "giro business" is not banking business in the sense of banking regulatory law.

2. The International Element

It was first planned that the Model Law would only apply when the originator's bank and the beneficiary's bank were located in different countries. Then it would have been apparent from the beginning which law would apply. Now the Law provides, however, that the Law shall apply whenever within the transfer chain a sending bank and one of the receiving banks are located in different countries. This is not a fortunate result because there is now the possibility that the applicable law can change during the execution of the transfer. This can lead to odd inconsistencies.

To make this clear, we can consider the following case: The originator, his bank, the beneficiary's bank and the beneficiary are all resident in the Federal Republic of Germany. The originator's bank and the beneficiary's bank are both branches of different foreign banks. The originator's bank transmits the order to its main office in the foreign country, which then passes the order to the main office of the beneficiary's bank. From there, the order arrives at the beneficiary's bank in Germany. "Branches" are deemed to be separate banks within the meaning of Art. 1 of the Model Law. Although the originator, his credit institution, the credit institution of the beneficiary and the beneficiary are all resident in Germany, the Law on International Credit Transfers should be applied. This will certainly not be apparent to the originator.

3. Paper-Based versus Electronic Execution

The Model Law is not restricted to payments made by means of electronic media. The original title, "Model Rules on Electronic Funds Transfers" was abandoned during the preparatory work. Instead, the transfer order can be given in any form and can be transmitted in whichever way is desired between the originator's bank and the beneficiary's bank.[13] However, the types of problems arising specifically through the use of electronic media are also dealt with, such as transfer orders on magnetic tape, data entry by unauthorized persons, (Art. 5 (2)), etc.[14] One criticism was that in many countries there are already legal rules governing paper-based transfers which have proved effective. Under this view, action would be necessary only with

[13] Under No. 1 of the savings banks' special business conditions for transfers, transfer orders "must, as a rule, be issued only on the forms provided by the savings bank". Special agreement must be made in advance for the use of other forms.

[14] The legal issues relating to the use of more recent technology are extensively analyzed by Hellner, in: Festschr. für Werner (1984), pp. 251 ff.; Blaurock, in: Neue Entwicklungen im Bankhaftungsrecht (Köndgen, ed., 1987), pp. 35 ff.; Hikel, Tragung des EDV-Risikos im Recht der Banküberweisung (1988). See also Köhler, AcP 182 (1982), pp. 126 ff.

respect to electronic transfers. If this proposal had been adopted, it would have led to the less convincing result that differing rules would apply, depending on the payment route and the techniques and media used.

4. Conditional Payment Orders

Under Art. 3, a payment order is defined as an unconditional instruction. Conditional orders or instructions are not deemed to be payment orders within the meaning of the Law. The Law shall, nevertheless, be applicable if the Bank executes the payment order by issuing on unconditional payment order.

5. The Unsatisfactory Result: the new disorder

The partially restricted scope of application of the Model Law leads to the unsatisfactory result that several independent bodies of rules are created and in specific cases it must be determined which body of rules shall apply.

- — For credit transfers within one country, the previously governing rules remain in effect.
- — For international credit transfers, the Model Law applies.
- — For international conditional credit transfers, the Model Law does not apply so that the issue arises as to whether the transfer remains under the general rules.
- — In addition, individual areas of the rules are supplemented by consumer protection provisions.

When one looks carefully, the harmonization effect appears doubtful.

V. The Rights and Obligations of the Originator and the Credit Institutions

1. German Contract Practice

In German banking practice, the individual payment order does not, as a rule, lead to an independent contract. Instead, it is common that a general "banking agreement" is entered into by the customer and his credit institution, which contains a service contract (giro or clearing agreement). Under this agreement, the customer acquires the right to bind the credit institution, by means of a unilateral instruction, to carry out a particular credit transfer.[15] Unless precise instructions are given, the bank may choose the means of execution at its discretion. If the originator's bank is not also the bank of the beneficiary, it must issue a payment order to an another bank (Art. 8). Only the originator's bank, however, contracts with the originator; there is no contract between the originator and the intermediary banks or the beneficiary's bank.[16]

When the payment order is issued to an intermediary bank, the originator's bank is not liable for the success of the transfer, i.e. that the amount is, in fact, credited to the beneficiary.

2. The Payment Order and the Duties of the Originator's Bank

a) The UNCITRAL Model Law is based on the primary assumption that each payment order leads to an independent contract even in the case where a general clearing agreement is in effect between the parties. In addition, the Model Law stipulates which necessary elements a payment order must include in order to elicit the corresponding duties.

b) It was first assumed that the acceptance of the payment order would create an agency agreement, which would not be a service contract but instead a contract for work. Under this concept, the originator's bank would fulfill its duties only if first it issued a payment order to an intermediary bank and second the beneficiary's bank "accepted" the order for execution. In other words, the receiving bank would undertake the duty to see that the beneficiary's bank accepted the transfer order.

This concept was criticized because the receiving bank is not in a position to be responsible for the actions of another credit institution if it has not itself selected this other credit institution. Also, a receiving bank cannot do more than select its correspondent bank with the usual degree of care required of a banker.

Now the Model Law follows a different path. The originator's bank is obligated only to issue the payment order including suitable selection of an intermediary bank. Separately from this main obligation, the Law provides for another duty, which will be described in more detail, namely to refund any payment received if the credit transfer is not completed (Art. 14).

---

[15] BGHZ 10, p. 322; BGHZ 84, p 374; BGH WM 1972, p. 308; Canaris, supra note 10, at margin no. 315.

[16] BGH WM 1958, p. 1078; BGH WM 1961, p. 78; BGH WM 1983, p. 410; OLG Karlsruhe WM 1988, p. 1330; Canaris, supra note 10, at margin no. 387, 392; Hadding/Häuser, Rechtsfragen des Zahlungsverkehrs (1984), pp. 71 ff. Contra, Möschel, AcP 186 (1986), pp. 211 ff.

c) If the payment order includes an instruction to issue the payment order to a specific intermediary bank or through a specific funds transfer system, the receiving bank must comply with this instruction. The receiving bank may deviate from this instruction, however, if it "in good faith" is of the opinion that it is not feasible to comply with the instruction or that compliance with the instruction would lead to excessive costs or delays in completing the credit transfer. The receiving bank can, in this case, also make inquiry to the sender before the end of the execution period, so that an issue arises as to whether and under what circumstances there is a duty to make such inquiry.

d) The receiving bank is free to accept or reject a payment order even if it has a general giro agreement or other standing business relationship with the originator. This idea was of particular significance for the Commission because the execution of a payment order can involve substantial risks for the receiving bank, particularly in cross-border transfers. If the credit institution does not wish to accept the payment order, it must, of course, so inform the sender no later than on the banking day following the end of the execution period, (Art. 7 (3)). Silence would constitute acceptance.

3. The Binding Nature of the Payment Order

Banks are required to strictly comply with accepted payment orders.[17] One example of an objective breach of duty under an agency agreement is where an expressly issued instruction to make payment to a specific account of the beneficiary is not heeded and payment is instead credited to a different account.[18] The originator may issue the order with additional instructions; in particular, he may specify which intermediary bank or funds transfer system should be selected or avoided in order to reach the beneficiary's bank. This so-called "routing" may be based on various reasons. The originator may have an interest in not having the transfer amount directed through a credit institution in a particular country because it would be subject to confiscation there. Especially important is the fact that routing by the originator can discharge the receiving bank from liability if a credit institution selected by the originator becomes insolvent.

---

[17] BGH WM 1962, p. 460; BGH WM 1976, p. 940; BGH WM 1991, p. 799 = WuB I D 1. Überweisungsverkehr 5.91 with comment by Sonnenhol.

[18] OLG Hamm WM 1989, p. 1321 = WuB I D 1. Überweisungsverkehr 1.90 with comment by Terpitz.

4. The Incomplete Payment Order

If the bank receives an incomplete payment order, it must inform the sender of this circumstance. This constitutes an accessory contractual obligation if a giro agreement or other standing business relationship exists between the parties. But even where there is no standing business relationship, this duty to inform the originator would constitute a statutory (professional) obligation (Art. 8 (5)).

5. Conflicting Payment Orders

Payment orders can contain conflicting information. The Law creates various classifications of cases, which are all dealt with in the same way:

— If in the payment order the amount is expressed in words and in numbers and if these amounts do not agree, the order may not be executed. The Model Law does not contain a stipulation that the amount in words or the amount in numbers shall be determinative. Instead, the Law requires that the sender be informed so that he will receive an opportunity to clarify the inconsistency (Art. 8 (5) and Art. 10 (3)). The fact that this may lead to delays must be accepted by the sender.
  This is not, however, a mandatory provision. The parties may contractually stipulate that the amount in words or in numbers shall be determinative.

— The same is true if the payment order specifies a beneficiary and an account number to which the amount should be credited, but the account holder is not the same party as the specified beneficiary. In this case as well, the beneficiary's bank, prior to execution, must first ask the sender to whom the amount should be credited (Art. 10 (4)). In other words: The beneficiary's bank must make a name comparison. The principle that the account number is determinative does not apply.[19]

  This differs from German law. The XI. Chamber of the Federal Supreme Court in its decision of October 8, 1991[20] recently confirmed its rule that in the case of a discrepancy between the name of the beneficiary and the specified account in paper-based credit transfers the beneficiary's name shall be determinative.

---

[19] On paper-based transfers: BGHZ 87, p. 376; BGH WM 1989, p. 1754 = WuB I D 1. Überweisungsverkehr 3.90 with comment by Möschel/Bartodziej. On transfers by non-documentary data media exchange, see OLG Cologne WM 1989, p. 93 = WuB I D 1. Überweisungsverkehr 2.91 with critical comment by Bülow.

[20] WM 1991, p. 1912; see also BGHZ 108, p. 386, 390 (non-documentary transfer) and BGH WM 1991, p. 1452, 1458.

VI. Payment Orders by Unauthorized Parties

A banks or savings institution has a right to compensation for its services only when the order to execute a credit transfer comes from its customer. The credit institution does not have the right to debit an account when an instruction carried out within the scope of a giro agreement is invalid because it was not originated by the account holder. The general view is that the credit institution bears the risk of counterfeit orders.[21] This principle is disputed only in the case of counterfeit by employees. In its decision of October 8, 1991[22], the XI. Chamber of the German Federal Supreme Court stated: "The general legal principle that a principal need not be responsible for criminal acts which his employees intentionally commit to his disadvantage is not applicable here". By contrast, the same chamber, in its former decision of October 3, 1989[23], held that a city as account holder need not bear the loss for criminal acts committed by a disloyal civil servant.

The Model Law contains a differentiating provision. A prerequisite for a binding payment order is that it be "authorized" by the originator (Art. 5). This means that not only the originator's own instructions and instructions by his representatives are imputed to the originator, but instead under certain circumstances also instructions by unauthorized third parties, such as disloyal employees. In general, no one must be responsible for instructions by third parties. The parties can, however, stipulate a specific authorization procedure in order to make it possible, for example, for a customer to carry out large numbers of payments by sending a magnetic tape containing the payment orders to the bank. It is obvious that this procedure involves a danger of misuse by unauthorized third parties. Here, the parties could stipulate a certain authorization procedure. In this case, under the provisions of the Model Law, the sender is bound by an unauthorized order only if the parties had stipulated "a commercially reasonable method of security against unauthorized payment orders" and this method was in fact used (Art. 5 (2)). The Law expressly excludes the right of the parties to stipulate a security system which is not commercially reasonable in the circumstances.

Even where a commercially reasonable authorization procedure is used, the sender is not bound by the payment order if he proves that the payment order was issued by an unauthorized third party who is not and has not been an employee of the sender. The sender thus has the possibility to show that a "hacker" broke into the system and was able to overcome the security system. Here, the bank bears the risk connected with counterfeit and

---

[21] BGH WM 1966, p. 396; BGH WM 1967, p. 1142; OLG Düsseldorf WM 1990, p. 1818 = WuB I D 1. Überweisungsverkehr 1.91 with comment by Peterhoff.

[22] WM 1991, p. 1912.

[23] BGHZ 108, p. 386, 392; but see BGH WM 1991, p. 1912, 1914.

transmission. This does not apply, of course, if the bank asserts and proves that the payment order was possible because the unauthorized party was able to gain access to the security procedure due to the negligent conduct of the alleged sender.

The decisive issue is therefore what constitutes a reasonable method of security. The discussions demonstrated that the various countries had different views concerning this issue. In paper- based transfers, the comparison of the signature with the signature sample originally submitted to the bank may be viewed as a reasonable security method — at least where small amounts are involved. To some extent, the general business conditions even provide that the account holder bears the risk that transfer forms which he provides to others may be used for counterfeit orders.[24] Others assert the view that signature comparison is not ever an adequate security method.

An originally planned limitation of risk under which the customer could be liable for payment orders by unauthorized parties only up to the amount of his account deposit or credit line is not contained in the present draft. The absence of this provision can be problematic because a credit institution could carry out a payment order by an unauthorized party within the scope of a standing business relationship and, where there is reason to hold the purported sender responsible for the order, can extend credit for the transfer amount to the account holder.

VII. The Time of Execution

The originator can specify in the payment order the date on which the payment order is to be executed. Where no such instruction is given, as a general rule, the payment order should be carried out on the same day ("same-day rule"). But in practice the bank's cut-off time must be taken into consideration, i.e. that all payment orders received after the cut-off time during the working day are handled as if they had been received on the following working day. If the cut-off time is set for 11 am and the transfer order is received at 11:15, then even using the "same day rule" the payment order need not be carried out until the following working day.

Criticism was expressed that one working day is not sufficient processing time; especially in cross-border credit transfers, there can often be substantial problems involved in finding a suitable intermediary bank and providing cover in the relevant currency so that the payment order can be executed. Particularly small and middle-sized banks would have had difficulty with the

[24] See OLG Düsseldorf WM 1990, p. 1818 = WuB I D 1. Überweisungsverkehr 1.91 with comment by Peterhoff.

same-day rule. It should also be pointed out that the EC Commission Recommendation of 14 February 1990 on the transparency of banking conditions relating to cross-border financial transactions[25] contains a different rule.

The 4th Principle states:

1. In the absence of instructions to be contrary and except in cases of force majeure, each intermediary institution should deal with a transfer order within two working days of receipt of the funds specified in the order or should give notification of its refusal to execute the order or of any foreseeable delay to the institution issuing the order and, where different, to the transferor's institution.
2. The transferor should be able to obtain a refund of part of the costs of the transfer in the event of any delay in executing his order.

The 5th Principle states:

1. The transferee's institution should fulfil its obligations arising from a transfer order not later than the working day following receipt of the funds specified in the order unless the said order stipulates a later date of execution.
2. If the transferee's institution is unable to execute the order within the time indicated in paragraph 1, it should, as soon as possible, inform the institution issuing the order and, where different, the transferor's institution of the reasons for its failure to execute the order or for the delay in execution.

The Model Law instead attempts a compromise. The "same-day rule" generally applies. But the bank is also granted the possibility of carrying out the payment order on the following day. In this case, the bank must pay interest for the additional day used (Art. 11 (2)).

In this context, there was a fundamental issue concerning the receipt of payment orders by branch offices of a bank. Here, the Model Law provides that for this purpose branches are deemed to be separate banks even if they are located in the same country as the main office. In this way, large credit institutions with an extensive network of branches gain extra processing days and can delay transmittal to an intermediary. In other words: In addition to the fee for the transfer, they also acquire the float for a longer time. The effects which this situation can have on the competition between banks are obvious.

[25] O. J. EC No. L 67/39 of Mar. 15, 1990.

VIII. Revocation of the Payment Order

1. The Rule in German Banking Practice

On the assumption that a giro agreement is an agency agreement and that the individual payment order represents a specifying instruction, the revocation is the mere counterinstruction as long as the order has not been carried out.[26] It is possible only until the beneficiary's bank credits the transfer amount to the beneficiary's account and thereby completes the transfer.[27] It is disputed whether the beneficiary's bank or an intermediary bank is required to comply with a direct revocation by the customer with which it does not have a business relationship. In the case of a revocation by the customer, this possibility should be rejected. As a rule, there is no contract between the customer and the intermediary banks or the beneficiary's bank. Also, the fact that it is quite difficult for the intermediary banks or the beneficiary's bank to verify the identity of the party issuing the revocation order should not be overlooked.[28] In doubt is only whether direct revocation by the originator's bank to the beneficiary's bank should be binding when intermediary banks have been engaged.

2. No Direct Revocation

The Model Law provides for the possibility of a revocation, although substantial opposition to such a provision was expressed in the Commission.

The revocation must be complied with by the sender's bank when it is received "at a time ... sufficient to afford the receiving bank a reasonable opportunity to act" before it further transmits the payment order (Art. 12). If the payment order has already been executed, the sender can require that the sending bank transmit the revocation order and instruct the next receiving bank to amend or not carry out the payment order. The Model Law is thus based on the idea of a "chain revocation". It does not provide for a direct revocation order by the originator to banks further down the line. The death, insolvency, the opening of a bankruptcy proceeding with respect to his assets or incapacity of either the sender or the originator does not affect the

---

[26] BGH WM 1986, p. 1409; BGH WM 1987, p. 986; BGH WM 1988, p. 321 = WuB I D 1. Überweisungsverkehr 2.88 with comment by Hadding/Häuser; Canaris, supra note 10, at margin no 352 ff.; Hadding/Häuser, Rechtsfragen des Zahlungsverkehrs (1984), pp. 60 ff.; Hadding/Häuser, WM 1988, p. 1149.

[27] On the issue of when settlement is made in an electronic credit transfer, see BGH WM 1988, p. 321; Hadding/Häuser, WM 1988, p. 1149.

[28] Schröter, ZHR 151 (1987), p. 118; Schwark, ZHR 151 (1987), p. 325, 339. Contra, Möschel, AcP 186 (1986), p. 187, 228.

validity of the payment order.[29] The originator who makes timely revocation of a transfer order must pay the sending bank only the fee for the costs incurred.

If the revocation has been validly communicated to a bank, which at the same time is the beneficiary's bank, that bank must comply with the revocation order only if the transfer has not been completed or the transfer amount has not yet been placed at the disposal of the beneficiary. This is understandable in the context of the special provisions regarding the acceptance of the payment order by the beneficiary's bank and the duties arising in connection with this acceptance.

There is, however, a serious inconsistency with the rule regarding discharge of the underlying contractual obligation; the underlying obligation is discharged when the beneficiary's bank accepts the payment order. But under Art. 12 (2), a revocation is still possible after that time. For this and other reasons, the provision relating to the underlying contractual obligation which was placed in a footnote to Art. 19 was strongly criticized by many delegations.

IX. The Liability of the Credit Institution

1. Risks and Losses

Losses can occur when, for the following reasons, it is not possible to transmit the payment order or to transmit it on time or to transmit it except in an amended form:

— incorrect conduct by the originator's bank, an intermediary bank or the beneficiary's bank, or

— technical failures, force majeure (e.g. political factors, etc.) or currency controls which prohibit the further transmittal of transfers in foreign currency, or

— the insolvency of one of the credit institutions. Possible damages are the loss of the transferred amount, interest losses, currency exchange losses and other consequential damages.

---

[29] By contrast, under German law the order lapses if the originator goes into bankruptcy, § 23 (1) and (2) KO (Bankruptcy Act); see BGHZ 67, p. 75, 76 f. The originator's bank is protected, however, by § 23 (2) in conjunction with § 23 (1) sent. 2 KO and § 674 BGB.

2. *Liability of Credit Institutions in German Banking Practice*

Based on the contracts commonly used in German banking practice, the originator's bank fulfills its obligations when it issues the payment order to an intermediary bank which it engages and makes the necessary cover available to this intermediary bank. The bank is then not liable to its customer for the loss of the transfer amount due to the insolvency or improper conduct of an intermediary bank. The intermediary banks and the beneficiary's bank are not the "agents" of the originator's bank within the meaning of § 278 German Civil Code.[30] The originator's bank is liable only for improper selection of the intermediary banks.

As a rule, there is no contract between the originating customer and the intermediary banks or the beneficiary's bank based on which the customer could derive direct contractual claims. Therefore, the customer must in part rely for claims against these institutions on the principle of violation of contractual duties with "protective effect for third parties".[31] Under a different view, the contractual partner of the negligent institution can assert claims for the customer on the theory of liquidation of third party damages.[32] The account holder can also demand that this right to assert claims be assigned directly to him.[33]

3. *Unclear Legal Situation in the Case of International Transfers*

In international transfers, the legal situation is completely unclear because direct claims by the customer suffering the loss against the negligent intermediary credit institution are dependent upon whether the concept of duties with protective effect for third parties is also recognized under the applicable legal system.[34] Claims by the contractual partner depend upon whether

[30] BGH WM 1991, p. 797 = WuB I D 1. Überweisungsverkehr 4.91 with comment by Horn. Details in Hüffer, ZHR 151 (1987), pp. 93 ff.; Hüffer, WM 1987, pp. 641 ff. Contra, Huber, in this volume, with additional references. Also different under British and American law, but these other contractual stipulations are permissible; see Equitable Trust Co. of New York v. Dawson Partners Ltd. (1927) 24 Ll LR 49; Ellinger, Modern Banking Law (Oxford, 1987), pp. 369 f.

[31] See e.g. OLG Düsseldorf WM 1982, p. 576; OLG Frankfurt WM 1984, p. 726 and OLG Munich WM 1988, p. 373; Canaris, supra note 10, at margin no. 395.

[32] Hadding, in: Festschr. für Werner (1984), pp. 165 ff.

[33] No. 9 sent. 3 Bank AGB; no. 19 savings bank AGB; BGH WM 1978, p. 367; BGH WM 1984, p. 834, 835.

[34] In American case law, a direct contractual relationship has been found to exist between the bank customer and the correspondent bank. See Evra Corporation v. Swiss Bank Corporation, 522 F. Supp. 820 (1981); for the differing result under English law, see Ellinger, Modern Banking Law (Oxford, 1987), p. 372.

liquidation of third party damages is possible. With regard to this situation, a limitation on liability would appear generally preferable. But the substance of such a limitation is problematic.

4. The Rule in the Model Law

In drafting the Model Law, one of the most disputed issues was that concerning the responsibilities of the credit institutions when the transfer does not reach the beneficiary or does not reach him on time. Here, the Model Law attempts to distinguish between

— the transfer amount,

— the interest loss, and

— other consequential damages incurred because the transfer amount is not received by the beneficiary or not received on time.

It was first stipulated that the contract between the originator and the originator's credit institution is an agency contract whose object is a work agreement. This would have had three consequences. First, the credit institution would have had no claim to be reimbursed for its services if the transfer broke down, e.g. due to the insolvency of an intermediary bank, and the beneficiary did not receive a claim against his bank for the transfer amount. Second, the originator's bank would have been liable for damages if it did not carry out the payment order with the proper care. Third, the originator's bank could claim the fee for the transfer only if the transferred amount in fact reached the beneficiary.

The Model Law still structures the contract between the originator and the originator's bank as an agency agreement, but one for services, not for a specific result. It does not contain only individual duties such as, of course, a duty to provide assistance, but in addition a mandatory duty to refund, which is so far unknown under German law although it was proposed by some authors recently. On the one hand, this can lead to substantial new risks for the credit institutions. On the other hand, it should not been overlooked, that liability for consequential damages is limited in a way which is quite favorable for the credit institutions.

An express rule is contained in the supplementary convention of Feb. 25, 1961 (CIV), regarding the liability of the railway company for unlawful death or injury of passengers in international travel (BGBl. 1974, p. 361). Under Art. 2 § 6, it is not the railroad company entering into the sales-contract but instead the one operating the route on which the accident occurs which is liable.

5. The Duty to Provide Assistance

Particularly in international transfers, it happens not infrequently that credit transfers to certain countries are not carried out for weeks or months because one of the intermediary banks, for whatever reason, does not transmit the order. An issue naturally arises with respect to compensation for damages. But this may not be the primary interest of the originator. His main interest is in having the transfer completed. The originator's bank, however, has already fulfilled its primary duties at this point. It has already executed the payment order. And under the concept of the Model Law, no contractual relationship exists between the originator and the intermediary bank. The Model Law provides for a special independent accessory duty for this situation in the form of a duty by the originator's bank to provide assistance by requiring the subsequent intermediary banks in the chain to comply with their obligations to further execute the payment order (Art. 13). This "duty to assist" should exist as a matter of course.

6. The Mandatory Duty of Reimbursement — the "Money-Back Guarantee"

a) Particularly disputed was the stipulation in the Model Law of the "money-back guarantee". The compromise contained in the present text is still not satisfactory at all. The claim for reimbursement of expenses arises only when the transfer amount reaches the beneficiary. This means that the originator's bank must refund the transfer amount to the originator if somewhere in the chain of intermediary banks one of these institutions becomes insolvent or if the amount is not transmitted for other reasons such as where it is attached at one of the banks. It is not relevant whether the intermediary bank involved is one which was selected by the originator's bank or one further along in the chain. It is thus not relevant whether the originator's bank acted negligently; under the wording of the model law this is a mandatory unconditional guarantee liability.

First, this so-called "money-back guarantee" was criticized because it burdens the credit institutions with unforeseeable risks. The receiving bank has no possibility to control the risk; it is liable for the solvency of institutions which it does not even select. Second, it was pointed out that this would create a new type of liability for banks which would have consequences for the law of bank supervision. The banks would have to cover these new risks with additional capital. Third, it was added that the mandatory guarantee will lead to serious distortions in competition. Globally active credit institutions carry out transfers internally worldwide. For these institutions, the problem of the solvency of intermediary banks arises only in the limited case where they do not have a direct relationship locally with the beneficiary's bank. By contrast, small and middle-sized credit institutions would have to rely on cooperation with intermediary banks. But these banks would not be in a position to guarantee the solvency of the intermediary banks. Fourth, it was clearly pointed out that bank directors would violate their duties owed to the bank if they accepted the risk of a credit transfer and the connected money-back guarantee without knowing all of the correspondent banks and having adequately analyzed their creditworthiness.

There was finally a consensus that the "money-back guarantee" would have to be taken into consideration in setting prices. The customer would, of course, have to pay for the additional liability. In order to avoid these costs, it was proposed that the credit institutions should be allowed the possibility of offering two types of transfers, namely one with the "money-back guarantee" and one without. This would demonstrate to the customer that he would have to pay an additional amount for a special service. But this proposal was not even seriously considered. One reason was that some countries wanted to enforce the rules of their national legal system worldwide — and were finally successful.

b) Two considerations convinced the Commission to provide at least for a small restriction. First, it was asserted with particular emphasis that the contraproductive result of the "money-back guarantee" would be that, in the future, credit institutions would simply reject payment orders directed to certain countries due to the risks involved. Second, it was pointed out that there is a danger that in the case of risky payments, the credit institutions would advise the customers to pay by check; here the customer would bear the full risk of delivery. For these reasons, it is now stipulated that in exceptional cases deviation may be made from the mandatory refund obligation. If an international transfer involves special risks, the "money-back guarantee" can be excluded "... when a prudent originator's bank would not have otherwise accepted a particular payment order because of a significant risk involved in the credit transfer" (Art. 14 (2)).

c) The refund guarantee also does not apply when the originator issues an instruction to engage a specific intermediary bank and this intermediary bank becomes insolvent or is prevented by reasons of law from executing the payment order. Credit institutions could, therefore, consider the possibility of accepting payment orders only on the condition that the customer consent to a specified chain of intermediary banks and issue the appropriate instruction. This possibility is expressly excluded in the Model Law in that the duty to make a refund is suspended only if the bank "does not systematically seek such directions".

d) The result of the "money-back guarantee" should be that each sender can demand refund of the transfer amount from the receiving bank. Within the chain of banks, the bank which selected the insolvent bank should finally bear the loss, even if it exercised proper care in this selection. It would, of course, require that the Model Law with its "money-back guarantee" be adopted in all relevant countries. In any case, the credit institutions would have to examine the solvency of their correspondent banks to a greater extent than in the past.

The Law also contains a special "skip rule". It is based on the concept that the originator has a contractual relationship only with the first receiving bank. However, he can demand the refund from any bank in the chain; and a credit institution within the chain is discharged with respect to the prior banks if it refunds the transfer amount to the originator.

7. Limited Compensation for Damages for Breach of Duties

a) It is obvious that credit institutions are particularly sensitive to those cases where transfers are not carried out on time and, as a result, substantial losses are incurred, e.g. where a contract between the originator and the beneficiary is rescinded due to failure to make timely payment or where an insurer does not provide coverage because the insurance premium was not paid on time. In this respect, the Model Law contains a limitation on liability which is quite favorable to credit institutions. The "banking system" — whatever this involves — is considered to be responsible for refunding the transfer amount to the originator if is does not reach the beneficiary. The "banking system" cannot, however, — it was argued — bear unforeseeable risks and damages resulting from delayed payments. We will not go into the justification of these deliberations here. In any case, it was stipulated that a bank which does not execute a payment order in a timely manner is liable to pay compensation. But the amount of this compensation is limited to the interest loss. All other forms of compensation claims of a contractual or statutory nature are to be excluded, unless a bank has improperly executed or failed to execute a payment order with the specific intent to cause loss or recklessly and with actual knowledge that loss would be likely to result (Art. 18).

b) In this way, the Model Law deals with the central issue of allocation of "float". Taking the contractual relationships into consideration, the claim for compensation for lost interest should belong to the originator. This would, of course, require that the respective credit institution have been responsible for the delay. The Model Law takes a different approach. The bank which does not execute a payment order within the time limit set in the Law — regardless of whether it was at fault for violating this duty — is liable to the beneficiary for the interest on the amount of the payment order for the period of delay, (Art. 17 (1)). The liability may be discharged by payment either to its receiving bank or by direct payment to the beneficiary. This does not represent a compensation claim or a claim for handing over of unjust enrichment, but instead it is a distinctive claim of "a special nature". The justification stated for this result is that is corresponds to banking practice in some countries.

X. The Practical Significance of the Model Law

In the drafting of the Model Law, consideration was given to the possibility of making it the object of an international convention. This approach was not adopted. In contrast, there is now substantial doubt whether all member states whose delegations exerted substantial influence in the drafting of the Model Law are prepared to accept the results.

In the European Communities, the situation is quite different.

— First, consideration is being given to the possibility of adopting the Model Law as a Directive. This would mean that the member states of the EC would be obligated to implement the Model Law. The working document of the Commission of the European Community "Easier Cross-Border Payments: Breaking Down the Barriers" of March 27, 1992, states, in a somewhat reserved manner, that the UNCITRAL Model Law should be "taken into consideration" during future work on eliminating differences in legal rules. But this is only one side.

— Second, one must keep in mind that the European Community has set the goal of achieving an internal market. This means that cross-border transactions should be handled in the same way as domestic transactions. A Directive would, therefore, not distinguish between international and national credit transfers. The result would be that adoption of the Model Law as a Directive would also determine the law of domestic transfers. In this way, the Model Law would achieve even more significance than originally thought. This is the other side.

International Initiatives for Rules Governing International Funds Transfers

By Uwe Blaurock and Peter Rennpferdt, Göttingen*

Contents

I. Delimitation of the Initiatives to be Examined

Execution of funds transfers across national borders touches on a number of issues in extremely varied legal areas, which have so far only partially been

* Translated by Dr. Frances Dielmann, Frankfurt/M.

dealt with in efforts by international or supranational organizations. An attempt to examine all of these efforts would substantially exceed the scope of this article. Most of the initiatives will only be mentioned here and a small selection examined in more detail.

1. Initiatives Not Analyzed in this Article

The sets of rules for international funds transfers which are the most significant at present and probably in the future as well are the S.W.I.F.T. communication system and the UNCITRAL Model Law on International Credit Transfers. These two systems are covered in separate articles in this volume.[1] The relevant initiatives by the EC to increase security, efficiency, and transparency in international funds transfers are also dealt with elsewhere.[2] We will, therefore, not go into those areas here.

The reform of funds transfer law in the U.S. in the years 1989-1990 are also described in another article.[3] The reform contained in Art. 4 A UCC and Regulation J are highly significant even outside the U.S.[4] because their application can under certain circumstances extend globally, i.e. it is not restricted only to transfers within the U.S. The American legal rules of liability in connection with funds transfers[5], which greatly differ from the respective German rules, cannot be covered here.

The harmonization of technical standards for international non-paper-based funds transfers[6], now progressing rapidly at various levels, can only be mentioned briefly here because these standards do not take direct legal effect but instead only indirectly when incorporated into a contractual relationship. A model of such a contract, a standard EDI (electronic data inter-

---

[1] See the articles in this volume by J. Etzkorn, on the S.W.I.F.T. rules, and U. H. Schneider on the UNCITRAL Model Law on International Credit Transfers.

[2] See e.g., Triumph für Europa: neue Kartenzahlungssysteme, KOM (86/754 of Jan. 12, 1987; Recommendation 88/590/EEC o. J. No. L/317/55 of 24. Nov. 1988); Recommendation 90/109/EEC, 14, Feb. 1990 (o. J. No. L 67/39 of 15 Mar. 1990).

[3] C. Felsenfeld, Article 4A of the United States Uniform Commercial Code.

[4] See 55 Fed. Reg. 40, 791, 40, 793 f. (1990).

[5] See Stockman, Liability of Intermediary and Beneficiary Banks in Fund Transfers: A Comparative Study of German and American Law, Masters Thesis, Los Angeles (1989) (unpublished).

[6] At the national level these are primarily the standards committee for offices [NBü] in the German Standards Institute (Deutsches Institut für Normung — DIN) and in particular the EDIFACT departments; at the international level: CEN/CENELEC as well as the International Organisation for Standardisation. See, e. g. ISO (ed.), Bank telecommunication — Funds transfer messages, at Part 1, Vocabulary and data elements, Reference No. ISO 7982-1:1987 (E) (new edition in preparation).

change) agreement[7] for the establishment of a communications order binding under civil law is presently being drafted at various national and international levels and is already partially in use. Electronic settlement by means of file transfer by the Hessian state central bank in the banking center Frankfurt/Main[8] is likewise based on an extensive EDI agreement. But the preparatory work in Germany[9], by the EC[10], by the International Chamber of Commerce[11] and in the United Nations Economic Commission for Europe[12] is still at such an early stage that no concrete model is yet apparent. Analysis of these initiatives would, therefore, not appear useful in this article.

All financial transactions, including domestic and international funds transfers, are subject to insolvency laws. In an age when many companies and private individuals have increasingly spread their assets throughout the world and these assets can be shifted from continent to continent by electronic means within seconds, it is obvious that national insolvency laws must be harmonized if the goal of uniform judicial execution is to be achieved or rather reestablished. For this purpose efforts have likewise been initiated at various international levels[13]; these have already been analyzed in

---

[7] EDI message: See definition from the „TEDIS" report (COM (90)) 361 ENDG. of July 25, 1990).

[8] On EAF see O. V., Neue Impulse im Zahlungsverkehr, Elektronische LZB-Abrechnung, Bankkaufmann, no. 8 1990, pp. 14-16; EAF, Bericht zum Abschluß des Pilotbetriebes (Landeszentralbank in Hessen ed., Frankfurt/Main 1990).

[9] In charge since 1991, the Arbeitsgemeinschaft für Wirtschaftliche Verwaltung e. V., in Eschborn, Germany, Working Group 10.3.

[10] Legal workshop within the TEDIS program of the EC Commission. See, Avant-projet de contrat-type règlant les modalités des échanges de données informatisées, Feb. 27, 1990, XIII-D-5 TED-LEG.

[11] Groupe de Travail Mixte, Comité juridique de l'EDI. The proposal by the International Chamber of Commerce of Sept. 22, 1987 can already be viewed as outdated because it did not go far enough. See, Uniform Rules of Conduct for interchange of trade data by teletransmission (UNCID), ICC Publication No. 452.

[12] Economic Commission for Europe (UN/ECE), Committee on the development of trade, Working-Party 4 (Facilitation of International Trade Procedures). The UN/ECE has so far received proposals by the delegations from the U.S.A. (Trade/WP.4/R 652 — 12/22/1985), Great Britain (Trade/WP.4/R 706 — 6/27/1990) and Canada (Trade/WP.4/R 732 — 12/4/1990).

[13] I. European Community. On June 26, 1980, the Commission of the European Community presented a draft convention on bankruptcy, reorganization and similar proceedings. This convention would supplement the convention on Jurisdiction and Enforcement of Judgments on Civil and Commercial Matters of Sept. 27, 1968. That "general convention" excludes bankruptcy, reorganization and similar proceedings from its scope of application. Also significant in this context: Amended Proposal for a Council Directive concerning the reorganization and the winding-up of credit institutions and deposit-guarantee schemes, O. J. EC No. C 36 of Feb. 8, 1988, p. 1.

II. The Council of Europe has also presented a draft for a European bankruptcy

detail.[14] Because this is an area of law not specifically limited to funds transfers, a brief reference should suffice here.

In addition to the UNCITRAL Model Law, the "Guidelines on International Interbank Funds Transfers and Compensation" of the International Chamber of Commerce in Paris are dedicated to the special legal issues of electronic funds transfers.[15] The common view is that these guidelines are not significant, at least for international transfers in industrialized countries, due to numerous defects.[16] For this reason, we will not examine them here.

No initiatives for legal provisions governing cross-border netting are apparent at this time, although substantial rationalization effects in terms of both time and costs can be expected.[17] The first apparent (private) proposal concerning the operation of multilateral settling of international payment obligations derives from Deeg[18] and has led to initial deliberations in this area.

2. *Objects of the Following Analysis*

The following analysis shall be limited primarily to the Conventions of the Council of Europe relating to the satisfaction of money debts and the corresponding initiatives by the Monetary Commission of the International Law Association (MOCOMILA).[19] In addition, proposals for harmoniza-

---

convention. It was prepared in 1984 and is published in German in Arnold, Entwurf eines europäischen Übereinkommens über den Konkurs, ZIP 1984, pp. 1152-1155.

III. International Bar Association. In June 1989 the International Bar Association adopted a Model International Insolvency Cooperation Act (MIICA). This is a model which enables national courts to participate in foreign insolvency proceedings.

[14] Thieme, Der Entwurf eines Konkursübereinkommens der EG-Staaten von 1980, RabelsZ 45 (1981), pp. 459-499; Thieme (ed.), Materialien zum ausländischen und Internationalen Privatrecht (v. 32, Tübingen 1988): proposals and analysis of the draft of an EC convention; Hoffmann, Banken- und Börsenrecht der EWG (Baden-Baden 1990), pp. 97 ff.; Arnold, supra note 13, at 1114-1152; Guillenschmidt, Projet de convention du Conseil de l'Europe sur certains aspects internationaux de la faillite, Banque et Droit 1989, pp. 191-194; Glosband/Katucki, Current Developments in International Insolvency Law and Practice, 45 Bus. Law. 2273, 2279 f. (1990).

[15] ICC (ed.), Publication No. 457, Paris 1990.

[16] Memorandum by the Bundesverband Deutscher Banken of July 27, 1988; Minutes of the meeting of the Legal Committee of the Fedération Bancaire de la Comunauté Européenne of Oct. 18/19, 1988, pp. 2 f. (both unpublished).

[17] See Polo, A perspective on the euronetting-Project, in: Payment Systems Worldwide 1990, pp. 46 f.: about 95 % of all currency transactions took place without a "real" basis, i. e. without an underlying exchange of goods and were not executed in fact but instead compensated by corresponding countertransactions.

[18] Deeg, A Proposal for a Multi-Currency Netting System, in: Payments Systems Worldwide 1990, pp. 40-45.

[19] Part II. below.

tion of laws for the protection of personal data will be described.[20] Finally, reference will be made to some lesser known or not yet completed initiatives.[21]

During the drafting of this article, two additional initiatives for the harmonization of contract law have made significant progress. One involves the work of the "Lando Commission" which is developing principles for uniform private law throughout the European Community. This work is being carried out for the EC Commission based on a resolution by the European Parliament of May 26, 1989.[22] The other is by a UNIDROIT working group on the same topic but in a global context. Both groups completed drafts for a uniform law of fulfillment at almost the same time. Both proposals are as yet unpublished and can therefore not be analyzed here with regard to money obligations. The two proposals differ little from the MOCOMILA models described below.

II. Initiatives for Harmonization of the Law Governing the Place of Performance for Money Liabilities

Any model of legal provisions regarding the place of performance for money liabilities must take three elements of performance into consideration, namely the place, the time and the object. With increasing physical distance between the creditor and the debtor, the significance of these elements increases because the duties involved in overcoming the distance and in the acceptance of the related risks and costs must be allocated between the parties. In cross-border funds transfers, the problems of contact with differing currency territories regularly arise as well.

By contrast, the recognition of deposit money as a fully adequate means of fulfillment of money debts is not a problem in international transfers. The mistrust in national legal systems against deposit money, expressed in the fact that payment by means of book money, as a rule, requires the creditor's consent if the effect of satisfaction of the debt is to be achieved[23], does not apply to cross-border payments. Unless otherwise stipulated by the parties,

---

[20] Part III. below.

[21] Part IV. below.

[22] O. J. EC No. 158, p. 400.

[23] This is the overwhelmingly prevailing view. See Soergel/Wolf, § 270 margin no. 2; Canaris, Bankvertragsrecht (3d ed., Munich, 1988) at margin no. 468 with further references; see also Schönle, Commentaire du projet de resolution du comité de droit monétaire-concernant l'harmonisation des dispositions légales nationales et des conventiones internationales régissant le moment de l'execution d'une dette d'argent (temps de paiement), Report of the ILA Conference 1984 in Paris, Part II. No. 25.

in international payment transactions the creation of an unconditional and irrevocable payment claim by the debtor in favor of the creditor in the underlying obligation against his bank is deemed to discharge the debt. A demand by the creditor for cash payment is generally viewed as an abuse of rights.[24]

The International Law Association and the Council of Europe are working on initiatives relating to the designation of the place of payment and the time of payment of (international) money debts as well as the handling of foreign currency obligations, which are intended to govern the cited performance elements for money debts in a uniform way internationally. None of these initiatives has yet been successful. The Conventions drafted by the Council of Europe have so far been ratified only by a few states.[25] But their provisions have achieved at least some practical effect due to their consistency with the corresponding provisions in the international uniform sales conventions[26] and their broad adoption in the law of the Netherlands.[27]

1. Reasons for Harmonization of the Law of Fulfillment of Money Liabilities

The minor success of legal harmonization efforts relating to the fulfillment of money liabilities within the past twenty years could lead to the assumption that harmonization in this area is not necessary. This assumption is not correct.

The volume of the cross-border flow of goods, services and capital is steadily rising and should increase even more in the common internal market in Europe. So far, little attention has been given to the fact that these streams of goods and services are generally matched by corresponding reverse flows of payments, which are subject to differing national legal systems. In the absence of stipulations to the contrary by the parties, these legal systems,

---

[24] Schönle, supra note 23, with additional references.

[25] The Convention on Foreign Money Obligations has so far been ratified only by Luxembourg, and the Convention on the Place of Payment by none of the member states of the Council of Europe.

[26] Hague Convention of July 1, 1964 on the Introduction of a Uniform Law on the International Sale of Goods, in Germany Art. 59 (1) Uniform Sales Act [EKG]; see von Caemmerer, in: Dölle (ed.), Kommentar zum einheitlichen Kaufrecht, (Munich 1976) at Art. 59 EKG, margin no. 7 f.; United Nations Convention of April 11, 1980 on the International Sale of Goods [CISG], in Germany Art. 57 CISG (BGBl. II 1989, p. 588); see Schlechtriem/Hager, Kommentar zum Einheitlichen UN-Kaufrecht — CISG, (Munich 1990), at Art. 57 CISG, margin no. 4 ff.

[27] See the reference in van Boeschoten/Smits, ILA Draft Rules on the Time of Payment of Monetary Obligations, ILA Warsaw Conference (1988), MOCOMILA Report, pp. 18, 19.

through statutes or case law rules, govern the rights and obligations, in particular the allocation of risks, in very different ways.

While the safety standards with which products in cross-border exchanges of goods must comply are usually contained in public regulatory law and are internationally equivalent to a great extent already, the gaps between the various national civil law models, at least in the area of optional law (provisions which may be modified by the parties to a contract), are still substantial.[28] For example, the failure to properly satisfy a money debt has substantial effects with respect to the corresponding performance obligation of the counterparty, e.g. bearing of costs and risks or, in the case of an insurance contract, regarding the existence of insurance coverage.[29] Because the place of performance serves in almost all legal systems as an important connecting factor for procedural and conflict of laws issues[30], the use of different methods in the debtor's and the creditor's country for fixing the place of performance leads to unsatisfactory consequences with regard to substantive law, procedural law, and conflicts issues.

As an illustration of the often paradoxical results, for example differing national rules governing the connecting factors for the determination of the applicable law, the case of a money debt between a Swiss debtor and his German creditor is often used[31]: Under Swiss law[32], the place of payment is the residence of the creditor, but under German law[33], it is usually the residence of the debtor. Therefore, a different result is reached depending upon whether the case is decided before a Swiss or a German court. In cases where the decisive connecting factor for the choice of law is the place of payment, the Swiss judge would look to the residence of the German creditor and apply German law to the contractual relationship. The German judge, on the other hand, would view the residence of the Swiss debtor as the place of payment and then apply Swiss substantive law.

The legal consequences of a single international set of facts thus differ depending upon which court hears the case, with the result that, for example, in a Swiss court insurance coverage would be held to exist based on the fact that money was sent but in a German decision loss of the money underway

---

[28] See also U. H. Schneider/Troberg, Finanzdienstleistungen im EG-Binnenmarkt: Sitzland- oder Gastlandrecht, WM 1990, pp. 165, 170 ff.

[29] See Schönemann, Der Erfüllungsort, dissertation Tübingen 1935 (Würzburg 1936), pp. 11 ff.

[30] See Schack, Der Erfüllungsort im deutschen, ausländischen und internationalen Privat- und Zivilprozeßrecht (Frankfurt/Main 1985).

[31] See Rabel, The Conflict of Laws, v. II, 473 ff. (2d ed., 1960); Schack, Internationales Zivilverfahrensrecht (Munich 1991), p. 103, with additional references to other foreign legal systems.

[32] Art. 74 (2) no. 1 Obligationenrecht (law of contracts).

[33] See § 269 German Civil Code [BGB].

would result in no coverage. With respect to legal certainty, this result is unacceptable; a harmonization of the rules for determining the place of performance would certainly be desirable.

2. Place of Payment

Following preparatory work by the MOCOMILA in 1966[34], the Council of Europe through the European Committee for Legal Cooperation (CCJ)[35] in the years 1966-1969 drafted the European Convention on the Place of Payment of Money Liabilities.[36] In contrast to the proposal by the MOCOMILA, the scope of application of this convention is not limited to international transactions, but is intended to cover domestic money debts as well. The reason for this extension was that the national or international character of a money debt under the Convention text is dependent upon the respective residences of both parties. It did not appear reasonable to have the law applicable to an obligation which was already in existence change in case one of the parties moved to a different country.[37]

a) The Determination of the Place of Payment under the Council of Europe Convention

The most significant provisions concerning the place of payment are the following[38]:

Article 1

Unless a different intention of the parties appears or a different usage is applicable, the place of payment of money liabilities shall be determined by the following rules.

---

[34] For the text of the proposal which was not formally adopted, see Küng, Zahlung und Zahlungsort im internationalen Privatrecht, dissertation (Freiburg, Switzerland, 1970), p. 116.

[35] Comité européen de Cooperation juridique = European Committee on Legal Co-Operation; since 1963 CDCJ (Comité Directeur Européen de Cooperation Juridique).

[36] For the text of the Convention and supplements, see Council of Europe (ed.), Explanatory Report on the European convention on the place of payment of money liabilities (Straßbourg, 1972) (in English and French). The most important substantive provisions are found in Appendix I to the Convention, printed in French in Schmelcher, Der Erfüllungsort von Geldschulden (Der Zahlungsort), dissertation Basel 1972 (typed manuscript), p. 136.

[37] Mezger, L'unifiction du lieu de paiement des obligations monétaires, Journal du Droit International 94 (1967), pp. 584, 586.

[38] These are found in Annex I to the Convention. It appears that there is not yet an official German translation of this convention. An unofficial translation of the explanatory report is printed in Rennpferdt, Die internationale Harmonisierung des Erfüllungsrechts für Geldschulden, dissertation Göttingen 1992, Appendix I (forthcoming).

Article 2

1. Payment shall be made at the creditor's habitual residence at the time of payment.

2. Nevertheless if the creditor so requires, payment shall be made at any other place in the State of the creditor's habitual residence at the time of payment or at any place in the State of the creditor's habitual residence at the time when the liability arose.

Article 3

1. Where the application of the provision of Article 2 would require payment to be made at a place other than the creditor's habitual residence at the time when the liability arose and the discharge of the liability would be rendered substantially more onerous in consequence thereof, the debtor may refuse to pay at such place.

2. In the event of such refusal, the place of payment shall be the place of the creditor's habitual residence at the time when the liability arose, provided that the debtor may defer payment at that place until the creditor shall have arranged for the payment to be received there by him or on his behalf. Nevertheless the creditor may designate another place in the State where the creditor had his habiltutal residence at the time when the liability arose, at which, subject to paragraph 1 of the present article, payment shall be made by the debtor.

Article 4

Where in accordance with the provisions of Article 2 or of Article 3, paragraph 2, payment is to be made at a place other than the creditor's habitual residence at the time when the liability arose, any increase in the expenses or any financial loss resulting from the change in the place of payment shall be borne by the creditor.

Article 5

Where the liability arises in the course of the creditor's professional or business activity, the "place of business" where this activity is carried on shall, in the preceding articles, be substituted for the "habitual residence" of the creditor.

b) Comparison with German Rules

The basic rule in the convention text is that the place of payment is at the respective residence[39] of the creditor. Although no unambiguous definition of the term "place of payment" is given, it is clear that it is consistent with the

[39] See also, Resolution (72) 1 on the Standardisation of the legal concepts of "domicile" and of "residence", of Jan. 18, 1972, published in Council of Europe (ed.), Resolutions and Recommendations of the Committee of Ministers in the fields of civil, commercial, public and international law, v. I (Straßbourg, 1983); the recommendation is consistent with German law.

"place of fulfillment" (Erfüllungsort) within the meaning of §§ 269, 270 German Civil Code [BGB], i.e. the place where the (last) characteristic act is performed by the debtor.

The concept of the place of fulfillment (Erfüllungsort) has gained a bad reputation due to its use in varied and conflicting ways in German substantive and procedural law.[40] In more recent scholarship, this term is usually reserved for procedural law and international conflict of laws. The term "place of performance" (Leistungsort) is also problematic. It is able to describe the spatial aspect of the substantive act of fulfillment as long as the location of the act of performance and that of the outcome are the same. This is true where the obligation is to be performed at the debtor's residence (in German: "Holschuld") or at the creditor's residence (in German :"Bringschuld"). For long-distance transactions, German law also recognizes a mixed form, the "Schickschuld" ("obligation to send"), in which the last act of performance by the debtor (sending payment) takes place at a location different from that where the result of the performance occurs, i.e. where the creditor is satisfied. Despite some diverging proposals in the legal literature[41], in the interest of clarity in the international discussion, separate terms for the place of the act of performance and the place where the outcome of the performance occurs should preferably be used.

In Anglo-American legal circles, the German solutions have encountered complete lack of understanding. Nußbaum has called the model of the "Schickschuld" a "complete distortion of the place-of-payment conception, nothing being actually paid at that place since the real payment is made at the place of destination".[42] But this objection would be valid only if the word "payment" could be understood only in the sense of the outcome of the payment. Weitnauer has previously shown that the terms "payment", "Zahlung" and "paiement" can refer to the act as well as the outcome.[43]

In contrast to German[44], French[45], Belgian[46], Luxembourg[47], Austrian[48], and Spanish[49] law, the Convention designates the place of payment as being

---

[40] See only Gernhuber, Die Erfüllung und ihre Surrogate pp. 8 ff. (Tübingen, 1983), with additional references; Schack, supra note 31, at margin no. 1.

[41] Id. with additional references.

[42] Nußbaum, Money in the Law, National and International (Brooklyn, 1950), pp. 147 f.

[43] Weitnauer, Das Urteil des Schiedsgerichtshof für das Abkommen über deutsche Auslandsschulden vom 3.7.1958 und die Frage des Zahlungsorts, WM 1960, pp. 1286, 1294.

[44] §§ 269 f. BGB.

[45] Art. 1247 Code civile.

[46] Art. 1247 Belgian Code civile.

[47] Art. 1247 Code civile of Luxembourg.

the respective residence of the creditor and thus chooses the system of the "Bringschuld". In the view of the commission of experts of the Council of Europe, "neither social nor other reasons [justify] the preference of the interests of the debtor or the creditor over those of the other".[50] Therefore the Council of Europe based its choice solely on the consideration that the majority of its member states[51] as well as the uniform international sales conventions[52] employ the "Bringschuld" system. Only with respect to obligations based on statutory debts is there a legal argumentation under which the delivery of the amount owed is viewed as a component of the principle of the restitutio in integrum.[53]

This decision runs diametrically opposite to the German dispositive law of money debts, at least under the presently prevailing view.[54] Under §§ 269 (1) and 270 (4) German Civil Code, in the absence of a stipulation to the contrary by the parties or other circumstances, the payment of money debts is to be made at the place where the debtor had his residence at the time the obligation arose. But in case of doubt, the debtor must send the money at his own cost and risk to the residence or place of business of the creditor.[55] Under German law, a money debt is a limited "Schickschuld" because in contrast to the pure "Schickschuld", the debtor bears the risk of loss during the transmittal of the money. The separation of the risk of delay, which the creditor must bear, is a special characteristic of German law, which has often been rightfully criticized[56], and which certainly cannot survive international harmonization.

---

[48] § 905 Austrian Civil Code.

[49] Art. 1171 p. 3. C. c.

[50] Council of Europe (ed.), Explanatory Report on the European Convention on the place of payment of money liabilities, par. 33.

[51] See e.g. for Switzerland and Turkey: Art. 74 of the Obligationenrecht; Greece: Art. 321 Civil Code [ZGB]; the Netherlands: Art. 6.1.9.A.4, 5 Civil Code [BWB]; Italy: Art. 1182 C. civ., Portugal: art. 774 C. civ. as well as the laws of the Scandinavian countries, Cyprus and England. (See the references in v. Caemmerer, Zahlungsort, in: Internationales Recht und Wirtschaftsordnung, Festschrift für F. A. Mann, Munich 1977, at 3, 4; Schönle, Ort und Zeit bargeldloser Zahlung, in: Festschrift für Werner (1984), p. 817; Schack, supra note 31, at margin no. 261, 268, 288.

[52] Art. 59 (1) EKG, and v. Caemmerer, in Kommentar zum einheitlichen Kaufrecht (H. Dölle, ed., Munich 1976), at Art. 59 EKG, margin no. 7 f.; Art. 57 CISG, and Schlechtriem & Hager, supra note 26, Art. 57 CISG; Schlechtriem/Hager, at Art. 57 CISG, margin no. 4 ff.

[53] Council of Europe, supra note 50 at no. 33.

[54] At first the legislative intent in Germany was also to structure money debts as "bringing obligations". The wording of § 270 (4) BGB was meant only to avoid having the place of payment establish jurisdiction in the courts at the creditor's place of residence in accordance with § 29 of the German Code of Civil Procedure [ZPO]. See in more detail, Schack, supra note 31 at margin no. 193 f.; v. Caemmerer, supra note 51, at 6-8.

[55] § 270 (1), (2) BGB.

The place of performance, in the sense of the place of the act of performance, has diverse functions in German law.[57] This was recognized by the committee of experts of the Council of Europe. The committee was of the opinion, however, that issues of jurisdiction and venue were outside the Convention's scope of application. This approach, which was also used with respect to the U.N. Sales Convention[58], merely shifts the problems. The Convention applies mandatorily in these areas and forces the national legislators to undertake extensive amendments in legal areas which are expressly not intended to be subjects of the Conventions.[59]

Because most other legal systems also tie important legal consequences to the place of performance[60], a Convention which demands a change in the corresponding national concepts encounters substantial problems in seeking acceptance in the national legal systems.[61]

c) Criticism of the Provisions in the European Convention

Substantial concerns exist regarding the provisions in the European Convention relating to the place of payment of money liabilities. The designation of the place of performance as the respective residence of the creditor at the time the debt falls due is not practical. It forces the debtor to continually check on where his creditors maintain their residences or places of business. The Convention text does not provide for a duty on the part of the creditor to give notice to the debtor.[62] And if the creditor's whereabouts at the time the debt falls due cannot be determined, no alternate place of deposit is stipulated.[63] The numerous choices of the place of performance

[56] Nußbaum, Das Geld in Theorie und Praxis des deutschen und ausländischen Rechts (1925), pp. 72 ff.; Klingsporn, WM 1972, pp. 1262, 1266; Fikentscher, Schuldrecht 145 at § 35 III 3 c (7th ed. 1985), v. Caemmerer, supra note 51, at 10, with additional references.

[57] See the references in Schack, supra note 31; Schönemann, supra note 29.

[58] See Schlechtriem/Hager, at Art. 57 CISG, margin no. 11.

[59] The implementation of the convention would also require extensive statutory amendments in Austria; see the list in Verschraegen, Gesamtevaluierung der Europaratskonventionen aus österreichischer Sicht — mit Prüfung der bisher von Österreich noch nicht ratifizierten Übereinkommen, in: Österreich im Europarat 1956 - 1986 (Hummer & Wagner, ed., Vienna, 1988), pp. 443, 449 n. 50.

[60] Id.

[61] On the significance of acceptance for success of the European legal harmonization generally, see Blaurock, Wege zur Rechtseinheit im Zivilrecht Europas, in: Rechtsvereinheitlichung durch Gesetze (Starck, ed. Göttingen, 1992).

[62] The U. N. International Sales Convention offers a solution in which under Art. 80 the creditor must accept payment at his original residence unless he gives notice to the debtor of a new residence. See Schlechtriem/Hager, at Art. 57 CISG, margin no. 6.

[63] Klingsporn, Das Europäische Übereinkommen über den Ort der Zahlung von Geldschulden, WM 1972, p. 1262, 1265.

provided to the creditor also appear unnecessary and are an unreasonable burden for the debtor. A flexible place of performance should also be rejected for reasons of principle because the place of performance is used in many conflict of laws rules as a (subsidiary) connecting factor; the place of jurisdiction and, in case of a cross- border move by the creditor the choice of law as well, are not foreseeable for the debtor. The MOCOMILA draft of 1966 provided for a fixed place of performance based on the place where the creditor resided at the time when the contractual obligation arose.[64]

In contrast to the view of the Council of Europe, the preponderance of reasons support fixing the place of performance for contractual monetary obligations at the residence of the debtor. Sending money is more convenient than collecting money at a foreign location[65]; therefore, it is quite reasonable, in the absence of a stipulation to the contrary by the parties, to assign to the debtor the duty to send the money. But the establishment of a principle under which the debtor would, as a rule, have to seek out the creditor at a foreign location, as is the case with a "Bringschuld", would overshoot the intended goal.

The codification of the "Holschuld", where the creditor must collect the money at the debtor's residence, should likewise not be considered. The appropriate means of payment, the debit transfer, is too complicated to be used for non-repetitive payments due to the necessity of prior (written) consent by the debtor.

It would make sense and would also be consistent with actual practice to codify a (limited) "Schickschuld": the debtor would be required to send[66] the money by a certain time, and he would be liable for the careful selection of an intermediary. The sending of the money would be timely only if in accordance with the ordinary course of events it could be expected that the amount would be received by the creditor or his receiving agent by the due date.

The question of a reasonable rule of liability with respect to the risks of loss and delay cannot be examined here in detail.[67] We would only like to point out that fixing the place of the act of performance, as derived from § 270 German Civil Code, does not by necessity also resolve the allocation of costs and risks. And it would scarcely make sense to assign to the debtor the duty to send the money based on the fact that it would be less of a burden for him than for the creditor to collect the money at a foreign location and then to also assign to the debtor all of the dangers arising in connection with this

---

[64] "Monetary obligations shall be paid at the place where the creditor resided at the time when the obligation arose."

[65] See Heck, Schuldrecht (Tübingen, 1929), at § 6.6 p. 24.

[66] As a rule by means of a credit transfer.

[67] For more detail, see Rennpferdt, supra note 38.

convenience for the creditor. In combination with the liability allocation rules of the sales shipment, a double privilege for the seller of the goods would arise; the seller is regularly released from liability upon proper handing over of the goods to the freight carrier so that he would not bear the transport risk for the goods or for the payment of the purchase price.

In long distance transactions, intermediaries are almost always engaged to overcome the distance between the creditor and the debtor. This fact should lead to a legal norm which does not presume that one or the other party will go to the residence of the other party in order to fulfill his obligation ("Bringschuld" system). Instead, rules should govern the duties of the parties at their respective residences as well as the allocation of costs and risks.

3. Time of Payment

The time at which a payment has to be made depends, among other factors, on the method of calculation of the time period. For this purpose, the European Convention on the Calculation of Time Limits[68] was drafted. It is consistent with German law.[69]

Where a "Holschuld" or "Bringschuld" is involved, an express stipulation of the time at which the payment is made or deemed to be made is not necessary. The time of payment is the time of the act of payment at the place of payment. Due to the diverse types of payment, the MOCOMILA did view it as necessary to include separate provisions for each type of payment instrument governing the time a payment is made or deemed to be made.

a) The Rules Governing the Time of Payment under the Draft by the Monetary Commission of the International Law Association

Rule 1: Basic rule on time of payment

Payment is deemed to be made at the moment when the amount due is effectively put at the disposal of the creditor.

Rule 2: Payment by bank or giro transfer

Payment by bank or giro transfer, including electronic funds transfer (EFT), is deemed to be made at the moment when the amount due has been unconditionally credited to the creditor's account.

---

[68] See the European Convention on the Calculation of Time-Limits, Europ. T. S. No. 76 of May 16, 1972; the convention has been in effect since April 28, 1983.

[69] §§ 186 - 193 BGB.

Rule 3: Payment by cheque

Payment by cheque is deemed to be made at the moment when the creditor received the cheque, subject to the condition that the creditor's bank[70] will credit the amount due to his account.

Rule 4: Payment by unconditionally guaranteed instrument of payment

Payment by an unconditionally guaranteed instrument of payment, such as guaranteed postal cheques, guaranteed Eurocheques and guaranteed credit cards, is deemed to be made at the moment when the creditor receives the cheque or, in the case of payment by credit card, has completed the appropriate procedures in respect thereof.

b) Analysis

These rules are primarily a particularization of the system of the "Bringschuld". But the rules would also be appropriate for a "Schickschuld" system and would be desirable in the interest of legal clarity. It is not fair to require that the creditor wait for an almost unlimited time for the money which has been sent, whether by transfer of deposit money or by check. With respect to his duty to minimize damages in accordance with § 254 German Civil Code, a precise date on which he must inform the debtor of the absence of the payment would be desirable. German law initially took this direction[71] but has been so extensively changed in case law rules and legal scholarship that the time of sending is now sufficient for compliance with the due date and any delay in receipt of the payment acts solely to the disadvantage of the creditor.[72] This result is unreasonable at least to the extent that the late receipt of payment by the creditor was foreseeable by the debtor and could have been avoided by timely sending of payment and proper selection of the means of transmittal. New rules governing the law of satisfaction of money obligations at an international level would be a welcome opportunity to shift the risk of foreseeable delay back to the debtor.[73]

---

[70] The wording of this provision is imprecise. In fact, whether the creditor's bank credits the amount (as a rule conditional upon receipt of cover) cannot be decisive, but instead the fact that the drawee honors the check. This is also the interpretation of the Chairman of the MOCOMILA; see Hahn, Grenzüberschreitende Umschuldungen bei bargeldlosen Geldbewegungen, ZfgK 1985, p. 190, 194.

[71] v. Caemmerer, supra note 51, at 9, with additional references.

[72] See only Palandt-Heinrichs, at § 270 margin no. 6, with additional references.

[73] The (actual) unforeseeable delay risks, such as political risks, should be classified in the same way as risks of loss. V. Caemmerer is also opposed to a distinction between risk of delay and risk of loss, supra note 51 at 10, with additional references.

The MOCOMILA proposal is not yet fully refined. First, payment by draft is not included at all. In addition, from a German perspective, a rule governing the time of payment of simple collection documents, such as the debit transfer which is very widely used in Germany[74], is lacking. The respective proposal by Schönle[75] also contained such a provision with a notice of the need for an agreement between the debtor and the creditor regarding the transformation of the money obligation into a "Holschuld". This proposal was consistent with German law presently in effect.[76]

4. Obligations in Foreign Currency

a) Drafting History of the Council of Europe Convention

The oldest international convention by the Council of Europe concerning issues of international[77] payments, the European Convention on Foreign Money Liabilities of Dec. 11, 1967[78], was similarly based on a 1956 draft prepared by the Monetary Commission of the International Law Association[79], in which Mann and Gutzwiller were significantly involved.[80] The Convention was promptly signed by the Federal Republic of Germany, but due to the necessary connection with the Convention on the Place of Payment of Money Obligations, ratification was initially postponed as in most other member states of the Council of Europe.[81] The compromise with respect to the designation of the place of payment of money obligations, which was found to be unsatisfactory by most member states, finally led to the failure of the entire project.[82]

---

[74] In 1990, more than 3 billion payments were carried out by means of debit transfers in Germany.

[75] Supra note 23 at no. 37 f.

[76] Canaris, supra note 23, at margin no. 628 f., 635 f.

[77] In accordance with its wording, the draft convention is not applicable only to international payments; but in practice the payments involved will usually be international ones because a contract for foreign currency obligations between two residents of Germany requires permission under § 3 of the Currency Law.

[78] European Convention on Foreign Money Liabilities, ETS 60 1967, printed in: Council of Europe (ed.), Explanatory Report on the European Convention on Foreign Money Liabilities (Straßbourg 1968), pp. 13 ff., and in French in Küng, supra note 34, at 126 ff., Appendix II.

[79] Preliminary work by the ILA began in 1926: the so-called "Vienna Rules" were adopted at the 34th Conference in Vienna (printed in French in Nußbaum, Vertraglicher Schutz gegen Schwankungen des Geldwertes (Berlin, Leipzig, 1928), p. 94 f.). The French text of the ILA "Dubrovnik Convention" of 1956 is found in Küng, supra note 34, at 123 ff., Appendix I.

[80] Weitnauer, supra note 43, WM 1960, p. 1286, 1291.

[81] Klingsporn, supra note 63, WM 1972, p. 1262, 1263.

[82] See part II, 2. above.

The beginnings had been quite positive. Following thorough preparatory work by the International Law Association, a draft by the Council of Europe for a convention on the payment of foreign money liabilities was completed in 1959.[83] The goal of this draft was the harmonization of legislation and case law rules in the European countries with respect to the requirements under which a foreign currency obligation can effectively be paid in foreign currency (true foreign currency liability) and which rate of exchange is determinative in the case of a quasi foreign currency liability.

Article 10 of this draft contained its own definition of the place of payment, which was doubly ambiguous and therefore unusable.[84] In particular, consideration was not given to the fact that in the legal systems of the member states of Germany and Austria money obligations are "Schickschulden", i.e. the place of the act of performance and the place where the result of the performance occurs are not the same. A provision under which the place of payment is the place where the payment is owed is too vague in this context. It was also unclear whether the determinative place is that where payment is in fact made or where it should have been made in accordance with the contract.[85]

Because the views regarding the concept of the place of payment had already irreconcilably collided[86] in a proceeding before the court of arbitration for the convention on German foreign debts[87], it can be presumed that this issue was first postponed and reserved for a separate convention. In any case, the final convention no longer contained an express provision on the place of payment. It was merely negatively stipulated, in contrast to the decision by the Reichsgericht (Supreme Court of the German Reich)[88], that the place where payment is actually made is not to be deemed the "place of payment".[89]

The Council of Europe Convention on Foreign Money Liabilities, like that regarding the place of payment, was unsuccessful. It was signed only by Germany and three other states and ratified only by Luxembourg.[90]

---

[83] Council of Europe Document No. 1023 of Aug. 27, 1959.

[84] See the five alternate interpretations in Weitnauer, supra note 43, WM 1960, p. 1286, 1292.

[85] Regarding the dispute, see RGZ 101, p. 312.

[86] See the excerpts from the arguments published in Weitnauer, supra note 43, WM 1960, p. 1262, 1268 ff.

[87] Decision of July 3, 1958; excerpts published in WM 1958, p. 1170.

[88] RGZ 101, p. 312.

[89] Annex, Art. 8 of the Convention in conjunction with the related explanatory report; see Council of Europe (ed.), Explanatory Report on the European Convention on Foreign Money Liabilities, No. 34 (Straßbourg, 1968).

[90] Loewe views disinterest on the part of the member states of the Council of Europe as the major reason; see Loewe, Europarat, Rechtsvereinheitlichung und Rechtsharmonisie-

b) The Most Significant Provisions in the European Convention on Foreign Money Liabilities

Article 1

1. A sum of money due in a currency which is not that of the place of payment may be paid in the currency of the place of payment, unless a different intention of the parties appears, or a different usage is applicable.

2. The debtor may not avail himself of this option if he knows or ought to know that payment in the currency of the place of payment would involve for the creditor a substantial prejudice.

Article 2

If a sum of money is due in currency other than that of the place of payment, the creditor may, if the debtor is unable, or alleges his inability, to make settlement in that currency, require payment in the currency of the place of payment.

Article 3

If, in accordance with Article 1 or 2, the debtor pays in the currency of the place of payment, the conversion shall be effected at the rate of exchange at the date of actual payment.

Article 4

1. If the debtor does not pay at the date of maturity and if after such date the currency in which the sum of money is due depreciates in relation to the currency of the place of payment, the debtor, whether he pays in the currency due or in the currency of the place of payment as provided in the preceding Articles, shall pay an additional amount equivalent to the difference between the rate of exchange at the date of maturity and the date of actual payment.

2. Nevertheless, the above-mentioned additional amount shall not be payable to the extent that the inability of the debtor is due to default of the creditor, or to force majeure, or the creditor has not suffered loss resulting from the depreciation. The debtor bears the burden of proof.

3. The provisions of paragraph 1 do not in any way limit other rights which the creditor may be in a position to claim from the debtor.

---

rung im Bereich des Zivilrechts, in: Österreich im Europarat 1969 - 1986 387, 392 f. (Hummer & Wagner, ed., Vienna, 1988).

Article 5

In the event of any proceedings for the recovery of a sum of money expressed in a currency other than that of the forum, the creditor may, at his choice, demand payment in the currency to which he is entitled or the equivalent in the currency of the forum at the rate of exchange at the date of actual payment.

Article 6

Article 4 remains applicable even if during proceedings instituted in conformity with Article 5, the currency in which the sum of money is due depreciates in relation to the currency of the place of payment.

Article 7

1. If a judgment entitles the creditor either to a sum of money in a currency other than that of the forum or the equivalent of such a sum in the currency of the forum, and a depreciation of the currency other than that of the forum in relation to that of the forum occurs between the date of the judgment and the date of actual payment, the debtor is obliged to pay an additional amount corresponding to the difference between the rate of exchange at the date of the judgment and the date of actual payment.

2. The provisions of paragraphs 2 and 3 of Article 4 shall apply mutatis mutandis.

Article 8

The place of payment referred to in the preceding Articles shall be the place where payment is due.

Article 9

For the application of the preceding Articles the rate of exchange shall be that intended by the parties, or, failing such intention, that which may enable the creditor to procure the sum due without delay. Usages shall be taken into account.

c) Criticism

In principle, the provisions in the Convention are consistent with the presently effective German law regarding foreign currency liabilities, in particular § 244 German Civil Code. The provision in Article 7 of the Convention conflicts with the principle of procedural economy. The stipulation of the permissibility of having the court decision state the debt owed in foreign currency is fully sufficient in the interest of the creditor if a forced execution is carried out on the basis of a quasi foreign currency liability converted at the foreign exchange rate in effect at the time of execution. The duty to pay the balance in accordance with Art. 7 (1), which applies in any case, would make the fixing of the respective exchange rate appear inappropriate.

5. Overall Evaluation of Initiatives Involving the Law of the Place of Performance

Harmonization of the law governing the place of performance for money obligations is, in principle, a worthwhile goal because it would help to facilitate international trade. But the cited initiatives by the Council of Europe and the International Law Association are not well-balanced and are partially outdated; therefore, they have no chance of success.[91] A redrafting of the texts of its conventions is now being recommended by the Council of Europe in light of economic developments[92]; for this reason, Switzerland, among other states, has ceased efforts to ratify the convention.[93]

Within the framework of this redrafting, efforts should be made to evaluate the usefulness of the various national legal solutions, including the German model of the "Schickschuld". Modernization and consideration of procedural economy would also appear desirable with respect to the handling of foreign currency obligations. Ideas are also present for changes in the German law of the place of performance regarding the issue of timeliness of the act of payment.

III. Initiative regarding the Law of Protection of Personal Data[94]

The customer data contained in transfer orders are personal data within the meaning of § 1 (2) of the Federal Data Protection Act [BDSG][95], which

[91] See Verschraegen, supra note 59, at 433, 449.

[92] See Conseil de l'Europe (ed.), Communication du comité des ministres relative à l'evaluation des certains traitées du Conseil de l'Europe, doc. no. 5427 of June 27, 1988, p. 8 (regarding the convention on foreign money obligations), and at 36 (regarding the convention on the place of payment).

[93] See 3. Bericht über die Schweiz und die Konventionen des Europarates vom 22.2.1984, Swiss BGBl 1984, v. I, p. 784, 809 ff.

[94] Initiatives in addition to those expressly cited below are found in Kilian, Datensicherheit in Computernetzen, CR 1991, pp. 73-80.

[95] Law to Protect Against the Misuse of Personal Data in Data Processing (Federal Data Protection Act) [BDSG], of Jan. 27, 1977 (BGBl. I, p. 201).

are stored in, amended, erased or transmitted from data files.[96] The Data Protection Act is, therefore applicable to (international) funds transfers.

The permissibility of cross-border transmission of personal data within the scope of funds transfers is dependent upon whether the transmitting party is a legal entity under public law or a private law institution, governed by part 2[97] or part 3[98] of the Data Protection Act. With respect to data processing by non- public entities for third parties, e.g. the SCHUFA which provides data regarding creditworthiness[99], § 32 BDSG must also be considered.

The cited provisions of the BDSG apply as national law only in Germany with the result that the level of protection for the affected parties in an international data transfer differs greatly. The diversity of legal provisions internationally can endanger interests of the parties worthy of protection, and the data transmission can be impermissible. The payment itself is, as a rule, carried out in accordance with the purpose of the contractual relationship between the affected party and the transmitting entity and is, therefore, permissible; it cannot be guaranteed, however, that the receiving entity will likewise use the data only for the intended contractual purposes.

From the perspective of the applicable law, data export on a contractual basis, even to countries with no data protection statute such as Belgium and Italy, is permissible.[100] But gaps in protection can occur here which make it appear advisable that the level of protection be harmonized internationally.

The OECD[101], which began in 1969 to examine the problems of data security and the international flow of data[102], soon began to point out the dangers of automatic processing of personal data to the individual's sphere of privacy. It was necessary to constantly attempt to achieve a balance between the directly conflicting economic interests in a free flow of data and the interests of the affected individual in the protection of his sphere of privacy. The OECD recommendations[103], which have been adopted in the

---

[96] Etzkorn, Rechtsfragen des Internationalen elektronischen Zahlungsverkehrs durch S.W.I.F.T., dissertation, Cologne, 1990 (Berlin, New York, 1991), p. 86.

[97] § 11 sentence 3 BDSG.

[98] § 24 BDSG.

[99] Schutzgemeinschaft für allgemeine Kreditsicherung.

[100] Bergmann, Grenzüberschreitender Datenschutz (Baden-Baden, 1985), p. 87.

[101] Further references regarding the historical development of international initiatives on data protection are found in Bergmann, supra note 100.

[102] Bergmann, supra note 100 at 143 with additional references.

[103] Guidelines Governing the Protection of Privacy and Transfrontier Flows of Personal Data, Doc. C (80) 58 (Final), of Sept. 23, 1980 = Empfehlung des Rates für wirtschaftliche Zusammenarbeit und Entwicklung über Richtlinien für den Schutz des Persönlichkeitsbereichs und den grenzüberschreitenden Verkehr personenbezogeener Daten, pub-

meantime, do not guarantee a sufficient level of protection[104]; they are almost meaningless at least in the European context. More significant are the initiatives by the Council of Europe, namely the European Convention No. 108 for the protection of persons in the automatic processing of personal data[105], which has been ratified or at least signed by the majority of the members of the Council of Europe. Following a long period of restraint, the European Community has now also offered a proposal for resolution of this issue[106], whose chances of success are uncertain because it would lead to a level of protection as yet unknown in most of the member states.

The only initiative directed toward the resolution of issues connected with the cross-border exchange of data related to funds transfers also comes from the Council of Europe, the recommendation for "Protection of Personal Data used for Payment and Other Related Operations".[107] The proposed provisions are characterized by a high level of protection without interfering with the funds transfer process. On many points, these provisions could be viewed as a particularization of the German Federal Data Protection Act. If this recommendation should be adopted in national legal systems, which already appears to be in doubt in some countries[108], international payments would no longer present a problem of data protection law at least between the member states of the Council of Europe.

The only moderate success of the legal harmonization efforts of the Council of Europe is in part a result of the low level of publicity of its work. For this reason, the recommendation by the Council of Europe for Protection of Personal Data used for Payment and Other Related Operations is included as a supplement to this article.[109]

lished in German in: Burhenne & Perband, EDV-Recht (looseleaf, Berlin, 1990 update) at no. 201 11.

[104] For more detail as to the reasons: Bergmann, supra note 100, at 174 ff.

[105] Of Jan. 28, 1981, in effect since Oct. 1, 1985. Ratified by the Federal Republic of Germany on May 13, 1985, BGBl. II, p. 538. Also ratified by Austria, Denmark, France, Ireland, Luxembourg, Norway, Sweden, Spain, Great Britain; signed also by Belgium, Greece, Iceland, Italy, the Netherlands, Portugal, Turkey (as of mid-1990). Recommended by the EC for adoption: see, EC-Recommendation, of July 29, 1981, No. L 246/31.

[106] See Proposal for an EC-Directive, (COM (90)) 314 final-SYN 287, of July 27, 1990, o. J. 90/C 277/03; legislative history published in: 1991 Datenschutz und Datensicherheit No. 1 at 24; see also: Proposal for an EC-Directive, concerning the protection of personal data and privacy in the context of public digital telecommunications networks, COM (90) 314 final — SYN 288 of July 27, 1990, o. J. 90/C 277/12.

[107] Council of Europe, Protection of Personal Data used for Payment and Other Related Operations, Recommendation No. R (90) 19 of Sept. 13, 1990 and Explanatory Memorandum.

[108] The representative from Great Britain expressly left open the question of whether his government would accept articles 3.3, 3.4, 5.1.c, and 7.1; see Council of Europe, supra note 107, at 4. For the wording of these provisions, see the appendix.

[109] See below.

IV. Other Initiatives Relating to International Funds Transfers

1. Initiatives by the Universal Postal Union

At its XIX. World Postal Convention in Hamburg on July 27, 1984, the Universal Postal Union adopted several conventions relating to international funds transfers. These included the Money Orders Agreement[110], the Postal Check Agreement[111], the Cash-on-Delivery Agreement[112] and the Collection Order Agreement.[113]

The Money Orders Agreement governs, among others, the issues of the currency in which postal orders and traveler's checks are to be paid and currency conversion (Art. 3) as well as the settlement procedure between postal authorities (Art. 28-30).

The Postal Check Agreement governs cross-border postal transfers, postal check deposits and payments by means of international order checks or postal orders. Art. 7 of the Postal Check Agreement governs the currencies in which payment can be made with the help of these payment instruments and the exchange rate for conversion. Under these provisions, the transfer must, as a rule, take place in the currency of the country of destination (par. 1) whereby the originating authority sets the exchange rate for the conversion of its currency into the currency of the country of destination (par. 3). For international postal orders, Art. 27 refers to Art. 7.

The Cash-on-Delivery Agreement sets the permissible collection amount at a maximum of 100 Swiss francs. In the absence of separate agreements, the amount is to be stated in the currency of the country of origin of the shipment; in the case of a deposit or transfer of the collection amount to a postal check account in the collecting country, this amount is to be stated in the currency of that country (Art. 4 of the Cash-on-Delivery Agreement). There is no express provision regarding the currency conversion.

The object of the Collection Order Agreement is the exchange of collection orders. These are enumerated as receipt confirmations, invoices, orders, drafts, interest and dividend certificates, and mature securities as well as all other commercial papers and other securities payable without fees (Art. 2 (1)). To the extent that no special agreement is made, the amount of the collection order is to be stated in the currency of the country of collection

[110] Acts of the Universal Postal Union, v. 4 (Bern); published as law in: Sammlung der eidgenössischen Gesetze, Nr. 50/1985, pp. 2175-2205.

[111] Id. at 2191-2206.

[112] Id. at 2207-2212.

[113] Id. at 2213-2218.

(Art. 4). There is, therefore, no special provision regarding currency conversion.

Common to all of the conventions of the Universal Postal Union are extensive provisions governing issues of liability. It is sufficient here merely to refer to these provisions. The other substantive provisions are so closely tied to the specific situation of postal authorities that it will not be necessary to discuss them here.

2. Initiatives for the Harmonization of Laws Relating to Credit Cards

The focus of international interest relating to individual payment instruments is presently the use of various forms of payment cards (credit cards). In particular the EC Commission has focused the emphasis in its initiatives in this area.[114]

A working group of the French Conseil national du crédit has also specifically undertaken the issues relating to credit cards; their report was submitted in March of 1988.[115] This report contains a comparative analysis of the respective national legal provisions governing credit card transactions as well as an extensive analysis of the conflict of laws implications.[116] This working group came to the conclusion that there is a need for legislative action with respect to international credit card transactions.[117]

Likewise concerned with issues relating to international credit card transactions is the "European Convention on the Use of Bank Cards", which was drafted in 1987 within the framework of the European Council for Payment Systems. The goal of this convention is cooperation in the credit card sector throughout Europe. Although the legal prerequisites for the achievement of this goal have not yet been met, the chances for success of the work of the European Council for Payments Systems is particularly promising because all banking groups in Western Europe are involved.[118]

---

[114] Commission Recommendation of 17 November 1988 concerning payment systems, and in particular the relationship between cardholder and card issuer, O. J. No. L 317/55 of Nov. 11, 1988; Commission Recommendation of 8 December 1987 on a European Code of Conduct relating to electronic payment (relations between financial institutions, traders and service establishments, and consumers), O. J. EC No. L. 365/72 of Dec. 12, 1987. See also the Discussion Paper-Making Payments in the Internal Market, COM (90) 447 final of Sept. 26, 1990, in particular No. 72 ff. with additional references.

[115] Conseil national du crédit (ed.), Aspects européens et internationaux des cartes de payement, v. 1: Rapport de groupe de travail; v. 2 Annexes au rapport de groupe de travail (Paris, 1988).

[116] Id., v. I at 91 ff.

[117] Id. at 96. See also Etzkorn, supra note 96, at 139.

[118] Etzkorn, supra note 96, at 140.

Appendix

Recommendation No. R (90) 19
of the Committee of Ministers to Member States
on the protection of personal data used for payment
and other related operations, Straßburg 13.5.1990

Appendix to Recommendation No. R (90) 19

1. Scope and definitions

1.1 The principles contained in this Recommendation apply to the automated processing of personal data linked to the provision of means of payment and of their use for payment or other related operations.

In addition, these principles apply to all parties involved in those operations (beneficiaries, bodies providing means of payment and communications network operators).

1.2 For the purposes of this Recommendation:

The expression "personal data" covers any information relating to an identified or identifiable individual. An individual shall not be regarded as "identifiable" if identification requires an unreasonable amount of time, cost and manpower.

The expression "means of payment" covers all payment instruments and other media for payment orders, in particular cheques, giro orders and payment cards as well as all other types of debit orders and credit orders whether or not initiated by an electronic signal.

The expression "beneficiary" includes all legal and natural persons who benefit from payment or other related operations, and in particular traders, retailers and service providers to the exclusion of the individual consumer.

The expression "bodies providing means of payment" covers all banking and non-banking undertakings which provide or manage means of payment whether regularly or intermittently.

Undertakings which receive instructions from the main providing body to provide or manage means of payment are also covered.

The expression "communications network operator" refers to the body which provides the transmission for processing the data which are used to carry out the payment or other related operation.

2. Respect for privacy

Respect for pricacy shall be secured during the collection, storage, use, communication and conservation of personal data linked to the provision or use of a means of payment. For that purpose, bodies providing means of payment, beneficiaries, and communications network operators shall take the necessary measures so as to secure the confidentiality of those personal data.

3. Collection and storage of data

3.1 In regard to the provision of a means of payment, personal data should only be collected and stored by the body providing the means of payment insofar as such data are necessary for making the means of payment available as well as the services linked to its use, including verification activities.

3.2 In accordance with provisions of domestic law, the body providing a means of payment should be able to entrust the collection, storage and processing of these data to a contractor insofar as the latter is instructed not to use the data for other purposes.

3.3 In principle, personal data should only be collected from the individual concerned. Where other sources need to be consulted, the individual should, prior to consultation, be fully informed about the categories of sources which may be consulted, as well as the consequences attaching to a refusal or withdrawal of consent.

3.4 Personal data may only be collected and stored by the beneficiary for the purposes of verifying the identity of the holder of the means of payment and for the determination of the validity and lawful nature of the payment or other related operation.

3.5 When an operation is carried out with a means of payment, the personal data relating to this operation should only be collected and stored by bodies providing means of payment to the extent necessary for validation and proof of the operation as well as for carrying out the services and fulfilment of any obligation laid down by domestic law associated with its use.

3.6 Payment systems should be designed in such a way as to avoid, in the course of a payment or other related opertion, personal data which are not necessary for the accomplishment of the purposes set out in principles 3.1 and 3.5 respectively being communicated to the body providing the means of payment and personal data which are not necessary for the accomplishment of the purposes set out in principle 3.4 being retained by the beneficiary.

3.7 The communications network operator should be able to collect and store only those personal data which are necessary for carrying out the services which he provides, or which are necessary for the purposes of proof and billing of such services.

3.8 The processing of personal data relating to the criminal convictions of an individual should only be carried out where the data are of such a nature that they are clearly justified for determining the suitability of that individual for receipt or continued use of a means of payment, and provided the individual has given his express and informed consent or the processing is in accordance with safeguards laid down by domestic law.

The collection and storage of the other categories of sensitive data referred to in Article 6 of the Convention for the protection of individuals with regard to automatic processing of personal data should not be permissible.

4. Use of data

4.1 Subject to the provisions of principle 4.2, personal data collected and stored in accordance with principle 3 should only be used to determine whether a means of payment should be provided to an applicant, for verification purposes, for managing the account concerned, including the provision of statements, or to avoid abuse in the case of loss or withdrawal of the means of payment.

4.2 Provided that the individual is fully informed in writing and unless he has objected, the body providing the means of payment may use the data collected and stored for the purposes referred to in principles 3.1 and 3.5 for marketing and promoting its range of services in regard to him.

The individual should be informed of the fact that if he objects to his data being used for marketing and promitional purposes this will not prejudice the decision to provide him with a means of payment or to allow him to continue using a means of payment already issued.

4.3 The interconnection of different personal data files resulting from the various uses of a means of payment by the individual should only be carried out by the body providing the means of payment for the purposes referred to in principle 4.1 or for the marketing and making available of services which the individual has accepted in accordance with principle 4.2.

Unless otherwise provided by domestic law, or with the express and informed consent of the individual, the interconnection of different personal data files for purposes other than those referred to in this principle, should not be permissible.

4.4 To the extent that the use of a means of payment gives rise to sensitive data, such data may not be used for marketing, promotion or any other purposes.

4.5 If a multifunctional card is also, among other things, a means of payment, and it is used for purposes other than those referred to in principle 1.2, sub-paragraph 2, it should be designed in such a way as to make impossible access to the type of personal data covered by this Recommendation when it is being used for such other purposes.

5. Communication of data

5.1 Personal data collected and stored for the purposes referred to in principles 3.1 and 4.1 may only be communicated in the following cases:

(a) in accordance with obligations laid down by domestic law;
(b) when it is necessary to protect the essential and legitimate interests of the body providing the means of payment;
(c) with the express and informed consent of the individual;
(d) in a case of a default in payment, where a system of reporting or recording of such information has been set up in accordance with domestic law to increase payment security within the sector covered by this Recommendation;

5.2 The conditions laid down in principle 5.1 shall not restrict the communication of personal data by the body providing the means of payment to contractors acting on its behalf or to the communications network operator insofar as communication is necessary for the issue and use of the means of payment.

6. Publicity

In accordance with domestic law and practice, bodies providing means of payment, as well as beneficiaries and communications network operators, should ensure that the individual is informed about the nature of data which they store, the purposes for which the data are stored, the categories of persons or bodies to whom the data may be communicated and the legal basis for such communication.

7. Rights of access and rectification

7.1 Each indivudual should, on request, be able to obtain in an intelligible form all data concerning him including such data as are contained on a means of payment.

7.2 He should be able to have such data rectified or erased where they are found to be inaccurate, irrelevant, excessive or have been collected or stored in disregard of the principles set out in this Recommendation.

7.3 Bodies providing a means of payment should take adequate measures so as to ensure that the data subject is aware of his rights in regard to his data as laid down in principles 7.1 and 7.2, as well as the ways and means of exercising them.

7.4 The body providing means of payment should ensure that the data subject can, without unreasonable delay or expense, exercise his right of access, in particular, where a system of distributed data processing involves the location of his data on several files.

8. Security of data

8.1 Each party to the payment or other related operation should take appropriate organisational and technical measures so as to safeguard the security, integrity and confidentiality of personal data against unauthorised access, use, communication, alteration or distortion.

8.2 Control measures which are sufficient to guarantee the protection of the data should be provided for by beneficiaries, bodies providing means of payment and communications network operators.

In particular, they should inform their staff of such measures and of the need to respect them. Measures should be taken within the organisation so as to designate by name those members of the staff who are entitled to have access to the data.

8.3 Bodies providing means of payment should give to their costomers advice regarding security, including advice on how to manage and keep safe means of payment and codes, and the procedures to be followed in case of loss or theft of a means of payment.

9. Remedies

Domestic law should provide a remedy in cases of breach of the principles laid down in this Recommendation, in particular where the rights laid down in principle 7 are not respected.

10. Transborder data flows

10.1 Where the provision or use of a means of payment requires the collection, storage and processing of certain personal data in two or more Parties to the Convention for the protection of individuals with regard to automatic processing of personal data, no obstacle should be created for the transborder flow of such data between and among them provided the principle of equivalent protection is guaranteed.

10.2 If the State to which the data are to be transferred is not a Party to the Convention, respect for the principles contained in this Recommendation in that State shall be regarded by the competent authorities in Contracting Parties as a strong justification for allowing personal data to be transferred to that State.

11. Conservation of data

11.1 Where personal data are no longer necessary for the accomplishment of the purposes referred to in this Recommendation, they should be deleted.

11.2 Contractors responsible for processing data on behalf of bodies providing means of payment should not retain them beyond the period necessary for carrying out their instructions.

11.3 Consideration should be given to the desirability of providing time limits for the conservation of personal data once a means of payment has been refused. Time limits should also be drawn up so as to take account of such matters as the need to retain data for the period necessary for the purpose of defending legal actions or for furnishing proof of transactions carried out by the individual.

12. Ensuring respect for the principles

12.1 Each State should institute a system of supervision making it possible to secure respect for the principles set out in this Recommendation.

12.2 For this purpose, each State should ensure that bodies providing means of payment are easily identifiable.

The Payment System in the Context of EMU
The Role of Central Banks[1]

By Franco Passacantando

Contents

I. Introduction

The creation of an integrated free trade area for goods and services in Europe will require an integrated payment system, i. e. a common set of rules and procedures to receive and execute payments across countries. Integration will be certainly enhanced by heightened competition resulting from customer pressure on financial intermediaries for efficient and reliable services throughout Europe. As in every domestic payments system, however, full integration can hardly be achieved without some form of public sector intervention. My remarks deal with the role central banks can play in this process.

In addressing this issue I will list what seem to be the major shortcomings of the present arrangements for international funds transfer and show the direction in which market forces are moving to overcome those difficulties, both worldwide and at a European level. Then I will isolate the area in which central banks should intervene, indicating what they could do at the domestic level to improve the European payment system and where the intervention of a supranational institution is needed.

[1] This is a revised version of the contribution published in: Banca d'Italia (1991), Proceedings of the Workshop on "Payment System Issues in the Perspective of European Monetary Unification", Perugia 22-23 November 1990, Roma, Banca d'Italia.

II. What is Missing in the European Payment System

No systematic study has ever been undertaken of the efficiency, reliability and soundness of the payment system in Europe. We know very little about the average time that it takes for a money transfer between two countries to be completed or for a check to be credited to the account of a foreign beneficiary. Nor do we have reliable estimates of the costs of international payments borne by the users and producers of the services, or of the risk to which banks are exposed because of settlement delays. Yet, from personal experience and the scattered information available, we have a clear perception that the present system for transferring funds across European countries is far less developed than the system operating within each country.

The shortcomings of European cross-border payment mechanisms are due to the absence of uniform and widely accepted rules and procedures for the transmission and settlement of payment instructions. The transfer of money is mainly based on bilateral links between banks and not on the use of multilateral facilities. Payments are settled not only in different currencies but also on the accounts of different banks for each currency. A payment might therefore take a long time to be completed because it has to go through a long chain of banks before reaching the account of the beneficiary.

So we don't know very much about the payment system in Europe, but we know that two things are missing: a clearing house for cross-border payments and a widely used settlement medium.

A clearing mechanism provides each bank with links with other banks with which it does not trade directly. The clearing house acts as an intermediary for a large number of banks in the exchange of payment instructions so that each bank deals only with that intermediary. The clearing mechanism therefore not only reduces bank costs — and, if well designed, risks — but, by streamlining the payment mechanism, it improves the quality and cost of the service for the ultimate users. Obviously, there are many clearing houses in Europe and some very efficient electronic systems for clearing payments originating abroad or in foreign exchange operations. But these clearing houses accept as members only institutions that operate in the country, and they only handle payments in domestic currency.

In domestic clearing systems the accounts of several banks can be used for settlement purposes, but by far the most common medium of exchange is central bank money. The use of a single instrument instead of many reduces transaction costs, simplifies accounting procedures and the whole settlement process.

III. Where Does the Need for Change Originate?

The need for a more structured international payment system is not felt only in Europe but worldwide. It is the result mainly of what is often referred to as the "globalisation" of financial markets. An ever larger amount of financial assets circulate outside the country issuing the currency in which they are denominated. Therefore, an ever larger number of currencies are used as settlement media.[2]

These market developments are generating severe strains in terms of costs and risks in an international payment based on arrangements that were devised when the number of international payments was small and the use of national currencies abroad limited. It is to provide an appropriate answer to these problems that market participants have introduced or proposed clearing mechanisms that handle currencies different from the one issued in the country in which they are located. In certain cases these mechanisms handle only one currency and in others two or more currencies, either for foreign exchange operations or for one-sided payments.

In Europe the intensity of the changes is stronger for two reasons. Firstly, the removal of barriers to cross-border movements of goods, services and capital flows is bringing about an increase in cross-border payments. Secondly, there is a widespread improvement in the quality of all individual European currencies because of the greater credibility of the EMS countries' commitment to exchange rate stability. This factor, together with investors' desire to diversify their portfolios, favours the use of European currencies in other European countries and elsewhere.

The BIS data confirm the picture. In international markets an increasing role as settlement medium is being played not only by the DM, the British pound and the Ecu, but also by currencies such as the French franc and the Italian lira.

Even though it is not easy to forecast developments in this field, it is highly likely that the completion of the internal market by 1993 and the progress towards EMU will give this process further impetus.

One should not draw the conclusion that since there is a strong market need for international clearing and settlement mechanisms within Europe, public authorities have nothing to do but wait until market participants create their own system. Several factors justify a public sector role. Interbank cooperation might be extremely complex when many banking systems, with very different operating practices and structures, are involved. This is particularly true for parts of the payment system such as the retail sector in

[2] See F. Passacantando (1991), The Payment System in the Context of EMU. The Role of Central Banks, in: Banca d'Italia (1991), ibid.

which banks do not feel an urgent need for change since volumes grow less than in the wholesale sector and liquidity and credit risks are less serious. Secondly, legal differences between countries might diminish the ability of netting schemes to reduce risk effectively. Thirdly, central banks are an integral part of any payment system; therefore any major changes in the payment system itself will require corresponding changes in central banks' acitivities.

The public sector can play a significant role by changing laws and regulations, providing a forum for interbank cooperation, ensuring oversight and supervision of the system and adapting the payment services that it directly produces.

It is particularly, on this last aspect, and specifically on central banks' scope for action, that I would like to focus. I will mainly refer to wholesale payment mechanisms since it is there that the issues of concern for central banks, such as systemic risks and potential liquidity problems, are greatest.

IV. Central Banks' Scope for Action

All central banks play a dual role in payment systems: acting as the authority responsible for the regulation and oversight of the system and as an operator offering services and payment instruments. In both roles the activity of central banks will have to change substantially in order to cope with developments in the international payment system. In both cases changes will require greater international cooperation.

Cooperation in the oversight field has been clearly defined by the Committee on Interbank Netting Schemes of the central banks of the Group of Ten countries.[3] For the first time, central banks have formulated a common policy with respect to payment systems based on:

- — A set of minimum standards for the design and operation of international clearing and settlement systems;
- — A set of principles for the allocation, or joint exercise, of the related oversight responsibilities.

Closer cooperation will also be required in central banks' settlement activity. Action in this field is much more complex, however: any change in the way in which central bank money is supplied to banks for settlement purposes directly affects all the aspects of central banking: monetary policy, supervision and payment system policy.

[3] See Lamfalussy A. (1991), The Report on Netting Schemes, in: Banca d'Italia (1991), ibid.

It is banks' demand for central bank money that gives central banks the necessary leverage for controlling money. Supervision is also a necessary consequence of the existence of central bank credit to commercial banks for settlement purposes. The payment system depends crucially on the provision of central bank money for two reasons: firstly, the use of one medium of exchange instead of a plurality of media reduces transaction costs and creates what economists call "positive externalities"; secondly, central bank money offers the advantages of a credit instrument for payment purposes without implying the credit risks that arise when the instrument is a liability of a private institution.[4]

Central bank settlement activity will have to change because, as I have already mentioned, individual currencies are increasingly being used in different countries and at different times from those in and at which central banks that issue them are willing to supply them. For example, European currencies are settled in the U. S. market when all European central banks are closed. The development of increasingly deep money markets reduces, but does not eliminate the possibility of liquidity shortages affecting individual banks, as the experience of the countries with the most developed domestic markets shows.

There are two types of change that central banks could make in their settlement activity in order to improve the efficiency and soundness of the European payment system: changes in their domestic systems and the supply of settlement services to international payment mechanisms.

Risks arising in foreign exchange markets depend, to a considerable extent, on the differences in the times of final settlement for the currencies involved. Therefore, if all central banks offered settlement services simultaneously, risks would be reduced, and in particular "Herstatt risk" would be eliminated. But in order to achieve this result central banks would have to operate before or after their standard business hours.

The second type of change in settlement activity concerns the provision of settlement services for netting schemes for multi-currency payments or foreign exchange operations. It is highly likely that these schemes will be structured around a clearing house and will probably involve a two-tier participation system, with only a relatively small number of banks having direct access to the settlement agent. In similar domestic arrangements

[4] The provision of central bank accounts for interbank settlement purposes is usually, but not necessarily, connected with some form of credit facility and creates therefore some form of moral hazard. This credit is provided because the clearing process typically entails a certain degree of uncertainty as to the quantity of central bank money needed for settlement purposes. By supplying this credit, central banks can therefore prevent a temporary liquidity problem in one commercial bank from disrupting the entire payment system.

central banks usually manage the accounts in central bank money for the direct participants and sometimes also for the clearing house.

If central banks are to provide the same kind of settlement service for these schemes, they will have to abandon either the practice of dealing only with institutions operating in their country, or that of supplying settlement services only in their own currency. For instance, in order to offer settlement services to a netting scheme in London, central banks would have to either establish direct links with the banks operating in London, or assign the role of settlement agent to the Bank of England, which would then open accounts denominated in all the currencies accepted in the system.

Both solutions pose many problems; let me briefly refer to a few of them. In the first solution, central banks would have to operate with institutions not subject to their supervisory powers; they would have to establish electronic links with a wide range of institutions, thereby duplicating facilities already put in place by other central banks; they would also have to overcome serious cooperation problems in connection with cross-currency settlement risk, i. e. the risk that arises in the event a bank faces a liquidity shortage in several currencies. A settlement delay in one netting system would hold up the operations of all the central banks involved.

The second solution would entail decisions on the quantity of money in circulation in the non-official sector being taken by a central bank different from that of issue; it could also lead to competition between payment systems — and perhaps between central banks — since international netting schemes could end up processing domestic payments as well.

All these problems derive from a very simple fact: central banks were designed to operate domestically and in their own currency. Any solution to the problem of supplying settlement services for netting schemes would require either very tight cooperation between central banks or the creation of a new institution whose jurisdiction would extend beyond national boundaries and individual currencies.[5]

V. The Evolution of the European Payment System in the Transition to EMU

As I mentioned earlier, the developments under way are mainly independent of the process of European economic and monetary unification. They

[5] See Padoa-Schioppa T. (1989), International Payment Systems: the Function Begets the Organ, speech given to the International Symposium on Banking and Payment Services, organized by the Board of Governors of the Federal Reserve System, Washington, 9 June 1989, in: Banca d'Italia, Economic Bulletin, no. 9, October, 67-74.

arise in a broader international context and are the expression of a market tendency to use currencies outside the country of issue. In Europe this tendency is stronger and the need to achieve greater central bank cooperation in payment systems even more pressing. However, any change in the European payment system, even if in response to factors that are not related to EMU, will have to be consistent with the policy decision that monetary union will be achieved, leading in the end to a common European currency, the Ecu.

In considering the transition to that final result, it is important that the activities of individual central banks and those of the European central bank be correctly defined. I will therefore consider the following two broad sets of questions:

— To what extent should the activity of national central banks in domestic payment systems and in domestic currencies be coordinated in the transition phase? Should there be some minimum harmonisation of rules and operations?
— During the transition phase, what should be the respective roles of national central banks and of the European Central Bank in the settlement services of cross-border and multi-currency payments, as well as in the Ecu settlements?

There is a lot that can be done even at the domestic level to reduce risks and improve the efficiency of the international payment system. Some standardisation of operating hours and of final settlement times on the accounts of central banks is probably the first objective to aim at. In Europe, differences in settlement times are not the result of time zones, but arise because of the lack of standardisation in central banks' practices. For instance, between Germany and France, which belong to the same time zone, there is a difference of four hours in final settlement cut-off times, since the Bundesbank closes its operations at 1.00 p.m. and the Bank of France at 5.30.[6] In these four hours banks are exposed to "Herstatt risk": the settlement of DMs in France cannot be completed by a transfer on the accounts of the Bundesbank. In other words, payments in DMs have a different degree of finality compared to those in French francs at certain times of the day.

Harmonisation of cut-off times is important not only to reduce "Herstatt risk" but also to pave the way for the integration of financial markets, and to effectively coordinate the use of monetary policy instruments. It would certainly not be easy to coordinate open market operations if domestic money markets operated at different hours of the day and if some central

[6] See BIS (1990), Large-Value Funds Transfer Systems in the Group of Ten Countries, Basle, May.

banks were active only in the morning while others continued to operate in the afternoon as well.

Some degree of coordination should also be achieved in the risk reduction policies followed for domestic systems. While a rigid harmonisation of rules is not desirable, or even conceivable, in view of the operational and institutional differences between the various systems, it would be dangerous not to seek any coordination at all. Risk reduction policies can alter the relative costs and benefits of using different payment systems and therefore can cause shifts in payment flows from one system to another, especially in the later stage of European unification. Consider, for instance, the extreme case in which, in order to reduce systemic risk, one country adopted a Fedwire-type of policy, but with no pricing of daylight overdrafts, and another country required banks to collateralise their exposures fully. In a situation in which exchange rates are almost fixed and interest rate differentials negligible, there would be a strong incentive to divert operations to the first payment system. What economists call currency substitution would be induced by differences not in the value of money but in the features of the payment industries.

There are other similar issues that I believe should be addressed, but to which I will not attempt to give an answer. For instance: should pricing policy be harmonised? Should the laws on bankruptcy presently in force in some countries be changed? To what extent should technical features, such as the communication protocols of individual systems or operating standards, be harmonised?

But it is with respect to cross-border payment and multi-currency systems that there is the greatest need for central bank coordination. The most important issue is the role that the ECB could play in these systems. Its first task could be that of acting as the settlement agent in the Ecu-netting system, taking over the functions now performed by the BIS. In doing so the ECB would of course have to rethink the architecture of the Ecu-netting scheme, which in the final stage of EMU is destined to become the main — if not the single — wholesale payment mechanism in Europe. This system should possibly utilize the facilities already existing in most European countries and which have required huge investment in recent years.

However, the ECB could also play a role in the settlement of cross-border payments and multi-currency transactions in individual European currencies. Let us assume that European central banks decided to provide an account for settlement purposes for cross-border payments in European currencies. Let us suppose also that their involvement was minimal and that all liquidity and credit risks were borne directly by the participants, consistently with the recommendation of the Lamfalussy Report. As I mentioned above, no national central bank could satisfactorily provide settlement services of the kind, since this would involve operating in other countries or in different currencies. By contrast, it is possible to conceive a system in which the ECB would play an operational role in the settlement process. One possibility would be that commercial banks open accounts in different currencies with every central bank and that the ECB manages settlement between central banks and strictly coordinates the activity of individual central banks. Another possibility would be that commercial banks open accounts directly with the ECB which would act as a sort of intermediary between central banks.

Obviously, solutions of the kind would pose many serious problems, which I will simply mention. Would commercial banks have to manage different accounts in the same currency, for domestic and international transactions respectively? How would they assess their risk exposures? How could reserve requirements be implemented? Furthermore, any system would have to be designed so as to be eventually transformed easily into a Ecu-clearing system, or combined with the existing one.

Even though any solution involving the ECB would give rise to many problems, it seems to me that the issue is not so much whether national central banks or the ECB should play a role in the settlement of multicurrency payments as whether this role should be played by the ECB or delegated to a large extent to the private sector. Banks and other institutions are in fact already developing projects for international clearing systems in which settlement would be managed by a limited number of banks operating in different European countries.

Whether settlement is to be made on correspondent or central bank accounts is still largely debated both on analytical grounds and practical terms. In my opinion, however, this choice depends very much on the context in which the system would operate. There is certainly no need for central banks to seek a role in the settlement of interbank transactions in every country of the world or, domestically, for every type of transaction, including those originating, for instance, in the retail sector or among smaller banks. But in a context in which the system for netting wholesale international transactions in individual EEC currencies is bound to become the future wholesale European payment system, there seems to be little doubt that settlement should be performed in central bank money.

VI. Conclusion

Let me summarize my remarks.

— First, there is a definite market need for international clearing and settlement mechanisms to reduce the risks and improve the efficiency of cross border payments. This trend in Europe will presumably be stronger than worldwide. It will also be largely independent of the accomplishment of economic and monetary unification;

— Second, central banks can contribute to this process by harmonising procedures for settlement in individual countries. Possible areas of intervention include the setting of common operating hours, the standardization of certain telematic procedures, the adoption of common principles for pricing and risk control, the promotion of changes in national laws;
— Third, if European central banks want to preserve a role in the settlement of interbank payments similar to the one that they generally play domestically, they will have to assign the responsibility of the settlement of cross-border transactions, both in Ecus and in individual currencies, to a supranational institution, namely the European central bank.

The task facing central banks is undoubtedly demanding; its completion could take years, just as it took many years to create todays' domestic electronic settlement system. But, it is highly desirable that the ultimate objective of European central banks' action is defined soon in order to make sure that uncertainty about the future does not discourage the private sector from undertaking the investments and initiatives that are indispensable to the creation of an integrated European payment system.

On the Future Organisation of Private Retail Payment Systems in the European Community

By Hannes Rehm, Bonn

Contents

I. Introduction

1. This paper starts by putting forward what may at first sight seem an improbable argument, but one which in the medium term may well turn out to be correct : If the common market becomes a reality, then cross-border payments in their traditional sense in this economic area will cease to exist. Instead international payment transactions within Europe will be equivalent, or at least very similar, to domestic payments. Or, seen from another angle : prosperity will only come about in the European Economic Area if the exchange of goods and services is not hampered by de facto barriers created by the monetary regulations that govern the real transactions. Payment systems in the Community must be rapid, sure and cost-effective.

2. Not surprisingly, therefore, the European Commission has over the past few years been taking initiatives in the field of European payments. Such initiatives date back to the year 1987 when the Commission addressed the problem of an enhancing the integration of payment card systems[1], its chief

[1] See "Triumph for Europe: New Card Systems" COM(86) 754 of 12th January 1987 (Communication from the Commission to the Council); Iris Vogel: "Zahlungsverkehr im

concern being to achieve "interoperability": cards issued in one country must be able to give access to cash dispensers, POS and other services in all other EC Member States.

But it soon became evident that progress could be achieved with the proper functioning of the internal market only if, in addition to looking at card payments by retail customers, the Commission turned its attention to the whole fabric of the general system of payments. "Interoperability" of payment cards was not the only area in which there was considerable room for improving the integration of payment techniques : cross-border payments cost many times more than domestic payments under similar conditions and take considerably longer to complete. The collection of a cheque sent by post from a foreign bank is complicated and expensive. It was on this and similar problems that the Commission focused when it presented a discussion paper on "Making Payments in the Internal Market" in September 1990[2].

3. This discussion paper which has since been the subject of a whole range of opinions by the credit sector associations, by consumer associations and individual institutions, drew largely on the work mentioned above in the field of payment cards. At the same time it extended the notion of "interoperability" to payments by cheque. The starting point and the model on which the extension of this integration method was based was the Eurocheque system with its guarantee rules and agreed procedures that already today make the cheque "interoperable" to a certain extent.

Even so, the main thrust of the 1990 "Green Paper" concerned interoperability not of retail payment systems, but in a wider and at least as important area : the establishment of better links between carriers of transfer payments or between other instruments of "paiement à distance" (or remote payments). While the approach in the 1987 document was to enable the payment card holder to enjoy the same facilities in all EC Member States as at home, the most important consideration in the 1990 Green Paper is that payments between any two points in the European Community — in particular payment transfers — should be transacted as efficiently and cheaply as domestic payments within one and the same Member State.

4. In March 1991, after public discussion of the 1990 document, the Commission adopted a Communication on "Payments in the Internal Market" in which it stressed yet again that in the interests of consumers the processing of retail payments by private individuals must be made faster, reliable and more cost effective. In pursuit of that aim Directorate General

EG-Binnenmarkt" (Payment systems in the internal market) in Bank-Informationen 1990, Volume 12, page 4 et seq.

[2] See EC Commission: Payments in the Internal Market COM (90) 447 final.

XV set up two Working Parties in April 1991, the "Payment Systems Technical Development Group"[3] and the "Payment Systems Users Liaison Group"[3]. Both Working parties submitted their reports in February 1992. These were summarised by the Commission in one concluding Report entitled "Easier Cross-Border Payments : Breaking down the Barriers — Commission Working Document"[4]. We shall be returning to this report several times throughout this paper. At this point, all that needs to be said is that the Commission is in favour of a structure that provides for the efficient and transparent processing of retail payments with individual national clearing houses working closely together throughout Europe[5].

5. Such collaboration of automatic clearing centres would also affect the stability of the financial system and the implementation of monetary and supply policy. This has raised the question of how to arrange the division of labour between the central banks on the one hand and the European Commission on the other when it comes to monitoring developments. It will be up to the central banks to prepare the role that the European Central Bank ("Eurofed") will have to play in a pan EC payments system, particularly since the draft statutes of the Eurofed make express provision for it to be responsible for payments. In particular when it comes to large payments, it will have a steering role to play in European monetary policy. To that extent it was logical for the group of Central Bank Governors of the EC to set up a Committee in March 1991 under the Chairmanship of Padoa Schioppa to determine what role the central banks should play in cross-border remote payments at European level. The work of this Committee is focused — unlike the central thrust of the Commission's role — on large-value payment systems, in other words it will concentrate primarily on ECU clearing at European level[6].

II. The Present Structure

1. If one wants to achieve structures that offer a better cost-benefit ratio, i.e. one that is more favourable to the consumer, then it is necessary first of all to identify the causes of the present dissatisfaction. To do so we must

[3] See the Reports of both working parties to Sir Leon Brittan of February 1992 which can be obtained as a DG XV document.

[4] See Commission of the European Communities: "Easier Cross-border Payments: Breaking down the Barriers" Commission Working Document, SEC(92) 621 final of 27th March 1992.

[5] See Geoffrey Fitchew: "The Development of EC Cross-Border Payments Systems" in National Westminster Bank (Ed.): European Integration — The Banking Issues, London 1992, p. 23 et seq.; David Barchard, Andrew Hill: Cash without Tears, across EC Frontiers, in The Financial Times of 20th March 1992, page 12.

[6] See Tommaso Padoa-Schioppa: The Risk in Large-Value Payment Systems, ibid., p. 35 ff.

examine the present position and the reasons behind it. And we can start by referring to a story that appeared in the Süddeutsche Zeitung on 23rd January 1992. Under the head-line "37 % bank transfer charges" it was explained how expensive it can be to transfer small sums of money abroad. A sum of 800 Schillings, so the story went, was transferred from an account with a German bank in Munich to an account in Vienna. The countervalue in German Marks was 113.84 DM but a sum of 166.34 DM was debited. That represented bank charges of nearly 50 %. The charges in question comprised a handling fee of 17.- DM, 3.- DM commission charged on the exchange from one currency into another, 2.50 DM postage and finally, and without any details given, a standard 30.- DM external fee which was charged to the remitter. When enquiries were made as to how it was possible for bank charges to be so enormous, it transpired that the 30.- DM had erroneously been set too high and that the external fee would be reduced to 20.- DM. Even so, the bank charges that remained after that reduction still worked out at 37 %. The article ended with the not wholly serious advice from a friendly bank employee that with such small amounts it was better to stick the money in an envelope and put it in the post. That is cross-border payments for you in the year 1992!

2. In order to piece together the reasons why prices are set in this way, it is necessary first of all to look at the technical procedures by which cross-border payments are processed. Unlike domestic payments, cross-border payments are subject to procedures that take two different forms. The communication of the payment information is a document-free operation conducted through the S.W.I.F.T. (Society for Worldwide Interbank Financial Telecommunication) telecommunications network. Here there exists since 1974 an internationally standardised payments order transmitted in the same form by all SWIFT Member banks throughout the world via dedicated lines (for further details of this, see the presentation of the SWIFT system by Etzkorn in this volume). The financial settlement between the participating banks, i.e. the bank of the remitter and the bank of the beneficiary, is conducted by the simultaneous debiting and crediting of accounts held with correspondent banks abroad. In cross- border payments there is basically nothing comparable to the national giro systems with batched settlements, say via the Bundesbank. Were a similar structure to operate domestically, then every German credit institution would have to maintain accounts directly with each and every of the 4,000 other German credit institutions. That simple comparison is enough on its own to show that in cross-border remote payments there is a clear need for action.

3. Returning to our example of the transfer of 800 Austrian Schillings, we must now consider what work processes and cost factors are involved and then see what impact they have on prices under present processing arrangements:

The written order given by the customer is fed manually into a data collection system and converted into an EDP message. Machine-readable documents do not yet exist in foreign payments. This is due in the main to the nature of the documents required by the Bundesbank for reportable payments. There then follows — according to our example — the electronic transmission of that message via the SWIFT telecommunications network from the German sending bank to its correspondent bank in Austria. Frequently the foreign correspondent bank is not the bank of the beneficiary. So, in our example, a further stage will be necessary in which the order is transmitted via the domestic Austrian banking network. Here it may well be necessary to make a print-out of the documentless SWIFT message as the format of the EDP message in the SWIFT process is not compatible with the documentless payment system in the receiving country. The result of this is that the document then has to be transmitted physically, i.e. through the post.

The SWIFT message transmitted to the correspondent bank contains, in addition to the payment data, an indication of the chosen method of settlement. Since in our example we are dealing with Austrian Schillings, the correspondent bank has the power to debit the Schilling account of the German sending bank. Were the payment to be transmitted in DM, the SWIFT message would contain a note to the effect that a credit had been made to the DM account of the correspondent bank with the German sending bank. Since the balances on accounts held by correspondent banks do not bear interest and since moreover balances in foreign currencies are always subject to an exchange rate risk, balances on correspondent bank accounts are kept as low as possible. This means for example that each day Austrian Schillings have to be purchased on the foreign currency markets in order to ensure that the account is adequately covered. Otherwise the account goes into overdraft and interest becomes payable. Purchasing foreign currencies on the market gives rise to a brokerage fee.

Since the remitter as a rule would have only a DM account and no account in any other foreign currency, funds have to be converted, in our example Austrian Schillings. Here the customer is entitled to the official asking rate on the foreign currency market which is uniform throughout the Federal Republic. The customer can therefore work out at any time whether the correct exchange rate has been applied, merely by consulting the financial press. In other countries it is customary for a house-rate to be applied that differs from bank to bank and can therefore not be verified by the customer.

4. So much is clear: in order for account to be taken of all the wishes of the customer in foreign payments, it is necessary to have a dense network of correspondent banks in many countries throughout the world. This involves the keeping of special foreign currency accounts and the observance of special notification procedures to the Bundesbank, such for instance as the

monthly return of a foreign position report. Over and above that there is the problem of foreign currency risk mentioned above and which has to be hedged against — at a certain cost. This requires the purchase of special hardware and software and, last but not least, well trained and therefore highly paid staff.

The result is high fixed costs and therefore substantial unitary costs. The actual level of these costs is determined by the way the costs are calculated in each case, though on average it works out at around 30.- DM per order. This part of the costs naturally adds an enormous percentage to transfers of small sums. In our example the charging of a handling fee of 17.- DM by the German bank merely serves to cover part of its costs. The result is a system in which the larger transactions subsidise the smaller. In the present case there was the additional factor that the remitter also bore the foreign bank charges, i.e. those costs which the receiving bank would normally charge the beneficiary. Here the deciding factor is whether to debit the actual costs that the foreign bank incurs which would involve monitoring and analysing each and every transaction or whether a standard fee should be charged which may sometimes work out to be too high and sometimes too low.

5. How is it, then, that cross-border payment transactions are processed in this way and not in any other? In the past, cross-border payments, their infrastructure and their procedures were primarily arranged for the financial settlement of import and export transactions. The original aim was to offer a service to corporate customers. Depending on the customer's position on the market, foreign commercial payments were made by letters of credit, cash against documents, bankers' orders, payment transfers, etc. These required a host of individual contacts between the banks of either party, frequently involving banking information which in many cases are essential for doing business with unknown partners.

6. Despite the existence of the SWIFT system, cross-border payments are more complicated under present settlement procedures than are payments that are effected within a single automated giro network. The reason for this is the series of steps that have to be gone through in unlinked systems and the absence of any uniform clearing procedure. And it is this that prompted the general approach of the Commission departments towards the integration of the European giro networks or indeed the construction of one or more international European networks. With that in mind, the 1990 Green Paper put forward some initial measures aimed at enhancing the degree of integration in the field of payments. Thus for instance the French banks, and in particular the French Co-operative banks headed by the Caisse Centrale du Crédit Populaire are looking for ways to achieve an international link-up. The European Community savings banks have set up a company called

EUFISERV (European Savings Banks Financial Services)[7] which has started by seeking to achieve mutual accessibility to all cash dispensers run by savings banks throughout the whole of Europe and will then turn its attention to establishing a link-up in the field of payments.

Individual institutions are coming onto the market with systems designed to facilitate the retail transactions of their major customers across international borders. Thus for example the Royal Bank of Scotland is now able to offer its customers payments to Spain through a computer link-up with the Banco Santander. Payment card organisations, such as VISA-NET, are developing plans to enable their card networks to cope with payment transfers as well.

III. The Present Environment

1. This means that for the mass of cross-border small value retail payment transactions typical of those made by personal customers, alternative procedures are becoming available. Here however it has to be borne in mind that retail payments in their normal sense still form an insignificant part of cross-border remote payments. Thus for example in Germany retail cross-border payments (payments involving sums of up to 5,000.- DM) currently represent no more than 0.2 % of the total volume of domestic payments. Furthermore, foreign payment transactions by personal customers have been dominated so far by what are called "face-to-face payments", i.e. direct payments made on the spot and not via a system of cross-border payment transfers which are initiated only on receipt of an invoice. Statistically the present situation can be summarised as follows (see also Tables 1 to 3)[8]:

- Table 1 shows the volumes of remote and face-to-face retail payments from and to four large Member States. Face-to-face payments dominate such payments, accounting for three quarters of their total. Within face-to-face payments, cards are much more important than eurocheques, except in Germany where Eurocheques are widely used. Total retail cross-border payments (RCBP) represent less than 1 % of domestic payments in France and the UK, but about 2 % in Italy.
- Table 2 shows intra-EC cross-border payments by cheques, cards and transfers as a proportion of domestic payments using the same media. The final column shows total intra-EC cross-border payments as a proportion of total domestic payments. The figures are markedly higher

[7] See the contribution by Müller in this volume.

[8] The sources for Tables 1 to 3 are: Bank for International Settlements: Statistics on Payment Systems in Eleven Developed Countries. Figures for 1990, Basle 1991; EC-Commission: Easier Cross-Border Payments, loc. cit.

Tabelle 1 : Hauptinstrumente im grenzüberschreitenden intra-EG-Massen-Zahlungsverkehr
(in Mio. Transaktionen, wenn nicht anders angegeben)

		Fernzahlungen		Persönliche Zahlungen		Massenz. Insges.	Gesamt
	Schwellen-betrag	Überwei-sungen	Schecks	euro-cheques	Karten		grenzüberschreitende Zahlungen*/Inlands-zahlungen insges. (%)
Frankreich	10.000 FFR	3,6	3,7	6,0	22,9	36,1	0,6
Deutschland	5.000 DM	6,2	1,9	16,4	11,6	36,1	0,5
Italien	3 Mio LI	2,4	n.v.	3,3	8,7	14,4	1,8
VK	[1.000 UK£]	4,6	5,8	5,0	24,8	40,2	0,8

* Der Zähler enthält alle innergemeinschaftlichen grenzüberschreitenden Zahlungen.
n.v. = nicht verfügbar

in the smaller Member States e.g. Belgium and Greece than in the larger ones such as the UK and France.

Tabelle 2: Hauptinstrumente innergemeinschaftlicher grenzüberschreitender Zahlungen

(Anteil der innergemeinschaftlichen an den gesamten (einschließlich innerstaatlichen) Zahlungen nach den jeweiligen Zahlungsinstrumenten. Klammern bedeuten, daß innergemeinschaftliche Zahlen nicht verfügbar sind und die gesamten grenzüberschreitenden Zahlungen verwendet wurden. Alle Zahlen in %.)

	Überweisungen	Schecks	Karten	insgesamt
Belgien	3,4	[1,5]	[10]	4
Frankreich	0.5	0,1	1,9	0,6
Griechenland	15	12	12	12
Italien	0,8	0,5	[24]	n.v.
Niederlande	[0,17]	[8,6]	[53]	[2,8]
Portugal	14,7	1,5	21,3	1,8
VK	0,5	0,4	2,7	0,8

— Table 3 finally focuses on retail cross-border transfers in the EC. The definition of retail that is used varies between Member States, ranging from 1,400 to 2,500 ECU. The aggregate of such transfers is around 35 million for the seven Member States concerned. Retail cross-border transfers in the EC account for a high proportion i.e. around a half of all cross-border transfers involving these Member States. However, they are dwarfed by total domestic transfers, accounting for only 0.2 % to 0.5 % of domestic transfers in the four largest countries in Table 3, though higher proportions in smaller Member States (e.g. 2.3 % in Belgium). The figures in the final column of Table 3 are of some global ones and conceal the fact that transfers between contiguous regions of different Member States are often a significantly higher proportion of total (including domestic) transfers from such regions than the figure in the final column for the Member State as a whole. This caveat applies to all types of RCBP.

The main conclusions from Tables 1 to 3 are:

— retail cross-border payments within the European Community represent a very low proportion of total transfers in those countries, especially in the large Member States;

— retail cross-border transfers within the European Community comprise a substantial proportion around half of all cross-border transfers;

Tabelle 3: Grenzüberschreitender intra-EG-Massen-Überweisungsverkehr (GMÜ)

	Schwellenbetrag (1.000 ECU)	Volumen (GMÜ) (Anzahl in Mio)	GMÜ/Auslandsüberweisungen inges.* (%)	GMÜ/Überweisungen insges. * (%)
Frankreich	1,4	4	50	0,3
Deutschland	2,5	8	65	0,2
Italien	2,0	2	40	0,5
Luxemburg	2,4	2	61	n.v.
Niederlande**	2,1	4	40	0,3
VK	1,4	5	40	0,3
Belgien**	2,4	11	69	2,3

* Gesamtzahl, nicht nur intra-EG-Überweisungen.

** Belgien und Niederlande: alle grenzüberschreitenden Massen-Zahlungen, nicht nur intra-EG-Zahlungen.

— remote cross-border payments are less common than face-to-face payments;

— face-to-face cross-border payments involve mainly cards.

Tables 1 to 3 are primarily concerned with intra-EC payments. The data for certain countries in the European Economic Area, e.g. Sweden, show that the volume of RCBP involving such countries and the European Community is significant and would therefore form a significant part of any global estimate of the volume of RCBP involving EC members. Of course any review of the volume of EC retail cross-border payments would include payments involving all third countries (whether within the European Economic Area or not), but such data are scarcer than those pertaining simply to the EC.

2. Despite the currently relatively small volume of retail cross-border payments, there can be no doubt that with the emergence of a single European market in goods and services, with the increasing mobility of people, jobs and capital, retail cross-border payments within the European Community are set to rise dramatically, particularly if, through the creation of a European Monetary Union and the establishment of a single European currency, the exchange rate risk will to all intents and purposes disappear. "Cross-border" transactions will then become "cross-network" transactions. The rate of growth of such payments will depend in the main on the progress achieved in eliminating other (e.g. tax) barriers on the one hand and on the other on the elasticity of retail payments with respect to the costs that will be charged for the services involved. But that in the end determines only the effective rate at which retail payments will grow; of its general growth and the accompanying need to iron out the weak points that are currently in evidence, there can at least in the long term be no doubt.

3. These weak points can be succinctly summarised as follows:

— There is as yet no cross-border payment network that can be compared with a national domestic giro network.

— At the moment it is not possible to integrate cross-border payments seamlessly into domestic payment systems.

— Even in the case of small-value transfers it is still necessary to involve correspondent banks.

— Other ways exist of transmitting funds in other currencies although the partners involved in the transactions merely keep accounts in the relevant currencies.

— There is a total lack of transparency with respect to prices, the time it takes for transactions to be completed and conversion rates.

— There is no difference between the technical infrastructures and procedures used to make retail payments on the one hand and large value commercial payments on the other.

4. In the past there was no reason to distinguish between these two types of transaction in the organisation and processing of cross-border payments. In simplified terms one can say that at the present time, on the basis of the numbers involved, 65 % of all cross-border payment transactions relate to sums below 5,000.- DM. In terms of the value of the transactions involved, the story is quite different. Here some 90 percent of the volume of funds transmitted can be attributed to corporate customers. With the development of the common market this ratio will change, for the reasons stated above. But it raises the question of how to take account of the prospect of an increase in the number of retail cross-border payments. In the search for an answer, it will be necessary to consider the possibility of creating new structures for the processing of transactions[9].

In order to make them rapid, cheap and therefore attractive price-wise and transparent as regards the cost and the time involved to complete them, retail payments should no longer be settled via correspondent banks. This does not mean we should do away generally with the well-tried correspondent bank system as it will remain essential for transactions by corporate customers. But as regards retail payments in the future the correspondent bank system is reaching the end of its useful life.

In saying that, however, it has to be admitted that it is impossible to draw a strict methodical line between small-value payments and large. Although it is certainly true that some countries have special systems to deal with retail transfers and others for handling large payments (thus for example in London the CHAPS system handles transactions of anything over 5,000 while the BACS system is typical of a system for smaller amounts), in other countries such distinctions do not exist. Even so, it has to be pointed out that measures to improve payments are often of a more general nature that affect both small and large amounts to the same degree. That is so in the case of the principles of law underlying payment transfers, the supervision of clearing systems or aspects of competition policy.

IV. Problems for the Future

1. When considering how to render payments more consumer-friendly by making them faster, safer and cheaper, one must not succumb to the

---

[9] See for example Michael Endres: "Demands for Payment Networks and Standardization" in: Karent-Zeitschrift für Zahlungsverkehr und Kartendienstleistungen, 1992, No 5, p. 10 ff.

temptation to view them primarily as a technical matter. Payments have evolved out of the banking practice of each individual country which means that there are bound to be substantial differences in procedure from one European country to another[10]. Payment services are banking services over whose price-performance ratio the market decides. The regulative policy questions of how to progress from the present situation as it is at the moment to how it should be in the future, are:

— How can competition in the field of payment services be organised along European lines?

— How much systematic and procedural cooperation is necessary in order to make the most of the rationalisation potential of payment infrastructures? In other words, how can the formula "as much competition as possible, as much cooperation as necessary" be transformed into a business reality?

— What steps must be envisaged in order to achieve a better cost performance ratio in cross-border payments in a reasonable time and at an acceptable cost in view of the different starting positions in the different European countries?

2. When seeking to improve the range of cross-border payment services offered to personal customers, the first point we have to bear in mind is the fact that some of these services are already directly catered for through the involvement of card based payment systems on the spot in the country being visited. This can be seen from Tables 1 to 3. Thus for example Eurocheque guarantees payment of sums of up to a countervalue of 400 DM per cheque. In addition, it has for many years been possible to draw eurocheques for higher amounts by a simplified procedure through the Eurocheque International network. The ceiling on this type of transaction was raised to 2,000.- DM with effect from 1st April 1992. The fees charged between the different banks are graduated. The top rate of charge for the customer is 12.- DM which is clearly less than the cost of a transfer order. In addition Eurocheque International plans to make it possible for customers throughout Europe to make payments with their eurocheque guarantee card without having to write out a cheque, along lines similar to the German electronic cash system.

Rates of growth which each year are substantially more than 100 % point to the withdrawals that are made from cash dispensers in foreign countries. In the Eurocheque International cash dispenser network alone, there were no fewer than 3.6 million withdrawals during 1991 throughout the Community as a whole worth nearly 1,000 million DM.

---

[10] See Bank for International Settlements: Payment Systems in Eleven Developed Countries, Frankfurt/M. 1989.

3. These examples show that progress can already be seen in the processing of retail payments. While this certainly puts the problem into perspective, there is however no reason for not examining the possibility of making further improvements.

V. Clearing Structures

1. This section considers the prospects for retail payments in Europe in the light of the status quo. It is broken down into the following parts:

— To start with, an explanation of possible technical clearing structures. A distinction is made between cheques on the one hand and transfers on the other.

— This is followed by a description of the infrastructural requirements necessary to reach uniform standards, norms and agreements in order to make the new structures operable.

— There then follows a discussion of the order in which the necessary steps should be taken to convert these requirements into guidelines for a European "judicial policy" in payment systems.

— Finally the problem is addressed of the "regulative policy" that must be aimed for in the field of European payments, with particular reference to requirements regarding competition policy, pricing policy, consumer and data protection and supervision.

2. So, to start with, let us turn our attention to cheques : In the eurocheque system, cheques issued abroad, both within the guaranteed limit and those for a countervalue of up to 1,000 ECU, are cleared through the "eurocheque international network". The German clearing centre is the "Gesellschaft für Zahlungssysteme" (Payment Systems Company) in Frankfurt. Figure 1 illustrates the connection.

As already indicated, from April 1992 onwards all eurocheques for sums between the guaranteed limit and a countervalue of 1,000 ECU are cleared through this network. Here it should be mentioned for example that in 1991 alone, German customers abroad issued nearly 20 million cheques to a total value of 5.8 billion DM. In the case of more than half of them the countervalue was collected without the establishment of any written documents. This means that the cheque as a rule remains in the country in which it is written and is required to be produced only in cases of protest by the bank with which the customer keeps his account. Document-free processing signifies a substantial simplification of the work involved and a considerable saving in costs. With this procedure it should be relatively easy to process according to the same criteria not only the pre-printed eurocheque forms but

Schaubild 1: ec-System

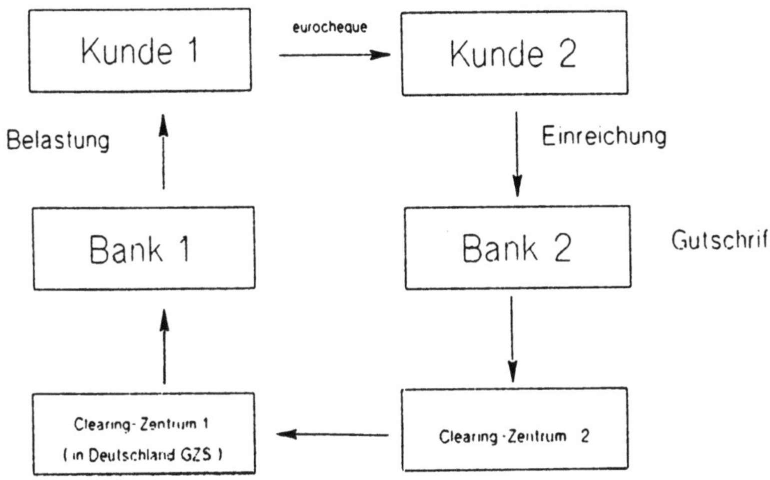

also all other cheque forms as well if the maximum amount were raised to 2,500 ECU or its equivalent.

While work was being carried out to ensure the technical feasibility of the system, efforts would also have to be made to clarify the legal requirements. German cheque law stipulates that the cheque must be physically presented to the drawee. However derogations are currently allowed in the case of cheque truncation, at least as far as cheques for sums of up to 2,000 DM are concerned. The plan to raise this ceiling in the Autumn of 1992 will broaden the usability of the cheque and thus make for a substantial improvement in retail cross-border payments.

3. In contrast, it will be more difficult to bring about improvements in remote payments by transfer:

As mentioned earlier, the SWIFT system transmits only messages about payments and does so mostly between correspondent banks. If in addition the banks were to fix values between themselves, a common clearing system would need to be set up, i.e. the banks would have to be linked up to each other through a cross-border electronic network. Moreover, it would be necessary for all credit institutions to be connected to one another as the important point is not merely to ensure the connection between one country and another, but rather to accelerate the procedure within each individual country. Practice suggests that problems arise not in the "international element" of the payment, but once the payment has entered the national clearing system. National systems differ sometimes quite radically from each other in their degree of automation and hence in their efficiency, i.e. in the speed and cheapness with which payments are processed within the country. What is required is a "mediating agency" to take on the tasks of transforming the payment format of the remitter into that of the beneficiary, of converting the payment order from the currency of the remitter into that of the beneficiary, and finally of clearing the payment by debiting the account of the sending bank and crediting the account of the receiving bank. From this it is clear that as has already been suggested it is not only a matter of linking together technical structures, but also of standardising and regulating the relevant procedural practices.

4. At present there is no such thing as a European central clearing agency for cross-border payments. Some countries, such as the United Kingdom or the Netherlands, have central clearing centres for domestic payments. In the Federal Republic, for instance, each banking group has its own specific giro centre, while the Bundesbank itself runs its own network.

In view of these different starting conditions, it would in principle be possible to consider the following four solutions[11]:

Model 1 :
Correspondent banking

Model 2 :
Linkages between national clearing centres

Model 3 :
Group-specific networks

Model 4 :
Third party networks.

Schaubild 2: Korrespondenzbank-Vereinbarung

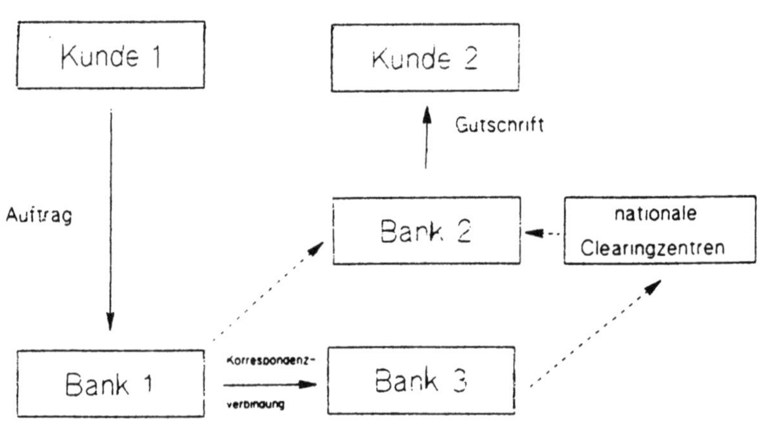

[11] See Commission of the European Communities: Source Documents for "Easier Cross-border Payments ...", XV/0105/92 in particular paragraphs 120 ff and Annex No 2.

Model 1 (Correspondent banking) would in principle be similar to the existing system of correspondent banks (see Figure 2). In principle it would be possible to imagine that for retail payment purposes only one correspondent bank were to be selected for each country. Since it is unlikely that agreement could ever be reached over which bank should be selected for the purpose, it is not worth pursuing this model that seriously.

Model 2 which is featured in the European Commission's 1990 Green Paper involves a linkages between national "automated clearing houses" and equivalent systems (ACHs). There are two possible variants : on the one hand the national ACHs could be linked to a "Super-ACH", on the other there could be a direct link-up between each of the national ACHs.

The first variant (Figure 3) is complicated and costly. At least in the short and medium term the chances of one ever being set up are extremely remote.

Schaubild 3: Super-ACH

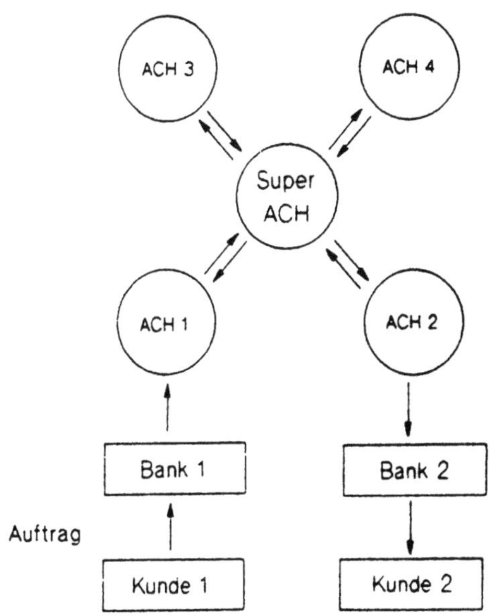

The second variant (Figure 4) involving a direct link-up between each of the national ACHs via so-called "gateways" would have the advantage of enormous flexibility. As and when technical progress was made, it would be possible to bring the ACHs of individual countries successively into the system as they achieved the required standards, and so clear retail payments through the international network thus created.

Just as national payment systems involve several giro-networks of individual banks or banking groups, it would also be possible to envisage the establishment of group-specific networks within the European banking market (Figure 5). The European savings banks have created such a network initially in respect of cash dispensers through their subsidiary company "EUFISERV". The European postal banks and the European co-operative banks also have plans to set up their own group-specific networks for their respective institutions, and so to be in a position to implement Model 3.

Schaubild 4: Direkte Verbindung der nationalen ACH's

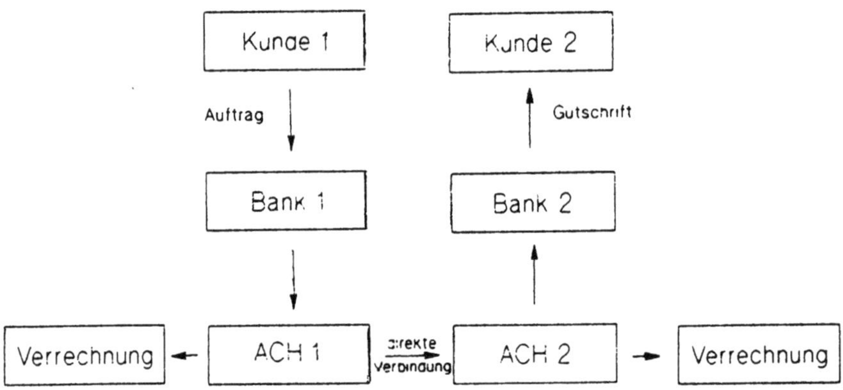

Schaubild 5: Gruppenspezifische Netzwerke

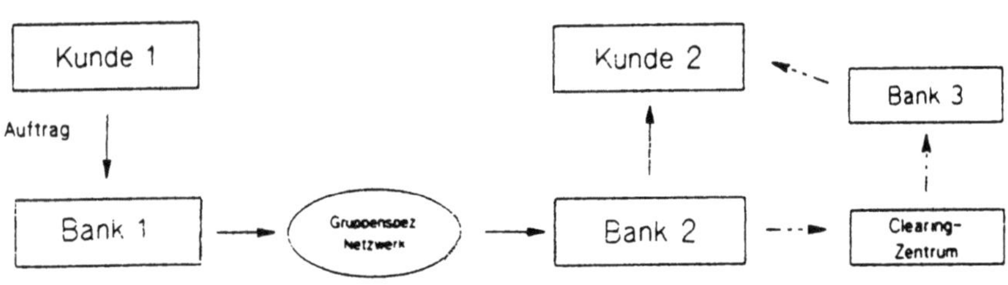

Lastly, it is possible to envisage Model 4 whereunder use would be made of third party networks to clear payments (see Figure 6).

The aim in all these approaches is to be able to by-pass the system of correspondent banks in the process of clearing retail payments. At this point it is worth asking whether the banks would be prepared to go along with this idea. In business policy terms it is a question of reciprocating services rendered, of examining the importance of managing current accounts as a potential means of acquiring customers and of coping with the effect on existing cost structures (which cannot be adapted in the short term) of deleting items in the balance sheet. This means that in view of the accumulation of costs (and charges) associated with the present structures, the industry will in the end be forced to accept these approaches.

Schaubild 6: Netzwerke Dritter

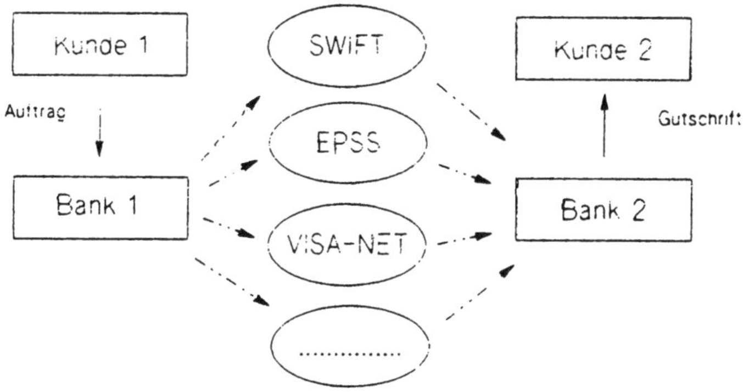

5. These new approaches will require agreement to be reached[12]

— on the common elements that have to be considered in constructing a system (the organisational structure of each infrastructure)

and

— on the common usage elements of the systems (the procedural organisation or practices within each infrastructure)

The common constructional elements include

a) the type of payment
b) the message format
c) the routing identifier
d) the carrier
e) membership of and access to the systems
f) security / liability / responsibility.

[12] See Hannes Rehm: Perspektiven des "Auslandszahlungsverkehrs" im europäischen Binnenmarkt (Outlook for foreign payments in the European internal market), in: Sparkasse, 1992, No 4, pp. 175 ff.; Ralf-Christoph Arnold und Andreas Martin, Zahlungsverkehr im Binnenmarkt — Initiativen der EG-Kommission in: Bank-Information, 1992, No 7, pp. 4 ff.

The common usage elements include

a) currency conversion
b) the settlement arrangements
c) the time cycle
d) charges
e) reporting requirements.

VI. Infrastructural Requirements

1. We shall now take a look at the common constructional elements:

a) the type of payment

For any system there needs to be agreement as to whether it will handle debit or credit items, or both, paper or automated/electronic items, individual items or batched items and whether there will be any maximum or minimum set for the value of items to be handled.

According to the European Commission, the maximum for retail payment transactions should be raised to 10,000 ECU. This would for instance be substantially higher than the reporting threshold set by the Deutsche Bundesbank (5,000.- DM). A hike of this kind would be important for the development of a simplified machine-readable electronically processable document for use in cross-border payments as well.

b) the message format

In the transmission of any payment between two parties, both sides have to be able to "understand" the message. This can be achieved either by using a common format for the message (i.e. the same "language"' is spoken), or by each party being able to convert the message sent into the recipient's format or convert messages received into its own format. The use of a common format offers substantial advantages because it can be adopted by new members without disrupting the system.

The future format should be based on existing international standards. The starting point should be the "SWIFT Bulk Payment" format (MT 102), while borrowing bits from "EDIFACT". EDIFACT (Electronic Data Interchange for Administration, Commerce and Transport) is a body of rules set up by the United Nations in which a model international payment instruction has been developed. On the one hand it is important that there should be agreement throughout Europe on a common format for messages, without the need to create new standards at considerable expense in time and money. On the other it is important to avoid the creation of European "standards islands", but instead, insofar as is possible, adopt international standards as the basis for a European solution. That has been done in Germany where the broader conception of the "electronic counter" opened by the Bundesbank in January 1992 provides for recognition of "SWIFT" domestic on-payments by banks.

c) the routing identifier

Similar to the German bank account number and sort code system, it is necessary to have a uniform system for identifying those involved in payment systems throughout the whole of Europe. The importance of uniform data and sort codes can be seen from the experiences made with the merging of the payment systems of the Federal Republic and the former German Democratic Republic. Certain systems already exist at international level such as the SWIFT "Banking Identifier Code" (BIC) in which each bank in each country is given its own identifier code. From an EDP point of view the BIC-code has the disadvantage of comprising a combination of letters and figures. The encoding of letters on magnetic stripes of cheque- and credit cards is not possible. It would therefore seem more sensible to look to the BIN-Tables that already exist under the eurocheque system and which also make it possible to achieve clear identification of the bank at which the account is kept.

d) the network operator

The details of more specific proposals are explored in greater depth below (in VII.5.). However it is important that each country adopt the solution that suits it best. That does not mean that it is necessary for all countries to adopt uniform criteria. Thus in individual countries several carriers can function while in other countries only one network may exist. Both public and private sector carriers should be allowed to operate.

e) membership of and access to the systems

The question of access is paramount for the management of "systemic risk". This is the risk that, through the inability of one of the partners to pay, the other partners are in turn unable to meet their commitments towards the system and so create the risk of a domino effect. This is one of the central questions concerning the establishment of cross-border payment systems since they necessarily lead to a bulking of payment flows and therefore raise the systemic risk. As a network of bilateral relationships, the correspondent-bank system excludes the systemic risk from the very outset.

As regards the question of authorisation one can assume from the start that on the basis of provisions contained in the EEC Treaty with respect to the freedom to provide services and the freedom of establishment, and in the light of the second banking directive and the European banking licence, that the way is open for providing services in the field of payments in the host country. This would mean that by virtue of the European passport, EC banks could be forced to join such systems. The host country is however entitled under Article 19(4) of the Second Banking Directive to limit access to a payment system with a view to maintaining its integrity, stability and efficiency, although any decision in that respect must be subject to objective criteria.

The comments above apply at any rate only if the government runs the cross-border payment system or cooperates in organising it: for only then will the EEC Treaty and the Second Banking Directive apply. If cross-border payment systems are run by the private sector then it is Articles 85 and 86 of the EEC Treaty that form the basis for assessing the competition aspects. The related prudential considerations are dealt with in a later chapter (see VIII.10).

f) security / liability / responsibility.

These are questions that can be dealt with only at a later stage of development. In the interests of both the customer and the participating bank, it is important to achieve a high degree of certainty in the law. Thus it ought to be possible to build on the existing security arrangements of national payment systems or on those of the SWIFT system.

2. Now let us consider the common user requirements :

a) currency conversion

As long as no single European currency exists, either for the orginator or for the beneficiary the funds transmitted will be denonminated in a foreign currency. The following points have therefore to be clarified:

— where the conversion takes place;
— what currencies are to be processed in a retail payment network; and
— how the conversion price is fixed.

The conversion into the currency of the recipient country can be made either in the country of the remitter in this case either by the sending bank or by the national or regional clearing centre or in the recipient's country in this case, too, either by the receiving bank or by the national or regional clearing centre. As far as the remitter is concerned, the desired highest level of transparency is assured when the conversion is made in his own country. This has the added advantage of substantially facilitating and accelerating the processing operation in the recipient country. The aim should therefore be to ensure that recipient countries receive sums only in their own national currencies. It must also be possible though under a different pricing arrangement to meet a customer's wishes to transfer funds in the currency of the remitter's country to a third currency or to debit a foreign currency account.

In the case of the first question as to whether the conversion should be carried out by the remitter's bank or by a clearing centre, there is much to be said for preferring conversion by a clearing centre. This facilitates the processing since then between the clearing centre and the participating domestic banks, settlement is in only one currency, e.g. the DM. All outgoing payments are debited to the remitter's bank in DM, all incoming payments, according to the above premise, are credited in DM as well. The other option of conversion by the receiving bank would require the clearing centre to acquire a large number of foreign currencies. In that case the clearing centre would have to maintain foreign currency accounts in all the currencies participating in the system.

The second question as to which currencies will be accepted is easier to answer at least insofar as the requirements set out in the foregoing paragraph have been met: the clearing centres involved would be obliged to accept the national currencies of all countries participating in the system.

As to the third question: conversion prices can be fixed according to present practice. Orders submitted to the clearing centre before dealing starts on the stock market are to be settled at the price for the day, while orders coming in later are settled at the rate of the following day.

b) settlement arrangements

With a view to international settlement arrangements there are many variants that can be considered. The following points need to be taken into account.

— systemic risks
— the amount of the set-off sums,
— the number of parties involved and
— the time-cycle required for settlement.

The odds are that preference will be given to constructing a gross clearing system. Net clearing systems are more difficult to manage as they require absolute synchronisation of all parts of the system. In contrast, gross clearing systems allow for graduated handling of individual sub-systems, e.g. through special priority lists or on a first-come-first-served basis.

Here it must be pointed out that the kind and scope of monitoring of net clearing systems is a matter for the central banks or the Bank for International Settlements (BIS) to consider. For the creation of such systems the BIS has drawn up a catalogue which broadly follows the list of criteria contained the Lamfalussy Report[13]. In particular

[13] See Bank for International Settlements: Report by the Committee for Interbank Netting Systems of the central banks of the Group of Ten countries, Basle 1990; see also the article by Le Guen in this volume.

— participants should be informed in detail of the influence of the system on all the financial risks arising out of the netting procedure;
— multilateral netting systems should have definite procedures for managing credit and liquidity risks; and in particular set risk ceilings for each participant;
— netting systems must provide a detailed report in good time on sums cleared during the day, even if the participant with the largest net debit position is unable to clear;
— objective access criteria must be fixed and published, guaranteeing fair and open access.

c) the time- cycle

The following timetables have to be fixed:

— the acceptance times of the clearing centre/s for same-day processing;
— the time taken to transfer sums to other countries;
— the normal end-to-end time-scale for processing a payment;
— the irrevocability of a payment / complaints possibility.

The question of how long it takes for a transaction to be completed is of prime importance to the consumer. But it can only be specified once an international consensus has been reached. In discussions at international level it has emerged that in retail payments the duration for which operators tend to strive is five to six working days (see also VIII.3 below). The fixing of the irrevocability of a payment is of decisive importance for the legal certainty of such systems, particularly against the background of different bankruptcy laws in the different countries[14].

d) charges

It is to be expected that between the participating credit institutions settlement charges will be established to enable them to cover the costs of processing payments in such a way that the cost will be borne by the originator of the payment. Unlike in national payment systems, the consumer will have to expect that in addition to the cost of managing his account, he will be charged with the costs of processing his payments. These ought however to be substantially less than those costs that are currently charged to consumers for transfers of small amounts through the correspondent bank system.

In the establishment of charges a distinction has to be drawn between inter-bank charges and the charges which are made to the customer. European competition laws (Articles 85 and 86 of the EEC Treaty) provide that

[14] See the article by Le Guen in this volume.

the charges to customers may not be determined by any international agreement. In inter-bank dealings, however, a general agreement on settlement costs is possible. The Community competition authorities nevertheless insist that bilaterally the option must remain open for lower settlement costs to be charged. To that extent settlement charges are always the highest declared charges (see also VII.5 below). As a starting point for these settlement charges it would be possible to adopt the rates that apply for the clearing of Eurocheques, i.e. maximum 4.8 ECU or around 10.- DM.

e) reporting requirements

In the past the reporting requirements of the central banks have hampered the rationalisation of cross-border payments. Thus for example until 1st August 1991 the reporting rules of the Bundesbank required it to be notified for statistical purposes of all payments of sums worth 2,000.- DM or more. That figure has now been raised to 5,000.- DM. In the EDP programmes of the banks and the savings banks it was and still is necessary to store comprehensive information not all of which is necessary for the processing of payment transactions. In addition they hinder the development of a simplified machine-readable voucher for foreign payments because the cost of developing such a voucher cannot be justified if it is to be used exclusively for low-value payments. Additionally there is the question of whether in a common banking market the statistical requirements of the central banks can be justified to the same extent that they could in the past. Indeed it is that consideration that has prompted the European Commission to recommend that the threshold be raised to 10,000.- ECU.

VII. Judicial Policy

1. All this raises the question of how a European "judicial policy" in payment systems should be framed. In other words, it is necessary to see what steps must be taken to ensure the transition from the status quo to a clearing structure that satisfies all concerned. The starting premise must be the fact already mentioned above that the different national systems differ with respect to their technical quality and speed of transmission and that at present the weak link in the chain lies not in the international stage of the transaction but in the transmission of the payment within the national systems of individual countries.

2. Bearing in mind the present situation, the following "programme" would be realistic and enable progress to be achieved:

— a policy of promoting transparent and uniform conditions;

— rapid and secure processing of payments in order to reduce the uncertainty over the time at which a payment will be completed to a minimum

— application of international standards and resources through the linkage of all relevant partners (the central banks as well as the credit institutions);

— control and management of systemic risk on the basis of a uniform body of law.

3. In order to attain these objectives, market forces must be brought into play if they are to promote efficiency, flexibility and a willingness to adapt. Competitors will exist in large numbers only if the conditions under which they can operate make sound business sense. This means that there must at all times be a sufficient volume of transactions at prices that cover the costs if a reduction in those costs is to be achieved.

At all events it would be possible to leave this process entirely to market forces only if the same technological requirements and unrestricted market structures were to be found in all countries. But since the strengths and the weaknesses of systems take different forms in different countries, the intentions of all those involved can probably best be expressed by the maxim "as much cooperation as necessary, as much competition as possible".

4. Cooperation is to be aimed at in order to reach agreement on those points that bring advantages to all participants.

Examples of such agreements on the offer side are the introduction of a uniform, pan-European system for identifying banks and banking groups, cooperation over the definition of a uniform data code for cross-border payments, and the fixing of clearing times.

In the interests of the consumer, on the other hand, there would be the agreements already described above as necessary over

— the type of payment instrument (transfer, debit, cheque, card);
— currency conversion procedures;
— clearing times;
— network settlement;
— the normal time-cycle;
— the maximum amounts for individual transactions.

Such accords and agreements are also necessary in order to meet insofar as is possible the customer's interest in having a binding commitment regarding the time that a payment will take to complete and the costs that will be charged to him. High charges and long delays are often due to the failure of the domestic system to meet with international requirements (as is the case for example in Italy, Ireland and Denmark). Here it would be appropriate to apply in the short term the minimum standards that have already been achieved with the SWIFT system. Uniform technical conditions that do not affect competition, uniform interfaces and uniform standards have the advantage of avoiding parallel and multiple developments and so between them help foster the rationalisation of payments. Such agreements between the banks should therefore not merely be tolerated, but actively encouraged.

If one wants to maintain and accept diversity in Europe as a source of competition, of innovation, of responsibility for the needs of consumers and of technical progress, it is no contradiction to say that in the long run there will only be suppliers and therefore competitors in large numbers if the conditions under which they can operate make sound business sense. All automated payment systems, whether national or international, are exceedingly costly to set up and run. The high level of investment required for the state-of-the-art technology and the lower unitary costs associated with large numbers may at first sight suggest the need for a single monolithic payments system. In the medium term, however, such an approach is less important than the need for competition : for competing systems are more innovative and more flexible; and they react faster to customers' wishes than a single system on its own[15].

5. Those fields where competition is necessary, which are therefore broadly free of regulation and in which cooperation should be kept to a minimum include:

— the range of products and services that each institution offers
— the price that each institution charges for its products and services
— network policy
— systemic risk management and control.

Thus, for example in the range of products and services, it makes sense to offer different services for debit and credit cards. Whereas in the case of credit cards suppliers have for the past twenty years been offering products that are accepted internationally or world-wide, it would be unrealistic to expect that to happen in the field of debit cards in Europe before 1993. Eurocheque International and Eurocard International are currently involved in developing an "Electronic Debit Card" (EDC) for use throughout Europe. Where possible, international agreements will be reached in order to underpin the system both legally and technically. Vis-à-vis the customer each bank will however be free to set the amount of overdraft and the conditions for it that it is prepared to grant. These can for example be linked to daily or weekly limits, but they can also depend on individual customer facilities. Those offering a narrow range of services will in the long run be forced to adapt to the higher standards of their competitors if they wish to remain in business.

[15] See Walkhoff: Sparkassen für Binnenmarkt gerüstet (Arming the savings banks for the internal market) in Betriebswirtschaftliche Blätter, 1992, Vol. 1, pp. 3 ff.

In the area of network policy a wide variety of possibilities must also be kept open for reasons of competition. Given the already existing networks, it is unnecessary to have a single European automated clearing house (ACH) linked to all European banks, or to construct a new European ACH linked up to all the national ACHs. To do so would involve substantial investment in software and systems, involving tremendous costs and long delays. A more sensible approach would be to build technical bridges, or "gateways", between existing ACHs. This would mean that payments between banks in different countries would be handled by the national ACHs while the Member States would remain sufficiently flexible with regard to the different stages of development reached by each other. Each country would be able to realise its best options within its own borders. The required standardisation of the interfaces with systems in other countries ought not to lead to insurmountable problems with respect to costs or time delays. Even from the point of view of systemic risk management, such a solution would have its advantages as the greater the number of systems, the easier it would be to spread the risk[16].

VIII. "Regulative Policy"

1. With a view to establishing a regulative policy in European payments the European Commission has in the past focused its attention on competition and charges. In particular the following three Commission Recommendations are relevant:

— Recommendation 87/598/EEC of 8th December 1987 (Official Journal No L 365 of 24th December 1987, page 12); this lays down as a code of conduct certain principles governing relations between card issuers and retailers;

— Recommendation 88/590/EEC of 11th November 1988 (Official Journal No L 317 of 24th November 1988, page 55); this grants the card-holder as a "consumer" special protection rights vis-à-vis the card issuer who is perceived to be in an economically stronger position;

— Recommendation 90/109/EEC of 14th February 1990 (Official Journal No L 67 of 15th March 1990, page 39); this lays down, among others, the following principles to be observed during the processing of cross-border payments:

  — information of the customer before he issues his instructions;
  — confirmation of the execution of the order;

---

[16] See Association for Payment Clearing Services: Infrastructure for Cross-Border Payments, London 1991 (unpublished paper); BACS: European Bulk Payments Feasibility Study Group Report to the Steering Committee, 15th June 1992 (unpublished paper).

— rapid processing of the order;
— conciliation before the courts in the case of complaints by the remitter.

2. In recent years consumer protection claims over the processing of retail cross-border payments have been voiced with increasing articulation. This is particularly so with the consumer protection associations who have called for the three above-mentioned Recommendations to be converted into binding Directives. So far the Commission has not yet finally rejected these calls. Instead it announced when adopting these Recommendations that it will examine after one year the extent to which they have been observed and their practical effect and then reconsider the possibility of drafting a Directive. That deadline (1988/89) has now passed. But in the meantime the Commission has been using its influence with the European banking associations to see that its Recommendations are put into effect.

3. In 1992 the European banking associations made a number of recommendations to their member organisations in a set of "European Banking Industry Guidelines on Customer Information on Cross-border Remote Payment"[17].

On the basis of the work carried out by the Payment Systems User Liaison Group mentioned above, the European Commission has indicated in its March 1992 document on "Easier Cross-border payments ..." that if efforts to implement the rights contained in the charter by the European banking sector by the end of 1992 are not satisfactory, the Commission will bring forward the necessary legislation to provide a statutory framework for such rights.

It has, once again, and as a yardstick so to speak, indicated five essentials which it wishes to see put into practice:

— The right of the user to appropriate information ("The Bank must inform the user of the most appropriate payment services available.")
— Prior information on the costs of the payment services ("The user must be given in advance full information regarding the total cost of a payment")
— The possibility for the customer to bear all the costs ("The user must have the option of paying all charges so that the beneficiary receives the full sum sent.")
— The same time-delay and reliability as for domestic payments ("Cross-border payments should be accelerated. The objective is to achieve the same time delay and reliability as for domestic payments by Stage Three of Economic and Monetary Union.")

[17] See for example European Savings Banks Group: European Banking Industry Guidelines on Customer Information on Cross-Border Remote Payment, DOC GB 33/92 fin. of 20th March 1992.

— Redress procedure for the customer ("The user should have access to a redress procedure at least equivalent to that existing for domestic payments.")

At the annual meeting of the European Banking Federation in June 1992, the Commissioner responsible, Sir Leon Brittan, stressed that the Commission expected this Users Charter to be implemented by the Banking sector by the end of 1992, failing which the Commission itself would take the initiative by drafting a Directive on the matter[18].

It is in particular the third and fourth points in the above list of rights that will cause problems for the banking sector. Concerning the third, it has to be pointed out that in certain countries it is banking practice to charge certain costs to the beneficiary of cross-border payments, costs over which the sending bank has no influence. Regarding the fourth point, it will be difficult to provide information on time delays, for example in those cases in which the receiving bank has no correspondent link with the sending bank. Furthermore, because of clearing regulations in the receiving country it will not always be possible for the sending bank to give precise information as to when the payment will be credited to the account of the beneficiary. The Commission has stopped short of fixing a maximum time delay for effecting payments in addition to the rule of two working days for each institution involved in the payment. It has at all events pointed out that the total time for the payment to be credited to the account of the beneficiary must respect this delay and that before the end of 1994 it will take steps to verify that this is the case.

4. The fact that the present regulative policy in European payments is not free of contradictions can be seen when it comes to data protection. The proposal for a Council Directive on the protection of individuals in relation to the processing of personal data (COM(90) 314) contains provisions which could have a direct impact on European payments and make matters particularly difficult. There are two major problems:

The first concerns the current wording of Article 24(1) and 24(3) of the draft Directive. Member States are required to provide in their laws that the transfer to a third country, whether temporary or permanent, of personal data which are undergoing processing or which have been gathered with a view to processing may take place only if that country ensures adequate protection. One can see immediately that a provision of that sort would bring payments to a standstill in those countries that have other ideas (or perhaps none at all) about data protection. For every transfer contains personal data. The text of the proposal must therefore be tightened up, and a clear message

---

[18] See EC Commission: Press Release (IP 92, 483) of 15th June 1992

to that effect has already come from the European Parliament which discussed the draft directive in March 1992.

A second problem concerns the protection of the remitter of a transfer order from unlawful communication of data concerning him on the transfer form. The principle is that personal data may be filed or processed only with the consent of the person concerned (the "data subject"). Articles 8 and 9 of the proposal for the Directive free the bank that has received a transfer order from the remitter from the obligation to inform him in this respect since in this case the introduction of a signed transfer order form can be construed as a tacit agreement on the part of the remitter that the personal data contained on the form should be processed. But it is doubtful whether that agreement applies in respect of other institutions that may be involved in processing the payment downstream and of whose existence the remitter may have no knowledge. If no consent has been given, it would have to be obtained by such institutions and that would not be practicable. Article 17 of the proposal is even stricter, prohibiting the automatic processing of data revealing "ethnic or racial origin, political opinions, religious or philosophical beliefs or trade union membership" on the transfer form. In such cases automatic processing would be prohibited unless the remitter had given his express consent in writing for the information to be processed. This rule, too, would be impossible to apply. So one must conclude that when the text was written, the particular aspect of payments was quite simply overlooked.

5. With a view to establishing the level and structure of charges in European payments, regulative policy should seek to create a business environment in which a pricing policy that favours the consumer can be implemented. This means first and foremost that, through a combination of cooperation and competition, conditions are created in which in numbers and average amount transactions can be batched in a way that allows individual institutions to lower their prices. This would also do away with the need for cross-subsidisation of cross-border remote payments through other activities, an aspect that gives rise to problems on both the business and competition fronts.

No rules governing prices should be set. Price differences as a rule reflect different services offered and are the sign of lively competition. No single price can exist as banks are not a single institution with a single range of products and services to offer. Prices are set individually by banks on the basis of different business policy considerations and in the light of their competitive position. If despite all that there emerges a distinct convergence of prices between the different institutions on the market, it must not be taken as a sign of restricted competition but rather as evidence that consumers are simply not prepared to put up with credit institutions that charge extortionate prices.

As regards payments between credit institutions (inter-bank transactions), it makes sense to have agreement on maximum prices. Here banks would remain free to charge lower inter-bank commissions on the basis of bilateral agreements. As far as relations between banker and customer are concerned, each individual credit institution should at all times remain free to fix the charges it makes to the consumer, a matter over which it alone should decide in the light of its competitive position.

6. An example of this dual pricing policy is the Package Deal which the Commission authorised in 1984 initially for five years for the "eurocheque community". The basis for this agreement is Article 85(3) of the EEC Treaty whereunder the Commission can grant derogations from the general prohibition on agreements that have the effect of limiting competition in those cases where the agreement or concerted practices of the undertakings involved have a positive effect and in particular where they bring advantages to the consumer. In the case of the eurocheque agreement the Commission accepted that the participating banks should charge each other the costs of processing cheques according to a fixed fee. A bank, say in Paris cashing a eurocheque for a German tourist from Munich may not retain any encashment fee from the amount for which the cheque is made out, but must instead pay out the whole amount. On the other hand it may charge the customer's bank in Munich a processing fee of up to 1.6 percent of the amount of the cheque. The bank in Munich is then free to pass on this charge in full to the account holder, debiting him with higher costs or, for customer-relational reasons, charging him less than the 1.6 percent. In other words a distribution of costs between the banks via an inter-bank fee which at all events may not be a fixed amount but must represent only a maximum amount, is considered as acceptable. In contrast the Commission vigilantly ensures that each and every bank pursues its own individual fee policy with respect to its customers so that as between banker and customer no price cartel can be established.

The French banks have modified the eurocheque agreement for their own purposes by charging the person presenting a eurocheque an additional encashment fee over and above the inter-bank fee. This procedure was agreed with the other partners to the eurocheque agreement in the so-called "Helsinki accord". In 1990 the Commission informed the French banks that it did not accept this additional agreement and in January 1992 imposed an appropriate fine on the eurocheque company and the French card company "Cartes Bancaires"[19].

7. Precisely in order to take account of the interests of consumers both as regards transparency and the price for the service, regulative policy in the

[19] See "Wettbewerbsverstoß bei Eurocheque" (Unfair competition at Eurocheque) in: Handelsblatt of 26th March 1992, p. 12.

field of European remote payments should give priority to the development of a European direct debit system[19a]. A system of this kind has been in existence in say the German banking sector for the past thirty years and, in view of its simplicity of operation, accounts for a large proportion of domestic payments in the Federal Republic. Standing orders for insurance premiums, telephone and electricity bills are now a standard part of the service German banks provide on current accounts. The reason the system is so widely used is its simplicity: the person required to pay gives the payee once and for all a written instruction to debit his current account at agreed intervals. The amounts may vary with the extent to which use is made of the service being paid for, such for instance as the telephone. But they can also be fixed sums, such as insurance premiums. If the customer disagrees with a particular sum, he has the right to contest it with his bank. The bank does not have the right to know the reasons for the protest or to make acceptance of the protest dependent on justification.

Because it also consists of a transmitted message and a funds settlement, the direct debit can be characterized as a reverse credit transfer. This procedure is likewise tied to the need to standardize the various systems of bank codes and account numbers. In addition, the following types of problems must be solved: "admission of payment recipients", "initialization of payments", "debit authorization" and "handling of rejected debit charges".

A pan-European direct debit system would do much to facilitate remote retail cross-border payments. But it would be necessary, in addition to solving a host of technical problems, to create the particular legal framework that would be required. One can therefore welcome the fact that in its March 1992 paper on "Easier cross-border payments ...", the Commission has announced its intention to "set in hand or support continuing work, in the course of 1992, research into the feasibility (standards, legal aspects) of direct debiting" (paragraph 73).

8. A further question relating to regulative policy is whether and to what extent technical standards in European payments should be harmonised. As set out in detail above (see V.3), the integration of the payments system will require uniform standards or norms. For example it will not be possible to grant cards from other countries access to EFTPOS terminals (Electronic

[19a] Regarding the general elements of the German debit charge procedure, see Jörg Schäfer, Die zivilrechtliche Qualifizierung der Interbankenabkommen (Berlin, 1990) pp. 44 ff.; for a European version, see Féderation Bancaire, Cross-Border Direct Debits, Report by the Cross-Border Direct Debits Working Group (unpublished paper, Brussels, July 20, 1992); Wilhelm Niehoff and Christian Westerhaus, Signale aus Brüssel — Stolpersteine eines grenzüberschreitenden Lastschriftverfahrens, in: Banking and Finance, 1992, no. 3, pp. 6 ff.

Funds Transfer at the Point Of Sale) until the technical standards for cards and terminals have been made compatible in all participating countries. The same applies in principle to the "protocols" according to which transfer instructions are framed electronically, including the system of bank sort codes which as mentioned above (V.3) must also be subjected to the same standards.

Are we therefore compelled to develop uniform EC standards for payment systems and must the banks be subject to binding regulations? The response to this question can be found in the Standards Directive (Directive 83/189/EEC of 28th March 1983 published in the Official Journal, No L 109 of 26th April 1983, page 8) and in the Principles of a European Standards Policy (OJ No L 136 of 4th June 1985, pp 2 ff) whereunder standards decided at European level override the equivalent standards of individual Member States. These documents also provide that work on the establishment of national standards in individual countries must stop as soon as work is begun on establishing European standards.

Against that it could be argued that these maxims merely describe the creation of technical norms and the relationship between European and national standards, but have nothing to say about the binding effect of such standards. Nevertheless the regulative policy of the European payments systems should restrict itself to stimulating and supporting the creation of uniform standards with the aim of making them available as a voluntary reference point. This was until now the approach adopted by the Commission and is one that makes sense for the future since, particularly when security factors have to be considered as for example is the case with cash dispensers competition leads to a *de facto* harmonisation at the highest technological level.

9. In doing what is necessary to harmonise the legal framework, it is also important to realise that in establishing the legal framework for European payments the Community, rather than ignoring international developments, in fact anticipates them. This is particularly the case with the model law on international credit transfers developed by UNCITRAL (United Nations Commission on International Trade Law)[20]. In this respect the question arises as to how the European Community will apply this model law which has been adopted during the course of 1992 by the competent bodies of the United Nations Organisation. Since it is no more than an international model law, each of the twelve Member States will be free (or not) to take it over in whole or in part or in a different form into its national legislation. The result is likely to be a situation in which the rules governing payments in the European Community will be even more fragmented than they are today. In addition to that there is the fact that the model law only applies to cross-

[20] See also the article by Uwe H. Schneider in this volume.

border payments and that it would therefore apply for instance to a transfer from Berchtesgaden to Bordeaux, but not necessarily to a transfer from Berchtesgaden to Bremen.

Regulative policy in the field of European payments therefore needs to perform in two respects:

- on the one hand all EC Member States must adopt a uniform approach to the model law and, either jointly or not at all, and if with amendments, then with the same amendments, transform it into national law.
- on the other hand, if the model law is adopted by all the Member States, it must apply to payments whether within individual Member States or between them.

This provides an argument in favour of integrating into Community law the principal elements of this model law. While it would provide a springboard for the harmonisation of the law on payments in the Community, it would in no way prevent individual Member States from codifying it into their own national laws. Harmonisation does not mean that solutions must be chosen which reflect legislation in one or more Member States. Harmonisation can also, far more effectively, be achieved by taking on board the salient points of a system operating world-wide. In the process the "neutrality" of an international body of law would probably be the best antidote to the legislative egotism that exists in certain countries of the Community.

Despite that it must not be forgotten that the EC Member States disagree on some of the basic principles contained in the model law. Thus, the so-called "money-back guarantee" is acceptable to most Member States but is rejected by the Germans. This provision determines the initiating liability of the sending bank for the proper conclusion of the order until it reaches the receiving institution. The German banks believe this provision is exaggerated since a German sending bank has no way whatever of exerting any influence over an independent bank involved somewhere along the way, e.g. a South American bank. It is in fact hard to understand why the sending bank should bear the risks inherent in the payment system and which may come about, say, as a result of the insolvency of one of the partners, through foreign currency exchange controls or because of other factors. The effects of such a rule can already be seen in the United States where the money-back guarantee has been incorporated into national law through Article 4A of the Uniform Commercial Code. In order to shift their own risk of the insolvency of their other correspondent banks, the US banks are now channelling doubtful foreign transfers through Europe. The point at issue when legislation in this field is harmonised, will be to prevent this provision in the model law from being taken over along with the rest, and so ensnaring the European banking sector as well in the risk chain of international payments.

There are also misgivings with respect to the same-day execution stipulated in Art. 11 of the Model Law. This cannot be made consistent with the mechanisms of foreign currency exchange presently being practiced internationally. The time of receipt of the order and receipt of cover can diverge. The practice in foreign currency exchange is a second day value date. The problem could be solved if one could assume that a "payment order" must be executed when the receiving institution has received cover — then it must provide same-day execution rather than a delayed value date. The Model Law does not take a clear position on this point.

10. In terms of bank supervision, the redefinition of remote retail cross-border payments within the European Community raises the particular question of how the so-called "systemic risk" is to be handled for prudential purposes. Here the problem is to meet the danger that in view of the transportation of large sums through world-wide data networks and computer-controlled transfer systems, break-downs or mere hiccups can spark off world-wide payment crises through the domino-effect. In the same way that traditional bank supervision requires credit or investment risks to be covered in varying degrees by own funds, it would be possible to argue that the risks of involvement in payment systems could also be covered for solvency purposes. The question outstanding however is how these risks are to be measured and whether, in view of the sums involved and the speed of the transactions which create open positions lasting for a matter of days, and in some cases for only a matter of hours, a solvency instrument of the traditional kind is at all appropriate.

Be that as it may, the BIS refers in its Annual Report for 1991 expressly to the need to limit for supervision purposes the risks involved in payment systems[21]. In the meantime it has been looking for appropriate solutions in different working parties. One worth mentioning here is the Farrant Committee — called after its Chairman — which, as part of its work on the prudential treatment of netting under the Basle Own Funds Agreement, has been looking into the treatment of risks of high-value payment systems and working out procedures for compensation of losses[22].

On the other hand in the early summer of 1992 the BIS put out a report on joint supervision of remote retail cross-border payments. This paper con-

---

[21] See Bank for International Settlements: Annual Report for 1991, Basle 1992, pp. 209 ff.

[22] See Bank for International Settlements: Die bankaufsichtliche Behandlung von Netting nach der Baseler Eigenkapitalempfehlung von 1988: ein Diskussionspapier (21. April 1992) (Prudential treatment of netting according to the Basle own funds Recommendation of 1988: a discussion paper) and, as a specific example: Exchange Clearing House Organisation: Netting Multilateral Netting for the Global FX Market, London, December 1991.

tains proposals for common rules on access and processing within such systems as well as basic rules for contingency provisions involving, among other things,

— reflections on common loss-sharing;
— the (agreed) fixing of securities for advance; and
— bilateral "caps".

These principles are now to be worked out in detail by a special working party of central banks and formed into operational arrangements, the purpose being to prevent an arbitrage of different systems in favour of "soft" supervision. This is necessary because from 1993 onwards, under the terms of the second banking directive, a European bank or its domestic subsidiary as is to be detailed below can in principle join the clearing system of the respective domestic central bank even though other bodies of civil law (notably bankruptcy) have not yet been harmonised[23].

In view of the complex nature of their provisions, prudential rules will determine the criteria for access to retail payments systems only in the medium term. As a first step a more probable solution is an early warning system by the central banks which will graduate those systems under which procedures do not observe the criterion catalogue of the Lamfalussy Report and so de facto exclude them from the market.

There are two outstanding issues which bank supervision still has to address:

1. Netting systems require a clear legal base: this could be achieved in the EC in the framework of proposal for a Directive on the reorganisation and winding up of credit institutions and deposit protection schemes (Commission proposal COM 85/788 published in the Official Journal No C 356 of 31st December 1987, page 55). For measures have to be taken to prevent an insolvent institution that leaves the market from according different treatment to its partners in the clearing system. In this connection it is worth recalling what has been said above (see VI.1).

2. The criteria for access to such systems must be fixed clearly and objectively:

— To the extent that the access criteria to a payments system are determined by agreement between the partners, the openness of the system must be governed only by Community competition rules (Articles 85 and 86 of the EEC Treaty).

---

[23] See Uwe H. Schneider and Peter Troberg: Finanzdienstleistungen im EG Binnenmarkt: Sitzland- oder Gastlandrecht? — Zum Verhältnis zwischen europäischem Bankvertragsrecht und Verbraucherschutzrecht (Financial Services in the Internal Market: Home country or host country control? — On the relationship between banking law of contract and consumer protection law), in: Wertpapier-Mitteilungen, 1990, pp. 165 ff.

— The prohibition on discrimination under the EEC Treaty can, like under the second banking directive be invoked only against restrictions imposed by the public sector, such for instance as in the case of supervisory measures. This is for instance the case when a payment system is established with a central bank and netting occurs on bank accounts with the central bank. Thus, for example, the Bank of England is prepared to open a netting account for a bank and offer it overdrawal facilities and the automatic call on central bank funds only after the bank has been subjected to a thorough examination and close observation. In actual fact all that the second banking directive will do, will be to restrict the discretion that the central banks have been able to exercise until now. For the practical scope of this directive can be limited by national laws only if, according to objective criteria, those national laws serve the general interest, guarantee the principle of proportionality and do not duplicate home country control.

IX. Conclusions

Even for European payments in the future, Victor Hugo's words still apply: "Nothing is as strong as an idea whose time has come." The time has come to remove existing barriers. Dogmatism, or confinement to one approach will not succeed. The path from multiplicity to uniformity will be decided by a show of strength. This must be stimulated. Payments are and always have been a matter of competition, and therein lies the real opportunity for the consumer. The decisive factor is a regulative policy of creative competition for customers along the lines of Schumpeters. This is particularly true of telecommunications[24], an area where enormous differences are to be found in price performance ratios from one European bidder to another.

Certainly, regulation will serve to protect the consumer from innovation. Indeed, the increasingly one-sided approach to consumer protection in banking matters may well remind one of Bertolt Brecht's observation that the enemy of good is not the evil, but the well-intentioned.

[24] See Commission of the European Communities COM (87) 290 final: Green Paper on the Development of the Common Market for the Telecommunications Services and Equipment, Brussels, 1987.

Bibliography

Albisetti Emilio ct. al. (ed.): Handbuch des Geld-, Bank- und Börsenwesens der Schweiz, 4th ed. 1987

Altmannsperger, Hans: Die Neuregelung der Posthaftung durch das Poststrukturgesetz, Postpraxis 1989, p. 204

Altmannsperger, Hans: Gesetz über das Postwesen, Kommentar, as of December 1989

Angelici, C.: La contrattazione d'impresa, L'impresa 1985, p. 185

Apice, U.: Revocatoria fallimentare e pagamento fatto dal terzo, Fallimento 1982, p. 1232

Arnold, Hans: Der Europaratsentwurf eines europäischen Konkursabkommens, ZIP 1984, p. 1144

Arora, Anu: Electronic Fund Transfers and the Law, 7 The Company Lawyer 195 (1986)

Association of Reserve City Bankers: Report on the Payments System, 1982

Aufricht, Hans: Comparative Survey of Central Bank Law, 1965

Augenti, G.: Conto corrente bancario, disposizioni di pagamento e morte del correntista, Notaro 1972, p. 1

Bac/Mathieu: La compensation pour dettes connexes après le jugement déclaratif peut-elle survivre à la loi du 25 janvier 1985, Jurisclasseur Périodique JCP 1991, p. 458

Baker, Donald I./Brandel, Roland E.: The Law of Electronic Fund Transfer Systems, 2nd ed. 1988

Ballen, R. B./Diana, N. H.: The Need for Article 4A, The Business Lawyer 1399 (1990)

Ballen, R. B./Diana, N. H.: Duties of the Beneficiary's Bank, The Business Lawyer 1467 (1990)

Ballen, R. G./Baxter, T. C. Jr./Davenport, W. B./Rougeau, V. D./Veltri, S. C.: Commercial Paper, Bank Deposits and Collections, and Other Payment Systems, 45 Business Lawyer 2341 (1990)

Banca d'Italia (ed.): Libro bianco sul sistema dei pagamenti in Italia, 1987

Banca d'Italia (ed.): Il sistema dei pagamenti in Italia: progetti di intervento, 1988

Banca d'Italia (ed.): Sistema dei pagamenti italiano: progetti in corso e prospettive di sviluppo, 1990

Banca d'Italia (ed.): Sistemi di pagamento in undici paesi industrializzati, a cura della Banca dei regolamenti internazionali, 1990

Banca d'Italia (ed.): Proceedings of the Workshop on „Payment System Issues in the Perspective of European Monetary Unification", 1990

Bank for International Settlements (ed.): Large-Value Funds Transfer Systems in the Group of Ten Countries, 1990

Bank für Internationalen Zahlungsausgleich (ed.), Report on Netting Schemes, 1989

Bank für Internationalen Zahlungsausgleich (ed.): Bericht des Ausschusses für Interbank-Netting-Systeme der Zentralbanken der Länder der Zehnergruppe, 1990

Bank of Japan Banking Bureau: Nichigin Net no Kinô to Yakuwari — Wagakuni Kessai System no Infrastructure (The Function and Role of BOJ-NET — The Infrastructure of Japanese Payment Systems), Nichigin Geppo (The Bank of Japan Monthly Bulletin), February 1991, p. 23

Bank of Japan: Japanese Transfer Systems in the Era of Financial Deregulation and Globalization, The Bank of Japan Report (No. 1), July 1989, p. 29

v. Bar, Christian: Internationales Privatrecht, 1987

Baumbach, Adolf/Duden, Konrad/Hopt, Klaus: Handelsgesetzbuch, 28th ed. 1989

Baumbach, Adolf/Hefermehl, Wolfgang: Wechselgesetz und Scheckgesetz, 17th ed. 1990

Baxter, Thomas C./Bahala Jr., Raj: Proper and Improper Execution of a Payment Order, 45 Business Lawyer 1447 (1990)

Beck, Heinz: Gesetz über die Deutsche Bundesbank, Kommentar, 1959

Becker, H.: Obligationenrecht, Allgemeine Bestimmungen, Berner Kommentar, v. VI/I, 1941

Bergmann, Michael: Grenzüberschreitender Datenschutz, 1985

Bialetti, G.: Deregulation valutaria: luci ed ombre, in: Commercio internazionale, 1990, no. 11, Inserto, XIX

Bianca C. H./Bonell, M. J.: Commentary on the International Sales Law, 1987

Bischoff, Jacques: Vertragsrisiko und clausula rebus sic stantibus. Risikozuordnung in Verträgen bei veränderten Verhältnissen, Zürcher Studien zum Privatrecht, v. 28, 1983

Blaurock, Uwe: Haftung der Banken bei Einsatz neuer Techniken und Medien, in: Köndgen, Johannes (ed.), Neue Entwicklungen im Bankhaftungsrecht, 1987, p. 35

Blaurock, Uwe: Haftung der Banken beim Einsatz neuer Techniken im Zahlungsverkehr, CR 1989, p. 567

Blaurock, Uwe: Wege zur Rechtseinheit im Zivilrecht Europas, in: Starck, Christian (ed.), Rechtsvereinheitlichung durch Gesetze, 1992, p. 90

Börner, Bodo: Die Fünfte Freiheit des Gemeinsamen Marktes: Der Zahlungsverkehr, in: Festschrift für Ophüls, 1966, p. 19

van Boeschoten, C. D./Smits, René J. H.: ILA Draft Rules on the Time of Payment of Monetary Obligations, ILA Warsaw Conference (1988), p. 18

Bonavera, E.: Pluralità di conti dello stesso correntista, giroconto e revocatoria fallimentare, Giurisprudenza commerciale 1989, p. 84

Bonelli, F.: La convenzione di Roma del 19 guigno 1980 e la legge applicabile alle operazioni bancarie, in: Treves, Tullio (ed.), Verso una disciplina comunitaria della legge applicabile ai contratti, 1983, p. 115

Brüggemann, Max: Die Banktechnik des Auslandsgeschäfts, 6th ed. 1983

Bucher, Eugen: Schweizerisches Obligationenrecht, Allgemeiner Teil, 1988

Bucher, Eugen: Wer haftet wem? Zum Problem der Tragung des Risikos betrügerisch veranlaßter Bankvergütungen, Zeitschrift recht 1984, p. 97

Bührer, Marc P.: AGB-Kollisionen, „the battle of the forms" und weitere Probleme beim Verweis auf Allgemeine Geschäftsbedingungen, Schweizer Schriften zum Handels- und Wirtschaftsrecht, v. 96, 1987

Bundeskriminalamt Wiesbaden (ed.), Macht sich Kriminalität bezahlt? — Aufspüren und Abschöpfen von Verbrechensgewinnen — Arbeitstagung des Bundeskriminalamtes Wiesbaden vom 10. bis 13. November 1986, BKA-Vortragsreihe v. 32, 1987

Bureau Européen des Unions de Consommateurs (ed.): Holiday money, BEUC/1/88, July 1988

Bureau Européen des Unions de Consommateurs (ed.): Transfer d'argent dans le CEE, BEUC/76/88, April 1988

Bureau Européen des Unions de Consommateurs (ed.): A Survey of the Implementation of the EC Recommendation Concerning Payment Systems, BEUC/CB/105/90, April 1990

Bureau Européen des Unions de Consommateurs (ed.): EEC Study on Credit Cards, BEUC/89, August 1989

Burhenne, Wolfgang E./Perband, Klaus: EDV-Recht, 1970 (looseleaf as of 1990)

Cabrillac, Henry: Le chéque et le virement, 5th ed. 1980

v. Caemmerer, Ernst/Schlechtriem, Peter: Kommentar zum Einheitlichen UN-Kaufrecht — CISG, 1990

v. Caemmerer, Ernst: Probleme des Haager einheitlichen Kaufrechts, AcP 178 (1978), p. 121 = Gesammelte Schriften v. III, 1983, p. 198

v. Caemmerer, Ernst: Verträge zugunsten Dritter, in: Festschrift für Wieacker, 1978, p. 311 = Gesammelte Schriften, v. III, 1983, p. 189

v. Caemmerer, Ernst: Zahlungsort, in: Internationales Recht und Wirtschaftsordnung, Festschrift für F. A. Mann, 1977, p. 3

Caltabiano, A.: L'accreditamento bancario, in: Portale, Giuseppe (ed.), Le operazioni bancarie, v. II, 1978

Campobasso, G. F.: Bancogiro e moneta scritturale, 1979

Campobasso, G. F.: Bancogiro, in: Enciclopedia giuridica Treccani, IV, 1988

Campobasso, G. F.: Il bancogiro. Profili strutturali, in: Portale, Giuseppe (ed.), Le operazioni bancarie, v. 2, 1978, p. 633

Canaris, Claus Wilhelm: Vertrauenshaftung im deutschen Privatrecht, 1971

Canaris, Claus-Wilhelm: Bankvertragsrecht, 4th ed. 1988

Capossela, E.: Liberalizzazione valutaria e direttiva CEE: un confronto, in: Commercio internazionale, 1990, no. 11, Inserto, IX

Carey: Electronic Funds Transfers: Model Rules, 16 International Business Lawyer 104 (1988)

Carriero, G.: Bonifico bancario ed onere di diligenza, in: Foro italiano, 1990, I, p. 128

Cavalli, G.: Conto corrente, in: Enciclopedia giuridica Treccani, VIII, 1988

Chaput: Droit du redressement et de la liquidation judiciaire des entreprises, p. 126 no. 114

Chorley, Lord: Opening the Account, and other Problems, 1955

Coing, Helmut: Zum Geldherausgabeanspruch gegenüber dem Treuhänder, JZ 1970, p. 245

Commission of the European Communities (ed.): „TEDIS", COM (90) 361 final, 25 July 1990

Commission of the European Communities (ed.): „Grünbuch: Zahlungsverkehr im Binnenmarkt", COM (90) 447 final, 26 September 1990

Conseil de l'Europe (ed.): Communication du comité des ministres relative à l'evaluation des certains traitées du conseil de l'Europe, doc. no. 5427 of 27. June 1988

Conseil national du crédit (ed.): Aspects européens et internationaux des cartes de payement, v. 1: Rapport de groupe de travail, v. 2: Annexes au rapport de groupe de travail, 1988

Costa, C.: „Astrattezza" ed eccezioni opponibili nel credito documentario irrevocabile, 1989

Council of Europe (ed.): Explanatory Report on the European Convention on the Calculation of Time Limits, 1983

Council of Europe (ed.): Explanatory Report on the European Convention on Foreign Money Liabilities, 1968

Council of Europe (ed.): Explanatory Report on the European Convention on the Place of Payment of Money Liabilities, 1972

Council of Europe (ed.): Protection of Personal Data Used for Payment and Other Related Operations, Recommendation Nr. R (90) 19, September 13th, 1990 and Explanatory Memorandum, Strasburg 1990

Council of Europe (ed.): Resolutions and Recommendations of the Committee of Ministers in the Fields of Civil, Commercial, Public and International Law, v. I, 1983

Cranston, Ross: Payment and Clearing Systems in the European Community, in: Cranston, Ross (ed.), The Single Market and the Law of Banking, 1991

Crawford, Bradley: The Legal Issues in EFTS, unpublished speech from the annual meeting of FELABAN, San Jose, Costa Rica 1988

Crawford, Bradley: International Credit Transfers: The Influence of Art. 4A on the Model Law, 19 Canadian Business Law Journal 166 (1991)

von der Crone, Hans Caspar: Rechtliche Aspekte der direkten Zahlung mit elektronischer Überweisung (EFTPOS) Schweizer Schriften zum Handels- und Wirtschaftsrecht, v. 109, 1988

Dach, Joseph: Payment in Cashless Societies, in: Festschrift für F. A. Mann, 1977, p. 707

Danovi, R.: In ricordo della revocatoria fallimentare degli accreditamenti sui conti correnti bancari, in: Fallimento, 1982, 1429

Deeg, Ernst: A Proposal for a Multi- Currency Netting System, in: Payment Systems Worldwide 1990, p. 40

Delaume, Georges R.: Transnational Contracts — Applicable Law and Settlement of Disputes, 4 volume looseleaf, 1980

Derrida/Godé/Sortais: Redressement et liquidation judiciaires des entreprises, 3rd ed.

Deutsche Bundesbank (ed.): Die Zahlungsbilanzstatistik der Bundesrepublik Deutschland; Inhalt, Aufbau und methodische Grundlagen; special publication no. 8, 2nd ed. 1990

Deutsche S.W.I.F.T.-Gruppe (ed.): Protokoll über die ordentliche Mitgliederversammlung der Deutschen S.W.I.F.T.-Gruppe of 12. May 1989

Di Meo, A.: I pagamenti internazionali, 1990

Dole, R. F., Jr.: A Japanese Insight with Respect to the Finality of Wholesale Wire Transfers, 1990 (unpublished)

Dölle, Hans (ed.): Kommentar zum einheitlichen Kaufrecht, 1976

Donadi, M.: Problemi giuridici del trasferimento elettronico di fondi, in: Contratto e impresa, 1988, p. 559

Dow, Steven B./Ellis, Nan S.: The Proposed Uniform New Payment Code: Allocation of Losses Resulting from Forged Drawers' Signatures, 22 Harv. J. on Leg. 399 (1985)

Dreher, Eduart/Tröndle, Herbert: Strafgesetzbuch und Nebengesetze, 45th ed. 1991

Drobnig, Ulrich: Allgemeine Geschäftsbedingungen im Internationalen Handelsverkehr, Festschrift für F. A. Mann, 1977, p. 591

Duboc, Guy: La compensation et les droits des tiers, 1989

Effros, Robert C.: A Banker's Primer on the Law of Electronic Funds Transfer 105 The Banking Law Journal 510 (1988)

Ehrenzweig, Albert A.: Private International Law — General Part, 1967

Ellinger, E.P.: Electronic Funds Transfer as a Deferred Settlement System, in: R. M. Goode (ed.), Electronic Banking. The Legal Implications, 1985

Ellinger, E.P.: Modern Banking Law, 1987

Emch, Urs/Renz, Hugo: Das schweizerische Bankgeschäft, 3rd ed. 1984

Endres, Michael: Sicherheitsanforderungen bei kundenbezogenen EDV-Anwendungen, Bank und Markt 1990, p. 1

Engelbracht/Zimny: Die Auswirkungen des Poststrukturgesetzes auf die Deutsche Bundespost Postbank und auf die Rechtsbeziehungen zu ihren Kunden, Postpraxis 1990, p. 35

Enneccerus, Ludwig/Lehmann, Heinrich: Recht der Schuldverhältnisse, 15th ed. 1958

Erman, Walter: Handkommentar zum Bürgerlichen Gesetzbuch, 8th ed. 1989

Esser, Jopsef/Schmidt, Eike: Schuldrecht, v. 1, 1984

Etzkorn, Jörg: Rechtsfragen des internationalen elektronischen Zahlungsverkehrs durch S.W.I.F.T., Recht des internationalen Wirtschaftsverkehrs, v. 6, 1991

Etzkorn, Jörg: Allgemeine Geschäftsbedingungen für Inhaber von Kreditkarten, WM 1991, p. 1901

Falcone, G.: Conto corrente postale, in: Digesto delle discipline privatistiche, Sezione commerciale, IV, 1989, p. 28

Federation of Bankers Association of Japan (ed.): Payment Systems in Japan, 1990

Federation of Bankers Association of Japan/Tokyo Bankers Association: Annual Report 1990 on Clearing Houses, 1991

Ferri, Giuseppe: Bancogiro, in: Enciclopedia del diritto, v. V, 1959, p. 32

Fikentscher, Wolfgang: Schuldrecht, 7th ed. 1985

Flume, Wolfgang: Allgemeiner Teil des Bürgerlichen Rechts, v. II, 3rd ed. 1979

Forstmoser, Peter: Allgemeine Geschäftsbedingungen und ihre Bedeutung im Bankverkehr, in: Forstmoser, Peter (ed.), Rechtsprobleme der Bankpraxis, 1976

Frignani, A.: Il contratto internazionale, in: Galgano, F. (ed.), Trattato di diritto commerciale e di diritto pubblico dell'economia, 1990

Fry, Patricia B.: Basic Consepts in Article 4A: Scope and Definitions, 45 Business Lawyer 1401 (1990)

Gablenz, Carl-Heinrich Freiherr v.: Die Haftung der Banken bei Einschaltung Dritter, 1983

Ganten, Reinhard/Jahn, Uwe: Neues internationales Wechselrecht vor dem Abschluß, Die Bank 1987, p. 394

Garioni, G.: Articolo per articolo il decreto valutario, in: Commercio internazionale, 1990, no. 11, Inserto, III

Garioni, G.: Posizione netta ed in cambi: cadono i divieti, in: Commercio internazionale, 1990, no. 11, Inserto, XXIII

Gautschi, Georg: Der einfache Auftrag, Berner Kommentar, IV/2/4, Art. 394-406 OR, 3rd ed. 1971

Gautschi, Georg: Besondere Auftrags- und Geschäftsbesorgungsverhältnisse sowie Hinterlegung, Berner Kommentar, IV/2/6, Art. 425-491 OR, 2nd ed. 1962

Gernhuber, Joachim: Das Schuldverhältnis, 1989

Gernhuber, Joachim: Die Erfüllung und ihre Surrogate, 1983

Gernhuber, Joachim: Austausch von Kredit im rechtsgeschäftlichen Verbund — zur Lehre von den Vertragsverbindungen, in: Festschrift für Karl Larenz, 1973, p. 455

Geva, Benjamin: CHIPS Transfer of Funds, 1987

Geva, Benjamin: International Funds Transfers — Performance by Wire Payment, 4 B.F.L.R lll (1990)

Geva, Benjamin: Payment into a Bank Account, 3 JIBL 108 (1990)

Giannantonio, E.: Trasferimenti elettronici dei fondi e autonomia privata, 1986

Giannantonio, E.: Trasferimenti elettronici di fondi e adempimento, in: Foro italiano, 1990, p. 165

Giardina, A./Villani, U.: Garanzie bancarie, commercio internazionale e diritto internazionale privato, 1974

Giardina, A.: Conflitti di leggi in tema di garanzie bancarie, in: Banca, borsa, titoli di credito, 1983, p. 447

Gilman, Martin G.: Auf dem Wege zur Währungskonvertibilität, Finanzierung und Entwicklung 1990, p. 32

Giorgianni, F.: I crediti disponibili, 1974

Glosband/Katucki: Current Developments in International Insolvency Law and Practice, 45 Business Lawyer 2273 (1990)

Goldschalk, Hugo T.C.: Computergeld, Entwicklungen und ordnungspolitische Probleme des elektronischen Zahlungsverkehrssystems, 1983

Goldstajn, Aleksandar: The New Law Merchant Reconsidered, in: Festschrift für Schmitthoff, 1973, p. 171

Goldstein, David B.: Federal Versus State Adoption of Article 4A, 45 Business Lawyer 1513 (1990)

Gotô, K.: Furikomi Fuikaeno Hôri to Shiharai Torihiki (Legal Principles on Credit and Debit Transfers, and Payment Transactions), 1986

Gramlich, A.: Ein ungewisser Übergang — Anmerkungen zu Folgen der Poststrukturreform, die sich hätten vermeiden lassen, Verwaltungsrundschau 1990, p. 82

Guggenheim, Daniel: Die Verträge der schweizerischen Bankpraxis, 3rd ed. 1986

Guhl, Theo/Merz, Hans/Kummer, Max: Das Schweizerische Obligationenrecht, 7th ed. 1980

De Guillenchmidt, Michel: Projet de convention du conseil de l'Europe sur certains aspects internationaux de la faillite, Banque et Droit 1989, p. 191

Gyler, E. U./Baker, J. C.: SWIFT: A Fast Method to Facilitate International Financial Transactions, 7 J. World Trade L. 458 (1983)

Hadding, Walther: Drittschadensliquidation und „Schutzwirkungen für Dritte" im bargeldlosen Zahlungsverkehr, Festschrift für Werner, 1984, p. 165

Hadding, Walther/Häuser, Franz: Gutschrift und Widerruf des Überweisungsauftrags im Giroverhältnis, WM 1988, p. 1149

Hadding, Walther/Häuser, Franz: Rechtsfragen des bargeldlosen Zahlungsverkehrs, RWS-Skript 127 (1984)

Hadding, Walther/Häuser, Franz: Rechtsfragen des Giroverhältnisses, ZHR 145 (1981), p. 138

Hadding, Walther/Schneider, Uwe H.: Bankgeheimnis und Bankauskunft in der Bundesrepublik Deutschland und in ausländischen Rechtsordnungen, 1986

v. Hahn, Carl: Commentar zum Allgemeinen Deutschen Handelsgesetzbuch, v. II, 2nd ed. 1883

Hahn, Hugo J.: Grenzüberschreitende Umschuldungen bei bargeldlosen Geldbewegungen, ZfgdK 1985, p. 190

Hahn, Oswald: Das Zahlungs- und Inkassogeschäft der Banken, 1970

Hamel, Joseph: Banques et operations de banque, 2nd ed. 1943

Hamel, Joseph/Lagarde, Gaston/Jauffret, Alfred: Traité de Droit commercial, 2nd ed. 1980

Hamel, Joseph/Lagarde, Gaston/Jauffret, Alfred: Droit commercial, v. 2, 1966

Hammann, Harald: Die Universalkreditkarte, 1991

Hannaway, Michael: The Jurisprudence and Judical Treatment of the Comments to the Uniform Commercial Code, 75 Cornell Law Review 962 (1990)

Hattori, K./Kato, K./Shibazaki, J.: Kaisei Naikokou Kawase (Domestic Fund Transfers), revised edition 1975

Hayashi, R.: CD Torihiki (Automated Teller Machine Transactions), in: Kato, I./ Hayashi, R./Kawamoto, I. (eds.): Ginkô Torihikihô Kôza Jôkan (Bank Transactions Law Course), 1976, p. 293

Hayashibe, M.: Songai no Futan tô (Loss Allocation), 1153 Kinyûhôjiô 26 (1987)

Heck, Philipp: Grundriß des Schuldrechts, 1929

Heini, Daniel: Rechtsstellung der am bargeldlosen Zahlungsverkehr Beteiligten, insbesondere Rechtzeitigkeit und Widerruf der bargeldlosen Zahlung unter Berücksichtigung internationaler Probleme, 1991

Heinrich, Gregor: International Initiatives Regarding the Harmonisation of Rules Having an Effect on Payment, Funds Transfers and Bankruptcy, RDAI 1991, p. 315

Heinrich, Gregor: Building A Universal Payments Law? The UNCITRAL Model Law on International Credit Transfers, Payment Systems Worldwide 1991, p. 4

Heinrichs, Helmut: Freizeichnung im Bankgeschäft, in: Köndgen, Johannes (ed.), Neue Entwicklungen im Bankhaftungsrecht, 1987, p. 115

Helbig, Claus: Die Giroüberweisung, deren Widerruf und Anfechtung nach deutschem und schweizerischem Recht, 1970

Hellner, Thorwald: Rechtsprobleme des Zahlungsverkehrs unter Berücksichtigung der höchstrichterlichen Rechtsprechung, ZHR 145 (1981), p. 109

Hellner, Thorwald: Rechtsfragen des Zahlungsverkehrs unter besonderer Berücksichtigung des Bildschirmtextverfahrens, in: Festschr. für Werner, 1984, p. 251

Herber, Dolf/Czerwenka, Beate: Internationales Kaufrecht, 1991

Hess, Martin: Rechtliche Aspekte der Banküberweisung, unter besonderer Berücksichtigung des Interbankzahlungsverkehrssystems Swiss Interbank Clearing (SIC), Schweizerische Zeitschrift für Wirtschaftsrecht 1991, p. 103

Hess, Martin: Die Rechtsgrundlagen des Swiss Interbank Clearing (SIC), Wirtschaft und Recht, 1988, p. 31

Hessler: Sachrechtliche Generalklausel und internationales Familienrecht, 1985

Heymann, Ernst: Handelsgesetzbuch, Kommentar, 1990

Hinsch, Christian L./Horn, Norbert: Das Vertragsrecht der internationalen Konsortialkredite und Projektfinanzierungen, 1985

Hitzel: Tragung des EDV-Risikos im Recht der Banküberweisung, 1988

Hoffmann, Diether: Banken- und Börsenrecht der EWG, 1990

Honold, John: Uniform Law for International Sales, 1982

Horn, Norbert: Uniformity and Diversity in the Law of International Contracts, in: Horn, Norbert/Schmitthoff, Clive M. (eds.), The Transnational Law of International Commercial Transactions, 1982, p. 3

Horn, Norbert: Codes of Conduct for Multinational Enterprises and Transnational Lex Mercatoria: An International Process of Learning and Law Making, in Horn, Norbert (ed.), Legal Problems of Codes of Conduct for Multinational Enterprises, 1980, p. 45

Horn, Norbert: Das Recht der internationalen Anleihen, 1972

Hoshino, E.: Minpô Gairon (Introduction to Civil Law) III, 1978

Houghton: Netting-off Agreements — The Legal Perspectice, 4 JIBL 241 (1987)

Huber, Ulrich: Der UNCITRAL-Entwurf eines Übereinkommens über internationale Warenkaufverträge, RabelsZ 43 (1979), p. 413

Hüffer, Uwe: Die Haftung gegenüber dem ersten Auftraggeber im mehrgliedrigen Zahlungsverkehr, ZHR 151 (1987), p. 93

Hüffer, Uwe: Haftungsfragen im Bankrecht, WM 1987, p. 641

Hull, Bryan D.: Common Law Negligence and Check Fraud Loss Allocation: Has Common Law Supplemented or Supplanted the U.C.C., 51 Ohio St. Law Journal 605 (1990)

Hummer, Waldemar/Wagner, Gerhard (ed.): Österreich im Europarat 1956-1986, 1988

International Chamber of Commerce (ed.): Uniform Rules of Conduct for Interchange of Trade Data by Teletransmission (UNCID), ICC Publication no. 452, 1987

International Organization for Standardisation (ed.): Bank Telecommunication — Funds Transfer Messages, Part 1, Vocabulary and Data Elements, Reference No. ISO 7982-1: 1987 (E), 1987

Ishiguro, I.: Kinyû Torihiki to Kokusaisoshô (Financial Transactions and International Litigation), 1983

Iwahara, Shinsaku: Denshi Shikin Torihiki Nikansuru Hôseiseibi no Hitsuyôsei to Kadai (The Need for and the Problems Associated with Enacting a New Electronic Funds Transfer Act) I-III", 1203 Kinyûhômujijô (1988), 1204 Kinyûhômujijô 17 (1988), 1206 Kinyûhômujijô 6 (1988)

Iwahara, Shinsaku: Denshiteki Shikin Idô (Electronic Funds Transfers), 385 NBL 14 (1987)

Iwahara, Shinsaku: Shikin Idô Torihiki no Kashi to Kinyûkikan (Unauthorized or Voidable Funds Transfers and Financial Institutions), in: Kokka to Shimin (State and Citizens), v. 3, 1987

Iwahara, Shinsaku: Computer o Mochiita Kinyû Kessai to hô (The Law of Computerized Financial Settlements), 1 Kinyûhô Kenkyu 9 (1985)

Jäger, Ernst: Konkursordnung, 8th ed. 1958

Jauernig, Othmar: Bürgerliches Gesetzbuch, 5th ed. 1990

Jayme, Erik: Komplexe Langzeitverträge und Internationales Privatrecht, IPrax 1987, p. 63

Jayme, Erik: Betrachtungen zur „dépecage" im internationalen Privatrecht, in: Festschrift für Kegel, 1987, p. 253

Jayme, Erik: Rechtswahlklausel und zwingendes ausländisches Recht beim Franchise-Vertrag, IPrax 1983, p. 105

Jayme, Erik: Kollisionsrecht und Bankgeschäfte mit Auslandsberührung, 1977

Joost, Detlev: Die Verteilung des Risikos von Scheckfälschungen, ZHR 153 (1989), p. 237

Joshino, E.: Minpô Gairon (Introduction to Civil Law), 1975

Jueterbock, Dietrich: SWIFT II für die 90er Jahre, Die Bank 1988, p. 329

Kämmerer, Ludwig: Die Rechtsgrundlagen des Weltpostverkehrs, Archiv für das Post- und Fernmeldewesen 1958, p. 99

Kato, K.: Kawase Torihiki Niokeru Tôjisha no Hôritsu kankei (Legal Relationships Among Participants in Fund Transfer Transactions), in: Horiuchi, M. (ed.), Hanrei Senrei Kinyû Torihiki Hô (Case Law and Precedents in Financial Transactions Law), 1979, p. 237

Kawamoto, I.: Kogitte no Ukeire to Yokin no Seiritsu (Checks, Deposits and Depositor's Claims), 176 Jurist 72 (1959)

Kegel, Gerhard: Internationales Privatrecht, 6th ed. 1987

Kegel, Gerhard: Die Bankgeschäfte im deutschen internationalen Privatrecht, in: Gedächtnisschrift für Rudolf Schmidt, 1966, p. 215

Kilian, Wolfgang: Datensicherheit in Computernetzen, CR 1991, p. 73

Kinami, A.: Shikin Idô System Niokeru Risk Eno Hôteki Taiô Notameno Ichishiten (A Viewpoint of Legal Strategies to Deal with Risks in Funds Transfer Systems), 1213 Kinyûhomlujijô 6 (1989)

Kindermann, Elmar: Zahlungsverkehr, BuB 6/129 (Looseleaf, as of 1990)

Kindermann, Elmar: Gutschrift und Belastungsbuchung im Geldüberweisungsverkehr, WM 1982, p. 318

Kleiner, Beat: Vertragsklauseln bei BankFremdwährungsschulden, EWS 1991, p. 53

Kleiner, Beat: Bankkonto und elektronische Transaktion, Festschrift für Max Keller, 1989, p. 715

Kleiner, Beat: Das neue IPRG — Ein vernachlässigtes „Detail", SAG 1988, p. 70

Kleiner, Beat: Bankkonto, Giro-, und Kontokorrentvertrag, Festschrift für Schluep, 1988, p. 273

Kleiner, Beat: Internationales Devisen-Schuldrecht, 1985

Kleiner, Beat: Die allgemeinen Geschäftsbedingungen der Banken; Giro- und Kontokorrentvertrag, 2nd ed. 1963

Kleiner, Beat/Schmid, Bernhard: Substitution im Überweisungsverkehr, SAG 1985, p. 178

Kleinknecht, Theodor/Meyer, Karlheinz/Meyer-Großner, Lutz: Strafprozeßordnung, Gerichtsverfassungsgesetz, Nebengesetze und ergänzende Bestimmungen, 40th ed. 1991

Klingsporn, Burkhard: Das Europäische Übereinkommen über den Ort der Zahlung von Geldschulden, WM 1972, p. 1262

Köhler, Helmut: Die Problematik automatisierter Rechtsvorgänge, insbesondere von Willenserklärungen, AcP 182 (1982), p. 126

Köndgen, Johannes: Bankhaftung — Strukturen und Tendenzen, in: Köndgen, Johannes (ed.), Neue Entwicklungen im Bankhaftungsrecht, 1987, p. 133

Kokumin Seikatsu Shingikai Shôhisha Seisaku Bukai (The Consumer Policy Committe of the National Life Council): Shôhisha Torihiki ni Mochiirareru Yaakkan no Tekiseika Nitsuite (Report on the Standard Contract Terms in Consumer Transactions), 1984

Koller, Ingo: Grundstrukturen des Bankhaftungsrechts unter besonderer Berücksichtigung des Zahlungsverkehrs, in: Köndgen, Johannes (ed.), Neue Entwicklungen im Bankhaftungsrecht, 1987, p. 21

Koller, Ingo: Die Verteilung des Scheckfälschungsrisikos zwischen Kunde und Bank, NJW 1981, p. 2433

Komachiya, S.: Hanrei Shôhô (Case Decisions on Commercial Law) II, 1953

Kreuzer, Karl: Ausländisches Wirtschaftsrecht vor deutschen Gerichten, 1986

Kümpel, Siegfried: Zur Anpassung der AGB der Banken an das AGB-Gesetz, WM 1977, p. 694

Küng, Joseph: Zahlung und Zahlungsort im internationalen Privatrecht, 1970

Kurusu, S.: Saiken no Junsenyû to Menseki Shôken (Apparent Creditor and Receipt), 33/4 Minshôhô Zassi 477 (1956)

Landeszentralbank in Hessen (ed.): EAF, Bericht zum Abschluß des Pilotbetriebes, October 1990

Lange, Hermann: Schadensersatz, 2nd ed. 1990

Langfeldt, Enno: Renaissance des Bargeldes in der Bundesrepublik Deutschland?, Die Weltwirtschaft 1989, p. 51

Larenz, Karl: Lehrbuch des Schuldrechts, 14th ed. 1987

Larenz, Karl: Allgemeiner Teil des deutschen Bürgerlichen Rechts, 6th ed. 1983

Lecchi, G. C.: Il servizio estero merci, 1982

Lehmann, Gerd D.: Zahlungsverkehr der Banken, 1986

Leitermann, Hubert: Drei Jahre S.W.I.F.T. — lautlose Revolution im Auslandszahlungsverkehr, Die Bank 1980, p. 418

Leverkus, Erich: Freier Tausch und fauler Zauber. Vom Geld und seiner Geschichte, 1990

Lew, Julian/Stanbrook, International Trade: Law and Practice, 1983

Libertini, M.: Pagamento cambiario e revocatoria fallimentare, 1983

Liesecke, Rudolph: Die Stellung der kreditgebenden Bank beim Dokumenten- Inkasso und beim Akkreditivgeschäft, Festschrift für Fischer, 1979, p. 397

Lingl, Herbert F.: Risk Allocation in International Interbank Electronic Fund Transfers: CHIPS & SWIFT, 22 Harv. Int'l L.J. 621 (1981)

Loewe, Roland: Europarat, Rechtsvereinheitlichung und Rechtsharmonisierung im Bereich des Zivilrechts, in: Hummer, Waldemar/Wagner, Gerhard (eds.): Österreich im Europarat 1956-1986, 1988, p. 387

Loh, Wolfram W.: Das S.W.I.F.T.-System, Die moderne Datenübertragung im internationalen Zahlungsverkehr, 1983

Lorenz, Werner: Fehlerhafte Banküberweisungen mit Auslandsberührung, NJW 1990, p. 607

Lüderitz, Alexander (ed.): Internationales Privatrecht, 1987

Luminoso, A.: Mandato, commissione e spedizione, in: Trattato di diritto civile e commerciale diterro da cicu e messineo, 1984

Maccarone, R.: I trasferimenti elettronici di fondi nel diritto italiano, in: Le operazioni della banca tra norme e prassi, 1988, p. 352

Maccarone, R.: I trasferimenti elettronici di fondi, in: Bancaria, 1981, p. 792

Maccarone, R.: Problemi in tema di responsabilità della banca per mancato pagamento di assegni, in: Maccarone, S./Nigro, A. (eds.), Funzione bancaria, rischio e responsabilità della banca, 1981, p. 177

Maeda, H./Kanda, H.I.: Obligation Netting, 6 Kinyûhô Kekyû (Shiryôhen) 1 (1990)

Maeda, H.: Tegata Koggitte Hô Nyûmon (Introduction to Bills, Notes and Checks Law), 1983

Maeda, S.: Shôhisha Hogo no Kanten Karamita Electronic Banking Nitairsuru Hôkiseijôno Mondai (Problems of Electronic Banking Laws from the Consumer Protection View Point), in: Kôdo jôhô Shakai no Hôritsu Mondai (Legal Problems in Technologically Informed Society), 1984, p. 236

Maeda, T.: Furikomi (Credit Transfers), in: Kato, I./Hayashi, R./Kawamoto, I. (eds.): Ginkô Torihikihô Kôza Jôkan (Bank Transactions Law Course), 1976, p. 313

Maffei, Alberti A.: Il danno nella revocatoria, 1970

Makuyama, I.: Comments on Kagoshima District Court Decision on Nov. 27, 1989, 1267 Kinyûhômujijô 14 (1990)

Maltese, D.: Azione revocatoria fallimentare e rimessa di terzo in conto corrente, in: Giurisprudenza italiana, 1972, I, 1, 1122

Marchesi, G. C.: Finanza e tecnica delle esportazioni, 1985

Marinoni, R.: Adempimento del debito altrui e gratutità dell'attribuzione: una nuova pronuncia della Cassazione sul tema, in: Giurisprudenza commerciale, 1990, II, p. 28

Martin-Serf, Arlette: L'interpretation extensive des sûretés réelles en droit commercial, Revue Trimestrielle de Droit Commercial 1980, p. 677

Martiny, Dieter/v. Dieken, Friedrich/Hausmann, Rainer/Joch, Bernd/Klein-Schmidt, Peter/Mertz, Franz/Rigaux, Francois: Droit international privé, Vol. II: Droit positif belge, 1979

Matscher, Franz/Siehr, Kurt/Delbrück, Jost: Multilaterale Staatsverträge erga omnes und deren Inkorporation in nationale IPR-Kodifikationen — Vor- und Nachteile einer solchen Rezeption, Berichte der Deutschen Gesellschaft für Völkerrecht 27, 1986

Matsui, M.: Nishi Doitsu Furikae Torihiki Niokeru Kashikata Kichô Nitsuite (Credit Entries in Funds Transfers in West Germany), 161 Dôshisha Hôgaku 361 (1980)

Matsumoto, S.: Shokai Naikoku Kawase (Details of Domestic Fund Transfers), revised ed. 1988

Matsumoto, S.: Furikomiki tô Kikai Niyoru Furikomi to Furikomikitei (Credit Transfers through Automated Clearing Machines and Proposed Standard Terms of Credit Transfers), 1153 Kinyôhômujijô 32 (1987)

Matsumoto, S.: Furikomi Torihiki Niokeku Shimuke Ginkô no Sekinin to Kumimodoshi no Toriatsukai (An Orginator's Bank's Liability and Revocation in Credit Transfers) II, 1138 Kinyûhômijô 1820 (1986)

Matsumoto, S.: The Zengin System, in: Suzuki, R./Takeuchi, A. (eds.), Kinyû Torihikihô Taikei (The System of Financial Transactions Law), v. 3, 1983

Matsumoto, S.: Shôkôihô (Commercial Transactions Law), 1929

Mattout, Jean-Pierre: Communication sur le netting présenté au colloque de Deauville en juin 1989, Revue de Jurisprudence Comerciale, special number, November 1989

Mendegris, Rogher: La nature juridique de la compensation, 1989

Mengle, D.L.: Real and Regulatory Reform in Electronic Payments: An Evaluation of Payment Finality Rules, in: Humphrey, D.B. (ed.): The U.S. Payment System: Efficiency, Risk and the Role of the Federal Reserve, 1990

Merkel, Helmut: Das Recht der Kreditkarte in den U.S.A., 1990

Merz, Hans: Vertrag und Vertragsschluß, 1988

Messineo, F.: Punti di vista sulla natura dell'accreditamento bancario, in: Banca, borsa, titoli di credito, 1963, I, p. 309

Mezger, Ernst: L'unification du lieu de paiement des obligations monétaires, Journal du Droit International (1967), p. 584

Meyer-Cording, Ulrich: Das Recht der Banküberweisung unter besonderer Berücksichtigung der steckengebliebenen Überweisungen, 1951

Meyer, Jürgen/Dessecker, Axel/Smettan, Jürgen R.: Gewinnabschöpfung bei Betäubungsmitteldelikten, Landesbericht Vereinigte Staaten von Amerika, 1989, p. 415

Miller, Fred H./Davenport, William B.: Introduction to the Special Issue on the Uniform Commercial Code, 45 Business Lawyer 1389 (1990)

Mimuro, T.: Gaikokukawase Yen Kessai Seido no Sôsetsu to Sono Toriatsukai (The Establishment and Organisation of the FEYSS), 404 Kinyû 62 (1980)

Minervini, G.: Mandato, submandato e sostituzione del mandatario nella prassi, bancaria e nella giurisprudenza, in: Portale, Giuseppe (ed.), Le operazioni bancarie, v. I, 1978, p. 217 = Revista dir. civ., 1976, v. I, p. 473

Minowa, S.: Zengin Sysytem Niokeru Shimuke Chôka Kanri Seido no Dônyû (Introduction of Net Debit Limits in the Zengin System), 519 Kinyû 11 (1990)

Möschel, Wernhard: Dogmatische Strukturen des bargeldlosen Zahlungsverkehrs, AcP 186 (1986), p. 187

Molle, G.: I contratti bancari, 1981

Morris, J. H. C. (ed.): Dicey and Morris on the Conflict of Laws, 8th ed. 1967

Mossa, F.: Il diritto dello check, I, p. 1919

Müller, Alfons: EUFISERV — Zusammenarbeit der EG-Sparkassen im Zahlungsverkehr, Die Bank 1991, p. 413

Münchener Kommentar zum Bürgerlichen Gesetzbuch Kurt Rebmann und Franz-Jürgen Säcker (eds), 2nd ed. 1984 ff.

Naikokukawase Uneikikô (The Domestic Fund Transfer Management Insitute)/TBA/ Zenkoku Ginkô Data Tsûshin Center (The National Bank Data Telecommunication Center): Zengin Shisutem Unyôjôkyô Hôkôku (Report on Activities of Zengin System), March 4, 1991

Nelson, N. R.: Settlement Obligations and Bank Insolvency, 45 The Business Lawyer (1990)

Neuhaus, Paul M.: Die Grundbegriffe des internationalen Privatrechts, 2nd ed. 1976

Nielsen, Jens: Das Inkassogeschäft, 1987

Nielsen, Jens: Grundlagen des Akkreditivgeschäfts, 1985

Nielsen, Jens: Auslandsgeschäft, BuB 5, looseleaf, 1980

Nigro, A.: Scoperto di conto, conto corrente assistito da apertura di credito e revocatoria fallimentare delle rimesse, in: Foro italiano, 1983, I, p. 69

Niizeki, T.: France Minpô Nioketu Saiken Senyû (Apparent Creditors under the French Civil Code), 41 Nagoya University Hô Sei Ronshû 84 (1967)

Nivarra, L.: Stanze di compensazione, in: Enciclopedia del diritto, XVIII, 1990, p. 651

Nobel, Peter: Devisenschuld: Realschuld oder Innominatschuld?, in: Festschrift für Schluep, 1988, p. 285

Nobel, Peter: Praxis zum öffentlichen und privaten Bankenrecht der Schweiz, supplementary volume, 1984

Nußbaum, Arthur: Money in the Law, National and International, 1950

Nußbaum, Arthur: Vertraglicher Schutz gegen Schwankungen des Geldwertes, 1928

Nußbaum, Arthur: Das Geld in Theorie und Praxis des deutschen und ausländischen Rechts, 1925

Oertmann, Paul: Bürgerliches Gesetzbuch, v. II, 3rd/4th ed. 1910

Ohse, Hermann: Die Devisen-Position des Bankiers, Bank-Archiv 1924, p. 299

Oser, Hugo/Schönenberger, Wilhelm: Obligationenrecht, Zürcher Kommentar v. V/I, Art. 1-183, 2nd ed. 1929

Ostler, Fritz: Umfang der Herausgabepflicht des Anwalts nach § 667 BGB für Fremdgelder auf Geschäfts- und Anderkonten, NJW 1975, p. 2273

Padoa-Schioppa, Tommaso: International Payment Systems: the Function Begets the Organ, speech given to the International Symposium on Banking and Payment Services, organized by the Board of Governors of the Federal Reserve System, Washington 1989, in: Banca d'Italia (ed.), Economic Bulletin, 1989, p. 67

Palandt, Otto: Bürgerliches Gesetzbuch, Kommentar, 50th ed. 1991

Paoli, G.: Operazioni di bancogiro e dichiarazione di fallimento, in: Diritto e giurisprudenza, 1981, p. 274

Passacantando, F.: Il sistema dei pagamenti in Italia, in: Il mutamento dell'attività bancaria: nuovi problemi monetari e organizzativi, 1988, p. 29

Patrikis, Ernest T.: Developments in the Law of Large Dollar Electronic Payments in the United States, RDAI 1987, p. 639

Patrikis, Ernest T.: UCC, 45 Business Lawyer 1389 (1990)

Pelichet, Michel: Note on Conflicts of Laws Occasioned by Transfrontier Data Flows, unpublished manuscript from the Hague Conference on Private International Law, 1987

Pelichet, Michel: Note on the Problem of the Law Applicable to International Credit Transfers, 1991

Peltier, F.: L'etendue des pouvoirs des administrateurs ou liquidateurs nommés par la commission bancaire, Banque et Droit no. 14, November/December 1990

Pennington, R.: Fraud, Error and System Malfunction, A Lawyer's Viewpoint, in: Goode, R. M. (ed.), Electronic Banking — The Legal Implications, 1985

Pennington, R./Hudson, A./Mann, E.: Commercial Banking Law, 1978

Perucci, U.: Dalla „canalizzazione“ al „monitoraggio“ al „monitoraggio“, in: Commercio internazionale, 1990, no. 11, Inserto, XVI

Phillips, A./Santomero, A.M.: Payment Risk, Network Risk and the Role of the Fed in: Humphrey, D. B. (ed.), The U.S. Payment Sytem: Efficiency, Risk and the Role of the Federal Reserve, 1990

Pico, G.: Ordine di bonifico ed accreditamento in conto, in: Banca, borsa, titoli di credito, 1971, II, p. 484

Planck, Gottlieb: Kommentar zum Bürgerlichen Gesetzbuch, v. II 1, 4th ed. 1914

Pleyer, Klemens/Wallach, Edgar: Erfüllungszeitpunkt und Gefahrtragung bei grenzüberschreitenden Überweisungen nach deutschem und englischem Recht, RIW 1988, p. 172

Polke, Heinrich: Widerrufbarkeit von Zahlungseingängen aus dem Ausland, ZIP 1985, p. 11

Polke, Heinrich: Der Zahlungsverkehr der Banken im In- und mit dem Ausland, 1978

Portale, Giuseppe: Le garanzie bancarie internazionali, 1989

Portale, Giuseppe: Delegazione „allo scoperto“ e revocatoria fallimentare, in: Giustizia civile, 1984, II, p. 451

Portale, Giuseppe: Diritto privato comune e diritto privato dell'impresa, in: Cento anni dal codice di commercio, 1984, p. 227

Portale, Giuseppe: Tra responsabilità della bance e „ricommercializzazione“ del diritto commerciale, in: Maccarone, S./Nigro, A. (eds.), Funzione bancaria, rischio e responsabilità della banca, 1981, p. 271

Porzio, Mario: I contratti bancari in generale, in: Trattato di diritto privato diretto, 12, 1985

Porzio, Mario: Il conto corrente bancario, il deposito e la concessione di credito, in: Rescigno, P. (ed.), Trattato di diritto privato diretto, 12, 1985

Prölss, Erich R./Martin, Anton: Versicherungsvertragsgesetz, 24th ed. 1988

Qualeatti, D.: Struttura e prospettive di sviluppo del sistema italiano dei pagamenti, in: Temi di discussione del servizio studi della Banca d'Italia, Quaderno no. 60, 1986

Rabel, Ernst: The Conflict of Laws, A Comparative Study, 1960

Radcliffe: Towards Uniformity in the Rules Governing Electronic Funds Transfers, 1988

Radicati di Brozolo, L.: Operazioni bancarie internazionali e conflitti di leggi, 1984

Radicati di Brozolo, L.: La legge regolatrice delle operazioni bancarie secondo la convenzione di Roma del 19 giugno 1980, in: Treves, Tullio (ed.), Verso una disciplina comunitaria della legge applicabile ai contratti, 1983, p. 83

Radtke, Klaus: Schuldstatut und Eingriffsrecht, ZVglRWiss 84 (1985), p. 325

Rehm, Hannes: Perspektiven des „Auslandszahlungsverkehrs“ im europäischen Binnenmarkt, Sparkasse 1992, p. 175

Reinhart, Gert: UN-Kaufrecht, 1991

Reithmann, Christoph/Martiny, Dieter: Internationales Vertragsrecht, 4th ed. 1988

Rennpferdt, Peter: Erfüllungsort und Erfüllungszeit von Geldschulden im internationalen Zahlungsverkehr, 1991

Rescio, G.: Clausola di modifica unilaterale del contratto e bancogiro di somma erroneamente accreditata, in: Banca, borsa, titoli di credito, 1987, II, p. 94

Rescio, G.: Revocatoria delle rimesse in conto corrente e situazione giuridica dell'accreditato, in: Banca, borsa, titoli di credito, 1984, II, p. 168

Ripert, Georges/Roblot, René: Traité de droit commercial, 12th ed. 1990

Rives-Lange, Jean-Louis/Contamine-Raynaud, Monique: Droit bancaire, 5th ed. 1990

Roth, Wulf-Henning: Internationales Versicherungsvertragsrecht, 1985

Rowe, Michael: Electronic Trade Payments, 1987

Ruozi, R. (ed.): Le operazioni bancarie, 3rd ed. 1989

Salanitro, Niccolo: Conto corrente bancario, in: Digesto delle discipline privatistiche, Sezione commerciale, IV, 1989, p. 15

Salanitro, Niccolo: Le banche e i contratti bancari, 1983

Sandrock, Otto: Die Bedeutung des Gesetzes zur Neuregelung des Internationalen Privatrechts für die Unternehmenspraxis, RIW 1986, p. 841

Sandrock, Otto (ed.): Handbuch der internationalen Vertragsgestaltung, v. 1, 1980

Santa, Maria A.: Diritto commerciale comunitario, 1990

Santini, G.: Giroconto, in: Novissimo digesto italiano, VII, 1965, p. 861

Santini, G.: Il bancogiro, 1948

Santoro, V.: Il conto corrente bancario, edizione provvisoria, 1988

Sawaki, T./Ishifuro K.: Kokusai Kinyû Torihiki (International Financial Transactions), 1986

Sawano, N.: Mukengen Shikinidô to Sonshitsu Futan (Unauthorized Funds Transfers and Loss Allocation), in: Iwahara, S. (ed.), Takeuchi Akeio Sensei Kanreki Kinen, Gendai Kinyûjô no Tenkai (Festschrift für Akeio Takeuchi, Developments in Modern Business Law), 1990

Sawano, N.: Electronic Banking to Hôteki Shoomondai (Electronic Banking and Legal Problems), in: Egashira, E. (ed.), Otori Tsuneo Sensei Kanreki Kinen, Hachijû Nendai Shôjijô no Shosô (Festschrift für Tsuneo Otori, Aspects of Commercial Law in the 1980's), 1985

Schack, Haimo: Der Erfüllungsort im deutschen, ausländischen und internationalen Privat- und Zivilprozeßrecht, 1985

Schack, Haimo: Internationales Zivilverfahrensrecht, 1991

Schinnerer, Erich: „Zum Leitfaden" — Entwurf von UNCITRAL über den internationalen elektronischen Überweisungsverkehr, Zeitschrift für Rechtsvergleichung 1985, p. 225

Schinnerer, Erich: Welthandelsrecht und internationaler Zahlungsverkehr, ÖBA 1975, p. 278

Schlegelberger, Franz: Handelsgesetzbuch, Kommentar, ed. 1960 ff.

Schlenke, Reinhard: Allgemeine Geschäftsbedingungen der Banken und AGB-Gesetz, 1984

Schluep, Walter R.: Innominatverträge, in: Vischer, F. (ed.), Schweizerisches Privatrecht, Bank VII/1, OR — Besondere Vertragsverhältnisse, v. II, p. 890

Schmelcher, Günter H.: Der Erfüllungsort von Geldschulden (Der Zahlungsort), 1972

Schmidt-Dencker, Hans-Michael: Die Korrespondenzbank im Außenhandel, 1982

Schmitthoff, Clive M.: Nature and Evolution of the Transnational Law of Commercial Transactions, in: Horn, Norbert/Schmitthoff, Clive M. (eds.), The Transnational Law of International Commercial Transactions, 1982, p. 19

Schmitthoff, Clive M.: The Harmonisation of Law by Means of Standard Contracts and General Conditions, 17 I.C.L.Q. 551 (1968)

Schmitthoff, Clive M.: The Unification of the Law of International Trade, Journal of Business Law 1968, p. 105

Schneider, Uwe H.: Das UNCITRAL Modellgesetz über den internationalen Überweisungsverkehr, WM 1989, p. 285.

Schneider, Uwe H.: Das Recht des elektronischen Zahlungsverkehrs. — Eine Darstellung des amerikanischen Rechts mit rechtsvergleichenden Bezügen zum deutschen Recht sowie dem Text und der Übersetzung des Electronic Fund Transfer Act 1978, 1982

Schneider, Uwe H./Merkel, Helmut: Preisaufschläge bei Zahlung mit Scheck, Kreditkarte oder an automatisierten Kassen?, in: Festschrift für Pleyer, 1986, p. 115

Schneider, Uwe H./Troberg, Peter: Finanzdienstleistungen im EG-Binnenmarkt: Sitzland- oder Gastlandrecht, WM 1990, p. 165

Schnyder, Anton K.: Das neue IPR-Gesetz, 2nd ed. 1990

Schöle, Otto: Das Recht der Überweisung, 1937

Schönemann: Der Erfüllungsort, 1935/36

Schönke, Adolf/Schröder, Horst: Strafgesetzbuch Kommentar, 22nd ed. 1985

Schönle, Herbert: Bank- und Börsenrecht, 2nd ed. 1976

Schönle, Herbert: Ort und Zeit bargeldloser Leistung (Zahlung), in: Festschrift für Werner, 1984, p. 817

Schönle, Herbert: Commentaire du projet de resolution du comité de droit monétaire-concernant l'harmonisation des disposition légales nationales et des conventions internationales régissant le moment de l'execution d'une dette d'argent (temps de paiement), Report of the ILA Conference 1984 in Paris, Part II, no. 25

Schönle, Herbert: Bank- und Börsenrecht, 2nd ed. 1976

Schröter, Jürgen: Bankenhaftung im mehrgliedrigen Zahlungsverkehr, ZHR 151 (1987), p. 118

Schubert, Mathias: Internationale Verträge und Eingriffsrecht — Ein Beitrag zur Methode des Wirtschaftskollisionsrechts, RIW 1987, p. 729

Schürenkrämer, Ulrich: Technologiebewertung des internationalen Datennetzes der Kreditinstitute: S.W.I.F.T. in Prognose und Realität, 1987

Schütze, Rolf A.: Kollisionsrechtliche Probleme des Dokumentenakkreditivs, WM 1982, p. 226

Schwark, Eberhard: 100 Bände BGHZ: Bank- und Wertpapierrecht, ZHR 151 (1987), p. 325

Scott, H. S.: Where Are the Dollars? Off- Shore Funds Transfer, 3 Banking & Finance Law Reviews 243 (1989)

von der Seipen, Christoph: Akzessorische Anknüpfung und engste Verbindung im Kollisionsrecht der komplexen Vertragsverhältnisse, 1989

Shea, Tony: Foreign Exchange Contracts and Netting in the UK, 9 Inter. Fin. Law Rev. 19 (1990)

Soergel, Hans: Bürgerliches Gesetzbuch, reedited by Siebert, Wolfgang, 12th ed. 1987

Spindler, Joachim v./Becker, Willy/Starke, Otto-Ernst: Die Deutsche Bundesbank, Grundzüge des Notenbankwesens und Kommentar zum Gesetz über die Deutsche Bundesbank, 4th ed 1973

Spinelli, M./Gentile, G.: Diritto bancario, 1984

Staudinger, Julius v.: Kommentar zum Bürgerlichen Gesetzbuch, 12th ed. 1978 ff.

Steuer, Stefan: Bekämpfung der Geldwäsche aus Bankensicht, Die Bank 1991, p. 138

Stevens, E.J.: Risk in Large-Dollar Transfer Systems, Federal Reserve Bank of Cleveland Economic Review (Fall 1984), p. 2

Straatmann, Kuno/Ulmer, Peter: Handelsrechtliche Schiedsgerichtspraxis, v. I 1975, v. II 1982; fortgeführt unter dem Titel: Rechtsprechung kaufmännischer Schiedsgerichte, v. III 1984, v. IV 1988

Suzuki, T. (ed.): Futsu Yokin, Teiki Yokin (Ordinary Deposits and Time Deposits), 1963

S.W.I.F.T.: Annual Report 1990, Brussels 1991

S.W.I.F.T.: Minutes of the Annual General Meeting, Brussels 1989

S.W.I.F.T.: Special Newsletter, Brussels 1979

Tanabe, M.: Furikomi Torihiki no Hôteki Shomondai (Legal Issues of Credit Transfers), 790 Kinyûhômu 4 (1987)

Tanabe, M.: Doitsu Niokeru Furikae Torihiki (Funds Transfers in Germany), 11/2 Hannan Ronshû-15 (1985)

Tanaka, K.: Tegatahô Kogittehô gairon (Introduction to Bills and Notes Act and Check), 1935

Tanaka, S.: Ginkô Torihikihô (Bank Transactions Law), revised edition 1979

Tarola, A./Qualeatti, D./ Di Blasi, P./Salamone, P.: Sistema dei pagamenti, prodotti bancari e reti telematiche. Aspetti tecnologici, realizzativi, di sicurezza e giuridici

Terranova, G.: Effetto estintivo e funzione solutoria delle rimesse in conto corrente bancario, in: Banca, borsa, titoli di credito, 1983, II, p. 8

Thalmann, Christian: Die Rechtzeitigkeit von Überweisungen und Einzahlungen auf ein Bank- oder Postscheckkonto des Gläubigers, Die Aktiengesellschaft, Schweizerische Zeitschrift für Wirtschaftsrecht 1990, p. 257

Thalmann, Christian: Überlegungen zur Haftung der Bank für indirekten Schaden aus Verspätungen im Zahlungsverkehr, in: v. Graffenried, Rudolf (ed.), Beiträge zum schweizerischen Bankenrecht, 1987, p. 161

Thévenoz: Error and Fraud in Wholesale Funds Transfers: U.C.C. Artikcle 4A and the UNCITRAL Harmonization Process, 1990

Thieme, Jürgen (ed.): Materialien zum ausländischen und Internationalen Privatrecht, v. 32: Vorschläge und Gutachten zum Entwurf eines EG-Konkursübereinkommens, 1988

Thieme, Jürgen (ed.): Der Entwurf eines Konkursübereinkommens der EG-Staaten von 1980, RabelsZ 45 (1981), p. 459

v. Thur, Andreas/Escher, Arnold: Allgemeiner Teil des Schweizerischen Obligationenrechts, v. I., 3rd ed. 1979

Toma, G.: Il nuovo look della „dichiarazione valutaria", in: Commercio internazionale, 1990, no. 11, Inserto, XXII

Toyama, H.: Problems of Risk in International Electronic Fund Transfer Systems, 2 Financial Services Yearbook 29 (1989)

Tutt, Nigel: Swift Tackles its Midlife Crisis, 5 Banking Technology 14 (1988)

Uchiike, K.: Saiken no Junsenyû to Uketori Shôsho (Apparent Creditors and Receipts), 34/1 Hogaku Kenkyu 49 (1961)

Ulmer, Peter/Brandner, Hans-Erich/Hensen, Horst-Diether: AGB-Gesetz, 6th ed. 1990

UNCITRAL (ed.): Legal Guide on Electronic Funds Transfers, New York 1987

Ungnade, Dieter: Die Geltung von Allgemeinen Geschäftsbedingungen der Kreditinstitute im Verkehr mit dem Ausland, WM 1973, p. 1130

Vassalli, F.: „Delegatio solvendi", adempimento di terzo e revocatoria fallimentare, in: Rivista di diritto commcerciale, 1967, II, p. 107

Vasseur, Michel: Informations sur les aspects juridiques des transferts internationaux de fonds par d'autres moyens que les cartes, in: Banque et Droit, no. 3/1989, p. 61

Vasseur, Michel: Droit et Economie bancaires, Opérations de banque, 4th ed. 1988 ff.

Verschraegen, Bea: Gesamtevaluierung der Europaratskonventionen aus österreichischer Sicht — mit Prüfung der bisher von Österreich noch nicht ratifizierten Übereinkommen, in: Hummer, W./Wagner, G. (eds.), Österreich im Europarat 1956-1986, 1988, p. 433

Vetter, Eberhard: Akzessorische Anknüpfung von Subunternehmerverträgen bei internationalen Bau- und Industrieanlagen-Projekten?, NJW 1987, p. 2124

Vischer, Frank: Probleme des Währungsrechtes nach dem Entwurf des schweizerischen IPR-Gesetzes, in Graffenried, Rudolf v. (ed.), Beiträge zum schweizerischen Bankenrecht, 1987, p. 425

Vischer, Frank: Internationales Vertragsrecht, 1962

Vital, Christian: Das elektronische Interbank-Zahlungsverkehrssystem SIC: Konzept und vorläufige Ergebnisse, Wirtschaft und Recht 1988, p. 9

Vroegop, J.: The Time of Payment in Paper-Based and Electronic Funds Transfer Systems, [1990] Lloyd's Maritime and Commercial Law Quarterly 64

Vroegrop, J.: The Role of Correspondent Banks in Direct Funds Transfer, [1990] Lloyd's Maritime and Commercial Law Quarterly 547

Wagatsuma, S.: Saiken Kakuron Jôkan (Details of Obligations Law, vol. 1), 1954

Weber, Rolf H.: Haftung für Schäden bei Ausführung gefälschter Zahlungsaufträge, Schweizerische Juristen-Zeitung 1985, p. 85

Weber, Rolf H.: Obligationenrecht, Allgemeine Bestimmungen, Berner Kommentar, v. VI/1/4, Kommentar zu Art. 68-96 OR, 1983

Weber, Rolf H.: Probleme bei der bargeldlosen Erfüllung von Geldschulden, Schweizerische Juristen-Zeitung 1982, p. 137

Weitnauer: Das Urteil des Schiedgerichtshofs für das Abkommen über deutsche Auslandsschulden vom 3.7.1958 und die Frage des Zahlungsortes, WM 1960, p. 1286

Weitnauer, W.: Der Vertragsschwerpunkt, 1981

Wengler: Die Anknüpfung des zwingenden Schuldrechts des internationalen Privatrechts, in: ZVglRWiss 54 (1941), p. 168

v. Westphalen, Die Banken-AGB in Rechtsprechung und Literatur, WM 1984, p. 2

Wettstein, Peter M.: Home Banking — Die Beziehungen zwischen Kunde und Bank aus juristischer Perspektive, Schweizer Schriften zum Handels- und Wirtschaftsrecht, v. 117, 1989

Wolf, Manfred/Horn, Norbert/Lindacher, Walter: Gesetz zur Regelung der Allgemeinen Geschäftsbedingungen, Kommentar, 2nd ed. 1989

Wood, Philip: Law and Practice of International Finance, 1980

Wood/Terray: Foreign Exchange Netting in France and England, Inter. Fin. Law Rev. 1990, p. 18

Wulf: Two ways to achieve the same goal — the model law on international credit transfers and the new UCC Article 4A in the national and international contexts, 9 Wisconsin International Law Journal 69 (1990)

Yamashita, T.: Ginkô Torihiki to Menseki Yakkan no Kôryoku (Bank Transactions and the Validity of Liability Exemption Provisions in Standard Contracts), in: Kinyûhô no Kadai to Tenbô (Problems and Perspectives of Finance Law), p. 189

Yazawa, M.: Jishû Shôhô 30 Mon (30 Questions for Independent Study of Commercial Law), 1963

Zahn, Johannes C. D./Eberding, Ekkehard/Ehrlich, Dietmar: Zahlung und Zahlungssicherung im Außenhandel, 6th ed. 1986

Zeller, Ernst: Auslegung von Gesetz und Vertrag, 1989

Zeno-Zencovich, V.: Clearing Houses informatizzate e irrevocabilità del pagamento, in: Il diritto dell'informazione e dell'informatica, 1987, p. 555

List of Authors

Dr. jur. *Jacques Bischoff*, Attorney at Law, Central Secretary of the TELEKURS AG, Zürich, Lecturer at the University of Zurich, Switzerland

Dr. jur. *Uwe Blaurock*, Professor, Georg August University, Göttingen, Germany

Michael Bruns, Regierungsdirektor, Federal Ministry of Justice, Bonn/Bad Godesberg, Germany

Debra W. Cook, Attorney at Law, Federal Reserve Bank of New York, U.S.A.

Concetto Costa, Professor, University of Messina, Faculty of Law, Messina/Catania, Italy

Ross Cranston, Professor, University of London, Faculty of Law, Queen Mary and Westfield College, Director of the Centre for Commercial Law Studies, London, England

Dr. jur. *Jörg Etzkorn*, Attorney at Law, Chief Legal Counsel, Wüstenrot Holding GmbH, Ludwigsburg, Germany

Carl Felsenfeld, Professor, Fordham University, School of Law, New York, U.S.A.

Klaus M. Gormanns, Ministerialrat, Directorate-General, Deutsche Bundespost POSTBANK, Bonn, Germany

Hervé Le Guen, Deputy Director, Legal Services, Banque de France, Paris, France

Dr. jur. *Walther Hadding*, Professor, University of Mainz, Director of the Institut für internationales Recht des Spar-, Giro- und Kreditwesens, Johannes Gutenberg-University, Mainz, Germany

Winfried Holzwarth, Attorney at Law, Corporation Counsel, Deutsche Bank AG, Frankfurt am Main, Germany

Dr. jur. *Ulrich Huber*, Professor, Institut für Handels- und Wirtschaftsrecht, University of Bonn, Germany

Shinsaku Iwahara, Professor, University of Tokyo, Faculty of Law, Tokyo, Japan

Eduard Kuß, Head of Konzern-Treasury Kontrolle, Volkswagen AG, Wolfsburg, Germany

Alfons Müller, Managing Director, European Savings Banks Financial Services Company [EUFISERV S.C.], Brussels, Belgium

Dott. *Franco Passacantando*, Director, Monetary and Financial Sector, Research Department, Banca d'Italia, Rome, Italy

Ernest T. Patrikis, General Counsel and Executive Vice President, Federal Reserve Bank of New York, U.S.A.

Dr. rer. pol. *Hannes Rehm*, Managing Director, Deutscher Sparkassen- und Giroverband, Bonn, Germany

Burkhardt Reichel, Kontrolle und Zahlungsverkehr, Volkswagen AG, Wolfsburg, Germany

Dipl.-Kfm. *Peter Rennpferdt*, Graduate Research Assistent, Georg August University, Göttingen, Germany

Mathias Rudnick, Kontrolle und Zahlungsverkehr, Volkswagen AG, Wolfsburg, Germany

Dr. jur. *Uwe H. Schneider*, Professor, University of Darmstadt, Director of the Institut für internationales Recht des Spar-, Giro- und Kreditwesens, Johannes Gutenberg-University, Mainz, Germany

Dr. jur. *Christoph von der Seipen*, Attorney at Law, Neumann, Krull und Partner, Düsseldorf, Germany

Jürgen Trosien, Director of Deutsche Bundesbank, Frankfurt am Main, Germany

Michel Vasseur, Professor, Université de Droit, d'Economie et de Sciences Sociales de Paris, Ancien Conseiller d'Etat en Service Extraordinaire, Paris, France

MIX
Papier aus verantwortungsvollen Quellen
Paper from responsible sources
FSC® C105338

Printed by Libri Plureos GmbH
in Hamburg, Germany